The Bona fide Hebrews of the Books of Moses

SECOND EDITION

Baba Chaitezvi Kanyuchi Dehwe

Vana VeNhaka Publishers

Vana VeNhaka Publishers
P.O. Box CY 221
Causeway
Harare
Zimbabwe

©Vana VeNhaka Publishers, 2008, 2015

All rights reserved; no part of this publication may be reproduced, stored in a retrieval system, or transmitted in any form or by any means, electronic, mechanical, photocopying, recording, or otherwise, without the prior written permission of the publishers.

First Edition Published in 2008

Second Edition Published in 2015

ISBN :   978-0-7974-3548-3

Contents

Contents	Page
Preface	1
Introduction	5
Chapter 1 Hebrew/African Culture	9

1.1	Kutanga kweNyika/ In the Beginning	9
1.2	Kutanga Kwezuva / The Start of a New Day	9
1.3	Mbereko / The Ability to Conceive and be Fruitful	10
1.4	Musikavanhu/ Umvelinqangi/ Mudzimu Mukuru/ Unkulunkulu/ The Creator	11
1.5	Mudzimu/ Mweya/ A Soul of a Departed Elder/ Ancestral Spirit	12
1.6	Kupira Mudzimu/Mweya / Perceived Intercession by the Ancestors	14
1.7	Good Deeds of the Ancestors (Madzitateguru) Interceding for their Children	15
1.8	Africa - the Domain Land of Hebrew Culture	16
1.9	Muti Usina Zita/ The Tree of Sustenance and Life - (The Tree of Knowledge)	20
1.10	Chisingarimwi / The Sabbath	21
1.11	Chisingarimwi/ Sabbath, a Hebrew/African Marker/Identifier	22
1.12	Musoro weMusha/ The Hierarchy of the Hebrew/ African Family	22
1.13	Wanano/ Marriage	24
1.14	Kupira/ Offering	25
1.15	Ngozi/ The Avenging Spirit	27
1.16	Murarabungu / Rainbow Symbolism	27
1.17	Zita raSekuru/ The Name of the Grandfather Passes onto a Grandson	28
1.18	Hebrew or African Culture Maintains Communication with the Spiritual Realm	28
1.19	African or Hebrew Blessings	29
1.20	The African or Hebrew Extended Family	32
1.21	Chikuva cheKupira/ An Alter of Offering	32
1.22	Kuoma Kwenyika/ Drought	33
1.23	Urombo Uroyi/ Poverty is not a Virtue	33
1.24	African Etiquette and Generosity	35
1.25	Zunde raMambo/ Tithes	36
1.26	Svikiro/ Dlozi/ Tenure of a Prophet	37
1.27.	Mwana Wedangwe/ Duties of the First Born	38
1.28	Africa the Land of the Children of Abraham	39
1.29	Barika/ Polygamy	39
1.30	Kupa Mbereko/ Assisted Conception	40
1.31	Chigaro chaVahosi Mubarika/ The Authority of the First Wife	41
1.32	Kudzingisa Vanakomana/ Male Circumcision	41
1.33	Mhondoro/ Angelic Entities	42
1.34	African Humility and Hospitality	43
1.35	Ungochani/ Sodomy	44
1.36	Zvinoera/ Taboos	45
1.37	Kuyeresa Denga/ The Fear of Heaven	46
1.38	Marriage Between Close Relations to Preserve Royalty or Family Integrity	47
1.39	Mabiko Emhuri/ Family Celebrations	47
1.40	Chitsidzo/ A Vow	48
1.41	Mupupuri/ Witness	48
1.42	Nzvimbo Yekupira (Dzimbahwe)/ Place for Offering (Shrine)	49
1.43	Mupiro/ Objects Suitable for an Offering	49
1.44	Makuva/ Family Burial Ground	50
1.45	Kuroorerana Vematongo/ Marriage within One People and Culture	51
1.46	Kupfimbirwa Nevabereki - Parental Involvement in Courtship	51

i

Contents

Contents **Page**

Chapter 1   Hebrew/African Culture

1.47	Kuroora Mhandara/ Virgin Marriage	52
1.48	Chiratidzo Cheumhandara (Chimandamanda/Chishava) /Token of Virginity	53
1.49	Place of Courtship	54
1.50	Kutambira Vakuwasha/ Receiving the In-laws	55
1.51	Roora/ lobola/ The Bride Price	55
1.52	Kudya Kwevakuwasha/ Food for the In-laws	56
1.53	Mai Vemba/ Qualities of a Wife	56
1.54	Bridal Coaching	57
1.55	Muperekedzi/ Bridal Escort	57
1.56	Bride Entering the Matrimonial Home	57
1.57	Pasichigare Kwaifa Vakweguru/ Death in Old Age	58
1.58	Seri Kweguva Hakuna Anoziva/ Nil Knowledge of Life After Death	59
1.59	Kutema Ugariri/ Working for the Bride Price	60
1.60	Kupa Zita/ Naming a Child	60
1.61	Manana/ Miracle	61
1.62	Unhu/ Ubuntu/ Morality	61
1.63	Mhiko Yerufu/ An Oath of Death	63
1.64	Madzitateguru/ The Link or Role of Ancestors or Fore bearers	63
1.65	Dzinza/ Lineage or Genealogy	64
1.66	Birth Right and Implications of Baptism	65
1.67	Remarkable Absence of the Name Israel in African Culture	66
1.68	Mhosva Inoripwa/ Restitution	67
1.69	Pwanyaruzhowa/ Damage Paid in Lieu of Lost Virginity	67
1.70	Zviroto/ Dreams	68
1.71	Conflict in a Polygamous Marriage	68
1.72	Kufa Nechigumbu/ To Die in Sorrow	69
1.73	Rufu Mubayiro Wezvivi/ Untimely Death is the Wage of Sin	69
1.74	Kurova Guva/ Kudzora Mushakabvu Mumusha/ Succeeding the Name of the Departed	70
1.75	Kugara Nhaka/ Inheritance Settlement	72
1.76	Muteyo/ Runyoka/ Ulunyoka/ Adultery Detection and Curse	74
1.77	Chimutsa Mapfihwa/ Inheriting a Wife	75
1.78	Tsvimbo Dzababa/ An Elder's Staff	75
1.79	Makomborero Anobva Kuna Musikavanhu/ Blessings Come from the Creator	76
1.80	Kusuma Nyikadzimu/ Apprising the Spiritual Realm	76
1.81	Vafudzi/ Shepherds	77
1.82	Kuraira Nhaka/ Unwritten or Oral Will	77
1.83	Mitupo/ Totems	77
1.84	Rufu/ Bereavement	78
1.85	African Endurance	78
1.86	Living in the Providence of the Creator	79
1.87	Kubvisa Tsapata/hwashu paDzimbahwe/ Taking off Shoes on Entering a Shrine	79
1.88	Zita raMusikavanhu/ Umvelinqangi, Unkulunkulu/ The Name of the Creator	80
1.89	Bira/ A Liquor Thanksgiving Offering	82
1.90	Natural Disaster Pre-warning Systems	83
1.91	Roast Meat Offering and Burning of Remains	83
1.92	Kutanga Kwemwaka/ The Beginning of Seasons	83
1.93	The Bitterness of African Vegetables	84
1.94	Universality/Inclusivity of the Hebrew Covenant	84

Contents

Contents   Page

Chapter 1   Hebrew/African Culture

1.95	Kusungira/ Redemption or Sanctification of the First Born	85
1.96	Kutungamirirwa neMhondoro/ Angelic Guidance	86
1.97	Bire naGanyire Cross the Zambezi in Leather Aprons	87
1.98	Masvikiro Echikadzi/ Female Priests	87
1.99	Zvisipiti/ Natural Wells, Fresh Waters and Springs from Providence	88
1.100	No Number Names for Years or Months	89
1.101	The Miracle Rock of Makate	89
1.102	MaDzishe nemaSadunhu/ Traditional Chiefs and Headsmen	90
1.103	Nzvimbo Dzinoera/ Sacred Places	91
1.104	Kuomba kweMhondoro/ Angelic Sounds	92
1.105	Mitemo yemaDzimbahwe/ Laws for the Services of Shrines	92
1.106	Makomo Anotsva Oga/ Mountains that Burn Naturally with Optimum Control	93
1.107	Musikavanhu Mumwechete/ Oneness of the Creator	93
1.108	Zviumbwa/ Graven Images	94
1.109	Kudaidza Zita raMusikavanhu Nhando/ Profaning the Name of the Creator	94
1.110	Kutanda Botso / Atonement for Dishonour to MOTHER and Father	95
1.111	Umhondi/ Murder	96
1.112	Upombwe/ Adultery	96
1.113	Kuba/ Theft	97
1.114	Basa Revakuru/ The Role of Elders	97
1.115	Nhoroondo/ African Oral Tradition	98
1.116	Ngoma, Mbira Nehosho/ Traditional Music Instruments	99
1.117	Drums and Horn Sounding for Communication	99
1.118	Nhapwa/ A Slave	100
1.119	Refuge for Accidental Killer	100
1.120	Kuroodza/ Marrying Off Daughter in Lieu of Poverty	101
1.121	Muroyi Ngaurayiwe/ Bulala Muthakathi/ Kill the Witch/Wizard	101
1.122	Mutorwa, Chirikadzi neNherera/ Treatment of the Stranger, Widows and Orphans	102
1.123	Chimbadzo/ Usury	103
1.124	Leader's Conduct Accountable to the Spiritual Realm	104
1.125	N'ombe Yakapirwa/ N'ombe yeMudzimu Mukuru/ A Sanctified or Offered Bull	104
1.126	No Names for Days of the Week	105
1.127	Dzimbahwe Guru/ The Great Zimbabwe Shrine	106
1.128	Gudzadungwe/ Following a Multitude	109
1.129	Murombo Munhu/ A Poor Person is Human	109
1.130	Inxwala/ The Offering of the First Fruits of Harvest	109
1.131	Rukoto/ Mukwerere/ Rain Offering/ Festival of Booths	109
1.132	Kuradza Minda/ Land Sabbath	110
1.133	No Buildings of Worship or Religious Doctrine in Africa	110
1.134	Makomo Anoyera/The Sanctity of Hebrew or African Mountains	111
1.135	The Great Zimbabwe Bird/ A Similitude of the Cherubim	111
1.136	Ndiro yeDzimbahwe/ A Stone Laver for the Oracle	112
1.137	Animal Skin for Spiritual Utilities	112
1.138	Mbatya dzeSvikiro/ Dress Code for Priests or Prophets	113
1.139	Kugadzwa kweSvikiro/Dlozi / Appointment of a Priest/Prophet	113
1.140	Mapiriro/ Finer Details of an Offering	114
1.141	Nyama Yezvirango/ Portion of the Priests/Prophets	114
1.142	Tenure of Offerings	115
1.143	A Census	115
1.144	Svikiro Harizi Tsvimborume/ Celibacy Vow	116

iii

Contents

Contents		Page
Chapter 1	Hebrew/African Culture	
1.145	Mono remaSvikiro / Holy Anointing Oil for the Priests	117
1.146	The Golden Calf and Similar Images of Worship	117
1.147	Remarkable Absence of the Devil/Satan in Hebrew or African Culture	118
1.148	Human Sacrifice	119
1.149	Gonan'ombe/ Chibako/ Nhekwe/ Snuff dishes	120
1.150	Animals Suitable for a Hebrew or African Offering	121
1.151	Sin Offering at National Level	121
1.152	Broken Earthen Vessels in African Culture	122
1.153	Consumption of Fat	122
1.154	Consumption of Blood	122
1.155	Instruments for Enquiring of the Creator Used by the Priests	123
1.156	Consecration or Sanctification of a Priest	123
1.157	Kubvumwa kweMupiro/ Acceptance of an Offering	124
1.158	The Use of Incense in Spirituality	125
1.159	Kutema Ruhau/ Making a Mark on Burial Ground of a Relation	125
1.160	Drinking While Doing Divine Work	126
1.161	Food and Non-food	126
1.162	Kutevera/ The Manner of Women	128
1.163	Muzvere/ Purification of Woman after Childbirth	128
1.164	Uncleanness Due to Flow of Seed in Man	128
1.165	Kurasira/ Kudzinga Mamhepo/ The Scapegoat	129
1.166	Kukanda Hakata/ Casting Lots	130
1.167	Approaching the Nakedness of Kinsman/Kinswoman	131
1.168	Bestiality	131
1.169	Gleaning for the Poor	132
1.170	Seka Urema Wafa/ Respect for the Disabled	132
1.171	Guhwa Harivaki Musha/ Tale Bearing Destroy Homes	132
1.172	Mingling Fabrics in One Garment	132
1.173	Use of Enchantment and Observing the Times	133
1.174	Cutting Hair and Beard in Weird Styles	133
1.175	Tattoos	133
1.176	Kuvhunzira Kumashavi Nen'anga/Sangoma / Consulting Familiar Spirits and Wizards	134
1.177	Mother-in-law and Son-in-law Boundary	136
1.178	Svikiro Guru/ The High Priest	136
1.179	Makunhakunha/ Incest	137
1.180	Basa raSekuru/ The Role of an Uncle	137
1.181	The Nazarite Vow	137
1.182	Defilement Due to Human Blood and Corpse	138
1.183	Kuvhunzira Kuna Musikavanhu/ Enquiring of the Creator	138
1.184	Mvura Yekuchenura/ Water of Separation	139
1.185	Nyaminyami / The Brass Serpent	140
1.186	Kugara Kwemwedzi/ New Moons and their Offerings	140
1.187	Kufumura Nyika/ Defilement of the Land	141
1.188	Hebrew or African Distress Call to the Creator	141
1.189	Kupinduka Kwetsika/ Cultural Dynamism	143
1.190	Kusarudza Nokugadza Mutungamiri/ Selection and Anointing of a Leader	143
1.191	Utongi/ Governance Hierarchy	146
1.192	Hoko/ Neighbour's Land Mark or Boundary	147
1.193	In Battle, the Creator Fights for the Africans or Hebrews	148

Contents

Contents		Page
Contents		**Page**

Chapter 1   Hebrew/African Culture

1.194	Male/ Female Dress Code	148
1.195	Proper Handling of Animals and Prevention of Cruelty to Animals	149
1.196	Cleanness Required in Battle	150
1.197	Mupoteri/ Refugee	150
1.198	The Hire of a Whore Unsuitable for Offering	151
1.199	Picking Corn in Neighbour's Field	151
1.200	Gupuro/ Token of divorce	151
1.201	Jinda raMambo/Induna / Assistants to the Leader	152
1.202	Kurova Manda/ Communication with the Dead	152
1.203	Death of a Leader Not Publicised	153
1.204	Kugiya/ Kudzana / African Dance	153
1.205	Basa reMasvikiro/Amadlozi muHondo / Role of Priests at War	153
1.206	Unsanctity of Corrosive Metals in Places of Spirituality	154
1.207	Language of an Offering and the Absence of Amen	154
1.208	Baal (Bari/ Mwari) in African or Hebrew Culture	155
1.209	Nzara/ Famine	156
1.210	Death Referred to as State of Slumber	157
1.211	Vana Gwenyambira/ Spiritual Musicians	157
1.212	Padare/ Court or Consultative Platform	157
1.213	Nhimbe/ Humwe/ Jakwara/ Communal Harvesting/Threshing	158

Chapter 2   Jewish Culture / Judaism   159

2.0	Introduction to Jewish Culture / Judaism	159
2.1	The Absence of the Creator in Judaism	160
2.2	The Absence of Monotheism	161
2.3	Redemption/Sanctification of the First Born / Kusungira	161
2.4	Lack of Knowledge and Practice of Sanctifying a Bull / Kupira N'ombe	162
2.5	No Names for Months and Years in Hebrew/African Culture	162
2.6	Traditional Chiefs and Headsmen/ MaDzishe nemaSadunhu	163
2.7	The Use of Graven Images - 'The Star of David'	163
2.8	Treatment of a Non-Jew (Stranger) in Judaism	163
2.9	Absence of the Oracle in Jerusalem	164
2.10	The Scapegoat/ Kurasira/ Kudzinga Mamhepo	165
2.11	Casting Lots/ Kukanda Hakata	165
2.12	Enquiring of the Creator/ Kuvhunzira Kuna Musikavanhu	166
2.13	Water of Separation/ Mvura Yekuchenura	166
2.14	Hebrew Law Compromised by the Law of the Strangers	166
2.15	Judaism is a Mixture of Foreign Cultures	167
2.16	The Term Jew Substituting Hebrew	167
2.17	Jews from Exile Ignorant of the Law of Moses	168
2.18	The Absence of a Prophet/ Priest among the Jews	168
2.19	Virgin Marriage/ Kuroora Mhandara	168
2.20	Bride Price/ Roora/ Lobola	169
2.21	Working for the Bride Price/ Kutema Ugariri	169
2.22	The Jews have Defiled the Once Holy Land and its Shrines	169
2.23	Genealogy/ Lineage in Judaism Follows the Mother	170
2.24	Duties of a Husband's Brother/ Kugara Nhaka	170
2.25	Totems/ Mitupo	171

Contents

Contents   **Page**

Chapter 2   Jewish Culture / Judaism

2.26   Hebrew Covenant not Exclusively for Jews Only   171
2.27   Appointment of a Leader in Judaism   172
2.28   In Battle the Creator Fights for the Hebrews   172
2.29   Jewish Cultural Dances   173
2.30   Enquiring of the Creator at War   173
2.31   Nehemiah Introduces Amen from Exile   174
2.32   Tishah b'Av Commemorating of the Fall of Jerusalem   174
2.33   Addition and Subtraction to the Law   174
2.34   The Purim Festival   174
2.35   The Messianic Concept / Ben David/ HaMoshiach   175
2.36   The Culture of Arrogance   176
2.37   Adonay the God of the Jews' Resemblance to Adonis of the Babylonians   177
2.38   The Use of the Term Saint   177
2.39   The Appearance of the Names of Angels   177
2.40   End of Times Prophets and Prophecies   178
2.41   Non Hebrew Terms   178
2.42   Resurrection of the Dead   178
2.43   Purity, Righteousness, Peace and Evil have no Colour   178
2.44   Pitum Haktoret/ Jewish Incense Offering or Recitation   179
2.45   Chanukah   179
2.46   The Pharisees and Sadducees   179
2.47   Zionism (Tsiyoniyut) / Tsaona / Disaster   180

Chapter 3   Linguistics   183

3.0   Language and Culture Linkage   183

3.1   Vanhu/Bantu Dialects – Jewish Hebrew Shared Roots   184

3.1.1   The African Language - The Vanhu/Bantu Language   184
3.1.2   The Linguistic Identity of People of African or Hebrew Descent   184
3.1.3   Unhu/Ubuntu Moral Code of Conduct   185
3.1.4   Spectacular Terms of African Dialects in the Hebrew Scriptures   185
3.1.5   Jewish Hebrew Dialect   186
3.1.6   The Ultimate Linguistic Milestone   186
3.1.7   Linguistic Medium of Communication and Worship   187
3.1.8   Trace Similarities Between Vanhu/Bantu Language and Northern Languages   187
3.1.9   Reasons for Linguistic Differences Between Vanhu/Bantu and Jewish Hebrew   187
        Dialects
3.1.10 Septuagint Mis-transliteration   189
3.1.11 Common Syllables for Jewish Hebrew and Vanhu/Bantu Dialects   190
3.1.12 Structure of the Vanhu/Bantu or Hebrew Language   191
3.1.13 Similarities Between Jewish Hebrew and Pre-Hebrew Languages of Canaan   192
3.1.14 Jewish Hebrew and Vanhu/Bantu Dialects Names Agreement in the Hebrew   192
        Scriptures
3.1.15 Linguistic Similarities - Vanhu/Bantu Dialects and Jewish Hebrew   197
3.1.16 Hebrew or African Common Spiritual Vocabulary   210
3.1.17 Linguistic Divergence Upon Return From Exile   211
3.1.18 Further Analysis of Vanhu/Bantu Terms in the Hebrew Scriptures   216
3.1.19 Conclusion on Vanhu/Bantu and Jewish Hebrew Dialects Analysis   218

Contents

Contents	Page

Chapter 3 Linguistics

3.1.20	Morality in Vanhu/Bantu Dialects and the Original Hebrew	219
3.2	Vanhu/Bantu Dialects – Arabi Shared Roots	220
3.2.1	Linguistic Similarities - Vanhu/Bantu Dialects and Arabi of Banu Arabia (Arabs)	220
3.2.2	Vanhu/Bantu Reference Dialects	220
3.2.3	Linguistic Similarities Comparison Table - Vanhu/Bantu Dialects and Arabi	221
3.2.4	Conclusion on Vanhu/Bantu and Arabi Dialects Analysis	231

Chapter 4 History — 233

4.1	History of the Hebrews or Africans	233
4.1.1	Introduction to Hebrew or African History	233
4.1.2	The Domain Land of the Hebrew or African Culture	234
4.1.3	The Grand Scheme of the New Testament	235
4.1.4	The Hebrew Links with Africa	235
4.1.4.1	Abram in Africa	235
4.1.4.2	The Hebrews Sustained by Africa During Famines	235
4.1.4.3	Midia and Sheba Home to the Children of Abraham	236
4.1.4.4	Moses Fled to Ethiopia from Pharaoh in Egypt	236
4.1.4.5	The Hebrew Nation Founded in Africa	236
4.1.4.6	At Exodus the Hebrews Craved for Egypt (Africa) - The Return	237
4.1.4.7	Hebrews Team up to Return to Egypt (Africa)	237
4.1.4.8	The Lost Tribes of Israel	238
4.1.4.9	The Dispersed Beyond the Rivers of Ethiopia	238
4.1.4.10	The Spiritual Wise Counsel from the Land Beyond the Rivers of Ethiopia	238
4.1.4.11	The Link Between Hebrews and Vanhu/Abantu	239
4.1.4.12	The Hebrew Population and Projected Growth	240
4.1.5	The Vast Mwene Mutapa Empire and the Great Zimbabwe Shrine	240
4.1.6	King Solomon Explorations in Africa	243
4.1.7	The Vanhu/Bantu Migration—The Hebrew Diaspora	247
4.2	History of the Jews	252
4.2.1	The First Return of the Jews from Exile	254
4.2.2	Anti-Semitism, the Blessings and the Number of the Jews	254
4.2.3	The Second Return of the Jews - the Search for a Jewish Residence	255
4.2.4	Peace in Israel	256

Chapter 5 Hebrew Scriptural Race Evidence — 257

5.1	Introduction to Hebrew Scriptural Race Evidence	257
5.2	Scriptural Race Evidence	259

Chapter 6 Prophecy — 269

6.1	Introduction to Prophecy	269
6.2	Modern Day Prophecies	269

Contents

Contents **Page**

Chapter 6   Prophecy

6.2.1	The Prophecy of Chaminuka	270
6.2.2	The Prophecy of Nehanda	271
6.3	The African Union	272
6.4	The Common Wealth	273
6.5	African People Fulfilling Hebrew Prophecies of the Books of Moses	273
6.6	African or Hebrew Salvation	281

Index   283

References / Bibliography   295

Preface

Preface

The author is a keeper of African Culture, who through this book, seeks to provide the link between African Culture, Hebrew Culture, Arabic Culture and Judaism by correcting misconceptions about the subjects of worshipping, spirituality and how they relate to culture, through the following:

1. African or Hebrew Culture is not a religion but simply the way in which people relate to each other on a day to day basis with a spiritual theme. How they raise their children with morality, how they relate to their land without defiling or polluting it, how they relate to their work, animals and their neighbour without doing that which no one would like done to them or by doing to others that which they would like to be done to themselves. When the neighbour's cattle stray, they bring them back to the owner's kraal as they would do to their own cattle. If a neighbour's children err, elders would discipline the erring children to bring them back to the moral fold like they would do to their own children. And when an enemy attacks the land, people defend their land. When one wants to travel or partake in enterprise, they apprise heaven to remove the stumbling blocks without trying to substitute hard work with begging or indolence.

2. Prayer was ideally like a good deed and there were no buildings where people would gather on frequent basis for prayer or for religious indoctrination but once in a week people would abstain from work and once in a year people would gather and dance, playing musical instruments, drinking, eating and thanks giving. The motivation for doing good was that heaven would open up and pour all blessings to the doer of good.

3. Religious schisms began in the north with the Romans, Greeks and later English and Dutch originating their religious doctrines that revolved around their identities like Roman Catholicism, Greek Orthodox or Anglicanism where the theme was to brainwash converts into thinking that they were Romans, Greeks or English so that these small and inconsequential states would create serious virtual empires stretching out of their own territorial borders. From that time prayer evolved from doing good to the neighbour, to some subjective and fruitless talk with a deity where every time a worshipper did the evil of annexing the neighbour's or third party territory, would make a prayer or talk to a deity to thank the deity for the committed brutality or when a slave master gets more slaves by brutality, would give a prayer to some deity and this day, as an example to demonstrate the fruitlessness of prayer, in a period of one day, people in Arabia make five prayers whose theme is thanking a deity for giving them authority or control over their underpaid alien employees from the four corners of the world or for any other misdeed which they understand to be a privilege granted as a result of a good prayer and not necessarily a result of a good deed. Prayer, which was a good deed has fallen so low today to the extent that in the same Arabia, the region with people who make more prayers than others per day in the whole world (the highest prayer per capita), all the suicide bombings in kindergarten schools recorded in the world are detonated in that region because prayer has been degraded from being a good deed to your neighbour as it was with the Hebrew fore bearers to some subjective and imagined talk to a deity. 'Oh great deity, do you not see that by worshipping you I am the greatest person on earth? Make me master of all people so that I have the most money, the most powers to subdue them so that your greatness manifest through me, thy prayerful servant', and the associated nonsense. During the author's sojourn in Arabia, witnessed pedestrians being hit and neglected by religious people in their high speed luxurious cars while rushing for prayer!! If there is a reward for such a prayer, then it is not from the Creator of life.

4. Hebrew Culture taught as an eternal covenant, was meant to be a universal culture/spirituality or covenant where upon exodus from Egypt under the leadership of Moses, the first tenet was about incorporation of the stranger or the non-Hebrew into the system, 'And when a stranger shall sojourn with thee, . . . One law shall be to him that is home born, and unto the stranger that sojourns among you', and therefore any literature or argument that says the Greek Testament was meant to accommodate all peoples of the world including the strangers (gentiles) that were not covered by the Hebrew Covenant is religious propaganda, Exo 12 vs 48-49. The Jews who are converts in Hebrew

Preface

Culture as shall be explained in this book, have over the years tribalised the universal Hebrew Culture and for that they have become one of the most resented groups of people this civilization has seen while the African people who have abandoned the Hebrew Culture / Covenant have become the most abused and exploited as prophesied by Moses, 'And thou shall become an astonishment, a proverb and a byword, among all nations whither the Creator shall lead thee',

Det 28 vs 37.

5. While the Hebrew Covenant was meant to be an eternal teaching, there was/is never a link or correlation between Hebrew Scriptures and Greek Scriptures which said that the former expired and was therefore to be superseded by the latter which was going to be all inclusive. The irony of the Greek Scriptures also known as the New Testament is unspeakable in that while the north claim that the New Testament is now the ruling covenant to replace the Hebrew Covenant, it trivialized some great names in Hebrew Culture like Judah and Simon by creating villains of the Greek Scriptures out of Judas Iscariot and Simon Peter making them betrayer and forsaker of Jesus the son of Joseph so that whoever reads or learns of the new covenant, would be conditioned to think that the esteemed Hebrew patriarchs Judah and Simon were the real and despicable villains. After condemning the patriarchs as villains, the New Testament does not end there, but it turns upside down the Hebrew Cultural tables by putting the harlots or social misfits onto the high table with Jesus the son of Joseph to try and break the fundamentals of the culture apart which teach that harlotry has no place in this civilization, so that the little girls will not make an effort to work on their morals but would rather settle for harlotry with the belief that should Jesus resurrect, they would be the ones gracing the high tables with him as his preferred harlots!! The Greek Scripture was a clear manifestation of cultural wars and was not in any way a part and parcel of Hebrew Culture. And while the Hebrew Scriptures were very clear about Ethiopia, Egypt, Canaan, Arabia, Syria, Lebanon, Persia and Babylon, the Greek Scriptures deliberately left out those places and then centred on Rome, Corinth, Colossia, Galatia, Philippi, Thessalonica – all of which are in the north and the domain of northern culture. The aim, strategy and scheme of things inherent in the Greek Scriptures were well planned by Greek philosophers to undo the popularity of Hebrew Culture so as to create the victorious Hellenic empire without much war. **The New Testament hardly agrees with anything African or Hebrew, it simply rebrands the millennia old traditions of the north like multiple deities, human sacrifice or use of human blood in worshiping albeit this time around with a Jew's name (Joshua the son of Joseph) attached thereto and there is nothing new in the 'New Testament'.**

6. The humility taught in Hebrew or African Culture which is symbolised by royal treatment of strangers or visitors, is the apex of the human civilization that if humans reach that stage where the second and third parties are considered kings as taught therein, then that would be the end of conflict, the end of envy and the individual survival instinct inherent in humankind would cease. But when the north rejected the inclusivity of Hebrew or African Culture, they went on a merciless rampage by forcing the growth of the church by brutality (inquisition), then slavery through to imperialism because they had rejected that strangers can come together as a family. The humility and peace inherent in African Culture still manifests even within the Africans who were victims to slavery, who fell to conflict. The Africans sing peace and reconciliation; Trevor Sutherland sang 'Are We A Warrior' and he sang that the Creator gave humankind wisdom and knowledge to understand love and peace not war. Joseph Hill sang 'fight down war and crime and build up righteousness'. Michael James Williams sang 'Stop the War'. Peter McIntosh sang 'We don't want no nuclear war; with nuclear war we wont get far'. These peace and love messages are coming from African victims of brutality not because the people of Africa cannot fight, but that peace and love is part and parcel of the African gene and culture but while such songs are playing for all to hear, the north are doing brisk business and making trillions of dollars on nuclear warheads, chemical and biological war (arms of barbarism). And to top-up that moral lead, the people of Africa lead human race for they are among the few peoples with no history of foreign territorial occupation, conquest, exploitation of a third party by slavery, looting of a third party resources, imperialism nor a history of colonization on planet earth. The reason behind these moral

Preface

achievements are the fundamental philosophy inherent in African or Hebrew Culture.

7. Linguistically, every attribute or constituent of Hebrew Culture has an equivalent term in Vanhu/ Bantu dialects as indicated in the contents section of this publication except for cultural matters that cannot be translated directly, which proves that Hebrew and African Culture are one culture. And as demonstrated in Chapter 3 Linguistics, Jewish Hebrew and Arabic terms appear shorter, truncated or with missing vowels or syllables in relation to Vanhu/Bantu dialects which indicate that the language spoken by the Jews and Arabs is Vanhu/Bantu dialects minus certain constructs, some syllables and vowels proving that Vanhu/Bantu dialects are closer to the language spoken by the Hebrew fore bearers than Jewish Hebrew and Arabi.

8. The people of Africa have a common culture, common language - the Vanhu/Bantu language spoken by the founding fathers before they separated and adapted to different habitats where they picked or dropped a syllable or so to result in the existing Vanhu/Bantu dialects. The people of Africa also have a common history and origin all of which is shared with the Arabs (the children of Ishmael or Banu Arabia) and the Jews (Bney Yisrael) to give a single identity which is a serious rallying point in these times of ever changing geo politics. Ethnic African conflicts between brother and brother, Hutu-Tutsi, Shona-Ndebele, Zulu-Xhosa, Igbo-Hausa, Kikuyu-Luo, Shia-Sunni, wars in Somalia, Sudan, Saharawi, Uganda, Congo, Nigeria, Libya, Kenya or any other African conflict will cease once the African people discover their common identity stretching back to the Hebrew fore bearers. The idea of leaders of Africa coming together to unite the African tribes through the African Union, based on the boundaries of Gen 2 vs 14 encompassing the rivers Orange in South Africa, Nile, through to the Euphrates in Iraq/Iran is a realistic target.

9. Racism partly emanates from religion and some cultures particularly on the subject of the colour of evil visa vis the colour of righteousness. In the north, righteousness was given the colour white while evil was given the colour black notwithstanding the fact that both righteousness and evil have no colour. The north have also associated white colour with Caucasian race while black is understood to refer to Vanhu/Abantu. The trouble makers like the Nazi are depicted in black colour in their cultural celebrations like D-Day while in children's play, there is the black sheep to the extent that people are brainwashed at early stages in life to be racist and no wonder the fight against racism is a challenge when northern children are brought up in racism. There is racism in most seemingly irrelevant issues like blood groupings. Blood group A is prevalent in Caucasian people while blood group O or zero (nothing) is prevalent among the dark skinned with African origin as if to suggest that when blood group O was picked, perhaps picking letters C, D, E were too close the Caucasian grouping A. Actually people with no melanin in their skin, require frequent visits to dermatologists to check skin cancer among other related skin ailments. The church has gone on to design priestly garments that are snow white in colour to suggest holiness, sanctity and righteousness they have associated with the colour white, yet among all Levite priestly garments, there is not a single white one. If the north are sincere in the fight against racism, they should begin to look even in their language at some words that have been built on racism against the dark skinned people like dark ages, blackmail, black market, black Monday and begin to replace such racist words with real words like barbaric ages, malicious exposure, parallel market and stern Monday respectively. The essence of the racism that has been seen lately of throwing a banana and start making monkey chants onto a football pitch in which Africans would be playing good football, which is meant to encourage them to literally lose focus of the ball and run for the fruit as done by monkeys, is not even a survival instinct on the part of racist proponents but is simply malice that aims to kill the African spirit but if the African spirit survived the brutality of slavery and imperial wars, would the same spirit succumb to a banana thrown on it, people underestimate the strength of the African spirit by a zillion times.

10. Within the domain of African or Hebrew Culture, human sacrifice or the use of human blood in spirituality either in real terms or in theory as a remembrance often practised in northern spirituality in relation to Jesus the son of Joseph who is now late, together with the use of associated accessories like incense are all abominations which are equivalent to witchcraft.

Preface

11. When it comes to the subject of teaching spirituality, morality or general goodliness, the north or west have no moral authority to teach especially Vanhu/Abantu for reason of a pervert moral resume. Morally, the north or west were the originators of the institution of slave trade in liaison with the Arabs to exert brutality on the guiltless people of Africa. Later, the same came to Africa among other international destinations to unjustly claim third party territory through imperialism. Today the north and west have legislated for sodomy on their land. And scientifically, the modus operanti is unethical where the products are barbaric nuclear, chemical and biological arms of war which are all against life and peace or serenity. The north or west are doing human stem cell science where they suffocate early life (foetus) to prolong the life of geriatrics who are better off dead than living thus offsetting the natural human life cycle. The same are doing gender conversion as well as designing the plastic garment of promiscuity. On the other hand, the students of northern teachings are African angels in righteousness and goodliness with no history of any of the above vices. It is Vanhu/Abantu who in fact should sent emissaries of civility, peace and goodliness to the pervert north and not the other way round otherwise that would be a travesty of morality and spirituality.

Introduction

Introduction

The object of the book, the Bona fide Hebrews of the Books of Moses is to present African Culture that has been kept by the people of Africa from their beginning and compare it to what was recorded in Hebrew Scriptures as Hebrew Culture in order to infer that African Culture and Hebrew Culture are one culture kept by one people.

The book not only compares the culture but it also looks into the Vanhu/Bantu dialects spoken by the people of Africa across the whole breath of Africa and compare those dialects to Jewish Hebrew spoken by the Jews (Bney Yisrael) and Arabi spoken by the Arabs (Banu Arabia) to conclude that the Vanhu/Bantu language spoken by the African fore bearers before they split and adapted to different habitats where they picked or dropped a syllable or so to result in the current dialects spoken in Africa today, was the same as the Hebrew language spoken by the Hebrew fore bearers. The basis of such a conclusion being that, a culture is executed in the language of its origin, and if the culture still lives it means the language of instruction is as old as the culture otherwise the loss of a language will automatically delete the culture with it and that the order of loss is that the culture is lost first before the language and then the language follows. The book compares the depth of Hebrew Culture in Africa on one side relative to that in Israel among the Jews which is now called Judaism and that among the Arabs on the other side to conclude that since African Culture kept in Africa today, is still nearly a faithful duplicate or mirror image of what was kept by the Hebrew fore bearers several thousands of years back, it therefore implies that those Vanhu/Bantu dialects which are spoken by the people of Africa today to execute the original Hebrew Culture, are the original language of the culture than Jewish Hebrew of the Jews and Arabi of the Arabs. From the dynamics of the language and culture of a people, culture is the first casualty if there is any followed by the language.

The book looks at African history, especially the Vanhu/Bantu migrations in relation to the history of the Hebrews to and from Africa recorded in the Hebrew Scriptures as generally Egypt and or Ethiopia and links the Vanhu/Bantu migration with the Hebrew Diaspora especially when viewed from the facts that only a handful of Hebrews (royals and artisans) were taken captive by Nebuchadnezzar to Babylon while the bulk who numbered in excess of six million at that time returned to the familiar Africa where they were brought up, under the leadership of Johanan and Prophet Jeremiah who actually died in Africa among his people while teaching African or Hebrew Culture. The book covers also the history of the Jews giving details of their origin from Assyria, Babylon, Persia, Canaan (pre-Hebrew inhabitants of Canaan) and converts from Europe, the Khazars.

The book analyses the prophecies made about the future of the Hebrews in the event of departure from the covenant with special attention given to Deuteronomy 28 and Leviticus 26 among other prophecies.

The book analyses the race of the Hebrews by looking at specific race references or evidence in the Hebrew Scriptures to infer that the Bona fide Hebrews of the books of Moses were not Caucasian like Jews nor mixed breed like the Arabs but were dark skinned like Vanhu/Abantu, the people of Africa.

In this book, the terms African people, Vanhu/Abantu or Hebrews have been used interchangeably for the reason that the book scholarly proves that indeed they are the same people. The name Israel, which means 'He who fights with god and angels and prevails' has not been used as frequent as it was referenced by the Jews in the Hebrew Scripture for the reason that the name is a Hebrew taboo in itself, the Creator in Hebrew Culture is an unfathomable entity and cannot be thought to sink low enough to fight with mortals and let alone sustain a defeat.

And not all of the African tribes, Jews or Arabs keep all the spiritual tenets inherent in Hebrew Culture, but that the level of observance varies with tribes and geography. During war times, circumcision and visiting the shrines are not practicable. In Babylon, the Jews could not keep the Hebrew tenets because they would risk their life from Nebuchadnezzar but the fundamental themes taught by Moses are very visible in African day to day life and to the effect that among the Hebrew prophets, none have

Introduction

in-subordinated the teachings of Moses and none among them have declared themselves greater than Moses and none have claimed revelations different and superior to those made by Moses except that subjects have tended to understand the Law of Moses differently in relation to the teachings of their prophets [Hadith - Al-Bukhari - Vol 3 - 594/5]. Even Muhammad in early phases of Islam (Hebrew Culture revival among Banu Arabia) would pray facing Jerusalem, the original Islamic Kiblah or direction of prayer before adoption of the direction of Makah Makarama.

The term Vanhu/Bantu language refers to all the combined African dialects spoken in Africa today which include dialects which have been classified either as Congo-Niger, Ethiopic or Afro-Asiatic by scholars external to Africa who are/were not well versed with the culture and its language. What has been classified in other books on African languages as languages are treated in this book as dialects in the sense that they all originate from one language—Vanhu/Bantu which was spoken by the founding mothers and fathers before they separated and adapted to different habitats, where they picked or dropped a syllable or so to result in the current dialects like Kikuyu, Mandinga, Garaginya, Herero, Hausa, Zulu, Shona, Xhosa, Tswana and Gorani among many others. Some of these dialects which have been called separate languages differ sometimes by one consonant where for example one dialect would use consonant 'R' while the other uses 'L' and therefore, the classification of language cannot be done on that basis and that kind of classification proves beyond doubt that either it was done by people with no knowledge of the language or by people with ulterior agenda to divide one people into imagined 'different tribes with a myriad of languages' when in fact the people are one with one history, one language, one culture and one origin. In that regard, Vanhu/Abantu have been grouped into Hamitic (whatever that is supposed to mean) or Asiatic sub-groupings without a reasonable linguistic or cultural basis for those classifications.

The people of Africa have never called themselves Africans nor Hebrews. The identity Africa or African is a foreign word which was used by the north to refer to Vanhu/Abantu. In the earlier days of the patriarchs to this day, they have never called themselves Hebrews. The name Hebrew was a third party reference associated with the patriarchs. The term Hebrew means 'from the other side of the river or to cross a river' and so other people external to Hebrew Culture would refer to the people as 'those from the other side of the river' and in that regard there was no way that the object would refer to self as 'those who are referred by others as belonging to the other side of the river'. In fact, like it is to this day, the people in the context have always referred to themselves as Vanhu/Abantu. Vanhu/Abantu is a name derived from their culture which is defined as a moral code of conduct and the people called themselves 'the people with or of a moral code of conduct', unhu/ubuntu. And if anyone of them fails the moral code of conduct, they call him a dog, not because he will be walking on four legs and wagging his tail, but that he will be lacking the fundamental morals upon which he has earned his name. The Vanhu/Bantu dialects spoken in Africa today were not as defined as they are today for the reasons that most were assigned by European settlers in the early stages of imperialism but by and large, they referred to each other as Vanhu/Abantu.

The author addressed the issue of identity very seriously in that identity is like a soul of a person and without identity, a person is without a soul and purpose in life. When identity is deleted in place of another, a person begins to identify with the new identity and begins to champion the causes of a new identity and if conflict arises between new and old identity, always a person will stand up and fight wars or objectives of her or his new identity and identity is a serious weapon where people deleted of their identity are often seen coming back to their roots, not to rediscover themselves but to fight as an alien would do. The first American Head of State to invade Africa to the extent of even mutilating and murdering a sitting Head of State was not a Caucasian, but a first generation African American deleted of identity. Moreover, there are people in Africa who call themselves Romans, Dutch or Anglican (English) all of which is derived from religious indoctrination and identity deletion yet these people have never been to Europe, have no European descent, nor nationality, nor assets and do not speak any of Roman, Dutch or English languages of the north but by identity deletion, people can do anything for those nations.

In order for critics to be able to satisfactorily analyse this book, they must be fluent with African Culture,

Introduction

Hebrew Culture, Jewish Culture (Judaism), Arabic Culture, Vanhu/Bantu Language (the current African dialects), Jewish Hebrew dialect, Arabi spoken by the Arabs, African History told especially by African Oral Tradition, Hebrew History and Jewish History. If there is no such a critic with those skills, a committee can be set up made up of members with any one of the referenced skills.

In the book, African or Hebrew Culture presented herein, was not classified into groupings relating to worshipping, the priests and shrines, or polity for the reason that every aspect of the culture has a spiritual theme and the current Hebrew Scriptures presentation did the same for there is no secular nor non-secular classification of African or Hebrew Culture and classifying the culture according to groupings may create schisms, which African or Hebrew Culture is not about.

Introduction

Blank Page

Hebrew / African Culture

Chapter 1   Hebrew / African Culture

1.1   Kutanga kweNyika/ In the Beginning

African or Hebrew Culture start with the story of creation where the Creator is understood to have created the universe and all that is therein, the stars, the planets, the plants, the animals and humankind. Well before the missionaries came to Africa with the bible, the Africans have always had knowledge of Musikavanhu/ Umvelinqangi/ Mudzimu Mukuru/ Unkulunkulu, which is the Creator of their fore bearers, heaven, earth, seas, rivers, vegetation and animals among other objects of creation. The Theory of Evolution was a matter unknown to Africa and it only came to light as it began to be preached to the continent by the north. The concept of creation in African terms is identical to that taught by Moses which opens the Hebrew Scriptures in the book of Genesis and the differences between the African story and that recorded in the Hebrew Scriptures occurs with respect of the name or designation of the Creator known to Vanhu/Abantu in comparison to that attributed to the Creator by the Jews given later in this work and also the reasons behind those different designations or names.

While Africa is known historically as the origin of civilization and technology by looking at the age and extent of the technologies that occurred at Giza in Egypt and the Great Zimbabwe, but nothing is considered to occur spontaneously without the design and scheme of creation. In other cultures, a devastating rain storm, earthquake, wild fire or human made disaster can be attributed to natural phenomenon but in African or Hebrew Culture, there is always a spiritual influence that people defiled their land for which the Creator sent a fire or an earthquake. And so while African or Hebrew Culture teaches of creation as the source of everything, in the north, scientists and scholars teach of the god particle which begot the big bang, which begot the dinosaur, which begot humankind. It is not imaginable in African or Hebrew Culture to say that things happen just randomly or from natural order without the scheme of creation. If the survival of a bird is analysed as an example, how it prepares a nest in a tree top and not on the wet ground, how it hatches the eggs, how it provides for its young, how it teaches them to fly and how it weans them into independent adults, it really is a well schemed set of events as said of creation than the way evolution tries to explain how it all began. Even the fish in the rivers know how to take care of their offspring and if they were not capable to do that in the first place, then most species would not have had time to adapt but would have all died. Even if two little birds are hatched in the laboratory and are made to live a secluded life where they do not learn from other birds these survival basics, when their adult cycle comes, they will do exactly according to the book. Can the evolutionists say that birds did not know about these survival instincts in their beginning but when they realized that they were approaching extinction then they thought of nursing their offspring round the clock to survive?

African Culture, Genesis 1

1.2   Kutanga Kwezuva / The Start of a New Day

A day in African or Hebrew Culture does not start at twelve midnight or the witching hour but at sunset. Often when a new moon or new year starts, it will be on the first day of the month or the year and that first day is the day upon which the new moon is sighted which happens at sunset and immediately an announcement of the new moon or new year follows and the first day of the month is not postponed until the midnight of the night upon which the moon has been sighted. The above description of a new day agrees with the following scriptural reference;

'And the Creator said, Let there be light: and there was light.
And the Creator saw the light, that it was good: and the Creator divided the light from the darkness.
And the Creator called the light Day, and the darkness called Night. And the evening and the morning were the first day'.

Gen 1 vs 3-5

And so the first half of the day is the night which starts exactly at sunset while the last half is the daylight at the end of which would be yet the start of another day. Most spiritual and cultural events, procedures and preparations leading to the execution of traditional fundamentals which include but not limited to Kupira (offering), Kurova Guva (inheritance settlement), bira (thanks giving offering), Kusungira (redemption of the first born), Kuvhunzira (enquiring of the Creator for guidance), Kuroora (marriage procedures) and many other African cultural procedures all begin in the evening/dusk or at dawn and not at midnight nor midday, thus coinciding with the start of a new day. The start of an African day conforms to the timeline written in the Hebrew Scriptures among a myriad of common attributes, for the reason that the two cultures are the same culture.

African Culture

1.3   Mbereko / The Ability to Conceive and be Fruitful

Mbereko or the ability to conceive and have children in African Culture is understood to come from the Creator as a blessing and failure to conceive is taken as a curse from the same. Culturally, the failure to conceive would mean that the name of him who cannot conceive will be discontinued from the face of the earth because the understanding in African Culture is the same as that in Hebrew Culture that every man must leave his seed to carry over his name;

'And the Creator blessed them, and said unto them, be fruitful and multiply, and replenish the earth, and subdue it: and have dominion over the fish of the sea, and over the fowl of the air, and over every living thing that moves upon the earth'.

Gen 1 vs 28

After creating humankind, the Creator instructs them to be fruitful and multiply and subdue the earth. Generations later, the Hebrew patriarchs are seen having problems associated with conception, the results of failure and emotions associated with their failure to conceive and have children is what still happens to the Africans today so many thousands of years after the departure of the fore bearers. Terminating pregnancies advocated by abortion lobby groups that is in practice in other nations is in total contrast to Hebrew or African Culture. No African or Hebrew was/is motivated to enter into a marital union with no prospect of conception of life because man and woman come together to have family and not fun but fun will come from the fruits of a marital union, the children. A marital union without children is considered to be like a fruit tree that is barren and always when a couple fails to conceive children the central discussion between the two is, what have we done against the Creator for the Creator to withhold the fruits of marriage from us. Even a miscarriage of pregnancy is a very painful experience, it is as bad as death in the family.

African or Hebrew Culture differs fundamentally from other cultures especially northern culture where womenfolk have rights to terminate or abort pregnancies yet constitutions give every mortal the right to life. And the selfishness of abortion lobby is that it is often pushed by the young women with such a short memory that if their mothers had been equally selfish and short sighted, the abortion lobbyist would not be anywhere lobbying for anything. Among all the living creatures; mammals, fish, birds among many, there is not a single one that has lost the desire for an offspring and the associated care involved in looking after an offspring to full maturity except the human female. Anything that appear to threaten the life of an offspring of any animal risks decimation from the mother but the human female will look for another animal that can eat her offspring if she has not thrown her in a sceptic tank or if she has not abandoned the offspring to starve to death or from weather elements.

The human female has sunk lower than any other females in terms of the morals associated with conception and childcare. The travesty of abortion lobby is that nations that have legalized abortion are top ranked cross border child adopting nations, they mutilate their own offspring in preference of third children. And it has been noticed that women who have consistently taken birth control medication or those that have aborted in their life, later often have problems associated with failure to conceive children and African or Hebrew Culture understand that as punishment that come from the giver of life and there is no original linguistic term to describe pregnancy termination because it is against the culture. Before the advent of Europeans in Africa, there have not been a single case of pregnancy

Hebrew / African Culture

termination even when the life of the mother was in great danger among Vanhu/Abantu. Rachel travailed and died during childbirth but the baby came out very healthy and alive (Benjamin). Abortion or infanticide is understood in African Culture to defile the land which in turn will bring curses on the people and their land.

There are myths that say that a few Vanhu/Abantu tribes used to kill infants who were born twins. Such myths are malicious and are without substance as there is no cultural reason, historical reference nor even a linguistic term for that practice. In the witchcraft domain, children are reported to die mysteriously in cases of making goblins and other devices of witchcraft and this practice of witchcraft is an abomination in African or Hebrew Culture and cannot be used to benchmark the culture.

And as shall be explained later in this work, Hebrew or African Culture has no celibacy among the priests; the African or Hebrew priest is a family head, a father of the family and not a celibate 'father' as is with the priests of the north. In the same regard, a bachelor for life in African Culture (tsvimborume) remains one of the least respected persons in society, the reason being that he has not lived up to the challenges of fruitfulness.

African Culture, Gen 15 vs 2-3, Gen 8 vs 17, Gen 9 vs 1-7, Judges 13 vs 2-3, 1 Sam 1 vs 2

1.4 **Musikavanhu/ Umvelinqangi/ Mudzimu Mukuru/ Unkulunkulu/ The Creator**

In African Culture, the entity of the Creator has no gender associated with that entity unlike the god and goddess of the north or the 'hu' or 'huwa' for he in Judaism and Islam respectively. There is therefore serious gender equality and neutrality in African or Hebrew spirituality. Women in the north are calling for equal gender rights, the right to priesthood and eventually they will question why and who said god is a he and not a she. Northern religions consider god to be a man or father as in 'Our father who art in heaven' and not as a mother or woman which is simply male chauvinism with no link at all to matters of spirituality;

'So the Creator created man in the image of the Creator, in the image of the Creator mankind were male and female'.

Gen 1 vs 27

In the referenced scripture, the author had to remove 'his and him' in order to give that scriptural reference its original meaning before it was changed when the current Hebrew Scripture was written post Babylonian exile by Ezra and compatriots. In the domain of African or Hebrew Culture, the Creator has no known form nor specific name but is known by various designations that revolve around the act of creation. If within the Vanhu/Abantu family, the Creator had a specific name, that name would have been preserved to the same extent that the term 'baba' for father has been preserved.

While among Vanhu/Abantu, the designation of the Creator is spot on commensurate with the awesome act of creation with terms like Musikavanhu which means the Creator of humanity, Umvelinqangi which means an entity with no beginning or ending, Mudzimu Mukuru which means the source of all souls, Unkulunkulu which means the great one without comparison, but on the other side, the Jews call their god El, which is the El of the Canaanites, the pre-Hebrew inhabitants of Canaan. The term El linguistically has not link to the act of creation as shall be described in Chapter 2 Judaism. The designations of the Creator mentioned herein which are spot on commensurate with the awesome act of creation were there in Africa from the beginning of the people and they are completely Vanhu/Bantu linguistic terms which are not in any way connected to the missionary teaching of the north when they came with the bible a few centuries ago. Meaning that before the advent of the missionary, the Africans were endowed with all the facets of a spiritual culture and a way of life that was well informed on the subject of the Creator and are therefore not the pagan or heathen race that has been preached at length by the north to justify their massive religious indoctrination that preceded imperial settlement in Africa. Vanhu/Abantu are one of the few people who have given the Creator the most befitting designation, that which details the momentous work of Creation and the Oneness of the Creator in just one word.

Hebrew / African Culture

The Jews also call upon 'the gods' (Elohim – or El, the Canaanite cult) in Gen 1 vs 1, a term they obtained from some of their origins - Canaanite. The much condemned abominations of the Canaanites by Hebrew Culture, operated on multi-god paradigm which the Jews (the converts to the culture of the Hebrews have inherited from part of their fore bearers (HaC'naani).

The Hebrew fore bearers, Moses and Jethro, the bona fide Hebrews priests taught about the Creator/ Musikavanhu/ Umvelinqangi/ Mudzimu Mukuru/ Unkulunkulu, the Great One as it is understood by the Africans today, but Ezra from exile, wrote 'the gods' (Elohim) because that is what he and other Jews like Nehemiah, Zerubbabel and those who had grown up in Babylon knew. The Creator in Jewish Hebrew is termed 'HaBore' but the Jews never use that designation, they have attached themselves to El of their Canaanite founding fathers.

The 'Nkosi Sikelela Africa/ Ishe Komborera Africa' in the African Anthem is an unsophisticated translation of 'God bless Africa' which reduces the entity of the Creator to a mortal king.

The term 'god' used by the north means an object of worship which is not necessarily the Creator, it could be molten image, a star, the sun, a dragon, a cow or even a man among other things.

> African Culture, Gen 14 vs 19, 1 Chr 17 vs 20, 1 Kings 8 vs 27,
> 2 Chr 2 vs 6, 2 Chr 6 vs 18, Hos 11 vs 9

1.5 Mudzimu/ Mweya/ A Soul of a Departed Elder/ Ancestral Spirit

It is critical to note that in the act of creation of humankind, the Creator breathes a soul from self unto humankind which differs from the other earlier creations where the Creator says a word and an object comes into being, in fact the soul of humankind comes from the Creator.

'And the earth was without form, and void; and darkness was upon the face of the deep. And the Spirit of the Creator moved upon the face of the waters'.

> *Gen 1 vs 2*

*'But there went up a mist from the earth, and watered the whole face of the ground.
And the Creator formed man of the dust of the ground, and breathed into his nostrils the breath of life; and man became a living soul'.*

> *Gen 2 vs 6-7*

The understanding in African Culture is that life comes from the Creator at birth and at death it returns to its source. The spirit/soul of the departed elder (ancestor or Mudzimu) returns back to the Creator or is reclaimed by the Source Soul or Mudzimu Mukuru or Mweya Mukuru where some form of reclamation by the source occurs. And so when offerings are made in African Culture to the ancestors, the implied destination of the offering has always been to the Creator and not worshipping the departed fathers (the ancestors) as overplayed by the north by labelling it heathen practice or worshipping the dead. It is actually in fact the north who are worshipping and also exhorting humanity to worship the person of a man called Joshua the son of Joseph who lived around two thousand years ago and is now late.

No human being has the actual picture of the Source Soul (the Creator) and the souls that are breathed in humanity. No human being knows the finer details of a returning soul in relation to the Source Soul, that is why Vanhu/Abantu in their offerings to the Creator sometimes say 'Vari kumhepo' for 'You in yonder place', it is from that understanding that the Creator (the Source Soul) and the departed elders are in some yonder place or Nyikadzimu. It is only in times of ngozi (avenging spirit) that the soul of the deceased is allowed by the Creator to appeal for vengeance as shall be explained on the subject the avenging spirit (ngozi) later in this work. Or alternatively an African priest doing work at a central shrine will direct the offering to the Creator but will not fail to reference the departed or the ancestors as in 'Musikavanhu/ Umvelinqangi/ Unkulunkulu/ Mudzimu Mukuru wakatungamirira madzitateguru edu muupenyu wavo wose, nhasi uno tatarisana nemuvengi, nenzara, toita seiko Mukuru-iwe'? Which

Hebrew / African Culture

means 'the Creator who guided our ancestors in all their days, today we confront an enemy, hunger, what shall we do'?

Reference to the ancestors is always made to ensure that the surviving children will not depart from the teachings of the fore bearers given in turn to them by the Creator, in pursuit of foreign myths, in that case it does not mean that Africans or Hebrews are worshipping their ancestors, but that the ancestors provide a pointer to the true form of spirituality, because it was them who were given authority to teach Hebrew or African Culture unto their children from Deuteronomy 6. A departed soul of a fore bearer will trace the normal after-death stage of life after the inheritance matter has been settled (Kurova guva), and nothing is heard again of them that died normally and in righteousness but a remembrance of their virtues. Any departed soul who will reappear as familiar spirit would not have navigated the normal after-death. Any priest who will not utter the voice/instruction of the Creator would in essence be a host to a familiar spirit of a departed person. A soul of a good/righteous departed person is reclaimed by the Source Soul and nothing of him is heard save for good works done on earth, that is why after the deaths of the patriarchs, no appearance of them in soul or physical form is known except for several references to their good works. It is the Creator's voice that manifests in a proper Svikiro/Dlozi (priest). There are other souls of departed persons that do not navigate the normal path of a departed person, such as those that are murdered, these are caused to linger till they have been appeased by way of justice/restitution. Thus an African priest (svikiro/dlozi) who fails to perform national priestly duties for the good of the nation would not be a priest of the Creator but would be a host to a familiar spirit of a departed elder, relation or stranger.

It is important to note that when the voice/instruction of the Creator is heard through a Hebrew or African priest (Svikiro reMudzimu Mukuru) at various shrines in Africa where Vanhu/Abantu make offerings, the voice/instruction is one, coherent and unambiguous, meaning it would not be coming from the myriad of departed elders but from the Creator. There is sometimes the confusion among inferior or less spiritual Hebrew or African priests who think that what is instructed from 'Vadzimu' – loosely translated as 'spirits' comes from a particular fore bearer for each clan, when in fact it would always be Mudzimu Mukuru (the Creator) at work. For that reason some priests are unable to visit a central or national shrine because they think that the instruction comes from a departed fore bearer when in fact those will be the works of Musikavanhu/ Umvelinqangi/ Mudzimu Mukuru/ Unkulunkulu except in instances of a familiar spirit, which will in fact come in a familiar voice of a known fore bearer, relation or stranger. It is important also when working with priests to verify their authenticity because a huge number of them today are magicians (n'anga/sangoma) and those that use or are host to familiar spirits (mashavi), these have no place at a shrine at all, because an offering that is presided by such personnel will not give a positive result.

Some songs in African Culture make appeals or supplications to the Creator (Mudzimu Mukuru) saying '... Mudzimu Mukuru chirege chinya' which is the same as Moses' plea before the Creator after people had murmured at the spies' report:

'Now if Thou shalt kill all this people as one man, then the nations which have heard the fame of Thee will speak, saying.
Because the Creator was not able to bring this people into the land which the Creator swore unto them, therefore the Creator hath slain them in the wilderness'.
Num 14 vs 15-16

Joel the prophet also says *'Let the priests, the ministers of the Creator, weep between the porch and the altar, and let them say, Spare Thy people, O Creator, and give not Thy inheritance to reproach, that the heathen should rule over them: wherefore should they say among the people, Where is their Creator'?*
Joel 2 vs 17

Readers need to note that the relationship between the Hebrews or Africans and their Creator is so close that, in the presence of a curse or lack of blessings the subjects can appeal to the Creator with

Hebrew / African Culture

quite a high and appealing tone (distress call) as seen above as well as from the song 'Mudzimu Mukuru chirege chinya'.

African Culture,

1.6   Kupira Mudzimu/Mweya / Perceived Intercession by the Ancestors

Spirituality in Hebrew or African Culture is heavily attached to the fore bearers or the ancestors and there is hardly anything that a Hebrew or African will say without a reference of the ancestors and ancestors play a very critical role as the departed teachers of the culture being followed by the living children this day. Often when things went wrong in Hebrew Scriptures or when a Hebrew took an oath, the names of the ancestors would be referenced in a supplication to the Creator or in the oath as clear proof that the ancestors left an indelible mark in the life of the people of Africa;

'Remember Abraham, Isaac, and Jacob, thy servants, to whom thou swarest by thine own self, and saidst unto them, I will multiply your seed as the stars of heaven, and all this land that I have spoken of will I give unto your seed, and they shall inherit it forever'.

Exo 32 vs 13

'And yet for all that, when they be in the land of their enemies, I will not cast them away, neither will I abhor them utterly, and to break my covenant with them: for I am their Creator.
But I will for their sakes remember the covenant of their ancestors, whom I brought forth out of the land of Egypt in the sight of the heathen'.

Lev 26 vs 44-45

As mentioned earlier, the souls of African or Hebrew departed elders are reclaimed by the Creator at death as they came from the same at birth. When Vanhu/Abantu make offerings, sometimes instead of directing their supplications to the Creator they say 'Our ancestors, may you pass our petition to the Creator of Heaven and Earth'. They say this for the reason above that indeed the souls of their departed fore bearers have been reclaimed back by the source (the Creator), and that they are now at one with the Source Soul. Or alternatively at a central shrine a priest will make an offering on behalf of all members of the African community and will therefore not go through the individual family ancestral hierarchy but will speak as follows; 'The Creator of heaven and earth of our fore bearers, who has guided our ancestors in their trials and tribulations, hear our supplications that we make before thee today, we have been hard hit by a drought, and our children are starving, show us our transgression that we may correct it, we seek thy mercy (Mudzimu Mukuru wakatungamirira madzitateguru edu munguva dzose, inzwaiwo nhuna dzedu dzetinopira kwamuri nhasi, onai Mudzimu Mukuru pasi raoma, vana vedu vava kufa nenzara, tirakidzei mhosho dzedu tizvichenure, Mudzimu Mukuru chirege chinya, tateterera Mukuruiwe).

This is a typical supplication from all time back as made by the fore bearers through to David and Solomon to the present day, which today has been labelled heathenism. And so when the central/ national offering system made up of the bona fide Hebrew or African hierarchy of the Priests, King and Chiefs fell as African or Hebrew heads converted to Christianity, offerings fell down to the family level as well where most priests or elders instead of referencing the Creator of their fore bearers as referenced herein to avoid getting lost spiritually, have put the names of their fore bearers in the offering hierarchy. If the central offering had been maintained, it would have been impossible to put the names of the fore bearers in hierarchy to the Creator but referencing would be ideal.

At family level, the matter of offering through the family departed elders hierarchy was also partly due to the understanding among Vanhu/Abantu that communication directly with the Creator was a preserve of the priests as happened at Sinai as it was them (Moses and Aaron) who had the proper sanctity/authority that befit communication with the Creator. At Sinai the same elders were afraid to communicate with the Creator directly and today in the absence of full throttle shrine procedures, the same people will not face the Awesome Creator directly but indirectly nekuti Mudzimu Mukuru unoera (because the Creator is holy) and any small mistake may result in fatalities. When the Hebrew High

Hebrew / African Culture

Priesthood could not be traced for several reasons, offerings came to the family level where African elders were quite informed on who had to address the Creator directly – the Levites and so the elders had to take the winding long route and avoid direct communication.

In the same regard, an enquiry at family level unto the Creator / Musikavanhu/ Umvelinqangi/ Mudzimu Mukuru/ Unkulunkulu, perceived by some Africans as enquiring unto to the fore bearers usually demands that the living make a bira offering accompanied by a beast offering, here most Africans misunderstand it altogether in that they dissociate themselves from such offerings thinking that such offerings are meant for the ancestors when such offerings (mapira) are for the Creator as detailed later under 'bira' for these must be done at appropriate times without fail. If they are not done accordingly the associated blessings to the family cease and upon enquiry, the failure to comply with 'bira' provisions are cited as the causes of the family misfortunes and calamities.

In the Hebrew Scriptures often are the departed fore bearers referenced by the living, the reasons are basically that the ancestors provide a role model to the living with regards to the work they did while they lived, and this in any way does not necessarily imply that Africans or Hebrews worship their departed elders. What in fact intercedes for Africans or Hebrews are the good works of the departed elders which made a distinguishing mark to the Creator to warrant everlasting blessings upon the children of the departed Africans or Hebrews to the extent that huge resources or riches were bequeathed to the Hebrews on the basis of the good deeds of the ancestors and when ancestors have such an impeccable track record, they do not need to be forgotten at any cost.

African Culture, Gen 2 vs 7, Gen 32 vs 9

1.7   Good Deeds of the Ancestors (Madzitateguru) Interceding for their Children

The good deeds of the fore bearers intercede for the children in African or Hebrew Culture. When an elder passes on with a good spiritual record, even the children will ride on that moral resume but should an elder be a cause of problems for everyone while he or she lives even the children will be affected sometimes in as simple as inheriting a bad name to as harsh as inheriting an avenging spirit;

'Remember thy servants, Abraham, Isaac and Jacob; look not unto the stubbornness of this people, nor to their wickedness, nor to their sin'.

Det 9 vs 27

'And the Creator said unto him (Moses on Mt Nebo), this is the land which I swore unto Abraham, unto Isaac, and unto Jacob, saying, I will give it unto thy seed: I have caused thee to see it with thine eyes, but thou shalt not go over thither'.

Det 34 vs 4

And so when the departed elders lived in righteousness, Vanhu/Abantu understand that by mentioning the good deeds of the fore bearers in an offering to the Creator, the good works will help bring positive results as seen on Moses praying for the children of Jacob after the sin of the golden calf, and the Creator responded accordingly by acknowledging indeed that were it not of the covenant sworn between the Creator and the Hebrew ancestors who did good in their time, the Creator would have decimated the entire generation. **As stated in the Preface, a good deed is an expression of righteousness and is the ultimate prayer.**

This is why in African or Hebrew Culture, the ancestors are very central, they have given the guidelines of life to their children, which they in turn obtained from the Creator of heaven and earth. The ancestral link is very visible even in the Hebrew Scriptures as it obtains also in African Culture. The Hebrews have survived the wrath of heaven or other nations for the reason of a perfect ancestral link/heritage/ blessings. To this perfect relationship the irony is that, the north have cried heathen worshipping of the dead to the Africans while at the same time applauding the works of the Hebrew patriarchs, when in fact

Hebrew / African Culture

they are the same people, living the same way but separated by race perceptions and time.

African Culture, 2 Kings 13 vs 23

1.8   Africa - the Domain Land of Hebrew Culture

The following scriptural references define geographically the land of Africa, the domain land of Hebrew Culture and nearly everything recorded in the Hebrew Scriptures revolve around that land;

'A river went out of Eden to water the garden; and from thence it was parted, and became into four heads.
The name of the first is Pison: that is it which compasses the whole land of Havilah (Chavilah, Chavira, Mavirira), where there is gold;
The gold of that land is good: there is bdellium and the onyx stone.
And the name of the second river is Gihon: the same is it that compasseth the whole land of Ethiopia.
And the name of the third river is Hiddekel: that is which goes toward the east of Assyria.
And the fourth river is the Euphrates'.

Gen 2 vs 10-14

The land of Hebrew Culture, Africa, is given here from the south where there is a lot of gold, roughly this area stretches from the Republic of South Africa to Ghana formerly known as the Gold Coast through the gold rich countries of Zimbabwe and the Congo. Therefore the first description of land in the Hebrew Scripture is Africa, meaning the whole Hebrew Culture centres around Africa and not Greece, nor Rome, nor any other land and the logic is that at that time, people were more interested in writing about themselves than digressing into third party history, culture or geography. If Hebrew Culture was for the people of Siberia or Mexico, the land that the Hebrew Scriptures would have described in the same detail would be Siberia or Mexico including climate and geographical features. There is no way that the people of Mexico would write about their culture, spirituality and history on Tibetan land if they have no link to Tibet. There is no argument here about the mineral riches bound by this region; the first river is therefore any of Orange, Vhembe (Limpopo), Kasambavezi (Zambezi) or the Congo rivers. The second river is Nile, which was split by the northern translators into the Blue and White Nile, where is the gold and other minerals along the Nile? If those minerals were all mined out, by what precision mineral extraction technology that cleaned every minute measure of mineral along the Nile? The exclusion of the first river emanating from the south may have been an attempt to exclude Vanhu/Abantu from their story—Hebrew Scriptures. The third river is the Hiddekel and the fourth river is Euphrates. The four rivers flow and water the land of Africa, the land of the Hebrews, the same is Eden. The Hebrew Scriptures start with mentioning the south and later the south is mentioned in relation to Abraham exploring further south, Moses' sojourn with Jethro, Joseph in Egypt, Hebrew nation born and bred in Africa, exodus out of Egypt and when Jerusalem fell to Babylon — the Hebrew Diaspora under the leadership of Prophet Jeremiah and Johanan went to Africa, not to Rome.

1.8.1   The Riches of The Land of Africa

The entire African continent is like a garden with the evergreen forests, good soil of high fertility, good rains that can support very high natural yields associated with a garden. The north have misconceptualized Eden as a point area somewhere in Iraq not remembering that the four rivers in question are not at one point. The African land is the richest land in all riches, not excluding agriculture, to give it the status of the garden. The land has very good soils, good rains, good sunlight, fresh waters that can support the most natural agriculture on intensive basis as befitting a garden all year round. Africa is rich, huge and good. The same region has vast oil reserves, gold, platinum, rare earth metals, silver, diamond, timber, iron, animals (game and domestic), fruits, honey, milk, abundant fresh waters and intelligent human resources. The level of mineral wealth obtaining on the African continent is to an extent that the gold, diamond, platinum, coal and other special minerals literally occur on the surface and usually extraction is by open cast mines. Africans literally walk on gold even when they visit a friend or when they take a walk in the wild. The author reminisces in childhood when hunting birds using

Hebrew / African Culture

catapult loaded with a rough stone that has now been discovered to be rough diamond.

The region defined by the boundaries mentioned herein is an economic power house, fully packaged and self sustaining region given to the Africans by heaven. As mentioned earlier it is a region of rich soils, good rains and abundant sunshine with ability to yield grain produce to feed the entire planet and a surplus yield if and only if the people were united. However for the reason of infighting between children of one family due to foreign influence, there is no time for agriculture and industrial production, for people are wandering from place to place afraid of war from fellow brothers. Africa depicted on the cover page of this book, is one region which if it were to close its borders to the other nations, will not run short of anything; in fact if it were to close its borders and promote trade among its states, the other races of the world would cry 'we have run short of this and that'.

Sunshine which is so abundant in Africa and is the most undervalued natural resource for the reason that sunshine is scientifically the source of food, air to breath, water, green habitat and life. There are no superlatives from existing words of the existing languages to describe fully the extent of beauty of Africa. The land can sustain agriculture twelve months a year compared to northern climates that are frozen for the larger part of the year. The rains are natural which makes farming cheaper. Sunshine, the critical ingredient for food, air and water cycles is twelve hours a day and intense. If Vanhu/Abantu have the belief, they can work on the land to produce unprecedented quantities of natural foods and huge economies with strong currencies and no target would be impossible. As the global population puts strain on the planet, the future belongs to those nations endowed with natural resources, there would be no nation that shall be sustained by third party natural resources or raw materials to prop up their industrial growth for the reason that all nations will evolve industrially and be able to add value to their natural resources and create jobs for their people. The fact that Europe's combined top ten countries (United Kingdom, Germany, France, Italy, Spain, Portugal, Switzerland, Belgium, Netherlands and Luxemburg — 2,259,167 sq km total land area, total GDP $14,401 billion, 2014) are smaller than the D.R. Congo (2,344,858 sq km total land area, total GDP 18.5 billion, 2014) in land resources but are economically bigger than the entire African continent, is just a momentary or instantaneous event necessitated by imperialism, Africa will for sure take the lead. While the land of Africa is very suitable for agriculture, the people of Africa are begging for food hand-outs of usually genetically modified junk food. Industrial pollution is nullifying the fresh water resources and people are dying of water born industrial poisons or the cost of purifying water is beyond reach yet the water falls in its freshest state.

While Europe can sustain a huge population in a land smaller than the D.R. Congo, any effort to control the population of Africa on the premise of alleviating poverty is like an act of conflict whose aim is to strategically restrict the population to a small and controllable number. And when two neighbouring African nations want to do business, why would they go to foreign nations to get other currencies to facilitate the transaction? In terms of value addition of African natural resources, there is no win-win situation between African countries with huge natural resources and third party countries that add value to those natural resources and sell for the reason that often adding value can be as simple as polishing a mineral or simply exposing fresh milk to bacteria which causes it to sour or rot and that cannot compare to the value of ownership of that resource. Oil trading benchmarks or indexes are in northern terms (Nymex or Brent) yet they are not the top producers of oil. If Africans think of partnership with foreign investors, investor equity must be linked to African equity in businesses outside Africa. The northern business proposals out of exploitation, have often brought investments proposals read between the lines of equivalent investment of a dollar with an expected return of a million dollars to expatriate home - economic sabotage, looting and fraud.

While this is true that Africa is the richest continent, the owner of the African inheritance, the Ndebele child, the Tswana child, the Shona child, the Chewa child, the Nyanja child, the Hutu child, the Tutsi child, the Amhara child, the Acholi child, the Ovambo child, the Herero child, the Mandinga child, the Congo child, the Ashanti child, the Kuyu child, the Hausa child, the Sotho child, the Zulu child, the Xhosa child, the Swazi child, the Tonga child, the Changani child, the Makhuwa child, the Sena child, the Lomwe child, the Bemba child, the Lozi child, the Lunda child, the Luvale child, the Kaonde child, the Sukuma child, the Gogo child, the Haya child, the Nyakyusa child, the Nyamwezi child, the Chaga child, the Luo child, the Yao child, the Tumbuka child, the Kalanga child, the Masai child, the Yoruba child, the Igbo child, the Arabi child, the Fulani child, the Akan child, the Dagomba child, the Ewe child, the Gurima child, the Mossi child, the Gurunsi child, the Sefuno child, the Lobi child, the Bobo child, the Mande child, the Balanda child, the Manjakwa child, the Guru child, the Gorani child, the Zaghawa child, the Kanembo child, the Kotoko child, the Bulala child, the Maba child, the Mende child, the Temne child, the Bioko child, the Bubi child, the Mina child, the Kabiye child, the Adja child, the Funi child, the Bariba child, the Jola child, the Sarahule child, the Bapunu child, the Nzebi child, the Obamba child, the Soninge child, the Bambara child, the Malinke child, the Baya child, the Banda child, the Mandja child, the Sara child, the Mbaka child, the Yakoma child, the Oromo child, the Tigrinya child, the Sidamo child, the Garaginya child, the Shangela child, the Kunama child, the Saho child, the Afara child, the Sango child, the Ovimbundu child, the Luganda child, the Basoga child, the Lango child, the Kalenjini child, the Luhya child, the Kisii child, the Embu child, the Kamba child, the Nyarwanda child, the Luba child, the Anamongo child, the Monokutuba child, the Sangha child, the Bateke child, the Gola child, the Gio child, the Somali child, the Juba child, the Dinka child, the Venda child, the Lingala, and each and every African child not mentioned here is tending her/his impoverished family's few remaining herd if any, after having left home in the morning upon eating the half stale remains of the previous night's family meagre meal. He will spend the whole day tending the animals feeding on the depleted wild fruits and when he returns home in the evening, it will be time for the family's half and meagre supper, while the north, east and west, have become the shareholders to the vast African resources and are living like kings in expensive hotels, are in board meetings or in executive planes, strategizing on how best they can maximize their profits from the rich continent. There is therefore no justification for African children, the children of the inheritance of the patriarchs - Vana Venhaka, to starve or long for any goodies for they have everything.

1.8.2   The Aftermath of Imperialism

What has alienated Vanhu/Abantu are the territorial boundaries drawn up by the north in their scramble for the African inheritance that started off as missionary incursions by the Christian missionaries whose main focus was to teach the successful Africans about the virtues of poverty, 'blessed are the poor' while other teams of explorers were exploring ways of getting the African wealth. Border disputes between Namibia-Botswana, Ethiopia-Somalia, Nigeria-Cameroon, Morocco-Saharawi and others must be resolved with the involvement of Traditional Chiefs. If a piece of land is agreed to belong to a particular chieftainship then it does not matter which side of which colonial border it is, what matters is that the owner Traditional Chief has the land for the reason that the African land was a continuous land with one people and no political boundaries. What is now known as the 'Middle East' today is North East Africa, and therefore the concept of a United Africa - the African Union, must never exclude the 'Middle East' or Arabia at any cost for reason of common history, language and culture. In the spirit of the African Union, the author has treated the matter of slave trade between mainland Africans and the children of Ishmael in North East Africa as an internal family matter which must not be referenced at all times concerning the re-union. The matters of African sub-boundaries like ECOWAS (Economic Community of West African States), SADC (Southern Africa Development Community), OPEC (Organization of the Petroleum Exporting Countries), PTA (Preferential Trade Area for some African states over other African states – business confusion), GCC (Gulf Cooperation Council), COMESA (Common Market for Eastern and Southern Africa) and other sub-groupings are trivial and divisive. The African family has been so divided that while the north talk of European Union on one side, Vanhu/ Abantu have lost the African togetherness and hospitality towards each other. Instead when you take a walk across Africa from the south to the north, the South Africans in the south have embraced the former imperialist - the Boer, to an extent that the foreigner is more citizen in that country than a fellow African, a Xhosa, Zulu or Ndebele who lives across the border! You go further north, the Congolese boast of more fluency in French than their African dialect.

To prove that the referenced sub-groupings are ineffective, they keep on being formed day after day to replace or complement one and the other. Issues of bilateral ties or friendships between any two African member states is like bilateral ties between members of the same family like brother1 – brother2 friendship, brother5 – brother3 friendship, sister4 – brother2 friendship; what is the motivation of such friendship that surpasses the overall family unity? If brothers in a given family begin to have preferred family member ties, where is the family heading to? Family friendship solves it all, when the family is a united entity, then there is friendship between each and every family member. If the African people unite under the background of such vast resources as the giant African Union with a single currency with no border from the Cape (South Africa) to the Caspian Sea (Iran), the northern currencies will plunge spot on and the success pendulum will swing this time in favour of Africa. In the absence of the African Union, trade and cooperation among Africans is isolated and marginal. Instead huge African resources like oil are benefiting the north, east and west who buy the unprocessed products in super bulk.

Concerning the African Union, it is common knowledge that over the years, the world has taken turns to exploit, abuse, cheat and fight the African people. There has not been a genuine win-win political and business partner for the African people. To make the best use of their potential and resources, Africans need to forge a relationship among themselves, consolidate fair trade among themselves wherein they will have respect for each other. Africa and Africans have always been an opportunity for exploitation by other races. In fact, there is a huge market for Africa within itself in business terms. Often the children of Ishmael empowered by oil revenue choose to buy their fruits and vegetables from remote bio-modified sources when within Africa, natural and quality produce would be available. The world's top stock markets, a handful in the north and a few in the west are all sustained by the African resources. If Vanhu/Abantu today were going to hold on to their oil, platinum, gold, diamonds and other resources, jitters will overwhelm the markets external to Africa, meaning that they are sustained by the African wealth. In the same token, the world's top economies are supported and hinged by the African wealth. There is therefore power in African Unity and not in the blood of the late Joshua the son of Joseph as often chanted by misinformed Hebrews on Sun Day worshipping schools. In fact, the future great nations will not be measured by the amount of arms of war technologies which they will own but by their natural resources and market. All nations will evolve industrially to be able to value-add their natural resources and sell to the market and there will not be any nation that will survive by adding value to third party natural resources to create value for themselves and jobs for their people.

The first stage of industrial development by all nations would be to own their market by providing for all the food and industrial requirements of their people without need for import and such capability depends on the availability of natural resources and therefore the future belongs to those nations endowed with natural resources and Africa is top of the list. And for Africa to develop, it must own the market by preferential acquisition where all nations within the continent will require all their needs to come from within by encouraging African scientists and entrepreneurs to produce for domestic consumption and if they cannot then they may have to starve. It will take quite long for Africa to develop to the level of other nations if the market is free for all. The people of Africa must take pride in consuming the products made by their children in order to develop the children. It is like a parent of a child who is crawling and beginning to walk, any attempt by the child to start walking must be supported and celebrated than for the parent to go to the neighbour's child who is already walking and start ululating. If other nations are making smart technologies while African children are making heavy brick technologies, those bricks must be consumed by the African technology market in order to technologically develop the children.

1.8.3   The Tribal Conflicts

It is easier for foreigners to buy minerals at super cheap prices from Africa or smuggle minerals out of the Congo or Darfur when the Congolese or those Africans from Darfur are at war with each other. It is easier for foreigners to exploit Iraqi oil when the Iraqis are at war with each other. Who will check on the extracting firm's oil meter when Sunnis and Shias take turns to bomb each other? The extracting firm is a usual northern, western or eastern business outfit, which takes every opportunity to make money and an unchecked oil meter is an opportunity to play with figures – 'look Abu Sunni, before Abu Shia attacked, the oil meter was showing that we extracted forty-nine million barrels of oil in the previous week, but when the Shia attacked and you ran away and disappeared for two working weeks, we faced challenges beyond our control to an extent that we only managed to extract two (2) barrels in the two weeks in question'. The manufacturers of arms of war literally thrive on African wars and conflicts among other nations. They sell guns and empower their entrepreneurs and create jobs for their folks at home

Hebrew / African Culture

from Africans at war or they exploit resources of Africa when Africans are fighting each other, so they heavily depend on African and other conflicts. The north or west do not fight war on their land for they do not want a single casualty on their people, rather they export war and its machinery to far lands for economic and political gains. It is very pertinent for Africans to realise that and make peace among themselves and begin to advance the welfare of Africa. Vanhu/Abantu need to learn that from times of recorded history, the north or west have been involved in all wars including the more recent ones; World War 1, World War 2, Cold War, African Liberation Wars, Gulf Wars and African Wars. In that regard it would be naive for Africans to engage the north in search for peace in Africa. Peace in Africa can only come from African brothers and sisters who realise and understand the value of their brotherhood. Northern arms factories are sustained partly by African conflicts and therefore peace for Africa is not a worthwhile cause for the north or west, it is a business liability. A United Nations peace initiative for Africa is not a solution for African conflicts for the reason that the United Nations was formed by the north, west and east, constituted by the same and decisions are made and broken by the north, west and east when and where it suits them.

Africans are reminded how the north and west dissented on Egypt and Libya recently, brutally murdering a sitting head of state and leaving the countries in turmoil, now arms of war made in the same north, west and east are filtering into the ensuing conflict and arms industries which contribute to their GDPs are recording brisk business with the impression that some wars are started to grow economies out of recession. On the other hand, it would be unimaginable for Vanhu/Abantu with their unhu/ubuntu to team up for whatever reason and invade a European state like Belgium or Luxemburg; that would mark the end of this civilization for the last vestiges of it are still in existence in Africa this day.

African governments need to be wary of economic formulae that lobby for privatisation of public infrastructure in Africa proposed by the north, east or west to give business opportunities for their business executives while back in Europe/West, public infrastructure remain in the hands of government to protect the ordinary people. And the economic advantage that the north and west have today is on the basis of slavery, imperialism, mineral and agro-exploration. One cannot define the northern infrastructure without the African foundation and backbone.

> African Oral Tradition, Gen 13 vs 14-15, Gen 15 vs 18, Exo 33 vs 3, Joshua 15 vs 4, 2 Chr 7 vs 8, 2 Sam 8 vs 3

1.9   Muti Usina Zita/ The Tree of Sustenance and Life - (The Tree of Knowledge)

Muti usina zita (tree without name), is a tree that occurs a few hundred kilometres to the north east of the Great Zimbabwe shrine. The tree, unlike any other fruit trees, is not accessible by any commoner for food or sustenance. There is in fact a protocol to access the 'fruit' of the tree for food or for use as a shrine;

'And the Creator commanded the man, saying, of every tree of the garden thou may freely eat:
But of the tree of the knowledge of good and evil, thou shalt not eat of it: for in the day that thou eatest thereof thou shalt surely die'.

Gen 2 vs 16-17

The tree is accessible in times of stress or drought; a priest accompanies the people to seek material and moral providence from the Creator. It is only after the procedure has been followed that life and sustenance are derived from the tree with no name 'Muti usina zita'. An ordinary person cannot go to this tree and start asking for sustenance from the Creator.

There are in fact matters that are forbidden in African Culture similar to the tree of knowledge in the Hebrew Scriptures and failure to uphold the protocol has serious consequences among the people in the same manner as what happened to humanity from the day when the forbidden fruit was eaten against a background of a prohibition. It is important to note that these spectacular similarities between African and Hebrew Culture confirm without any doubt that the two are indeed one culture. The concept of Muti

Hebrew / African Culture

usina zita in providence terms is identical to;

'Then said the Creator unto Moses, behold, I will rain bread from heaven for you; and the people shall go out and gather a certain rate every day, that I may prove them, whether they will walk in my law, or no.
And it shall come to pass, that on the sixth day they shall prepare that which they bring in; and it shall be twice as much as they gather daily'.

Exo 16 vs 4-5

Thus in times of famine or food insufficiency, the hand of the Creator would manifest as in the exodus or in more recent times at a tree known as Muti usina zita (a tree without name) for sustenance, which was then later desecrated by the European missionaries who often visited most African shrines without the requisite sanctity, authority or cleanness.

African Culture, African Oral Tradition, Gen 21 vs 19, 1 Kings 19 vs 5-7, 2 Kings 4 vs 3-6

1.10   Chisingarimwi / The Sabbath

One day in seven, on a day called Chisingarimwi (literally the day of no work), is a day of solemn rest. In fact the Sabbath, Chisingarimwi, in African Culture is so revered to the extent that failure to abide by it invites punishment from the spiritual realm to the offender of the form of being bitten by a snake or being harassed by a mental patient or being gored by own cattle or even struck by lighting on the very day of violating the Sabbath or sometime thereafter;

'And on the seventh day the Creator ended the work of creation and rested on the seventh day from all work of creation.
And the Creator blessed the seventh day, and sanctified it: because in it the Creator had rested from all work which the Creator had made.'

Gen 2 vs 2-3,

The Sabbath among some Africans does not occur on a Saturday perse due to a few changes that have happened over the years as people moved from one place to another and made adaptations to their habitats but Saturday is regarded as the national or universal Sabbath among most tribes which coincides with the Jewish Sabbath. The various Sabbaths that most tribes have adapted to range among communities from Wednesday to Saturday, the Sabbath range which includes that of the children of Ishmael in Islam. In Hebrew or African Culture, the Sabbath day requires people to abstain from work which relates to earning of income or sustenance but work that relates to day to day chores like cooking for the family or for the visitor or stranger and tending animals is exempted. People do not congregate to pray or sing but they simply rest and on the day of rest they can visit their extended families.

The Sabbath though has come under threat from the teachings of Christianity which have sanctified Sun Day for the purpose of sun worshipping which has defiled the land. A defiled land will inherit the curses of droughts, natural disasters, hunger and pestilence among other calamities.

In place of the Sabbath, the north keep the Sun Day in honour of the Sun and if the Sun Day is not dedicated for sun worshipping, why call it Sun Day? Why would the north call the first day of the week Sun Day if they are very sure that its not dedicated to worshipping the sun on Sun Day, what is the point in calling something with one title when it is the opposite of the implied sense? Or perhaps that is the only day in the north that the sun shines. If the Greek Scriptures were meant to supersede Hebrew Culture as the future of spirituality or as the new covenant for all civilizations, the north would not have gone back to pagan days of worshipping the sun which was done by their founding fathers as implied in Sun Day, instead a compromise day of rest could have been selected perhaps. The fact that the Greeks settled for their original day of worship meant that the so called 'New Testament' was not new at all, but was simply an expression of cultural wars or religious propaganda to try and displace the popular

Hebrew / African Culture

Hebrew Culture without a single battle.

African Culture, African Oral Tradition, Exo 16 vs 25-30, Exo 20 vs 8-11,
Exo 23 vs 12, Exo 31 vs 13-17, Exo 34 vs 21, Exo 35 vs 2-3, Lev 19 vs 3,
Lev 19 vs 30, Lev 23 vs 3, Lev 26 vs 2, Num 15 vs 32-36, Det 5 vs 12-15,
1 Kings 12 vs 32-33, 2 Kings 4 vs 23, 1 Chr 23 vs 31, 2 Chr 8 vs 13, Eze 20 vs 20

1.11 Chisingarimwi/ Sabbath, a Hebrew/African Marker/Identifier

The Sabbath is a marker, sign, identifier or a pointer to a Hebrew or a convert. It is a discernible lifestyle of a Hebrew or a convert, the children of Ishmael have kept it from the days of the patriarchs, Vanhu/ Abantu have kept Chisingarimwi from their beginning and the Jews keep the Sabbath;

'Wherefore the children of Abraham shall keep the Sabbath, to observe the Sabbath throughout their generations, for a perpetual covenant.
It is a sign between Me and the children of Abraham forever: for in six days the Creator made heaven and earth, and on the seventh day was refreshed'.

Exo 31 vs 16-17

The strangers keep the Sun Day and not the Hebrew Sabbath. The spectacular aspect of the Sabbath in Africa is that it was not by coercion or by conversion but it traces itself back to the days of the fore bearers. All the oral evidence that is there in the culture agrees to the fact that the Sabbath has been there in African Culture from the beginning of the people themselves.

The European missionaries found the Sabbath in full force. Upon conversion, most Africans have taken the habit of following two days of rest in a week, the Sun Day, the day that the north have dedicated to their sun god, as well as the Sabbath (Chisingarimwi) of the Creator so that they keep and conform to the traditions of the fore bearers. This is so for the reason that any African, a convert of northern mythologies or an adherent African is fully informed on what it means to breach the Sabbath. The Sabbath has not ceased to be with the Africans or the Bona fide Hebrews as it was a covenant forever. As an identifier of the Hebrews, a snap survey among the Africans today in Africa will tell of the Sabbath, one day in seven being kept without fail. The actual and original Hebrew Sabbath needs to be harmonized among the Hebrew family on their land by an enquiry of the Creator through a priest to enable the family to pursue spiritual and business matters as it was during the days of the fore bearers and abstain from keeping the Sun Day. **A more physical identifier over and above the dark skin, is the ability of hair to lock into a Nazarite hair lock shown of the book cover** as shall be seen in Chapter 5 Hebrew Scriptural Race Evidence.

African Culture, African Oral Tradition

1.12 Musoro weMusha/ The Hierarchy of the Hebrew/ African Family

The African family has a head who is the man and the woman is the assistant as given in the referenced scripture;

'And the Creator said, it is not good that the man should be alone; I will make him an help meet for him'.

Gen 2 vs 18

'And the Creator caused a deep sleep to fall upon Adam, and he slept: and the Creator took one of his ribs and closed up the flesh instead thereof;
And the rib, which the Creator had taken from man, made a woman, and brought her unto the man.
And Adam said, this is now bone of my bones, and flesh of my flesh: she shall be called woman, because she was taken out of man.
Therefore shall a man leave his father and his mother, and shall cleave unto his wife: and they shall

become one flesh'.

Gen 2 vs 21-24

The African family has over centuries been united and peaceful under the referenced hierarchy, but of late has been under siege from the cultural values of the north and west which tend to undo the hierarchy in question. The advent of cultural values external to African Culture, under the guise of equal 'rights' have created two viciously competing persons in one family; the result has been endless fights, divorces and sometimes murder in the family. African or Hebrew Culture acknowledges the issue of rights of all parties to a marriage but under strictly the given hierarchy. Institutions with two equal leaders often have decision making deadlocks for two leaders will always have differences in opinion. There is always tremendous teamwork between the two parties to a marital union to raise up a family of high moral values with full acknowledgement of the fact that man is the leader of the family. The issue of gender equality is an external agenda to create an uneasy atmosphere in the African family as the head and his assistant begin to compete unnecessarily. The women of the north and west were given all the 'rights' and the result was moral decadence.

By design the anatomy of the female is tender and less muscular and is well articulated for the growth of the foetus and child upbringing while the male is stronger, resilient and more muscular to suit the demands required of the man to fend for and protect his family. The female gender is naturally designed to nurture the offspring. Assigning strenuous duties like those of the army to women or engaging them in heavy sporting activity offset the female reproductive health. There are army or war drills that require soldiers to crawl on their stomach and breast, how are women supposed to handle that given the tenderness/sensitivity of their breasts. Some women are known to develop reproductive cycle temperaments that affect their normal operation, how much worse does that put them in a heavy battle? War assignment are for man and when women who bring up children become war experts, so shall it be with children they will raise and the children will not be afraid of spilling human blood as a result of teachings derived from the mother. Conception of life occurs in the mother and when the mother goes to war and start destroying the life that she conceived, then that is extremism. Is there any role that is greater than nurturing life? If women continue to clamour for male roles while ignoring nurturing life then it is unbelievable ignorance of the grand scheme of life usually championed by illiterate gender lobby groupings. Sending women to war assignments interrupts the crucial bonding process between mother and child and often later in life some of these children may fail to take good care of children, may even abandon their children for they will not understand the value of the bond between mother and child for they never experienced it in the first place.

Actually, sending women to war away from their children interrupts or destroys the bonding process that is necessary between young children and their mother which in future may cause children to throw away or give away their own offspring because they would lack an understanding of mother and child bond and how that bond has survived the human race. Children survival and growth is enhanced within the reach of the mother and in the absence of the mother children lack food, love, education and morality and these are issues that should be best understood by the women of all the people. Modern female liberalism is detaching the woman away from nurturing life towards the abyss of human extinction as the female rejects her role in the human survival scheme of things. The real fall of the modern female from civility, is her reluctance to breast feed her offspring in order to maintain the fullness of the breasts so that in her imagination, men will look at her with 'more interest' while the offspring is given some junk milk formulae which may negatively affect child development.

Interchanging gender roles in cases like a) reversing the family hierarchy by making the mother head will cause the males to lose interest in family which all along was done to preserve his name and if his name no longer has any guarantee of survival, why would he bother venture into family anyway? If there are any gender indulgences he needs from women, he may choose to do that without a marital or family commitment. b) If society fundamentally changes the role of women to fending for the family and not nurturing life, what it will mean is that women will preoccupy themselves with survival other than conceiving children if there is no guarantee that someone will help them fend for the children. Most women today who are taking demanding

careers hardly have any time for family and such scenarios will lead to the demise of a civilization. So these established trends were not out of patriarchy or male chauvinism but were well thought order.

On the job market, a balance or compromise can be struck by employing much more women in the equally awarding professions of teaching and nursing while men can handle the army and security assignments. Readers are reminded of how many children are abused by male teachers or nurses, how would the face of educational systems change if all teachers were to be women in terms of safety of children and the general tenderness or hospitality associated with motherhood? Women do not use force when they raise up children and when children adapt to that, it has the potential to change a civilization for the better in that children will learn to do good not from fear of punishment. The male and female are different but they complement each other. If two or more objects choose to do one role, there will remain a role undone. And being the head of the family does not translate to a king or the better part of the house bearing in mind that in anatomy, the head will be of no use if the nose refuses to breath.

In matters of spirituality, the man leads his family in that he has the knowledge of how to prepare for an offering at family level and the execution thereof. The wife may do so in the absence of the family head and always will do so with the requisite sanctity for example the manner of women must not be upon her or must not visit her during the execution of the offering, such qualifications naturally make men appropriate but not necessarily more suitable because a woman who has ceased to be with the manner of women can equally do the job. The problem with gender lobbying is that it is being led or championed by divorcees and their hangers on - the estranged spouses and the single for life/celibates. These are the ones who have not lived up to the challenges of raising up a family in the presence of both heads. They have sometimes opted for a divorce in matters of petty misunderstandings and sometimes have regretfully wished they had endured longer in the marriage or have not divorced at all. An ideal champion or leader in gender matters must be a woman in a thriving marriage, who has managed to hold together a family unit in sometimes turbulent phases and such candidates would be well informed on how to strike the compromises that build up families as gender matters get addressed. A divorcee usually would strive to settle old scores encountered with a single spouse but now against the entire opposite gender.

African Culture, Num 30 vs 7-8

1.13   Wanano/ Marriage

In African or Hebrew Culture a marriage is a requirement and not an option and if one is not married he/ she is not considered to be in the ideal mode, because an unmarried person, has not fulfilled the responsibility laid upon him by the Creator to be fruitful and multiply;

'And Adam said, this is now bone of my bones, and flesh of my flesh: she shall be called woman, because she was taken out of man.
Therefore shall a man leave his father and his mother, and shall cleave unto his wife: and they shall become one flesh'.

Gen 2 vs 23-24

If a person chooses celibacy, the name of that person will not be continued or carried forward for he will have no children to carry his name. The referenced scripture says a man 'shall' and not 'may' leave his father and mother and 'shall' cleave and not 'may' cleave unto his wife if he can as suggested by Paul when he was trying to justify the unjustifiable – celibacy. In some Christian denominations (Catholicism) the entire clerical hierarchy are celibate all the days of their life while the designer of the human body (the Creator) designed the human body with the following requirement which the Hebrews or Africans have adhered to with all due care;

'**It is not good that the man should be alone; I will make him an help meet for him'.**
'**Therefore shall a man leave his father and his mother, and shall cleave unto his wife: they shall be one flesh'.**

Hebrew / African Culture

Thus humankind being of the quoted design, those in the priesthood are thus caught in the unspiritual instances of undergoing the flow of seed while they sleep due to overstressing the human body by anxiety caused by longing for the bed of marriage, or being exposed to the possibility of coveting daughters and wives of the members of their congregation, it is because by design the human body cannot be configured for celibacy. Marriage is therefore a must and not an option. It is by the design of heaven that a human being requires the physiological and psychological benefits that come out of a marriage. It is also important to note that the African or Hebrew marriage is bi-gender (it involves man and woman and not man and man nor woman and woman) and not sodomite as given later in this work.

The threat to the African marriage today is that it is lightly recognized in African constitutions which are largely derived from the northern justice systems where the African marriage falls under 'customary law', where it is often considered an inferior marital union. More recognition is given to the paper one, the more 'legally binding' marital union which is not necessarily a higher commitment marriage for commitment is in the heart and not on a paper certificate.

Marriage, the building block of a civilization is under threat from lose unions where partners are free to walk away as and when they feel so without a commitment to the other party. In a marriage there are roles which are shared by men and women which one person may fail to fully cover which may result in development of a population with children short of certain fundamental human requirements. Children who grew up in a single parent home may lack bonding with the missing parent and that lack may affect the way in which they will raise their children. The role of the wife in African Culture is not restricted to her husband and children but that when she is married the whole extended family look up to her as a mother or daughter-in-law. When people see her, they refer to her as the wife of so and so family, (mukadzi wekwanhingi) and she becomes totally committed to the new family in word and deed and most families in Africa are strengthened or stabilised by the wife. When Ruth' husband died, she was inherited by a kinsman in another aspect of African or Hebrew Culture called Kugara Khaka which ensures that once a woman becomes a wife to one family, she becomes wife forever even if the husband dies. Even when husband dies, the wife does not feel lonely as she is given the companionship of her husband's next of kin as happened to Ruth. The wife can only be exempted from her duties of being a wife through divorce which was rarely given and only for one reason – adultery. Ruth promised Naomi her mother-in-law that she was there to stay with or without her husband because she was now part of the family. The Arabs introduced a temporary marriage to accommodate their soldiers on duty away from home but in essence that is prostitution on part of the men and abuse to women.

Africa Culture, Ruth 1 vs 11-17

1.14   **Kupira/ Offering**

In a Hebrew or African offering, the following need to be provided; a suitable place with the requisite sanctity (connecting point), a place befitting a shrine (a prerequisite) has to be identified, timing of offering is a prerequisite, which could be early in the morning or at even and never midnight or midday, an altar is erected (may be optional), an animal may be slaughtered, burnt on fire or cooked (optional), snuff (optional), beer may be brewed (optional) or farm produce but what constitutes it (an offering) are words of praise, thanks giving, supplication or of seeking guidance that are made by the person making the offering as an acknowledgement of the fact that the providence of the Creator of the fore bearers is being seen to be at work and as such deserve thanksgiving and praise (prerequisite). Though most of the offering requirements are optional, the common practice is to avoid offering nothing to heaven and the minimum is usually snuff.

'And the Creator appeared unto Abram, and said, unto thy seed will I give this land: and there built he an altar unto the Creator, who appeared unto him'.

Gen 12 vs 7,

Hebrew / African Culture

'Unto the place of the altar, which he had made there at the first: and Abram called the name of the Creator'.

Gen 13 vs 4,

The language of the offering is strictly the language of the fore bearers, African or Hebrew dialects and not the 'modern day prayers' by Africans which are in a foreign language usually of the north or in a linguistic confusion called 'speaking in tongues' – the Habra dadada nothing.

Vanhu/Abantu have kept this tradition of an offering to this present day where offerings are still done at a bira (family gathering and thanks giving) where a beast is offered, slaughtered, blood spilled to the ground accompanied by a supplication from a family elder. This is the exact manner of the offerings that were done by the African or Hebrew fore bearers. The offering may also be of the first fruits of the harvest (Inxwala).

The detailed offering procedures are not knowledgeable to the Jews, it is an aspect of the culture that is directly linked to the priesthood (masvikiro - Vaera Mwoyo, vaRozvi) of the tribe of Levi. The Jews would not qualify to make offerings at national level for the reason that they are strangers in the culture, this is an area including that of the king or leader that a stranger or a convert will not be able to partake. The Jews who take it from the script of Ezra have no exact details of a Hebrew offering for the reason that often Ezra did not go into details, he simply wrote **'the patriarch made an offering'** without giving details and that is as far as the Jews know, the detail is in Africa among Vanhu/Abantu, **the Bona fide Hebrews of the Books of Moses.**

The north are now teaching the traditions of their fore fathers of a human substitute for the offering. The approach to substitute the farm produce or stock in the African or Hebrew offering with a human offering of the north has two fundamental problems:

1. Not at one instance is a human offering at play in Hebrew or African Culture. Abraham the patriarch was tested by the Creator to offer his son, but at the moment of offering his son, a ram was given. If human sacrifice was the right offering, his son would have been spared for Abraham's sake, and one of the two servants left afar with the ass would have been offered. Besides even the Hebrew youngster (his son) had an idea of an offering, for he asked his father where the animal of the offering was. The summary to this is that within African or Hebrew spirituality, human offering is an abomination to the Creator and any suggestions linking this type of offering to a high level of spirituality serves to show the pagan origins of the designers of Christianity. Jephtah's vow to offer anything that came out of his house was a foolish man's vow which has no link to Hebrew Culture.

2. If a human offering was given through the person of Joshua the son of Joseph (known as Jesus Christ in the north) as claimed by the north, why do men continue to die individually at their individual sins? He who decides to go whoring and commit all sorts of sin must be ready to die for the reasons of his iniquities for only his blood will be required for his transgression and not a third party's blood for Moses had given himself up for the children of Jacob at the sin of the golden calf *'Yet now, if Thou wilt forgive their sin-; and if not, blot me, I pray thee, out of thy book which Thou hast written'.* to save the children of Jacob but this was rejected as follows: *'And the Creator said unto Moses, whosoever hath sinned against me, him will I blot out of my book'.*

The foundation of Christianity is the blood of Joshua, who is said to have redeemed the entire human race on the cross as a human sacrifice. This is a declaration of the pagan origin of the faith. What will save the people is a full adherence to the culture or laws contained therein as it was given in the beginning as an everlasting covenant as what some practising Africans or Hebrews are still doing today. Human sacrifice is abominable and defiles the shrine, altar and land upon which it is performed. If human sacrifice was a spiritual requirement, the poor would be extinct by now, they would be sacrificed by the overzealous religious sects at lightning speed. The last supper recitation which instructs followers to *'eat; this is my body'*, is in African Culture like a witchcraft ritual and is unimaginable to drink human blood in real terms or in theory for *'The fathers shall not die for their children, neither shall the children*

Hebrew / African Culture

die for the fathers, but every man shall die for his own sin'.

> African Culture, Oral Tradition, Gen 4 vs 3-4, Exo 32 vs 32-33, Gen 46 vs 1
> Exo 17 vs 15, Exo 18 vs 12, Judges 6 vs 19-21, Judges 6 vs 26, 2 Kings 23 vs 16,
> 1 Kings 13 vs 1-2, 1 Chr 16 vs 40, 2 Chr 28 vs 3-4, 2 Chr 25 vs 4, Eze 16 vs 36

1.15   Ngozi/ The Avenging Spirit

After Cain had murdered his brother Abel;

'And the Creator said unto Cain, Where is Abel thy brother? And he said, I know not; Am I my brother's keeper?
And the Creator said what has thou done? The voice of thy brother's blood crieth unto me from the ground.
And now thou art cursed from the earth, which hath opened her mouth to receive thy brother's blood from thy hand'.

Gen 4 vs 9-11

The referenced scripture is typical ngozi (avenging spirit) in African or Hebrew Culture which is an aggrieved spirit of the departed soul that cries unto the Creator seeking vengeance, and indeed it gets the vengeance and gets appeased when the blood of the murderer is shed. The matter of the avenging spirit of a murdered innocent person is a living aspect of African Culture today. When an African murders an innocent person and manages to evade conviction in the courts pursuant to the law/justice system of the north, he/she knows fully well that the avenging spirit will be with him sooner or later, in most instances, such a matter is settled by African elders where the guilty party will admit to the murder and is tried according to the Hebrew or African laws. The avenging spirit will only rest when the murdered soul is appeased. Without appeasement, the entire family of the guilty party may die in very mysterious circumstances. Christianity has been quick to label this as the work of demons, the fortunate aspect of this matter is that all the Africans who have converted to Christianity know about it and they acknowledge its existence. When things happen this way, they come home to African or Hebrew Culture to settle the matter the African or Hebrew way and later return to Christianity. In Arabia, the avenging spirit is appeased by either death to the murderer or through payment of restitution called blood money.

In African Culture, the procedure for appeasement of the avenging spirit has been changed for the convenience of powerful or rich murderers. Instead of taking away the life of a murderer, an innocent girl is often handed over to the family of the deceased so that a kinsman will take her as wife and the children that will be born will carry on the name of the deceased and this practice is abuse of women and children. Trying to appease the spirit of the murdered victim by handing over a girl to the family of the deceased is a law of convenience which is deviant from the culture. The Acholi of Uganda cleanse a murderer of innocent blood by giving him/her an egg to crush as it is thought to cleanse but again these are inconsequential rituals and the solution is restitution with life for life, people who have spilt human blood often will spill again and again as they lack the respect or the sanctity of life and ejecting them from this life is often the way to go.

> African Culture, Gen 4 vs 8, Gen 9 vs 6, Gen 42 vs 21-22, 2 Sam 21 vs 1-10,
> 1 Kings 2 vs 31-34, Judges 9 vs 23-57, 1 Sam 19 vs 5, 2 Sam 3 vs 28-39,
> 2 Sam 21 vs 1-9, 1 King 2 vs 5-6, 1 Kings 2 vs 28-33, 1 Kings 21 vs 14-29,
> 1 Kings 22 vs 33-40, 2 Kings 9 vs 7-10,24-26, 30-37, 2 Kings 10 vs 7,
> 2 Sam 3 vs 27-39, 2 Kings 9 vs 22-37, 2 Kings 10 vs 11, Eze 33 vs 6

1.16   Murarabungu / Rainbow Symbolism

The appearance of a rainbow in a raining sky, in Africa Culture signifies that the rains have ceased and this compares well to the story of Noah where it signifies the same;

Hebrew / African Culture

'And it shall come to pass, when I bring a cloud over the earth, that the bow shall be seen in the cloud: And I will remember my covenant, which is between me and you and every living creature of all flesh; and the waters shall no more become a flood to destroy all flesh'.

Gen 9 vs 14-15,

The symbolism of the rainbow in Hebrew or African Culture differs from the Christian doom's day theory. The doom's day theory agrees also with Jewish messianic 'end of days' theses. There is no literature in Hebrew or African Culture on the end of this civilization, what is known to end is the life of a human/ creature/plant when his/her or its time has come. Covenants of the Creator last forever as there have not been another flood. If the destruction of the earth/universe comes, it would be man-made for reason of global pollution, the use of unproven biogenetics or effects of barbaric/nuclear arms among others.

Oral Tradition, 2 Sam 3 vs 26-39

1.17   **Zita raSekuru/ The Name of the Grandfather Passes onto a Grandson**

*'**Nahor** lived nine and twenty years, and begat Terah: And **Nahor** lived after he begat Terah an hundred and nineteen years, and begat sons and daughters. And Terah lived seventy years, and begat Abram, **Nahor**, and Haran'.*

Gen 11 vs 24-26

Hebrew or African Culture has several cases of grandfather's name passing onto a grandson and anyone else after that generation and not from father to immediate son as in Nahor-junior. In most cases when father and son share one name, the other family members have a dilemma in how they treat father's namesake.

African Culture, African Oral Tradition

1.18   **Hebrew or African Culture Maintains Communication with the Spiritual Realm**

There is always a spiritual link between Africans or Hebrews with the spiritual realm. When Vanhu/ Abantu embark on a journey or need to partake in enterprise, or when they have a problem among them, the norm is always to apprise the spiritual realm in order to get a good result or to get a revelation of the cause of problems;

'Now the Creator had said unto Abraham, get thee out of thy country, and from thy kindred, and from thy father's house, unto a land that I will shew thee':

Gen 12 vs 1

'And the Creator came down upon mount Sinai, on the top of the mount: and the Creator called Moses up to the top of the mount; and Moses went up. And the Creator said unto Moses, go down, charge the people, lest they break through unto the Creator to gaze, and many of them perish. And let the priests also, which come near to the Creator, sanctify themselves, lest the Creator break forth upon them.'

Exo 19 vs 20-22

The communication channel is not one way but clearly two way in that if there is no priest to relay back what is coming from heaven, a dream often comes which gives the instructions on the way to go and how to approach an impending problem. And most cultures call this superstition or some even said Moses and the elders of the children of Jacob did not hear the voice of the Creator at the mountain of Sinai perse but that the people had taken a herb that caused them to hallucinate.

There is always a link or communication channel between heaven and Vanhu/Abantu. The conditions that govern the access to the channel are adherence to the culture always, holding the shrines of the Creator where the voice or communication signs appear with high sanctity. In the Hebrew Scriptures, Sinai and several others were places where a priest or prophet or the people themselves would communicate with the Creator. In most instances the communication is restricted to the Creator and a priest or prophet for the reason that the general members may not necessarily meet the sanctity required to visit a shrine and hear the voice. Anyone who made contact with a woman with her manner is prohibited, or any man who was with his wife within a certain time neighbourhood of visiting a shrine, or any man who has had the flow of seed in the time neighbourhood of visiting a shrine is prohibited, or anyone who has made contact with a dead body especially that of humankind and has not been cleansed the hyssop way or anyone who is defiled by eating forbidden food especially that of the swine sort, him/her must not come near the shrine for he/she will defile it and suffer the wrath of the heaven. All these conditions automatically meant that special people well acquainted with the shrine matters had to visit the shrine and hear the voice. In Africa such places are Matonjeni, Great Zimbabwe shrine, Chirorodziva, Mapungubwe and many others scattered across the face of Africa including North East Africa. This is a sign associated with the Bona fide Hebrews, that they are always in contact with the Creator of their fore bearers, any person who claims to be a Hebrew, but is without this ability is not a genuine Hebrew. Communication may be severed for reasons of spiritual impurity on the part of the Hebrews or Africans but sooner or later communication re-establishes to give the Hebrews guidance always.

The Arabs have not had a two way communication channel with the spiritual realm after the death of Muhammad for the reason that there has not been an inspired person among them to provide the link thereof to this day. If there was a communication link between the Creator and the Arabs today, them and their converts would not be detonating themselves among the innocent folks in the name of Jihad or this and that for they would be told by heaven in clear terms to unbutton the explosive devices and neutralise them for there is no place for barbarism in the spiritual realm. Which holiness empowers people to kill others with brutal injustice? There is nothing like that in African or Hebrew Culture, the elders in Arabia must sit down and carefully teach both converts and children on what it means to embark on a spiritual journey inherent in Hebrew Culture.

African Culture, Gen 17 vs 1-14, Gen 22 vs 1-2, Exo 3, 19, 20, Num 11 vs 17
Det 4 vs 33, Det 5 vs 24-26

1.19   African or Hebrew Blessings

An analysis of world events from the time of recorded events by oral tradition or otherwise in relation to the treatment of the Africans or Hebrews by other races will acknowledge the vast strength, ability, tolerance, robustness and endurance of the people;

'And I will make of thee a great nation, and I will bless thee, and make thy name great, and thou shalt be a blessing'.

Gen 12 vs 2

1.19.1 Vanhu/Abantu Resilience

In number terms, the dark skinned people of African origin, the children of the patriarchs are today in excess of a billion people out of over seven billion people of the world. The ability to grow as a population against such world vices is a blessing of endurance otherwise if Vanhu/Abantu were cursed and weak, they would be extinct by now from brutality. The Hebrew strength told in the Hebrew Scriptures especial in the Egyptian sojourn is a real tale because the people are there to see right in the depth of Africa and across the globe with their resilience. The African people have been blessed not with a frail physical body infrastructure but are strongly built and are a resilient race. Highly immune to diseases to the extent that while other races would wear nose covers as a way to protect themselves from infections like bird flu, Vanhu/Abantu would actually share the same shelter with infected birds without exhibiting any symptom of infection at all. Given the vices that have been applied against them by races of the world, a frail infrastructure would have helped exterminate the entire African race. When the Pharaoh issued a decree to kill first born sons born to Hebrew women in Egypt, the Hebrew women had to do without Egyptian midwives, they simply delivered the infants by themselves in spectacularly similar events to what happened during slave trade. African women in slavery in America were required to work in the plantations by the slave masters up to their delivery day and would go under a tree to deliver the infant, breast for the first time and thereafter return back to the plantations to work while the newly born infant would sleep under the tree!! Was that not miraculous and amazing? The Africans used that strength to navigate a dry wilderness for forty years and prevailed. In terms of natural ability, innovation and ingenuity they do exceptionally well even under very difficult conditions usually in the form of double standards and unfair practices by other races. After many centuries of abuse, over the years the African people have by blessing and miracle re-established themselves. It is now known to the oppressors of Vanhu/Abantu that no matter how much pressure one exerts down on them, they continue to rise to the top. They do very well against all odds.

1.19.2 **The African Resources**

It is not by coincidence that Africa with boundaries from the Cape to the Caspian Sea including North East Africa (the Middle East) is the richest continent, it is by the design of heaven, the children of the patriarchs have the richest inheritance in fulfilment of the promise made to the forefather by heaven.

In material terms the children of the patriarchs were given the entire garden of Eden, from the Cape to the Caspian Sea (Iran), which is a rich land, the land has the most abundant mineral wealth on earth, gold, platinum, iron, cobalt, tungsten, diamond, rare earth metals, uranium, oil, coal, gas, timber, wildlife and many other riches. The continent has the best soils, best rains, best sunshine, and the combination of which can produce enough natural food to feed the entire world. The continent has one of the freshest waters, waters that come out of the earth's springs that can be consumed directly without purification at all. The continent has the most natural wonders of the world, the Mosi-a-tunya (Victoria Falls), the Nile river, Mount Kilimanjaro, the rift valley, the Drakensberg mountains, the Vhumba mist mountains. The continent has vast wildlife of any form at Virunga in the D.R. Congo, Malindi in Kenya, the Serengeti in Tanzania, the Trans-frontier Park in South Africa-Mozambique-Zimbabwe just to mention a few. In summary it is the only continent on earth that can close its borders from the outside world and still sustain itself. A blessing indeed. **The continent has more than sixty-five percent of earth's natural resources mentioned herein for a population of about a fifth of the world. Resource ratio per population being 65/20 equalling at least 3.25 against 35/80, about 0.4375 for the remaining population. The overall resource ratio of Africans to others is thus 3.25/0.4375 equalling 7.4285, yet the north will say Africans of the richest continent are the poorest people. How is that possible? Because the African riches are not in the hands of the owner, they are being manipulated by a third party. How do African currencies supported by such huge resources become so weak? At the same time how do northern currencies, supported by very little resources become that strong? The reason is that, the weighting rationale is improper so as to exploit the Africans. The reason why African currencies, which are supported by huge natural resources of gold, diamond and platinum among many Africa's riches are perceived weak is that those with no natural riches have formulated a currency benchmarking system. In that benchmark, the currency support comes in the form of goods and services which they have derived from processing of African mineral riches which they do not have. They have changed the rules that govern currency support from the traditional base resources to 'goods and services' that they have. If it had been them with the huge natural resources as in Africa they would not changed the currency benchmarks. The north will postulate that an African kilogram of pure gold is of less value than their kilogram of 'value added' iron ore and their currencies will go a hundred fold. They use economic propaganda which they jiggle around to short-change others. Speculation and economic propaganda are the key merchandise. Sometimes to offset rising oil prices, they will claim fake discoveries of oil.** Unfair practices sometimes extend to African agricultural produce which is natural, wholesome and not bio-modified. The pricing of African livestock, poultry, grain, fruit and vegetable which are naturally grown to their full maturity period of about four times that of bio-modified foods may be priced the same or less than that of bio-modified foods. Their business practices are sometimes so insincere that doing business with them is a result of sheer

Hebrew / African Culture

desperation on the part of Africans and if that is the only scope of business partners around, it is better to keep the said resources and trade later at own terms, there is no wisdom in walking into a partnership where one will lose.

A part of Africa is a desert which is quite hot and arid but ostensibly surrounded by the sea. Temperatures that approach sixty degrees Celsius provide a natural greenhouse for the desert to grow high yield multiple harvests per year. Vanhu/Abantu will benefit more if they do research on how they can desalinate sea water by application of solar energy by pumping it to a high potential and let it be desalinated by reverse osmosis exerted by gravity. Pump it into the desert fields by solar energy, irrigate by solar, harvest by solar and store by solar. It is an agricultural potential that has not been fully explored for the reason that there is not as huge hot desert in other destinations as that which occurs in Africa.

Today the African continent is sustained by natural agriculture which is largely irrigated by natural rain, the above scenario has not yet been applied yet Africa is self-sufficient while other continents have to survive on bio-modified - quantity without quality food engineering – biotechnology. The danger with their bio-modified foods is that as much as the food speeds up maturity in livestock and vegetation so shall it be with human consumers of such foods. There is high possibility of people starting to age at twenty-four years of age. Greying of hair is already starting as early as eighteen years and the manner of women is now visiting infants as young as five years and these are serious issues of concern. Considering the small size of Europe by land mass relative to its people and climate, GMOs maybe justifiable but not for Vanhu/Abantu with their gigantic Africa. The people of Africa are spending billions in purchasing arms of war (Saudi Arabia, Libya, Egypt, Nigeria, Congo, Zimbabwe, South Africa among others) from the north, west and east instead of researching on natural agriculture, desalination and other worthwhile sciences.

The desert is rich agricultural land in reserve, who ever thought that one day the same desert would yield trillions of barrels of oil for the same people in question? **As the world population grows and put strain on food resources, land and natural food shall become more critical and valuable than silver and gold.**

Africans are the originators of globally friendly technologies ranging from architecture, masonry, metal working (excluding the use of barbaric technologies out of radioactive metals— nuclear arms), natural agricultural technologies, and natural sciences, mathematics that have given birth to living testimonies such as the pyramids of Egypt and the Great Zimbabwe pure stone architecture which have left other civilizations without any clue to this day relating to how such technologies were developed. In spite of the vices of slavery, imperialism and today's scourge of racism against Vanhu/Abantu by other races, they have done exceptionally well against the odds. Is it unimaginable that Africans who were taken to the west as slaves are doing exceptionally well in all fields of life – sciences and academy, sport, music and art. In the game of football, which is the largest sporting event of the world, the Africans in South America were the champions before the game was commercialised, today nations awash with money are buying football players and their citizenship like groceries. Even if monkey chants and other racist malice are exerted on Africans, the African spirit is resilient and will not yield to that. If they survived imperial and slave injustices, how can a monkey chant or a banana thrown on the football pitch kill that mountain peak African spirit and resilience? If you are made of the strength of diamond, how much less harm would you incur if a mosquito limb was thrown at you to disturb your peace?

1.19.3 The Future of Vanhu/Abantu

The people resident within the African continent are the greatest single cultured people, who if united will conquer the world without firing a bullet for reason of their common values, which are imbedded in their culture. The goal of a United Africa has not been achieved so far for reason of penetration by imperial nations, who came and divided Africa on basis of foreign religious schisms or cultures. The Africans have never oppressed any nation from their beginning, they have been used, kicked, oppressed, massacred and yet still they remain the friendliest of all the peoples.

Hebrew / African Culture

The consolation to all Vanhu/Abantu is that, once the Sumerians, Acadians, Assyrians, Babylonians, Persians, Greeks, Romans, Turks, British, and Americans have all dominated the world at one point, and have fallen or will fall. It is only Africans who have not, and when they do so it will be forever. The children of Abraham will indeed rise, as indicated by the African Union momentum. The children of Ishmael (Banu Arabia/Vanhu veArabia) in North East Africa, the 'Middle East' must be part of the African Union initiative for their commercial crude oil friendship with the north and west will not last long. The eventual and perpetual giant is in the making. What is required to achieve that is not only unity but also full proof and impermeable unity. Let not the north find a weakling among the African brothers, for they will penetrate through that brother. Such weaklings today are those that are allowing the north to build their military bases on African soil to create uneasiness among the African family.

African Oral Tradition, Gen 12 vs 3

1.20　The African or Hebrew Extended Family

African Culture has a well established extended family which is well knit by relative descriptors such as brother, sister, 'babamudiki - junior father' (father's younger brother), or 'mainini - junior mother' (mother's younger sister) and not by way of the more remote cousin, nephew and niece as characteristic of the northern family;

'And Abram took Sarai his wife, and Lot his brother's son, and all their substance that they had gathered, and the souls that they had gotten in Haran; and they went forth to go into the land of Canaan; and into the land of Canaan they came'.

Gen 12 vs 5

In Hebrew or African Culture, one's brother's son is not one's nephew but one's true son, the bone of one's flesh, no wonder the patriarch Abram took it upon himself to raise Lot like his own son. A younger brother in the event of the death of his elder brother who would have died without man child, will give his biological son to continue the name of his deceased brother. However, due to foreign influence among other things, the African extended family is under threat. The African family has been divided chiefly by political and religious affiliations. Families are shrinking, interaction is diminishing, the richer members of a family are getting richer while other members are waxing poorer.

African Culture, Gen 11 vs 31-32, Gen 29 vs 14

1.21　Chikuva cheKupira/ An Altar of Offering

An altar (chikuva) is part of each and every African observant home in conformity with the following;

'An altar of earth thou shalt make unto me, and shalt sacrifice thereon thy burnt offerings, and thy peace offerings, thy sheep, and thy oxen: in all places where I record my name I will come unto thee, and I will bless thee. And if thou will make me an altar of stone, thou shalt not build it of hewn stone: for if thou lift up thy tool upon it, thou hast polluted it. Neither shalt thou go up by steps unto mine altar, that thy nakedness be not discovered thereon'.

Exo 20 vs 24-26

The altar is permanently built in each round hut reserved for family cooking, the kitchen. It is important for readers of this work to verify this for their information. Activities that occur on this altar include communicating with the spiritual realm in search of blessings in the event of travelling, in search of livelihood and in other matters that concern the family. The other altar is housed in a central shrine like at the Great Zimbabwe, Mapungubwe, Makah Makarama in North East Africa and any other African pure stone shrine scattered across the face of Africa. In the latter shrines, matters of national importance take place; enquiries on war, drought, pestilences and any other matters that concern the entire nation. It is also important to look at the specifications of the altar and make a direct comparison of the pure stone altars that obtain in Africa with what the Jews now call the 'temple of King Solomon' where blocks of stone were bound by mortar. The original shrine by King Solomon was a pure stone shrine, not hewn

Hebrew / African Culture

by a metal tool and whose stone were not bound together by mortar. The altar of earth can also be used for thanksgiving just before a goat or sheep is slaughtered in a household to give thanks unto Mudzimu Mukuru (the Creator), where the beast is laid thereon while a brief thanksgiving is offered. Note that in African Culture, it is taboo to step on the altar of earth, which is much in conformity with Exo 20 vs 26. When the family is making an offering at the altar, it is the eldest in the family who speaks, and takes the role of a priest at family level as a result of the decentralization of the Hebrew offering.

African Culture, Gen 12 vs 7-8, Gen 13 vs 4, Judges 6 vs 24-26

1.22 Kuoma Kwenyika/ Drought

A drought is understood as the expression of heaven on the people's deteriorating morals in Hebrew or African Culture and does not come when people are morally doing good, it is a curse inflicted on the people and their land for the transgressions of some or all the people who inhabit that land. In the case of the three years of famine in the time of King David, the land had been defiled by the blood guilt of Saul and the usual blessings from the Creator ceased.

'And there was a famine in the land: and Abraham went down into Egypt to sojourn there; for the famine was grievous in the land'.

Gen 12 vs 10

'Then there was a famine in the days of David three years, year after year; and David enquired (akavhunzira) of the Creator. And the Creator answered, it is for Saul, and for his bloody house, because he slew the Gibeonites'.

2 Sam 21 vs 1,

In all matters of redressing curses, the root cause of the curse has to be established and addressed, in the matter in context, the blood of Saul's family was required to atone for the innocent blood of the fallen Gibeonites thus automatically cleansing the land. When a drought occurs today in Africa, it affects an entire region like Southern Africa, East Africa or North Africa, which in earlier years, African fore bearers in Southern Africa like South Africa, Botswana, Zambia, Namibia, Swaziland, Lesotho, Mozambique, Malawi, Tanzania and a few others would convene at Matonjeni and make an offering/supplication/ request for a good season of good rains. Under such circumstances droughts were very rare, however today when Africans have abandoned their culture and embraced Christianity of the north, droughts are now part of Africa. Some Africans especially the 'academics' schooled in the north are very good at defending the northern thesis of climatic/global warming related changes that link droughts to rising temperatures notwithstanding the fact that although temperatures are rising, some areas are receiving devastatingly high rains while other areas within the same global domain are receiving devastatingly low rains which in summary is an indicator that morally people have sunk low enough to attract the wrath of heaven in the exact sense implied by Hebrew or African Culture. There are more floods and droughts today which scientifically means that the overall global annual rainfall is the same but the distribution is not uniform but devastating. So instead of Africa receiving hundred percent of its annual rain, it is getting maybe fifty percent while another continent is getting two hundred percent with an overall scheme of creating disasters and scientists do not want to consider that the globe has begun to warm up at the zenith of man's iniquities.

African Culture, Oral Tradition, Gen 26 vs 1,
Gen 41 vs 56, Gen 43 vs 1, Rut 1 vs 1, 2 Kings 8 vs 1

1.23 Urombo Uroyi/ Poverty is not a Virtue

Poverty is given the same moral weighting as witchcraft in that it is considered not a virtue but a curse. Poverty may compromise a person's morals seriously in that a poor mother may be lured easily into harlotry just for the need of providing food to her dear children and a poor man can kill another man to wad off poverty no wonder poverty is understood to be of the same weight as witchcraft. If riches were unacceptable, the inspired African or Hebrew fore bearers would not have worried themselves with

Hebrew / African Culture

personal wealth, instead all their history is spent hunting for sustaining their families not just modestly but comfortably as well.

'And Abraham was very rich in cattle, in silver and in gold'.

Gen 13 vs 2

'Thou shalt therefore keep the commandments, and statutes, and the judgments, which I command thee this day, to do them.
Wherefore it shall come to pass, if you hearken to these judgments, to keep, and do them, that the Creator shall keep unto thee a covenant and the mercy which the Creator swore unto thy fathers:
And will love thee, and bless thee, and multiply thee: will also bless the fruit of thy womb, and the fruit of thy land, thy corn, and thy kine, and thy oil, the increase of thy kine, and the flocks of thy sheep, in the land which the Creator swore unto thy fathers to give thee.
Thou shalt be blessed above all people: there shall not be male or female barren among you, or among your cattle.
And the Creator will take away from thee all sicknesses, and will put none of the evil diseases of Egypt, which thou knowest, upon thee; but will lay them upon all them that hate thee'.

Det 7 vs 11-15

Hebrew or African Culture rewards good deeds and adherence to cultural values always with peaceful and prosperous life, and poverty is a known curse from the Creator. Christianity teaches the opposite that poverty is a prerequisite for people to go to heaven 'For it is easier for a camel to go through a needle's eye, than for a rich man to enter the kingdom of heaven' is the interpretation of the Greek Scriptures in relation to richness or wealth. When the European settlers came to Africa with the bible while scouting for African wealth, they taught such double standards with all their hearts while at the same time were busy making mining claims in the land of Vanhu/Abantu.

The European settler missionaries acquired the rich fertile lands of the Africans to enrich themselves while impoverishing the Africans so as to make it easier for Vanhu/Abantu to enter 'the kingdom' of poverty. Poverty was taught to Africans by the north to psychologically empower the Africans with a promise of heaven and the heavenly mansions while the imperial north took all that belonged to Vanhu/Abantu including the African's children for the north to use as slaves and farm labourers. Were the north not keen on going to heaven together with the Africans by first having to share the trials and tribulations associated with poverty? Not at all were the north interested in impoverishing themselves in preparation for heaven for the reason that the issue of mansions in heaven was not fact and that poverty leads to a people's oblivion. Poverty is a human scourge that takes out humanity from humankind and when humanity is gone, you will see a mother selling off her innocent thirteen year old daughter into prostitution. The mother will turn herself into the agent to look for harlotry clients for her daughter so that the two will not starve from poverty. The author saw poverty at close range, poverty has no comparison to any tribulation that a human can endure especially to people with children. The psychology that came along with Christianity was tremendous, they taught of the virtues of poverty and the near impossibility of the rich to enter heaven vis-a-vis the possibility of a camel to enter the eye of a needle which made it impossible for Africans to reflect on their welfare state. And to teach that poverty is the requirement for people to go to heaven, contradicts what Vanhu/Abantu knew in relation to poverty especially drought which are associated which defilement of the land as a result of sin and when the same poverty becomes the passport to heaven, every norm and standing rule is violated which also caused people not to enquire on the reason of their poverty which the new faith championed.

By expounding on the virtues of poverty, Christianity has earned a place among the poor as a religion of poverty instead of encouraging followers on how to better their life economically.

Africa Culture

Hebrew / African Culture

1.24 African Etiquette and Generosity

Lot and Abraham had a misunderstanding by way of fights between their herdsmen, how they resolved their conflict was unparalleled human etiquette of all times;

'And Abram said to Lot; Let there be no strife, I pray thee, between me and thee, and between my herdsmen and thy herdsmen; for we be brethren.
Is not the whole land before thee? Separate thyself, I pray thee, from me if thou wilt take the left hand; then I will go to the right; or if thou depart to the right hand, then I will go to the left'.

Gen 13 vs 8-9

'Then Lot chose him all the plain of Jordan; and Lot journeyed East: and they separated themselves the one from the other'.

Gen 13 vs 11

Whichever way the land falls among one people is immaterial, for the reason that it still remains their land or property. The settlement made herein between the patriarchs was generous, humble, exemplary and should therefore serve to motivate Africans today in issues that may arise between them especially on land and territorial boundaries. The bottom line used here was brotherhood, 'why should brothers fight?' was a theme that brought peace to them. Abraham and Lot did not invite a third party to resolve their differences. In the same manner, Africans are advised to sit among themselves and settle any matter that may arise among themselves. Strangers should not be party to the solution for the same have a lot to gain when Africans fight. Abraham resolved the referenced disagreement with Lot like someone with deeper knowledge of the land in question which to him were the same which compares with history of Vanhu/Abantu in relation to imperial conquest who understood that if Caucasians take the north, Vanhu/Abantu will take the south but then the former do not share the same level of civilization for the reason that they wanted it all.

Critical decision making in African Culture is carefully thought-out before decisions are made, as opposed to lighting speed decision making that often has caused unnecessary conflict or war and to this behaviour, some northern researches classified Africans as people of low intelligence quotient on the basis of non-philosophical tests like how fast a person can switch on a light if told to so. Added on to that, the African value system is less commercial than other cultures as more time is spent on the moral aspect of the culture than the hurry to make profit which is very visible in Asia, Europe and West.

How do Africans seek for a solution to their conflicts between themselves from the manufacturers of arms of war? Like going to a butcher seeking a remedy for an obsession for meat? Mr butcher, please help me I am addicted to meat, how can I solve that problem? Mr butcher will tell you that it is not a problem to have an obsession for meat but an honour, because out of that obsession the butcher is in business.

Socially Africans have been a closely united entity in that in times of famine no one person would die because people identified themselves as a unit. In that case a famine would kill all or none. A problem to one member of the family was viewed as a family problem and not as his/her problem. People were bound together by their oneness until the stranger came among them. Shia and Sunni are slight religious differences or schisms to Hebrew brothers born largely to Ishmael and converts. The motivation in conflict resolution is given herein by the forefathers. If the Arabs refuse to understand that they are brothers and insist on fighting each other over the 'Sunni/Shia nothing', the end result is that the land/resources upon which they are fighting shall remain and they will extinct as a result of conflict. Their children will grow up in war and die in war while other nations' children only know the joy of children's play or children's wonderlands. The children of Abraham were blessed with a huge land and huge resources which the children will not exhaust, if Lot and Abraham had decided to solve their small problem the way it is being done largely in the Arab world, none will be here to inherit the huge inheritance that is there today for the children of Abraham, the strangers would be mining the oil

Hebrew / African Culture

resources from Angola to the Gulf, the diamonds in Southern Africa, the gold, platinum, the rich land and many other riches. The challenge to that shall lie on Arab elders to rein in on their children before it is too late. In the same token, if the north had the same Hebrew or African etiquette described herein, then imperialism would not have occurred for the north will keep the north while they leave the south for Vanhu/Abantu but alas things are not like that, sometimes this world can be much lower than the human code of conduct.

African Culture, Exo 23 vs 5

1.25 Zunde raMambo/ Tithes

The Zunde raMambo concept in African Culture is in fact the Hebrew tithes system. The practice is in existence to this day in Africa where a traditional chief, those instituted on the advice of Jethro the Hebrew Priest of Midian, levies a tithe from among his subjects usually in the form of grain and other tithes which when collected to the chief will be the Levite's portion (the priests - masvikiro), the poor, the widowed and the orphans' sustenance, for they have no inheritance (the Levite). In most areas in Africa, the Levites still man the Hebrew shrines across Africa to this day, their sustenance comes from the tithe levy.

'Wherefore Levi hath no part nor inheritance with his brethren; the Creator is his inheritance, according as thy Creator promised'

Det 10 vs 9,

'Thus speak unto the Levites, and say unto them, when you take of the children of Abraham the tithes which I have given you from them for an inheritance, then you shall offer up an heave offering of it for the Creator, even a tenth part of the tithe'.

Num 18 vs 26,

'At the end of three years thou shalt bring forth all the tithe of thine increase the same year, and shalt lay it up within thy gates:
And the Levite, (because he has no part nor inheritance with thee) and the stranger, and the fatherless, and the widow, which are within thy gates, shall come, and shall eat and be satisfied; that thy Creator may bless thee in all the work of thine hand which thou doest'.

Det 14 vs 28-29

Alternatively Zunde raMambo (the tithe) can be administered through a system of agricultural land which would be worked by the people for free on selected days of the week whose produce would feed the priests, orphans and widows. Africa had a well organised system of charity. Until recently, the tithe system was administered by the genuine priests but today in the absence of the bona fide priests, the tithe system has been hijacked by the fly by night and brief-case people of non-priestly origins largely from Pentecostal church who have transformed it into a money generating business to fish-out every cent from their poverty stricken and misinformed congregation who are promised paradise after death when they live in abject poverty on earth. The tithe system is one Hebrew Culture law that has outlived others not for reason of piety but greed which has converted tithes collection to some thriving enterprise.

The brief-case priests or tithe merchants usually have a lot of tricks they use to maximize their illicit tithe revenue. Sometimes they cast evil spells on the congregation which they would reverse if a church member submits to them with heart and pocket where upon the subjects would start worshipping not the Creator but these tithe merchants and paying to the brief-case priest all their family income. Some are very popular for making death prophesies and nothing else when there are so many problems affecting the common people. Sometimes these tithe merchants use magic enchantment to attract personal wealth, the consolation to the victims is that most uninformed congregation are opening their eyes to see these cheats.

African culture, Oral Tradition, Gen 14 vs 20, Det 14 vs 28-29, Det 18 vs 1-2, Det 26 vs 12-19

Hebrew / African Culture

1.26 Svikiro/ Dlozi/ Tenure of a Prophet

A number of inspired people in African Culture continue to see visions from the Creator pertaining to the course of life of the people. Such visions were more prevalent during the liberation struggles in Africa against imperialism where priests/prophets (masvikiro/amadlozi) would either see visions or would enquire of the Creator on the direction of battle as Saul, David and other Hebrew kings did in their times;

*'A prophet will thy Creator raise up unto thee, **from the midst of thee, of thy brethren**, like unto Me; unto him you shall hearken';*

Det 18 vs 15

The ability to prophesy is in contrast with Israel today, the Jews are not the direct descendants of Abraham and they do not have the gift of prophecy for this gift was bestowed among the children of Abraham. This is why there is no prophet in Israel today against the word of the Creator that said a prophet shall always be raised among Hebrews for communication between the Hebrews and the Creator. In like manner, the great prophets were Hebrews and not Jews, like Moses, Isaiah, Jeremiah (who died in Africa at work while exhorting the Hebrews or Africans to abide by their culture), Ezekiel, Samuel among others. The Jews, from the Chief Rabbi to the common Jew who happen not to be the descendants of Abraham have no prophets being raised among them by the Creator in conformity with the referenced scripture. **The office of the priest and the Hebrew leader/king are two offices in Hebrew Culture that cannot be assumed by strangers or converts for these posts are the symbols and foundation of Hebrew Culture and any effort to try and install a convert may threaten the survival of the culture by changing the fundamentals of the culture as done by the Jews that has given the impression that the Bona fide Hebrews (Vanhu/Abantu) are the strangers or gentiles while Hebrew Culture has been relegated to Canaanite mythologies in Babylonian descent.** Nevertheless, strangers or converts must not feel segregated but are very welcome indeed, tinokugamuchirai nomufaro, marhaba bikom.

There are priests or prophets (Masvikiro/ Amadlozi eDzimbahwe) at Matonjeni, Mapungubwe, Great Zimbabwe among other sites installed for the purposes of making offerings (kupira) in exact manner and form as was done by Abraham, to offer direct communication with the Creator on matters concerning subjects like rain making or other offerings or ceremonies. The Africans have continued to communicate with the spiritual realm because they are the very people who were endowed with the ability to prophesy pursuant to the culture; and to other cultures, the matters of prophecy and prophets sound like fairy tales.

In Arabia, they currently do not have a prophet and in place of a prophet they have religious leaders called mufti with no prophetic authority. The Arabs affirm that their last prophet was Muhammad and there will be none else after him, this of course is their version because Muhammad said he was a prophet but he did not say that he was the last prophet for Hebrew Culture is very clear about prophets; the Creator will always send a prophet among the Hebrews wherever they are to solve a lot of issues for the people.

Today, the Arabs are in need of a prophet more than any other time because Arabia is a melting pot of conflict; the monarchs in Arabia are sponsoring religious conflict or terrorism in their backyards in order to draw personal benefits from those wars while on the other side there are religious schisms causing Shia-Sunni conflicts which are results of disagreement on who should have succeeded Muhammad when he died and surely if they can be prophetic authority today linked to the Creator to lead the people, the Shia-Sunni conflict would not be there at all but of course Islam doctrine is based on the belief that the last prophet came and died and there wont be any other and if that dogma is resolved or modified only then will the people begin to see the absurdity of Shia-Sunni conflict, as for now the blood will continue to spill. On the other side, there is a sect of religious warriors, Jihad fighters fighting for their god perhaps on the assumption that the god is not powerful enough to fight for self.

There will always indeed be a prophet among the Hebrews in their life unless if the Arabs have

Hebrew / African Culture

intermarried beyond Hebrew identity, and it is definite that Muhammad would not have said that there will not be other prophets after him, it was the same selfish clique of Arabic elders who originated the Shia-Sunni schism in their greed to succeed Muhammad, who were responsible for making such selfish statements to the effect that there will not be any prophet after Muhammad. **When one splinter group proclaimed a new prophet after Muhammad, then the opposing splinter group preached of nomore prophet after Muhammad to try and counter the other group, simple as that**.

A prophet will be necessary to explain to the referenced Jihad group that the entity of the Creator is greater than the universe as suggested by Solomon when he was apprising heaven of the completion of the oracle in Jerusalem where he said;

'But will the Creator indeed dwell on the earth? Behold, the heaven and heaven of heavens cannot contain thee; how much less this house that I have built'?

1 Kings 8 vs 27

And so the Creator being that great, the jihad soldiers need a prophetic authority to explain to them that their services do not even compare to a drop in the ocean in power in relation to the Creator and therefore their war for god is wasted effort. The war that Jihad soldiers are required by heaven to fight is the war of love, compassion, mercy and goodliness against self. Everyone knows how hard it can be to discipline self to be good, merciful, compassionate and to be just to others, yes that is the war against self that the new prophet in Arabia is required to explain to the Arabs day and night. And in that war there is no need for use of guns or bombs but a sincere heart.

African Culture, Oral Tradition, Gen 15 vs 1,18, Gen 15 vs 12-16, Gen 17,18,19,
Gen 31 vs 3, Gen 31 vs 11-13, Gen 35 vs 1, Exo 4 vs 12,14,15, Det 28 vs 37,
Exo 18 vs 1, Num 11 vs 26, 1 Sam 3 vs 4-15, 2 Sam 7 vs 4-17, 2 Sam 12 vs 1-12,
1 Kings 3 vs 5-15, 1 Kings 18 vs 9, 1 Kings 19 vs 12-16

1.27. Mwana Wedangwe/ Duties of the First Born

The first born is the beginning of another generation, inherits the privileges of birthright and is the symbol of the father and mother's pride for the reason that through the first born, they become father and mother for the first time, Vanhu/Abantu still feel the same pains endured by the patriarchs in the event of failure to conceive especially a son;

'And Abram said, O Creator, what will thou give me, seeing I go childless, and the steward of my house is this Eliezer of Damascus?
And Abram said, behold to me thou hast given me no seed: and, lo, one born in my house is mine heir.
And, behold, the word of the Creator came unto him, saying, this shall not be thine heir; but he that shall come forth out of thine own bowels shall be thine heir."

Gen 15 vs 2-4,

The first born is the administrator of the family estate and also like other sons he carries on the name of his father. Some African states have constitutionally changed the provision of this African or Hebrew tenet by awarding family inheritance to the surviving spouse. Often have children of a deceased hard worker been impoverished when their inheritance is passed on to some lazy worthless men who court widows with the aim of inheriting their estate. When a marriage fails to conceive a male child to carry on the name of the father, that is the major reason for polygamy in African or Hebrew Culture as happened to the patriarch Abraham. In the event of a family failing to conceive a male, the name the family head risk being erased in the whole African or Hebrew family unless a younger brother marries the elder brother's wife and the first born named after the departed brother to carry on or continue his name in yet another African or Hebrew tradition known as kugara nhaka which shall be explained later in this work. The first born male child carries on the name of his departed father not for the reason of a system of patriarchy but for scientific principle of the y-gene and how it survives or extinct. True all children male and female are equal but when it comes to carrying over the name of the father to the next generation,

Introduction

that aspect is possible through the male child, the children of the son-in-law born by the girl child will not count, for they will take after the name and gene of their own father and not the name of their mother's father. The name of such a man will only be referenced later in historical terms as so and so who died without man child to continue his name or will be forgotten, for there will be no bearer of his name. While it is fact that the boy child carries on the name of his father, that does not deprive the girl child of her rights and privileges in a Hebrew or African context.

African Culture, Gen 25 vs 32-33, Num 27 vs 4, Det 21 vs 15-17,
1 Sam 1 vs 11, 1 Chronicles 5 vs 1, 1 Chr 26 vs 10,

1.28 Africa the Land of the Children of Abraham

The following scriptural verse defines the land of the inheritance of the children of Abraham;

'And in the same day the Creator made a covenant with Abram, saying, unto thy seed have I given this land, from the river of Egypt (Nile) unto the great river, the river Euphrates'.

Gen 15 vs 18

The upper boundary of the land demarcated by the river Euphrates is clear but what needs a clarification is the south and western border of the domain land of the children of the patriarchs. Nile is a river that starts partly in Central East and West Africa. And so the river Nile makes its footprint on a larger part of Africa which includes the north, east, central and west of the continent and that alone is a statement to say Africa not excluding the south was the land of the domain of Hebrew Culture and also the inheritance of the children of the Hebrew fore bearers.

And so the land given to Abraham and his children was not confined to Canaan but the entire African continent with original boundaries from the Cape to the Euphrates as given in the story of creation in Gen 2 vs 10-14. The subcontinent of the 'Middle East' is a divisional creation of the north with a prime aim of weakening Vanhu/Abantu.

African Oral Tradition

1.29 Barika/ Polygamy

The original polygamous marriage in Hebrew or African Culture was not a matter of a husband's propensity/desire for many wives but was necessitated by matters of barrenness on the part of the first wife (Vahosi) or alternatively for the need of a larger family;

'Now Sarai Abram's wife bare him no children: and she had a handmaid, an Egyptian, whose name was Hagar.
And Sarai said unto Abram, Behold now, the Creator has restrained me from bearing: I pray thee, go in unto my maid; it may be that I may obtain children by her. And Abram hearkened to the voice of Sarai.
And Sarai Abram's wife took Hagar her maid the Egyptian, after Abram had dwelt ten years in the land of Canaan, and gave her to her husband Abram to be his wife'.
Gen 16 vs 1-3

Failure by the first wife to conceive a son or the demands or need of a large family always triggered the first wife to give authority or to look for a suitable second wife for her husband. The first wife was highly involved in this matter, which if improperly handled might break up the family. The first wife had the responsibility of looking for a suitable partner in marriage, a unifying partner like her brother's daughter was sometimes a preferred choice by most African women, for there can never be war between the first wife and her brother's daughter. The polygamous marriage that is in practice today is in most cases a deviant from that of the fore bearers and is sometimes influenced by some men's insatiable search for

Hebrew / African Culture

women or greed of the bed. The process of taking a second wife is subject to approval by the first wife because she is special to the husband in that she has bonded with him and the man owes the title of father to her. The approval process resembles the bridal courtship until the first wife approves or rejects for very valid reasons like prospective wife being known for harlotry or family destruction. Today the first wives are fighting serious battles to suppress polygamy but then polygamy has gone underground not only in Africa but everywhere with the second wife having to live outside her husband's home, which has resulted in infidelity on the part of the second wife as a result of loneliness and rejection and often brings gender diseases to the first wife. **In countries where polygamy is not allowed by law, often polygamy manifests through multiple cases of adultery by men implying that monogamy is very possible on paper or in theory but in practical it is polygamy all around the world.**

Jacob's marriage to his first two wives was as a result of a technicality raised by Laban on behalf of Leah. Subsequent wives, three and four were to try and raise a larger family. In the scriptural context, Sarai who upon failure to conceive, authorized her husband Abram to take a second wife Hagar for the purposes of raising an heir to the family name. Abram agreed like any other Hebrew or African man without raising any questions because that was/is very acceptable in the culture. Sometimes when the first wife realizes that she has passed her active life while her husband is still in need of the bed, she excuses herself and thereupon authorises her husband to seek another wife. Women of the north take hormonal therapies to prolong their active lives but at the expense of breast cancer among other illnesses. In earlier years, the north would marry another wife only after killing or divorcing the first wife for polygamy was unacceptable among them and they saw killing the first wife as a lesser evil in order to marry another wife than polygamy.

Today in Arabia due to wealth from oil, open polygamy is no longer housed in one home but multiple homes where the husband inhabits on time division basis, a few days in one home and thereafter moves to another home or wife and that way the bonding process with the wife and children becomes a challenge. Sometimes the husband can lie all his life that he needs three weeks in every month to attend to business meetings abroad in which time he visits the other wives.

<blockquote>
African Culture, Gen 29 vs 28, Judges 8 vs 30, 1 Sam 1 vs 2,
1 Sam 25 vs 42-44, 2 Sam 3 vs 2-5, 2 Sam 5 vs 13-16,
2 Sam 11 vs 27, 1 Kings 11 vs 3, 2 Chr 11 vs 23
</blockquote>

1.30   Kupa Mbereko/ Assisted Conception

When a man fails to get children in his life, he keeps on trying until his death in the sense that scientifically the male remains active up to a very advanced age or even up to death but the woman tries until the manner of women ceases. Thereafter she approaches a kinswoman from her maiden extended family to conceive on her behalf but strictly not on the basis of surrogate motherhood but on the basis of second wife with shared motherhood to the child in exact manner and detail as done in the quoted scriptural verse;

'And Sarai said unto Abram, behold now, the Creator has restrained me from bearing: I pray thee, go in unto my maid; it may be that I may obtain children by her. And Abraham hearkened to the voice of Sarai'.

Gen 16 vs 2

As mentioned previously, most of the original polygamous marriages of the patriarchs were driven by the need to conceive children who would carry on the family name and the first wife was often in support of the marriage. In the referenced verse, is another application of Hebrew or African Culture called Kupa Mbereko or assisted conception where a kinswoman conceives children on behalf of the first wife. The aspect of African or Hebrew Culture depicted herein remains in force to this date, and is well understood as stated by Sarai that the children born will be biologically the children of Hagar but they will also belong to Sarai. Hagar will enter the marriage arrangement above fully aware and informed of the implications. A 'modern' woman in the position of Hagar may raise the issue of rights over one's

Hebrew / African Culture

children, but it must be remembered that an African family is a unit where collective living is paramount.

African Culture, Gen 30 vs 3-13

1.31 Chigaro chaVahosi Mubarika/ The Authority of the First Wife

When the first wife fails to conceive and opts in a second wife, the position and authority of the first wife must not be compromised by the over excited second wife who may think that being the biological mother of the heir and administrator to the name and estate of the family then she should be exempted from the authority of the first wife. In African Culture, the protocol is very clear to all the members in the marriage, and failure to abide by that protocol may result in the expulsion of the second wife on the instruction of the first wife in exact manner and format as what happened to Hagar;

'And the angel of the Creator said unto her (Hagar), return to thy mistress, and submit thyself under her hands'.

African Culture, Gen 16 vs 9

1.32 Kudzingisa Vanakomana/ Male Circumcision

Circumcision of male children, keeping the Sabbath, Nazarite hair lock and communicating with the Creator through the priests/prophets continuously and not historically are the hallmarks of the Bona fide Hebrews. Readers must note the gender of the candidates for circumcision prescribed in the quoted scriptural reference. Female circumcision is not part of Hebrew or African Culture, it is a misapplication/ deviation from the culture. **It must also be noted that in the Hebrew Scriptures, the first two candidates for circumcision were Abraham and his first born Ishmael, the father of the Arabs (Vanhu veArabia/ Bantu beArabia/ Banu Arabia) and therefore any means which try to isolate the children of Ishmael from the Hebrew family is misplaced and divisive. Ishmael grew up in the Hebrew family, witnessing, learning and practising all Hebrew laws applicable to his age before him and his mother Hagar were sent off as a result of the conflict between the matriarchs. Hebrew Culture was therefore in practice among the children of Ishmael from their beginning. Muhammad re-established parts of Hebrew Culture.**

'And the Creator said unto Abraham, thou shalt keep my covenant therefore, thou, and thy seed after thee in their generations.
*This is my covenant, which you shall keep, between me and you and thy seed after thee; Every **man child** among you shall be circumcised.*
And you shall circumcise the flesh of your foreskin; and it shall be a token of the covenant between Me and you.
*And he that is eight days old shall be circumcised among you, every **man child** in your generations, he that is born in the house, or bought with money of any stranger, which is not of thy seed.*
He that is born in thy house, and he that is bought with thy money, must be circumcised: and my covenant shall be in your flesh for an everlasting covenant.
*And the uncircumcised **man child** whose flesh of his skin is not circumcised, that soul shall be cut off from his people; he has broken my covenant'.*

Gen 17 vs 9-14,

'And Abraham was ninety years old and nine, when he was circumcised in the flesh of his foreskin.
And Ishmael his son was thirteen years old, when he was circumcised in the flesh of his foreskin.
In the selfsame day was Abraham circumcised, and Ishmael his son'.

Gen 17 vs 24-26,

Most African tribes in Africa still abide by the circumcision tenet. Besides being a spiritual requisite, it is a very high health law, it improves male immunity to gender diseases by substantial measure. HIV and AIDS have taken a huge toll on the Vanhu/Abantu yet in most instances Africans have lower rates

Hebrew / African Culture

of promiscuity relative to other cultures. By design, the Hebrew or African anatomy had not developed a high immunity to gender diseases on account of the clean state of the male gender part due to circumcision to the extent that the natural immunity was not under attack often, resulting in the body lagging the dynamics of resistances to gender diseases. However the uncircumcised to this day, were being attacked with any disease that came in through their gender anatomy and so they developed a better immune system with the result that the originally uncircumcised are dying in less numbers. When an African is not circumcised, any degree of promiscuity will find the immune system unprepared for any infections whose entry point is the reproductive organs. In order for Vanhu/Abantu to survive the scourge of pestilence, they must return to the covenant—circumcision and those who will reject the covenant will be cut off, not by an army of course but by gender diseases among other curses.

Women by nature of their gender anatomy are the worst affected by gender diseases which may be at their peak while they behold an uncircumcised spouse in a marriage. If elders renege on the upkeep of circumcision tenet, the onus falls upon women to demand upon marriage a circumcised husband. This shall not be an instance of subjugating the covenant but it will be enhancing it. The spirituality of circumcision is not in the blood flow but in the sign, else it may be misconstrued as the use of human blood in matters of spirituality. Keepers of the circumcision tenet must note that while circumcision reduces the prevalence of the gender infections, it is not a license for promiscuity among men but a reward for keeping one of the fundamental tenets of the covenant.

Due to Vanhu/Abantu movements across the breath of Africa necessitated by droughts and conflict, circumcision had to be postponed until conducive conditions prevailed but sometimes it was postponed forever. During the forty year sojourn in the wilderness, Joshua did not circumcise the males, the prevailing conditions were not favourable. A whole Canaanite tribe of Hamor was exterminated soon after the wounds of circumcision by the children of Jacob for the reason of defilement of their sister Dinah at the hands of Shechem.

> African Culture, Gen 21 vs 4, Gen 34, Det 10 vs 16, Det 30 vs 6,
> Josh 5 vs 2-8 Judges 14 vs 3, Judges 15 vs 18

1.33 Mhondoro/ Angelic Entities

Most discussions or opinions have depicted angels as human males when in fact they can take any form as given in the following scriptural reference;

'And the king of Assyria brought men from Babylon, and from Cuthah, and from Ava, and from Hamath, and from Sepharvaim, and placed them in the cities of Samaria instead of the children of Jacob: and they possessed Samaria, and dwelt in the cities thereof.
And so it was at the beginning of their dwelling there, that they feared not the Creator: therefore the Creator sent lions (mhondoro) among them, which slew some of them.
Wherefore they spoke to the king of Assyria, saying, the nations which thou has removed, and placed in the cities of Samaria, know not the manner of the Creator of the land: therefore the Creator hath sent lions among them, and, behold, they slay them, because they know not the manner of the Creator of the land.
Then the king of Assyria commanded, saying, carry thither one of the priests (svikiro/dlozi) whom you brought from thence; and let them go and dwell there, and let him teach them the manner of the Creator of the land'.

> *2 Kings 17 vs 24-26*

Angelic entities or angels manifest in different forms such as human beings, animals of the form of lions, snakes, eagles among other animals or natural phenomenon as in wind, fire, cloud, hail storm, hurricane, typhoon or any other which are all sent by the Creator to redeem people in need of redemption or inflict punishment or justice. The animals that are sent do not necessarily exhibit normal animal behaviour.

Hebrew / African Culture

The lions that were sent by heaven to inflict punishment on strangers that were sent by the king of Assyria in the referenced scriptural verse were not ordinary lions which could be handled the usual way of dealing with animals but were angelic entities (mhondoro) in the form of lions which needed to be handled by addressing the issue for which they were sent. The strangers had defiled the land for they did not know the spiritual requirements of that land in relation to Hebrew or African Culture. And so the solution was to carry a Hebrew priest to that land where angelic lions were killing people for defiling the land to teach people how to conform to Hebrew Culture. The king did not say lets carry arms to go and kill those lions because it was very clear that the lions were not the usual animals that everyone was accustomed to. Such angelic entities which come in the form of lions will make serious effort to kill their prey but strictly they do not eat the carcass thereof, remembering also that ordinary lions only hunt and kill their prey when they are hungry, in other words, lions do not kill to store food for tomorrow's consumption.

Other examples of angelic entities on a mission in the form of natural phenomenon today are fires, floods , tsunamis and hurricanes that are ravaging numerous parts of the globe for reason of unprecedented level of evil. Academics would argue that natural disasters have no scientific connection to morality but in Hebrew or African Culture the link is known and can be demonstrated and fires that are sent to punish immorality would disappear for any value of fire hazard index/rating when the moral issue for which they were sent to address is corrected. Readers must understand that African Culture can administer a lightning bolt on a clear cloudless sky against all scientific theories.

And when angels come in the form of human beings, they definitely come with no names as those that appeared to the patriarch at Mamre;

'And the Creator appeared unto him in the plains of Mamre: and he sat in the tent door in the heat of the day;
And he lifted up his eyes and looked, and, lo, three men stood by him: and when he saw them, he ran to meet them from the tent door, and bowed himself toward the ground'.

Gen 18 vs 1-2

'And there came two angels to Sodom at even; and Lot sat in the gate of Sodom: and Lot seeing them rose up to meet them; and he bowed himself with his face toward the ground';

Gen 19 vs 1

And when a person makes an encounter with an angelic entity, most lay people may not even notice it but elders in the culture know for sure, there are specific benchmarks that are experienced. The Jews have taught of arch angels by the names Gabriel which means 'El, (the Canaanite cult) is my hero' and Michael which means 'who is like El? or El has no comparison'. In African Culture to this day as was in the days of the fore bearers, angels continue to be seen in action but have never carried a name let alone one that salutes the Canaanite cult El, for that matter. In view of the ongoing Jewish-Palestine hostilities, there may not be peace without engagement of the Bona fide Hebrews of the Books of Moses in much the same way as was done by the king of Assyrians to consult the Hebrew priests.

African Culture, Oral Tradition, Exo 7 vs 12, Exo 12 vs 29, Exo 13 vs 21-22, Josh 5 vs 14-15, Judges 2 vs 1, Judges 6 vs 12, Judges 13 vs 6-22, Dan 6 vs 16-22, 1 Kings 13 vs 24-28, 1 Chr 21 vs 16,

1.34   African Humility and Hospitality

Most tribes in Africa give water to a visitor as a welcome gesture in exact manner and form as was done by Abraham, to their visitor who has appeared even without notice or appointment;

*'And (Abraham) said, **my lord**, if now I have found favour in thy sight, pass not away, I pray thee, from* ***thy servant****.*

Hebrew / African Culture

Let a little water, I pray you, be fetched, and wash your feet, and rest yourself under the tree'.

Gen 18 vs 3-4,

'Kupa mvura kumuenzi' or giving water to a visitor as a welcome gesture is typical African humility and hospitality by the humble people of Africa as they behold another or a stranger who comes in peace. In an African dialect it becomes 'Abarahama akati, **Changamire wangu**, kana maona ndakakodzera mumaziso enyu, musaenda kure, ndapota, kubva ku**muranda wenyu',** and such expressions of humility are **complemented by clapping of hands in sympathy with the tone of the quoted words**.

Humility is the zenith of the human civilization and without humility, animism or survival of the most brutal becomes the order. If one person considers another with high esteem, that is not worshipping the other. The expectation is that when one person respects the other then the same is expected of each other. If Africans considered the north as the land and possession of the people of the north then in the same human token, the north was expected to consider the south as the possession of Vanhu/Abantu but that did not happen because of lack of respect or consideration of the other as taught at length in Hebrew or African Culture. When the north came to Africa, they had more respect for their pets than the people of African descent they met and Africans were shuttered how on earth or from which civilization another people can be so disrespectful to the extent that was demonstrated by northern settlers as African minors and their fathers and mothers were treated the same without respect for the elders. If Hebrew or African Culture gives so much respect for the strangers in African or Hebrew territory, how much more respect would Africans give to strangers in the land of the strangers? The current civilization would have been a different landscape altogether if it were Africa who had gone to the north first before the north came to Africa, then it would have been possible to teach other nations the African or Hebrew code of conduct which is at play in the referenced scripture by the patriarch.

At one point in Arabia, the author tried to demonstrate the referenced expression of humility and hospitality but the Arabs showed a lot of contempt for that for the reason that such gestures of unhu/ubuntu or humility in general are extinct among Banu Arabia and the necessary step to do now is strip them of the title 'banu' for it is earned from works of unhu/ubuntu and without such works men are given the title of a dog not for the reason of walking on four legs like dogs but for the reason of lack of unhu/ubuntu.

African or Hebrew Culture welcomes a visitor or stranger with genuine sincerity. Once a visitor announces arrival, is ushered into a comfortable place, given water to quench thirst while baggage is off-loaded and kept well in a safe place. Later food is served and all these offers are given to the visitor regardless of invitation or not or whether he or she has asked for food provisions or not. The majority of European settlers and Asians who came to Africa in the past centuries lived peaceful and prosperous life for reason of African hospitality. After embracing the strangers to the full breath of Unhu/Ubuntu, it was in fact the settlers who segregated (Apartheid) Vanhu/Abantu.

African Culture, Gen 44 vs 16-34, 2 Sam 9 vs 6, Gen 18 vs 4-8
1 Sam 30 vs 11, 1 Sam 28 vs 23-25

1.35   Ungochani/ Sodomy

Sodomy has no place or accommodation in African or Hebrew Culture, it is as unacceptable today as it was during the days of Lot;

'And they (men of Sodom) called unto Lot, and said unto him, where are the men which came in to thee this night? Bring them out unto us, that we may know them'.

Gen 19 vs 5,

'There shall be no whore of the daughters of Jacob, nor a sodomite of the sons of Jacob'.

Det 23 vs 17

Hebrew / African Culture

Man lying with another man in African Culture is taboo. The culture of sodomy is only creeping slowly into Africans from the influence of the north and west through television programs produced for markets in the north and west, which have been allowed by African leaders on African television channels as well as the internet. Strangers in the land of Africa have lobbied for the legalization of sodomy in South Africa and the African leaders in that part of Africa have agreed to that. They have scored a first in wickedness against Africa and the land is defiled. A defiled land will not give the blessings to its people, peace, good rains, sufficient food, health to its people among other benefits associated with Hebrew Culture and the land will start consuming its people.

The north and west have accommodated sodomy sufficiently among themselves and their brothers and have enacted laws in their national constitutions that legalise sodomite marriages. They claim to be democracies and their laws follow the will of the majority. If the majority of people in the north consider that sodomy is morally unacceptable, how would democratic constitutions approve? If they are to say a fair democracy also considers the human right needs of minorities then they need to be informed that sodomy is not a human right nor is it an animal right but some gender preference disorder which must be treated and not encouraged. Sodomy is against the essence of creation, it will exterminate humankind.

At the moment of writing this work, the north were at laboratory level teaching male rats to be sodomite, which is as devastating as global pollution and poorly researched biogenetics in relation to the habitat earth. When sodomite rats are released onto the natural habitat or ecosystem, they will not reproduce and that failure will offset the natural ecosystem.

The number of natural disasters like tsunamis, hurricanes and heavy devastating floods or wild fires have increased especially in the north, west and far east in direct proportion with the number of sodomite legislations in those countries.

African Culture, Lev 18 vs 22, Det 23 vs 17

1.36   Zvinoera/ Taboos

There are matters in Hebrew or African Culture that are taboo or prohibited without detailed explanation or which cannot be understood using all the present scientific knowledge base which if followed as prescribed, would give positive result but if breached may cause fatalities as happed to Lot's wife;

'And it came to pass, when they had brought them forth abroad, that he said, escape for thy life; look not behind thee, neither stay thou in all the plain; escape to the mountain, lest thou be consumed'
'But his (Lot) wife looked back from behind him, and she became a pillar of salt'.

Gen 19 vs 17-26

Lot's wife out of curiosity and failure to adhere to instructions became a pillar of salt, which in African Culture is not a new phenomenon for the reason that there are sites and shrines which need strict adherence to instruction of highest order to get optimum results like when climbing Africa's high and holy mountains like Mt Nyangani, one has to conduct self with due humility and avoid speaking the forbidden as one progresses else the climber risks disappearance in the mountain. The same is applicable to most African or Hebrew shrines where one risk being swallowed by the shrine on uttering or doing the prohibited in the land.

When the son of the Shunamite woman died, Elisha instructed Gehazi to go to the lad with his staff to lay it upon the boy so that he can come back to life and Elisha instructed Gehazi not to greet or talk with any man on the way. There are a myriad of similar rituals in African Culture which have no known scientific explanation where a person requiring spiritual assistance is given instruction such as not to look back, nor to talk to anyone, nor to touch this or that, nor to look at this or that before executing a healing instruction and failure to follow such instruction would not bring positive results. When sending away the escape goat, there is a similar procedure that has to be followed and failure to do so will send the goat without the curses, it would be like a wasted exercise or effort.

It is forbidden also to defile some holy ground or virgin forests and other mountains by way of speaking obscenities, making comments of faithless disbelief or mating on such holy ground for what may befall a trespasser may range from disappearance for life to being eaten by beasts.

Trade in wild fruits which occur naturally and are not watered by anyone in Africa is a taboo that can cause serious poverty to the trader and when harvesting such fruits from providence if a rotten fruit is sighted, no inappropriate comments can be said of the rotten fruit and moreover harvesting of wild fruits disallows the felling of unripe fruits and is only limited to picking the ripe fruit on the ground, any effort to try and shoot down fruit will cause the harvesting stick or log of become a snake that will bite the harvester, Hebrew or African Culture sound like fiction to outsiders but real.

African Culture, Oral Tradition, Num 11 vs 1-3, Num 11 vs 32-34, Num 16,
Num 20 vs 12-13, Num 21 vs 5-7, Num 25 vs 6-9, Num 27 vs 14, Det 11 vs 6,
1 Sam 5-6, 1 Sam 13 vs 8-14, 1 Sam 15 vs 8-35, 2 Sam 6 vs 6-7, 2 Kings 4 vs 29

1.37   Kuyeresa Denga/ The Fear of Heaven

The underlying theme of African or Hebrew Culture is the fear of heaven and every deed partaken therein revolves around that theme. The implied fear of heaven is not the literal sense of fear but awe of heaven and the rules and guidelines of life in the culture as demonstrated by the patriarch in the quoted scriptural reference;

'And Abimelech said unto Abraham, what sawest thou, that thou has done this thing?
And Abraham said, because I thought, surely the fear of heaven is not in this place: and they will slay me for my wife's sake'.

Gen 20 vs 10-11

Even the subject on heaven which is highly regarded as the abode of the Creator is hardly discussed and no theories on heaven are postulated by Africans. There are no jokes about the spiritual realm.

Ever since the matter of the tower of Babel, all people bound by the African continent, the children of inheritance have not partaken in any matter that seeks to explore or demean heaven. There are no Hebrew or African tales that explore a journey whose destination is heaven for in the same culture heaven is known in clear terms that it is not the abode of mortals. It is only from the northern or eastern cultures that depict several human looking deities where Africans see, read about deities, their mansions and their beloved and only begotten sons. Today, the north are exploring or searching for the 'god particle' which in African or Hebrew terms is taboo. Often other nations make space explorations for unclear reasons and if space missions can be said to be for the reason of better understanding the universe as a habitat and how to best balance that ecosystem, the same explorers who claim to have better knowledge of the universe from their space studies are the ones who are into devastating barbaric nuclear technology and other globally unfriendly technologies.

The depletion of the ozone layer has come as a result of numerous globally unfriendly experiments. The north, east and west have also littered the universe with artificial debris. The destination heaven story only comes up from the no fear heaven who wrote about a man called Joshua the son of Joseph whom they presume to have died on the cross and went to heaven, the question the enlightened will ask is, if indeed he was going to glory, to the 'heavenly mansion' then why did he cry 'my god, my god, why have you forsaken me?' The feeling of going to heaven, the abode of the Creator should not have been considered as being forsaken. No mortal has ever had knowledge of heaven including the prophets. In spite of claims of paradise and the glories of heaven, no prophet has died joyfully in anticipation of heavenly glory. There is no knowledge of life after death. Moses preferred to be allowed to go over to Canaan and see the land here on earth before his death. He craved for the land here on earth. It cannot

Hebrew / African Culture

be argued that because the Creator made prophets out of the ordinary men and hence their fear of death. It must not be forgotten that the same ordinary men (prophets), have been given access to information/revelations no other ordinary people have been given and therefore that privilege should have equipped prophets with 'anticipation' when they behold their deaths.

The Hebrews or Africans' mention of heaven is from the fact that when a person dies, the soul is reclaimed by the Creator (the Source Soul) whose abode is heaven (undefined) and nothing beyond that is said. The north have added that Joshua went to heaven to reside on the right hand side of the Creator as if to suggest that they have a clear picture or graphic of the awesome Creator. The north have portrayed the Creator graphically or pictorially as an old white haired and bearded Caucasian male whereas Hebrew or African Culture gives no gender nor form of the Creator.

Due to foreign influence brought in by Christianity, Africans now believe that the earth is not their home but heaven; 'Hatina musha panyika - we have no home on this earth'. They normally sing such ideas at funerals applauding the premature deaths of their children whilst consoling themselves. They then claim that children who die in infancy would have been taken to heaven, instead of asking themselves why the Creator has taken a young soul after introducing it on earth and before it had lived life to its fullness.
They forget the story of creation where humankind are made from dust and given a breath of life by the Creator. In life, humankind are admonished to be good and live a prosperous and long life here on earth. On death they are buried in the ground because indeed humankind came from the earth (Adamah). Imaginations of heaven as mankind's eternal abode are overzealous and misinformed.

African Culture, Oral Tradition, Gen 11

1.38   Marriage Between Close Relations to Preserve Royalty or Family Integrity

In very few exceptions, African or Hebrew Culture did not discourage marriage between relations when the aim was to preserve the royal family from penetration by the enemy or when an esteemed family was surrounded by the morally and culturally wayward people like the situation of Abraham and Lot;

'And Abraham said, because I thought, surely the fear of the Creator is not in this place; and they will slay me for my wife's sake.
And yet indeed she is my sister; she is the daughter of my father, but not the daughter of my mother; and she became my wife'.

Gen 20 vs 11-12

Terah's family, father to Abraham did that in Ur when they were surrounded by idol worshippers and those who sacrificed their children to their gods. Samson was a strong man who was weakened by the enemy because the enemy came through contacts with his wife who was kin to the enemy. Without condoning it, in Africa, the occurrence of such a marriage is influenced by the need to preserve the royal line of inheritance, but rarely occurs.

African Culture, Oral Tradition, Exo 2 vs 1, Judges 14 vs 15-18, Judges 16 vs 5-20

1.39   Mabiko Emhuri/ Family Celebrations

Occasions in a Hebrew or African family that have always warranted a family celebration or feast are the birth of a child, circumcision after 8 days, redemption of the first born (masungiro) in the case of a man-child, weaning at about 3 years and marriage (chimandamanda/ chishava). The birthday celebration and wedding reception which originate from the north are conspicuously absent in Hebrew or African Culture for the reason that these are foreign events in the culture which even linguistically bear no African terms. The spiritual feasts or celebrations have been abandoned in pursuit of those of the strangers. In some instances of marriage, an African couple worry so much about the wedding before the important cultural marriage pre-requisites like 'n'ombe yeumai', the fundamental of the bride price

Hebrew / African Culture

are paid. The matters that are being taken casually have been seen by African elders to sometimes affect the life of the children born in the marriages where 'n'ombe yeumai', has not been settled, the mother of the bride will murmur for life against the in-law, and perse, that is an offering unto the Creator against the in-law and the children so born in such a marriage may sometimes find it difficult in life.

African Culture, Oral Tradition, Gen 21 vs 2, Gen 21 vs 4, Gen 21 vs 8

1.40   Chitsidzo/ A Vow

A vow is an unbreakable spiritual promise or undertaking that one intends to fulfil without fail. Jephthah's vow of burnt offering whatever would come out of the doors on his triumphant return was not a Hebrew or African vow for it was not spiritually objective, it was a foolish man's vow similar to promising to throw self down the cliff if the anticipated result does not happen. Not all animals kept indoors are suitable for offering to the Creator. Once a person has made a vow, it means a promise has been made to the spiritual realm which if broken has fatal consequences to the person who made that vow.

'And she (Hannah) vowed a vow, and said, Oh Creator, if thou wilt indeed look on the affliction of thine handmaid, and remember me, and not forget thine handmaid, but wilt give unto thine handmaid a manchild, then I will give him unto the Creator all the days of his life, and there shall no razor come upon his head'.

Sam 1 vs 11

In the same regard, a Hebrew or African oath is symbolized by an act of irrevocable commitment as performed between Abraham and his servant and is not necessarily written on a piece of paper and yet it is so binding that a misfortune will be bound to occur to the party that breaches it. An oath bound here on earth by two parties is believed to be bound in heaven also and the parties to the oath are aware of this and can only breach it in the event of death of one party at the least. In that regard a vow/oath taken by an African to speak the truth in a traditional court of law is highly regarded for the reason that if breached will definitely have far reaching consequences to the party that breaches that vow and Africans are well informed.

African Culture, Gen 21 vs 23-24, Gen 24 vs 2-3, Lev 5 vs 4, Det 23 vs 21-23, Josh 9 vs 18-21, Josh 15 vs 16-17, 1 Sam 14 vs 24-28, 1 Sam 20 vs 16-17, 1 Sam 20 vs 42, 1 Sam 23 vs 18, 2 Sam 15 vs 8, 1 Kings 2 vs 42-46, Josh 9 vs 19-20, Judges 11 vs 31, , 2 Chr 6 vs 22-23

1.41   Mupupuri/ Witness

The fear of heaven being the underlying philosophy in Hebrew or African Culture, a witness is not a subject of deceit as heaven is understood to be watching and in that case it is better to incur the costs of telling the truth than be liable to false witness under oath;

'And he (Abraham) said, for these seven ewe lambs shall thou take of my hand, that they may be a witness unto me, that I have dug this well'.

Gen 21 vs 30,

The habit of lying under oath is a commercial stance prevalent in Roman/Dutch/English law but not in African or Hebrew Culture. Most transactions in Hebrew or African Culture are always supported by a witness to certify the sincerity as opposed to northern law where the performance of an advocate in a court of law has more bearing than a witness, where a couple of witnesses who saw a crime being committed with their own eyes will be vexed before the judge of a court by an advocate by way of frivolous questions such as 'what makes you so certain that you saw what you saw? Did you really see something or it was an illusion?'

African Culture, Det 19 vs 15-19

Hebrew / African Culture

1.42 Nzvimbo Yekupira (Dzimbahwe)/ Place for Offering (Shrine)

In African or Hebrew Culture, there are specific places with certain characteristics that are suitable for making offerings and therefore not all places can be a shrine. A suitable place for making offerings, a shrine, a connection point or gateway to the spiritual realm is of the referenced scriptural specifications;

'And Jacob awoke out of his sleep, and he said, surely the Creator is in this place; and I knew it not.
And he was afraid, and said, how dreadful is this place! This is none other but the house of the Creator,
and this is the gate of heaven (a shrine - a communication point - a gateway).
And Jacob rose up early in the morning, and took a stone that he had put for his pillows, and set it up for
a pillar, and poured oil upon the top of it'.

Gen 28 vs 17-19,

Such places are very prevalent in Africa, for Vanhu/Abantu are always in constant communication with the spiritual realm but in Israel among the Jews, these experiences have ceased upon the departure of the Hebrews together with the ability to prophesy. In Africa, there are places like Matonjeni, Great Zimbabwe, Nyangani, Mapungubwe, Chirorodziva and many others where the unordinary experiences are witnessed, places of the highest spirituality where an African can experience or detect such a place when he/she passes by it. An African can relate spiritually with the place where a stranger will not feel anything, such is an example of a place synonymous with a shrine. These shrines will cease to connect people to the Creator when they are desecrated or defiled. When the north invaded Africa, they made researches to that effect whereupon they defiled a bulk of Hebrew shrines, so as to break the communication channel between Vanhu/Abantu and the Creator.

Africans or Hebrews understand that the Creator requires a sanctuary, a place on earth where people would come in on instituted seasons or in times of problems and communicate with the Creator.

The place suitable for a Hebrew or African offering or sacrifice is a mountain or a hilly area and therefore stone or rock is the key word. The central shrine that Solomon built was on a hill. The African or Hebrew shrine specification contrast with the flat ground or any place without a special attribute synonymous with an oracle where strangers especially the missionaries who came to Africa to preach Christianity have built their churches on.

In Makah Makarama, a place where the Arabs do pilgrimage (Hajj), is a hilly area and the centre of that Makah shrine is a stone (kabah) or kabwe in Vanhu/Bantu dialect or the stone (bwe) in the Great Zimbabwe shrine.

African Culture, Oral Tradition, Exo 25 vs 8, Lev 19 vs 30, Lev 22 vs 3-8

1.43 Mupiro/ Objects Suitable for an Offering

Hebrew or African Culture has specific objects that can be offered within the spiritual realm and the following scriptural reference will help to discount a popular offering in northern spirituality;

'And when the king of Moab saw that the battle was too sore for him, he took with him seven hundred
men that drew swords, to break through even unto the king of Edom: but they could not.
Then he took his eldest son that should have reigned in his stead, and offered him for a burnt offering
upon the wall. And there was great indignation against the Hebrews: and they departed from him and
returned to their own lands'.

2 Kings 3 vs 26-27

An animal offered in Hebrew or African Culture has always been a goat, sheep, beef or fowl and never at one time a human being for even Abraham's son upon noticing no animal for the offering at Moriah enquired;

Hebrew / African Culture

'And his son spoke unto Abraham his father, my father: and he said, behold the fire and the wood: **but where is the lamb** *(not the man) for the burnt offering'?*

Gen 22 vs 7

Human sacrifice taught by the north which is presumed to lead to the expiation of sin is not in accordance with African or Hebrew Culture but was associated with a number of pagan deities with northern origins. Joshua the son of Joseph is presumed to be the ultimate sacrifice for the expiation of all sin but humankind today continue to die for their individual sins. Hebrew or African Culture understand that no person can die or be killed on behalf of other people for that will not be just but complete disorder or chaos. Punishment is exerted on people to reform them by making them accountable to their misdeeds but if according to human sacrifice, one person is sacrificed for the omissions of other people, how are people going to correct their misdeeds?

The fundamental tenet or pre-requisite of pagan worship is human sacrifice and the associated use of human blood in reality or in symbolism. In fact the use of human blood or flesh is the work of sorcery, witchcraft and goblins, which are sustained by human blood or flesh only and not the flesh or blood of animals. Human sacrifice is such a cardinal abomination before the Creator that even the land upon which it is performed will be defiled and a curse will descend upon it. African or Hebrew Culture was the beginning of an informed relationship between the spiritual realm and people and Africans or Hebrews were the originators of that level of spirituality and the travesty today is that northern culture which actually is premised on some aspects of Hebrew Culture to the extent that northern scholars learnt spirituality from Hebrew Culture and how can the same students of Hebrew spirituality master the Hebrew Culture better than the Hebrews themselves and begin to make addendums to the culture such as human sacrifice and begin to teach such matters to their teachers?

Northern religious scholars often reference the use of muti done by Vanhu/Abantu as human sacrifice. When Africans use muti portions derived from parts of human anatomy or animals, that practice is purely witchcraft and magic enchantment used to pursue ill wealth which all have no link to worshipping but greed and all such devices are prohibited in African or Hebrew Culture.

African Culture, Oral Tradition, Exo 12 vs 3, Exo 24 vs 5-8, Exo 29 ,
Lev 1-9, Lev 16 vs 27, Lev 23 , Num 7, Num 23, Det 28

1.44   Makuva/ Family Burial Ground

Every Hebrew or African family has a family burial ground where all deceased members of the family are interred by the surviving family members in accordance with the following scriptural reference;

'I am a stranger and a sojourner with you: give me a possession of a burying place with you, that I may bury my dead out of my sight'.

Gen 23 vs 4

The commercialization of death and burial through development of funeral parlours, funeral services and cemeteries are foreign to Africa. A dead body defiles the person who handles it and so funeral parlours will naturally ensure that certain Africans employed by the parlours would be defiled all the days of their working life rendering them unsuitable for spiritual undertakings. When cemeteries were introduced to Africa most Africans rejected the idea of being buried away from the family burial ground with songs to describe that rejection sung as, '...Torai hama muende nadzo, Kambuzuma (name of a cemetery) handidi, ndondovigwepi? Ndondovigwa kumusha, torai hama, torai hama muende nadzo - kumusha', which is translated 'when I die, take my body to the family burial ground and not to a municipal cemetery for that I do not want'. Even with the advent of urbanization where people dwell in areas where a family burial ground is not permissible, Africans make serious effort to bury their people at their rural homes like what was done by the Hebrews to enable them to rest with their fore bearers.

Hebrew / African Culture

Africans or Hebrews do not cremate their dead. Cremation is like a burnt/roast offering of a human body to the gods which definitely defiles the land upon which it is performed in Hebrew terms. African chiefs to this day continue to be buried in caves. Traditionally in Hebrew or African Culture, people were buried in caves (ninga), however with the increase in the population, it is now chiefs or members of the royal families who are now being buried in caves. Some northern historians who wrote their story with their agenda have said that maDzimbahwe (shrines) are places where Africans bury their dead. This is incorrect because it tends to suggest that African spirituality has a lot to do with the dead, notwithstanding the fact that in the same culture, a dead body defiles a shrine itself or humankind.

In Egypt today the tombs where the Pharaohs or royals were interred are being excavated by vagabond historians in the name of Egyptology while also vandalizing very precious Egyptian historical records while the Egyptians watch. In Arabian cities there are no longer burial grounds but cemeteries like in Africa, the difference though is that in Arabian cemeteries graves can be reopened to squeeze in another departed kin.

African Culture, Oral Tradition, Gen 47 vs 29-30, Gen 49 vs 30, Gen 50 vs 25,
2 Sam 21 vs 11-14, Judges 8 vs 32, Judges 16 vs 31, 2 Sam 2 vs 32

1.45 Kuroorerana Vematongo/ Marriage within One People and Culture

The ideal African or Hebrew marriage is among one's kindred for the reason that introducing strangers into the family especially those of non-Hebrew origins would bring foreign or sometimes no fear of heaven practices in the family. Abraham made his servant swear;

'And I will make thee swear by the Creator of heaven, and the Creator of earth, that thou shalt not take a wife unto my son of the daughters of the Canaanites, among whom I dwell:
But thou shalt go unto my country, and to my kindred, and take a wife unto my son Isaac'.

Gen 24 vs 3-4, 1Kings 11 vs 1-2

The referenced tradition is in force today in Africa, but of course is being eroded with the influence of partly the Diaspora of Vanhu/Abantu abroad, and Christianity which give too much responsibility to the clergy to match marriage couples than the traditional African or Hebrew family. Children who come from cross cultural marriages have serious identity problems as they find it difficult to choose between mother and father's culture of origin and spouses that constitute a cross cultural marriage have to sacrifice certain aspects of their original culture to ensure that their marriages works.

Some families are known for witchcraft, whoredom, sodomy and general notoriety which sometimes manifest in the children born from such backgrounds and for those reasons, African elders have insisted on marrying their daughters or sons to/from families they are well informed about. Some African families have curses of the avenging spirit (ngozi) and children born therein may be afflicted by such.

African Culture, Gen 26 vs 34-35, Gen 27 vs 46, Gen 28 vs 1-2, Gen 34, Num 36 vs 5-13,
Det 7 vs 3, Josh 23 vs 12-13, Judges 14 vs 1-4, 1 Kings 11 vs 1-2

1.46 Kupfimbirwa Nevabereki - Parental Involvement in Courtship

Parents play a very important role in finding the most suitable bride for their children in Africa Culture and they do so without imposing a life partner for their children in similar fashion to what Abraham instructed his servant;

'And the servant took ten camels of the camels of his master, and departed; for all goods of his master were in his hand: and he arose, and went to Mesopotamia, unto the city of Nahor.
And he (servant to Abraham) made his camels to kneel down without the city by a well of water at the time of the evening, even the time that women go out to draw water'.

Gen 24 vs 10-11

Parents who raised a child to adulthood, would know the weaknesses of their child and in those circumstances would know who best suits their child to avoid marital problems in the future. In the event that the bride is found the African way, issues of infatuation that normally drive a young couple to a marriage are taken care of by the mature and experienced people. The sad story is that Africans have copied the dating system of other cultures and the immediate result is the prevalence of very high divorce rates which was never part of the African or Hebrew Culture, where men and women of the north as an example are known to be in their eleventh or twelfth marriage after having divorced ten or so times for the reason that their marriages are based on love on first sight or general infatuation where elders do not play a role in courtship. Often spouses are taking their lives upon being shocked after they discover that their partners are cheaters or abusers. The principal reason behind this is having very little information about their partners and lack of experienced advice on life partner selection. When parents are involved in courtship such disasters are avoided.

African Culture, Gen 24 vs 3-15

1.47 Kuroora Mhandara/ Virgin Marriage

Hebrew or African Culture emphasize strongly on a young man to marry a virgin maid. A woman may only be married not as a virgin without raising questions in the culture if she was divorced or widowed, otherwise the act of losing virginity by girls before marriage will bring shame to her family. Society will label the girl as one of loose morals and the family she hailed from will be looked down upon as a family incapable of raising moral children.

'And the damsel was very fair to look upon, a virgin, neither had any man known her: and she went down to the well, and filled her pitcher, and came up'.

Gen 24 vs 16,

A relaxation of virginity pre-requirement in a Hebrew marriage by Africans by encouraging their children to put on garments of whoredom/fornication designed by the west and north, to de-stigmatise whoredom at universal level to an acceptable norm, will not save African children from the scourge of HIV and AIDS caused by whoredom.

The traditional African woman referenced in the verse above will become a model of morality – 'amai, um or ima' when she settles in her marriage. She will start her family life as a virgin wife and dies with the knowledge of one man at gender level, the whole of her life unless the catastrophe of losing a husband occurs early in life. She becomes a role model in both her maiden family and matrimonial family, the Sarai, Leahs and Rachels. The younger girls are always reminded of her virtues and encouraged to emulate her. Teaching children to use the garment of whoredom before marriage would devalue the marriage package. Prior knowledge of the bed devalues a marriage.

Chastity and morality have a link to good health and security especially for women. The female gender anatomy is very prone to gender infections that may kill the woman all in the name of liberty and therefore restrictions made to women are meant to protect them and the entire population. Female gender anatomy is a moist and warm cavity which retains the gender seed or residue after interaction and that provides a perfect habitat for incubation of any little infection. Any slightest infection on the female gender would be incubated to a full pathogen colony that would kill the woman all in the name liberty; graveyard liberty perhaps and African elders had serious scientific knowledge of these facts and therefore they instituted restrictions on reckless mating whose aim was not to deprive women of their rights but preserve both men and women. Even before a woman chooses to mate recklessly, infection can attack her when taking a bath in infected water and most women are not well informed on what it means to be a woman. If women were prohibited to mate reckless, it meant that men also were deprived, women were the benchmark because they are usually the target by men and are the ones to agree to those advances or reject. It is like fighting against drug abuse, emphasis is always on the sources of drugs, the barons than the market, if there is no drug on the market, no one will take drugs, by the same token if there are no harlots on the land, no man will commit adultery. Morality also gives security to women, if they engender with a man with whom they are in marital contract then they will not

Hebrew / African Culture

be left alone as single mothers struggling to raise children of absentee fathers. In Vanhu/Abantu dialect, a girl is called 'mukunda' which translates to moral invincibility or infallibility in the sense that morality is a challenge in which the girl has to be victorious. Every now and again men of all sorts come to make advances on the girl and she has to turn down all those proposals and that means invincibility as men often consider a woman who could not turn them down as some easy conquest of some sort.

African Culture, which is considered by people external to it as abusive to women, consider casual gender interaction between man and woman without marriage contract as exploitation of woman which puts women at risk of gender diseases such as cervical cancer as well as the single responsibility of bringing up the offspring that come out of casual relationships. When one party to a marriage brings in experience related to the bed, that experience often exposes the other inexperienced party and that often causes marriage breakdown but when both parties are inexperienced, it means the best that they know are themselves and everything would be perfect.

Gender liberalism comes along with ill-health which affects males as well and of what value would gender liberalism be if it diminishes human survival. There is a trade off between liberalism and good health, the better is any of the two, the lesser is the other. There is a lot to learn from animals, the female is not very keen on mating and mating is never done as sport or entertainment but as a survival instinct and humans were like that until they started eating gender enhancement concoctions and every norm broke loose. Anabolic steroids used in today's agriculture to grow food are having a negative ripple effect on the growth of children, thirteen year olds are exhibiting characteristics of fully grown up adults thus taking a huge toll on chastity and morality among the minor children. A minor child in junior school too immature in the mind shows signs of a fully developed gender ready for mating.

Moreover, women change drastically anatomically with age and most men prefer not very aged women and the patriarchy system ensures that before women attain old age they must be in durable relationships with a lot of cheering grandchildren and the larger extended family and such durable relationships are incubated while women are in their prime time for no one will look at a ninety year old woman who spend all her life hopping from one bed to the other. At ninety years a women cannot attract any stranger for a serious relationship but must do so at the peak of her life and African Culture requires women to abstain from being used and opt for a serious relationship while the sun shines for grandchildren do not drop from heaven like manna but are nurtured early in a woman's life.

African Culture, Det 22 vs 13-21, 2 Sam 13 vs 1-19,

1.48   Chiratidzo Cheumhandara (Chimandamanda/Chishava) /Token of Virginity

The token of virginity is one of the facets of the Hebrew or African Culture that meant that no single child was ever to engage in the premarital bed of immorality. **The occasion of being married whilst a virgin remains one of the most virtuous experiences in Africa to both parents of the children and the children themselves. It is understood in African Culture that a wife who was married as a virgin is by default a virtuous woman and every man understands that, and therefore there is no occasion in the marriage for a man to utter words unbefitting of the woman in that regard.**

'If any man take a wife, and go in unto her, and hate her,
And give occasions of speech against her, and bring up an evil name upon her, and say, I took this woman, and when I came to her, I found her not a virgin:
Then shall the father of the damsel, and her mother; take and bring forth the tokens of the damsel's virginity unto the elders of the city in the gate:
And the damsel's father shall say unto the elders, I gave my daughter unto this man to wife, and he hates her;
And, lo, he hath given occasions of speech against her, saying, I found not thy daughter a virgin; and yet these are the tokens of my daughter's virginity. And they shall spread the cloth before the elders of the city'.

Det 22 vs 13-17

Hebrew / African Culture

Practising African readers of this work are quite fluent with the form of the cloth of the token of virgin and how it is handled and the author is not going into the details. In the event of virgin marriage, a feast would be called soon after marriage where a beast (n'ombe yechimandamanda/chishava) would be slaughtered in honour of the virtuous wife, and all this would be sponsored by the husband. In the event of the damsel being married not a virgin, that is not publicized but confidentially the token of no virginity would be transferred from the family of husband to the family of the maid for future use and reference, and no feast would be offered. This is one of the numerous spectacular facets of Hebrew or African Culture that have survived the years and test of time. A spectacular living testimony of a Hebrew tenet that has been preserved in African Culture to the last detail.

Only the husband would check after marriage and see whether the maid was a virgin or not and not necessarily other authority. Parents are not necessarily authorized by the culture to do so, all they need to do is raise up children under conditions conducive to chastity throughout the life of their children up to marriage. The ceremony of the reed dance (Umhlanga) administered by elderly African women and performed by African tribes today especially in southern African countries is not a parading of half-nude young girls for commercial purposes as done by beauty or modelling shows, but is a celebration by African or Hebrew girls of the virtues and the spirituality of being a virgin up to the day of marriage - a massive weapon against HIV and AIDS. Virgin girls and boys are holy, including those that lost their virginity through gender abuse and the rest are notorious and disobedient children. The reed dance ceremony is administered by women and is about women and is not a public event, therefore the appearance of photographers of any kind and men is not permitted and is not the motivation of the reed dance. Today misinformed gender activism is crying foul against the rights of the girl child, they lobby for more freedom for the girl to make it easier for the girl child to catch the gender diseases and die very young. The anatomy of woman is more vulnerable to diseases of the bed, though women may be more behaved and are less involved in multiple bed relations, any few times they do so imposes a high risk on them. African or Hebrew Culture had in a way factored that prudently and misinformed activists will rage on. The choice is individual, he who has a daughter and wants his daughter to live life to its fullness must be wise. There is no wisdom in giving one's daughter the freedom to die. HIV and AIDS infections and their effects are very low among the Arabs, because they uphold that aspect of culture. And there is no room or provision in African or Hebrew Culture for a girl under parental guidance to shout 'its my life'. When Africans are sick they are nursed by the family, when they die they are buried by the entire family, so it is not your life, it is collective family affair and every piece of advice from family counts!

It is prudent for parents to note that sometimes the human body and its sundry requirements may outgrow the brain function. A sixteen year old body may deem itself ready for anything, but the brain will be far behind, that is the time a parent's brain must work on the sixteen to twenty year old. A sixteen year old is like a machine powerful enough to run itself down the cliff to ruin, so control of the machine is very important. The author witnessed a dying woman on death bed who was admonishing her father for not disciplining her enough to abstain from immorality, she was adamant that everything she did was a result of the father's failure to rein her in. Her point was that she was not mature enough to understand the consequences of her commissions and in giving her all the liberty, the father was like giving her the noose to hang herself.

African Culture, African Oral Tradition

1.49   Place of Courtship

Though there is parental involvement in courtship in African or Hebrew Culture, children are only given guidelines in regard of what kind of a man or woman will make a long and happy marriage and so the other part of the work that relates to the actual courtship is a responsibility of the children working in liaison with uncles and aunts and most of those procedures occur in strategic places;

'And he (servant to Abraham) made his camels to kneel down without the city by a well of water at the time of the evening, even the time that women go out to draw water'.

Gen 24 vs 11,43

Hebrew / African Culture

The place of courtship (kutsvetsva/kupfimba) remains the well for thousands of years because it is at the well where any Hebrew or African damsel would go unattended because it is regarded as feminine territory. Most Africans are well aware that when it comes to making a marriage proposal, the well is the right place. It is important to preserve male and female roles for the reason that interchanging them may dis-orient the children or bring up sodomite children in a normal family.

African Culture, African Oral Tradition

1.50   Kutambira Vakuwasha/ Receiving the In-laws

It is a Hebrew or African custom to test for humility on the in-laws, traditionally the in-laws are tested up to the end of their tolerance to try and measure what kind of people they are and to what extent they would be able to tolerate the wife. And so when they introduce themselves, every step they take must be according to the book like in the following scriptural reference, they come and stand like 'stooges' as if they did not know what to do next and Laban was watching carefully for that and he instructed them to take the next step;

'And he (Laban) said, come in thou blessed of the Creator; wherefore standest thou without? For I have prepared the house, and room for the camels.
And the man came into the house: and he ungirded his camels, and gave straw and provender for the camels, and water to wash his feet, and the men's feet that were with him'.

Gen 24 vs 31-32

When the in-laws arrive at the family home of the bride for settling the bride price, they do everything by instruction. It is amazing to note that detail on these cultural procedures has not changed by a bit from the times of the patriarchs to this day in Africa, the Jews do not keep the referenced tradition, they come from other cultures surrounding the Hebrews which included the Canaanites (HaC'nani) and it was not easy for them to totally lose their origins while picking up every nitty-gritty of their adopted culture.

African Culture, Africa Oral Tradition

1.51   Roora/ lobola/ The Bride Price

Roora, lobola or the bride price has always been a modest price whose motivation was the measurement of the son-in-law's ability to fend for his new family and if a man was unable to get that modest price, there was high chance that his wife and children might starve to their death and such a candidate was better to live all his life without a wife or any children;

'And the servant brought forth jewels of silver, and jewels of gold, and raiment, and gave them to Rebekah: he gave also to her brother and to her mother precious things'.

Gen 24 vs 53,

The presents given in the referenced scripture relate largely to a royal marriage in Hebrew or African Culture for Abraham, the patriarch was a great man, however marriages between the common people are characterized by modest bride prices which largely come in the form of beasts and other things as obtaining in Africa this today. The male provides the bride price and not the woman and the bride price is a must, and if a man cannot pay the price he will have to work for it (kutema ugariri) as done by Jacob for Leah and Rachel. The only problem with roora/ lobola today is that people are commercialising it especially in Africa and Arabia among the Arabs, causing serious debts to the son-in-law which strain relations in the new marriage that have often caused divorce and what binds people together is not the size of the bride price but the procedures, protocols and introductions that bring the two families together. After the young man and maid intending to marry have acquainted themselves to the idea of

Hebrew / African Culture

marrying each other, the messenger (munyai) of the in-laws introduces the family he is representing and immediately he lays down their intention to marry the daughter of the host family to which he has been sent. When the marriage proposal has been accepted, the bride price is paid (customary gifts to the family of the damsel);

The settlement of the bride price is one of the numerous Hebrew customs that have been preserved by the African people to the last detail. It is also a Hebrew pointer. It is miraculous how the African people have managed to preserve the Hebrew or African Culture to the last details even amid the onslaught of foreign influence and propaganda. Readers are reminded that Jews do not perform these procedures in their marriages as detailed here, but that their children date like the north or west and they do not pay the bride price.

African Culture, Gen 24 , 1 Sam 18 vs 25

1.52 Kudya Kwevakuwasha/ Food for the In-laws

The following detail relating to the time when the in-laws are served food serves to illustrate the extent of detail that has been preserved in African Culture in relation to the life lived and celebrated by the Hebrews of the Books of Moses in order to provide an irrefutable link between the same people;

'And there was set meat before him to eat: but he said, I will not eat, until I have told mine errand. And he said speak on'.

Gen 24 vs 54

There are matters in African Culture where people can eat and dine before those matters are discussed and settled, but not with the marriage procedure. The procedure has to be done and concluded before the in-laws can eat food. Food is synonymous with the mother or wife and the in-laws cannot get the benefit of a wife through food without being accepted as representing an acceptable husband but this is an exceptional requirement which does not imply that hospitality is given only to people with a link to the husband.

African Culture, Gen 24 vs 33, 53-53

1.53 Mai Vemba/ Qualities of a Wife

There are certain attributes that men look for in a wife to assure of a stable and lasting marriage. Marriages in African or Hebrew are not casual relationships but are required to end forever and therefore the process of selection of a wife is a careful procedure that looks at sincerity, humility and a good upbringing as done by Abraham's servant when he was scouting for a wife for Isaac;

'And she (Rebekah) said, drink, my lord: and she hasted, and let down her pitcher upon her hand, and gave him drink.
And when she had done giving him drink, she said, I will draw water for thy camels also, until they have done drinking.
And she hasted, and emptied her pitcher into the trough, and ran again unto the well to draw water, and drew for all his camels'.

Gen 24 vs 18-20

The servant of Abraham watched every detail of Rebekah's conduct in his pursuit for a befitting wife for his master's son. In African or Hebrew Culture, what matters most are the manners of the damsel, her hospitality, her reception of guests or strangers, her humility and many other attributes of a mother and not how good she can swing her hip in a modelling show.

All Rebekah did for the stranger was from the bottom of her heart, she did not expect a present for it, it was in fact part and parcel of her life, to be courteous, moral, helpful and of good heart and that by definition is what Hebrew or African Culture looks for in a wife.

African Culture

Hebrew / African Culture

1.54   Bridal Coaching

After the marriage formalities are complete, before the newly married bride is sent away with the in-laws, the maiden family would stay a few more days with the bride in order to coach her on the significance of a marriage, which is a building block of a civilization without which the same can extinct;

'And her brother and her mother said, let the damsel abide with us a few days, at least ten; after she shall go'.

Gen 24 vs 55

The maiden family would emphasize the folly of both male and female chauvinism and that there are always sacrifices to be made in order to sustain a marriage. And that there is more to marriage than to spent a whole life hopping from one marital bed to the other. When a woman has gone through multiple marriages with children in each marriage scattered across a geographical space, there can never be as complicated a task for that woman like bonding with all the children.

During the coaching days, the damsel family would impress upon the damsel to be an exemplary wife, and to teach her all that is required to raise a successful family and to sustain and hold a marriage and make divorce not an option.

African Culture,

1.55   Muperekedzi/ Bridal Escort

The newly married damsel is given a woman escort (muperekedzi) to assist the newly married damsel here and there as is with African or Hebrew tradition. After a few days the escort may return, but if the escort is in the form of a housemaid, she will tarry there for much longer. The escort helps the bride to cope with separation from her family in her initial days in a space outside her maiden family as there are issues that women require to share with a close relation which she cannot keep to self or pick any member of her new family and start sharing her issues. In trying times like these, women are very strong and determined out of which result in the survival of the human civilization and they need to be appreciated;

'And they sent away Rebekah their sister, and her nurse, and Abraham's servant and his men'.

African Culture, Gen 24 vs 59

1.56   Bride Entering the Matrimonial Home

The extent of detail in the marriage traditions in African or Hebrew Culture would give the impression that Hebrew life was frozen in time only to be de-frozen to today's setting in Africa;

'And Rebekah lifted up her eyes, and when she saw Isaac, she lighted off the camel.
For she had said unto the servant, what man is this that walketh in the field to meet us? And the servant had said, it is my master: therefore she took a veil, and covered herself'.

Gen 24 vs 64-65

These procedures remain in force today here in Africa among the Bona fide Hebrews of the Books of Moses, the children of the inheritance. The ceremony of welcoming the bride into her new home concludes the marriage rite and readers should note the conspicuous absence of a wedding in the Hebrew or African marriage. The wedding came with European settlers especially the missionaries who considered the African or Hebrew marital procedures stated herein without a wedding as mere prostitution and often Christian converts have refused to release their daughters who have been married the African or Hebrew way to the in-laws on the basis that marriage without wedding is prostitution and some in-laws actually moved on to leave the converts and their beloved daughters.

African Culture,

Hebrew / African Culture

1.57   Pasichigare Kwaifa Vakweguru/ Death in Old Age

When death occurred, it was always to the elderly and the children were not informed of it, instead they would be taken to a safe haven until the burial was complete and all the mourners had returned to their homesteads. Children did not even know of death or of dead bodies or even graveyards. Today things have changed drastically to the extent that children's games and motion picture is all about death or merciless killing and no wonder some of the little children are murderers courtesy of the motion picture mafia who will live no stone unturned to produce anything that makes them money;

'And these are the days of the years of Abraham's life which he lived, an hundred three score and fifteen years (175).
Then Abraham gave up the ghost, and died in a good old age, an old man, and full of years; and was gathered to his people'.

Gen 25 vs 7-8

'And the days of Isaac were an hundred and fourscore years (180).
And Isaac gave up the ghost, and died, and was gathered unto his people, being old and full of days: and his sons Esau and Jacob buried him'.

Gen 35 vs 28-29

Death was a rare event in Hebrew or African Culture in any given family and when it occurred, it would be to an old person in his/her good old age, on the contrary today Africans are dying in their tender ages and the misinformed bereaved family think that their relative has been taken by the Creator to glory or to the heavenly abode. When people die in their youth, it is not a blessing from heaven, it is a curse for one such curse was pronounced to Eli;

'And thou shalt see an enemy in my habitation, in all the wealth which the Creator shall give Jacob: and there shall not be an old man in thine house forever'.

1 Sam 2 vs 32

The death of a young person is understood as a curse caused by misdeeds of the elders or the deceased, and for that reason an enquiry for a redress unto the Creator must be done else another death will occur sooner. Heaven is only the Creator's abode, when people die they are not understood to go to heaven from the perspective of abiding in glory but from the perspective of the soul being recalled by its Creator. One of the ways in which the Christian missionary managed to console Africans when they came to Africa as a front to imperialism was to preach to people dispossessed of their land and resources of the glories of heaven and good prospects of a prosperous life in heaven especially when one lived a poor and miserable life here on earth, yet they did not ask the preachers of paradise why they were amassing earthly riches, were they not interested in the paradise theory that he preached about?

The patriarchs for the reason of their good, lived life to its fullness and died in good old age.
When King Hezekiah was told of his impending death, he was disturbed, for he had known himself to be a good man not deserving death at that age;

'In those days was Hezekiah sick unto death. And the prophet Isaiah the son of Amoz came to him, thus said the Creator, set thine house in order; for thou shalt die, and not live.
Then he turned his face to the wall, and prayed unto the Creator, saying,
I beseech thee, O Creator, remember now how I have walked before thee in truth and with a perfect heart, and have done that which is good in thy sight. And Hezekiah wept sore.
And it came to pass, before Isaiah was gone out into the middle court, that the word of the Creator came to him, saying, Turn again, and tell Hezekiah the captain of my people, thus said the Creator of David thy father, I have heard thy prayer, I have seen thy tears: behold, I will heal thee: on the third day thou shalt go up unto the house of the Creator.
And I will add unto thy days fifteen years; and I will deliver thee and this city out of the hand of the king of Assyria; and I will defend this city for mine own sake, and for my servant David's sake'.

2 Kings 20 vs 1- 6

Humankind are reminded that they may cause the death of their innocent children when they sin over and above their own lives, in this day the AIDS scourge is killing mother and child because the sins of the parents may invite curses upon the innocent children, and so it is important for a parent in whatever he/she partakes in, to think of what that may cause to later generations (posterity).

When the unexpected happened, the death of children, African Culture prohibits the mother to bury her child, it is a heart wrenching and unbearable exercise which may cause the mother to lose the meaning of life and opt to join the child. Dead infants are not mourned, African Culture prohibits the family of the deceased child from mourning the death thereof especially if the child was under one year. The family can show distress before the child passes on while nursing the sick child but once the child is gone, people meet quietly and bury the deceased. David prayed and fasted for his ill child but when the child died he returned to his normal person as if nothing had happened.

African Culture, African Oral Tradition, Judges 8 vs 32,
1 Chr 29 vs 27-28, 2 Sam 12 vs 14 - 23

1.58   Seri Kweguva Hakuna Anoziva/ Nil Knowledge of Life After Death

Very little is known in African or Hebrew Culture on the subjects of life after death and heaven. As soon as a person dies, references are made about that person by the living in as far as the life lived on earth and not much is said or known about their abode after death. There is no talk of heavenly mansions in Hebrew or African Culture for the dead save for 'the yonder place' contrary to volumes and volumes of literature taught in Christianity.

Hebrew or African Culture contrasts ancient Egyptian Culture that heavily embalmed the dead in preparation or in anticipation of a form of physical existence after death. The African burial involves the simple washing of the body in water, wrapping the body in papyrus and burying the corpse thereafter without any chemical treatment.

Moses at the end of his life aspired to see the land of Canaan. When he was told that his time of death was approaching, he did not celebrate the 'impending heavenly glory' which is preached today, his insistence was on the land of milk and honey which he had an idea about. He was a great prophet by all standards, was privy to more divine information than the ordinary man, but when it came to matters of heaven, after-death and other matters pertaining to the Creator he was an ordinary man. No prophet at the moment of sickness leading to death has celebrated the coming moment of death. Many prophets have run away into caves or mountains to escape any death possibility from the world leaders or kings.

And when people die, they are considered guiltless. David lamented the death of Saul and his sons and spoke wonders though during the life of Saul, David was always on the run from Saul. The understanding in the spiritual realm is that as soon as people die, no one fully understands the specifics of their situation and to condemn such souls which have been reclaimed by their Creator is taboo, only the good concerning the departed is admissible.

There is so much literature by the Arabs on the after-life, most of which pertain to the physical which include unlimited number of wives a man can get notwithstanding the fact that the after-death is spiritual realm and not the physical, the body is interred into the ground where it originates while the soul is reclaimed by its source. And if the spirits of men and women are in equal numbers in 'paradise' then some of these thoughts about multiple wives may never be realized and prophets would be confronted by their followers. Heaven sounds like a man's domain if that is added to gender bias of the form 'lord god our father' and not 'lady goddess our mother'!!

African Culture, Oral Tradition, Gen 25 vs 7-8, Gen 35 vs 28-29,
Judges 8 vs 32, 1 Sam 2 vs 32, 2 Sam 1 vs 17-27, 2 Kings 20 vs 1- 6,

Hebrew / African Culture

1.59   Kutema Ugariri/ Working for the Bride Price

Jacob worked for Laban his uncle in lieu of the bride price for Rachel's hand in marriage and for reasons given by Laban at the end of the seven years, Jacob ended up working for the two sisters. The settlement of the bride price/ roora/lobola is an important aspect of an African or Hebrew marriage in that a damsel will not go for free nor for a fortune, but for some token price;

'And Jacob loved Rachel; and said, I will serve seven years for Rachel thy younger daughter.
And Laban said, it is better that I give her to thee, than that I should give her to another man: abide with me.
And Jacob served seven years for Rachel; and they seemed unto him but a few days, for the love he had to her'.

Gen 29 vs 18-20

The tradition of working for the bride price enables any man to marry the woman of his aspiration regardless of his wherewithal. It is also a cultural test of a man's ability to fend for his future family, if a man cannot raise a token bride price for his wife's hand in marriage, then he may not marry because the chances are high that he will not be able to sustain or fend for his family.

The Jews do not keep this practice among themselves, those Jews who have seen it in practise, have seen it in Africa, among the Bona fide Hebrews of the Books of Moses.

African Culture, Exo 2 vs 21, Hos 12 vs 12

1.60   Kupa Zita/ Naming a Child

A Hebrew or African name is not just a means of identifying one person from the other but it is a means of telling a story of praise unto the Creator, a story of a complaint, a story of one's misfortunes to the world or to the Creator as in names like Kukutendai, Tafara, Nhamoinesu, Khumbulani, Nkululekho and many others. Naming a child is an occasion for prayer, supplication or praise unto the Creator. It is where a parent gives a name to a child that says something every time that name is called. Descriptions of such names include Judah (praise the Creator), Dan (the Creator has judged me), Gershom (stranger in a strange land), Simba (the Creator's power is manifest in Creations), Kukutendai (praising you) as suggested by the following scriptural reference;

'And Leah conceived, and bare a son, and she called his name Reuben: for she said, surely the Creator hath looked upon my affliction; now therefore my husband will love me'.

Gen 29 vs 32

Never at one instance has an African or Hebrew given a name to his child that declares a deity upon his child as the Septuagint translation of Isaiah 9 vs 6;

'For unto us a child is born, unto us a son is given: and the government shall be upon his shoulder: and his name shall be called wonderful, counsellor, the mighty god, the everlasting father, the prince of peace'.

Isa 9 vs 6

Such a name in African or Hebrew Culture would be an idolatrous nomenclature which by itself would kill the child in infancy. The proper translation of Isa 9 vs 6 is a name that says unto the Creator;

'Wonderful in counsel is the Mighty Creator who is everlasting and the source of peace'.

So each time the parent calls the name in Jewish Hebrew 'Pele yoets el gibor avi-ad shar-shalom' he or she acknowledges the wonderfulness of the Creator of heaven and earth and never the 'wonderfulness' of his son. Such translations demonstrate fundamental cultural and linguistic weakness of the Septuagint which shows that the translators were using beliefs they knew in their cultures to translate the Hebrew Script whose underlying culture they did not know and understand. To the north, deifying an object or a child was in order but not within Hebrew Culture, it is an abomination unto the Creator. The translation of the Septuagint is in African or Hebrew Culture, a blasphemy that can result in the destruction of the entire family all in the name of a child.

Another interpretation of the Septuagint translation was that the north wanted to create a deity from a Hebrew child (Joshua the son of Joseph) and superimpose him in the Hebrew Scriptures for him to be understood by the Hebrews and thus be authenticated as the other party to their trinity story.

African Culture, Oral Tradition, Gen 21 vs 3, Gen 29 vs 33-35, Gen 30 vs 6-24, Exo 2 vs 22, Isa 9 vs 6

1.61 **Manana/ Miracle**

Manana is a Vanhu/Bantu dialect term for miracles which agrees well with what happened when the Hebrews saw miraculous food for the first time, they did not know that it was bread until Moses said so but what they concurred was that its appearance was in conformity with miracle and so they called it a miracle (manna) and readers need to note that even after so many thousands of years apart, the Vanhu/ Bantu dialect term carries the double 'n' and the associated vowels but the Jewish Hebrew term has lost the vowel along the way as shall be explained in Chapter 3 Linguistics;

'And when the children of Jacob saw it, they said one to another, it is manna: for they wist not what it was. And Moses said unto them, this is the bread which the Creator gives you to eat'.

Exo 16 vs 15

African or Hebrew Culture is the domain of miracles. Abraham was given a son through Sarah when it had ceased with her as with women in old age, Moses amazed the Pharaoh with the miracles and wrestles the children of Jacob from the Pharaoh and crossed the Red Sea and David defeated Goliath when the odds were against him. In modern times, it was a miracle how African slaves en route to the north and west survived the Trans-Atlantic voyage piled like wood in ships, and how Africans reclaimed their heritage in the wars of liberation against heavily armed settler forces and it is a miracle how Vanhu/Abantu are re-establishing themselves as a people of great renown against centuries of abuse and identity deletion by the other races.

African Culture, Gen 21 vs 2, Gen 30 vs 37-43, Exo 3, Exo 4 vs 3, Exo 4 vs 7-9, Exo 5-13, Exo 14 vs 21-31, 1 Kings 17 vs 3-24, 1 Kings 18 vs 38, 1 Kings 19 vs 62 Kings 4 vs 4-7, 35 2 Kings 5 vs 10,

1.62 **Unhu/ Ubuntu/ Morality**

Jacob worked for Rachel's hand in marriage for seven full years, and in that time he and Rachel never knew each other on the bed, they only did so after the marriage procedure was complete when the damsels (Leah first then Rachel) were presented to Jacob for that purpose. Today, across global cultures very young girls and boys engage in premarital gender activities well before they are ready for marriages which is causing all sorts of worries to the parents. Unhu/Ubuntu is a moral code of conduct taught by African elders to their children and to the entire African community with such themes as 'thou shalt not commit fornication; thou shall not walk nude; thou shall not approach the nakedness of thy father, mother, sister, or kin; thou shall not sacrifice a human being to thy Creator; there shall be no sodomites among thy brothers nor whores amongst thy daughters'. The Unhu/Ubuntu code is the entire culture as kept by Africans. It is that code that sends a shiver into an African when she/he beholds a same gender couple.

Historically, Africans have been enslaved, colonised, exploited, impoverished by other nations of the world, but Vanhu/Abantu have remained accommodating, kind, sincere and neighbourly even to those who have exploited, enslaved, impoverished and harassed them. After all kind of vices were done against Africans, they still embrace other races as colleagues but the same strangers even with full knowledge of African sincerity and good will, will continue to exploit and short-change the African people. The bottom line is Unhu/Ubuntu.

Vanhu/Abantu have reached a spiritual and level of righteousness that other races have not yet reached. That is why today the strangers feel safer in their backyards when they stock mega tonnes of nuclear arms of barbarism and not by the use of goodwill, good neighbourliness and sincerity to other nations of the world. What if their barbaric arms of war were to explode naturally and kill them and their children and also destroy their habitat? What level of safety does a stockpile of nuclear war-heads give to a nation that surpasses good relations with the neighbours? Do they know that if the Hebrews begin to keep their full-throttle spirituality on their land those nuclear arms will not detonate on holy ground?

Africans, the north and west concur that when the north first landed in Africa in the middle of the second millennium through missionary incursions through to the late nineteenth century, Africa was overflowing with serious levels of morality among the youth, women and men. Trust, goodwill, brotherhood and general goodliness described the people at that time and African Culture was at its peak or zenith and so was morality and that time Christianity was not in existence. **Then the missionary started converting Vanhu/Abantu into Christianity to this day most Africans are now Christians and they have forsaken the bulk of African or Hebrew Culture and its moral teaching and in place of morality there are unspeakable evils being committed in Africa like abortion, baby dumping, promiscuity that has caused unprecedented levels of gender diseases among other vices and such immoral ills are coming at a time when Africa is at its Christian peak or zenith and at its lowest in terms of African or Hebrew Culture and the obvious and unambiguous inference is that there is a direct link between Christianity and immorality in Africa on one side and morality and African or Hebrew Culture on the other side.**

As a sign of morals under invasion in Africa, South Africa approved same gender marriage in their national constitution as a result of influences from the north and such laws defile the land of Africa.

And in relation to Banu Arabia (the children of Ishmael), prayer is one aspect of spirituality that should be able to transform the person's human shortfalls to some high principled person. As stated in the preface, prayer was/is ideally a good deed to the neighbour or self and in that regard even without going to a prayer room to kneel down and pray, a good deed is a more practical approach to goodliness and good world order. The Arabs have the highest prayer per capita in the whole world. The Arabs have five prayer sessions in each day but morally Arabia is a land of blood shed, a land of no pity no mercy where brother kills brother as easy as a flea. Arabia is a place where a full grown man can easily arm self with explosives to detonate in kindergarten school with other people shouting 'god is great'!

Unhu/Ubuntu code is all about goodliness before anyone thinks of visiting a shrine to make an offering, goodliness must be seen to be in practice first. Before prayer and deeper spirituality was revealed to Abraham, he was generally a good man. In Arabia among the children of Ishmael, it is not like that. The author saw people of Arabia high speeding and hitting pedestrians without stopping in their luxury cars while rushing for a prayer session!! The author saw Arabs abusing workers from all parts of the globe in scenes reminiscent of slave trade but what was astounding among the Arabs was that they would take a prayer session with a rosary in one hand, in the middle of those savage abuses and then continue with the abuses after the prayer without any remorse.

There is also the issue of holy war which they call Jihad. There is no war that is holy for the reason that every war has the potential to mutilate the objects of creation including the innocent women and children. Jihad, like any other war is below the human moral code of conduct, if people see what is happening in Iraq as examples of war (Jihad or non Jihad), it is humankind's fall into the abyss of savagery and barbarism. What is heart wrenching is that some of these wars are financed by fellow Arab states. The Arabs have exported the Jihad savagery and barbarism to other parts of the globe

Hebrew / African Culture

including Africa and religious thugs are running riot on innocent people. The highest prayer per capita made by the children of Ishmael would make a huge difference to the world if those prayers are complemented by deeds of kindness and mercy. There must definitely be respect for life among the children of Ishmael that equates to the spirit of Unhu/Ubuntu/Ubanu. The war tactic of exploding oneself in the middle of a market place largely made up of innocent women and children is a teaching from an unknown world. The war with the enemy is not won by taking the life of the innocent especially that of women and children. The fore bearers had a few battles with enemies but suicide tactics were unheard of and where these traits come from now and their motivation among their children is a cause for concern. Prayer is a free-will and non physical offering unto the Creator which seeks to enhance the individual relationship between humankind and their Creator and for that reason is not enforceable. What is enforceable are the observance of the Sabbath and other laws which if violated will cause the land upon which they are committed to be defiled, and the defiled land will be deprived of the usual blessings of good rains and associated food that comes from the land. If these laws are not enforced, a few people that will defile the land will cause a curse to afflict all the people.

Prayer is an extra spiritual relationship between humankind and the Creator which is not measured by the length or the frequency of prayer necessarily but by sincerity and works of kindness, mercy and general goodliness. Prayer without works is hypocrisy, shallow and empty and the author that category of prayer in Arabia at range. When prayer is hastily and frequently done especially without the requisite sanctity, it loses its significance as is obtaining in Arabia and neighbourhoods where prayer per capita is the highest in the land with the highest suicide detonations and associated lack of the sanctity of life as a result of unnecessary wars being fought by the Arabs and their converts, prayer will yield no positive results if performed under the said setting and the worshippers thereof will become a laughing stock.

A true prayer must inspire a manufacturer of nuclear arms of barbarism to realise the dangers and irrelevancy of nuclear war, after a true prayer, a manufacturer of nuclear arsenal automatically will begin to think of dismantling the arsenal for such systems are not in line with the essence of creation of the Creator to which the manufacturer is offering a prayer. Nuclear arms of war will annihilate creation.

African Culture, Gen 29 vs 20-30

1.63   Mhiko Yerufu/ An Oath of Death

Jacob unknowingly made an oath of death against his wife Rachel and indeed Rachel died during childbirth when in fact she had given birth to her first son Joseph normally;

'With whomsoever thou findest thy gods, let him not live: before our brethren discern thou what is thine with me, and take to thee, for Jacob knew not that Rachel had stolen them'.

Gen 31 vs 32

In African or Hebrew Culture, an oath made will stand pursuant to the matter upon which it has been made. If it is an oath or vow of death, it will stand even if it means death to the maker of the oath. Oaths or vows must be objective, Jephtah's vow/oath of burnt offering anything that came first out of his door was subjective in that offerings are of certain animals and not anything and that his door was home to his family including his daughter who was eventually trapped in a foolish man's vow.

African Culture, Oral Tradition, Gen 35 vs 16-20, Josh 9 vs 19-20, Judges 11 vs 31, 1 Sam 14 vs 26-39, 2 Chr 6 vs 22-23

1.64   Madzitateguru/ The Link or Role of Ancestors or Fore bearers

The ancestors or the fore bearers are the link or the pointers for the living to spirituality, the role models that guide the living as tales that revolve around the ancestors are nearly guiltless and evil seem to emanate from the current generation and Hebrew or African Culture will cease to exist if the link with the ancestors is broken. The African people will always try to connect at human and spiritual level with

Hebrew / African Culture

ancestors even if they are no longer physically there as done by Jacob;

'And he (Jacob) blessed Joseph, and said, the Creator, before whom my fathers Abraham and Isaac did walk, the Creator which fed me all my life long unto this day, The angel (mhondoro) which redeemed me from all evil, bless the lads; and let my name be named on them, and the name of my fathers Abraham and Isaac';

Gen 48 vs 15

The African or Hebrew link to her/his Creator is always attached to the fore bearers/ancestors (Madzitateguru/ Midzimu/ Mweya). The blessings that the Africans have today, a rich continent, with good rains, offering good crop yields are blessings that came upon the African or Hebrew people for the reason of the good deeds of their fore bearers. Those good deeds are not the object of worship but should inspire the children who are benefiting from the good deeds of their fore bearers. Those good deeds should provide a reference to the Africans for generations after generations never to follow the ways of strangers but to abide by the culture or good deeds of the fore bearers which have brought blessings to the children. There was no possibility in Hebrew or African Culture for a person to worship a a pagan image or deity which were external to their culture as it was pre-requisite to worship the Creator of one's fore bearers. The link only got distorted when the missionaries came with Christianity and started teaching northern heroes, angels, saints and value system. **The link with the ancestors is the identity and loss of which results in a person without identity.**

The African link to the fore bearers is inherent in each and every African today and the north have called it worshipping the spirits of the dead by the Africans and the irony is that the north have not said so to the Hebrew patriarchs who did exactly what Vanhu/Abantu are doing this day. The names Abraham, Ishmael, Isaac, Jacob, David, Isaiah, Jeremiah and later Nehoreka, Chaminuka, Mulimo, Nehanda, Kaguvi always strike a spiritual and physical tone each time they are sounded by the living. In fact the deeds of the fore bearers provide the spiritual synchronization to each Hebrew or African each and every time one begins to get lost, one should always ask himself/herself that this new thing he has accepted, is it what the Hebrew or African fore bearers taught down the line, if it is not then one should quickly abandon it for it may be a wrong belief. And above all, the Hebrew elders stood together with Moses at Mount Sinai to receive the law and they have passed on that tradition to this day.

The culture, language and names of the African fore bearers provide a link to the Creator. Even the language of a prayer should always be in an African dialect as it is at any African shrine where no foreign language is uttered when an offering is being made. The north have not abandoned the languages of their fore bearers in preferences of foreign languages; they have not changed their names either. There are no names as Thembinkosi Van da Mer, Farai Cooper, Mabua Smith, Ngugi waBotha and others among the Europeans or Americans but among the Africans there are names as James Muti, Lucy Sibanda, Winston Khumalo, Laughter Mwanga, Nwankwo Martins and many others, which have no trace to the fore bearers. The north have kept the religious doctrines of their fore bearer like the matters pertaining to the trinity, no matter how awkward they may sound to people who are external to northern culture.

> Det 7 vs 2-8, Gen 31 vs 51-54, Exo 3 vs 6, Exo 3 vs 13, Exo 3 vs 15-16,
> Exo 5 vs 3, Exo 32 vs 13, Det 1 vs 11, Det 6 vs 10, Det 7 vs 8,12, Det 9 vs 5
> Det 9 vs 27, Det 32 vs 7, Det 34 vs 4, Judges 2 vs 11-23, 1 Kings 8 vs 57-58,
> 1 King 18 vs 36, 1 Chr 29 vs 18

1.65   Dzinza/ Lineage or Genealogy

Dzinza/ lineage or genealogy links the Hebrew or African to the ancestors or fore bearers and that link provides the source of identity, values, language, culture of an individual or a group of people and it defines a people in terms of past, present and future. Hebrew or African Culture has remained undistorted for thousands of years for the reason of a traceable ancestry. Genealogy tells the Hebrew or African a line of his/her fathers from creation, their history and culture as obtaining in the Hebrew Scripture to this day of the form 'Shem begot Arphaxad who begot Salah who begot Eber who begot Peleg who begot Reu who begot Serug who begot Nahor who begot Terah who begot Abraham'.

Hebrew / African Culture

And up until the advent of European missionaries in past few centuries, these genealogy trees were well known and defined through African Oral Tradition and it was the duty of the elders to teach the children of their lineage including the totems. When Christianity came and started teaching of new identities to Vanhu/Abantu through baptism or religious brainwashing, most people lost their identities and the associated lineage. The arguments under debate in this book that link African Culture to Hebrew Culture were much clearer among African elders prior to the arrival of the Christian missionaries prior to religious indoctrination. The Hebrew or African lineage passes through the male and not the female. The Jews who were converts from Persia and Babylon brought in non Hebrew provisions into the African or Hebrew Culture and one such aspect among others is that their lineage comes from the woman, the reason for this is derived from the Jews that came from Babylon. When Nebuchadnezzar took Judah in 586 BCE, he took with him the king, princes, artisans, loot and women, and out of those women, the Babylonians fathered children known today as the Jews. The Hebrew traits of these children came through the mother for it was the mother who was Hebrew and it was the mother who taught the child some bits of Hebrew Culture in exile and this is how the genealogy was passed over to the women by the Jews. The people affected by that genealogy change were largely the people that returned to Judah after about fifty years of exile with Ezra, Nehemiah and Zerubbabel (which means the seed of Babel/ Babylon in Jewish Hebrew or the generation or age of Babylon in Vanhu/Bantu dialect).

Hebrew law stipulates that when a Hebrew woman conceives a child with a stranger, a Spaniard, a Briton or a Portuguese or any other stranger, the child takes after the father and becomes a Spaniard, a Briton or a Portuguese and not the other way round in accordance with the following;

'And the son of a Hebrew woman, whose father was an Egyptian, went out among the children of Jacob: and this son of the Hebrew woman and a Hebrew man strove together in the camp';

Lev 24 vs 10

And from the African or Hebrew Culture point of view, a child born out of a Hebrew woman with a non Hebrew man is without doubt non Hebrew.

African Culture, African Oral Tradition, Gen 11,
Gen 38 vs 6-8, Det 25 vs 5-10, Ruth 4 vs 17-22

1.66   Birth Right and Implications of Baptism

There are privileges that come along the first born or being of a particular lineage. Over and above the heir and administrator of the father's estate, these privileges include inheriting the values, madzinza, culture, language and land. Esau was born once with the rights of a first born and later sold them out for a plate of pottage and he never got the rights back. The entire blessings associated with his birth got lost the moment he gave up his birth right. People do not choose to be first or last born but they can choose to forsake all the privileges that come along that status especially when they have unstable tendencies, in that case the spiritual realm will not hesitate to withdraw everything entrusted on them.

'Then Jacob gave Esau bread and pottage of lentils; and he did eat and drink, and rose up, and went his way: thus Esau despised his birth right'.

Gen 25 vs 29-34

There is no concept of multiple birth or the idea of being born again in African or Hebrew Culture and once one is born and injected into the world that is it. When an African is 'born' again as implied by Christianity, that person forfeits the birth rights. When Africans are born, they are born with blessings of a good and rich continent from the Caspian (Iran) to the Cape (South Africa), with the capacity of being self sustaining and the blessing of a cultural heritage of unbreakable ties to the ancestors and spiritual realm but as soon as they renounce their identity and all links to African Culture through baptism, they in fact reject their birth right and begin a new identity and the life of singing blues.

Baptism is the beginning of a new culture and value system called Christianity and is a straight ticket to

65

religious indoctrination and the philosophers who originated Christianity knew very well that to teach people to embrace a new cultural dispensation would be difficult as people would compare their existing culture to the new doctrine and therefore it became a requirement to delete the identity associated with the old culture. If a person agrees to reject original identity as a first step then indoctrination would be easier and to that effect baptism has no spiritual standing.

African Culture, Gen 25 vs 29-34

1.67   Remarkable Absence of the Name Israel in African Culture

In Judaism, which is a Jewish version of Hebrew Culture, the name Israel means *'He who fights god and man and prevails'*, where the implied fight is not metaphorical but real show of physical strength as happened to Jacob when he wrestled a man until the breaking of the day in the following scriptural reference;

'And he said unto him, what is thy name? And he said, Jacob.
And he said, Thy name shall be called no more Jacob, but Israel: for thou has striven with god and with men, and has prevailed'.

Gen 32 vs 27-29

The name Jacob or Yaakov in Jewish Hebrew, agrees linguistically with the African dialects names such as 'Yakovo/Yako - your inheritance' and the context of what transpired between Jacob and Esav or Esau (Aisave - he who was not to be heir to the inheritance') as given in Chapter 3 Linguistics. However the name Yisrael or Israel is non-existent in African Culture, it only came into the picture with the writings of Ezra from exile.

The Jews literally confirm that the patriarch Jacob blasted their deity El in a fist fight. The name Israel is remarkably missing among the Bona fide Hebrews, the Africans, for the reason that it is a pagan identity in the sense that;

1) It tries to equate the Creator with man as one that can at one point physically stoop low enough to be man, fights with man and sustain a defeat

2) It is similar to the combination of three pagan deities a) **Is**is the queen mother of an ancient Egyptian deity, b) **Ra** of the ancient Egyptians and c) **El** the deity of the Canaanites, another origin of the Jews. The name Israel is therefore a trinity of pagan deities worshipped by the Jews and ancient Egyptians.

Vanhu/Abantu who inhabit Africa today worship the Creator of their fore bearers, the Creator of heaven and earth and not to the pagan deities of ancient Egyptians or Canaanites. Today the name Israel has attracted a lot of hate or hostilities for the reason that there is no spirituality in the name. It is a pagan identity, which has nothing to do with the Creator of heaven and earth - Musikavanhu, Mudzimu Mukuru/ Umvelinqangi, Unkulunkulu or the implied patriarch Jacob. It is unimaginable in Hebrew or African Culture for a man to fight with the Creator and let alone prevail. Ezra wrote that which is taboo in Hebrew or African Culture as a testimony to disastrous influences of exile.

The Jews must begin to learn the Hebrew Culture from the Bona fide Hebrews of the Books of Moses. In the same context when Joshua the son of Joseph practised his work and at the time of his death, he called upon the name of El for mercy before crucifixion. The Bona fide Hebrews who had left Canaan half a dozen centuries earlier to this day, do not know nor have any testimony about El – 'Elohey HaC'nani' – the god of the Canaanites.

The land that the Jews inhabit this day (Israel) is always under spotlight for the wrong reasons, it is a land where the inhabitants or visitors sleep with their eyes wide open for the lack of peace. A soul searching Jew will not begin to label the author an enemy and a threat to the state of Israel, but is a moment for searching for true spirituality, and if the Zionist insist on stiff necked-ness, let El fight for himself (v' im haTsiyoni amor betokef, harsheh El, lachmo), indeed let him try - Ngaaedze tione iye El

Hebrew / African Culture

wacho). In fact the author is an enemy of El as was the forefather Jacob and not the enemy of the Jews because the Jews are now part of the inheritance (Exo 12 vs 47-48) and El must be conquered and the author shall be the conqueror of El whom Jacob fought and conquered among his Canaanite neighbours but has now reappeared among the Hebrew sister's children - 'vazukuru'.

Both the Zionist and any ordinary person will concur with the author on the fact that the El implied in the fight with Jacob in the context is not the Creator of heaven and earth, the Awesone One, the Holy One, not the object of worship that Ezra portrayed as in fighting with man and sustaining a defeat. These are the foreign influences that Ezra went through that the author is exhorting the Jews to forfeit for there is no spirituality therein. How often have the Jews implored the Canaanite Cult to bring peace to Israel but without result? (Sim shalom, tovah, uvrachah, chen, vachesed verachamim aleynu veal kol Yisrael amecha - Establish peace, goodness, blessing, graciousness, kindness and compassion on us and upon Israel, your people.)

African Culture, African Oral Tradition, Hos 12 vs 3-4

1.68   Mhosva Inoripwa/ Restitution

Jacob left his brother for Haran with a pending inheritance matter, he sincerely believed that he had cheated Esau and when he returned, he felt duty bound to pay back and appease his brother Esau who in the same spirit appreciated the gift and they reconciled.

In that regard, eye for an eye will not make the world blind but will make each person realize the gravity of another person's eye. If people understand that before they go out to take off other people's eye, they will lose their eye soon after, then they will not even contemplate such a move, and no person on this earth will ever lose an eye, and how good and perfect it would be for people to dwell together in peace.

The problem that confronts the Africans is that they have adopted the law of the north where any cold-blooded murderer who has enough money to hire an attorney can get away with the most gruesome murder or crime and there is now no accountability. The consolation to the keepers of the Hebrew or African Culture is that though under the northern law a well represented murderer may get away with it in a court of law, the same murderer if acquitted by the courts will still face the avenging spirit (ngozi) sanctioned by the Creator.

African Culture, Gen 33 vs 8-11, Exo 21 vs 19-26, Exo 22, Lev 24 vs 18-21,

1.69   Pwanyaruzhowa/ Damage Paid in Lieu of Lost Virginity

The subject compensation applies either when a man impregnates a damsel before the marital rites have been performed or when a man deflowers a maid without intending to marry her (kubvisa umhandara) which conforms to the following scripture;

'And if a man entice a maid that is not betrothed, and lie with her, he shall surely endow her to be his wife.
If her father utterly refuse to give her unto him, he shall pay money according to the dowry of virgins'.

Exo 22 vs 16-17

The father had the right to refuse marriage of his daughter to some men because there are some brutal thugs who do not deserve a woman near them other than a mother. It is an issue of serious concern in Hebrew or African Culture when a maid loses virginity out of marriage. It attracts a hefty penalty if the two parties are never to marry at all, and a more lenient penalty if they choose to get married. The form of the penalty in the case of impregnating the damsel before marriage is termed pwanyaruzhowa which literally means that a man who takes away a maid's virginity before marriage has broken a family boundary, intruded, transgressed and must be penalised. **This is a law that penalises men for abusing women and there are hardly any laws in Hebrew or African Culture that penalise women**

Hebrew / African Culture

for abusing men yet there is so much criticism of the patriarchy inherent in African or Hebrew Culture. Critics may argue that there were no such laws meant to penalise women for abusing men because women never abused men but it is known well in the same culture of women who abused their husbands but the abuses though were not physical perse, rather a lot of them were verbal but strong enough to encourage a full grown adult and head of family to hang himself and often the African justice courts would not raise any issues with women but would pass a comment to suggest that the men who hanged themselves under any conditions were weak.

The act of deflowering maids outside marriage is a punishable offence for it is considered abusing women. Most men prefer women with their full features, sincerity, humility, chastity and innocence and if another man will come and steal his way into any of those attributes will put the woman at a disadvantage and the woman must be compensated and the feminists from the blues of confusion may disagree.

African Culture, Gen 34, Det 22 vs 28-30

1.70 Zviroto/ Dreams

Dreams play a very important spiritual role in Hebrew or African Culture. A blessing or a curse just about to befall the people may be shown unto them in a dream, and most African people have the ability to see matters in their lives through dreams and can interpret dreams. Dreams have the purpose of alerting a good person of the malice that they may meet along the way or can give them consolation in hard times with dreams of a future prosperous life when people are under distress but an evil schemer will not dream of the prospects of evil schemes but maybe shown of the futility of his trade.

Readers should note that while Hebrew or African Culture can indicate impending events in advance but the business of predicting the future using the signs of the zodiac or the constellations of the stars used by other cultures is prohibited. Life will be to obvious and boring if each one person knew of the future in every detail but that every day brings its surprises.

Joseph had dreams which did not tell the future openly but needed interpretation and the gift of interpretation he rightfully declared came from the Creator.

African Culture, Gen 37 vs 6-10, Gen 40, Gen 41, Judges 7 vs 13-15

1.71 Conflict in a Polygamous Marriage

Children from a polygamous family are sometimes involved in vicious inheritance conflicts or petty jealousies which often come from the mothers and nowhere else. The culture neither condones nor discourage polygamy, it merely states in clear terms the conflicts that sometimes arise between women of a polygamous marriage or between the children of a polygamous family;

'And they said one to another, Behold, this dreamer cometh.
Come now therefore, and let us slay him, and cast him into some pit, and we will say, Some evil beast hath devoured him: and we shall see what will become of his dreams'.
Gen 37 vs 19-20

Warning is done to alert any person who hopes to enter such a marriage for the wrong reasons and using the wrong procedure on the challenges involved so that all those who enter into such marriages gear themselves up for the challenges. When the first wife is consulted on the need for the second wife, she prepares for her welcome and even the children born therein would be like children of one woman. If resources are limited to the women and children in a polygamous family, they engage the survival gear and then proper family order and etiquette may be lost as family members struggle to survive in sometimes very trying and difficult episodes of their life.

Hebrew / African Culture

The lessons derived are that it may harm the unity of the family if some children are loved more than others, the less preferred children will become jealousy and act in a similar or worse manner.

African Culture

1.72 Kufa Nechigumbu/ To Die in Sorrow

In the most emotional, sincere, loving and compassionate scene in the Hebrew Scriptures, Judah offered to be taken bondman by Joseph in place of Benjamin and his motivation was to avoid the possibility of his father Jacob dying in sorrow against Judah if anything wrong would happen to Benjamin;

'It shall come to pass, when he (Jacob) seeth that the lad (Benjamin) is not with us, that he will die: and thy servants shall bring down the gray hairs of thy servant our father with sorrow to the grave.
For thy servant became surety for the lad unto my father, saying, If I bring him not unto thee, then I shall bear the blame to my father for ever.
Now therefore, I pray thee, let thy servant abide instead of the lad a bondman to my lord; and let the lad go up with his brethren'.

Gen 44 vs 31-33

In African or Hebrew Culture, an elderly person especially father or mother like Jacob must not die in grief caused by another person, for whoever caused that grief attracted penalties equivalent to those invoked by ngozi/ avenging spirit and such are matters to avoid in life when one is dealing with the elders. And so when Jacob insisted that if anything was to happen to his youngest son Benjamin, the son of his old age, he will die in sorrow brought by whoever would be responsible and Judah like a true leader well knowledgeable on Hebrew Culture and the consequences pertaining to an elder who dies in sorrow, opted to be taken bondman. Judah knew very well that whatever was going to happen to him while in bondage in Egypt, was nothing compared to allowing an elder to die in sorrow for Judah knew that it was much better for him to die a slave than to go free and cause his father to die in sorrow, for an elderly's sorrow would not only bring a curse on him (Judah), but also upon generations after him.

And if society would today raise children of the moral mindset of Judah, the goodwill and good human relations that will come from such children would be ideal especially when people reflect on the today's hateful world.

African Culture, Oral Tradition, Gen 37 vs 35, Gen 42 vs 38, Gen 44 vs 14-34

1.73 Rufu Mubayiro Wezvivi/ Untimely Death is the Wage of Sin

Evil is always associated directly or indirectly to every instance of untimely death of people in Hebrew or African Culture. Directly, an offending person can die untimely while committing evil like robbery, theft, adultery among other transgressions and indirectly as an offspring, beneficiary or accomplice to a person committing evil. Even children are not spared of death from iniquities of their fathers as scourges like HIV AIDS kill both parent and child;

'And Er, Judah's first born, was wicked in the sight of the Creator, and the Creator slew him'.

Gen 38 vs 7

In fact there are hardly any tales of untimely deaths due to exceeding righteousness and neither are there any tales of righteous persons who have supplicated the Creator to die prematurely nor are there any righteous who were sacrificed to atone for the sins of the evil people which is taught extensively in Christianity. An example of a righteous life which lead to good and long life was demonstrated through King Hezekiah;

'In those days was Hezekiah sick unto death. And the prophet Isaiah the son of Amoz came to him, and

said unto him, thus said the Creator, set thine house in order; for thou shalt die, and not live.
Then he turned his face to the wall, and prayed unto the Creator, saying,
I beseech thee, O Creator, remember now how I have walked before thee in truth and with a perfect heart, and have done that which is good in thy sight. And Hezekiah wept sore.
And it came to pass, before Isaiah was gone out into the middle court, that the word of the Creator came to him, saying,
Turn again, and tell Hezekiah the captain of my people, thus said the Creator, the Creator of David thy father, I have heard thy prayer; I have seen thy tears: behold, I will heal thee: on the third day thou shalt go up unto the house of the Creator.
I will add unto thy days fifteen years; and I will deliver thee and this city out of the hand of the king of Assyria; and I will defend this city for mine own sake, and for my servant David's sake'.

2 Kings 20 vs 1-6

Hebrew or African Culture acknowledges that people who die in their youth are as a result of sin and that they live to good old age due to credits of goodliness that they acquire in life. Most Africans are taught in Christianity that when a small child dies in a family, that child was so righteous and has been claimed by the Creator, when it is written *'for I thy Creator am a jealousy Creator, visiting the iniquity of the fathers unto the children unto the third and fourth generation of them that hate me'.*

Life is understood to be a gift and blessing from the Creator, the longer the life, the bigger is the Blessing. Loss of life is the loss of the blessing. Death is therefore not an expedition to the heavenly mansions and glory of the Creator as taught in some religions.

As a result of the teachings that applaud untimely death as passage to heaven, most people who lose their children do not soul search themselves to find out where they may have gone wrong to warrant the death of their young. Hebrew or African Culture requires the family to enquire the cause of death for any untimely death where children who often die earlier than their elders are subsequently buried by their elders.

There are situations which cause people to opt for an abortion to save the life of the mother, that would be an act of transferring the sins of an adult onto an innocent soul. For every calamity that happens to humankind, there is always a sin associated with it. Horrendous fires, droughts, earthquakes, floods, typhoons, hurricanes and other natural phenomenon that destroy humanity are not by coincidence but by design of heaven as a result of iniquities of humankind.

African Culture, Exo 20 vs 5, Exo 12 vs 29, Lev 10 vs 1-2, Num 16, 1 Chr 10 vs 13

1.74 Kurova Guva/ Kudzora Mushakabvu Mumusha/ Succeeding the Name of the Departed

In African Culture among Vanhu/Abantu and not among the Jews, about one year after the death of a married man with or without child, people gather to facilitate the succession of the name of the departed known in Vanhu/Bantu dialect as 'kurova guva' or 'kudzora mushakabvu mumusha'. The quoted scriptural reference did not give the details, it simply mentioned the theme of what happens in the culture when a married man dies;

'If brethren dwell together and one of them dies, and have no child, the wife of the dead shall not marry without unto a stranger: her husband's brother shall go in unto her, and take her to him to wife, and perform the duty of an husband's brother unto her.
And it shall be, that the first born which she bears shall succeed in the name of his brother which is dead, that his name be not put out from among the Hebrews'.

Det 25 vs 5-10

The process of inheriting the wife of the deceased by the surviving younger brother is the last part of the process which is another application of African or Hebrew Culture called 'kugara nhaka' or the

Hebrew / African Culture

inheritance assumption which is given in this work under article 1.75 hereafter where also linguistically the Vanhu/Bantu dialect terms 'kugara nhaka' concur well with Jewish Hebrew as given chapter 3 Linguistics.

The fundamental theme of the 'kurova guva' is the process of succeeding the name of the departed man. When a man dies and leaves a surviving man child, after other rites like adultery detection that may have occurred between the death of the husband and the time that the inheritance matter is settled have been done: 'Pamusi wekurova guva, rupasa runowaridzwa, mudzimai ane murume akashaya anogara parukukwe apo anopiwa tsvimbo dzemurume wake onzi ngaasarudze uyo waanoda kuti asimudzire zita romurume wake, kana ane mwana wechikomana ndowaanonopa tsvimbo idzi zvichireva kuti zita romurume wake richadeedzwa mumwana wake, ipapo mwanakomana anonzi anogara padyo nababa mudiki avo vanozoita sara pavana. Mushure mazvo madzimai anosimuka achipururudza achiti "Auya ari iye, auya ari iye", zvichireva kuti zita romufi harichatsakatiki mumhuri nekuti adzoka ava mumwana wake (the wife of the departed brother is requested to choose who will succeed or carry over the name of her departed husband. The wife would take the staff of her departed husband and hand it over to her son which in African Culture means the name of the departed man will be succeeded by the his son and the women in the vicinity of these procedures would chant 'the departed man has come back to live like he did before').

And when the departed husband did not leave a man child, the wife would choose one of her preferred younger brothers of her husband to whom she will hand over her departed husband's staff and that in African Culture means the brother will inherit the wife out of which union will come a man child who will be named after the name of the departed to carry on or succeed the name of the departed man like it is stated in the quoted scriptural reference which is translated in Vanhu/Bantu dialect as 'kana mufi akanga asina mwanakomana, mudzimai anopa tsvimbo dzababa kuna babamudiki avo vanobva vatora mudzimai uyu kuti vaite vana vanozomutsa zita romufi semanyorerwe azvakaitwa mundima yapiwa iyo'.

Alternatively the procedure of succeeding the name of the departed married man is in African Culture called 'kudzora mushakabvu mumusha' which means that when a married man dies, before the name succession procedure is performed, his name would be in some sense of undefined state (pending continuance or discontinuance) so to speak, in other words there remains a disconnection up until the name succession fundamental has been settled.

When Christianity began to infiltrate Africa, kurova guva was a major casualty of the laws or provisions of Hebrew or African Culture, for it was labelled heathen, when in fact it is clear in the Books of Moses. Kugara nhaka (inheritance assumption) and kurova guva (succession of the departed man's name) are inter-connected events done by the living on behalf of the departed. In other words, an ailing elder brother who prior to his death would be without man child cannot assign his wife to his younger brother for the purpose of the continuance of his name. It is a matter that can be settled by the surviving relations as done by Judah to his son Onan when Er died. In fact it is a cultural right of the departed brother that the living must perform else his name will vanish. Now what has happened is that when the north began to teach Christianity to Vanhu/Abantu, they also discouraged Africans from settling these procedures in question on behalf of their departed kin for the reason that the north labelled the practice heathen yet these procedures conform very well with Hebrew Culture. Like it is with the matter of avenging spirit, the soul of the departed brother whose name succession matter was not performed, is given justice by the Creator in that the surviving relations will not have peace or prosperity in their enterprises for as long as the inheritance matter of the departed brother remains outstanding.

Overzealous Christian pastors have tried to 'cast out demons' foolishly against the departed soul but in vain, because the inheritance law is a living spiritual requirement to which the concerned parties must conform without fail, for the departed soul will continue to murmur, linger and cause havoc on the stubborn surviving relatives. In fact Onan died for refusing to succeed the name of his departed brother. It was actually him whose name was discontinued for refusing to continue the name of his brother. This is one of the cardinal pointers to the Hebrews of the Books of Moses; the Jews have no idea how this is done. Sometimes African Christian converts who have forsaken the spiritual culture of their fore bearers

Hebrew / African Culture

have often given instruction to the living upon their time of departure never to perform the name succession procedure (kurova guva) for they have been brainwashed by the north to believe that the practice is heathen. The surviving relatives would obviously heed the instruction of the misinformed African only to be tormented viciously by the soul of the departed relation for not settling the inheritance matter on his behalf, for in this case it sometimes occurs after death that the state of misinformation is undone. 'Mufi anozochiona kuti kurova guva kwakakosha ave kuseri kweguva ochizotanga kushupa vapenyu kuti vamupinze mumusha'.

The tradition of succeeding the name of the deceased brother involved the younger brother for the continuance of the elder brother's name and not otherwise. The elder brother will not inherit the surviving wife of his departed younger brother to raise a child to succeed the name of the deceased younger brother for he is a virtual father in an African or Hebrew family. The eldest brother inherits the status of the father and the authority to administer the estate of the father and to every family member, he is a father as detailed in article 1.27 **Mwana Wedangwe/ Duties of the First Born**, and he cannot therefore uncover the nakedness of his younger brother or ideally his 'son's wife. However the eldest son cannot inherit his father's wives for that will be uncovering the nakedness of his father, Reuben erred on this matter and lost the status of the first born.

Some families in Africa upon noticing that their elderly son is failing to conceive child, have organized for the younger brother to interact at gender level with the wife of his elder brother without the knowledge of the elder brother only for the sake of conception to continue the name of the elder brother whilst he still lives and eventually when he dies. This is improper, and must only be done in line with the tradition, that is after a total failure of conception of man child by the elder brother and only after his death.

The wife of a deceased husband may not remarry without the conclusion or settlement of the succession of the name of her husband. If she remarries before the settlement of the matter, then she will in essence be a woman of two husbands and she will not have peace in her new matrimonial home until the settlement of the matter.

Readers need to note that the name succession procedure is only performed for married men and not bachelors for the reason that if a married man dies without man child to carry on his name, it means the deceased had personal interest in the continuance of his name and so when he fails to get man child during his life, the living relations will solve his problem but if the deceased was a bachelor, there is no requirement in African Culture to succeed his name because during his life he did not show any interest in the continuance of his name and so when he is buried, African elders tie an object on his body and in eulogy, they instruct him never to bother the living relatives over the issue of name succession for during his time, he did not take his name seriously no wonder he had no wife. The central theme in Kurova Guva is not taking the spirit of the deceased into the home because after death the spirit navigates the spiritual realm (nyikadzimu) and also Kurova Guva is performed only for married men; if the central theme was that of taking the spirit of the dead to the home, then it would mean that the deceased wife, bachelor, spinster or children for whom the procedure is not performed have no spirit to bring in the home.

What is complicating this aspect of Hebrew or African Culture today is the scourge of AIDS in that sometimes the elder brother would have died of HIV and AIDS and inheriting his wife may spell a disaster for the younger brother or alternatively the younger brother would be infected and inheriting his departed brother's wife may pause a serious health risk to the widow.

African Culture, Gen 38 vs 8-9, Det 25 vs 5-10, Ruth 4 vs 5-17

1.75 Kugara Nhaka/ Inheritance Settlement

The matters that deal with inheritance settlement upon the death of a family head follow the procedure for **Kurova Guva/ Kudzora Mushakabvu Mumusha/ Succeeding the Name of the Departed** detailed

Hebrew / African Culture

in article 1.74 and the inheritance settlement are secondary matters which relate to how the estate of the deceased is administered or distributed after the key name succession procedure has been completed for the reason that the name continuation is more important than his estate.

When the deceased family head left a man child, that child will be the administrator of his late father's estate in such a way that all family members would benefit in exact manner and format as if the departed father was still alive as detailed in article 1.27 **Mwana Wedangwe/ Duties of the First Born** in which case the inheritance law does not entrust father's estate to the surviving spouse but to the whole family under the auspices of the first born with the assistance or advice of the uncle (father's younger brother) and the mother. If the deceased left a man child to succeed his name, the mother was exempted from the inheritance issue, she would naturally not necessarily marry again for her husband would ideally be manifesting on the son in all matters of family save for the bed. Most African governments have adopted northern justice systems which entrust the estate of the deceased spouse to the surviving spouse. When the surviving wife inherits the estate of her deceased husband, she usually remarries outside the extended family to a stranger and when she dies, all the family estate will be inherited by the surviving spouse to the extent that indolent and worthless men in Africa are scouting for old widows for marriage in order to inherit their estates when the widows die or when the worthless men suffocate the old widows to their deaths!! African families have encountered unprecedented hostilities between the mother and the male children in the event that the widowed mother has opted for a husband out of the extended family and rejected the provisions of inheritance laws. Male children are naturally quite comfortable with their uncle marrying their mother than to deal with a stranger as their mother's spouse. Often such hostilities have sometimes been fatal, these are the testimonies of the results of rejecting the provisions of African or Hebrew Culture.

In the event that the family head leaves no man child, the deceased's younger brother will inherit the wife largely for the sake of succeeding the name of the departed brother and not for beneficiation from his late brother's estate and therefore the estate remains in the family with the mother and uncle (father's younger brother) making decisions that would have been made by the departed brother if he were alive. African Culture acknowledges the inheritance of the girl child within the family and that she is entitled to all the privileges that come with it within the family context but upon marriage, the fathers' inheritance is not generously given-out to the son-in-law for the understanding that if the son-in-law does not sweat for his income, he becomes so good in amassing extra women other than the daughter of the source of fortune and in doing so will bring in gender diseases to the girl. The more the son-in-law sweats for his income, the less he is generous with his income in relation to other women. The door is always open for the girl child when things go wrong in the marriage and if the father-in-law's resources had previously been invested in the reckless son-in-law, what would be the fallback position when the girl returns home? Father, mother or elders in the extended family are not allowed to inherit the estate of their son or daughter to discourage the lazy ones from killing their wealthy and hardworking children but if a son kills his father to inherit his estate then it is the father who failed to raise his child to the expected standards and there will not be an avenging spirit against the son due the father, not at all.

Disagreements that sometimes erupt between the relatives of the departed member over estate are a result of greed caused by the reluctance by some family members to work for themselves - total laziness and nothing more. As mentioned earlier, the estate of the departed father is given to the eldest son to administer for the benefit of all the children as ideally as it would have been in the presence of the father. The eldest son would administer the estate with the advice of the uncle (sara pavana) and the mother. Ideally the inheritance is not split and distributed among the entitled members of the family as that would split the family. When a younger brother thinks of his own family then can he be given his lot for the bride price and other associated requirements for his new family, the younger family members will continue to look up to the elder brother as the 'father' who would be administering the estate just as the father would have done it.

African Culture, Gen 38 vs 8-9, Num 27 vs 4-11, Num 36, Det 25 vs 5-10, Ruth 1 vs 12, Ruth 3-4

Hebrew / African Culture

1.76   Muteyo/ Runyoka/ Ulunyoka/ Adultery Detection and Curse

The bitter water adultery detection procedure detailed in the Hebrew Scriptures in Numbers 5 is one of the few procedures in Hebrew Culture that were written to a reasonable detail that tries to compare with African Culture but there are no details on the actual bitter water cocktail which in African Culture is well known even by some little boys or girls. Even though there is that extent of detail in the Hebrew Scriptures, still the Jews have no idea about that, in fact the bitter water adultery detection procedure is one of the several provisions of Hebrew Culture that the Jews just read about without a clear picture about the actual administration of such procedures.

Actually, the bitter water adultery detection procedure is one of several procedures used to detect adultery in African or Hebrew Culture.

A)   Jealousy Offering Adultery Detection

The jealous offering bitter water for adultery detection given in the referenced scripture is always initiated by a living husband, causes the stomach of the guilty party to swell that may be fatal only to the guilty party where the innocent party will vomit by the scheme of spirituality. Adultery detection can be applied before or after the act of adultery has been committed even by a jealousy or suspicious husband with the consultation of a priest which in Vanhu/Bantu dialects is called Muteyo/ Runyoka/ Ulunyoka whose aim is to guard against adultery among Vanhu/Abantu. Critics of African Culture have labelled this practice as an act of witchcraft yet it is the same tenet taught by Moses and kept by the Hebrew fore bearers with the same moral theme to fight adultery;

'Then the priest shall charge the woman with an oath of cursing and the priest shall say unto the woman, the Creator make thee a curse and an oath among thy people, when the Creator doth make thy thigh to rot, and thy belly to swell;

And this water that causes the curse shall go into thy bowels, to make thy belly to swell, and thy thigh to rot':

Num 5 vs 21-22

B)   Adultery Detection Prior to Kurova Guva/ Succeeding the Name of the Departed

Prior to the procedure for '**Kurova Guva/ Succeeding the Name of the Departed'**, another application of adultery detection is performed and initiated by the elders of the family to try and determine if after the death of her husband, the widow was mourning or whoring and this latter application of adultery detection is not fatal but only seeks to establish the facts. If the widow is guilty, she would be reprimanded in accordance with cultural laws related to that act of misconduct;

'Then said Judah to Tamar his daughter in law, remain a widow at thy father's house, till Shelah my son be grown: for he said, lest peradventure he die also, as his brethren did. And Tamar went and dwelt in her father's house'.

Gen 38 vs 11

'And it came to pass about three months after, that it was told Judah, saying, Tamar thy daughter in law hath played a harlot; and also behold she is with child by whoredom. And Judah said, bring her forth, and let her be burnt'.

Gen 38 vs 24

Engaging in gender relations after the death of wife or husband out of marriage is considered as an act of disrespect first to the departed and secondly to the matrimony in African Culture and the widowed woman is forbidden to have any relations before the inheritance matter is settled. **[Emphasis was on checking widow adultery because men often died earlier than their wives]**. In the event that the widow was not caught playing harlot and did not get pregnant, African Culture will detect that for sure,

Hebrew / African Culture

prior to the inheritance ceremony, the widow would be made to pass an adultery detection procedure administered through a walk through procedure. The widow would be requested to confess of any improper activities post the death of the husband so as to avoid unnecessary embarrassment that may be encountered in a walk through procure of walking across the staff of the departed husband, where if she passes without incident then she would be clean and the ceremony would proceed, but if she fails the test, then she fell into the Tamar catch, Tamar was lucky in that it was Judah himself who was the accomplice. Hebrew or African Culture does not condone the manner in which Judah conducted himself as an accomplice, but Judah himself later acknowledged that Tamar in committing adultery was more righteous than him, but in summary the harsh penalty that had been laid down on Tamar was/is deterrent in that if women reject advances by man, there would never be a single case of adultery. African or Hebrew law puts more restrictions on woman for the reason that the female gender is more vulnerable to gender diseases, so the law seeks to preserve and advance the welfare of woman lest it be misconstrued by some gender lobbyists as double standards. Like a parent of two children would do if one child is a fast runner and a shrewd dealer in wild life and the other is not, a prudent parent would be more strict on the latter child not to be found in a wild animal infested jungle. A parent is more likely to say to the latter, what will happen to you if a predator animal was to appear before you? But to the former, a parent would at least have an assurance of safety. Or if men and women choose whoring and each one goes his/her way thereafter, in the end it will be the responsibility of the mother to fend for the child alone and this, Hebrew or African Culture does not encourage.

The gender lobbyists have said that such matters as adultery detection infringe on the rights of the woman and in doing so have created an African female of lower morals. Gender lobbyists try to create the impression that they care and are greatly concerned about the African woman yet African women suffer numerous diseases from immorality and morally the reference/benchmark set by the Hebrew mothers Sarah, Hagar, Rebekah, Leah, Rachel and others become mythical and unrealistic targets by empowering the contemporary African woman by rights to unaccountable adultery.

Though men are the accomplices in harlotry but instinctively they discourage harlotry not only to their wives and daughters but to every women for nearly all men have no respect for harlots even when they often enjoy the indulgences offered by harlotry.

African Culture, Gen 38 vs 11-24, Num 5,

1.77   Chimutsa Mapfihwa/ Inheriting a Wife

When the wife dies earlier than the husband in African Culture, which is very rare like the death of Rachel and the daughter of Shuah, the kitchen flame in the home is considered to be extinguished and the in-laws would offer the widower another wife usually the younger sister to the deceased wife to comfort the husband for the rest of his life and provide the best mother to her sister's children and actually in African Culture, the mother's younger sister is literally called 'younger mother' or 'mainini' in Vanhu/Bantu dialect and she will bond very well with the children for the reason that she is known by the children from the beginning as 'younger mother' when compared to opting in a step-mother into the family. When the 'younger mother' comes in as described above, the scenario is called 'chimutsa mapfihwa' which literally means 'reviving the fire place'. Jacob was not given another wife to revive the fire place for he already had the two sisters over and above their maids upon the death of Rachel while Judah was married to the Canaanites, he was not given a wife in conformity with Hebrew Culture for the Canaanites did not keep Hebrew Culture.

Gen 35 vs 19, Gen 38 vs 12

1.78   Tsvimbo Dzababa/ An Elder's Staff

An African elder identifies himself with a staff as was with Judah in the matter between him and his daughter-in-law Tamar and the staff is the symbol and power of an elder which can be used to represent that elder even in his absence. Tamar demanded the staff from Judah for the reason that she

Hebrew / African Culture

understood the significance of the staff and later when she produces Judah's staff as her alibi, Judah accepted the full responsibility of his lapse in moral conduct.

The staff is a trade mark symbol of a Hebrew or African man everywhere he happens to be, it is not necessarily a supporting stick for the elderly and it is unusual for an African adult male to walk about without a staff as done by a newly married bride.

When the elder dies, most ceremonies or procedures that require the physical presence of the departed, the staff will stand in for him.

African Culture, Gen 38 vs 18, Num 17 vs 1-4, 2 Kings 11 vs 10

1.79 Makomborero Anobva Kuna Musikavanhu/ Blessings Come from the Creator

Good fortune or luck does not come by chance or randomly in African or Hebrew Culture, it is always attached to blessings or providence from the Creator as testified by Joseph's brothers;

'And they (children of Jacob) laded their asses with the corn, and departed thence (Egypt).
And as one of them opened his sack to give his ass provender in the inn, espied his money; for, behold, it was in his sack's mouth.
And he said unto his brethren, my money is restored; and, lo, it is even in my sack: and their heart failed them, and they were afraid, saying one to another, what is this that the Creator hath done unto us'?

Gen 42 vs 26-28

Bad luck is understood to either come from the Creator as punishment for evil or may be incited by a third party with permission from heaven.

African Culture, Det 7 vs 13-24, Det 8 vs 18, Det 11 vs 13-15,
Det 28 vs 3-14, Det 30 vs 9, Det 32 vs 12-14, Ruth 1 vs 6

1.80 Kusuma Nyikadzimu/ Apprising the Spiritual Realm

Prior to partaking in any enterprise or setting on a journey or raising an army for battle, African or Hebrew Culture requires people to apprise the spiritual realm of the course of action that people intend to take and always in conclusion, a request for success can be sought as done by Jacob before he went to Egypt and usually all enterprises or journeys which would have been set before the Creator have good results and journey or enterprise done without apprising the spiritual realm is often met with insurmountable stumbling blocks;

'And they told him all the words of Joseph, which he had said unto them: and when he saw the wagons which Joseph had sent to carry him, the spirit of Jacob their father revived:
And Jacob said, it is enough; Joseph my son is yet alive: I will go and see him before I die.
And Jacob took his journey with all that he had, and came to Beersheba, and offered sacrifices unto the Creator of his father Isaac.
And the Creator spoke unto Jacob in the vision of the night, and said, Jacob, Jacob. And he said, here am I.
And said, I am the Creator of thy father: fear not to go down into Egypt; for I will there make of thee a great nation'.

Gen 45 vs 27-28, Gen 46 vs 1-3

By the same token, upon attainment of victory or achievement of a goal which had been previously set before the Creator, an African or Hebrew will advise the same and give thanks as done by Jacob when he sought to go to Egypt to see his son Joseph. African liberation movements did set their course of action of fighting the imperialists before the Creator through the priests, but when the northern army was delivered upon the hands of the Africans, the same did not report the matter back to the Creator and

Hebrew / African Culture

re-establish the pre-colonial governance system and for that failure, there is no reasonable progress in Africa among Vanhu/Abantu post the victories that Africans attained against the imperial armies.

African Culture, 1 Kings 8 vs 13-53

1.81 Vafudzi/ Shepherds

Hebrews or Africans have for a very long time been shepherds, the Masai tribe of Kenya and others are still shepherds to this day. Up until the arrival of Europeans, almost every African animal species was surviving with the correct ecological balance as a result of expertise inherent in African or Hebrew Culture relating to keeping or co-existing with animals as the assistants of humankind without which human life would not be sustainable.

African Culture, Gen 46 vs 32

1.82 Kuraira Nhaka/ Unwritten or Oral Will

A Hebrew or African elder due to a higher level of spirituality, knows when his time of death is near and for that reason he/she does not write a will, but simply senses it through dreams and revelations from the Creator and summons his/her family together and give the last instructions, and thereafter sleeps with the fore bearers as done by Jacob when his time was nigh;

'And the time drew nigh that Jacob must die: and he called his son Joseph, and said unto him, if now I have found grace in thy sight, put, I pray thee, thy hand under my thigh, and deal kindly and truly with me; bury me not, I pray thee, in Egypt'.
Gen 47 vs 29-31,

African Culture, Oral Tradition, Gen 49,
Num 27 vs 13, Num 31 vs 2, Det 31 vs 14-16

1.83 Mitupo/ Totems

Totems are a means of identifying the original African or Hebrew tribes as done by Jacob to his children. The totems remain in force to this day among Vanhu/Abantu except in cases of cross racial marriages where children born out of foreign fathers and African or Hebrew women have no totems, for the child's totem follows after the father.

There are however some Bona fide Hebrews of the family of Ishmael and the children born to Abraham through Keturah who were not there when Jacob gave the totems. These may have or may not have totems but they remain Bona fide Hebrews. The following summarises the core totems found in Africa today which the north have called animism when they wrote their story about Vanhu/Abantu;

1. Water and associated animals that live in water totem for Reuben (Vaera Dziva nedzimwe mhuka dzinogara mudziva)
2. The lion and associated cat family totem for Judah (Vaera shumba)
3. The zebra/ass and the associated family of animals totem for Issachar (Vaera mbizi)
4. The snake and associated family of animals totem for Dan
5. The deer and associated family of animals totem for Naphtali
6. The wolf/hyena and associated family of animals totem for Benjamin (Vaera bere nedzimwe mhuka dzinokwarakwata kana kudya nyama yasiyiwa nedzimwe mhuka).
7. The fish and associated family of animals totem for Zebulun (Vaera hove)
8. The fat totem for Asher (Vaera beta).
9. The heart totem for Simon and Levi (Vaera mwoyo) that emanated from the emotional conduct of Levi and Simon when their sister Dinah was defiled or the core or heart of the Hebrew family, the priests.

Hebrew / African Culture

The totem system is a family or tribal identity or marker that prohibits people within one totem to intermarry which ensures hybridization of offspring which produces stronger and healthier children. People within one group identify as one family even if they are not related but down the family line, they understand that they originate from a particular forefather. The totem system unifies the people and it creates a sense of identity and self belief as most totems are tactful animals like lions which motivate people within a tribe.

Jews are ostensibly totemless for they do not have a direct link back to Abraham for the reason that their Hebrewness comes from the mother who if married to a stranger will not transfer her totem to the children. The genealogy of the patriarchs is Terah begot Abraham, who begot Isaac, who begot Jacob and so on but not Sarah, who begot Rebekah, who begot Leah and Rachel because these did not beget each other. There is no lineage from the mother side.

African Culture, Oral Tradition, Gen 49

1.84 Rufu/ Bereavement

Bereavement is a moment of loss and great pain for the entire African family for the reason of family unity. An African or Hebrew funeral is characterised by a multitude mourning with great lamentation for a couple of days until interment is complete as opposed to other races who do not gather at all but meet (a few of close relations) at the chapel, a few minutes before the burial, the same applies to the Jewish burial.

African Culture, Gen 50 vs 10-11, Num 20 vs 29, Det 34 vs 8, 1 Sam 25 vs 1

1.85 African Endurance

Nations will concur without much debate that indeed the people of Africa have tremendous endurance and resilience when their history can be analysed in relation to how they have withstood brutality, malice and abuse from other races in the form of slavery, imperialism and racism, in fact the more they were abused, the stronger they became as a population as what happened to the Hebrews in Egypt when Egyptian taskmasters set over them more work;

'Therefore they did set over them taskmasters to afflict them with their burdens. And they built for Pharaoh treasure cities, Pithom and Raamses.
But the more they afflicted them, the more they multiplied and grew. And they (Egyptians) were grieved because of the children of Jacob'.

Exo 1 vs 11-12

In the same token, the Egyptian midwives were assigned by their king to kill all male Hebrew deliveries but the midwives were shocked;

'And the king of Egypt called for the midwives, and said unto them, Why have ye done this thing, and have saved the men children alive?
And the midwives said unto Pharaoh, Because the Hebrew women are not as the Egyptian women; for they are lively, and are delivered ere the midwives come in unto them'.

Exo 1 vs 18-19

The Hebrew women did not wait for the Egyptian midwives, they delivered themselves as a sign of amazing strength which is reminiscent of African life in American plantations during slavery where African women would work on the fields up to the day and time of delivery, feel the labour pains while doing hard labour, retire to some tree shade to give birth, breastfeed for some few minutes and return to work immediately thereafter, unbelievable but real.

Vanhu/Abantu have comparatively a higher birth rate and a higher population growth, which is contrary to the level of poverty and malnutrition that prevail on the continent.

Hebrew / African Culture

However due to a drastic change in lifestyle and deviation from African foods to northern junk foods, the resilience and endurance is dying. Africans are now giving birth by Caesarean section where sometimes it is not necessary. African men no longer do demanding tasks that were often associated with men, they no longer walk long distances as in old days but now use machine transport.

African Culture

1.86   Living in the Providence of the Creator

Critics of African Culture and people say that life in Africa was very easy among all the nations of the world in that the continent has abundant wild fruits and animals for food, the continent has good climate with no extreme weather which is like living and benefiting from the providence of the Creator which caused Africans not to advance in technology after the successes of Giza and the Great Zimbabwe.

And when stories of miraculous survival like how Moses as a child was hidden in a basket in the mighty river Nile without the risk of torrents and the predator animals of the river to Moses, it all adds up to the providence of the Creator every step of the way;

'And when she could no longer hide him, she (Yocheved) took for him (Moses) an ark of bulrushes, and daubed it with slime and with pitch, and put the child therein; and she laid it in the flags by the river's brink.
And his sister (Miriam) stood afar off, to wit what would be done to him.
And the daughter of Pharaoh came down to wash herself at the river; and her maidens walked along by the river's side; and when she saw the ark among the flags, she sent her maid to fetch it.
And when she had opened it, she saw the child: and, behold, the baby wept. And she had compassion on him, and said, this is one of the Hebrews' children'.
Exo 2 vs 3-6

The irony was that Pharaoh had issued a decree against the Hebrew male children, but his daughter who was supposed to be highest custodian of the decrees of Pharaoh violated the decree on baby Moses. The reason for that was the hand of the Creator which was also seen by the oppressed Africans in the liberation struggles against the northern army where the Creator at the thickest of things would warn Africans by the acts of an eagle making a sign in the sky or save them by a whirlwind or by a mist. The sad news is that these acts of providence have remarkably vanished when Vanhu/Abantu forsook the culture on a massive scale especially after independence.

Providence sometimes comes to a travelling hungry African in the form of miracle food provision that is usually accompanied by water.

Oral Tradition, Exo 3 vs 17, Exo 6 vs 1, Num 11 vs 7-9, Num 11 vs 31,
Num 21 vs 8-9, Det 8 vs 2-4, Det 29 vs 5

1.87   Kubvisa Tsapata/ hwashu paDzimbahwe/ Taking off Shoes on Entering a Shrine

Vanhu/Abantu across the entire continent including the children of Ishmael (the Arabs) still maintain this tradition of taking off their shoes upon entering a shrine or holy ground as Moses was instructed to do, the Jews do not take off their shoes on entering places of worship;

'And when the Creator saw that he (Moses) turned aside to see, the Creator called unto him out of the midst of the bush, and said, Moses, Moses. And he said here am I.
And the Creator said, draw not nigh hither: put off thy shoes from off thy feet, for the place whereon thou standest is holy ground'.

Exo 3 vs 4-5,

Hebrew / African Culture

Actually when Moses was instructed to take off his shoes at a holy ground, he was herding the flock of his father-in-law Jethro in Africa and therefore critics cannot argue that that tradition was introduced by Arabs when they brought Islam to Africa but even though, not all African tribes embraced Islam.

African Culture, Oral Tradition, Exo 30 vs 19, Josh 5 vs 15

1.88   Zita raMusikavanhu/ Umvelinqangi, Unkulunkulu/ The Name of the Creator

The actual name and form including gender of the Creator remains an unknown subject to the Hebrews or Africans and all humanity. In the Hebrew Scriptures it is written;

'And the Creator said unto Moses, I AM THAT I AM: and the Creator said, thus shalt thou say unto the children of Jacob, I AM (Ini/Ani/Ana) hath sent me unto you.
And the Creator said moreover unto Moses, Thus shalt thou say unto the children of Jacob, the Creator of your fathers, the Creator of Abraham, the Creator of Isaac, and the Creator of Jacob, hath sent me unto you: this is my name for ever, and this is my memorial unto all generations'.

Exo 3 vs 14-15

In African Culture, the entity of the Creator has no specific name but a range of designations with one theme of creation. The referenced scripture gives credence to such titles as Mudzimu/Mweya Mukuru (the Source Soul), Musikavanhu (the Creator), Nyadenga (Whose abode is heaven), Umvelinqangi (One who was there in the beginning and with no ending), Unkulunkulu (the great one with no comparison) which are used by Vanhu/Abantu to refer to the Creator and that no actual name has been passed-on to the Africans by their fore bearers and these designations are by no means heathen or pagan. In African Culture, the Creator is called by a designation related to powers or acts of creation as in the Creator of heaven and earth. The Creator is not called a father, king, prince, lord, master or any other title that is shared by objects of creation (humankind), instead the Creator is called by designations commensurate with the awesome act of creation. Other nations including the north have deities which have names and which appear in human forms. The Creator in Hebrew or African Culture is understood to live in a yonder point (infinity) and nothing more to that subject is known. Any other literature on the subject of the Creator is just human imaginations out of curiosity and therefore anyone who will teach humankind on the form, name, mansions of the Creator based sometimes on dubious dreams or 'revelations' shall be a very false prophet - a liar.

A name is necessary often when objects of one kind appear in numbers exceeding one in order to distinguish them by identity. The Hebrew or African fore bearers were told 'I am who I am', and Moses did not further enquire on how the Creator would be distinguished from other 'who I ams', for the Creator is one and a name is not necessary, but only a designation that is commensurate with the awesome work of creation as the Bona fide Hebrews have spot on called so among other designations Musikavanhu - The Creator of heaven and earth or Unkulunkulu - the Great One, for no entity compares to the greatness of the Creator, including the sun that is now worshipped over Sun Day in the north. The Jews have inherited a number of names, El and Elohim (god and the gods) from the Canaanites, El Shadai and El Elyon, and the other names such as Adonay (our master) and YHVH are all clearly absent from Hebrew or African Culture. The discussion between the Creator and Moses ended without a name but a designation, meaning these names by the Jews will help the world to trace their non-Hebrew origins. Though a term exists in the Jewish Hebrew dialect for the Creator of heaven and earth, which is 'HaBore lehashamayim vehaarets', but the Jews do not use that designation which is commensurate with the awesome act of creation as done by the Africans, they prefer the Canaanite cult El and his variants as explained earlier, because there is very little Hebrew Culture in Judaism of the Jews.

Linguistically, the term 'El' means 'to' or 'not/nothing' and has no connection at all with the act of creation except that it is the name of a Canaanite deity. However to give it some semblance of power and

Hebrew / African Culture

strength synonymous with a deity, the Jews have given a non-original meaning of 'El' to mean 'strength or power' so that among the gods or deities 'El' would not sound powerless. The north who were used to deities with names like Zeus, Horus, Mars, Apollo, Jupiter and many other unholy names sought to translate what has been written by Ezra about the Creator in the Hebrew Scriptures by Yod Hay Vav and Hay (Hebrew letters for YHVH) got it all wrong for the designation of the Creator was given to Moses only in the manner of the referenced scripture.

If the north cannot decode basics in ordinary life like the fact that nuclear energy is better not used at all for it is highly toxic or that swine meat is not food but a poison known as cholesterol or that sodomy will lead to extinction of humankind, what will give the uncircumcised the intellect to decode the HOLY NAME? The result of the translation written by Ezra has given many forms of the name without a clear cut meaning - causing confusion - as was with the tower of Babel, which is what happens each time humankind try to dig deep into fruitless research.

The Jews have given the Creator a name synonymous with Canaanite culture like El (the chief god of the Canaanites) and also Elohim (which mean gods), implying that there is no monotheism in Jewish Culture. Vanhu/Abantu, the Bona fide Hebrews have accorded the Creator the actual title because it is the Creator who created heaven and earth and all that is therein. There is a universal concurrence there, because even all the pagan polytheist cultures of the world do not have instances of god 1 who created heaven in the beginning, god 2 who created the earth, god 3 who created the stars, god 4 who created the air and so on, rather what prevails in those cultures is simply some statues moulded from the clay which the Creator made being used to denote the god of vegetation, or rain, or river and so on without out-rightly declaring that it was those idols that created the objects they represent.

The Hebrew or African designation, Musikavanhu and other designations imply the Creator of heaven and earth and are spot on and if there was a distinct name taught by the fore bearers, that name would have survived as much as the term 'baba' for father has survived even after tribes have adapted to different habitats. Note a distinction between ancient Egyptians and the bulk Africans or Hebrews in terms of spiritual beliefs; while the Africans are resolute about their belief in the Almighty Creator/ Musikavanhu, as is given in the Hebrew Scriptures, the Egyptians were very renowned before Muhammad preached Islam for worshipping idols such as Amen Ra or objects like the sun and the river Nile. When Muhammad taught Islam the bulk of them converted to Islam. A number of professors of African and Religious Studies at most African universities and abroad are very fond of referencing pre-Islamic Egyptian culture as representing general African Culture yet the two were in matters of spirituality different before Islam was taught unto the Egyptians.

There is no information in Hebrew or African Culture relating to the form of the Creator including gender to the extent that Vanhu/Abantu do not use any gender pronoun or superlative to refer to the Creator unlike the Jews and Arabs who use 'hu' and 'huwa' for 'he'. There are no known partners like holy spirit that work in collaboration with the Creator as implied by the Christian trinity which attaches son and holy spirit to the father as if to imply that in the absence of the holy spirit, the father is as spiritually empty as dead wood. Though the Creator is known to have angels of different forms which are sent to punish or redeem when it is necessary. The Creator is not known to have a family and making such family assumptions also means that people are giving the Creator gender and the popular one given to the Creator is the male gender as in father of all creation and not mother of all creation which is just male chauvinism at the minimum. If man begin to associate themselves with god, what will womenfolk do? There is no gender conflict in African Culture as the Creator is neither man nor woman and neither are priests or prophets exclusive to a particular gender and therefore African or Hebrew women like Miriam, Deborah, Queen of Sheba, Nehanda have been prophets/priests/judges. Women of the north need to lobby seriously to be able to be priests like their menfolk, who said a woman cannot be a priest anyway? And if they succeed, the author advises them to force their menfolk to remove gender on god.

African Culture, Oral Tradition, Exo 6 vs 3, Exo 6 vs 7, Exo 7 vs 15, Exo 8 vs 20, Exo 10 vs 3, Exo 10 vs 16

Hebrew / African Culture

1.89   Bira/ A Liquor Thanksgiving Offering

The strong drink offering is universal in Africa and it dates back to the beginning of the people. Though Vanhu/Abantu have separated and adapted to different habitats but the tradition of strong drink offering has not vanished from each and every tribe and the methodology is summarily still the same and the associated sanctity required of people who prepare it has not changed. The Jews do not keep the strong drink offering Hebrew tradition for many reasons that include lack of knowledge of the offering, the details given in the Hebrew Scripture are just a statement relating to the need for a strong drink offering but not the methodology which is in Africa this day and the Arabs stopped the tradition by way of a decree from Muhammad for the reason that the Arabs had commercialised it and were brewing beer on daily basis and cases of intoxication were now part of their life;

'Thou shalt not delay to offer the first of thy ripe fruits, and of thy liquors: the first of thy sons shalt thou give unto me'.

Exo 22 vs 29

In principle a bira or strong drink offering is a thanksgiving offering performed by Africans as an expression of gratitude to a peaceful life, prosperity at home, success at school, successful hunting, success at war, good harvest and for good health among the people as an acknowledgement of the providence of the Creator in the life of the Hebrews. A common offering at a bira is a traditional brew (liquor) accompanied by fruit, grain or animal offering of cattle, goat or sheep.

Priests, kings or elders lead the events and the requirements are that leading to the offering there must be spiritual cleanness of the place of an offering, the people preparing the items of the bira and those who will utter the words of thanksgiving that form part of an offering and the ordinary people who will attend else the offering would be defiled and fruitless. Those who have had contact with human blood, or dead body need to sanctify themselves. Women with their manner or those undergoing purification after child birth are not required. Men who have had the flow of seed need to sanctify themselves to qualify. Prior to an offering with respect to those preparing and leading the offering and the ordinary people who will attend the offering, matters of the bed are not partaken of.

It is important to note that African families that still keep the statutes of bira offering of the Creator are doing quite well, however the Hebrew Christian converts would be quick to say the practising Africans 'enrich themselves by evil, they will not see heaven'. Feasts (mapira) for thanksgiving unto their Creator have always been occasions for family gatherings and celebration with song and dance. Fewer Africans still abide by these feasts, for the reason of brainwashing or indoctrination by the north, who have called nearly every African Cultural festival heathen/animist without first checking whether it conforms to the Hebrew Culture (the benchmark) or not. In the same way the Africans who have converted to Christianity did not check the spirituality of the foreign abominations of the north before they agreed to convert to a foreign faith, especially the matter of human sacrifice. In summary the majority of Africans who have converted to Christianity are very misinformed. In terms of spiritual matters, they are not sure which is right or left.

Usually amid afflictions in life, Vanhu/Abantu enquire of the Creator as to the causes of their tribulations. When an enquiry is done the wrong way through a man with a familiar spirit, the remedial message will be real but misleading in that the familiar spirit will prescribe a bira to the departed fore bearers. The reason for such a recommendation is that a familiar spirit does not interface with the Creator, but it interfaces with pre-known life or others and in that regard an offering to the departed fathers is prescribed. However an enquiry of the Creator through a bona fide priest will prescribe a bira to the Creator and if the offering is done the results would be tremendous.

Though the north have adopted the term bira into pray/prayer but the content of their prayer is not the same as that of African or Hebrew Culture for the reason that human sacrifice, use of human blood in worshipping, trinity or multiplicity of deities or use of incense among other devices used in their prayer are abominable in Hebrew Culture. And while the technology of brewing beer was known for thousands

Hebrew / African Culture

of years by Vanhu/Abantu, brewing beer was not commercialized on the basis that continuous consumption of beer is not good for health, morality and is a source of conflict among the people and therefore ideally beer is consumed once and moderately during the thanks giving strong drink offering.

African Culture, Exo 5 vs 1, 1 Sam 20 vs 6, 1 Chr 29 vs 21-22, 2 Sam 6 vs 19

1.90   Natural Disaster Pre-warning Systems

In observant communities, there is no need to invest in disaster warning systems, African or Hebrew Culture has inherent natural disaster warning systems. A drought, pestilence, an earth quake, locust attack, a flood or any other disasters are made known to practising Africans for the reason that those practising people would be in high spirituality level and such disasters would not be meant for them but are foretold together with a remedy. If locusts are to come in the land of practising Africans, a priest will inform the people to put in preventive mechanisms. However for the reason of conversion by the bulk of Africans, such warnings are no more forth coming and the consequences are disastrous unchecked agricultural losses leading to hunger and starvation.

Oral Tradition, Exo 7-12, Exo 10 vs 4, Exo 10 vs 15

1.91   Roast Meat Offering and Burning of Remains

The accuracy of detail and manner of the offering and disposal of remains which is done according to the book by practising Africans would give an impression that Moses or Jethro or the fore bearers were in the community teaching the culture the previous evening prior to the offering.

'Eat not of it raw, nor sodden at all with water, but roast with fire; his head with his legs, and with the purtenance thereof.
And you shall let nothing remain until the morning; and that which remaineth of it until the morning you shall burn with fire'.

Exo 12 vs 9-10

The referenced scripture gives the details of the ceremony of the succession of the name of the deceased (kurova guva) which is performed after the acceptance procedure of the goat to be offered, the entire goat is roasted and consumed and all the remains, the bones, head, legs, hide and the dung are all burnt up in the same fire until all are ash.

African Culture,

1.92   Kutanga Kwemwaka/ The Beginning of Seasons

In Africa, the year or the beginning of seasons starts at some period which is characterised by a particular event on vegetation or crops or natural phenomenon, for example the beginning of the year given in the scriptural verse starts off around March/April, a period characterised by green corn (nguva yezhizha) or sometime in August/September where vegetation start vegetating again (pfumvute/ nhenhere).

'And the Creator spoke unto Moses and Aaron in the land of Egypt, saying,
This month shall be unto you the beginning of months: it shall be the first month of the year to you'.

Exo 12 vs 1-2

There is no instance in the African/ Hebrew calendar where the year just starts in the middle of a particular activity as it does in January. It may sound sensible for the north if the first of January is the start of one of their four seasons, but to Africa the first of January is not the beginning of any season, it is simply an instance of imitating the north.

On the other end, the Jews have named their months with symbols or deities of Babylonian origin

Hebrew / African Culture

giving more credence to the assertion that they are indeed the grandchildren of Nebuchadnezzar (Babylonians), Achashverosh (Persians) and the Assyrians among others sired out of Hebrew women who were taken into captivity as war booty.

The Arabs had a similar Hebrew year which started on the start of vegetation but was changed and now their year can start on any day of any season without a complete cycle and before the change was made, their month of Ramadan was consistent with the hot season and did not change all year round like now.

African Culture, Oral Tradition,

1.93   The Bitterness of African Vegetables

A large variety of African vegetables eaten by Africans today are bitter. Sometimes the same vegetable that can be prescribed for an ailment or medication will be part of African dietary vegetable and the origin of that diet is spiritual;

'And they shall eat the flesh in that night, roast with fire, and unleavened bread; and with bitter herbs they shall eat it'.

Exo 12 vs 8

Africans who naturally eat their traditional foods have lower instances of dietary related diseases than those that have adapted to northern junk food in the form of soft, sugary, processed and sometimes seedless or bio-modified food. The Vanhu/Abantu diet, over and above the referenced bitter vegetables, consists of the small grain cereals and wild fruits. Naturally the small grains consisting of pearl millet, finger millet and sorghum are very resilient to extreme weather especially droughts and plant diseases compared to maize, wheat and rice largely staples of the north and the east. If maize and small grains are grown in the same area, a dry spell of as little as three weeks will cause the maize to wilt beyond recovery while the small grains will show very minimal stress signs, if at all. And Africans have derived their resilience and strength from such a diet and any shift from this diet to the northern cereals will take away the African resilience no wonder today Africans have dietary health problems and general frailties which they never used to have before the dietary switch to northern foods.

African Culture,

1.94   Universality/Inclusivity of the Hebrew Covenant

The main justification for the 'new covenant' taught chiefly in Christianity is that the Hebrew Covenant was not universal or inclusive of the strangers (the gentiles) but was only between two parties; the Creator on one side and the Hebrews on the other side. Christianity further states that there was therefore need for a universal covenant. Such teachings are notwithstanding the following provision for non-Hebrew entry or assimilation into Hebrew Culture;

'And when a stranger shall sojourn with thee, and will keep the Passover to the Creator, let all his males be circumcised, and then let him come near and keep it; and he shall be as one that is born in the land: for no uncircumcised person shall eat thereof.
One law shall be to him that is home born, and unto the stranger that sojourns among you'.

Exo 12 vs 48-49

And so one of the first laws drafted at exodus from Egypt was about the stranger and for the stranger in order to accommodate any willing race to embrace Hebrew Spirituality and Culture and moreover when the Hebrews had settled in Canaan, Solomon built the temple and on the very first day of inauguration of the temple when he apprised the Creator of job completion, he supplicated on behalf of the strangers to the Creator to equally hear and champion the requests of strangers as well as those of Hebrews;

Hebrew / African Culture

'Moreover concerning a stranger, that is not of thy people, but comes out of a far country for thy name sake; For they shall hear of thy great name, and of thy strong hand, and of thy stretched out arm; when he shall come and pray toward this house; Hear thou in heaven thy dwelling place, and do according to all that the stranger calleth to thee: **that all people of the earth may know thy name**, *to hear thee as do thy people; and that they may know that this house, which I have built, is called by thy name'.*

1 Kings 8 vs 41-43

With the universality or inclusivity of Hebrew Culture defined in the referenced scriptures, the north rejected assimilation into Hebrew Culture as provided for in Exodus, and later through the Greek Scripture they wrote the religious script of their origins – human sacrifice, human deification all of which were the symbols of worship of their founding fathers.

The Jews did not help the situation either, instead of encouraging assimilation of non-Hebrews into the culture, out of selfishness synonymous with overzealous converts, they narrowed the universal Hebrew Culture to some tribal religious sect and closed possibilities for the strangers to assimilate no wonder the global animosity they have earned. Instead of being part of the huge family after conversion, the Jews made sure that there were not going to be any further conversion after them and the Hebrew Covenant has never been popular thereafter. The Arabs have used brute force to convert people to their version of the script thereby making enemies with virtually every living soul while the people of Africa have remained very accommodative and reconciliatory. Conversion is natural and is not forced but in Arabia, some converts and some Arabs are using extremism or terrorism to enforce a culture or religion but for how long can you force people to hold on to what they do not prefer, you need to be eternally stronger than all the people to be able to subdue them forever which of course is not possible? And Christianity was grown by brutality and savagery meant to convince the people that Joshua the mortal son of Joseph was god because at first most people did not take that, but after sufficient force, they had to.

An audit of salvation that comes along Christianity is open for all to see, the world that humankind live today is all war and weapons of mass destruction caused by suspicion between people of different creeds, diseases unwritten in the scriptures and hunger caused by endless droughts and floods are the summary of life at the zenith of Christianity. The Christian doctrine was modelled on nationalist schism inclined to the Romans, Greeks, English and Dutch among others which competed for religious conquest and that did not help to unite the people of the world as would have been achieved through Hebrew Culture which taught of one family begotten of the patriarch Abraham.

African Culture, Num 9 vs 14, Num 15 vs 14-16, Det 23 vs 7-8, 1 Chr 16 vs 17, 1 Chr 16 vs 23-35, Jer 50 vs 4-5

1.95 Kusungira/ Redemption or Sanctification of the First Born

The practice of sanctification/redemption of the first born in African Culture is literally called attaching the child to heaven and in the child's life all the challenges that confront him will be solved for him because he has been sanctified to the Creator and he lives a nearly effortless life.

'And the Creator spake unto Moses, saying,
Sanctify unto me all the firstborn, whatsoever openeth the womb among the children of Jacob, both of man and beast: it is mine'.

Exo 13 vs 1-2

'That thou shalt set apart unto the Creator all that openeth the matrix, and every firstling that cometh of a beast which thou hast; the males shall be the Creator's.
And every firstling of an ass thou shalt redeem with a lamb; and if thou wilt not redeem it, then thou shalt break his neck: and all the firstborn of man among thy children shalt thou redeem'.

Exo 13 vs 12-13

Hebrew / African Culture

It is African tradition that upon the birth of a firstborn child, the woman prior to the birth of a first child is sent to her maiden home to fulfil the redemption rite where the husband will provide a goat or lamp to be slaughtered for the redemption and thus the firstborn is redeemed, and this practice is done only on the birth of the first child and births that follow, the second, third born children and so on are born normally at their new homes. The problem though is that this tradition of Hebrew or African Culture of high spiritual significance is slowly giving up to Christianity which does not sanctify first born children to the Creator. The consequences of reneging on such key laws is that if the firstborn child is not redeemed, will grow up a hard life full of misfortunes and inexplicable trials and tribulations summed up in the 'mwana wedangwe anofanira kushinga nekuti nhamo dzeupenyu dzinenge dzakaringana naye' which means, the first born child has to be of an enduring heart for worldly trials and tribulations are always in front of him/her. It is partly due to the responsibilities that befall a first born child when parents die in the first born's childhood, leaving him with the insurmountable task of raising up the family. A child who has not been redeemed will not have the blessings of the Creator in life. In the same token a child born out of a marriage where the mother-in-law's dues (n'ombe yeumai) have not been honoured or in which dues to the in-laws for the upkeep of children have not been settled will have a hard road travelling in life.

A dissatisfied mother will murmur to the Creator and that in itself is an offering against the children indirectly. Vana vanokura kunge vakafuratirwa neMudzimu Mukuru (the children will grow up the hard way as if they were forsaken by the Creator), vachikwira gomo risina michero (while they attain fruitless targets) when other children seem to have easy and nearly effortless life. Every target for these unsanctified children or those children whose mother-in-law is murmuring seem elusive. At school they could be very brilliant, passing with distinctions up to university, but when the time for employment comes, they struggle to get decent jobs and when they finally get them, they do not rise remarkably, they have modest rises if they come at all. When they try to venture into business, their business proposals are water tight and risk free, but come implementation time, merchandise does not sell for reasons beyond business rationale. Thus by sanctifying the first born, all channels and avenues to navigate in life in search of a prosperous life are opened. And if the children are not sanctified scripture recommends breaking their necks and the statement is not literal but it means the act of not sanctifying the first born is like burdening his neck with very challenging trials and tribulations that may break his neck.

African Culture, 12-13, Exo 20 vs 5, Exo 22 vs 29-30, Exo 34 vs 19-20, Num 3 vs 40-51, Num 8 vs 17-19, Num 18 vs 15-19

1.96   Kutungamirirwa nemhondoro/ Angelic Guidance

Divine guidance has always been with the Hebrews in all their life for wonders in the verses quoted herein will always be with them in their trials and tribulations against the enemy nations. This is one of the vivid signs that the Hebrews or Africans are with the Creator and that the Creator is happy or merciful for them. Hebrew or African Culture acknowledges the existence of angels which are sent by the Creator for a purpose, to bless or to inflict punishment on humanity, but no names are attached to the angels considering that sometimes they come not only as human but animals or natural phenomenon as referenced herein and therefore such names given to angels as Gabriel or Michael as explained earlier are non-Hebrew.

'And they (children of Jacob) took their journey from Succoth, and encamped in Etham, in the edge of the wilderness.
And the Creator went before them by day in a pillar of a cloud, to lead them the way; and by night in a pillar of fire, to give them light; to go by day and night:
The Creator took not away the pillar of the cloud by day, nor the pillar of fire by night, from before the people'.

Exo 13 vs 20-22

'And the angel (Mhondoro) of the Creator, which went before the camp of Jacob, removed and went

Hebrew / African Culture

behind them; and the pillar of the cloud went from before their face, and stood behind them':

Exo 14 vs 19

Readers with knowledge on Africa during the colonial era leading to the conclusion of the liberation struggles will not dispute that the African people had living encounters with divine guidance; liberation fighters would evade the northern armies in inexplicable circumstances to the northern armies but to Vanhu/Abantu who were familiar with the works of Mhondoro dzaMusikavanhu (angels of the Creator) were not surprised at all.

Earlier in the initial wars with the imperialists that occurred centuries earlier when the continent was not yet defiled by European settlers, wonders would happen of the resemblance of the Red Sea crossing where Africans under threat from the enemies would have the earth open for them (ninga) and close before their adversaries, whereupon the Africans would take refuge underground for days. Today such instances are not as much in occurrence as in the said period for the reasons that Africa has been defiled by both Africans and strangers. After winning the war against the north, the same Africans who were guided by angels (Mhondoro) of the Creator, instead of offering thanks giving (mapira) for success at war, exalted Anglicanism or Roman Catholicism, the same forces that they fought.

African Culture, Oral Tradition, Exo 14 vs 19-28, Exo 23 vs 20-23,
Exo 33 vs 2, Num 9 vs 15-23, Det 9 vs 3, Gen 18, Gen 19,
Josh 3 vs 10, Josh 3 vs 14-17, Josh 4 vs 21-24

1.97   Bire naGanyire Cross the Zambezi in Leather Aprons

On their journey from Egypt at Exodus, the Hebrews who were confronted with the insurmountable task of crossing the Red Sea, were assisted by the powers of the Creator that split the sea into two to create a dry land. In exact fashion later as they travelled southwards during the Vanhu/Bantu migrations, the same people this time led by Bire and Ganyire crossed the crocodile infested Kasambavezi river (Zambezi), using their leather aprons to stop the vicious flow of water as their colleagues crossed the river like what was done by Elijah in the referenced scripture. It was not the aprons that stopped the waters, but the works of spirituality.

'And Moses stretched out his hand over the sea; and the Creator caused the sea to go back by a strong east wind all that night, and made the sea dry land, and the waters were divided.
And the children of Jacob went into the midst of the sea upon the dry ground: and the waters were a wall unto them on their right hand, and on their left'.

Exo 14 vs 21-22,

'And Elijah took his mantle, and wrapped it together, and smote the waters , and they were divided hither and thither, so they two went over on dry ground'.

2 Kings 2 vs 8

The Hebrews or Africans, with the blessings of the Creator can conquer the world without firing a single bullet, the Hebrews while fully practising their culture can cure the most deadly disease, the Hebrews in full adherence of their culture can stop the times, but things can go wrong the moment they forsake the culture or the covenant that the Creator entered into with their fore bearers in pursuit of wanton abominations.

African Oral Tradition, 2 Kings 2 vs 8,14, Josh 3 vs 13-17,

1.98   Masvikiro Echikadzi/ Female Priests

There is substantial literature written by writers who are external to African Culture about the patriarchal system and its 'abuses' to women but when African Culture is critically analysed, most of what is called abuses are embedded features that protect the woman for example when women are forbidden from

Hebrew / African Culture

premarital gender interaction, that prohibition affects men as well with the key objective of making sure that no woman is exploited by men.

African Culture does not associate the entity of the Creator with a particular gender male nor female, in other words the Creator is not male as popularly believed in other cultures and in this context, priests and prophets in African or Hebrew Culture have been male and female from the beginning yet in northern culture, women are still fighting for the priesthood let alone ascribing a genderless god.

'And Miriam the prophetess, the sister of Aaron, took a timbrel in her hand; and all the women went out after her with timbrels and with dances'.

Ex 15 Vs 20,

'And Deborah, a prophetess, the wife of Lapidoth, she judged the land at that time'.

Judges 4 vs 4

Prophets can be either men or women in Hebrew or African Culture who are married and not celibate. The priests or prophets are largely from the tribe of Levi or any other among the spiritually capable persons within the Hebrew family. The prophetesses of the Hebrews did not end with Miriam, but the Hebrews or Africans continued to be inspired by way of Deborah up to Nehanda (a Zimbabwean 1st liberation war chief architect) - at the end of 19th century who used high level spirituality to outdo the imperial army. To this day there are African women who are practising priests among the people. Moreover when the Queen of Sheba and Cleopatra ruled in Africa, such feats by women were unheard of elsewhere.

African Culture, Oral Tradition, Judges 4 Vs 8-10

1.99   Zvisipiti/ Natural Wells, Fresh Waters and Springs from Providence

In African or Hebrew Culture, there are no outright tales of people who died of hunger and thirsty even when they were navigating the most barren place on the planet for the reason that water or food would very often be offered from providence as happened to Ishmael and his mother when the they ran short of water, somehow somewhere water will be provided;

'And they (Children of Jacob) came to Elim, where there were twelve wells of water, and threescore and ten palm trees: and they encamped there by the wells'.

Exo 15 vs 27

The bulk of African waters are fresh spring waters or natural wells from underground water which are ready for drinking even without the minimum purification. In the process of extraction of water, what is important in the culture is the proper extraction procedure that does not desecrate the naturals wells of the Creator, because as soon as people desecrate the wells, the water will cease to be with the well and such scenarios are inexplicable even by science where matters such as water-table recession or non-recession will not make a point.

Life is made easy in the land of observant Hebrews or Africans for fresh waters sprout out of the earth at various points in the neighbourhood of Africans. Living examples are described in the verse quoted herein but today there are famous fresh water sources across the face of Africa, Pungwe water is a typical example in Zimbabwe where fresh water falls against a mountain and by gravity and it travels for kilometres in a tunnel like the tunnel of Hezekiah to supply spring fresh water to the people of a town called Mutare in the eastern district of Zimbabwe.

'This same Hezekiah also stopped the upper watercourse of Gihon, and brought it straight down to the west side of the city of David. And Hezekiah prospered in all his works'.

2 Chr 32 vs 30,

Hebrew / African Culture

'And the rest of the acts of Hezekiah, and all his might, and how he made a pool, and a conduit, and brought water into the city, are they not written in the book of the Chronicles of the kings of Judah'?

2 Kings 20 vs 20

When an engineering survey of waters of providence is made, dimensions are not important, what is important is cultural observance and requisite extraction procedures; a small spring that seem suitable only for small community consumption can supply adequately the entire metropolitan city. However as a result of degenerate industrial technology that came with the north, most of these waters have been polluted by industrial waste.

And while the works of providence are always seen in the life of Vanhu/Abantu but the people never stop worrying or planning for tomorrow contrary to what is taught in Christianity where humankind are required not worry about tomorrow but should emulate the birds of the air when the irony was that the north fronted by the missionary, occupied Africa among other destinations as some form of future territorial planning for their unborn children. The extent of insincerity is huge.

African Culture, Gen 21 vs 19

1.100 No Number Names for Years or Months

The original Hebrew year had no continuous number identity, it was simply a finite number of years referenced to/from a great historical or spiritual event similar to 'in the 40th year after departing Egypt'. The same is done with respect to month naming/numbering, which simply identify months with respect to events that occur in those months like mwedzi wembudzi (the month of goats - November - the breeding month for goats) and years in relation to a great event or catastrophe for example gore remhashu, gore renzara (the year of locust and hunger respectively).

'And they (children of Jacob) took their journey from Elim, and all the congregation of the children of Jacob came into the wilderness of Sin, which is between Elim and Sinai, on the fifteenth day of the second month after their departing out of the land of Egypt'.

Exo 16 vs 1,

The Jews have given names to their months like Nisan (their first calendar month), Ayar (second calendar month), Sivan (third calendar month), Tammuz (fourth calendar month), Ab (fifth calendar month), Elul (sixth calendar month), Ethanim (seventh calendar month), Tishret (eighth calendar month), Kislev (ninth calendar month), Tebit (tenth calendar month), Shebat (eleventh calendar month), and Adar (twelfth calendar month). The Jews derive the name of the fourth month from Babylon where Tammuz was a pagan god of pastures and livestock, who is understood to have died in the summer sun. The Jews got this name from Babylonians because as stated in this book, much of the Jews are descendants of Babylonians as a result of the fall of Jerusalem to Nebuchadnezzar around 586 BCE.

The name Ishtar is the same name that the Jews got for their book of Ester (written by a Hebrew woman called Hadassah meaning an evergreen aromatic flower bearing purple black berries) which sounds like African Ruvarashe (the king's flower), changed her name upon marriage to King of Persia Achashverosh, this marriage and other subsequent marriages between Hebrews and Persians, yielded some of the present Jews who insist that they are the Bona fide Hebrews when every manner of their life is foreign.

African Culture, Oral Tradition, Exo 19 vs 1, Num 1 vs 1,
Det 16 vs 1, Ruth 1 vs 22

1.101 The Miracle Rock of Makate

An African king by the name Makate upon being cornered by his adversary king Nehoreka in Mutoko (north east of Zimbabwe), gathered his family and property and fled to a nearby mountain, split and

Hebrew / African Culture

entered a rock and left an iron hoe at the site of entry, to this day at the point at which Makate entered, has not been available to strangers for observation because any planned visits by them have failed to locate the point in question while Africans, the children of the inheritance literally walk there without any difficulty. Some schools of thought question whether it was by the power of the Creator that Makate entered the rock as Moses did induce the waters of Meribah from the rock.

What is important to note is how Africans are synonymous with power to perform miracles;

'Behold, I will stand before thee there upon the rock in Horeb; and thou shalt smite the rock, and there shall come water out of it that the people may drink. And Moses did so in the sight of the elders of Jacob'.

Exo 17 vs 6,

African Oral Tradition, Num 20 vs 8-11

1.102   MaDzishe nemaSadunhu/ Traditional Chiefs and Headsmen

Moses who had grown up in the house of Pharaoh soon after he was weaned by his mother Yocheved, learnt quite a lot from Jethro the Hebrew priest of Midian, his father-in-law. Jethro who was a descendant of Midian, son to Abraham through his wife Keturah was a practising Hebrew.

Jethro taught Moses the Hebrew or African traditional governance system which is still in practice today in Africa, thousands of years from inception;

'Hearken now unto my voice, I will give thee counsel, and the Creator shall be with thee: be thou for the people to the Creator-ward, that thou mayest bring the causes unto the Creator:
And thou shalt teach them ordinances and laws, and shalt show them the way wherein they must walk, and the work that they must do.
Moreover thou shalt provide out of all the people able men, such as fear heaven, men of truth, hating covetousness; and place such over them, to be rulers of thousands, and rulers of hundreds, rulers of fifties, and rulers of tens.
And let them judge the people at all seasons: and it shall be, that every great matter they shall bring unto thee, but every small matter they shall judge: so shall it be easier for thyself, and they shall bear the burden with thee'.

Ex 18 vs 19-22,

The referenced system of governance which is still in place in Africa this day and is very intact as if Jethro was in Africa yesterday. Readers need to note that when the Hebrews sojourned in Egypt, they could not practice some of their laws for they were under the Egyptian rule and they did not have much autonomy to operate as an independent system. The Hebrews reported to the Egyptian system and that broke the traditional governance hierarchy that was later taught by Jethro. Moses had to be reminded by Jethro how to do it the Hebrew or African way.

Besides teaching Moses the Hebrew governance hierarchy, Jethro also made Hebrew offerings in the presence of Moses and Aaron and the Hebrew elders who had come from Egypt. Notwithstanding such huge evidence to the Hebrew origins of Jethro and his expertise in the Hebrew Culture, the converts (the Jews) have recorded that Jethro was a pagan priest of Midian who was the first to convert to Judaism. The Jews even went on to portray Jethro, the Bona fide Hebrew priest in motion picture as a pagan priest who gave up on pagan worship in pursuit of Jewish culture.

The Jews have made this inference based on the known fact that Jethro was an African priest who lived around the land of Ethiopia, which was later ruled by his descendant, the Queen of Sheba. A number of ordained African chiefs have fallen to Christianity and the problems encountered when they do so is that the authority vested in them is compromised when the African or Hebrew Culture 'becomes the shadow

90

Hebrew / African Culture

of Christianity' while ironically they are required for the administration of the Hebrew tithes systems - the Zunde raMambo that feed the priests, the orphans, the widowed, the stranger and the poor among many other laws under their traditional jurisdiction which have been condemned by Christianity. An African Chief or King is also supposed to lead the offerings and spiritual ceremonies unto the Creator (Musikavanhu) together with the priests, it is impossible for him to split himself between his cultural requirements and those of the northern faith. He will end up doing services of African or Hebrew Culture for the sake of it without being spiritually involved and profane the Creator of heaven and earth and cause the Creator to smite him, that is how some of these chiefs have ceased to die in old age.

The hierarchy quoted herein is the African or Hebrew judiciary/governance system, with all the laws and institutions to deal with any matter as taught by Jethro the Hebrew priest of Midian. The same structures are still intact in Africa but wield no power/authority, for all the power has been taken over by a parallel hierarchy based on the culture/law of the north - to the extent of running African or Hebrew institutions using the Roman/Dutch (Nether) law. The Roman/Dutch/English laws are the same laws that have declared that witchcraft does not exist, and have enacted laws that bar Africans from dealing with those practising witchcraft under the witchcraft suppression acts, to make sure that Africans exterminate themselves by witchcraft, while rendering the African judiciary ineffective and powerless in dealing with witchcraft and related vices. According to the law of the north, the most cold blooded known murderer is presumed innocent until proven guilty, yet in the African or Hebrew legal system, justice begins to work from the moment that the crime is committed, the avenging spirit in exact manner as the matter between Cain and Abel is in typical occurrence in African or Hebrew Culture in Africa today.

The laws of the north have a legal practitioner, a commercial spokesman/representative/ or 'super witness' of the accused. African or Hebrew Culture has no such an officer, matters are/were judged based on the witnesses. If there was/is no consensus on the matter, a priest would enquire of the Creator, so as to identify the actual criminal, and indeed the system was/is so doubtless that the convicted party would hasten to apologise, for the institution is/was flawless and spot on. The judicial system in application by the north is such that he who has a more consistent statement (the speciality of seasoned criminals) and a more efficient advocate will win the day no matter how criminal. The system of the north is based on frivolous loopholes on the part of the witness like 'what makes you so certain that the killer killed someone?', in other words to the no fear heaven, a statement by the witness supporting the fact that he saw murder being committed is not enough. Northern law is sustained by a lot of probabilities, reasonable doubt, false oaths and blatant lies – 'so help me god'.

African Culture, Oral Tradition, Det 1 vs 13-17, Det 16 vs 18, Det 31 vs 28

1.103 Nzvimbo Dzinoera/ Sacred Places

African or Hebrew Culture makes a distinction between sacred and ordinary places where the former are held in high esteem which require to be kept by laws and procedures that ensure that such places are not defiled;

'And the Creator said unto Moses, go unto the people and sanctify them today and tomorrow and let them wash their clothes.
And be ready against the third day: for the third day the Creator will come down in the sight of all the people upon mount Sinai.
And thou shalt set bounds unto the people round about, saying, take heed to yourselves, that you go not up into the mount, or touch the border of it: whosoever touches the mount shall be surely put to death':

Exo 19 vs 10-12

There are holy mountains or holy places in Africa to this day where there are prohibited areas. These bounds have been relayed to the Africans by the fore bearers. To ensure that such places are not defiled, African or Hebrew Culture has put in custodians of such places, the priests and laws that preserve such places where ordinary people are not allowed to access unless authorised by the priests.

Hebrew / African Culture

Often people have tried to make unapproved entries to sacred places but have died or disappeared forever with no trace of them at all. **The author advises visitors from other cultures to abide by laws that govern the sanctity of sacred places as failure to do so can have fatal consequences.**

After the departure of the Hebrews through the Diaspora, holy grounds are no longer present in Israel and the Jews will acknowledge that there are indeed holy sites in Africa this day among Vanhu/Abantu where the extra-ordinary are felt and Vanhu/Abantu know the procedures that are required to bring back the awe of Mount Sinai as an example.

African Culture,

1.104 Kuomba kweMhondoro/ Angelic Sounds

In all moments of high spirituality where Africans transact with the spiritual realm especially at offerings, angelic sounds with the likeliness of a roaring lion in a populated African hilly neighbourhood or the sound of drums emanating from a mount are heard in the same manner as quoted in the Hebrew Scriptures. It is a synchronisation protocol between heaven and the people;

'And it came to pass on the third day in the morning, that there were thunders and lightings, and a thick cloud upon the mount, and the voice of the trumpet exceeding loud; so that all the people that were in the camp trembled'.

Exo 19 vs 16

Often such sounds bring in some element of fear or awe among the people in the sense that direct encounter with the Creator by humankind has never been an easy event. Later in the same day it was learnt that the Hebrew elders requested that Moses exempt them from dealing directly with the Creator for the Hebrew elders knew the strict requirements needed by human to interface with the Creator.

In that regard when the Hebrew Chief Priest could not be traced in the Hebrew family, African elders have brought the office of offerings into their homes vis-a-vis at a central shrine. They have sometimes put in the offering hierarchy, their fore bearers who have been called from above, for the reason of awe associated with heaven, they feel that they do not have the requisite sanctity or authority to communicate directly with the Creator. There is therefore a tribe (the Levites/ VaRozvi), who were ordained to serve as interface between the people and the Creator with special training on rules and protocols in that regard and not an ordinary person can communicate with Heaven for it is awesome.

The Jews have no experience with such signs to an extent that a Jewish psychology professor at Canaanite 'Hebrew' University in Israel claims that the Hebrews or Africans could have taken a hallucinating plant at Mt Sinai when Moses taught the ten commandments. The Canaanite professor says the thunder, lightning and blaring of a trumpet which the Book of Exodus says emanated from Mt Sinai could just have been the imaginings of a people in an 'altered state of awareness'. A testimony of a stranger in the Hebrew family. Another Jew has made a claim that the 'awe' associated with the ark of the covenant was a result of accumulation of electrostatic charge on the golden ark which could have killed Uzzah when the oxen pulling it stumbled. A total lack of knowledge of the Hebrew or African spirituality or value system by Jews in general.

African Culture,

1.105 Mitemo yemaDzimbahwe/ Laws for the Services of the Shrines

Services or offerings at shrines always require ritual purity, women with their manner are forbidden and sometimes women still in their childbearing age yet not with their manner, or men who have had the flow of seed are forbidden at an African shrine;

'And Moses went down from the mount unto the people, and sanctified the people, and they washed their clothes.

Hebrew / African Culture

And he said unto the people, be ready against the third day: come not at your wives.
And it came to pass on the third day in the morning, that there were thunders and lightning, and a thick cloud upon the mount, and the voice of the trumpet exceeding loud; so that all the people that were in the camp trembled'.

Exo 19 vs 14-16,

The people who will perform the services of the shrines will not come unto their wives prior to the shrine services, this is still in practice in African shrines, on those still undefiled shrines that are still in operation. If the ritual purity of that level is required of the congregation, what of the priest? And will a sodomite priest administer an offering of the Creator? In as far as Hebrew or African Culture, that is not possible for he will surely be smitten by spirituality.

Therefore the issue of ritual sanctity is not a new concept in African Culture. It is also forbidden in African Culture to lie with a woman in a sacred hill, forest or place; such act will defile the land and bring misfortunes upon the people. It is advisable for African tour guides of the tourism and hospitality industry to check on some visitors who have a habit of interacting with their women anywhere or any time regardless of the sanctity of a place. To ensure that rules that pertain to sanctity of the shrines are kept, the king/chief works in close liaison with the priests usually as a combined custodian of the shrines, the children of Ishmael (Banu Arabia / Bantu beArabia) have done well with regards to the upkeep and guardianship of the shrines.

African Culture, Num 9 vs 6-10, Josh 3 vs 5, 1 Sam 20 vs 26, 1 Sam 21 vs 3-6

1.106   **Makomo Anotsva Oga/ Mountains that Burn Naturally with Optimum Control**

Fires do ignite themselves every year in African mountains and the fires are so naturally controlled that it is ample proof that they are not the usual veldt fires like the ones that usually burn America or the north which burn up to the cities inhabited by humankind, killing and destroying as they go, but fires in African mountains burn differently, without upsetting the environment, and when they burn it does not require a state of emergency, for people will be busy doing their day to day business; these are fires of high spirituality associated with the land of the Hebrews or Africans. These are the kind of fires that are mentioned in the quoted scripture, where no livestock or people or their dwellings are burnt by it, because they are holy fires at work;

'And mount Sinai was altogether on a smoke, because the Creator descended upon it in fire:
and the smoke thereof ascended as the smoke of the furnace, and the whole mount quaked greatly'.

Exo 19 vs 18

The fires that ravage the west and the north every year are a curse on sodomy, as soon as the inhabitants of those lands abandon sodomy so will the fires disappear.

African Culture,

1.107   **Musikavanhu Mumwechete/ Oneness of the Creator**

The oneness of the entity of the Creator is a discernible feature in almost all the designations of the Creator in Vanhu/Bantu dialects; Musikavanhu is singular which means the Creator of heaven and earth, Umvelinqangi is singular which means One (Um) who was always there and will always be there, Unkulunkulu which is singular and means the great one with no comparison, Mudzimu Mukuru is singular which means the Source Soul as implied by the following scriptural reference;

'And the Creator spoke all these words saying,
I am thy Creator, which have brought thee out of the land of Egypt, out of the house of bondage.
Thou shalt not have gods before me'.

Exo 20 vs 1-3,

Hebrew / African Culture

The quoted scriptural reference tells the fundamental attribute of the Creator as understood in Hebrew or African Culture. The oneness of the Creator is clear in contrast with other cultures which have a multiplicity of deities so numerable that they had to be given names to distinguish one from the other, which include, Zeus, Mars, Jupiter, Apollo, Cupid and many others which of course are not the same entity of the Creator given different names but are totally different deities symbolizing different things like the god of war or the god of love among others.

There are no tales of three in one Creator or the Queen Creator in Hebrew or African Culture. The Creator is one and the source of all life and death, blessings and curses, rain or no rain, and in the process of executing all these to humankind, there is no helper attached to the Creator from the African point of view save for angels as opposed to the story of the trinity of deities. The designation that Africans have given to the Creator is spot on in that it tells the story of creation and the oneness of the Creator in just one word Musikavanhu, Umvelinqangi or Unkulunkulu - the Great One without comparison.

African Culture, Exo 23 vs 13,24,32, 33, Exo 34 vs 14 , Det 5 vs 6
Det 17 vs 1-7, 1 Sam 2 vs 2

1.108   Zviumbwa/ Graven Images

While there is no known form or image of the Creator in African Culture, in the north or east there are statues everywhere and of any form and any likeness, the nude ones, the Colossus, the Statue of Liberty (though there is no link between liberty and a motionless statue which has zero freedom of movement, sight, hearing and any other aspect of life identifiable with a free body).

In Christianity and Buddhism as examples, there are known images of god, Joshua the son of Joseph popularly known as Jesus, Mary the mother of Joshua and Buddha which are often made and displayed in places of worship. While elsewhere there are statues, which depict gods of all sorts, but in Africa, the land of the Hebrews; there are no statues of any form that depict the deities in compliance with the following scriptural prohibition;

'Thou shalt not make unto thee any graven image, or any likeness of anything that is in heaven above, or that is in the earth beneath, or that is in the water under the earth.
Thou shalt not bow down thy selves to them, nor serve them: for I thy Creator am a jealous Creator, visiting the iniquity of the fathers upon the children unto the third and fourth generation'.

Exo 20 vs 4-5,

The South Africans intended to build a statue of King Tshaka on the banks of Thukela river to compete with the idols above, this is a result of influences from the people of Netherlands.

Today images of other forms are now in full production by Africans primarily to sell to the northern tourists who visit Africa often but Hebrew Culture does not condone that. Traditionally art in Africa produced artefacts for use in life and not artefacts for idolatry. Drums for music, Hebrew staff for elders, furniture and other technologies appear artistic but the purpose of making them is not for vanity or idolatry but for day to day applications and therefore the fabrication of a god to worship was/is out of the question. The matter of northern images does not end at solid images, but ascends to pictorial representation of an old bearded white haired Caucasian male, whom they call god, and on his right hand sits his Caucasian son who died on the cross.

African Culture, African Oral Tradition, Exo 34 vs 13-17, Lev 19 vs 4, Lev 26 vs 1
Det 4 vs 15-23, Det 5 vs 7-10, Det 16 vs 22, Det 27 vs 15, Josh 23 vs 7

1.109   Kudaidza Zita raMusikavanhu Nhando/ Profaning the Name of the Creator

The designations of the Creator of the forms Musikavanhu/ Umvelinqangi/ Unkulunkulu/ Mudzimu

Hebrew / African Culture

Mukuru are not spoken or mentioned in trivial matters nor are they used to make false oaths for people of the culture know well of the consequences which conforms well with the following reference;

'Thou shalt not take the name of thy Creator in vain; for the Creator will not hold him guiltless that taketh the name in vain'.

Exo 20 vs 7

The designation is mentioned only for a purpose and is permissible to pronounce while teaching others about the Creator, or while making an offering, supplication or when making an enquiry or while thanking the Creator. When an African makes a joke that has a deity in it, that deity is always Bari or Baal and never Musikavanhu/ Unkulunkulu/ Umvelinqangi for every African knows that the designation is holy, awesome and sacred.

African Culture, Lev 19 vs 12, Lev 22 vs 32, Det 5 vs 11

1.110 Kutanda Botso / Atonement for Dishonour to MOTHER and Father

Honour to parents is compulsory and unconditional even if the mother is a harlot or father is a murderer. Children if they disrespect parents they will not be exempted from Kutanda Botso/ Atonement for Dishonour to mother and father for the reason of father being murderer or mother being harlot for father and mother will be judged not by the children but by another hierarchy. Respect to elders is not limited to father and mother but transcends all elders and African children are accountable to every elder and if found misbehaving in public may be disciplined by any nearby parent. Children who disrespect or abuse their parents especially the mother, are known to live a short life full of misery and misfortunes in line with the following scriptural reference;

'Honour thy father and thy mother: that thy days may be long upon the land which thy Creator giveth thee'.

Exo 20 vs 12,

The parent is called mubereki in Vanhu/Bantu dialect who is a source of blessings mubarak in Arabi and in the absence of respect from the children to the parent will come the curses. Disrespect to parents by children is one of the most feared misconduct in African or Hebrew Culture for it carries a personal redemption so morally demeaning that no man ever dares disrespect them, (Kutanda Botso) and any rebellion against the parent is rebellion against heaven and it spells doom for the child. A deceased parent who died in sorrow caused by a child pauses the same curse as that inflicted by the avenging spirit, no wonder Judah in fear of causing sorrow to his father unto death opted to be taken bondman instead of Benjamin, for it would have been more honourable and more comfortable for him to die a slave devoid of any rights than see his father die in sorrow. In the case of Judah, if he had died a slave, while his father was a happy man that would have meant nothing worse, but if Jacob had died in sorrow, Judah and all his generations after him would have paid dearly for that and Judah knew clearly of all the possibilities like any other African would do and this is not worshipping parents but is strict adherence to the tenets of the spiritual realm, for it is a good thing and full of blessings to do so.

That is why in African Culture the child remains under the control of the parents till death; there is no room for independence from the parent of any African.

Warnings to would be violators of this statute are; ngozi yaamai hairipike, unofa uchishupika (avenging spirit due to your late mother is irreparable, you will live a miserable life and die a miserable death.) or nhamo inhamo, amai havaroodzwe (No matter how severe poverty deals you, you can never trade your mother for it).

Key in the actual process of atoning for dishonour to parents is humiliation and shame to the disrespectful child. The person atoning for dishonour to parents is required to gather a quantity of small grain that can brew the strong drink required to offer in the atonement. He/she is required to put on sack

Hebrew / African Culture

clothes and carry a small bag into which he/she will gather the grain. The grain cannot be bought but must be collected the humiliating way where the parent molester has to move around the communities chanting in public that 'I am the idiot that harassed dear mother, I beg for forgiveness from my mother, give me some small grain for the strong drink offering'. When the members of the community hear the matter, they are only allowed to donate a few grams but before they can donate, they are required to insult and molest the thug after which they will pour just a few grams of their grain into the sack of the thug and the thug will be required to thank joyfully. The process will be repeated to so many people who will donate so little but giving so much beating and insults to the thug. When the thug has collected enough grain, he will go back home and hand over the grain to the elders who will do all the preparations for the offerings. At the end of the offering, the mother will forgive and heaven will answer immediately by restoring the things that the thug would have lost as a result of murmurings from the mother. If the thug lost a job, employers will by miracle start looking at his resume. As long as parents have been dishonoured, mother and child cannot sweet talk or spoil each other with expensive presents for the mother to forgive the child for the dishonour was not only to parents but to the spiritual realm and the full humiliating atonement must be done to free the erring child from the curses. A living and intriguing testimony of African or Hebrew Culture kept for thousands of years.

The mother is a well respected figure in African or Hebrew Culture, and if she unjustifiably fights or hates her own child, the child cannot fight back, for that will be like fighting heaven and that will not be a winnable war. An African warrior can conquer the whole universe but not the mother and the only way to deal with a malicious mother is for the child to set self aside or hide until the mother begin to miss her offspring. After Adam and Eve were created by the Creator, the mother was delegated to carry it on, she is awesome, isn't she?

African Culture, Exo 21 vs 15-17, Lev 19 vs 3, Lev 20 vs 9,

Det 5 vs 16, Det 21 vs 18-21, Det 27 vs 16

1.111 Umhondi/ Murder

Although most cultures condemn murder but in African Culture what stand up on top are the consequences of killing another person as well as the inherent system in the culture that can detect the murderer for a murder committed in the absence of any witness where an enquiry can readily be made unto the spiritual realm to catch the criminal spot on else the avenging spirit with the authority of heaven (the Super Witness) will work on the offender effectively and decisively.

Often murderers have escaped punishment in the courts of Roman/Dutch/English law but the avenging spirit will not let go until fully appeased and often Vanhu/Abantu have witnessed murderers under going a series of inexplicable catastrophes which they truly attributed to murder of an innocent person. Roman/Dutch/English law has more interest in protecting trouble makers like murderers than the children of murder victims who will not get any compassion while the referenced law is defending the murderer under human rights provisions which tend to suggest that when trouble makers murder a bread winner, the law and human rights protection must revolve around the murderer.

African Culture, Exo 20 vs 13, Lev 24 vs 17, Det 5 vs 17, 2 Sam 11 vs 17

1.112 Upombwe/ Adultery

Like murder, adultery is not condoned by many cultures but African or Hebrew Culture puts in extra mechanism to prevent the proliferation of adultery. In other cultures, as long as there is no evidence or a witness to prove that two persons committed adultery, there is no other way that can compel the law to put blame on anyone on unfounded suspicion of adultery. However in African or Hebrew Culture, if there is suspicion among any party to a marriage that the other party may have committed adultery, the adultery detection procedure would be set in motion as described in article 1.76 **Muteyo/ Runyoka/ Ulunyoka/ Adultery Detection and Curse.**

In other cultures, there is a business or industry that relates to prostitution, pimping, flirting, dating and

Hebrew / African Culture

fornication where companies advertise their services in the full view of the law and every day millions of people spend hours chatting, flirting, fornicating and committing adultery with strangers.

One French female has written about her gender liberalism, 'its a simple matter of demand and supply, pick a group of males, test sales pitch, have a face to face interview, hire on spot and dismiss without notice – a case of ultra-liberalism meets romance. And low cost fornication.'

The northern culture has gone a step further in pursuance of fornication, adultery and general immorality, they have designed the garment of whoredom to promote fornication, adultery and immorality amongst themselves and their children. They have spent huge resources, monies, several hours of time in their laboratories doing research, scientists working in plastics, fluids and associated technologies to make immorality a resounding success amongst their kindred.

African Culture, Exo 20 vs 14, Lev 20 vs 10, Det 5 vs 18, 2 Sam 11 vs 4

1.113 Kuba/ Theft

In African or Hebrew Culture, theft of another person's property is punishable among other things by restitution of the stolen property by at least two-fold and it is known practically that stolen wealth brings more trouble and poverty to the thief for the owner will murmur and cry to the Creator - I have worked so hard to earn this thing, I have deprived myself of good things to save this money but someone just walks in and takes it without doing any work, may the Creator, the giver of this law against stealing execute justice. Often thieves die inexplicably while in the process of stealing or after the act. Sometimes they do not die but the proceeds of theft do not make any material change in their life, the stolen wealth vanishes or stolen wealth put them in a troublesome life. **And once someone starts a career of stealing in Africa, usually they do not live long, thieves in Africa have a life span of about twenty-five to forty years and no later than that for reason of curses thieves earn while on duty.**

African Culture can put an invisible fence on valuable property against thieves where a thief once he picks an item from the fenced property will lose memory and start moving around the property from which he stole merchandise until the return of the owner who will free him or take him to the traditional court for justice. Stolen food if eaten by the thief can cause stomach to swell until the thief atones for the theft and if the stolen property is sold to some innocent person will not cause any problem to the new owner but curses will be carried by the thief.

Critics have often labelled some of these features of African Culture as witchcraft but the theme is very visible, the fight against the underworld. All civilizations agree that stealing is unacceptable and in all civilizations there are laws that guard against theft including African Culture, the difference though is that African Culture uses the spiritual realm very easily where other civilizations have to start designing and fabricating closed circuit television cameras and access control to deploy around valuable estate. The methodology of fighting theft is different but the motive of the methodology and desired results is the same like other cultures and the issue of witchcraft is misplaced.

African Culture, Exo 20 vs 15, Det 5 vs 19

1.114 Basa Revakuru/ The Role of Elders

African Culture has survived to this day to this level of detail for reason of the role of Oral Tradition and how it has transcended generations teaching the value system from elders to children continuously without a break;

'Go, and gather the Hebrew elders together, and say unto them, the Creator of your fathers, the Creator of Abraham, of Isaac and of Jacob, appeared unto me, saying, I have surely visited you, and seen that which is done to you in Egypt'.

Exo 3 vs 16

Hebrew / African Culture

Elders in African or Hebrew Culture play a central role in the culture, they provide the guide, advice, teaching and they authenticate an assertion by a prophet, priest or king to his subjects. Later they become the reliable and undisputed source of oral tradition, (vakuru vakare vaiti) - 'our elders used to say', and once a saying references the elders its stands without further debate. Naturally in the culture the elders are a generation earlier and are closer to the time origin of the culture than the later generations and are therefore more informed when it comes to the administration of the culture.

However the African elders are slowly losing their status because a bulk of them have converted to the value systems of other cultures, including African heads and chiefs, the custodians of Hebrew Culture and the African child born therein has lost the guide and is now easy target of any sweet sounding myths.

African Culture, Num 11 vs 16, Det 31 vs 28, Det 32 vs 7

1.115 Nhoroondo/ African Oral Tradition

African Culture has no written record and the primary store is the human memory which then uses oral tradition to transfer what is stored in human memory to the next generation through teaching and the extent of the accuracy of African Oral Tradition is incredible for the reason that the same data that was recorded in the Hebrew Scripture was able to be preserved to more detail and content than the written copy. The Jews who have had the written copy of Hebrew Scriptures acknowledge that the bulk of Hebrew Culture is kept by Vanhu/Abantu albeit without a written copy but through Oral Tradition.

'And it shall come to pass, when your children shall say unto you, what mean you by this service?
That ye shall say....',

Exo 12 vs 26-27

Coupled to the use of Oral Tradition was a requirement for parents to teach their children the culture diligently, Det 6. Key to an unadulterated Oral Tradition is to close any possible loopholes where children may be indoctrinated. If indoctrination is allowed among the children from a third party as happened through Christianity, the teachings from Oral Tradition will fail and the following generations of Africans will be brainwashed and the succeeding generations would start teaching of Roman/Dutch/ English descent when there is no figment of northern descent among the people of Africa.

African Culture has a very rich Oral Tradition which has preserved the culture to this day. There is/was no formal education of culture but that culture is taught from father to son or within the community and in this regard the author remembers all the teaching in graphics when as a little boy would go herding cattle with the elder brothers and how the elder brother would teach how to be a good herd boy where eventually they would retire to let you take over. At community or family level, there would be thanks giving offerings, sanctification of bulls, celebrations of birth of children, marriages, offerings for rain and all these systems are administered by the elders while the entire community would participate with shared responsibilities but critical for the success is teachings from the fathers and mothers is conformity with the following requirement;

'And these words, which I command thee this day, shall be in thine heart:
*And **thou shalt teach them diligently unto thy children**, and shalt talk of them when thou sittest in thine house, and when thou walkest by the way, and when thou liest down, and thou risest up'.*

Det 6 vs 7

Hebrew or African Culture places the responsibility of teaching children all the facets of the culture upon the parent. A Hebrew or African parent is considered a failure if his/her children acquire little or no knowledge of their culture in other words if the parents allow their children to be brainwashed by other people or cultures. Once a people depart from the teachings taught unto them by their fore bearers, they become vulnerable to any sweet sounding myth no matter how unspiritual.

Hebrew / African Culture

There was no room for a child to pursue some foreign culture as seen today that in a family living under one roof, the father will be an African cultural adherent while one child will be Anglican (British), another Italian (Catholic) and the other Dutch. That would be clear proof that the family is divided in all facets of family. A foreign cultured son should be a cause for concern to any parent, because that child will be synonymous with a stranger/foreigner in the family who would be more likely to cause disharmony and disunity in the family.

African Oral Tradition had preserved the Hebrew Culture inherent among the African people to the level it is today, because all what the children learnt came from the parents, but with the advent of the European missionary, the child who got admitted for school would come home with a new identity preaching the culture and faith of the north - the blessedness of poverty, the cleanness of a swine, the sanctity of human blood and the spirituality of human sacrifice thereby deleting thousands of years of culture.

African Oral Tradition, Det 6 vs 1-7, Det 11 vs 18-25,
Josh 4 vs 6-7, 1 Sam 3 vs 13, 2 Chr 17 vs 3-4

1.116 Ngoma, Mbira Nehosho/ Traditional Music Instruments

African Spirituality is inseparable from its music and music is possible through the instruments ngoma (drum), mbira and hosho shown on the cover page. Every African event has a spiritual significance and there is no event that can be called circular and in those events there are specific songs and dances for those events. There are songs and dances for marriage, war, offerings, bereavement, harvest, herding cattle, courtship, lullaby and each and every event in life of the people of Africa and these songs are always accompanied by an instrumental beat and music invokes or brings spiritual realm back
to the human level which conforms to the following Hebrew life style;

'And Miriam the prophetess, the sister of Aaron, took a timbrel in her hand; and all the women went out after her with timbrels and with dances'.

Exo 15 vs 20,

'And it came to pass, when the evil spirit from the Creator was upon Saul, that David took an harp, and played with his hand: so Saul was refreshed, and was well, and the evil spirit departed from him'.

1 Sam 16 vs 23

When Vanhu/Abantu converted to Christianity, they have tended to associate the African instruments with magic enchantment and not true spirituality and for that reason, the use of such instruments has been restricted largely to only the practitioners/keepers of African Culture. Almost all Christian concerts organised by Africans play foreign instruments like guitars and pianos which are deemed to be highly spiritual. The mbira or metallic music instruments has more than five thousand (5000) years in use in African Culture. The mbira instrument was a feat of serious sound engineering so many thousands of years back where every musical note was realized.

African Culture, 1 Chr 16 vs 42, 2 Sam 6 vs 5, 2 Kings 3 vs 15

1.117 Drums and Horn Sounding for Communication

African communities still use drums and horns to communicate with the people at various events. It cannot be attributed to the lack of technological advancement, for the reason that Africans are the originators of modern technology and the retention of the instruments above is cultural and traditional and also for the reason that most of today's technology is not environmentally friendly and in that respect cannot be seen to be an advancement in the use of science and engineering but rather degenerate and backward.

'There shall not a hand touch it (the bounds set upon the mountain of Sinai by Moses), but he shall

Introduction

surely be stoned, or shot through; whether it be beast or man, it shall not live: when the trumpet sounds long, they shall come up to the mount'.

Exo 19 vs 13

African Culture, Num 10 vs 1-10, 2 Sam 18 vs 16, 2 Sam 20 vs 1

1.118 Nhapwa/ A Slave

A slave/assistant in an African or Hebrew home was a helper who was more of a member of the family than a slave as opposed to the slavery that the Africans were exposed to in the west and elsewhere by the north including the Jews and Arabs, which was hard labour for life for all generations, meaning if a father was a slave so were the children and great grand children yet in the Hebrew Culture, the slave after six years of family work would be freed on the seventh year together with his children and wife if he had some. He was only incorporated into the family forever at his own plea by boring his ear (through a court of judges for justice) as a sign that he refused to be freed, to discourage slaves who would aspire to be slaves for life. In Africa the slave had the privilege to marry even his master's daughter (kutema ugariri) should she be willing as in;

'And if he (master) have betrothed her unto his son, he shall deal with her after the manner of daughters. If he take him another wife; her food, her raiment, and her duty of marriage shall he not diminish",

Exo 21 vs 9-10

It was unheard of in the days of slavery of the Africans at the hands of the north or west for an African slave to have relationship with slave master's kin, in fact getting involved in a relationship with a daughter of the master by an African slave was punishable by death and the unborn pregnancy would be terminated by abortion or by killing the damsel.

The Arabs had one of the most savage and brutal history of slave trade. The Arabs came to Africa in the middle of the second millennium with the Quran in their cargo to harvest Vanhu/Abantu for sale to the west and slaves for their own use in Arabia and it is fact that while slaves that the Arabs sold to the west would be retired at advanced age, but in Arabia they did not retire their slaves for they considered the retired slaves a feeding liability and therefore slaves were pensioned off to death.

Today slave trade has morphed into the work place where the Arabs entice expatriate labour from Africa and Asia with liveable salaries only to change the conditions of service when the expatriate lands on Arabia then slavery begins in earnest in the full view of the international community which largely consists of friends of the Arabs who will keep their mouths shut at every evil that the Arabs commit against humanity because the international friends of Arabs want to keep their commercial crude oil friendship firm and any matter that may sever that crude oil friendship must be suffocated at all costs.

The author saw the Arabs praying in thanksgiving to their god for the gains that they had made while underpaying or giving their employees slave wages, they were supplicating the usual 'god is great' while counting their profits of brutality.

African Culture, Oral Tradition, Exo 21 vs 1-11, Det 15 vs 12-18

1.119 Refuge for Accidental Killer

African Culture requires an accidental killer of his fellowman to be kept at a distant place for a defined period of time then allowed to come back among his kindred and live a normal life, though in the Hebrew Scriptures, the period of exile is indefinite, and depends on the death of a chief priest, otherwise the concept is one;

Hebrew / African Culture

'And if a man lie not in wait, but the Creator deliver him into his hand; then I will appoint thee a place whither he shall flee'.

Exo 21 vs 13,

Notable practising tribes in Africa include those from East, Central and West Africa. An act of being killed accidentally means the victim had a case of blood guilt to answer on his part as suggested by the quoted scripture for such death is by the Creator for a reason and can never be by accident.

African Culture, Oral Tradition, Num 35 vs 6,11-28, Det 4 vs 42, Det 19 vs 1-10, Josh 20

1.120 Kuroodza/ Marrying Off Daughter in Lieu of Poverty

African or Hebrew Culture considers poverty a curse or the results of reluctance to work and the practice of the quoted scenario was not a cultural tradition and is/was never condoned. It was an effect of poverty;

'And if a man sells his daughter to be maidservant, she shall not go out as menservants do.
If she please not her master, who hath betrothed her to himself, then shall he let her be redeemed: to sell her unto a strange nation he shall have no power, seeing he hath dealt deceitfully with her'.

Exo 21 vs 7-8

Kuroodza in African Culture involves an exchange of a daughter by a poor father with money or food from a rich member of society for the damsel's hand in marriage. A slight variation is recorded herein where initially the poor damsel is sold as a slave and later she is betrothed to him.

Kuroodza had no age; a girl from a poor family could be exchanged at a tender unmarriageable age whereupon she would be attached to her new family. Upon maturity, she would become wife to the man himself or his son. Poverty is not a virtue in African Culture neither is there spirituality attached to poverty contrary to what was taught by the north when they occupied rich Africa of the Africans. Poverty is like a curse and things such as these that emanate from applications of poverty are not emulated, but are mentioned here for the purposes of comparison.

African Culture,

1.121 Muroyi Ngaurayiwe/ Bulala Muthakathi/ Kill the Witch/Wizard

African or Hebrew Culture has never been soft on witchcraft, for the practitioner of such had to be killed for the good of humanity.

A witch is identified by the process of casting lots administered by a priest (svikiro) whose result is without any doubt even from the culprit. With the advent of the Europeans in Africa, legislations were enacted like the witchcraft suppression acts, which have declared illegal the Hebrew or African way of identifying and punishing witches and that has resulted in the proliferation of witchcraft in Africa. Most scholars who have written about African Culture have summarized the culture as witchcraft and related vices notwithstanding the fact that there are a lot of laws that fight witchcraft and were only rendered ineffective upon the advent of European settlers in Africa.

Ritual killing is not some form of African spirituality but some evil within the culture related to witchcraft which most writers also are often happy to benchmark as the fundamental theme in African Culture.

In African Culture, if a child or any other person dies prematurely and there is suspicion that death was not from natural causes, an enquiry through a priest would be made (gata/gumbwa) where through various procedures similar to the bitter water test of the suspected adulterous person or casting lots would be used to catch the sorcerer. A prohibitive punishment would be applied to the guilty person.

Hebrew / African Culture

All these accurate and doubtless attributes of the African judiciary have been replaced by the probability justice system of the north. An inferior justice system is in practice in Africa today so many years after independence for the reason that the mind of Africans is under massive northern influence, which has often divided Vanhu/Abantu.

The referenced Hebrew tenet has been rendered difficult to enforce among the African elders partly due to government laws and the church. Most witches today thrive in the church, the church which has no witchcraft detection infrastructure and jurisdiction to handle witchcraft matters, has become a safe haven for witches. The wicked who deserve to die in Hebrew or African Culture have found a safe haven in the church. These practitioners of witchcraft have found it difficult to abide by African Culture for the reason that the cultural detection mechanism is spot on. The witch would be told when she bewitched, how she bewitched and how many casualties were involved in the witchcraft detection test. Practitioners of witchcraft do not kill each other necessarily, they form night hunting clubs that prey on the innocent people, but sometimes they kill their children on rotational basis.

Most African governments have modelled their laws in accordance with northern law wherein the practitioners of witchcraft are protected by human rights clauses, the rights that protect a notorious witch who has eaten a dozen innocent victims. One wonders what kind of justice and human rights these are. When the day of Atonement/ Yom Kippur / Musi weKupupura was in place among Vanhu/Abantu, evil doers that included wizards would come open and reveal their transgressions before the priest in return for expiation of sin and during those times iniquities were well checked.

African Culture, Exo 22 vs 18, Lev 20 vs 27

1.122 Mutorwa, Chirikadzi neNherera/ Treatment of the Stranger, Widows and Orphans

'Muenzi haapedzi dura' is an African statement of hospitality which means that a visitor's food requirements will not exhaust the host's food store, which is an African expression of hospitality to a stranger for such kind of treatment to strangers bring blessings to the host. A harsh treatment to a widow or orphan will bring widows and orphans to the host family;

'You shall not vex a stranger, nor oppress him: for you were strangers in the land of Egypt.
You shall not afflict any widow, or fatherless child.
If thou afflict them in any wise, and they cry at all unto me, I will surely hear their cry;
And my wrath shall wax hot, and I will kill you with the sword; and your wives shall be widows, and your children fatherless'.

Exo 22 vs 21-24,

An African orphan may miss his/her real father or mother, but every male member of the African or Hebrew community assumes the role of father to the orphan, and the result is that the orphan grows up like an ordinary child without longing for much else in life. In the same way ill treatment to any member of society which causes him/her to murmur is known to be a prayer or offering to the Creator against the offender and a redress will soon follow.

African hospitality to strangers was abused by the strangers who had come to Africa for the purposes of imperialism. The Africans did not confront the strangers/imperialists but rather were advocating for a peaceful co-existence, which was rejected by the strangers for the reason of selfishness and greed of unparalleled proportions. The African fore bearers on the advent of the imperialists were confronted with the need to keep their tradition of hospitality to the strangers and at the same time did not want to lose their inheritance, they therefore sometimes settled for a compromise, meaning they offered the stranger peaceful co-existence in their land, but the strangers refused that, they wanted it all and in South Africa through apartheid laws, the majority Africans were squeezed in finger-nail sized Bantustans while the bulk of the African land was reserved for a European minority. The story is sung in African songs as 'takamuudza kuti ngatigarisane asi mupambepfumi akaramba, nekuti aida pfuma yevamwe iri yose!'

Hebrew / African Culture

In the same context, African people are known never to have occupied any foreign land or annexed any property from strangers, that kind of conduct, civility or spirituality was based on teachings from the culture in relation to treatment of strangers, it was out of the question for Vanhu/Abantu to invade Europe and possess it for the reason that Europe was the inheritance of Europeans.

African Culture, Exo 23 vs 9, Lev 19 vs 33-34, Det 10 vs 19, Det 15 vs 7-11, Det 16 vs 11, Det 24 vs 17-22, Det 26 vs 12-19, Det 27 vs 19, Ruth 2 vs 2, Zec 7 vs 10, Mal 3 vs 5,

1.123 **Chimbadzo/ Usury**

Critics of African Culture will concur that the subject of commerce was not as developed to the extent of charging interest rates or applications of usury. Though people used to exchange goods either by barter trading or with some form of currency such as cowries in west and central Africa but that did not advance to a full commercial aspect as life in African Culture was communal. The author remembers as a young boy being sent next door to ask for salt or other accessories with promises to return them when they become available and never on usury basis. The lack of commercial development in African Culture was not for reason of lack of skills thereof but was spiritual as stipulated by the scriptural reference;

'If thou lend money to any of my people that is poor by thee, thou shalt not be to him as an usurer, neither shalt thou lay him usury.
If thou at all take thy neighbour's raiment to pledge, thou shalt deliver it unto him by when the sun goeth down:
For that is his covering only, it is his raiment for his skin: wherein shall he sleep? And it shall come to pass, when he crieth unto me, that I will hear; for I am gracious'.

Exo 22 vs 25-27

The Jews are quite popular globally for their understanding of commerce most of which understanding negates the referenced scriptural prohibition and much of their economic fortunes were derived from that basis and not from the basis of the blessings of the children of the patriarch. Actually there are quite a number of documented money lenders of Jewish descent who sometimes earned themselves notorious reputations in their application of usury.

The referenced usury law is opposite of the basis of laws governing the business ethics of the north, which Vanhu/Abantu have embraced upon rejecting traditions. If an indebted person dies without settling his debts, the law or business practices of the north will have the house taken and sold to settle the debt. In America the term fore closure brings trauma to any indebted person because their culture is very commercial for most of their trust is not in god but on the piece of paper (money) upon which that statement is writ. No due care is taken to cover the children and spouse of the indebted deceased against shelterlessness, when in fact the Hebrew law goes to the extent of protecting sometimes a living careless debtor, but the law of the north will not only humiliate the debtor, but also his innocent children and wife. With such unethical business practices today, the gap between the rich and poor is widening, these are the matters that were checked by Hebrew Culture that sometimes in business some debts just have to be termed bad debts and not pursue them to the extent of selling the house which is the only inheritance left to the poor debtor's children. The Hebrew business ethics quoted herein ensure that not a single person would wax exceedingly rich while others struggle in abject poverty as witnessed in today's societies.

In the event of the indebted fathers' death, the business law of the north has an institution of debt collection with a notorious messenger of court who bears no respect, nor pity, nor mercy for the poor, homeless orphans and the widowed. The same messenger will dispose the property and house of the deceased to leave the orphans and their mother homeless. The obvious results have been the proliferation of street children, which in essence is a measurement of communal irresponsibility. The

Hebrew / African Culture

higher the number of destitutes in society, the more irresponsible is the community.

African Culture, Lev 25 vs 36-37, Det 23 vs 19-20, Det 24 vs 12-13

1.124 Leader's Conduct Accountable to the Spiritual Realm

When chiefs, rulers or leaders err, there is no provision for subjects in Hebrew or African Culture to dishonour them for their misconducts are dealt with at spiritual level for the same leaders are appointed by spirituality. If historically an analysis of African leaders is made, they have led by example when compared to the northern leaders some of whom were hanged by their subjects for notoriety and abuse of office.

When David took Uriah's wife and caused Uriah to perish in battle, his subjects did not dishonour him, he was dealt with by the Creator.

Earlier David had advised Abishai against taking the Creator's anointed Saul, showing high regard with which Africans or Hebrews behold their leaders. Emperor Haile Selasie the African king of Ethiopia was murdered by an army general in Ethiopia, a fear heaven general would have at the worst exiled the Emperor and not to kill him for the anointed one only falls to the Creator. Today the same general languishes in exile for that and other transgressions.

African Culture, Exo 22 vs 28, 1 Sam 26 vs 7-25, 1 Sam 24 vs 4-12

1.125 N'ombe Yakapirwa/ N'ombe yeMudzimu Mukuru/ A Sanctified or Offered Bull

The sanctification/offering of a bull unto the Creator is one of the most amazing applications of Hebrew or African Culture that have survived among the Africans. The awesome aspect of the sanctification is the acceptance gesture by the bull that has been accepted by the Creator for reason of being of the right specifications and also for the reason of the sanctification process having been done the proper and exact way. When heaven acknowledges the offering, the Africans are humbled whereupon they automatically go into song as done by Miriam after crossing the dry Red Sea. The offered/sanctified bull is not castrated nor is a yoke placed on its neck throughout its life for it is sanctified to the Creator and it is held with high esteem but not worshipped. The sanctified bull is given the same sanctity as a Hebrew or African shrine or any other spiritual utility but is strictly not worshipped. What constitutes worshipping in respect of the sanctified bull is the observance of the Hebrew tenet that stipulates bull sanctification unto the Creator. The bull will not be sold for money but will be offered at a family or shrine thanks giving accompanied by liquor pursuant to Exo 22;

'All the firstling males that come of thy herd and of thy flock thou shalt sanctify unto thy Creator: thou shalt do no work with the firstling of thy bullock, nor shear the firstling of thy sheep.
Thou shalt eat it before thy Creator year by year in the place which the Creator shall choose, thou and thy household'.

Det 15 vs 19-22

'Thou shalt not delay to offer the first of thy ripe fruits, and of thy liquors: the first born of thy sons shalt thou give unto me.
Likewise shalt thou do with thine oxen, and with thy sheep: seven days it shall be with his dam; on the eighth day thou shalt give it to me'.

Exo 22 vs 29-30,

Like the escape goat, the sanctified bull is an intriguing aspect of African or Hebrew Culture which continue to perplex even Vanhu/Abantu themselves. The sanctified bull (n'ombe yemudzimu) literally means the spiritual bull. Prophet Chaminuka kept a deeper version of the sanctified bull which was like a Spiritual companion or assistant with a higher sense of communication and understanding of any situation than an animal.

Hebrew / African Culture

At the end of its life, the bull is slaughtered at a family bira gathering or central shrine with its blood sprinkled on the ground as is with the manner of an offering and another bullock sanctified in its place in accordance with the referenced scripture. This is in essence giving or sanctifying the first born of the African or Hebrew's herd to the Creator, which has been labelled animism by the north, with full knowledge of the custom's scriptural concordance. Such a bull sanctified for the Creator may not behave like an ordinary animal, but like some sensible creature beyond a beast, sometimes the beast that has been sanctified to the Creator may cross a good person's field of corn without eating or destroying anything, but will look for a village notorious candidate's field of corn and begin to dine from it, which of course has a meaning. Sometimes people may fail to chase away the sanctified bull unless they call an elder or the owner who will make a small Hebrew or African offering - 'maoko', then the beast will return to the herd without incident and the sanctified bull prefers to be herded by small boys or girls who have not come of age.

These peculiarities are usually synonymous with a sanctified bull and not any other, for in any given herd that includes a couple of bulls exhibiting ordinary animal traits but once one of the bulls is sanctified unto the Creator it changes dramatically and establishes itself among the entire herd even in terms of physical structure, strength and similar traits. Sometimes the sanctified bull can opt to leave the normal kraal for his habitation and will come to the family home by the door side and sleep or literally live there. African elders know the meaning of this gesture by the Creator's sanctified bull.

The author witnessed one African family who tried to slaughter the sanctified bull outside the cultural provisions, things can really go wrong. The family tasked the son-in-law to do the slaughtering job but all what everyone remember was seeing the slaughtering axe landing not on the head of the bull but severing the leg of the son-in-law into two pieces. Compensation was paid to the son-in-law for he was misled that the bull was not sanctified. An elder who has broken a taboo in African Culture is always the bull's obvious target for goring yet the same bull can be a friend to the innocent people. When someone is gored, usually elders would read that as a problem with the victim that needs to be addressed. If the family sanctifies a bull that does not qualify for sanctification, the bull will be very notorious with the neighbour's cereals as well as with its host family.

The greatest experience of the author was herding the sanctified bull as a little boy and understanding the spiritual realm through seeing spiritual manifestations on the bull. The author also had an opportunity to see the effects of rejecting the tenet of bull sanctification by a practising family in pursuit of Christianity or the selling of the sanctified bull for money by a stubborn African; things can really go wrong - misfortunes to the family get on the unprecedented rise, the cattle herd will diminish to nothing in record time, for the Creator will have the following matter - 'I blessed you with a prosperous life, gave you a large herd of cattle that you may eat flesh and milk and be satisfied, and in turn I gave you a law concerning the sanctification of the first of thy herd and of thy flock but you have rebelled against Me, wherefore shall I give you more herd?'

African Culture, Lev 27 vs 26

1.126 No Names for Days of the Week

Like months and years, days of the week have no names in Hebrew or African Culture save for the seventh day which is called Shabat (Jewish Hebrew) and Chisingarimwi (African dialect) which means a day of no work which is a holy day of the Creator.

Other cultures like the north as an example, have given names to the days of the week in honour of their deities famous among these days is the Sun Day in honour of the Sun which they perceive as their source of everything especially when coupled to their creation story - the Theory of Evolution and the big bang. Saturday is named after a northern deity by the name Saturn. The names of days which Africans now have today are translations or transliterations of the pagan names of days given by the north;

'Remember the Sabbath day, to keep it holy.
Six days shalt thou labour, and do all thy work:

Hebrew / African Culture

But the seventh day is the Sabbath (Chisingarimwi) of thy Creator: in it thou shalt not do any work, thou, nor thy son, nor thy daughter, thy manservant, nor thy maidservant, nor thy cattle, nor thy stranger that is within thy gates:
For in six days the Creator made heaven and earth, the sea, and all that is in them, and rested the seventh day: wherefore the Creator blessed the Sabbath day, and sanctified it'.

Exo 20 vs 8-11

In essence days are counted in sevens in Hebrew or African Culture as in day 1, day 2 up to day 6 and the seventh day is known to be the Creator's holy day (Chisingarimwi/ Shabat) and people desist from doing work. The day is so holy and sanctified that whoever desecrates it by doing work therein is punished not only by humankind but by heaven.

African Culture, Oral Tradition, Gen 1,2

1.127   Dzimbahwe Guru/ The Great Zimbabwe Shrine

1.127.1 The Shrine

The Great Zimbabwe shrine was built by Vanhu/Abantu and not by Phoenicians as a central pure stone shrine for making a variety of offerings at national or regional level in accordance with the following scriptural references;

'And there shalt thou build an altar unto the Creator, an altar of stones: thou shalt not lift up any iron tool upon them.
Thou shalt build the altar of the Creator of whole stones: and thou shalt offer burnt offerings thereon unto the Creator:
And thou shalt offer peace offerings, and shalt eat there, and rejoice before the Creator'.

Det 27 vs 5-7

'An altar of earth thou shalt make unto me, and shalt sacrifice thereon thy burnt offerings, and thy peace offerings, thy sheep, and thy oxen: in all places where I record my name I will come unto thee, and I will bless thee.
And if thou will make me an altar of stone, thou shalt not build it of hewn stone: for if thou lift up thy tool upon it, thou polluted it.
Neither shalt thou go up by steps unto mine altar, that thy nakedness be not discovered thereon'.

Exo 20 vs 24-26

And to this day there are remains of animal bones which were the referenced burnt offerings unto the Creator that were sacrificed by the priests, the Levites - VaRozvi, when it was in full operation years back. However when northern historians/archaeologists made excavations at the Great Zimbabwe, for reason of lack of knowledge on African or Hebrew spirituality, they called the Great Zimbabwe a 'ritual initiation centre' while some have called it a 'royal butchery', a deduction obtained from a heap of cattle bones found inside the Great Enclosure. Such is a story that the African children will learn when their elders surrender the institution of teaching their children to a foreign historian who will teach his story to the African children. African children will be given a foreign perspective of Africa - 'a land of ape-like human species of animist spirituality'.

These shrines of pure stonework scattered across Africa are points or spiritual gateways that can link Africans to their Creator, the spiritual realm and are highly regarded but a majority of them have been defiled after Africa fell to the north and the African governments have not restored the shrines to their pre-colonial status with a fully functional African governance system led by the leaders and the priests as it was during the days of David (Mudavadi) and Solomon (Chiromo),

Hebrew / African Culture

1.127.2   **Technology of the Great Zimbabwe**

The Great Zimbabwe shrine is the greatest architectural and mortarless pure stone design with the appealing grandeur and size of the pyramids of Egypt of all times, not only in Africa, but the world over. The pure stone Hebrew or African shrine is a combination of African architectural ingenuity and inspiration as quoted herein about Bezaleel the son of Uri.

The original Hebrew shrine in Jerusalem was of the same architecture but was smaller than this spiritual centre of the over four thousand miles long Great Mwene Mutapa Empire whose founder was Mambo Chiromo (Melech Shlomoh in Jewish Hebrew, King Solomon in English transliteration) who was referred to as Amenhotep (Munhu Mutapa/Mwene Mutapa) by the Egyptians, more detail is given in Chapter 4 History.

'And the Creator spake unto Moses, saying,
See, I have called by name Bezaleel the son of Uri, the son of Hur, of the tribe of Judah (muera shumba
- of the lion totem):
And I have filled him with the spirit of heaven, in wisdom, and in understanding, and in knowledge, and
in all manner of workmanship,
To devise cunning works, to work in gold, and in silver, and in brass,
And in cutting of stones, to set them, and in carving of timber, to work in all manner of workmanship'.

Exo 31 vs 1-5,

The Hebrews or Africans were inspired with very high skill architecture. Readers should note that these people were not exposed to intensive architectural studies but were gifted by spirituality with such skills as the quoted verses state. The same knowledge of architecture was used to build Jerusalem the city and its walls. The same skills of stonework were used at the Great Zimbabwe and various stone constructions in Africa which world explorers are still wondering who did the construction work thereof and how. The work is too advanced for critics to believe that the lowly regarded Africans could have attained that level of engineering so many thousands of years earlier than other races.

The Great Zimbabwe shrine provides a classical pure stone work of highest skills of a Hebrew or African altar. It is the largest pure stone altar ever known to the Hebrews or Africans and surrounding the shrine are other stone shrines around Zimbabwe and Africa, which tell an unbelievable story of high level spirituality. The mortar bound 'Western Wall' of Solomon's temple was not original as well as the wall of the modern city of Jerusalem. The original wall was pure stone work well balanced to evade the effects of time, weather and war like the timeless Great Zimbabwe. Centuries of weather have not had an impact on the pure stone and mortarless architecture at Great Zimbabwe. Cyclones have come that destroyed dam walls, bridges and modern buildings equipped with anti-cyclone designs but the Great Zimbabwe has stood for thousands of years highlighting a timeless Creator inspired architecture of the Hebrews or Africans - the children of the inheritance - bney nachal - vana venhaka/bwana bwenhaka, those with irrevocable title deeds to the world's richest continent - which is not by coincidence but by blessedness – the promise of the covenant to the children of the patriarch.

The technologies that Africans have pursued over the years are globally and ecologically friendly as well as inspired technologies. The African people have not made research or will not make research in;

1.	Nuclear or barbaric arms of war	5.	Bio-modification
2.	Design of the garment of whoredom	6.	Abortion
3.	Human Cloning	7.	Gender conversion
4.	Human stem cell		

These are trademarks of the north with uncontested northern patents. Africans will not pursue such researches as these are against the essence of creation, immoral and unethical. Ecologically friendly technologies were originated by the African fore bearers ranging from the architecture of the Pyramids

Hebrew / African Culture

of Egypt, the Great Zimbabwe shrines and others, the irrigation systems in Egypt, the number systems, geometry and many other fields of engineering. When these technologies were stolen by the north that became the start of global pollution; catastrophes of nuclear power and their effect on the natural habitat, the emission of global warming gases. The African technologies always combined nature effects, ingenuity, ecology and inspiration.

Today a collection of mobile metal pieces run on globally unfriendly energy (automobile) is considered technology whereas a walk in an unpolluted African well balanced eco-jungle is more advanced than the most sophisticated computer processor, because it requires tremendous ingenuity to maintain and balance the ecosystem as obtained in Africa before the north brought pollution to the continent. Technologies that occur at Chernobyl Nuclear Station, Fukushima or Kennedy Space Centre are massive global pollution by an inferior mind which has a tendency to want to be seen to be the biggest or the most dreadful.

And the absurdity of human stem cell science is to deprive or suffocate new organisms of their life to support the life of rich geriatrics who are better dead than alive. What use are these geriatrics in the human life cycle except passing on to the after-death? Human stem cell mutilates an important constituency of the human life cycle by the rich when they learn that they cannot carry their money to the after-death and so they prefer to live forever. And Bio-modification especially in food, is a rushed enterprise motivated by profit other than need, where modified food is hurriedly sent to the market without safety guarantees but profiteering, most GMO farmers do not eat their produce, it is strictly for sale. Natural agriculture can still sustain this planet if performed efficiently while research on food agriculture can be done at the right pace to yield good and safe foods.

Northern technologies are generally self destructive with the object of trying to create artificial growth necessary to keep their populations content for now. When one technology makes landmines, the other one will de-mine the infested lands. When one technology creates information technology viruses, the other one will clean the viruses. When one technology makes agricultural chemicals, the other one will be necessary to remove those chemicals from food and drinking water. When one technology makes biological war germs, one will be made to try and fight the germs but often the counter technologies have failed to neutralise human made diseases. One technology makes arms of war that decapitate people's limps while another technology makes prosthetic limps. If the enlightened ones were to say, prosthetic limp technology is not the solution but that the solution is to close all the factories of war that make war machinery which decapitate limps, they will not understand that when the spirit of greed and artificial growth is upon them. In summary northern technologies sound like uneducated or illiterate technological approach to industrial growth without any due care about the adverse ramifications of the manufactured technologies while people want shot term gains. There is a problem when everyone wants to be a billionaire anyhow when an individual needs a much less portion of those billions to survive adequately. The danger in human nature is the lack of a spiritual insight into the future and therefore in the survival scheme of things, people lack deep knowledge of what need and what need not be done.

The tragedy of African shrines today is that the leaders of Africa are allowing people to defile them at will. International events that depict foreign cultures like beauty exhibitions are now being done near or inside these holy shrines, with females even with their manner, just walking through profaning every aspect of African holy sites, with the African beaurocrats who in most instances were schooled or brainwashed in the north just watching – akangoti tuzu. Sometimes when national events are done by Africans themselves in or around the shrines, teenagers are allowed to bed their mates around the shrines literally littering the entire shrine with used garments of whoredom/fornication/adultery or devices of whoredom. The result of such gross negligence on the part of Africans and their leaders is a spell of national disasters, hunger, pestilence and poverty among the Africans for profaning these shrines of high spirituality.

The country Zimbabwe obtains its name from the Great Zimbabwe pure stone shrine which has given the country a name synonymous with a virtual shrine and the people of Zimbabwe are like priestly children. It is expected of the priestly children to lead the African family to retrace its identity and

Hebrew / African Culture

spirituality. A leader/head of such a virtual shrine of a state must be well versed with the level of spirituality of the country that he/she is entrusted to lead. Any visits to the north by the head especially to the Vatican and start bowing down to the senior uncircumcised celibate priest and start worshipping - father I come as a sinner to confess my iniquities, be merciful to me, et al - will bring curses to his/her reign and his/her country.

African Culture, Oral Tradition, Det 27 vs 5-10, Josh 4 vs 8-10,
1 Kings 6 vs 7, 1 Kings 8 vs 29-50, 1 Kings 22 vs 48, 2 Chr 8 vs 17-18,
2 Chr 20 vs vs 8-9, 1 Chr 29 vs 4, Eze 44 vs 7-9

1.128 Gudzadungwe/ Following a Multitude

To promote integrity and innovation in the use of own intellect, Hebrew or African Culture condemns crowd followers or hangers on but strongly encourages teamwork.

African Culture, Exo 23 vs 2

1.129 Murombo Munhu/ A Poor Person is Human

When dealing with a poor person, it is understood well in African Culture that justice, respect or his general treatment must not be overtaken by his state of poverty in favour of the rich.

'Neither shalt thou countenance a poor man in his cause'.   *Exo 23 vs 3*

African Culture, Exo 23 vs 3-6, Det 24 vs 12-16

1.130 Inxwala/ The Offering of the First Fruits of Harvest

At the beginning of ripening of fruits or the harvest of the land, a select of the first fruits is picked by a family head and is either presented to the priest at a shrine for an offering or is presented to the traditional chief who would make the offering on behalf on his subjects. After that form of offering only then can individual families begin to consume the fruit of their labour in Africa;

'The first of the first fruits of thy land thou shalt bring into the house of thy Creator'.

African Culture, Exo 23 vs 19

1.131 Rukoto/ Mukwerere/ Rain Offering/ Festival of Booths

In some communities in Africa, around the months of August/September/October, African families make contributions in the form of small grain and other requirements for the rain offering. When sufficient grain has been gathered, it is deposited in an empty rocky hole (guvi) or dry river bed. Natural rains would pour sufficient enough to malt the grain. A brew is prepared in the booths made by green leaves and grass by women past their child bearing age as an offering to the Creator for good rains in the coming season. When this festival is done properly by practising Africans, rains begin to pour before the people have dispersed to their homes. Such is a living testimony of Vanhu/Abantu when they choose to keep their traditions.

In the same period in booths made of green vegetation called succah, the Jews pray for dew or rain during the Succot festival;

'And the feast of harvest, the first fruits of thy labours, which thou hast sown in the field: and the feast of ingathering, which is in the end of the year, when thou hast gathered in thy labours out of the field'.

Exo 23 vs 16,

Hebrew / African Culture

'Also in the fifteenth day of the seventh month, when you have gathered in the fruit of the land, you shall keep a feast unto the Creator seven days: on the first day shall be a Sabbath, and on the eighth day shall be a Sabbath'.

Lev 23 vs 39

'And you shall dwell in booths seven days; all that are Hebrews born shall dwell in booths'.

Lev 23 vs 42

Critics may dispute the spirituality of the ceremony and the subsequent rains that fall thereafter, but they will acknowledge that rains come from heaven, and if they accept that, then they will have no problems in accepting also that the Creator of heaven and earth is still in tangible communication with the beloved subjects.

African Culture, Num 29 vs 12-40, Det 16 vs 13, 2 Chr 8 vs 13, 2 Kings 4 vs 42

1.132 Kuradza Minda/ Land Sabbath

Leaving the land fallow for a period of time among Vanhu/Abantu was an application of both agricultural science and spirituality. When the land is left fallow to sustain the full eco-system, it means Hebrew law ensured the survival of all species that are necessary to supplement or support human survival especially now when critical species are nearly extinct for reason of failure by humankind to balance the ecosystem. Leaving the land fallow would restore fertility while at the same conforming to the land Sabbath;

'And six years thou shalt sow thy land, and shalt gather in the fruits thereof:
But the seventh year thou shalt let it rest and lie still; that the poor of thy people may eat: and what they leave the beasts of the field shall eat. In like manner thou shalt deal with thy vineyard, and with thy oliveyard'.

Exo 23 vs 10-11

Land in Africa is no longer left fallow on the seventh year at this point but some portions of it are left idle the third, fourth or any other year and any crops that grow therein are left for strangers, the poor and the animals, which is in contrast to the highly commercial life of the north who burn leftovers or dump grain in the sea in full view and knowledge of the world's poor to dictate a favourable price for themselves, they will not give to the poor because they understand that donation to offset the demand-supply chain which may mark down the price of their merchandise.

When the land is deprived of its Sabbath, the land will be given rest by the Creator, for example from about the years 1945 to 1980, a period of thirty-five (35) years there were about five droughts in the land of Zimbabwe. One drought for each seven year cycle. In other words if people refuse to abide by the rule of the Sabbath of the land, it will be enforced on the land by the giver of the law.

African Culture, Lev 25 vs 2-5

1.133 No Buildings of Worship or Religious Doctrine in Africa

The temple, the jewellery of the temple and associated items are conspicuously absent in African Culture, which were synonymous with the lifestyles of the Hebrews from the times of Solomon. What is in place are shrines/oracles like the Great Zimbabwe, Mabweadziva/Matonjeni, Mapungubwe and others as the resemblance of the shrine of King Solomon. A weekly prayer house such as the synagogue/shul of the Jews is not a Hebrew matter. In the life of the Hebrews or Vanhu/Abantu, gatherings are largely seasonal and national events, the Sabbath/Chisingarimwi is not a day of gathering perse, but it is a day of abstaining from doing any work and that level of observance in African/Hebrew Culture is spirituality.

The idea of worship in Hebrew or African Culture is not to choose one day in a week of trying to do good

Hebrew / African Culture

in the eyes of a sizeable crowd or congregation, but true Hebrew worship/spirituality occurs at every moment of life. It starts at birth, where the father circumcises his male children on the eighth day, abstaining from work on the seventh day, looking after the poor, the widowed, the orphans, the stranger, keeping the yearly festivals of thanks giving, of the first fruits, of the booths, what to say and what not to, holding the designation of the Creator with reverence, marrying one's daughters the right way to the fellow circumcised and many other matters that happen in the lives of the people which have to be handled the spiritual way constitute worshipping. The north have defined worshipping as a one day event out of seven days, where those who spend the entire week stealing, coveting, committing adultery, fornicating, sodomising, witching, economic sabotaging, money laundering and other world vices would gather in a building including those defiled by their uncleanness, and start bellowing like bullocks in 'dubious tongues or linguistic confusion' *Bradadd   hardsddnuuuuu rababa haya, siriya wakafawo devender* or the habradada nothing.

African Culture, Oral Tradition, Exo 24-27, Det 12 vs 10-14, Det 14 vs 22-26

1.134   Makomo Anoyera/ The Sanctity of Hebrew or African Mountains

All African mountains are sacred or were sacred at one time and there is hardly any mountain in Africa with no tales of high spirituality attached to them in much the same as mountains navigated by Moses all of his life, when he abode in Africa with Jethro, a voice from heaven told him that the place upon which he stood was holy, then he set bounds upon the holy mountain of Sinai and before he expired, his last communication with the spiritual realm was in a mountain;

'And Moses went into the midst of the cloud, and got up into the mount: and Moses was in the mount forty days and forty nights'.

Exo 24 vs 18,

'When I was gone up into the mount to receive the tables of stone, even the tables of the covenant which the Creator made with you, then I abode in the mount forty days and forty nights, I neither did eat bread nor drink water':

Det 9 vs 9

In the present day, there are several holy mountains in the land of Vanhu/Abantu where Africans have climbed and were abode the mountains for weeks, without eating, without getting weary and clothes not getting worn-out. Some of these Africans have descended from the mountains to tell a spiritual story of a day's tour, only to be reminded by the others who would have remained behind that they have been abode the mountain for weeks. Such is a living spiritual story of Mount Nyangani in the east of the Great Zimbabwe. A story of a living voice that instructs the African in the mountain in search of Hebrew or African spirituality. The voice and the guidance can only be experienced by the African people, the children of the inheritance, where sometimes visitors may either perish in the mount or are made to loiter in the mount many days with dizziness when they violate the protocols that govern the holy mountains. Mount Nyangani is a mountain which if climbed by the spiritually unclean, those with the manner of women, or those who have made contact with such, or men who have had the flow of seed, or those who have eaten the swine or have made contact with such, or those overloaded with forbidden artefacts, will be tempted to break the rules by objects that will be revealed to them as they travel, and when they break the rules it becomes terrible for them. Seeing strange objects or having to loiter with dizziness in the mountain are proof to the mountain climber that he/she is not spiritually pure and clean enough to climb the mount.

African Culture, African Oral Tradition

1.135   The Great Zimbabwe Bird/ A Similitude of the Cherubim

Though the cherubim remain one of the least revealed features of the Hebrew Scriptures, the Great Zimbabwe shrine is conspicuous for the discernible equivalent design and make of the cherubim in the form of the Zimbabwe birds which have always remained attached to the shrine as were the cherubims

Hebrew / African Culture

of the ark of the covenant. Readers need to note that there is an instruction to make cherubims in the Hebrew Scriptures/Culture as a shrine utility lest it be misconstrued as idolatry or image worshipping;

'And thou shalt make two cherubims of gold, of beaten work shalt thou make them, in the two ends of the mercy seat.
And make one cherub on the one end, and the other cherub on the other end: even of the mercy seat shall ye make the cherubims on the two ends thereof.
And the cherubims shall stretch forth their wings on high, covering the mercy seat with their wings, and their faces shall look one to another; toward the mercy seat shall the faces of the cherubims be'.

Exo 25 vs 18-20

Though the Ezra script is silent on the spiritual role of the bird/cherub, African elders especially those from Southern Africa understand in full detail the spiritual significance of the bird/cherub and its applications. The cherubim whose residence is the oracle compares well with the Zimbabwe bird in the Great Zimbabwe Oracle. The Zimbabwe birds which were tempered with by two world powers which themselves are now history (one power fell in the second world war and the second power fell in the cold war) serve to demonstrate the spirituality of these birds which compares to what happened to the Philistines (HaPelishtim) when they took the ark of the covenant from the Hebrews. The other bird is in the Republic of South Africa - A fellow African nation with the same heritage as Zimbabwe - there is no harm in them having access to it but with regards its custody at a proper shrine/oracle, they are answerable.

African Culture, African Oral Tradition, Exo 37 vs 6-9

1.136 Ndiro yeDzimbahwe/ A Stone Laver for the Oracle

The Hebrew Scriptures give details of brass lavers, however the Great Zimbabwe lavers are stone lavers which comply well with the general design of the shrine itself which is made of pure stone;

'Thou shalt also make a laver of brass, and his foot also of brass, to wash withal: and thou shalt put it between the tabernacle of the congregation and the altar, and thou shalt put water therein.
For Aaron and his sons (Masvikiro/Amadlozi) shall wash their hands and their feet thereat:
When they go into the tabernacle of the congregation, they shall wash with water, that they die not; or when they come near to the altar to minister, to burn the offering made by fire unto the Creator':

Exo 30 vs 18-20,

The northern historians, who made excavations at Great Zimbabwe, for reasons of lack of knowledge in African or Hebrew spirituality, have labelled the lavers as beef serving bowls of the ruling class for reason of their large size and also for the need to support their earlier position that the Great Zimbabwe shrine was a butchery.

African Culture, Oral Tradition, Exo 38 vs 8, 1 Kings 7

1.137 Animal Skin for Spiritual Utilities

Animal hides/skins feature prominently in African or Hebrew spiritual dress codes, these dresses are still in use in African spiritual procedures. African Culture thrives in harmony with animals and use or dependence on animals will make sure that people will need animals as long as they want the culture to survive. And Vanhu/Abantu have totems symbolised by a variety of animals and killing those animals to Africans is like killing self let alone hunting the animals to extinction. Most offerings are from domestic animals over and above spiritual animal utilities like the sanctified bull and no wonder there are more surviving animal species in Africa than any other place;

Hebrew / African Culture

'And thou shalt make a covering for the tent of rams's skins dyed red, and a covering above of badgers's skins'.

African Culture, Exo 26 vs 7-14

1.138 Mbatya dzeSvikiro/ Dress Code for Priests or Prophets

African priests are known to always perform their holy work while dressed in their priestly garments and none of these garments are white to try ascertain any link between spirituality or holiness with the white colour;

'And thou shalt make holy garments for Aaron thy brother for glory and for beauty'.

Exo 28 vs 2

And coupled to the above dress code, the African priests have diverse decorative ornaments that they wear when they perform their services and in their day to day ordinary life, they wear something that include breast plates, neck laces, leg rings among others;

'And they made upon the breastplate chains at the ends, of wreathen work of pure gold.
And they made two ouches of gold, and two gold rings; and put the two rings in the two ends of the breastplate'.

Exo 39 vs 15-16

The African priests (masvikiro/amadlozi) today do put on some kind of ephod itemised herein necessarily, and bracelets or rings are part of their usual jewellery dress.

African Culture, Exo 28

1.139 Kugadzwa kweSvikiro/Dlozi / Appointment of a Priest/Prophet

The priesthood in African or Hebrew Culture follows family lines that were appointed from the beginning among the Levites, there is no voting system nor appointment by an application letter based on religious academic credentials but by heaven and the priesthood would follow a family line or men of great spiritual renown;

'And take thou unto thee Aaron thy brother, and his sons with him, from among the children of Jacob, that he may minister unto me in the priest's office, even Aaron, Nadab and Abihu, Eleazar and Ithamar, Aaron's sons'.

Exo 28 vs 1,

The appointment system quoted herein contrasts how the priesthood is bestowed upon a person in other cultures, where they train students from any background, criminal, sodomite or from any other unspiritual attribute. Noticeable in these handpicked priests is their inability to prophesy as opposed to the spiritually and culturally ordained Hebrew or African priests/prophets whose core characteristic is the ability to prophesy for the good of the common people and maintain a communication channel between the Hebrews and the Creator.

A true priest of the Creator will not speak with the familiar voice of a departed relation or stranger, because that would be a familiar spirit and not a priest. In fact a true Hebrew or African priest is unmistakable, for he/she speaks with authority of the Creator and speaks of issues that pertain to the entire families of the area about rain, pestilence, national issues, defilement of the land and how to cleanse the land and he/she speaks in a language understood by the people present, and not bellowing Italian or Latin *'dominus vobiscum'* at a shrine in South Africa, Kenya or Zimbabwe.

Most evangelical pastors or clergy derive their power not from Christianity but from their Hebrew descent where some are of the tribe of Levi but some with spiritual powers are magic enchanters or n'angas/

Hebrew / African Culture

sangomas who have picked the bible to make money and often such candidates eat more and earlier than their followers when previously scarce food become available unlike Moses and the bona fide priests who would not eat at all even if food becomes available for they are sustained spiritually.

African Culture, Num 1 vs 50, Num 3 vs 6-13, Num 16, Num 17,18,
Num 20 vs 23-25, Num 27 vs 15-23, Det 10 vs 6, Det 34 vs 9, 1 Chr 6 vs 1-15

1.140 Mapiriro/ Finer Details of an Offering

The finer details relating to the actual offering have been included as a separate item from an offering in general to demonstrate the extent of Hebrew Culture detail that is inherent in African Culture which the Jews have either read about or seen it in execution in Africa among Vanhu/Abantu;

'And thou shalt cause a bullock to be brought before the tabernacle of the congregation: and Aaron and his sons shall put their hands upon the head of the bullock.
And thou shalt kill the bullock before the Creator, by the door of the tabernacle of the congregation.
And thou shalt take of the blood of the bullock, and put it upon the horns of the altar with thy fingers, and pour all the blood beside the bottom of the altar.
And thou shalt take all the fat that covers the inwards, and the caul that is above the liver, and the two kidneys, and the fat that is upon them, and burn them upon the altar'.
Exo 29 vs 10-13,

The procedures quoted in the referenced scripture are known in African Culture to more detail than what is quoted. Prime in these procedures is the slaughtering of a bullock, the pouring of blood on the ground and the strict handling of the inner parts that include the kidney, inner fat and the fore or hind leg among other parts.

Visitors who have come to Africa are familiar with the referenced scriptural details who most of the times are intrigued by African Culture and Traditions.

African Culture, Exo 29 vs 27, Lev 1-7, Num 19, Det 12 vs 27

1.141 Nyama Yezvirango/ Portion of the Priests/Prophets

Even in cases where a beast has not been slaughtered for the purpose of an offering, African elders have always handled these parts with high regard to an extent that they are left to be handled or consumed by the elders only after a few procedures have been performed over them as detailed;

'And Aaron and his sons shall eat the flesh of the ram, and the bread that is in the basket, by the door of the tabernacle of the congregation.
And they shall eat those things wherewith the atonement was made, to consecrate and to sanctify them: but a stranger shall not eat thereof, because they are holy'.
Exo 29 vs 32-33

In that regard, there are portions of an offering, be it liquor or an animal offered in African Culture today that are reserved for the priests/masvikiro/amadlozi or for the elders in general. Those portions are understood in clear terms by Vanhu/Abantu even by the greediest or glutton or hungry commoner that they are exclusively for the mentioned hierarchy and can never be consumed by anybody else. Even when an animal is slaughtered for family consumption, those specific priestly portions are handled by elders in a special way. Usually an African child grows up to adulthood with the understanding that such parts if consumed by the young will cause them to 'forget their friends and relatives' (chikanganwa hama) or that they will be 'lost in the rain or wilderness' as a means to discourage children from breaking these rules.

African Culture, Lev 2 vs 10, Lev 6 vs 16,
Lev 7 vs 4-6, Lev 7 vs 32-35, Det 18 vs 3-4

Hebrew / African Culture

1.142 Tenure of Offerings

The offerings in the form of the liquors (mapira), animal offerings, grain offerings, first fruits and others have not ceased among the Vanhu/Abantu, they are in practice to this day and their tenure is forever. Offerings have only ceased among those Africans who have converted to the faith of the strangers.

'This shall be a continual burnt offering throughout your generations at the door of the tabernacle of the congregation before the Creator: where I will meet you, to speak there unto thee'.

Exo 29 vs 42

Strangers are preaching to the Hebrews that the Hebrew system of offering is old and has been replaced by the much older human offering (the blue print of pagan worship) of the strangers in the form of the one off sacrifice of Joshua the son of Joseph, when the Hebrew Scriptures are very clear on the tenure of these sacrifices, for they shall be in place for all generations.

The Hebrew system of offerings was brought about through a covenant entered into between the parties, the Creator on one side and the Hebrew fore bearers on the other side. And if the same covenant needs to be repealed so as to make any necessary changes, then those changes will be by way of the same two parties agreeing on an amendment and not through a third party, let alone with a completely different culture.

In Africa today, it is particularly the burnt offering that is not necessarily in place, the reason is that the burnt offering was/is a preserve of the Chief Priest or of the top priestly hierarchy and without the Chief Priest in clear picture today, the burnt offering has not been easy to execute. Saul erred in offering a burnt offering instead of Samuel and by so doing he lost the throne of the Hebrews. The burnt offering is awesome, it is a kind of an offering that can cause the earth to open up and consume he/she who is offering if done the wrong way. Nadab and Abihu erred in the administration of an offering and they fell before the Creator.

African Culture, Oral Tradition,

1.143 A Census

In African Oral Tradition, there is no memory or record of the counting of people before the advent of the European settlers for the reason that humankind are not considered as objects of commerce but should an instruction come for people to be counted, a ransom is required of every person to redeem self else the nation will be struck by a plague;

'When thou taketh the sum of the children of Jacob after their number, then shall they give every man a ransom for his soul unto the Creator, when thou numberest them; that there be no plague among them, when thou number them'.

Exo 30 vs 12,

David counted the Hebrews without authority from the Creator and brought a plague to his people and seventy thousand men died. In most parts of Africa, it has been statistically proven that there is always a drought or any other catastrophe each time there is a census. In Zimbabwe as an example, there have been censuses at the instigation of an African government in 1982, 1992 and 2002 and in each of these years, there have been terrible droughts that have killed people.

A planner will insist that the number of people at any given time and location is necessary for infrastructure planning and development, but then the danger is to dissociate providence and the principles of spirituality in the affairs of humankind.

African Culture, Oral Tradition, Num 1 vs 2, Num 26 vs 2-51, 2 Sam 24

Hebrew / African Culture

1.144 **Svikiro Harizi Tsvimborume/ Celibacy Vow**

African or Hebrew priests/prophets (amadlozi) were not, are not and will not be celibate. The tribe of Levi was chosen to be priests among their generations, and if the Levites were to be celibate, how were they going to continue the priesthood? If Aaron and his Levite generation had opted for celibacy, both the name of Levi and the priesthood would have long been discontinued from among the Hebrews within their first generation which would have violated the scheme of creation of being fruitful and multiply. And the designer of the human body confirmed in the very beginning that it was bad for a man to be celibate in his life but certainly needs a partner of the opposite gender as clearly stated without ambiguity in the following scriptural reference;

'And the Creator said, it is not good that the man should be alone; I will make him an help meet for him'.

Gen 2 vs 18

'And the Creator caused a deep sleep to fall upon Adam, and he slept: and took one of his ribs, and closed up the flesh instead thereof;
And the rib, which the Creator had from man, made a woman, and brought her unto the man'.

Gen 2 vs 20-21

'Therefore shall a man leave his father and his mother, and shall cleave unto his wife: and they shall be one flesh'.

Gen 2 vs 24

'And take thou unto thee Aaron thy brother, and his sons with him, from among the children of Jacob, that they may minister unto me in the priest's office, even Aaron, Nadab and Abihu, Eleazar and Ithamar, Aaron's sons'.

Exo 28 vs 1,

With celibacy ruled out of humankind with the designer of humankind, Paul's letters cannot be used to justify the unjustifiable. African literature even says that it is better to have a granny for a wife than celibacy (Chembere mukadzi hazvienzani nokurara mugota).

The referenced scriptures mean that it is wrong/improper that man should be alone all the days of his life while longing for woman every minute of his life (dai ndine nemukadzi wanguwo sevamwe)! The danger of setting aside the requirements and regulations that govern the life of humankind against the word of the designer of the human body, who knows in all manner of detail of the requirements and the optimum conditions for the survival and psychological and physiological requirements of humanity, is that the celibate priests that come out of that negation, are those spiritually unclean for the reason of flow of seed caused by the longing of woman each time they go to bed, or instead of teaching spirituality to an unsuspecting congregation, the celibate priest will be covetous each time he looks at someone's fair wife in the congregation, 'If only I was allowed to marry, that fair woman would be mine by all means, or even in my celibacy how can I have a relationship with that maid'? That is the mind of a human being that has been configured wrongly while at the same time expected to operate normally.

Some celibate priests of the church have over centuries sodomised a wide section of their congregation or have helped themselves among sisters in convents.

The simple rule is that celibacy is against the essence of creation. Gender anatomy is for a purpose and if it is mature enough, the appropriate or enabling environment (marriage) that is necessary for the fulfilment of the role of that anatomy need to be provided. The sad news about celibacy is that usually it is the little children who get abused by celibate priests at the expedience of unnatural laws by elders. It is a pertinent matter for the Vatican to understand the negative effects of those unnatural laws to society and normalise the situation – allow their priests to marry and their sisters to mother. Motherhood and

Hebrew / African Culture

fatherhood are an important part of human life, without that a human being would be considered a wasted seed. It is spiritual to marry, raise or suckle a baby for it enhances the theme of creation - be fruitful and multiply and celibacy is against that. A celibate person is like a hen that lays eggs but does not hatch them or abandons them and by doing so angers the farmer and naturally qualifies itself for slaughter.

In fact, there is no link between celibacy and holiness, who said there is a link? (Ani iyeye)?

Medically it is known that women who either have their first conception at thirty years or more (late) or who do not conceive at all have higher risk of breast cancer. It is also known that women who use hormonal therapies to prolong among other things their active gender life also have a higher risk of breast cancer. The lesson derived here is that the human body was designed for a purpose and it has requirements and optimum operating conditions, trying to change those attributes of creation is usually met with heavy consequences. The woman's breasts were meant to sustain a baby, if 'modern women' think otherwise and refuse to conceive and suckle a baby, breast cancer is a heavy and enduring ailment. The Catholic sister needs to be more informed.

African Culture, Judges 4 vs 4

1.145 Mono remaSvikiro / Holy Anointing Oil for the Priests

Mono is a special oil prepared for African priests (masvikiro/amadlozi) for them to use while they do their spiritual duties which conforms well to the following scriptural reference;

'And moreover the Creator spoke unto Moses, saying,
Take thou also unto thee principal spices, of pure myrrh five hundred shekels, and of sweet cinnamon half so much, even two hundred and fifty shekels,
And of cassia five hundred shekels, after the shekel of the sanctuary, and of oil olive an hin:
And thou shalt make it an oil of holy ointment, an ointment compound after the art of the apothecary: it shall be a holy anointing oil.
And thou shalt anoint the tabernacle of the congregation therewith, and the ark of the testimony,
And the table and all his vessels, and the candlestick and its vessels, and the altar of incense,
And the altar of burnt offering with all his vessels, and the laver and its foot.
And thou shalt sanctify them, that they may be most holy: whatsoever touches them shall be holy.
And thou shalt anoint Aaron and his sons, and consecrate them, that they may minister unto me in the priest's office'.

Exo 30 vs 22-30,

A priest cannot commence his priesthood without being ordained by way of the anointing oil. The oil is exclusive to priestly use but tithe merchants of Pentecostal incline in Africa are using it to their congregation to create awe that will boost tithes revenue.

African Culture, Oral Tradition, Exo 37 vs 29, Lev 8 vs 12

1.146 The Golden Calf and Similar Images of Worship

The scriptural golden calf remains one of the few known instances of image worshipping among the Hebrews. The punishment that was meted upon the parties involved was so prohibitive that today no images of that sort are seen in the culture or any likeness of it thereafter.

Images that are moulded and carved from wood are household utensils used on day to day basis which are not meant for worshipping.

African Culture, Oral Tradition, Exo 32

Hebrew / African Culture

1.147 Remarkable Absence of the Devil/Satan in Hebrew or African Culture

1.147.1 The Devil or Satan

There is a conspicuous absence of the devil/Satan in Hebrew or African Culture as the influence to sin. In fact in most African dialects, the vernacular equivalent name for the devil is non existent, the only available terms are the borrowed terms 'Satani or Dhiyabhorosi' for Satan and diabolic respectively. Of course Vanhu/Abantu are sinful like any other mortals but when they do so, they do not see the imagined entity of the Devil as a source of their evil but themselves;

'And it came to pass on the morrow, that Moses said unto the people, You have sinned a great sin: and now I will go up unto the Creator; peradventure I shall make an atonement for your sin'.

Exo 32 vs 30,

'For the Creator had said unto Moses, say unto the children of Jacob, you are a stiff-necked people: I will come up into the midst of thee in a moment, and consume thee: therefore now put thy ornaments from thee, that I may know what to do unto thee'.

Exo 33 vs 5,

The root of sin in Hebrew or African Culture is humankind, that is why David pleaded 'I have sinned before the Creator' before Nathan the prophet on the matter of Uriah and Bathsheba. It is important in matters of spirituality for one to accept one's own guilt when seeking forgiveness from heaven for the devil is in the mirror and nowhere else. When a sinner refuses to take the blame for his sin and create another body (Devil) to blame for his iniquitous mind, then that person is definitely beyond redemption.

David in response did not heap the blame on the pseudo character Satan or Devil but he confessed 'I have sinned before the Creator' - 'Chatati (Ndashata ini) la HaBore', he did not say, Satan has caused me to sin before the Creator, which in Hebrew or African Culture means that Satan/Devil is a non existent concept. A logical rendering of Satan in this sense which also agrees with African dialect is 'Ndashata ini' meaning 'I have sinned'. In that regard Satan is the personification of the evil intent inherent in humankind and not an independent and external entity that influences humankind to sin. In fact when a sinner refuses to take blame for the things that he has done, that sinner is beyond the redemption and the mercy of the Creator, such a sinner is stubborn and stiff-necked. Forgiveness of sin starts by the sinner accepting that he (and none else) has sinned, without that there can never ideally be expiation of sin no matter how many characters are nailed on the cross for his/her sins.

It is important to note that when David accepted his sin and that none else caused it, he later became the most faithful servant of the Creator.

When man sins, it is man who is punished by the spiritual realm and not "Satan", because Satan is non existent. Each time man sins, the Creator confronts man and never at one single time have humankind heard that Mr Devil was held accountable for humankind's iniquities and punished by the Creator.

Adam and Eve could have changed the course of life humankind are living today if they had not blamed a third party but themselves for their sin, to this day humankind continue to die no matter how near righteous one can be. Theories of some men going to heaven alive are myths, based on the wrong beliefs of the presumed form of the Creator. If the Creator is not known in terms of which form of existence the Creator lives, why would myths portray humankind ascending or being called in flesh. Righteousness is humankind's ability to tame the evil intent inherent in them and abstain from sin. If a man depends on a third party to control the evil intent inherent in him, that man is spiritually empty.

1.147.2 Good and bad spirits all from the Creator

African Culture holds that everything comes from the Creator, good and bad fortune, good and bad

Hebrew / African Culture

spirits and that the devil is a non-existent entity, which agrees wholly with the verse quoted herein.
The good and bad spirits all come from the Creator under different circumstances, when an individual does well spiritually in will come the blessings, and when an individual descends spiritually in will come the curse and its associated bad spirits (mhepo).

'But the spirit of the Creator departed from Saul, and an evil spirit from the Creator troubled him.
And Saul's servants said unto him, behold now, an evil spirit from the Creator troubles thee.
Let our lord now command thy servants, which are before thee, to seek out a man, who is a cunning player on an harp: and it shall come to pass, when an evil spirit from the Creator is upon thee, that he shall play with his hand, and thou shalt be well'.

1 Sam 16 vs 14-16

It is important to note that in African Cultural rites, music generated by instruments such as mbira, ngoma (drums), hosho and similar scriptural instruments, play a very important part in these ceremonies in the similar manner as music played by David did to the state of Saul.

African Culture, Oral Tradition, Det 8 vs 19-20, Det 9 vs 8 ,
Det 11 vs 16-17, Det 11 vs 26-32, Det 28 vs 15-68,
Det 32 vs 39-43, Judges 9 vs 23, 1 Sam 2 vs 6-10,
1 Sam 16 vs 14-16, 23, 1 Sam 18 vs 10, 1 Sam 19 vs 9,

1.148   Human Sacrifice

When a cornered Moabite king offered his son as human sacrifice to the gods, there was great indignation against the Hebrews for the act was an abomination. Human sacrifice is abominable and defiles the shrine, altar upon which it is performed and land. If human sacrifice was a spiritual requirement, the poor would be extinct now, they would be sacrificed by the overzealous religious sects at lightning speed. The last supper recitation which instructs followers to 'eat; this is my body', is in African Culture like a witchcraft ritual and is unimaginable ritual to drink human blood or any blood in real terms or in theory;

'And when the king of Moab saw that the battle was too sore for him, he took with him seven hundred men that drew swords, to break through even unto the king of Edom: but they could not.
Then he took his eldest son that should have reigned in his stead, and offered him for a burnt offering upon the wall. And there was great indignation against the Hebrews: and they departed from him and returned to their own lands'.

2 Kings 3 vs 26-27

Human sacrifice was a preserve of most pagan cultures surrounding Hebrew Culture and Hebrew Culture affirms that, *'the fathers shall not die for their children, neither shall the children die for the fathers, but every man shall die for his own sin'.*

2 Chr 25 vs 4,

A dead body especially that of humankind defiles a spiritual person like a Nazarite or utility like a shrine. How then would a human body be used as an eternal offering to the Creator? If the Hebrew law says the swine defiles humankind, then did that mean the swine could be offered to the Creator? If the same law says a man who has had the flow of seed is defiled then would the same man be allowed to do the services of the shrine in that defiled state? If the answer is no to the referenced questions why would a dead body which defiles a mortal sound the right item of an offering to the Creator? These are the abominations akin to those of the Canaanites and Sodomites that the Creator through Moses, condemned in all the strongest terms.

In Hebrew or African Culture there is no instance of one party being punished, sacrificed or afflicted on behalf of others but children may be caught in the iniquities of their parents. A thoughtless war by parents may catch the children in the cross-fire or children born to adulterous parent/s may be born with

AIDS or effects of diseases of the bed of whoredom. The matter of redemption of other people's sin by sacrificing a third party is a non-Hebrew concept with high pagan connotations. The use of muti which uses human or animal body parts by some Africans is not human sacrifice as usually referenced by northern religious scholars, but is an evil search for wealth powered by witchcraft and magic enchantment.

Within the African or Hebrew Cultural domain, any teachings anchored on human sacrifice that seek for the expiation of sin is in summary the blue print of pagan worship. The patriarch Abraham was called from the land of Ur where the people of that time and place were sacrificing their children to their numerous deities for the same reasons as expounded by Christianity. If human sacrifice itself was spiritual, then the patriarch Abraham for his faith would have been spared of his son at the mount with another person being sacrificed instead of a ram.

African Culture, Exo 32 vs 31-33, Num 6 vs 5-6, 1 Sam 2 vs 25, 1 Kings 13 vs 1-2, 2 Kings 3 vs 26-27, 2 Kings 23 vs 16, 2 Chr 28 vs 3-4, Eze 16 vs 36

1.149 Gonan'ombe/ Chibako/ Nhekwe/ Snuff dishes

Snuff and its associated snuff containers or dishes (shown on the cover page) are widely used in spiritual services and procedures in Africa among Vanhu/Abantu and usually at the centre of use of snuff are the priests/prophets (masvikiro/amadlozi) or the common people who are still keeping the African Cultural values and traditions. Readers should note that no detail was given by Ezra with regards to matters pertaining to the snuff, snuff dishes and the associated offerings, yet in African Culture, snuff is used extensively at offerings by the priests, or at family level, showing that there is more detail in African Culture among the Africans today pursuant to the Hebrew Culture than what Ezra wrote and what the Jews know;

'And he (Bezaleel) made his seven lamps, and his snuffers, and his snuff dishes, of pure gold'.

Exo 37 vs 23

The north and the Jews are conspicuous with their use of the abominable incense which Hebrew Culture condemned in all possible terms.

The appearance of sweet incense and frankincense in the Books of Moses concerning a number of offerings was a catastrophe influenced by exile which misplaced snuff for incense. Incense is foreign in Hebrew or African Culture and particularly in Africa, incense is unknown, the author got to know about incense at a school which was administered by Romans where little African children were brainwashed to identify themselves as Romans.

The manner of the incense offering practised by the north to this day that among other details involves burning it, was an offering that caused Aaron's sons Nadab and Abihu to die before the Creator and such an incense offering cannot then be seen to be spiritual now. Incense offering was a pagan offering of pre-Hebrew inhabitants of Canaan yet in 1 Chr 23 vs 13 in writings made post exile by writers like Ezra who had been brought up in exile, ratified it yet on the contrary prior to exile priestly sons of Aaron, Nadab and Abihu died when they made a strange incense offering of fire. Actually incense defiles the spiritual realm.

Readers need to note that though the north use snuff this day, it originates from Hebrew or African Culture as a spiritual utility. The north use snuff as a miscellaneous flavour and not for religious purposes, their religious utility in that regard is the abominable incense and when the north started using snuff in the middle of the second millennium, the Pope threatened to excommunicate the snuff takers.

African Culture, 1 Kings 11 vs 7-8, 1 King 13 vs 1-2, 1 Kings 22 vs 43, 2 Kings 23 vs 5, 11, 2 Kings 12 vs 3, 2 Kings 12 vs 13

Hebrew / African Culture

1.150　Animals Suitable for a Hebrew or African Offering

In spiritual offerings, not all animals or objects can be offered; cattle, flock or bird can be offered and never a human being as taught by other cultures like in the north the majority of northern temples had altars for human offering or sacrifice. And when the north began to teach Christianity, they encrypted human sacrifice as the backbone or the fundamental theme in Christianity which they learnt from their fore bearers and not from Hebrew Culture;

'And the Creator called unto Moses, and spake unto him out of the tabernacle of the congregation, saying,
Speak unto the children of Jacob, and say unto them, if any man of you bring an offering unto the Creator, you shall bring your offering of the cattle, even of the herd, and of the flock'.

Lev 1 vs 1-2

The swine is neither suitable for an offering nor for food in Africa as it was brought in by the north who have expertise in grinding it into rows and slicing it into a morning fast cholesterol fry, notwithstanding the health risks caused by the consumption of the swine.

If an animal meets the offering specification quoted herein, it is further inspected by African elders for any defects. A bullock necessarily and not a castrated draught animal is fit for an African or Hebrew offering. Even the bullock that is sanctified by Africans for the Creator has to pass an inspection for any defect by the family elders before it is sanctified. If it fails the test and the elders insist on sanctifying it, the bull will not be accepted by the spiritual realm, sooner it would become very notorious with the neighbour's corn and would be slaughtered and replaced and the said inspection for defects conforms with the following scriptural reference;

'Blind, or broken, or maimed, or having a wen, or scabbed, you shall not offer these unto the Creator, nor make an offering by fire of them upon the altar unto the Creator.
Either a bullock or a lamb that hath any thing superfluous or lacking in his parts, that mayest thou offer for a freewill offering; but for a vow it shall not be accepted'.

African Culture, Lev 22 vs 22-23,

1.151　Sin Offering at National Level

Transgression can be committed in Africa by as simple as making an inappropriate comment when walking in a holy mountain or forest or when one is in a shrine and often when such transgressions are made they may cause the offender to get lost or loiter in the wilderness but when none of that happens enquiries are made prior to a thanks giving offering. In order for an offering to give positive results, such transgressions committed sometimes in ignorance must be resolved by sin offerings at community or national level;

'And if the whole congregation of the Hebrews sin through ignorance, and the thing be hid from the eyes of the assembly, and they have done somewhat against any of the commandments of the Creator concerning things which should not to be done, and are guilty;
When the sin, which they have done against it, is known, then the congregation shall offer a young bullock for the sin, and bring him before the tabernacle of the congregation.
And the elders of the congregation shall lay their hands upon the head of the bullock before the Creator: and the bullock shall be killed before the Creator.
And the priest that is anointed shall bring of the bullock's blood to the tabernacle of the congregation:
And the priest shall deep his finger in some of the blood, and sprinkle it seven times before the Creator, even before the veil'.

Lev 4 vs 13-18

Hebrew / African Culture

Prior to offerings, African elders make enquiries to find out if anyone of the people defiled a shrine, the land or violated any taboo and often the offenders will pay for the animals that are offered for such sin offerings and these specific details on Hebrew Culture are not found in Israel among the Jews but in Africa among Vanhu/Abantu, the Bona fide Hebrews of the Books of Moses.

African Culture, Oral Tradition,

1.152 Broken Earthen Vessels in African Culture

Around some African shrines or mountains, there are fragments of broken earthenware in support of the scriptural verse quoted. These are some of the awesome offerings that require chief priests which have not been observed for the reason of the unavailability of the office of the chief priests among Vanhu/Abantu.

'Whatsoever shall touch the flesh thereof shall be holy: and when there is sprinkled of the blood thereof upon any garment, thou shalt wash that whereon it was sprinkled in the holy place.
But the earthen vessel wherein it is sodden shall be broken: and if it be sodden in a brazen pot, it shall be both scoured, and rinsed in water'.

African Culture, Oral Tradition, Lev 6 vs 27-28

1.153 Consumption of Fat

The African staple diet consist of wild fruits and other derivatives like honey, green vegetables, milk, nuts, fish, small grain cereals and sometimes meat. When meat was prepared the African way, it was often always roasted with fat allowed to burn in the fire but the small grain cereals were cooked in earthen wares but not the meat and therefore such a diet ensured that Africans ate very little of fat and even their bodies reflected that diet prior to the advent of the Europeans.

When domestic animals were slaughtered often fat was hang outside their houses for it to waste on its own in agreement with the quoted scriptural reference;

'And the Creator spake unto Moses, saying,
Speak unto the children of Jacob, saying, you shall eat no manner of fat, of ox, or of sheep, or of goat.
And the fat of the beast that dies of itself, and the fat that which is torn with beasts, may be used in any other use: but you shall in no wise eat it.
For whosoever eats the fat of the beast, of which men offer an offering made by fire unto the Creator, even the soul that eats it shall be cut off from his people'.

Lev 7 vs 22-25

Actually some African families of the Beta (fat) totem do not eat fat at all for that is their totem. The consumption of fat only came when abattoirs were introduced in Africa by the north where they extracted fat and processed it into a cholesterol brand called drip and then sold it to the Africans, then came cholesterol related illnesses among Vanhu/Abantu. And the people who consume fat will not be literally cut their necks off but will succumb to fat related ailments like heart attack or hyper tension.

African Culture,

1.154 Consumption of Blood

The meat that was eaten often in Africa was not of beef or flock, most meat came from wild animals and in that regard there was no easy means of extracting blood from a wild animal hunted in the depth of the jungles, often the hunters did not bring fresh meat but dried meat after spending some weeks on hunting sprees. However when domestic animals were slaughtered blood was allowed to flow onto the ground;

Hebrew / African Culture

'Moreover you shall eat no manner of blood, whether it be of fowl or of beast, in any of your dwellings. Whatsoever soul it be that eats any manner of blood, even that soul shall be cut off from his people'.

Lev 7 vs 26-27,

Blood was only consumed unknowingly by Africans who bought their meat from abattoirs managed by European butchers who slaughtered their meat by the bullet shot into the brain to cause death of the beast without bleeding.

The blood would then solidify in the body of the beast and those who bought the meat thereof would then eat the blood. The lesson learnt here is; for Africans to keep their culture ideally, they need to administer all the systems that produce their day to day requirements, should they choose to delegate that to the stranger, the stranger will do what he/she knows or believes in. The Jews and the Arabs have the requisite slaughter systems to meet the requirements of the tenet in question which produce kosher and halal products respectively.

When Hebrew Culture prohibited the consumption of any blood in real terms, it did not mean that blood had to be eaten as in symbolism of the last supper, 'he took a cup of wine and said drink ye my blood, the blood of the new covenant shed for you'.

Medically blood contains both supplies to the body as well as the waste some of which are poisons and prolonged consumption of such poisons will negatively affect the eater which links to a soul being cut of from the people not by a holy army but by diseases derived from eating blood. **African or Hebrew diet has well proven scientific approach to eating where not everything that fly across the mouth can be eaten with clearly spelt out consequences for those who refuse to follow the dietary laws and that is not religious indoctrination but clear scientific approach to living.**

African Culture, Det 12 vs 16-25, Det 15 vs 23, 1 Sam 14 vs 34

1.155 Instruments for Enquiring of the Creator Used by the Priests

Priests in Africa today use a variety of instruments with complex procedures and interpretation which are exclusive to them to enquire at spiritual level on behalf of the people. Part of those instruments are used for casting lots, the instruments used thereof and the interpretation of the result are a preserve of the priests;

'And he (Moses) put the breastplate upon him (Aaron): also he put in the breastplate the Urim and the Thummim'.

Lev 8 vs 8

The Urim and the Thummin were instruments for enquiring of the Creator used by the priest, and remained one of the closest guarded secrets in Hebrew or African Culture for it was/is only the priest who knew/knows how to conduct an enquiry and these instruments are clearer to people who have had a close encounter with African Culture.

African Culture,

1.156 Consecration or Sanctification of a Priest

The following scriptural reference is another example of Hebrew Culture and Spirituality that will be found in African Culture in exact form and extent and such are the aspects of the Hebrew Scriptures which the Jews (the converts to African or Hebrew Culture) would testify that they have seen it in Africa among Vanhu/Abantu and if there are any variations, the variations would be very minor. A number of observers especially those from other cultures have labelled such procedures as either backward or animist but to Africans, these procedures are easier and familiar to understand and appreciate because they are part of the culture and they identify with the people;

Hebrew / African Culture

'And he (Moses) brought the other ram, the ram of consecration: and Aaron and his sons laid their hands upon the head of the ram.
And he slew it; and Moses took of the blood of it, and put it upon the tip of Aaron's right ear, and upon the thumb of his right hand, and upon the great toe of his right foot'.

Lev 8 vs 22-23,

All matters of Hebrew or African spirituality such as making an offering, communicating with the spiritual realm or other peripheral duties like making or cleaning priestly garments or tools have to be done with the requisite prequalification of sanctification and these procedures or duties are not free for all. The prequalification involves sanctifying oneself by eating the right food, being hygienically clean, being spiritually clean by abstaining from the women or men, contact with the flow of men or women or with people or objects who/which have made such contact or with a dead body and only after achieving that sanctity can a person or priest proceed to conduct matters of spirituality.

Often critics especially from the north have questioned why the spiritual realm in African or Hebrew point of view does not interface with the flow of seed, women with the manner of women, contact with the dead body or men who have made contact with other men (sodomy) and to that effect have not found it a requisite to sanction sodomy even in their clergy. The answer to such questions is that there are a number of issues in the spiritual realm that are undefined in the physical realm while making sense or giving positive results to the physical, in other words, the current knowledge of science cannot give a logical conclusion to matters of the spiritual domain yet African Culture, using the spiritual realm can deliver a lighting bolt which can be measured and certified by modern science.

African Culture, Num 8

1.157   Kubvumwa kweMupiro/ Acceptance of an Offering

In any offering that is offered within the realm of African Culture, there is a physical discernible event that shows or proves whether an offering has been accepted. Like the Mukwerere/Rukoto or Rainmaking offering, rain begins to rain when people making the offering are making the concluding procedures. And when sanctifying or offering a bull, there is a physical discerning event that is known by Vanhu/Abantu which tells them that the sanctified bull has been accepted and is of the right specification and that the sanctification procedure was done the proper way. When offering the goat of **Succeeding the Name of the Departed (Kurova Guva),** there is also a discernible physical event that is performed by the goat which will trigger Vanhu/Abantu into clapping hands, celebration with all sorts of ululations for these are awesome occurrences that are amazing about African Culture and Spirituality.

In the Hebrew Scriptures, similar examples were of the following;

'And Moses and Aaron went into the tabernacle of the congregation, and came out, and blessed the people: and the glory of the Creator appeared unto all the people.
And there came a fire out from before the Creator, and consumed upon the altar the burnt offering and the fat: which when all the people saw, they shouted, and fell on their faces'.

Lev 9 vs 23-24

In African offerings today, the portions reserved for the Creator which are offered at a shrine are consumed in the similar manner, the priest will go later to the shrine to collect the utensils that would have previously contained the consumed beer (bira in Jewish Hebrew) and the meat. Such an occurrence is living testimony that the offering would have been accepted by the spiritual realm. If upon inspection it is found that the offering has not been consumed, that would mean that something went wrong with regards the offering preparation or procedure. An enquiry of the Creator would be done by the priest whereupon the cause of offering rejection will be revealed and a redress would be done

Hebrew / African Culture

followed by a repeat of the offering.

African Culture, African Oral Tradition, Judges 6 vs 21-23,
1 Chr 21 vs 26-28, 2 Chr 5 vs 13-14, 2 Chr 7 vs 1,

1.158 The Use of Incense in Spirituality

There is no place for incense, censers (utilities for burning incense) and associated incense offerings in Hebrew or African Culture for the reason that such undertakings are not spiritual for they do not harmonize humankind with the spiritual realm, incense actually defiles the spiritual realm. While the sons of Aaron fell for making an incense offering, the Jews make a recitation of incense offering called Pitum Haktoret at every Jewish service while the church performs the same abominable incense offering at each church service and worshipping in the north is literally sustained by incense. More detail on Pitum Haktoret is given in **Chapter 2 Jewish Culture / Judaism**. It will not be a church service without an incense offering, Pentecostal services have seen the irrelevancy of incense and have stopped the use of it in their services;

'And Nadab and Abihu, the sons of Aaron, took either of them his censer, and put fire therein, and put
INCENSE *thereon, and offered strange fire before the Creator, which the Creator commanded them not.*
And there went out fire from the Creator, and devoured them, and they died before the Creator'.

Lev 10 vs 1-2,

It is in fact snuff and its associated dishes (gonan'ombe/ nhekwe/ chibako) that are used and offered in Hebrew or African Culture and strictly snuff offering is not a burnt offering. Making a burnt offering of snuff is not spiritual but vicious and is some form of witchcraft, it is an abomination. In spite of the lessons drawn from the tragedy that befell the sons of Aaron for offering incense, the north and Jews cannot conduct a service without the abominable incense offering or its recitation respectively. The death of Aarons' sons that occurred after the incense offering was one of the few instances other than the death Korah and Dathan where instant justice came from heaven to punish the living upon commission of a grave mistake in spirituality. And with incense use prohibited to that extent prior to the Hebrew exile, its reappearance in the post exile writings by Ezra and compatriots showed to what extent exile in Babylon completely changed the culture of children born in exile, Zerubbabel—the seed of Babylon.

Services of the shrine in African Culture are conducted with a high level of observance by taking finer detail of instructions, speaking words befitting the business of an offering and abstaining from making comments not befitting one born in the culture. Any failure to abide by such conduct in African traditions may cause the subject to be swallowed by the ground or by the waters on which he stands or disappearing in mysterious circumstances. On enquiring of the Creator the relatives of the victim would be told through a priest (svikiro) the offence for which the subject was consumed or was made to disappear. The European settlers from the north who sought to defile/desecrate various spiritual shrines in African countries have disappeared and to date remain untraceable. Such places include Mount Nyangani, Matonjeni and Chirorodziva in Zimbabwe among others.

African Culture, Oral Tradition, Num 3 vs 4

1.159 Kutema Ruhau/ Making a Mark on Burial Ground of a Relation

In African Culture, when a relation dies, it is the responsibility of another related person like an uncle to take charge of the burial that involves, identifying the burial ground (kutema ruhau), managing the digging of the grave, cleaning the body and burying it in similar fashion to the following;

'And Moses called Mishael and Elzaphan, the sons of Uzziel the uncle of Aaron and said unto them,
come near, carry your brethren from before the sanctuary out of the camp (for burial).
So they went near, and carried them in their cots out of the camp; as Moses had said'.

Lev 10 vs 4-5,

Hebrew / African Culture

That was the task that Moses assigned to the two uncles of the deceased; this is being done in African Culture this day. More detail is in African Culture today than in the Ezra script.

African Culture, Gen 50 vs 5-13

1.160 Drinking While Doing Divine Work

Beer or strong drink is used in African or Hebrew Culture. Seasonal offerings usually include beer whose preparation and consumption is regulated by the following law;

'And the Creator spake unto Aaron, saying,
Do not drink wine nor strong drink, thou, nor thy sons with thee, when you go into the tabernacle of the congregation, lest you die: it shall be a statute for ever throughout your generations: And that you may put difference between holy and unholy, between clean and unclean';

Lev 10 vs 8-10

In Africa, spiritual services are done by sober people, from the priest down to the common person. For all the procedures relating to rain offering (Mukwerere), thanks giving among others that are accompanied by beer or strong drink, the preparation of the strong drink itself and the spiritual offerings that are performed using beer by spilling it on the ground or rock as examples are performed by sober people until completion and all those that drink beer are very fluent with this requirement.

People will only drink beer at the end to celebrate the success of the offering only when instruction to drink beer is given and priests usually take the introductory sip and thereafter they retire to their places.

African Culture,

1.161 Food and Non-food

Hebrew or African Culture clearly distinguishes between food (what people can eat) and non-food (what people cannot eat). Though Africa is abundant in a variety of plant and animal species but not everything is recommended by the culture as food no matter how appealing those species may be to the sense of sight, smell and taste. The following quoted scripture summarises the general specification for food and non-food;

'Whatsoever parteth the hoof, and is cloven footed, and chews the cud, among the beasts, that shall you eat'.

Lev 11 vs 3,

'These shall you eat of all that are in the waters: whatsoever hath fins and scales in the waters, in the seas, and in the rivers, them shall you eat'.

Lev 11 vs 9,

African tribes in Africa adhere to these eating habits notwithstanding the absence of the spiritual written manual, the law of Moses. A snap survey of African foods will comply with the referenced food specification; the donkey is non-food in Africa for it is not cloven footed and does not chew the cud, the swine is cloven footed but does not chew the cud and has a digestive gut identical to humankind and the excretory waste of a pig are like that of humankind and so the swine is like humankind on four legs and eating such is like cannibalism.

The crab is non-food to the extent that when an African goes out for fishing and catches a crab, she/he considers that as a bad omen on a bad day. The crab is a delicacy in the east which carries disease causing parasites but is strictly non-food in Africa.

Hebrew / African Culture

These eating habits cannot be termed coincidence and natural for the reason that other nations who are without the law of Moses eat anything from snakes, scorpions, monkeys, octopi, crabs, snails, shrimps, crocodiles, tortoises and other items but most African tribes do not eat these. There is a remarkable absence in Hebrew or African Culture in the field of animal husbandry of the matters that pertain to pig industry, the rearing and processing thereof. Equally the pig is absent on the altar, shrine and in all matters of spirituality. Ostrich and duck farming were never part of the Hebrew or African agricultural domain. The African swine is the warthog which is wild and was never tamed for the reason that the fore bearers called it non-food for reason of fat among other features. The north came to Africa with a breakfast sliced swine fry (heavy in cholesterol), to an extent that a large number of Africans have to fry the slice of no spirituality before going to work, and their authority and audacity to eat cholesterol is derived from the 'new testament' of the north. The swine by anatomy has a thick layer of fat that protects it against cold weather and this shows that it is an animal that is adapted to northern weather and climate from where it originates but is now in Africa as a result of movements that ensued imperialism.

The Arabs do not allow the rearing, consumption or the shipment of swine products on their land and neither do they allow other people to defile their land on their behalf.

Besides the spiritual requirement associated with keeping the dietary laws, abstaining from eating swine products is a guard against heart and cholesterol related diseases. The eagles and vultures are tertiary consumers with a lot of poisons in their bodies, the dietary laws provided a very healthy diet upon the Hebrews. Rodents of the family of rats and mice carry a number of disease causative agents and for that reason are unsuitable for human consumption. Any item that is not as given herein, is in Hebrew Culture non-food item, such items include the swine, the rats, mice and others. Thus if a Hebrew or practising African is given a swine dish to eat, to him/her that would not be food, because the swine in the culture is non-food, is like serving a dead donkey or chameleon.

Isolated incidents in Africa where people eat chimpanzees, donkeys or rodents is unAfrican but is a result of poverty and hunger. Earlier in the life of Africans when the land was not defiled, small animals such as hares, rabbits or mice did not constitute what a hunter would call a catch because during that time game animals were quite plenty and consumption of the referenced rodents was quite rare. African folk tales and children songs sung when children want to identify someone who has released digestive gas consider most rodents as big as the hare to be smelly and not worth eating in such songs as 'amutsa tsuro ndiani, anoidya ari oga achinhuhwirwa' translated 'who has awoken up a hare? he is going to eat it alone while enduring its bad rodent smell'. The hare only became food when push came shove as food became scarce and non food items had to be eaten else people would die. When an African embarks on a walk, the instance of stepping on a snail let alone eating it would be considered a bad day because the quality of life has always been quite high until a few tens of years back.

Eating or getting in contact with dead animals is also prohibited, in fact it is taboo in Africa to eat an animal that has died on its own illness other than by slaughter. Such laws provided checks against the spread of infectious diseases that would have killed those animals. There is a lot of scientific knowledge in African or Hebrew Culture especially when a reflection on other laws like restricting liberal and promiscuous mating especially on women.

If there are people today who eat directly the food that they produce, then they are blessed people indeed for the majority of people are teetering beyond their redeemable status due to consumption of poisonous foods that is entrusted to greedy food merchants who will sell anything ingestible in order to earn money. People who own pieces of land upon which they are producing their family food needs must hold on to that land for as long as they live. Africa must be very careful in urbanization as such settlements will take a huge toll on African Culture and associated health life especially when reflected upon the quality of food and environment.

African Culture, African Oral Tradition, Len 11 vs 13-47, Det 12 vs 15, Det 14

Hebrew / African Culture

1.162   Kutevera/ The Manner of Women

African or Hebrew Culture exempts a woman in her separation from partaking in the services of the shrine or holy work, cooking for any event or family and meeting her husband on her matrimonial bed.
In some communities in Africa that include those in Ethiopia, a woman in her separation will not stay in the same room with the family for the duration of her separation;

'And if a woman have an issue, and her issue in her flesh is blood, she shall be put apart seven days: and whosoever toucheth her shall be unclean until even.
And every thing that she lieth upon in her separation shall be unclean: every thing also that she sitteth upon shall be unclean'.

Lev 15 vs 19-20,

Abstaining from the wife during her manner creates the compulsory break and the subsequent anxiety required on any matrimonial bed. Knowing a wife with her manner takes away the pleasure in a marriage. It is not good for the body of a man to know his wife during her manner; it weakens the man and kills enthusiasm or interest, is not pleasant and not worth looking forward to and when a man remembers that displeasure, he loses interest in that particular woman among other health issues. Even an African harlot knows that when the manner of women is upon her she makes no contact with men for even in the middle of her iniquities she still understands in clear terms issues which are taboo in the culture.

African Culture, Lev 18 vs 19, Lev 20 vs 18

1.163   Muzvere/ Purification of Woman after Childbirth

After giving birth, an African woman will not know her husband on bed during her recovery duration, she will not be allowed to be part of the traditional spiritual ceremonies. She is required to stay at home most of the time and most domestic chores like cooking are done for her till she has completed her purification process. Most un-noticing Africans do not know exactly why most tasks are done for her by senior women, those beyond child bearing age, other than for the need to help out an exhausted body.

'Speak unto the children of Jacob, saying, if a woman have conceived a seed, and born a man-child: then she shall be unclean seven days; according to the days of the separation for her infirmity shall she be unclean.
And in the eighth day the flesh of his foreskin shall be circumcised.
And she shall then continue in the blood of her purifying three and thirty days; she shall touch no hallowed thing, nor come near the sanctuary, until the days of her purifying be fulfilled'.

Lev 12 vs 2-4

There is a reasonable time that African Culture discourages mating between husband and his pregnant wife from the time that pregnancy is noticeable to the time that the wife completes her recovery and such restrictions provided the sufficient rest the woman required especially during the first trimester where miscarriages are occurring in excessive numbers these days.

African Culture,

1.164   Uncleanness Due to Flow of Seed in Man

The spirituality of an African or Hebrew becomes heavily compromised by matters of the bed but that does not licence celibacy among humankind for it leads to the extinction of humankind from the face of the earth. Spiritual requirements are that prior to holy work man must have the requisite sanctity and prime among that aspect is the need to abstain from matters of the bed and their peripherals like seed. In times of war, or fasting for an objective, spiritual uncleanness will deter the required result;

'And if any man's seed flows from him, then he shall wash all his flesh in water, and be unclean till even.

128

Hebrew / African Culture

And every garment, and every skin, whereon is the seed shall be washed with water, and be unclean until the even.
The woman also with whom man shall lie with, they shall both bathe themselves in water, and be unclean until the even'.

Lev 15 vs 16-18

When an African is unclean due to flow of seed or otherwise, he will not partake of the procedures of the oracle or an offering for he is unclean. He is not allowed to walk on holy ground till his uncleanness is corrected or if he goes to battle in that state of uncleanness, he may not come back from battle alive but a dead man. A celibate priest, for the natural necessity for womankind, is more likely to have the flow of seed unnecessarily and thus render him unsuitable for the services before the congregation in Hebrew or African terms.

African Culture, Lev 15 vs 1-4, Gen 2 vs 18

1.165   Kurasira/ Kudzinga Mamhepo/ The Scapegoat

The referenced scripture is typical African Culture and most practising readers of this work know the scapegoat procedure in detail, how the goat is driven away and how it is left in the wild and the conduct of him that sends the goat away, all in detail. Readers must note that Ezra did not write the exact details of casting lots and procedure for releasing the goat into the wild and the Jews know only as far as the Ezra script, the rest belongs to the Africans, the Bona fide Hebrews of the Books of Moses. And with regards to the procedure of releasing the scapegoat, if an omission is made on the procedure, the curses will not be transferred to the goat but will remain where they would be;

'And he (the priest) shall take two goats, and present them before the Creator at the door of the tabernacle of the congregation.
And Aaron shall cast lots upon the two goats; one lot for the Creator, and the other lot for the scapegoat.
And Aaron shall bring the goat upon which the Creator's lot fell, and offer him for a sin offering.
But the goat, on which the lot fell to be the scapegoat, shall be presented alive before the Creator, to make an atonement with him, and let him go for a scapegoat into the wilderness'.

Lev 16 vs 7-10,

'And Aaron shall lay both his hands upon the head of the live goat, and confess over him all the iniquities of the Hebrews, and all their transgressions in all their sins, putting them upon the head of the goat, and shall send him away by the hand of a fit man into the wilderness:
And the goat shall bear upon him all their iniquities unto a land not inhabited: and he shall let go the goat in the wilderness'.

Lev 16 vs 21-22

Vanhu/Abantu know also the recommended type, colour and age range of the goat in question. Such goats which are let free in the wilderness are there in Africa today for anyone to see, they usually reside in mountains as wild goats which were previously tamed goats before a lot fell on them and were later driven into the wild. In Israel or Arabia, there are no such goats for the reason that the said Hebrew Culture procedure of the scapegoat is not easy to understand and let alone implement unless if it is done by the owner of the culture or those born in it. In fact there is a cocktail of what is permissible to do and what is not, relating to the person who sends away the scapegoat before, while and after sending away the scapegoat which includes what to talk, who to talk to and where to look and where not to.

An African would rather starve to death than slaughter a goat of this category for the consumption thereof will bring curses loaded on the goat to the consumer of that goat. When any object, animal, money or cloth takes the role of scapegoat, whoever takes such items for a possession will inherit the curses loaded on the scapegoat as happened to Gehazi when he inherited the leprosy of Naaman and that is why all objects of scapegoat are never eaten or taken by anyone in Africa who is informed of the culture. The custom of the scapegoat gives provision in African or Hebrew Culture to exorcise the

Hebrew / African Culture

family of ill-fortune (mamhepo) caused by reasons other than avenging spirit or a tormented innocent soul for these will definitely require restitution or appeasement or a settlement prescribed in the same culture. A malicious person may send misfortune to a third party due to petty jealousy and such are issues among others that can be handled by kurasira (the scapegoat). Or when a person undertakes to travel a long journey, he or she may be prompted to take a rest sometimes under a tree or on a rock where a soul of an innocent person was murdered for which restitution was not paid or a person who has not been appeased spiritually whose is loitering, such souls would easily attach themselves to any living host when an opportunity arises and these souls need to be cast away as they cause a lot of problems on their human hosts.

Usually the hand is one part of the human body through which the spiritual realm can be propagated or transmitted as in passing on a blessing or a curse and to that effect traditionally Vanhu/Abantu do not greet each other by the hand for the reason that curses may be transferred to the innocent ones from the notorious people. Instead when people greet each other, it is by word or hand gestures such as clapping hands in the air or on ones' chest and the actual process of a hand greeting is done to the relatives of the deceased through a process called kubata maoko where hands are touched deliberately to the mourning to share or off-load their ill-fortunes through the spiritual conductor—the hand.

Upon the advent of the church in Africa and the subsequent conversion en masse to Christianity by Vanhu/Abantu, the matters pertaining to the scapegoat have been abandoned gradually to this day to the extent that all matters that used to be carried by the scapegoat from the people to the wild now are being carried by most African families and the tormenting effects are heavy and catastrophic to the people. The Christian pastors especially of Pentecostal church, largely of doubtful credentials have simply transferred such heavy loads from one member of the congregation to the other creating a vicious circle of such matters, while refusing to accept that kurasira (the scapegoat solution) is the answer to such matters. The more one goes to church and bring the pastor or church leader goodies, the less likely is one to carry such loads, a scenario that has sometimes resulted in some members of the congregation worshipping the pastors - 'he is surely a man of god, sent to take away my tribulations', et al. The author advises Vanhu/Abantu to abstain from 'demon casting' events for they risk being burdened by matters meant for the scapegoat for evil spirits/curses cannot be cast into the air or vacuum but that they need a host to abide on and they only die/vanish upon the death of their host. Curses loaded on the goat will disappear/die upon the natural death of the goat, but should the goat be stolen or killed by another person, the curses would come back to humankind through that person.

African Culture, African Oral Tradition, 2 Kings 5 vs 27

1.166 Kukanda Hakata/ Casting Lots

The system of casting lots is used to determine usually the cause of a misfortune, a problem or to identify a culprit among the Hebrews or Africans especially when the culprit is unwilling to tell the truth, or when dealing with objects which will not be able to speak out for themselves, or in times of doubt among the people. Lots are cast in front of all parties to pick out the culprit or to identify the cause of a problem/curse/misfortune. This is in contrast to the trial and error probability method employed by the north through their system of justice to determine the culprit where eloquence and coherence of a statement usually wins the day in place of innocence;

'And Aaron shall cast lots upon the two goats; one lot for the Creator, and the other lot for the scapegoat'.
Lev 16 vs 8,

'So the shipmaster came to him (Jonah), and said unto him, what meanest thou, O sleeper? Arise, call upon thy Creator, if so be that the Creator will think upon us, that we perish not.
And they said every one to his fellow, come, and let us cast lots, that we may know for whose cause this evil is upon us. So they cast lots, and the lot fell upon Jonah'.
Jonah 1 vs 6-7,

The referenced scriptures do not go into the details of casting lots, the specifics of casting lots that

130

Hebrew / African Culture

include the devices that are cast or thrown, the method of casting and the way to interpret the results and be able to determine that one event was caused by one specific person and not the other and all this detail is found in Africa among the people who live in Hebrew Culture and not the Jews in Jerusalem, Bethlehem, Paris or London for that system is foreign to them.

Lots are cast by a priest (svikiro/dlozi) of genuine credentials whose result will be true and inspired by spirituality, though this spiritual aspect of the culture has been hijacked in most instances by the magicians of Africa or by the genuine Hebrew priests who have fallen to the lure of money by using their priestly privileges in fortune telling to earn money. It is important to note that a priest still makes a determination where there is doubt and requires the casting of lots, nevertheless he/she may not necessarily cast the lots practically but uses an inspired method of determination. When a lot falls on the culprit, the later will accept blame and a remedy will be applied basing on the result of the cast lots. Lots can also be administered by a leader to distribute resources equitably and without favour as was done by Joshua in distributing land to the Hebrew tribes.

African Culture, Josh 18 vs 10-11, 1 Sam 10 vs 20-23,
1 Sam 14 vs 41-42, 1 Chr 24 vs 30-31, 1 Chr 26 vs 13-18

1.167 Approaching the Nakedness of Kinsman/Kinswoman

Critics of African Culture have said that before the arrival of European settlers, every African walked nude and it was therefore not possible to keep the tradition given in the referenced scripture yet it is known that Vanhu/Abantu wore a variety of clothing ranging from animal skins, tree bark to cotton garments bearing in mind that Africans have a very long history in cotton agriculture and that cotton was not grown for export but for weaving clothes;

'None of you shall approach to any that is near of kin to him, to uncover their nakedness: I am the Creator. The nakedness of thy father, or the nakedness of thy mother, shalt thou not uncover: she is thy mother; thou shalt not uncover her nakedness'.

Lev 18 vs 6-7

In African or Hebrew Culture, it is taboo to uncover or approach the nakedness of one's near kin, whereas in other cultures, Judaism included, it is part of culture to walk almost bare naked in homes in the presence of all near kin or at the sea beaches. In times of sporting activities, which include swimming, near nakedness is a must and male adult children do not blink at the sight of their mothers' bare bodies.

Prior to the advent of European settlers, some African communities used to wear animal hides that only covered half the body, true it is but the same critics need to note that with respect to that clothing standard, no African looked more bare/naked than the other, it was uniform. Actually African children are taught that looking at the body of a nude person will cause their eyes to develop a sudden eye defect called 'showera', which was a way to instil that sense of morality among the African children.

Today centuries later and clothing industries are in full throttle, some of the people in other cultures dress normally, and some half-naked and the remainder constitute the nude club.

African Culture, Lev 20 vs 11-12, Lev 20 vs 17, Lev 20 vs 19-20

1.168 Bestiality

Bestiality is a problem with shepherd tribes especially now when survival is a challenge to the extent that it is more difficult for young men to get married early in their right age and sometimes they help themselves with animals against the following statute;

'Neither shalt thou lie with any beast to defile thyself therewith: neither shall any woman stand before a beast to lie down thereto: it is confusion'.

Lev 18 vs 23

Hebrew / African Culture

Lying with a beast is taboo in African Culture and is forbidden.

African Culture, Lev 20 vs 13, Lev 20 v2 15,16, Exo 22 vs 19, Det 27 vs 21

1.169 Gleaning for the Poor

After the first harvest, it is known in African Culture that the second one is free for all, strangers, the poor and animals which agrees with the following;

'And when you reap the harvest of your land, thou shalt not wholly reap the corners of thy field, neither shalt thou gather the gleanings of thy harvest.
And thou shalt not glean thy vineyard, neither shalt thou gather every grape of thy vineyard; thou shalt leave them for the poor and the stranger: I am thy Creator'.

Lev 19 vs 9-10,

The provision for the poor was compromised when the European settlers occupied Africa, they gave land title deeds unto themselves and designed trespass laws that made it criminal for anyone to walk or do anything including gleaning in their yards or fields that they confiscated from Africans. Strangers, the poor or stray animals that intrude into the confiscated property of the north will invite the action of a bullet. In their morals, and in their culture, the poor and the stranger are not treated with the manner as prescribed in the Hebrew Scriptures, yet the same people came to preach to the Hebrews, the blessedness of the poor, and how near impossible it would be for a rich man to enter 'heaven'.

African Culture, Lev 23 vs 22

1.170 Seka Urema Wafa/ Respect for the Disabled

Cursing the disabled is seriously discouraged to the extent that the saying 'seka urema wafa' literally means laugh at the disabled in your after-death, which means it is not possible to abuse the disabled and that conforms to the following scriptural reference;

'Thou shalt not curse the deaf, nor put a stumbling block before the blind, but shalt fear thy Creator: I am the Creator'.

Lev 19 vs 14,

It is taboo in African Culture to vex the disabled like the blind, the deaf and the lame, for tradition says the same disability will come to your own family if you cannot treat them well so that when you have a disabled member in your own home, then you will be bound to learn to be courteous to the disabled.

African Culture, Det 27 vs 18

1.171 Guhwa Harivaki Musha/ Tale Bearing Destroy Homes

African literature teaches that tale bearing destroys homes in expressions such as 'guhwa harivaki musha', which is the summary of the following Hebrew tenet;

Thou shalt not go up and down as a talebearer among thy people: neither shalt thou stand against the blood of thy neighbour: I am the Creator'.

African Culture, Lev 19 vs 16

1.172 Mingling Fabrics in One Garment

African garments are either wholly animal skin or wholly cotton or any other fabric and not a combination of two or more. A critique may attribute this to lack of modern clothing technology among the Africans, but the same must note that if Africans had architectural technologies thousands of years as old and as complex as the Egyptian pyramids at Giza, the Shaduf irrigation systems, the Great Zimbabwe among

Hebrew / African Culture

technologies, would clothing technology appear more complex? Again there is a lot of science in not mixing different fabrics. When fabrics of different strength are used in one garment, they age or wear and tear differently which is wasting the stronger fabric;

'You shall keep my statutes. Thou shalt not let thy cattle gender with a diverse kind: thou shalt not sow thy field with mingled seed: neither shall a garment mingled of linen and woollen come upon thee'.

Lev 19 vs 19

In like manner, Africans have not ventured into animal cross breeding, though they are known to be great animal breeders, because it is against their spiritual law. The north besides making explorations into space as Nimrod tried to do, they are duplicating animals and humans against the normal reproductive cycles of animals as ordained by creation, to the detriment of the natural ecosystem.

African Culture,

1.173 Use of Enchantment and Observing the Times

Observing times or use of the signs of the Zodiac to fortune tell is not part of African Culture, it is a concept that came with the north who were well versed with the science of the constellations of the stars leading to signs of the Zodiac, there is no equivalent name of this practice in African dialects for the reason that it is foreign although Vanhu/Abantu can foresee the coming of rains or any weather pattern based on observations in the atmosphere;

'You shall not eat anything with the blood: neither shall you use enchantments, nor observe times'.

African Culture, Lev 19 vs 26, Det 18 vs 10-14

1.174 Cutting Hair and Beard in Weird Styles

Vanhu/Abantu are known by all nations of the world to keep their hair and letting it grow into a lock and a beard that never knew a shave;

'You shall not round the corners of your heads, neither shall thou mar the corners of thy beard'.

Lev 19 vs 27,

Africa is well known for skills in iron working and processing, a key raw material needed for making hair shaving/cutting devices, but the understanding in African Culture is that there is spirituality in the hair as shown in the laws of the Nazarite. Cutting hair in the heads and shaving the beard among the Africans is purely an imitation by Africans of the north; it is not part of African Culture and besides, the African man is not a fanatic of good looks as that is culturally accepted as the female domain; men should ideally look tough and rugged.

African Culture, Lev 21 vs 5, 2 Sam 10 vs 4-5

1.175 Tattoos

Vanhu/Abantu have markings on the skin for two reasons; medical treatments that leave marks especially on the face or other parts of the body (nyora) and for compulsory tribal identity for people found in places like Kenya and Sudan among other places in Africa but clear and outright tattoos are not common in Africa and that characteristic of Africans complies with the following;

'You shall not make any cuttings in your flesh for the dead, nor print any marks upon you: I am the Creator'.

Lev 19 vs 28

It is quite a heart sore for a parent to see a child bring home a savage tattoo on the face, hand or belly.

Hebrew / African Culture

But Africans who were dispersed into exile through slavery (especially African Americans), have made huge tattoos onto their bodies and the summary of tattoos among Africans is that they have a link to the strangers by way of imitation, but that is not condoning a deviation/breach of the Hebrew or African Culture by Africans when they imitate other nations.

Not only have the Africans in exile tattooed themselves but they are also on drugs and similar intoxicants or substances. Not only have they gone on drugs, but they have also become sodomites like their hosts. These are the grim realities and catastrophes of exile, that befell Vanhu/Abantu when they were separated from the larger family on mainland Africa.

African Culture,

1.176 Kuvhunzira Kumashavi Nen'anga/Sangoma / Consulting Familiar Spirits and Wizards

The business of consulting those with familiar spirits and wizards is a perennial trade with unending clients in African Culture as humankind have serious interest in knowledge of their social and economic life in the future or the future of their adversaries in breach of the following Hebrew tenet;

'Regard not them that have familiar spirits, neither seek after wizards, to be defiled by them: I am thy Creator'.

Lev 19 vs 31

African or Hebrew Culture holds in high esteem enquiring of the Creator through priests of the lineage of Levi (Svikiro/Dlozi) in times of need, but the same culture condemns enquiring unto persons with familiar spirits or unto wizards for the reason that these people do their trades in pursuit of money. In that context a man or woman with familiar spirits or a wizard can cause harm to another person using his or her trade under the instruction of a paying client. However a priest (svikiro/dlozi) performs his/her duties with high level adherence to the laws governing the spiritual aspect of enquiring of the Creator and is thus not influenced by money but by the nature of the problem to humanity in relation to the Creator.

A familiar spirit is a soul of a departed person which did not navigate the normal after-death for some reason. Proof that familiar spirits have not navigated the full spiritual realm but are somewhere between the physical world and spiritual realm is that:

a)   Sometimes when a familiar spirit descends on a living human host, it asks for water for reason of excessive thirst as a sign of lack of peace and rest in the domain of its abode
b)   When a harlot is murdered while plying her trade, she often comes back to pick clients of her original trade as a sign that she is somewhere between the physical and spiritual realm. Most of her clients have often given testimony that the moment they entered the house and switched on the lights, the deceased harlot would just disappear without trace like the wind.

Familiar spirits being souls of the departed who did not navigate the normal after-death, can be seen in Hebrew Culture when Saul requested Samuel's spirit to be brought up through the woman with familiar spirits, Samuel felt disturbed from his after-death rest but souls that have not navigated the normal after -death actually come on their own without invitation for reason of lack of peace in the abode of their after -death. In the absence of the voice of heaven for reason of sin, people in Africa will consult those with familiar spirits (n'anga, sangoma) as happened to Saul with the woman of Endor for the reason that the Creator had rejected him and was not answering him anymore;

'And when Saul enquired of the Creator, the Creator answered him not, neither by dreams, nor by Urim, nor by prophets.
Then said Saul unto his servants, seek me a woman that hath a familiar spirit, that I may go to her, and enquire of her.
And his servants said to him, behold, there is a woman that hath a familiar spirit at Endor'.

1 Sam 28 vs 6-7

Hebrew / African Culture

Familiar spirits usually complain of a number of issues associated with the places they come from which is a sign of lack of peace in the spiritual realm. Such failed spirits cannot be role models to provide spiritual consultancy to the living, such spirits defile humankind. In African Culture there is clear distinction between the act of familiar spirits (mashavi) and wizards on one side and the priestly duties of masvikiro/amadlozi. It is known without any doubt that the priestly duties by the priests are acts of proper spirituality while the use of familiar spirits and wizards are abominations unto the Creator and to that effect those who consult or use familiar spirits are viewed with the appropriate contempt as people with familiar spirits use a lot of concoctions that defile humankind. All African services of the oracle like conduction of a bira (thanks giving offering), rain offering and many other spiritual works are never conducted by those with familiar spirits (mashavi) or wizards or magicians (n'anga/sangoma), in fact their presence at shrines is prohibited; not only do the ordinary people or the priests know that but the same unspiritual candidates know it, they sense it or are caused not to linger in such sites by the spiritual realm. In the event that those prohibited to do such services find themselves leading the services in question, there will be no positive result from such offerings, they will be rejected for they would lack the requisite spiritual sanctity.

Familiar spirits were used in the days of Saul in exactly the same manner as they are used today in Africa, with the person host to the familiar spirit always confirming that he/she has no gift or knowledge of fortune telling except the spirit that sits on him/her, as was the manner of the woman to whom Saul enquired upon, when she was back to herself, she found Saul disturbed, a sign that what had come from the familiar spirit was not good news for Saul.

Those with familiar spirits and wizards are the African or Hebrew candidates who have illegally taken over the business of casting lots, and they have commercialised it, sometimes manipulating results or sometimes not knowing how to do it altogether. Sometimes authentic Hebrew or African priests have fallen spiritually to the lure of money and became n'anga/sangoma and magic enchanters with gifts of casting and interpreting lots.

Physicians (doctors) have always been in existence in Hebrew or African Culture with the name 'merape'/ 'murapi', (equivalent linguistic terms in Jewish Hebrew and Vanhu/Bantu dialects respectively) with knowledge to source medicine, make medical researches and use it on appropriate applications. The knowledge of medicine in Hebrew or African Culture was acquired through dreams or revelations from heaven, general knowledge or were passed on from father to son through an apprenticeship or housemanship and not necessarily through familiar spirits. The issue of enquiring unto familiar spirits has become popular under the background that humankind have a propensity for wanting to know beyond the ordinary or beyond the present day, and the temptation is there for those with familiar spirits to earn a living because the customers for that trade are naturally there though the practice is forbidden and is not spiritually acceptable. Yes it is proper to practice medicine in Hebrew or African Culture, from the perspective of 'merape'/'murapi' as explained herein but not from the perspective of n'anga/sangoma and familiar spirits. The practice is not spiritual and it renders the practitioner and patient impure. The trade of witchcraft, the use of goblins and other unspiritual devices by man are tradable merchandise of a magic enchanter (wizard). Innocent people who visit the magic enchanter for fortune enquiries or general enquiries end up being loaded with these devices by the wizard or some clients literally buy devices of witchcraft from these magic enchanters/ witchdoctors/ n'anga/sangoma.

That is why magic enchanters or wizards are considered highly unspiritual. They are manipulated by money. A n'anga/sangoma can cause the death of an innocent person from an instruction of a paying client and are feared by the general people but not the priests. Usually he/she will not look at the rationale or ethics of his action, to him its the money that matters, no wonder such professions have no place nor respect in the culture. The priests though for telling the truth and exposing immorality, are usually avoided by the ordinary people.

African Culture, Lev 20 vs 6, Lev 20 vs 27, 1 Sam 28 vs 6 -21,
2 Kings 1 vs 2, 2 Kings 21 vs 6, 2 Kings 23 vs 24,
1 Chr 10 vs 13

Hebrew / African Culture

1.177 Mother-in-law and Son-in-law Boundary

African Culture maintains one of the most formal and strictest interactions between mother-in-law and her son-in-law for these two are not allowed to be in close proximity of each other; the son-in-law when he meets his mother-in-law by the roadside will leap some several metres away from the road, take a crouching position, make a quick greeting largely enquiring on health and welfare of mother-in-law and dismiss. The two do not share a room even for a meeting and these restrictions come from the following scriptural prohibitions;

'And if a man take a wife and her mother, it is wickedness: they shall be burnt with fire, both he and they; that there be no wickedness among you'.

Lev 20 vs 14

African Culture gives extra high respect to the mother of one's wife to an extent that the son-in-law cannot stand in front of his sitting mother-in-law for the fear that he may uncover her head. The son-in-law cannot look at his mother-in-law directly in the face, he looks aside peradventure for some reason of insanity or some other, the mother-in-law becomes bare, the son-in-law must see nothing. When there are such restrictions in African Culture between son-in-law and mother-in-law, the chances of the two knowing each other on the bed is out of the question, it is taboo (chisionekwe), and if a man marries a woman who has a daughter, her damsel becomes the man's daughter also, and all laws governing father and daughter apply. While the relationship between father-in-law and daughter-in-law is like the simple father and daughter relationship but that between mother-in-law and son-in-law is another realm.

African Culture,

1.178 Svikiro Guru/ The High Priest

Each shrine in Africa is manned by a priest (svikiro/dlozi) who permanently resides by the shrine and performs all the services of the sanctuary. The priest ideally is one of the beneficiaries of the tithe system, Zunde ramambo for his life is dedicated to the services of spirituality and has no time for other work to sustain his family. The priests keep a Nazarite hair lock all the days of their life and this and other life style conform to the following spiritual tenets;

'They shall not make baldness upon their head, neither shall they shave off the corner of their beard, nor make any cuttings in their flesh'.

Lev 21 vs 5

'And he that is the high priest among his brethren, upon whose head the anointing oil (Mono remasvikiro) was poured, and that is consecrated to put on the garments, shall not uncover his head, nor rend his clothes;
Neither shall he go in to any dead body, nor defile himself for his father, or for his mother;
Neither shall he go out of the sanctuary, nor profane the sanctuary of his Creator; for the crown of the anointing oil of his Creator is upon him: I am the Creator'.

Lev 21 vs 10-12

Most of these priests who do not put a razor on their hair and are also anointed with oil do not attend funerals or interact with ordinary people nor put themselves at risk of spiritual defilement, it is for the reason that they are the Levim, their entire life is dedicated to the Creator. In Judaism, the Chief Rabbi is an ordinary man, whom you can meet in any public place while pushing his luck and counting his profits like any other ordinary person but not the Bona fide Hebrew priests in the depth of African shrines.

Historically, the office of the high priest in Africa could not be traced for among other reasons, the movements that Vanhu/Abantu have gone through and in that regard the keeping of the Day of Atonement (Yom Kippur) or Musi weKupupura among the people has not been possible for that service requires the chief priest. Linguistically there is concordance between Kippur and Kupupura and as usual

Hebrew / African Culture

the Jewish Hebrew dialect has lost two vowels but Vanhu/Bantu dialect is still the full original word.

African Culture, Lev 21, 1 Sam 13 vs 9-14, Eze 44 vs 11

1.179 Makunhakunha/ Incest

It is taboo (chisionekwe) in African Culture for one to take his sister or brother or any near kin person to bed. It is one transgression that can cause heaven to withhold rain, or cause a pestilence to afflict the people, it defiles the land and often African elders banish the culprits from the land they have defiled;

'Cursed be he that lieth with his sister, the daughter of his father, or the daughter of his mother'.

Det 27 vs 22

A variation of this law has developed in African Culture when people were confronted with that anomaly/ breach between them, instead of executing judgement on the parties to the forbidden marriage, they created a law of dissolution of kinship of the two parties to accommodate for a normal marriage (Cheka ukama nemombe chena). These are laws of convenience, to justify the forbidden; kinship cannot be dissolved like dirt in soap, for it is in the blood.

Children born out of incest, are not hybrids, they are biologically weak and frail. Usually they die in infancy or are born disabled.

African Culture, Lev 20 vs 17, Det 27 vs 20-23, 2 Sam 13 vs 11-17,32

1.180 Basa raSekuru/ The Role of an Uncle

The uncle (sekuru/babamudiki) plays a multifaceted role in Hebrew or African Culture in marriage matters, burial matters and other matters pertaining to the trial and tribulations of kinsmen as quoted herein, in an ideal extended family, which gives the individuals in a community that interdependence that binds the African extended family together.

'Either his uncle, or his uncle's son, may redeem him, or any that is nigh of kin unto him of his family may redeem him; or if he be able, he may redeem himself'.

Lev 25 vs 49,

African Culture, Lev 10 vs 4

1.181 The Nazarite Vow

Before the advent of European settlers in Africa, Vanhu/Abantu kept their hair locks shown on the cover page for reason of spirituality inherent in the hair lock and not because they did not have instruments for cutting hair as often said by critics of African Culture, for Africans had serious expertise in the working of iron or metals that could have yielded blades (chisvo) for shaving and cutting their hair and above all, the Vanhu/Bantu dialect term for scissors called chigero is a very old word which is the same in Jewish Hebrew used by the people before they separated and adapted to different habitats;

'All the days of the vow of his separation there shall no razor come upon his head: until the days be fulfilled, in which he separated himself unto the Creator, he shall be holy, and shall let the locks of the hair of his head grow'.

Num 6 vs 5

It is encouraging that hair locks are coming back among the Africans today in the search of their African identity and spirituality but to make a Nazarite vow means to choose to dedicate one's life to spirituality as was done by Samuel. It is not just a matter of growing one's hair lock for fashion as done by a number of Africans today. There are strict adherence laws to go along the hair lock. Failure by a

Hebrew / African Culture

Nazarite to keep those laws is a breach of the Nazarite vow and that can have fatal consequences. Samson breached the laws and the readers are well informed of his story, the same fatalities are happening to Africans who are just keeping the lock for fashion without full adherence to the Nazarite laws. When a Nazarite fails the conditions that are required of his/her state - dedication to the Creator - he/she has to cut the hair without fail. As explained in Chapter 6, Scriptural Race Evidence, African hair is the only hair that can lock itself naturally as it grows, other hairs flow or curl slightly. When African hair grows, it automatically locks and when it has done so the lock cannot be unlocked save by shaving, **that is why it is called a hair lock.** The Africans of Jamaica or the Caribbean Islands keep the locks of their hair. When an African who keeps the hair lock is defiled by the dead, that is when a family member dies in his or her proximity, he/she will cut the hair lock after the funeral to let it grow again.

Actually when African hair is allowed to grow naturally without combing it to try not imitating Caucasian hair which is a violation of the African identity, it locks. In the same token, Caucasian hair is straight and does not lock naturally and forcing a hair lock on it would also be a violation of Caucasian identity. African or Hebrew priests are born Nazarites dedicated to spiritual services all the days of their life and they do not shave their hair. The author pities largely African women who spend billions of dollars as a collective, of their meagre incomes in hair formulae that mimic Caucasian hair and skin bleaching chemicals as a clear indicator of lack of self belief and identity.

African Culture, Num 6, Judges 13 vs 3-25, Judges 16 vs 17,
1 Sam 1 vs 11, 2 Sam 10 vs 5, Amos 2 vs 11

1.182 Defilement Due to Human Blood and Corpse

In spirituality, Hebrew or African Culture consider human blood and corpse over and above the flow of seed in men and the manner of women as among the most defiling situations to the extent that a priest or commoner will not make offerings when he/she has had contact with human corpse or human blood before being cleansed which agrees with the following scripture;

'And those men said unto him (Moses), we are defiled by the dead body of a man: wherefore are we kept back, that we may not offer an offering of the Creator in the appointed season among the children of Jacob'?

Num 9 vs 6-12,

On the contrary, the north believe the human body can be used as an offering and human blood can be symbolised as the eternal drink of salvation in their spirituality which shows the extent of difference between Hebrew and northern spirituality which in summary are opposites. **It is therefore not possible to substitute Hebrew Culture with northern culture to the extent taught in the Greek Scriptures without violating fundamentally the tenets of one of the cultures.**

In summary Hebrew or African Culture and European cultures are so fundamentally different that one cannot stand in for the other, and for the Greeks to proclaim that their testament was now superseding Hebrew testament, that was simply religious propaganda with no substance at all to back it.

African Culture, Lev 12, Num 19 vs 11, 1 Chr 22 vs 8,
1 Chr 28 vs 3, Eze 44 vs 25, Hag 2 vs 13

1.183 **Kuvhunzira Kuna Musikavanhu/ Enquiring of the Creator**

When confronted with a problem like a drought, a pestilence or defeat in war or any matter of uncertainty, Africans go to the various shrines scattered across Africa and enquire of the Creator on what would be the cause of the problems. Africans have the full details of Hebrew communication protocol to heaven and today only Africans can communicate with their Creator in vivid language for the Creator gave an assurance that a prophet/priest will always be among the Hebrews, as a

Hebrew / African Culture

communication gateway;

'If there arise a matter too hard for thee in judgment, between blood and blood, between plea and plea, and between stroke and stroke, being matters of controversy within thy gates: then shalt thou arise, and get thee up into the place which the CREATOR shall choose;
And thou shalt come unto the priests the Levites, and unto the judge that shall be in those days, and enquire; and they shall shew thee the sentence of judgment':

Det 17 vs 8-9

When the Jews require to enquire of the Creator, they do it through a Hebrew or African priest here in Africa, who on their behalf will reveal what is required of them at that time by the Creator. They are aware that any attempt to usurp the Hebrew priest will not give them access to the Creator. This is the proper way to do things on their part. It is a good thing to know and to do. It is wrong to enquire through the familiar spirits and wizards, for these have no such authority.

When a priest of the correct lineage has been consecrated, often the spirit of heaven inspires upon him/ her on enquiry of the Creator or when the Creator deems it necessary to inspire the priest. The process of inspiration by the Creator is calm and not of trance in nature unlike that which happens on a person with a familiar spirit. When a familiar spirit descends upon its human host, the process resembles death or some form of a trance, where for example when a man expires sometimes the departure of his soul can be a struggle (untimely death or death of a wicked person). In the case of descent of a familiar spirit onto the living host, the host soul is for the period of descent/visitation, displaced by the familiar spirit. After completion of the business of the familiar spirit, the host soul returns and when it does so the host person is usually unaware of what he/she would have said or done during the time duration of the familiar spirit visitation.

However when the spirit of the Creator is upon a priest, the priest will be aware of the happenings and the process is a near normal life scene in which a priest wields high inspiration and knowledge of what the ordinary person will not know.

African Culture, Num 9 vs 7-8, Det 17 vs 8-13, Det 19 vs 16-19, Judges 20 vs 28, 1 Sam 9 vs 6-20
1 Sam 14 vs 36-38, 1 Sam 23 vs 1-13, 2 Sam 2 vs 1, 2 Sam 5 vs 19-23, 1 Kings 22 vs 7-8
2 Kings 3 vs 11, 2 Kings 22 vs 13, 1 Chr 14 vs 10-14, 1 Sam 30 vs 7-8, 1 Kings 14 vs 3

1.184 Mvura Yekuchenura/ Water of Separation

The water of separation (mvura yekuchenura) prepared by the elders from hyssop (muzeze) is a common feature at every traditional African funeral. After the burial procession, it is assumed that everyone involved was in contact with a dead body directly or indirectly. Thus a bowl of water is laid before a funeral procession just after burial before any member of the procession returns back home or re-enters the bereaved homestead. Each member washes his/her hands with the water specially prepared by the elders. It is a requirement for everyone who was part of the funeral procession to come back home and do the rite;

'Whosoever touches the dead body of any man that is dead, and purifies not himself, defiles the tabernacle of the Creator; and that soul shall be cut off from among the Hebrews: because the water of separation was not sprinkled upon him, he shall be unclean; his uncleanness is yet upon him'.

Num 19 vs 13

With the people involved made clean in the quoted manner, the cleaning procedure is transferred on to the clothes, the vessels that could have been in contact directly or indirectly with the dead body. In exactly the same manner taught by Hebrew Culture, water of separation is sprinkled on the vessels, the clothing, the house and anything else that could have been defiled by the dead body among African tribes. Africans do not refer to the book when they practise these laws of the Books of Moses, but the

Hebrew / African Culture

laws are in them, these procedures have been relayed down the people generation after generation to this day and agrees with the following scriptural reference;

'And a clean person shall take hyssop, and dip it in the water, and sprinkle it upon the tent, and upon the vessels, and upon the persons that were there, and upon him that touched a bone, or one slain, or one dead, or a grave':

Num 19 vs 18

Scientifically hyssop is an antiseptic which means that there is a possibility of infection of mourners that may emanate from the corpse or among mourners themselves and African or Hebrew Culture has scientific checks and balances to suppress infections when there is possibility of spread of disease and the culture is not a religious schism but serious scientific philosophies meant to improve life and environment.

African Culture, African Oral Tradition

1.185   Nyaminyami / The Brass Serpent

The powers associated with a snake are imbedded in Hebrew or Africans Culture in that even today in the waters of the great river Kasambavezi (Zambezi), are the same powers associated with a giant serpent with sustenance giving attributes - the Nyaminyami which in times of drought, the Africans surrounding the river would ideally be sustained by it and be self sufficient and live and not die in much the same manner as the life begotten from the bite of the brass serpent;

'And the Creator said unto Moses, make thee a fiery serpent, and set it upon a pole: and it shall come to pass, that every one that is bitten, when he looks upon it, he shall live'.

Num 21 vs 8

Readers need to note that in much the same way as the bite that heals, the Nyaminyami perse is not the healing or sustenance giving power, but the power comes from the spiritual realm. The mistake of Africans or Hebrews as what happened to Moses' brass serpent is to worship the snake. At a later stage, Moses' brass serpent had to be destroyed for the reason that some mis-informed Hebrews had started worshipping it in much the same way as some of Vanhu/Abantu associated with the Kasambavezi Nyaminyami may be doing this day.

African Culture, African Oral Tradition

1.186   Kugara Kwemwedzi/ New Moons and their Offerings

The new moon remains one of the recognizable spiritual days in African Culture to this day;

'And the beginnings of your months you shall offer a burnt offering unto the Creator; two young bullocks, and one ram, seven lambs of the first year without spot':

Num 28 vs 11

The new moon is announced on its sighting by African elders/authorities, those appointed by Moses with the advice of Jethro among the children of Jacob. Though the system of a new moon offering may not be in place in exact details as given in the scriptures, the new moon is highly regarded as one of the sacred days and markers in African spirituality.

African Culture, Num 28 vs 11-14, 1 Sam 20 vs 5, 1 Sam 20 vs 18-24,
2 Kings 4 vs 23, 1 Chr 23 vs 31, 2 Chr 8 vs 13

Hebrew / African Culture

1.187   **Kufumura Nyika/ Defilement of the Land**

The spilling of innocent blood, dumping of newborn babies to die on their own, sodomy, human sacrifice, incense offering and similar matters are some of the most abominable deeds that defile the entire land. When the entire land is defiled, the blessings to humankind will cease and all people will starve or suffer due to acts of a few individuals among them. Thus it is a communal responsibility to see that the land is not defiled, else all will suffer the consequences of the iniquities due to one or few individuals;

'And you shall take no satisfaction for him that is fled to the city of his refuge, that he should come again to dwell in the land, until the death of the priest.
So you shall not pollute the land wherein you are: for blood it defiles the land: and the land cannot be cleansed of the blood that is shed therein, but by the blood of him that shed it.
Defile not therefore the land, which you shall inhabit, wherein I dwell: for wherein I the Creator dwell among the Hebrews'.

Num 35 vs 32-34,

If people are to agree to allow those acts that defile the land to be performed on their land so as to cater for the needs of a few with a gender preference disorder (sodomy), then the entire land will be defiled and all the people including the sources of defilement of the land will suffer for those few people.

Any point in Africa whereupon innocent blood has been spilt needs cleansing. If the murderer is found he has to be dealt with according to the law before the cleansing ceremony could proceed, if the murderer is unknown a cleansing ceremony has to be conducted for fear of bringing a curse upon the land. However with the coming in of Christianity among Africans, the cleansing ceremonies have been labelled heathen and have sometimes in some places been stopped depending on the level of brainwash Christianity has done to that section of Africans. Terrible or unpleasant incidents will continue to occur on the defiled places, till the Africans go back to the shrine and enquire of the Creator. There they will be told of the cause of the curse and its remedy. That is why today certain points on national trunk roads are called accident spots, an innocent soul was killed, and the area was not cleansed. The cleansing ceremony is simple, it starts off with finding he who caused the loss of innocent life, when found he/she will pay restitution or tried according to manners that will pacify the deceased and the family of the deceased would perform a ceremony to retire and send away the aggrieved spirit. If the evil doer is not found then the ceremony of elders washing their hands refuting responsibility will occur, thereafter another offering would be made to enable the deceased to go in peace for all people around the place would be guiltless or to seek vengeance from the Creator against the actual culprit elsewhere. When the procedure has been done accordingly, the spot will not be termed the accident spot anymore, it will become a quiet spot as original as it was before.

There are many of these spots that are claiming a lot of life because Vanhu/Abantu have left their land defiled and uncleansed for too long and they are dying for that.

African Culture, Gen 18 vs 20, Exo 30 vs 12, Exo 32, Lev 18 vs 24-30
Det 21 vs 1-9, Gen 4 vs 8-12

1.188   **Hebrew or African Distress Call to the Creator**

In times of war, famine, pestilence, tribulation or any other national disaster, Africans or Hebrews would supplicate/sound before the Creator a distress call **for the Creator has a special ear for the children of Abraham** for wherever they would be, they would be heard for Abraham's sake;

'When thou are in tribulation, and all these things are come upon thee, even in the latter days, if thou turn to thy Creator and shall be obedient unto the voice;
Thy Creator will not forsake thee, neither destroy thee, nor forget the covenant of thy fathers which thy Creator sware unto them'.

Det 4 vs 30-31

Hebrew / African Culture

'If I shut up heaven that there be no rain, or if I command the locusts to devour the land, or if I send pestilence among My people;
If My people, which are called by my name, shall humble themselves, and pray, and seek Me, and turn from their wicked ways; then will I hear from heaven, and will forgive their sin, and will heal their land'.

2 Chr 7 vs 13-14

The referenced scripture should provide high motivation for the children and try to discover what kind of deed did the forefather do before heaven to warrant eternal blessings to the children for generation after generation. The Hebrew patriarch was a great man yet so humble and righteous man who impressed the Creator. A moment of reflection upon every father is; will the Creator be impressed by him when he jostles for every opportunity to get wealth and power? If the children will sin against the Creator, will they be spared for their father's sake? Or the children would suffer for their fathers' iniquities as in visiting the iniquities of the fathers upon the children unto the third and fourth generation?

A distress call is a call for the Creator to have mercy and compassion to the children of the inheritance. An example of a distress call that Africans sounded to the Creator during the times of oppression or imperialism by the north was 'Mudzimuwe (Mukuru), Mudzimuwe (Mukuru), ho here Mudzimuwe (Mukuru) vana tatambura, ho here Mudzimuwe (Mukuru)', which is translated 'Oh Great Soul or Source Soul (the Creator), the children of the fore bearers with whom You entered into a Covenant, are in great tribulation, we seek Your intervention for on our own, we are finished, we are overlooking total decimation from the enemy, the northern army has come with savagery, brutality, barbarism and with vile.' This is one kind of a distress call that will move a mountain or split the sea as happened to Moses and the children of Jacob at the Red Sea when the Pharaoh had come with malice. It is fact that when the Hebrews transgress against heaven they are punished as a corrective measure only and not with an aim of decimating the entire people, but when they seek the mercy and forgiveness of the Creator by sounding a distress supplication, heaven's response is spot on for Abraham's sake – for the covenant will live forever.

A Hebrew distress call is resultful plea of redemption. No matter how difficult things can be, the redemption plea or distress call, once sounded in total supplication will get a spot-on response from the Creator of heaven and earth, for the reason of the covenant which is real and the children of Abraham, Vana Venhaka yeDzitateguru, will never be forsaken, ever.

The answer or redemption will not come to the Africans by the recitation of the last supper memorial;

'And as they were eating, he took bread, and blessed it, and broke it, and gave it to his followers, and said, Take, eat; this is my body.
And he took the cup, and gave thanks, and gave it to them, saying, Drink ye all of it;
For this is my blood of the new testament, which is shed for many, for the remission of sins.'

For this is a pagan recitation which has no merit in matters of spirituality as taught in Hebrew or African Culture. It is a recitation or religious ritual that will not harmonize humankind and their Creator. It is a recitation that will invoke the wrath of heaven especially when it is sounded by Vanhu/Abantu. Munofa vana imi - you will surely die.

And in the same token, any African in distress in any part of the globe, South America, Europe, Asia or in the African peninsula itself must first sanctify self by abstaining from eating foods that defile humankind in search of spirituality and matters of the bed and on third day at dawn (mambakwedza/ runyanhiriri) or dusk (ruvhunzavaeni), take the snuff dish and make a call or supplication, not forgetting to reference the fore bearers who stood at Sinai and their later generations, emphasizing the hardships and refusing to be the tail, things will change for sure.

African Culture, African Oral Tradition, Det 4 vs 28-31, 1 Sam 12 vs 9-11, 22; Judges 10 vs 10-18

Hebrew / African Culture

1.189 Kupinduka Kwetsika/ Cultural Dynamism

Cultures do not survive by dynamism but that they try to adapt in order to preserve themselves. When a culture changes quickly as implied by cultural dynamism, it loses its fundamentals and a culture without its fundamentals is a dead or extinct culture and so African or Hebrew Culture had to be preserved by shunning dynamism;

'Now therefore hearken, O Vanhu/Abantu, unto the statutes and unto the judgements, which I teach you, to do them, that you may live, and go in and possess the land which the Creator of your fathers giveth thee.
You shall not add unto the word which I command you, neither shall you diminish ought from it, that you may keep the commandments of thy Creator which I command you'.

Det 4 vs 1-2,

If Hebrew or African Culture says that offering can either be grain, fruits, strong drink, cattle, flock or bird, and substituting those offerings with human offering is not cultural dynamism but cultural mutilation that will bury Hebrew or African Culture forever. Hebrew or African Culture has laws on offerings (kupira), thanks giving feasts (mapira), treatment of strangers, widows and orphans, agricultural practices, keeping of the Sabbath (Chisingarimwi), how to marry one's daughters, the system of justice and many others that are all within the culture and substituting some of these laws with sodomy and gender liberalism means extinction of Hebrew or African Culture and the founding fore bearers were taught that no one shall add or subtract a word on the existing culture else it would confuse the people.

The importation of ordinances or judgements from other cultures is condemned, thus the scriptures according to Paul, of a Greek way of life are an addition or subtraction to the African or Hebrew Culture and these additions do not advance the culture but suffocate it while promoting the Greek way of life which in summary was the whole business of the so called New Testament—to fight and extinct Hebrew Culture on a philosophical technicality.

If an audit of Hebrew Culture is taken today, it is clear that the New Testament has taken a huge toll on Hebrew Culture as people were being told to let go the old things to embrace a new culture which is all against the Hebrew Culture's guiding tenet of not adding or subtracting not even a word. Hebrew or African Culture and Greek Culture or northern culture are so fundamentally different that they cannot complement each other but are opposite and one cannot supersede the other without completely exterminating the other and neither can people attach these two opposing documents into one document as the present bible, it is like binding together the United Nations human rights charter to the Mein Kampf and start preaching of the 'new human rights philosophy'!!

African Culture, Det 6, Det 8 vs 1-2, Det 8 vs 6-20

1.190 Kusarudza Nokugadza Mutungamiri/ Selection and Anointing of a Leader

1.190.1 Kusarudza Mutungamiri/ Selection of a Leader

A Hebrew or African leader is ordained by the Creator, will not be a stranger but one born in the lineage, is guided by a code of conduct enacted by the Creator, and failure to uphold that leadership code will cause the leader to fall by the wayside as happened to Saul and Solomon. Thus in Hebrew or African Culture democracy comes from the Creator (theocracy), being the Creator of every thing knows the most suitable candidate in accordance with the following scripture;

'When thou art come unto the land which thy Creator giveth thee, and shalt possess it, and shalt dwell therein, and shalt say, I will set a king over me, like as all the nations that are about me;
Thou shalt in any wise set him king over thee, whom thy Creator, shall choose: one from among thy brethren shalt thou set king over thee: thou shalt not set a stranger over thee, which is not thy brother.
But he shall not multiply horses unto himself, nor cause the people to return to Egypt, to the end that he

should multiply horses: forasmuch as the Creator has said unto you, you shall henceforth return no more that way.
Neither shall he multiply wives to himself, that his heart turn not away: neither shall he greatly multiply to himself silver and gold'.

Det 17 vs 14-17,

Usually when a leader is selected as specified herein, he/she would be modest, humble, loving, compassionate and wise. Other cultures had kings without fear of heaven or kings who were not chosen by heaven, these kings brought torment to the people to an extent that their rule was rejected by their subjects through revolutions. Some kings and their queens were hanged by their discontented and poverty stricken subjects after recommending to the hungry subjects to eat cake if they had no bread, like advising a homeless person to live in a mansion than sleep in the streets. The north want to impose their way of choosing a leader premising on the past performance of their kings notwithstanding the fact that in this diverse world of cultures, there are different governance systems to suit that diversity. Some African heads have adopted democracy models being taught by the former imperial masters, when the African or Hebrew Culture itself has various models of applicable democracies should the need arise.

The northern model of democracy divides the people into viciously competing groups, the ruling group and the opposition and there have been a myriad of conflicts in Africa and elsewhere which have emanated from northern democracy models. The northern model of democracy is based on at least 51% of registered adult voter population who turn up for an election to impose their minority over the adult registered voters who do not turn up for an election, plus eligible adults who are not registered, plus adult voters who turn up to vote but are of the other view, plus nearly 50% of the population consisting of the aged and those below majority adult age. Statisticians are at liberty to evaluate the percentage minority in real terms of the northern democracy model that wins the election.

Appointment of a leader is by the Creator (Musikavanhu/Mudzimu Mukuru), through the priest (svikiro/ dlozi) and the ballot is not necessarily the answer to the matter of governance in Africa. The Africans have jumped onto the ballot system of the north, which is benchmarked by the north. A spiritual selection process will give the people a wonderful leader, endowed with the fear of heaven, just, humble, generous, innocent and wise among other attributes of a good leader whereas the northern democracy is simply a means of selection where a horde of thieves, malicious, cruel, power hungry, selfish and arrogant among other attributes of a bad leader may enter an electoral race and may win by massive fraud, vote buying, intimidation and murder among other unholy means of attaining a win. The Africans do not reflect at each electoral result on the matters above because they have adopted northern benchmarks and for the reason of brainwash will not ask any question because the north say it is alright.

The African or Hebrew selection process of a leader is simple, the adjudicator is a priest, the contestants are any willing citizen of a country and the costs are equal to zero. The selection process has no monetary overheads, no ballot papers or boxes, no budget allocation or electoral staff/college. The process is open, all candidates have full access to the process and the selected candidate will not be queried through a court of law. A simple test or task is laid before the candidates which by design of Heaven only one will pass. When one passes the test, all the other candidates will be humbled by the attributes of the winning candidate and they will not even contemplate to contest the result. Then came the north first with imperialism – imposed rule on other nations by brute force. When the north were dethroned through liberation struggles, they brought their democracy model, made it a United Nation convention and instructed all members to sign. Any other nation found not practising their model will be accused of having breached the norms of United Nations and they lobby for barbarism against that member – launch missiles till the 'dictator' is dead, they do not care how many innocent people die even women and children when they defend their model of democracy.

An African leader selected by the process of spiritual selection like Moses and Aaron, in the event of hunger and thirst will be the last to eat or drink when the previously scarce commodities become available. Today the African head chosen using northern democracy has hardly a neck for the reason of fatness, he lacks the good heart, he will eat the few resources available and leave bits and pieces for his subjects. The subjects will grow thinner and thinner for reason of hunger while the leader grows fatter and fatter for reason of abundant resources. In most cases, when an African head socialises with his subjects once in a while, a clear story of abundance in resources on the part of the leader is clearly visible and that of trials and tribulations on the part of his subjects.

Northern democracy presupposes that anyone, a thief, a thug, a murderer, albeit with access to lots of money can steal his way up by vote buying, rigging or intimidation. When he/she rules nothing comes out of him. And so any citizen is assumed to have the potential to be a national leader and a platform is given in that regard for anyone willing to lead and with enough resources to launch an electoral campaign, anyone can win an election regardless of whether he/she can lead or not. In African or Hebrew Culture, not everyone can be a leader. Leaders come from the Creator in not very big numbers, they are therefore not made from the book by reading a manual or any write-up on leadership. Humankind over the years have had experiences with textbook leaders and the consequences were catastrophic. Northern democracy also place the responsibility of electing a leader upon an eighteen year old's shoulders whose choice may largely be influenced by emotions of one month's unemployment spell than the actual issues of leadership. An ideal minimum age for universal suffrage can be set at forty years of informed elders to choose a leader.

Today a lot of money is spent in financing Electoral Commissions, administering elections, running political parties which could otherwise be used for economic empowerment had Africans opted for the spiritual selection process. In the process of electoral campaigns, many are killed, maimed, raped and coerced, all in the name of northern democracy when the same Africans have a smarter way which they are not using because the policy maker knows he is so corrupt and will not win power the spiritual way. It is fact that the candidate with more money to campaign and give bribes to supporters will win an election, even if he/she has very little or no leadership traits let alone the brains. The ordinary people, the innocent civilian is obviously trapped in these greed vices. Ko zvino isu vanhunje toita seiko Mukuruwe?

When the issue of leadership is reflected against those resident in Israel, the Jews have not raised the prospect of a spiritually selected leadership since 1948, when their stay was recognised by the United Nations, for none of them will qualify to be a king in Israel for no stranger shall hold that post, to this the Jews are well informed, for any stubborn stranger who will dare sit on the Hebrew throne will be struck by heaven.

1.190.2 **Kugadza Mutungamiri/ Anointing of a Leader**

When a leader is selected in African or Hebrew Culture through the procedure given in article 1.189.1, by heaven through a priest, the act of anointing the leader is done by a priest (svikiro/dlozi) on the most suitable candidate among a group of righteous, humble, wise, virtuous, and candidates endowed with the fear of heaven. The selector is the Creator and not a bunch of sometimes misinformed or malnourished or discontented or restless electorate who will stop at a candidate holding a plate of cooked millet. No hostilities will erupt among opposing camps prior, during or after the selection. The candidate who will come out winner will be so suitable that even contestants themselves will not argue about his/her qualification but will confirm his/her suitability - a righteous, fear heaven, kind, generous, fearless and wise person;

'Then Samuel took a vial of oil, and poured it upon his (David) head, and kissed him, and said, is it not because the Creator hath anointed thee to be captain over the inheritance thereof'?

1 Sam 10 vs 1,

'Then Samuel took the horn of oil, and anointed him (David) in the midst of his brethren: and the spirit of the Creator came upon David from that day forward. So Samuel rose up, and went to Ramah'.

1 Sam 16 vs 1-13

Hebrew / African Culture

In summary, the inferior governance system from the north which selects a popular and not necessarily a true leader is now the universal benchmark for leadership selection. What has gone wrong today is that Africans have adopted foreign leadership structures which do not put befitting power to the traditional leadership. The African leader ruled in collaboration with the priests, his generals and the regional chiefs. All matters of African Culture were well taken care of within that leadership. Today the African head who is supposed to be the leader, rules along with northern schooled beaurocrats with no idea of matters of African spirituality; the traditional African leaders have been demoted to some mediocre state officials, with responsibilities of bits and pieces of their original role. To make matters worse, the traditional leaders have converted to northern spirituality and have no idea on how to govern the Jethro way, some have lost the rich African Oral Tradition from the fore bearers to an extent that they now only know the names of their father and grandfather and nothing more, the same knowledge that is wielded by a five year old infant. Sometimes African beaurocrats schooled and brainwashed of their culture in the north would want to officiate matters that do not fall under their jurisdiction on flimsy basis that they would happen to be a member of parliament for the constituency upon which the chieftainship lies, not wanting to accept that part of their constituency or the whole of it falls under the chieftainship.

Around 1890 CE Zimbabwe was occupied by the British Imperialists and thereafter the priests and traditional leaders mobilized war against imperialism. During the war many priests and traditional leaders were tortured and killed and eventually the war was won against imperialism in 1980 CE where popular democracy selected a head. The selected head was quite familiar with the role played by the priests (masvikiro/amadlozi) and traditional leaders in achieving the war objectives, but at lighting speed, the elected head linked with the Vatican to get priests to anoint him the head of Zimbabwe after which he enacted laws not based on African or Hebrew Culture but based on Roman/English/Dutch law and spirituality, the very same imperialists that Vanhu/Abantu fought in the war against imperialism which made it impossible for the people to abide by even one cultural tenet and thereafter Zimbabwe was relegated by Creator to some hungry village defiled by the human blood of innocent civilians mutilated and murdered for rejecting the leader's directionless rule.

African Culture, African Oral Tradition, 1 Sam 8, 1 Sam 9 vs 16-27, 1 Sam 10 ,
1 Sam 11 vs 11-15, 1 Sam 16 vs 1-13, 1 Sam 24 vs 6-11, 1 Sam 26 vs 9-11,
2 Sam 1 vs 14, 2 Sam 7 vs 21, 2 Sam 14, 1 Kings 1 vs 23-39, 2 Kings 9 vs 5-6,
Hos 8 vs 4,

1.191 Utongi/ Governance Hierarchy

In matters of governance and spirituality among the Hebrews, the king, priests, army generals and traditional leaders work hand in hand. At war the king will lead in very close consultation with the priests who constantly enquire of the Creator about the course of events leading to the war, during the war and after the war. In matters of spirituality the priest leads but works closely with the king, and sometimes the king may lead the spiritual matters in consultation with the priest as what Solomon did;

'So King Solomon was king over all the land of the Hebrews.
And these were the princes which he had; Azariah the son of Zadok the priest,
Elihoreph and Ahiah, the sons of Shisha, scribes; Jehoshaphat the son of Ahilud, the recorder.
And Benaiah the son of Jehoiada was over the host: and Zadok and Abiathar were the priests:
And Azariah the son of Nathan was over the officers':
1 Kings 4 vs 1-6

'And King Solomon, and all the Hebrew congregation, that were assembled unto him, were with him before the ark, sacrificing sheep and oxen, that could not be told nor numbered for a multitude.
And the priests brought in the ark of the covenant of the Creator unto his place into the oracle of the house, to the most holy place, even under the wings of the cherubims'.
1 Kings 8 vs 5-6

Hebrew / African Culture

The quoted scenario was in practice when most African liberation movements were fighting against the imperial north before independence. This alliance was abandoned by most African Heads upon attainment of independence.

Today African heads have converted to the northern religious schisms, and instead of leading the congregation with the priests as done by Solomon (Mambo Chiromo) and David (Mambo Mudavadi), the African head will plead to the celibate priest of the north 'Thy servant hereby comes before thee in his humility, oh my lord, we have no rain and food, your assistance my lord is required, else your congregation will starve'. This supplication is done every Sun Day while kneeling before a celibate priest, on the day that the north have dedicated to their Sun deity; the African head virtually surrenders the throne on Sunday to the north. He now tries futilely to communicate with the Creator through the northern priests, an overseer of northern mythologies, and synchronization or an answer from the Creator will be out of the question, no chance!

Wars are fought to impose a philosophy on a given piece of land upon which battles are waged, if people go to war, incur a lot of casualties but eventually win. And after winning, the winner allows the polity and philosophy of the loser to rule, then what was the foolish point of going to war? The reason why foolish men fight or go to war is nothing. If the British knew that after the war Vanhu/Abantu would swallow the English governance and spiritual philosophy, the imperialists would not have gone to war at all, they would have allowed anyone to rule only with the assurance that their philosophy would rule the day.

African Culture, 1 Kings 8, 1 Kings 1 vs 32-35, 1 Chr 18 vs 14-17, Lev 8-9

1.192 Hoko/ Neighbour's Land Mark or Boundary

In African traditions, a landmark (hoko) still remains a means to demarcate boundaries between adjacent properties, and removing such a landmark is a great fraud which can result in the other party losing all or part of the family inheritance;

'*Thou shalt not remove thy neighbour's landmark, which they of old time have set in thine inheritance, which thou shalt inherit in the land that thy Creator giveth thee to possess it'.*

Det 19 vs 14,

A reflection of African history will show that there have been massive movements of people in Africa and elsewhere and when the people were confronted with land that had land marks or claimed by others, Vanhu/Abantu have not invaded that land but cross tribal skirmishes were quite prevalent. The Hebrew or African laws have moulded Africans to be among the few nations that have not occupied, annexed or taken a third party's land or territory.

The laws relating to boundaries or borders also include good neighbourliness in that a neighbour's problem is shared by the whole community. If a neighbour's child misbehaves, African Culture empowers a neighbour or any other elder on the spot of the misbehaviour to discipline.

David and Solomon, the Hebrew kings made friendships with a bulk of their neighbours including the king of Tyre and even Pharaoh of Egypt in line with the Hebrew tenet of good neighbourliness but today the Jews have turned all those good friendly neighbours into enemies. The Jews' argument is that all their neighbours including Lebanon who had a wonderful relationship with the Hebrews are a potential threat to their survival. What has changed of fundamental significance that has seen original and genuine friends and neighbours become arch enemies? No African/Hebrew state today has any hostility/ misunderstanding/ enmity with any of the Jew's neighbours.

African Culture, Oral Tradition, Det 22 vs 1-4, Det 27 vs 17

Hebrew / African Culture

1.193 In Battle, the Creator Fights for the Africans or Hebrews

In battle the Creator fights for the people and not the other way round otherwise that would be a presumption of the impotency of Heaven. Confronted with a great army with sophisticated war machinery, the Africans or Hebrews do need faith and cultural observance to win against the world's largest army;

'And there was no day like that before it or after it, that the Creator hearkened unto the voice of man; for the Creator fought for the Hebrews'.

Joshua 10 vs 14

'When thou goest out to battle against thine enemies, and seest horses, and chariots, and a people more than thou, be not afraid of them: for thy Creator is with thee, which brought thee up out of the land of Egypt'.

Det 20 vs 1

Young and unarmed Hebrew David defeated the Philistine army by killing the heavily armed Philistine Goliath by one pebble thrown from a sling, while today the Jews with modern war machinery straight from the northern arms factories of their kin are encountering heavy casualties due to unarmed Palestinian (Philistine) stone throwing youths. The reason being that the Creator is not on the side of the Jews and also not for their cause.

In the 20th century, the Africans fought battles of liberation against multiple dozens of northern armies, who had modern war machinery, on the other side the Africans fought the hide and seek warfare, for reason of inferior war machinery, but had the faith in that the Creator of their fore bearers, the Creator of heaven and earth was on their side and ten of them chased a thousand of the northern army.

The Africans won the war, but got lost spiritually after independence, and the enemy is back on their throat, this time it is with economics.

What therefore matters most to the Africans or Hebrews when confronted by an enemy at war is not the size of the enemy but cultural observance of the African or Hebrew spirituality. An observant Hebrew or African will enquire before the battle starts of the Creator and the response will come as a victory or defeat. If the enquiry warned of defeat then the African or Hebrew will negotiate peace, if it is a victory, the African will go to war and win for the Creator will make it possible for him/her to chase a thousand and therefore the size of the enemy becomes immaterial. The sad development among Africans is that the bulk of African heads are not observant with respect to the culture and the northern army maintains an upper hand.

In the same regard, Jihad which according to Arabs and their religious converts is war waged by the subjects to fight for the causes of a deity is a statement of impotency about a deity by its followers when they mobilise wars to fight and defend the impotent deity instead of a deity redeeming its people. Africans or Hebrews fought a number of wars with a few adversaries but the Creator actually fought for them and not the other way round where sometimes hardly armed Vanhu/Abantu won wars by miracle as a statement of omnipotence and providence of the Creator on behalf of beloved subjects.

> African Culture, Oral Tradition, Det 31 vs 5-8, Josh 6, Josh 8 vs 18-29, Exo 14 vs 19-31,
> Josh 10 vs 14, Josh 11 vs 8, Judges 4 vs 7, Judges 6 vs 16, 36-40, Judges 7 vs 9,
> 1 Sam 7 vs 8-14, 1 Sam 13 vs 22, 1 Sam 14 vs 12-23, 1 Sam 17 vs 34-58, 1 Sam 23 vs 27-29,
> 2 Kings 19 vs 32-37

1.194 Male/ Female Dress Code

In African Culture, dress codes are gender exclusive, men have their clothes and women have theirs, however women of the north have developed fashions that take after male dress code and the African

Hebrew / African Culture

women have fallen for it;

'The woman shall not wear that which pertaineth unto a man, neither shall a man put on a woman's garment: for all that do so are abomination unto thy Creator'.

Det 22 vs 5

If women were to go full time onto the male dress code, that may compromise the female's appeal to men. Or if men were to put on female dress and related utilities, women would perceive them as sodomites and that also compromises the male's natural appeal to womankind. In health terms, the female gender anatomy requires more ventilation as provided for by the traditional female dress code.

If women begin to put on a fake beard and male dress, while men shave their beards in female dresses, that will confuse people in terms of gender preferences and so these gender specific features have a role to play in the survival plan of humankind. Women today think it is smarter to put on some trousers which for a very long time have been regarded as male dress code and when they do so, the femininity dies off. A woman who looks feminine is like a flower to a bee and without the feminine look, she is as unattractive to a bee as a sand dune. That is the reason why man have certain distinguishing features that separate them from women. And by rejecting female dress code women refuse the feminine look as if to suggest that it is worthless to look female without understanding that there is no super role than that of conception and nurturing life where even animals like hens once they have new chicks, they start walking in slow motion as a manifestation of holiness and the need to protect the sanctity of life once a female is in life nurturing mode, there is no greater role than being a mother.

A woman can be socially accomplished person but as long as she is not a mother, then she has no awe.

While most animals can harm or kill an intruder when they have new offspring but the human female will throw away the offspring or request a passer-by to take away their offspring and that is how low humanity have sunk morally in that all other primates still bear their original instincts or natural characteristics. A human female sounds confused and inconsistent when compared to other female primates.

Though dress is exclusive to gender but the covering of the face as demanded by Arabs of their women is not part of African or Hebrew Culture, it is unreasonable jealousy that suspects that every male is after the women.

Critics of African Culture have often said that Africans did not put on much of clothing except animals skins notwithstanding the fact that cotton growing and weaving has been in Africa as early as Egypt but animal skins were more eco friendly, popular and easier to grow and process than cotton.

African Culture, African Oral Tradition,

1.195   **Proper Handling of Animals and Prevention of Cruelty to Animals**

Africa is an ecosystem with thousands of thriving animal and plant species as proof that the culture handles animals well unlike other cultures where most animal species are now extinct. Actually animals play a part in the culture providing totems to Vanhu/Abantu, food, offerings among other needs and without the animals, the culture may not survive, moreover animals are assistants to humankind and they make human life sustainable and easier and without animals, human survival would be very limited in both scope and time;

'Thou shalt not plough with an ox and an ass together'.   *Det 22 vs 10*

An ox and ass are domestic animals that have different strengths, speeds and modes of harnessing. Combining these two together will cause the ass to be overburdened. Thus a chapter against cruelty to animals was imbedded in the Hebrew or African Culture given thousands of years back, while other

Hebrew / African Culture

cultures have just realised it now that humans need to be gentle with animals and are thus coming up with organizations for the prevention of cruelty to animals, when in fact they have inflicted more harm (slavery) to human beings. Or when they breed horses, an African horse attendant sleeps in the same stable with the horses, because the horse owner has more respect for his horses than to the African.

African Culture,

1.196 Cleanness Required in Battle

In battle, African Culture requires cleanness on any warrior in the camp even the cleanness due to food eaten, there are food items that are forbidden for men of war to eat for they will render them unclean and unsuitable for battle. Failure to uphold such laws will result in heavy casualties upon the host in any battle. Uriah was well informed of the consequences of going into battle with all sorts of uncleanness and when David tried to persuade him to breach the laws of battle for David's selfish schemes, Uriah rejected out-rightly;

'When the host goes forth against thine enemies, then keep thee from every wicked thing.
If there be among you any man, that is not clean by reason of uncleanness that chances him by night, then shall he go abroad out of the camp, he shall not come within the camp':

Det 23 vs 9-10

'And Uriah said unto David, the Ark, and Jacob, and Judah abide in tents; and my lord Joab, and the servants of my lord, are encamped in the open fields; shall I then go into mine house, to eat and to drink, and to lie with my wife? as thou livest, and as thy soul liveth, I will not do this thing'.

2 Sam 11 vs 11

African freedom fighters who indulged in matters of the bed often especially with women with their manner or seeing women before battle, or those who have bedded women in holy mountains or on holy ground, such fighters breached or did not follow the rules of the cleanness required of a warrior before battle and such warriors did not see the end of the war, they succumbed in battle and fell by the wayside, they did not live to see the fruit of the independent Africa, which they were fighting for.

African Culture, African Oral Tradition, Det 23 vs 9-14, 2 Sam 11 vs 8-14,

1.197 Mupoteri/ Refugee

African Culture has a saying that sums up the refuge law, a runaway person who seeks refuge with you, has hidden away from his adversary (apotera avanda). Meaning if a person runs away from his/her adversary and comes to you to seek refuge, it is assumed that he/she has found a hiding place from the adversary and the host will be duty-bound to take care of the refugee and never to alert the adversary.

'Thou shall not deliver unto his master the servant which is escaped from his master unto thee:
He shall dwell with thee, even among you, in that place which he shall choose in one of thy gates, where it liketh him best: thou shalt not oppress him'.

Det 23 vs 15-16,

During slave trade, the north, west and Arabs, the teachers of Christianity and Islam respectively, ran a network of associations to arrest and return run-away slaves to their brutal masters.

In the same culture when a dove under pressure from a pursuing eagle, takes shelter in any person's house, that bird will not be slaughtered for flesh but will be freed when the eagle has gone. Or when a parent decides to punish his/her child with a whip, if the whip is blocked by any object, the parent will not proceed to punish the child but will stop.

150

Hebrew / African Culture

In their recent wars with the Palestinians (Philistines), the Jews or the children of Zerubbabel son to Babylon, even went into refuge shelters for women and children to kill and brutalize the innocent inmates with unparalleled brutality and savagery unimaginable and unspeakable in African or Hebrew Culture. The Jews broke the brutality record previously held by the Nazis.

Seeking refuge is a statement of conceding defeat and rules of compassion and mercy should apply to both ordinary people who meet the refuge as well as the victor. In America war captives are suffocated in water to force the captives to divulge even things that the war captives have no knowledge of, as a real demonstration of brutality and savagery.

African Tradition, 1 Sam 30 vs 15; 1 Kings 1 vs 50-53

1.198   The Hire of a Whore Unsuitable for Offering

African Culture does not collect a contribution for a national offering from a known harlot as these are naturally exempted from such duties;

'Thou shalt not bring the hire of a whore, or the price of a dog, into the house of thy Creator for any vow: for even both these are abomination unto thy Creator'.

Acceptance of the income derived from harlotry would be in contradiction with the culture which does not allow whoredom. In fact it would be encouraging harlotry if the price thereof was accepted in matters of spirituality. In the church, harlots can bring the proceeds of whoredom as freewill vows/offerings, the archbishop does not ask any question relating to the source of income while Joshua the son of Joseph shared the high table with a harlot as if to encourage harlotry. Yes harlots need to be reformed but they cannot be top of the high table list when the moral women are yet to have their chance.

African Culture, Det 23 vs 18

1.199   Picking Corn in Neighbour's Field

When people travel very long journeys which cause their travel food provisions to become stale or where travel food get exhausted, they are not required to carry large quantities of food to consume along the way, for they are allowed to pluck from any field that they find along the way but they are not allowed to carry the left-overs but one has to be a traveller or a stranger to benefit from this tenet, this is so to discourage the lazy ones from feeding freely from the produce of the hard working neighbour;

'When thou comest into thy neighbour's vineyard, then thou mayest eat grapes thy fill at thine own pleasure; but thou shalt not put any in thy vessel.
When thou comest into the standing corn of thy neighbour, then thou mayest pluck the ears with thine hand; but thou shalt not move a sickle unto thy neighbour's standing corn'.
Det 23 vs 24-25

The orphans, widows and priests do not go direct into their neighbour's field and reap as they like for the tithe of the farmer (Zunde ramambo), which is administered by the king/chief is their share.

African Culture,

1.200   Gupuro/ Token of divorce

'When a man hath taken a wife, and married her, and it comes to pass that she find no favour in his eyes, because he hath found some uncleanness in her: then let him write her a bill of divorcement, and give it in her hand, and send her out of his house'.
Det 24 vs 1

Hebrew / African Culture

In African Culture, the husband does not write a bill of divorce necessarily, but he gives a token thereof (gupuro). The divorced wife will carry with her to her maiden home the token as proof that indeed she has been divorced and that token authorises her to make other marital pursuits without hindrance.

African Culture,

1.201 Jinda raMambo/ Induna / Assistants to the Leader

Jinda ramambo assists the king at war as captain of the host, as a bodyguard, as an adviser and at the king's court while trying various cases brought by subjects. Abner or Joab performed all these roles identically in the context of a jinda ramambo/ induna in African Culture;

'And the king sat upon his seat, as at other times, even upon a seat by the wall: and Jonathan arose, and Abner sat by Saul's side, and David's place was empty'.

1 Sam 20 vs 25

Abishai, Joab and Asahel were among the top most generals of the army of the Hebrews in the time of David. Such relations so close yet are not heirs to the kingship were installed by David to be his closest lieutenants. The trend continues in Africa where traditional chiefs still make such appointments. The same is happening with African heads of state, but the north have labelled that nepotism with respect to political appointments, yet the benefits of security and stability that the hierarchy brings are tremendous.

African Culture, 2 Sam 14 vs 32-33, 2 Sam 15 vs 12, 1 Chr 27,

1.202 Kurova Manda/ Communication with the Dead

The living people may try to communicate where they deem applicable with the dead as done by David in the quoted scripture or as done by Saul to Samuel previously or when a person is killed without cause, Africans feel sometimes that the avenging spirit is not prompt enough to act on the offender whereupon they go on the grave site of the deceased and give the following instructions, 'You were murdered without cause by your assailant whom you know very well, rise up and revenge yourself' - (Kurova Manda).

'And David called one of the young men, and said, go near, and fall upon him. And he smote him that he died.
And David said unto him, thy blood be upon thy head; for thy mouth hath testified against thee, saying, I have slain the Creator's anointed'.

2 Sam 1 vs 15-16

David was speaking to the spirit of the dead justifying why he (David) had instructed the deceased to be killed, so that the deceased soul will lie in peace and not cause an avenging spirit. The communication done with the dead in this context is an example of doubtful humanity. The avenging spirit will always seek vengeance from the Creator regardless of whether the surviving relatives have pleaded with the dead or not. The facts are, the avenging spirit is a responsibility of the spiritual realm, because sometimes the victim may not see who has killed him but the Creator who instituted the command against murder is always on guard, and so whether Africans give instructions to their deceased to revenge or not, the avenging spirit (ngozi) will act without fail.

Sometimes the murderer may approach a n'anga/sangoma to make the avenging spirit null and void, but this will not work for this law is from the Creator so that humankind respect life that came from the same. Often magicians (n'anga/sangoma) have died while trying futilely to exorcise a family from avenging spirit by evading the laws that govern loss of innocent life.

African Culture,

Hebrew / African Culture

1.203   Death of a Leader Not Publicised

The death of a leader or king is an issue unfit for the public in its early stages. When leader dies, those close to the leader will perform all the necessary burial procedures, bury the expired leader and anoint another and thereafter make announcement of the two issues, death of the former leader and appointment of the new leader;

'And David lamented with this lamentation over Saul and over Jonathan his son:
Also he bade them teach the children of Judah the use of the bow: behold, it is written in the book of Jasher.
The beauty of Jacob is slain upon thy high places: how are the mighty fallen!
Tell it not in Gath, publish it not in the streets of Askelon; lest the daughters of the Philistines rejoice, lest the daughters of the uncircumcised triumph'.

2 Sam 1 vs 17-20

A nation in mourning is a nation in disarray and unstable and easy to subdue by adversaries.

African Culture, African Oral Tradition

1.204   Kugiya/ Kudzana / African Dance

The dancing prowess of King David is known among many civilizations that have had access to Hebrew Culture. Such dancing extra abilities are found mostly among African tribes who have body infrastructure which can support any dance as well as adjust to any dancing style in the shortest possible time compared to other races whose body infrastructure seem more stiff and less flexible to be able to sustain the dancing abilities of King David;

'And David danced before the Creator with all his might; and David was girded with a linen ephod.
So David and all the house of Jacob brought up the ark of the Creator with shouting, and with the sound of the trumpet'.

2 Sam 6 vs 14-15

Mambo Mudavadi akatamba nesimba rake rose; hazvinganzi nesimba rake rose kana aiita 'ballet dancing' yevana vekuMaodzanyemba, asi kutoti aigiya/aidzana, nokuti ndiko kunoda simba rose (It cannot be said that King David danced with all his might while he did ballet dancing of the north peradventure, because ballet dancing as an example of a northern dance is soft, in fact he danced the hectic way - African dance/kugiya/kudzana). Ballet dancing is played with caution rather than might. When African or Hebrew Culture was in full practice, diseases associated with overweight or lack of exercise were rare for the reasons that such hectic dances and doing a lot of chores kept body weight in check and also ensured that people were healthier than the cabbages that they are this day.

African Culture, 2 Sam 6 vs 14,20

1.205   Basa reMasvikiro/Amadlozi muHondo / Role of Priests at War

Besides providing the communication link between the Hebrews or Africans and the Creator, the priests (masvikiro/amadlozi) always play a proactive role at wartime as demonstrated by Zadok and Abiathar herein. In modern battles with imperialists, examples of the role of priests at war came in the form of Mulimo, Sekuru Kaguvi and Mbuya Nehanda - the inspiring Zimbabwean 20th century priests (masvikiro/amadlozi) in the first Chimurenga war against the imperialists. These priests fought so hard and inspired later generations to the highest order, and when Mbuya Nehanda finally died she gave a premonition of the war out-turn, she said 'my bones will rise', meaning that her children with the blessing of spirituality, would to rise and prevail against the enemy. However upon independence, Africans opted for northern governance hierarchies which do not recognise priests and the aspirations of independence

Hebrew / African Culture

were lost. Mbuya neHanda (great grand mother at that time) was amazing as she was actually the architect of the armed against imperialism;

'And lo Zadok also, and all the Levites were with him, bearing the ark of the covenant of the Creator: and they set down the ark of the Creator; and Abiathar went up, until all the people had done passing out of the city.
And the king said unto Zadok, carry back the ark of the Creator into the city: if I shall find favour in the eyes of the Creator, the Creator will bring me again, and show me both it, and its habitation':

2 Sam 15 vs 24-25

The African priests started and led the liberation war up to independence but when they won the war, the African political leaders converted to Christianity and started giving themselves names of the imperialism that they fought and are still subjects to the Roman/Dutch/English law or polities which they fought against. Wars are fought to defend territory or have dominion over territory and if Vanhu/Abantu fought and won the war but are still subjects to their adversaries' polities, then they are the real losers, why would a nation go to war if after victory will surrender its dominion to the loser?

Masvikiro/Amadlozi do their work free of charge but the tithe merchants (evangelical pastors) of Pentecostal inclination have transformed religion into money spinning enterprises. The tithe merchants are prevalent in Ghana, Nigeria, Zimbabwe and in the Diaspora, they own airplanes, mansions and expensive cars of vanity with the money that they milk from their poverty stricken congregation while promising them the mansions in heaven.

African Culture, Oral Tradition, 1 Sam 3, 1 Sam 15 vs 32-33,
2 Kings 5 vs 15-16, 2 Chr 13 vs 9, 2 Chr 18

1.206   Unsanctity of Corrosive Metals in Places of Spirituality

Corrosive metals of iron and its alloys are not allowed in African places of high spirituality, which include shrines, and other places;

'And the house, when it was in building, was built of stone made ready before it was brought thither: so that there was neither hammer nor axe nor any tool of iron heard in the house, while it was in building'.

1 Kings 6 vs 7

An African well of high spirituality (from providence) will dry up as soon as prohibited metal objects are used to extract water or are used to fence the area.

For the record, the Great Zimbabwe shrine which is the greatest known pure stone African or Hebrew shrine ever, was built of stone which was not only cut by metal tool elsewhere far from the shrine but was built from stone cut beyond human technological ability and comprehension because it was through inspired architecture that has stood the test of time and weather for a couple of millennia. The north will give testimony to what happened to their settlers or corporations when they tried to extract minerals whose seams passed through or originated from holy African or Hebrew mountains; they were simply swallowed by the holy ground for reason of unsanctity of tools among other things.

African Culture, African Oral Tradition

1.207   Language of an Offering and the Absence of Amen

A culture is executed in the language of its origin and most features of a culture are imbedded in its language and when the language is changed or dies so will the culture. And so all the offerings, prayers, procedures, supplications, instructions, teachings of African or Hebrew Culture are administered in the language of origin—Vanhu/Bantu language which today consists of the Vanhu/Bantu dialects spoken in

Hebrew / African Culture

Africa this day and when a language of a culture is changed, the people will be guaranteed to pick the abominations of the new language;

'When thou art come into the land which thy Creator giveth thee, thou shalt not learn to do after the abominations of those nations'.

Det 18 vs 9

'When thy Hebrew people be smitten down before the enemy, because they have sinned against thee, and shall turn again to thee, and confess thy name, and pray, and make supplication unto thee in this house (oracle).
Then hear thou in heaven, and forgive the sin of thy people, and bring them again unto the land which thou gavest unto their fathers.
When heaven is shut up, and there is no rain, because they have sinned against thee, if they pray toward this place, and confess thy name, and turn from their sin, when thou afflictest them'.

1 Kings 8 vs 33-35

Today Vanhu/Abantu now do most of their offerings and their business in foreign languages. Africans now boast of their ability to communicate in foreign languages while looking down upon their own language to the extent that African leaders address their own people in foreign languages even when all the listeners on a particular gathering are all African who happen to speak the same dialect spoken by their leader, but the leader due to a high level of foreign influence finds it more respectable to communicate in a foreign language. One leader from Southern Africa is famous for good English but his subjects are starving for reason of poor leadership.

Dominus Vobiscum/Et cum spiritu tuo is therefore of no relevancy to the Hebrews or Africans but is quite appropriate in Rome.

The African language is a high level spiritual language used to communicate among Africans themselves as well as communicate with the spiritual realm. It is impossible for an African to shout obscenities in his/her language because the language and its culture do not allow for that, while it is very easy for strangers especially of the north to say anything in broad day light to anyone without hesitation because the languages of the north have no taboos. And when they choose to sing in their languages, the key words are tonight and mating and in their motion picture or gaming, the language is guns or war.

When King Solomon made an offering quoted herein after the construction of the shrine in Jerusalem, he did it in the original Hebrew, the original Hebrew similar in form to the dialects spoken and so shunned by Africans today as outlined in Chapter 3 Linguistics.

In his conclusion, Solomon did not in real terms salute with Amen, a salutation introduced by Nehemiah and Ezra after exile. Amen-Ra was the state god of ancient Egypt. Therefore each prayer made to the gods at that time had to conclude with a seal of Amen in honour of the god or as a belief that Amen was the source of everything including the requests that such a prayer sought for. Nehemiah must have been heavily influenced by exile to come up with such a seal in Jewish prayers. Abraham, Ishmael, Isaac, Jacob, Moses, Aaron, Samuel, David, Solomon or any Hebrew prophet in their times did not conclude prayers in honour of Amen-Ra as taught by Nehemiah. Amen is a non-Hebrew concept. In like manner in African offerings, the seal of Amen is very absent for the reason that the Africans did not return to hear the teachings of Nehemiah and Ezra.

African Culture, African Oral Tradition,

1.208   Baal (Bari/ Mwari) in African or Hebrew Culture

The actual name of the Creator of heaven and earth is not known in African or Hebrew Culture, in fact designations that are commensurate with the act of creation which are Musikavanhu, Umvelinqangi, Unkulunkulu, Mudzimu Mukuru or Nyadenga among other designations exist as explained earlier.

Hebrew / African Culture

Such designations agree with what Moses was told by the Creator when he asked by whom am I sent will I tell the children of Jacob? *'Thus shall you say unto the children of Jacob I or I Am* (Ini/Ani/Ana - linguistic terms for 'I' in Vanhu/Bantu dialect, Jewish Hebrew and Arabi dialect respectively) *has sent me to you'.*

But over and above the stated designation is Baal which has morphed into Mwari against the following lessons;

'And he (Ahab) reared up an altar for baal (bari/mwari) in the house of baal, which he had built in Samaria.
And Ahab made a grove; and Ahab did more to provoke the Creator to anger than all the Hebrew kings that were before him'.

1 Kings 16 vs 31-32

The name mwari, which can refer to any deity, comes from the prohibited baal, which linguistically concur. The abominations associated with baal (mwari) have not ceased to be with the Hebrews or Africans because in the middle of their iniquities, the Hebrews or Africans fail the spiritual requirements of the Creator and the associated blessings at peace and war vanish, whereupon they are quick to follow after the easy baal whom they have known to require no spiritual purity to appease.

Linguistically 'ba' and 'mwa' are one syllable in African dialects and 'r' and 'l' are interchangeable, thus mwari is the same as baal. Practising Africans need to note that at all offerings of the shrines, oracles or even at family level, the term mwari is never used by informed elders but by the spiritually illiterate.

Among many spiritual low moments of the Hebrews like the pursuit of pagan abominations, foreign myths like the acknowledgement of human sacrifice as a means to total forgiveness of sin or the use of human blood in symbolism or in reality, the worshipping of baal remains the zenith of Hebrew's lowest fall from spirituality. It is a matter that has made the Hebrews or Africans the tail and not the head among all the nations of the world. It is the straying of the Hebrews that has brought vicissitudes in the life of a once people of great renown to become the most down trodden of all races and they have become *'an astonishment, a proverb, and a byword, among all nations'.*

The matter of baal worshipping is an area that all the Hebrew prophets stood so firm to discourage the Hebrews from, and it is a matter where some of them lost their lives while exhorting Hebrews to abandon baal. It is a subject matter that the author of this work may risk his life against his fellows, for baal is now part of their filthy lives. 'Oh naBari/mwari Oh ndapika ini. Bari/mwari ndiye chete anoziva. Tongozviisa mumaoko aBari/mwari' which is translated (In the name of Baal, I trust sincerely). Where has the knowledge of Musikavanhu, Umvelinqangi, Mudzimu Mukuru or Unkulunkulu/ the Creator taught by the fore bearers gone among Vanhu/Abantu?

African Culture, African Oral Tradition, 2 Kings 10 vs 19-36, 1 Kings 18 vs 21,

1.209 Nzara/ Famine

Famine and other curses like early death, poverty and many others are all understood to come from the Creator as curses due to human transgressions;

'Then spake Elisha unto the woman, whose son he had restored to life, saying, arise and go thou and thine household, and sojourn wheresoever thou canst sojourn: for the Creator hath called for a famine; and it shall also come upon the land seven years'.

2 Kings 8 vs 1,

Vanhu/Abantu in times of such curses always make supplications in their hearts or even loudly to the effect that 'they have done wrong before the Creator, their wish is that they get pardon for their sins and get rain as in all seasons'. There is clearly no mention of Satan or the Devil in all the instances that

Hebrew / African Culture

Africans bear a curse for it is known that Satan is a non-existent entity, and that only the Creator of heaven and earth inflicts suffering upon people in the middle of their transgressions.

African Culture, 2 Chr 6 vs 26-30

1.210 Death Referred to as State of Slumber

African or Hebrew Culture refers to one dead as one who has slept with his/her fore bearers. Usually while giving a eulogy on the grave side before burial, African elders normally refer to the deceased as 'uyo arere apa uyu' meaning he who sleeps here today.

'And Hezekiah slept with his fathers: and Manasseh his son reigned in his stead'.

2 Kings 20 vs 21

African Culture,

1.211 Vana Gwenyambira/ Spiritual Musicians

Musicians (vana gwenyambira) play a very important part in African spiritual procedures. Musicians are part of rain making offering, an enquiry of the Creator at the shrine, at thanks giving offerings of the Creator (mapira) or in the king's court to provide entertainment in exactly the same manner as referenced in the Hebrew Scriptures and actually music facilitate the visitation of the spirit of heaven on priests in exact manner and fashion;

'And Elisha said, as the Creator of hosts lives, before whom I stand, surely, were it not that I regard the presence of Jehoshaphat the king of Judah, I will not look toward thee, nor see thee.
But now bring me a minstrel. And it came to pass, when the minstrel played, that the hand of the Creator came upon him (Akasutswa kana kumukirwa neMudzimu Mukuru).
And he said, Thus says the Creator, make this valley full of ditches.
For thus saith the Creator, you shall not see wind, neither shall you see rain; yet that valley shall be filled with water, that you may drink, both you and your cattle and your beasts'.

2 Kings 3 vs 14-18,

'And these are they whom David set over the service of song in the house of the Creator, after that the ark had rest.
And they ministered before the dwelling place of the tabernacle of the congregation with singing, until Solomon had built the house of the Creator in Jerusalem: and then they waited on their office according to their order'.

1 Chr 6 vs 31-32,

A number of instruments ranging from mbira, ngoma, hosho shown on the cover page and related instruments are played to provide the best music and these instruments have been played from the beginning of the people in question.

African Culture, 1 Chr 25 vs 1-7

1.212 Padare/ Court or Consultative Platform

African or Hebrew leaders/kings rule/ruled in full consultation with their chiefs and elders (vakuru) as done by David herein. They hold consultative meetings to make their decisions above board and they also receive inputs from priests, who in the event of pressing and more demanding matters, enquire of the Creator for advice, this way they would never go wrong;

'And David consulted with the captains of thousands and hundreds, and with every leader.

Hebrew / African Culture

And David said unto all the congregations of Jacob, if it seem good unto you, and that it be of our Creator, let us send abroad unto our brethren everywhere, that are left in all the land of the Hebrews, and with them also to the priests and Levites which are in their cities and suburbs, that they may gather themselves unto us':

1 Chr 13 vs 1-2

The result of such good governance system was that all the people lived by the rule of the king and that is why in the times of African traditional monarchs/leaders there were very few or no insurrections, coups or revolutions as contrasted to the revolutions of the north in the last few millennia where a number of them (northern kings) were hanged by their subjects. In Hebrew or African Culture, subjects have no such authority, kings are appointed by the Creator, are answerable to the Creator for the people and thus can only be demoted the same way - 'captain of my people, I put you on the Hebrew throne to guide my flock, what is this that you have done against one of the most humble of them?' as happened to Saul.

African Culture, African Oral Tradition,

1.213   Nhimbe/ Humwe/ Jakwara/ Communal Harvesting/Threshing

Communal work in Hebrew or African Culture is usually done to help widows or renowned farmers who would not be able to complete their work on time and during such communal work people meet to socialise, share ideas, give advice and help those in need of help;

'Then Naomi her mother-in-law said unto her, my daughter, shall I not seek rest for thee, that it may be well with thee?
And now is not Boaz of our kindred, with whose maidens thou were? Behold, he winnows barley tonight in the threshing floor.
Wash thyself therefore, and anoint thee, and put thy raiment upon thee, and get thee down to the floor: but make not thyself known unto the man, until he shall have done eating and drinking'.

Rut 3 vs 1-3

These communal floor threshing of grain are still in practise in Africa today in the same manner as they were done in the time of Boaz and Ruth.

African Culture,

Jewish Culture / Judaism

Chapter 2   Jewish Culture / Judaism

2.0   Introduction to Jewish Culture / Judaism

Among other Hebrew Cultural laws detailed earlier in Chapter 1 that the Jews do not keep or have no knowledge of, the following will help the readers to understand better a people called the Jews or the Israelites. If among the readers of this work there are Jews, they should not take this work as a source of hostilities with the Africans or with the author - the Bona fide Hebrews, but that this work should provide a turning point for the Jews and encourage them to keep the Hebrew law as taught by Moses as lived by the patriarchs and as encrypted in African Culture today.

Hebrew Culture is very clear on the conversion laws, that if a stranger chooses the Hebrew Culture, all laws that pertain to the Hebrews shall apply to the convert. However when a convert comes into the culture, **modify/change** laws to suit himself most and later start calling himself more original than the Bona fide Hebrews, it is an abomination unto to the giver of the law (The Creator). The Jews need to reflect on why in converting, instead of getting the blessings associated with the children of Abraham, the patriarch, they have attracted all the international hostilities against themselves to become the world's most hated and restless. A soul searching Jew should begin to understand that one of the world's harshest calamities that almost exterminated them by the hand of Hitler warrants an enquiry of the Creator. The result of the enquiry must provide a moment of reflection on the part of the Jews. The author understands well that the Jews are part of the Hebrew family, and that is given and cannot be contested, but for them to want to hijack the whole inheritance is being stubborn and stiff necked and for that the Hebrew Culture is clear on the consequences.

All the write-up in this work on the Jews' affinity for El – the Canaanite Cult, is a corrective measure and not an irrevocable condemnation for life .The Jews should also reflect on the absence of peace in the land they inhabit now even when they have the support of one of the present day's biggest army. The Hebrew boy David conquered a vicious army while armed with a sling and pebbles with the guidance of the Creator but today, the Jews are having problems in dealing with unarmed descendants of the same army, this time the Jews are heavily armed but are not winning at all. The land they are inhabiting is a holy land and has procedure of how it can be inhabited. The Assyrians occupied it at the end of the eighth century BCE, and when they did not follow the Hebrew laws, when their presence defiled the land, lions ate them up (Vakamedzwa neMhondoro dzaMusikavanhu/ Mudzimu Mukuru).

When the Jews associate themselves with the name Israel (which means he who fights with man, god and prevails) and the Canaanite cult El and his angels MichaEl (who is like El) and GabriEl (El is my hero/power) in the land, they definitely will encounter the same fate that befell the Assyrians. The remedy for the fall out will be the same, enquire of the Creator and seek a Bona fide Hebrew who will teach them ways on how the land is sanctified. Their association with today's largest manufacturer of arms of war or barbarism is not foolproof protection from the wrath of Heaven.

The Jews need to abandon El and begin to keep the Hebrew laws as well as become their brother's keeper – good neighbourliness. Simple.

America can provide all the jet fighters, the atom/nuclear/chemical arms to assist the Jew but a non-observant Jew who also happen to be not his brother's keeper will be the one to cry. How many times have they pleaded with El to 'establish peace, goodness, blessings, kindness, mercy and compassion on them and upon all Israel *his* people? (Sim shalom, tovah, uvrachah, chen, vachesed verachamim aleynu uvechol Yisrael amecha). And how often has El complied?

How often have the Jews recited the abominable Incense offering (Pitum Haktoret), the offering which caused the death of the priestly sons of Aaron – Nadab and Abihu before the Creator?

The children of Abraham are a huge family now which is not only made up of the Jews. If the Jews were to understand and accept that, then they will not even need a single bird gun pellet to defend and have

Jewish Culture / Judaism

peace among themselves and their neighbours. But for them to claim irrevocably and exclusive right to the Hebrew heritage and add that to the sanctification of the Canaanite cult El in the land of the fore bearers, that is a spiritual disaster that will cause the land to consume their children.

The Jews need to understand that each time that they call upon the name of El, they are reciting the very same ritual that the Canaanites recited to warrant heaven to invoke upon them the curses of their time.

2.1　The Absence of the Creator in Judaism

The Jewish Hebrew Scriptures start with the opening verse which relates to creation;

'Bereshit (In the beginning) bara (created) Elohim (gods) et-hashamayim ve-ethaarets (the heaven and the earth)'.

Gen 1 vs 1,

The name or designation given by the Jews to refer to the Creator as outlined in Chapter 3 Linguistics, does not in any way suggest that Elohim which in real terms means gods, is the Creator of heaven and earth as clearly outlined in the designations given to the Creator by Vanhu/Abantu, the Bona fide Hebrews. Africans call the Creator Musikavanhu, a term which literally means the Creator of humanity, heaven, earth and all that is therein or Umvelinqangi which means One with no beginning and ending or Unkulunkulu which means the Great One and with no comparison or Mudzimu Mukuru which means the Source Soul among many designations that Africans call the entity of the Creator that all relate to the awe of heaven and creation. The Jews assign to the 'Creator' a name El that they share with the Canaanites, whose abominations have been condemned out-rightly in the Hebrew Scriptures. The Jewish Hebrew dialect has a verb 'bore' which means to create, but when it came to the matter of giving the Creator a designation commensurate with the act of creation such as HaBore (the Creator), the Jews chose 'Elohim' which means 'the gods' of the Canaanite mythologies. El is the chief deity in Canaanite culture.

By origin, Jews descended from largely children born out of Hebrew women to Babylonians and Persians. The remainder of the Jews converted later in the second millennium common era from the Euro strangers called the Khazars (of East European descent) who chose to convert to Judaism and not Christianity nor Islam for political rather than spiritual reasons. With that background, the Jews have so much been influenced by foreign cultures and have not found any anomaly in calling the 'Creator' El for the reason that the Jews as mentioned later in this work in Chapter 3 Linguistics, are descendants of people heavily influenced by Canaanite culture. Readers also need to note that the adherence to El of the Canaanites can also help them to trace or benchmark the origins of some of the Jewry, no wonder they have held tenaciously to the beliefs of the Canaanite forefathers who strongly believed in El/Elohim, religious concepts which are totally non-Hebrew.

Besides Elohim, there are designations that the Jews assign to their gods, one of which is Adonay meaning our master which can be a title for any man and does not send awe and message of creation. The north, those who are related to the converted Jews call a person of renown among themselves a lord ('Adon' in Jewish Hebrew, which when terminated with 'ay' forms the Adonay in question and becomes our lord or master). Other titles that the Jews ascribe to their god are Melech (king), El Elyon and El Shadai all of which bear no message of Creation and can be shared by any mortal.

For the actual name of the Creator, the Jews call Yahveh, an unknown term, a designation which complicates an individual's understanding of the Creator. When contrasted to African Culture, such designations show that the Africans are the people who have given the Creator a proper designation. Besides the act of creation, the title ' I AM WHO THAT I AM' should teach humanity that the actual name of the Creator is a subject of great awe, a matter that should be best kept quiet about save for a designation commensurate with the awesome act of creation.

160

Jewish Culture / Judaism

While the above is true for the Jews, the north have names of deities like Zeus, Mars, Jupiter and others which are objects of creation or imaginations rather than the Creator.

Exo 3 vs 14, Canaanite Culture

2.2   The Absence of Monotheism

The quoted scriptures tell how polytheistic Jewish Culture is. It is clear that their god is a set of gods (Elohim) who are discussing the supposed creation story. The Jews have explained that the plural form of the designation Elohim (gods) together with the 'let us make man in our image' is an expression to demonstrate the Creator's plenitude of might. Their argument here perhaps is if the Creator is one, the powers may not sound as plentiful as that attributed to the Creator, ironically this is the obvious basis or motivation of polytheism used by any pagan/heathen worshipper throughout the history of humankind that the more they (gods) are, the greater are the powers they wield;

'And Elohim (gods) said: 'Let us make man in our image, after our likeness; and let them have dominion over the fish of the sea, and over the fowl of the air, and over the cattle and over all the earth, and over every creeping thing that creepeth upon the earth'.

Gen 1 vs 26,

Polytheism in Judaism is buttressed by the Canaanite influence in Jewish Culture mentioned earlier for the reason that Elohim as obtaining in Jewish faith today is exactly as what the Canaanites have always meant thousands of years back, without the semantics of plenitude of might and their variables. However pertinent to note in African Culture is the fact that the respect or plenitude of might that is used to refer to the Creator is very careful about the number term of the Creator (one) Musikavanhu (singular) and not Vasikavanhu (plural for the Creators) nor Abankulunkulu nor Abavelinqangi.

Let it be stated in no unclear terms that in fact, the Jews are the people whose myths have given momentum to the three in one polytheism taught by the north. The north thought that the Jews being the Hebrews and them talking of the gods, then a multitude or trio is befitting of the gods. Ki hem (Yehudim), lo Bney Avraham, hem bney hagoyim, haC'nani, haChatsar, Nevuchadnetsar vechol (For they (the Jews), are not the children of Abraham, they are the children of the strangers, the Canaanites, the Khazars, Nebuchadnezzar and all.)

Gen 3 vs 22, Canaanite Culture

2.3   Redemption/Sanctification of the First Born / Kusungira

These laws are as intact in African Culture among the Africans as they were taught by Hebrew fore bearers thousands of years back, but on another end the Jews are at a loss, they have no idea what this redemption is all about;

'And the Creator spoke unto Moses, saying, sanctify unto Me all the firstborn, whatsoever openeth the womb among the children of Jacob, both of man and of beast: it is mine'.

Exo 13 vs 2

'That thou shalt set apart unto the Creator all that openeth the matrix, and every firstling that comes of a beast which thou hast; the males shall be the Creator's.
And every firstling of an ass thou shalt redeem with a lamb; and if thou wilt not redeem it, then thou shalt break his neck: and all the firstborn of man among thy children shalt thou redeem'.

Exo 13 vs 12-13

The few Jews that know or have seen redemption of the first born, have seen it in Africa being practised by the Bona fide Hebrews of the Books of Moses. Sometimes the Jews actually find the Hebrew laws as practised by Africans today and as taught by Moses thousands of years back as backward, because the

Jewish Culture / Judaism

culture is not theirs. When Africans fail to perform these laws in their life they get dejected by society and the feeling on an African who has failed on these fundamental African or Hebrew Cultural practices is devastating.

African or Hebrew Culture, Exo 13 vs 1-13

2.4   Lack of Knowledge and Practice of Sanctifying a Bull / Kupira N'ombe

Sanctification of the bull is one of the most awesome and complex aspects of African or Hebrew Culture which continue to perplex even the very same people who have kept this tradition from the beginning;

'All the firstling males that come of thy herd and of thy flock thou shalt sanctify unto thy Creator: thou shalt do no work with the firstling of thy bullock, nor shear the firstling of thy sheep.
Thou shalt eat it before thy Creator year by year in the place which the Creator shall choose, thou and thou household'.

Det 15 vs 19-20

'Thou shalt not delay to offer the first of thy ripe fruits, and of thy liquors: the first born of thy sons shalt thou give unto me. Likewise shalt thou do with thine oxen, and with thy sheep: seven days it shall be with his dam; on the eighth day thou shalt give it to me'.

Exo 22 vs 29-30,

There are a number of Jewish farmers in Israel and the world over, but none of them has an idea of sanctifying the bullocks that break the matrix unto the Creator as taught by Moses and as is in practice among the Africans, the Bona fide Hebrews, to this day. These are some of the aspects of Hebrew Culture that the Jews have found impossible, difficult to understand and to implement because the culture is foreign to them and also for the fact that the sanctification is a string of procedures which need to be completed faithfully for a successful result.

African or Hebrew Culture, Det 15 vs 19-22, Lev 27 vs 26

2.5   No Names for Months and Years in Hebrew/African Culture

In African or Hebrew Culture as mentioned earlier, months have no names, but they are given designations which have something to do with the events that occur in those months and the same is done to the years, years have no number identity, they are simply counted from a latest major national event like the year of pestilence or great hunger or the eleventh year after the year of pestilence;

'And they took their journey from Elim, and all the congregation of the children of Jacob came unto the wilderness of Sin, which is between Elim and Sinai, on the fifteenth day of the second month after their departing out of the land of Egypt'.

Exo 16 vs 1,

The Jews have carried with them Babylonian names for months, sometimes the same names are names of Sumerian pagan deities, famous among them is Tammuz which is the god of pastures and flocks for the name of the Jewish fourth month. The other names of the months Nisan, Ayar, Sivan, Ab, Elul, Tishret, Kislev, Tebit, Shebat and Adar have a lot to do with the unspiritual constellations of the stars, the forbidden signs of the Zodiac. The use of such names or symbols is unknown to the Africans, it only became known due to the influence of the north upon imperialism, but not to the extent of Africans having to change their spirituality fundamentally in line with the Zodiac signs - no. The Hebrew calendar system starts at Creation and generations are counted from the date of Creation. After some known time came Noah's ark and the flood, the new reference will defer from the date of Creation to the flood. The call of Abraham and the covenant were the next major events. After the call of Abraham, the next major event was exodus from Egypt and there are known years between the call of the patriarch and exodus, then came the fall of Jerusalem, then Modern day slavery of the Hebrews at the hands of the north, then imperialism, then independence and soon would be the day of Return of the Hebrew Family to the

Jewish Culture / Judaism

covenant, where the number of years between each event is known. Such a calendar would be more informative compared to the number Gregorian or Julian calendar as in 1944 – one needs to remember what would have transpired in that year. The Hebrew calendar was more informative for it referenced a point in time in relation to an event and in number years from the previous major event as written by Ezra.

Exo 19 vs 1, Babylonian Culture

2.6   Traditional Chiefs and Headsmen/ MaDzishe nemaSadunhu

The offices of Traditional Chiefs and Headsmen (Madzishe/Igwes and Masadunhu), that were instituted by the teachings of Jethro, the Hebrew teacher, the priest of Midian, a descendent of Abraham through Midian born to Keturah are still intact in Africa and not in Israel among the Jews and they (such African structures) remain custodians of Hebrew or African Culture;

'And thou shalt teach them ordinances and laws, and shalt show them the way wherein they must walk, and the work that they must do.
Moreover thou shalt provide out of all the people able men, such as fear Heaven, men of truth, hating covetousness; and place such over them, to be rulers of thousands, and rulers of hundreds, and rulers of fifties and rulers of tens: And let them judge the people at all seasons: and it shall be, that every great matter they shall bring unto thee, but every small matter they shall judge: so shall it be easier for thyself, and they shall bear the burden with thee'.

Exo 18 vs 19-22

African or Hebrew Culture,

2.7   The Use of Graven Images - 'The Star of David'

While among Africans there is a remarkable absence of graven images, the Jews have a conspicuous six-edged star they term the Star of David;

'Thou shalt not make unto thee any graven image, or any likeness of anything that is in heaven above, or that is in the earth beneath, or that is in the water under the earth.
Thou shalt not bow down thyself to them, nor serve them: for I thy Creator am jealous, visiting the iniquity of the fathers upon the children unto the third and fourth generation of them that hate Me';

Exo 20 vs 4-5

The star is not mentioned anywhere in the Hebrew Scriptures or Oral Tradition, and such images are only mentioned in the law that strongly forbids such use and symbolism. The Jews engrave all their religious, political, social and economic symbols with this graven image. Almost every item of Jewish Culture bears this graven image.

While King David is known for his unparalleled skills in battle, extra abilities, shrewdness, music, dancing and good looks, there is no mention or association of him in relation to the graven star that the Jews today attribute to him. King David had his low moments like in the case of Uriah and the insurrection by his beloved son Absalom but other than that, he is not known to have gone low enough to pursue images like the graven star all the days of his life.

Judaism, Amos 5 vs 26

2.8   Treatment of a Non-Jew (Stranger) in Judaism

Jewish Culture with some tints of Zionism is very clear on the treatment of a non-Jew, he is quickly referred to as a gentile (goy) and his or her under-privileges and restrictions are clearly visible. He or she is given a set of rules and the reason to that is, he is told by the convert (the Jew) that the laws say so when in fact the Hebrew law says otherwise about the stranger. No wonder the world writers have

Jewish Culture / Judaism

called the Jews the world's most vicious racists;

'Thou shalt not vex a stranger, nor oppress him: for you were strangers in the land of Egypt'.

Exo 22 vs 21

The Jews through Judaism have amended Hebrew conversion laws and made it very impossible for willing people to assimilate, and they will tell a prospective proselyte that to convert it is necessary for the wife to start and through the wife the proselyte will become a Jew when conversion laws have nothing to do with husband or wife!! In doing so the Jews have transformed the universal Hebrew Culture into some narrowly defined tribal sect or schism.

In African or Hebrew Culture, a stranger is treated like a king or queen if he or she comes in peace. In most poor African families, the single lamb of the story of Nathan against David for the matter of Uriah is willingly slaughtered by an African just to make the stranger feel at home and that is what the Hebrew Culture teaches. The Jews have not found it appropriate to treat the stranger the correct way for they were never strangers in Egypt, they therefore do not know exactly how it feels to be a stranger. After so many years after being oppressed by the north, Africans have forgiven and are now living peacefully with the grandchildren of the imperial north, the strangers.

Judaism, Exo 22 vs 21-24, Exo 23 vs 9

2.9   Absence of the Oracle in Jerusalem

Wherever the Hebrews or Africans are, they always have an oracle or gateway where they communicate with the Creator. Today in Africa there are oracles in Matonjeni (Mabweadziva), Great Zimbabwe, Nyangani, Mapungubwe (South Africa) among other places where Vanhu/Abantu make offerings or enquire of the Creator as done by the fore bearers in their time but the oracle is absent in Jerusalem;

.
'And let them make a sanctuary; that I may dwell among them.
According to all that I shew thee, after the pattern of the tabernacle, and the pattern of all the instruments thereof, even so shall you make it'.

Exo 25 vs 8-9,

The Jews know very well that such a shrine can only be constructed with the Hebrews and the offerings that can be performed therein are to be done by the Hebrew priests and no one can fake that aspect of spirituality because it can have very fatal repercussions. Saul made a burnt offering when he had no authority and he lost the Hebrew throne. King David (Mudavadi), one of the Creator's faithful servants, a true Hebrew, was disqualified from constructing the oracle on a technicality of blood on his hands, let alone a non-Hebrew of foreign descent for that matter (Jews), Solomon built the oracle, and it fell to Babylon for the reason of sin.

In the same context Ezra introduced a non-Hebrew who proclaimed that the Creator of heaven and earth had given him charge to build the oracle, proving to the world how much foreign influence had crept into the Jews.

The Jews have all the money to build a building as large as stretching from Jordan river to the Western sea, but they do not have the right lineage, to this they are well informed and that is why the matter of the messiah as shall be explained later in this work is so important in Judaism. All the Jews have is the Wailing Wall from the remnants of Herod's Temple (the original temple was destroyed by Nebuchadnezzar), where they call upon the name of the Canaanite cult nekuti vazukuru, vana vaNebuchatinetsa havazivi nezveMudzimu Mukuru (for the Jews have nil knowledge of the Source Soul).

African or Hebrew Culture, Det 12 vs 10-14, Ezra 1 vs 2, Ezra 5 vs 16, Jer 52 vs 13

Jewish Culture / Judaism

2.10   The Scapegoat/ Kurasira/ Kudzinga Mamhepo

There has never been a culture that has imitated the Hebrew or African way of life for reason of both high spirituality and complexity in the world. The Jews do not do this tradition and do not know the finer details of this procedure save for that which was written in summary in the books of Moses by Ezra, the finer details are in African Culture, it is not written anywhere but it is in the elders of Africa, those upon which it was taught extensively for years and years;

'And he (the priest) shall take two goats, and present them before the Creator at the door of the tabernacle of the congregation.
And Aaron shall cast lots upon the two goats; one lot for the Creator, and the other lot for the scapegoat.
And Aaron shall bring the goat upon which the Creator's lot fell, and offer him for a sin offering.
But the goat, on which the lot fell to be the scapegoat, shall be presented alive before the Creator, to make an atonement with him, and let him go for a scapegoat into the wilderness'.

Lev 16 vs 7-10,

'And Aaron shall lay both his hands upon the head of the live goat, and confess over him all the iniquities of the Hebrews, and all their transgressions in all their sins, putting them upon the head of the goat, and shall send him away by the hand of a fit man into the wilderness:
And the goat shall bear upon him all their iniquities unto a land not inhabited: and he shall let go the goat in the wilderness'.

Lev 16 vs 21-22

The referenced scapegoat procedure has the object of off-loading unjust curses or ill fortune onto an animal without abusing the animal for the reason that any animal upon which the lot fell will be released in the wild and will die naturally to its full life span and will not provide meat for humankind. The procedure has to be performed by a Bona fide Hebrew priest in order for it to deliver its objective and in the absence of a Hebrew priest, the result will not come and therefore such Hebrew laws were impracticable outside the Hebrew domain.

People may imitate or try to fake the practice but for what benefit when a faked system produces no result? The referenced procedure gives typical Hebrew or African cultural complexity that a stranger or one not born in the system will not comprehend.

African or Hebrew Culture

2.11   Casting Lots/ Kukanda Hakata

The Jews like any other people, have seen lots being cast in Africa by Vanhu/Abantu and like everyone else have wondered how the system of casting lots is administered;

'And Aaron shall cast lots upon the two goats; one lot for the Creator, and the other lot for the scapegoat'.

Lev 16 vs 8,

'So the shipmaster came to him (Jonah), and said unto him, what meanest thou, O sleeper? Arise, call upon thy Creator, if so be that the Creator will think upon us, that we perish not.
And they said every one to his fellow, come, and let us cast lots, that we may know for whose cause this evil is upon us. So they cast lots, and the lot fell upon Jonah'.

Jonah 1 vs 6-7,

When Ezra wrote the system of casting of lots of the Hebrews, he wrote the basics that he knew for he was not writing the detailed Hebrew Scriptures for use by the Bona fide Hebrews and he left out finer details with regards objects used in casting lots, the method of casting lots and how to interpret the

Jewish Culture / Judaism

results. All what he mentioned is as far as the Jews know, the finer details are in African Culture today and in practice to this day.

African or Hebrew Culture, Lev 16 vs 8, Jonah 1 vs 6-7

2.12 Enquiring of the Creator/ Kuvhunzira Kuna Musikavanhu

In order to enquire of the Creator, a culture must have the infrastructure; the priests, the shrines and the methodology all of which are at large or missing among the Jews;

'If there arise a matter too hard for thee in judgment, between blood and blood, between plea and plea, and between stroke and stroke, being matters of controversy within thy gates: then shalt thou arise, and get thee up into the place which the LORD thy God shall choose;
And thou shalt come unto the priests the Levites, and unto the judge that shall be in those days, and enquire; and they shall shew thee the sentence of judgment':

Det 17 vs 8-9

Confronted with such dilemmas, Africans still enquire of the Creator through a priest (Svikiro/Dlozi), and readers should note again that here details of enquiring of the Creator are not given, but Africans do enquire today, Jews do not, for they are not endowed with such skills and can only do so through the Bona fide African priests, the children of Levi of Hebrew descent.

African or Hebrew Culture, Num 9 vs 7-8, Det 17 vs 8-13

2.13 Water of Separation/ Mvura Yekuchenura

The water of separation is a requirement at every Hebrew funeral which cleanses the mourners, the home, the utensils and the clothes among other items that would have had contact with the dead body;

'And a clean person shall take hyssop, and dip it in the water, and sprinkle it upon the tent, and upon the vessels, and upon the persons that were there, and upon him that touched a bone, or one slain, or one dead, or a grave':

Num 19 vs 18

As Africans do the finer details of this part of the Hebrew Culture, the Jews simply wash their hands in tap water put in a small plate after the funeral provided by the Chevra Kadisha (Jewish Burial Society).

African or Hebrew Culture, Num 19 vs 14-19

2.14 Hebrew Law Compromised by the Law of the Strangers

Within the neighbourhood of the land of the Hebrews, there was hardly any people with a law or culture that was identical or at least could complement Hebrew Culture and so when the Persian Jews were required to abide by both Persian and Hebrew law, it was like being required to keep opposing laws;

'And whoever will not do the law of thy Creator, and the law of the king (of Persia - Artaxerxes), let judgement be executed speedily upon him, whether it be unto death, or to banishment, or to confiscation of goods, or to imprisonment'.

Ezra 7 vs 26

Hebrew Culture is a complete entity which requires no supplements and thus the Jews of Ezra's time by allowing the king of Persia to do so under any trying circumstances, were erring, the results of which have resulted in a mediocre culture as practised by the Jews today. Africans have maintained the entire Hebrew Culture as an integral system up until one century ago for the reason that they did not factor into

Jewish Culture / Judaism

it other cultures, Vanhu/Abantu did not compromise the spiritual culture of their fore bearers by ways of the strangers they met along the way.

Persian Culture,

2.15   Judaism is a Mixture of Foreign Cultures

The following scriptural reference from the book of Ezra summarises the Jews, their cultures and how they have evolved;

'Now when these things were done, the princes came to me, saying, the people of Israel (Jews), and the priests, and the Levites, have not separated themselves from the people of the lands, doing according to their abominations, even the Canaanites, the Hittites, the Perizzites, the Jebusites, the Ammonites, the Moabites, the Egyptians and the Amorites.
For they have taken of their daughters for themselves, and for their sons: so that the holy seed have mingled themselves with the people of these lands: yea, the hand of the princes and the rulers has been chief in this trespass'.

Ezra 9 vs 1-2

The culture of the Jews when analysed today lacks those attributes practised by the patriarchs that are inherent among the Africans; this was as a result of excessive foreign influence. A line could not be drawn between Judaism and other cultures for the reason that the bulk of the Jews were children of those foreign people. Most Jews today find the Hebrew Culture in practice in Africa old fashioned and backward, because the culture is not theirs, theirs is Canaanite and other foreign cultures. Anything in those cultures no matter how backward, odd or weird will never sound awkward to the Jews except for the culture of the patriarchs because it was never Jewish culture from the beginning.

When the Jews interacted with the strangers in the referenced manner, then in came the beliefs of the Canaanites, the deities of the Canaanites and the result was that Judaism in practice among the Jews is far different from the Hebrew Culture that was kept by the patriarchs and as kept by Africans to this day.

Judaism

2.16   The Term Jew Substituting Hebrew

While the Hebrew Scripture has very few instances of the term 'Jew', the quoted scriptural reference provides some of the initial incidents of the term 'Jew' which effectively transformed the universal Hebrew Culture into a some narrow tribal sect of the tribe of Judah and Benjamin;

'That Hanani, one of my brethren, came, he and certain men of Judah; and I asked him concerning the Jews that had escaped, which were left of the captivity, and concerning Jerusalem'.

Neh 1 vs 2

It is very noticeable in the books written in exile (Ester and others) or those written upon return from captivity that the term Jew was taking more centre stage than the term Hebrew, it is because the Jews who returned knew that they were not the same in descent and culture as the bulk of the Hebrews who had gone to Africa and had not returned and those who were already in Africa like Jethro.

On the onset of captivity (Assyrian), the Hebrews were still around Canaan and the Jews only became a people or established themselves upon return from exile which was more than two centuries later.

Judaism

Jewish Culture / Judaism

2.17   Jews from Exile Ignorant of the Law of Moses

In Africa nearly every elder is quite fluent with each and every provision of African or Hebrew Culture including those that have converted to Christianity yet the Jews of Nehemiah's time did not know the law of Moses which means that the Jews had to be introduced to Hebrew Culture at some point of their life;

'Also Jeshua, and Bani, and Sherebiah, Jamin, Akkub, Shabbetai, Hodiah, Maasejah, Kelita, Azariah, Jozabad, Hanan, Pelaiah, and the Levites, caused the people to understand the law: and the people stood in their place.
So they read in the book of the law of the Creator distinctly, and gave the sense, and caused them to understand the reading.
And Nehemiah, which is the Tirshasha, and Ezra the priest, the scribe, and the Levites that taught the people, said unto the people, this day is holy unto thy Creator, mourn not nor weep. For all the people wept, when they heard the words of the law'.

Neh 8 vs 7-9

The quoted scripture shows the extent to which the Jews were ignorant of the law. The same can be extended to the Africans who have fallen to Greek mythologies (Christianity).

The Jews were shocked by their ignorance of the Hebrew laws, how deviant they had gone and how lacking they found themselves in comparison to the requirements of the law. The restrictions of exile among other reasons were to blame for those in captivity were not at liberty to sing a Hebrew song or perform other Hebrew cultural requirements.

Judaism

2.18   The Absence of a Prophet/ Priest among the Jews

The Jews will be the first to acknowledge that there are no prophets/priests among their entire kindred from the grassroots Jew up to the Chief Rabbi. They have no gift of prophecy nor can they be priests for they are not of priestly lineage. In Africa there are men of renown for their ability to state things as they would have been revealed unto them. These can be tested by any person who may be in doubt in line with Hebrew prophet authenticity tests;

'Thy Creator will raise up unto thee a prophet from the midst of thee, of thy brethren, like unto Me, unto him you shall hearken'.

Det 18 vs 15

The reason why the Jews have not been endowed with the gift of prophecy is as per Det 18 vs 15, they are not Hebrews. The Hebrew tribe that Jews have associated themselves with is through the mother for those Jews that originated from Babylon, Assyria or Persia arbitrarily picked a tribe of choice and prime among these were strangers from Khazars of largely East European Caucasian origin. **Strangers cannot be appointed king/leader or priest or prophets for these are the pillars of Hebrew Culture which if mishandled will without doubt extinct the culture.**

Judaism

2.19   Virgin Marriage/ Kuroora Mhandara

Virginity remains the topmost expectation/attribute when an African or Hebrew looks for a wife. A non-virgin maid at marriage is exposed to her family and close relations by way of the token of virginity;

'And the damsel (Rabekah) was fair to look upon, a virgin, neither had any man known her: and she went down to the well, and filled her pitcher, and came up'.

Gen 24 vs 16

Jewish Culture / Judaism

Like in the northern culture, virginity is not an important attribute for a wife as in Jewish Culture, it does not matter how many times a Jewish girl has known men before marriage, no man will ask of her virginity. Jewish girls have a carefree night life in places such as night clubs like any other northern girls wherein they give themselves and their virginity away quickly and cheaply but not with African or Hebrew girls especially girls from Arabia.

African or Hebrew Culture

2.20   Bride Price/ Roora/ Lobola

The bride price is a vital component of a Hebrew or African marriage. The Hebrew patriarch Jacob who did not have the bride price was not exempted, but had to work for it for fourteen years in yet another Hebrew or African cultural marvel yet in practice today among the Africans detailed earlier in Chapter 1 Hebrew / African Culture – Working for the Bride price/ Kutema Ugariri. Jewish grooms do not pay the bride price at marriage;

'And it came to pass, as the camels had done drinking, that the man took a golden earring of half a shekel weight, and two bracelets for her hands of ten shekels weight of gold'.

Gen 24 vs 16-22,

'And the servant brought forth jewels of silver, and jewels of gold, and raiment, and gave them to Rebekah: he gave also her brother and to her mother precious things'.

Gen 24 vs 53

Settling the bride price the African or Hebrew way is one aspect among many that Jews look down upon, they have not adapted to the culture.

African or Hebrew Culture, Gen 24 vs 16-22

2.21   Working for the Bride Price/ Kutema Ugariri

The poor are catered for in Hebrew or African Culture for they will not fail to marry for reason of poverty. The practice is still intact in Africa today, the Jews have no knowledge of its practice among themselves;

'And Jacob loved Rachel; and said, I will serve thee seven years for Rachel thy younger daughter'.

Gen 29 vs 18

African or Hebrew Culture

2.22   The Jews have Defiled the Once Holy Land and its Shrines

Mount Sinai is still there but no such spiritual events of meeting or hearing the voice of the Creator still occur. The reason is that the land has been defiled for there are conditions upon which the Creator reside/communicate with the people and failure by the people to abide by those rules, the Creator will not be experienced in goodness save for wars, defeats, pestilence and any other disasters that humankind fear;

'And the Creator said unto Moses, go unto the people, and sanctify them today and tomorrow, and let them wash their clothes.
And be ready against the third day: for the third day the Creator will come down in the sight of all the people upon mount Sinai.
And thou shalt set bounds upon the people round about, saying, take heed to yourselves, that you go not up into the mount, or touch the border of it: whosoever touches the mount shall be surely put to death':

Exo 19 vs 10-12,

Jewish Culture / Judaism

Israel and its environs are now the Jews' hunting grounds for their perceived enemies and in the process a lot of blood has been spilled on the land and that blood among other abominations have defiled the land. There is a procedure to cleanse that land, but this again is unknown to the Jews.

African or Hebrew Culture, Gen 28 vs 17-19

2.23   Genealogy/ Lineage in Judaism Follows the Mother

The genealogy or lineage of Hebrews or Africans passes from father to son and not from mother to child. The quoted scripture shows a son of a non-Hebrew father and Hebrew mother not being referred to as a Hebrew. The referenced genealogy of David also is with respect of fathers and not mothers for the reason that while it is known that Abraham begot Isaac, and Isaac begot Jacob, and Jacob begot Judah, meaning there is lineage among the fathers, it is not true that Sarah begot Rebekah, that Rebekah begot Leah and that Leah begot the daughter of Shuah/Tamar for there is no lineage among mothers in Hebrew or African Culture. In Jewish Culture, Jewishness comes from/through the mother. A child can only be a Jew if the mother is a Jew; the lineage of the father does not matter. If the father is Jewish and the mother is non-Jewish, the resultant child is non-Jew unless if the mother converts to Judaism which is in contrast to the following;

'And the son of a Hebrew woman, whose father was an Egyptian, went out among the children of Jacob: and this son of a Hebrew woman and a man of Jacob strove together in the camp'.

Lev 24 vs 10,

'These are the generations of Pharez: Pharez begat Hezron,
And Hezron begat Ram, and Ram begat Amminadab,
And Amminadab begat Nahshon, and Nahshon begat Salmon.
And Salmon begat Boaz, and Boaz begat Obed,
And Obed begat Jesse, and Jesse begat David'.

Ruth 4 vs 18-22,

The reason for this lineage discordance is that most Jews from exile were children born out of captured Hebrew women and victorious men of the armies of Babylonians, Assyrians and Persians. Thus the Hebrew woman was solely responsible for teaching the child the Hebrew Culture and language because the father was non-Hebrew. The Rabbis then sat down and passed a law to the effect that Jewishness comes from the mother when in fact the child might be a child of a stranger. In African Culture, when a child is born of an unmarried woman, loosely translated as a child without a father, because the father did not take up the challenge of marriage and the associated responsibilities of being a father, the child takes after the mother in relation to family name and culture, but such a child will be known to be a child of a stranger and will not be a determinant factor in the inheritance matters. In that context, some Jews especially those that came out of Babylon were a result of unrecognised marriages in terms of Hebrew or African Culture because the mothers did not enter into a formal marriage but were captured and forced to mother children for strangers. In the book of Ezra, priests who intermarried with strangers and adopted foreign names of their wives lost their inheritance/priesthood.

Gen 11, Gen 38 vs 7-12, Ezra 2 vs 61-62, Judaism

2.24   Duties of a Husband's Brother/ Kugara Nhaka

The Hebrew tradition concerning younger brother inheriting wife of the deceased elder brother is part and parcel of African Culture;

'And Er, Judah's first born, was wicked in the sight of the Creator, and the Creator slew him.

Jewish Culture / Judaism

And Judah, said unto Onan, go in unto thy brother's wife, and marry her, and raise up seed to thy brother'.

Gen 38 vs 7-8,

The Jews do not practice this tenet, they find it awkward and backward to do so but when it comes to worshipping El, the Canaanite cult, naturally it is quite odd and backward but the Jews keep their tenet and embrace it without qualification because El is a religious trade mark of their fore bearers. To them there is nothing backward or odd about El of the Canaanites, but when it comes to keeping Hebrew traditions like in this context, kugara nhaka, it becomes unfamiliar to them and backward too.

African or Hebrew Culture, Num 27 vs 4-11

2.25 Totems/ Mitupo

At the end of his life, Jacob gathered his twelve sons to address them. During the address, he gave totems unto each tribe to identify each tribe. Today in Africa, save for some of the children of Ishmael and the children of Abraham born to Keturah, it is very easy to identify to which tribe one belongs by way of his/her totem. The Jews have no totems, they address themselves by the twelve tribes of Jacob arbitrarily, however in reality families who either converted or those who originated from Babylon or exile chose the tribes of the captured Hebrew mother, otherwise all other associations with a particular tribe were arbitrarily picked.

African or Hebrew Culture, Gen 49

2.26 Hebrew Covenant not Exclusively for Jews Only

The Hebrew Covenant is today associated with racism for the reason that when the Jews converted, they closed all the channels for other strangers to assimilate and they have also made conversion very difficult when it is as simple as given in the referenced scripture that when a stranger sojourns with the Hebrews and is willing to convert, circumcise his males but **sojourning with Hebrews by the prospective converts is necessary for them to learn and have an in depth understanding of the culture which contrasts with Islamic conversion which requires recitation of one line (Shahadah), without necessarily any understanding on anything else relating to Islam no wonder the religion is now the epicentre of religious conflicts and unnecessary wars. In Islam, the emphasis is on numbers and not the quality of the converts, any thug with no clue on Islamic rules who can recite the Shahadah in one second becomes a Moslem at the click of a button;**

'And when a stranger shall sojourn with thee, and will keep the Passover to the Creator, let all his males be circumcised, and let him come near and keep it; and he shall be as one born in the land: for no uncircumcised person shall eat thereof.
One law shall be to him that is home born, and unto the stranger that sojourns among you'.

Exo 12 vs 48-49

The Jews have put in laws which do not relate to Hebrew conversion laws, they now require all males to convert through their wives; even if a male comes with a willing heart and get circumcised, the Jews will not accept him and such laws have reduced the universal Hebrew Culture into a Jewish racist religious sect intolerant to other people.

Through such referenced laws of cross cultural accommodation, Africans who were even oppressed for centuries by strangers, they still remain the most tolerant among all peoples of the world even to their oppressors. They easily accommodate a stranger even when sometimes a stranger ends up short-changing them; Africans have a good heart, as required by the law quoted herein. All nations of the world can be united under the Hebrew envelop, in fact that is the entry point of non-Hebrews into the inheritance. The impression given by the Jews on conversion laws is that of exclusivity, that is, the law of Moses was for the Jews and always for the Jews yet the entry point for non-Hebrews was provided

Jewish Culture / Judaism

for as the first tenet at/after exodus. The overzealousness of a convert is ironical, if upon conversion, a convert would block the other non-Hebrews from converting then there would be no convert thereafter.
It is the selfishness of a misinformed person for the inheritance of Abraham is huge and it comes from the Creator, for as long as one converts he/she automatically benefits and that will not diminish individual portions for each member. And therefore the salvation of the gentiles through the blood of Joshua the son of Joseph taught in Christology is a misunderstanding of Hebrew spirituality and culture which must die a natural death.

To prove that the Hebrew Covenant was universal and all inclusive, Saul and his sons died and subsequently lost the Hebrew throne over and above other curses like droughts that were inflicted upon the land for killing the Gibeonites, one of the first converts to Hebrew Culture and spirituality, among other reasons for his demise. And when Solomon apprised heaven of job completion at the inauguration of the temple, he made a compassionate supplication for the strangers but ironically the non-Hebrews in Israel today will resist any strangers into the Hebrew Covenant!

On the other hand in Arabia, the children of Ishmael want quantity of converts, even if they can get all the religious thugs into their version of Hebrew Culture and Spirituality, to them it does not matter for as long as they are more than others and this quantity acquisition of converts is breeding terrorists that are detonating themselves inside their own kindergarten schools in the name of religion. It is better to have no converts or companions at all than to be surrounded by a bunch of religious thugs that are coming especially from Pakistan, Afghanistan, Somalia and Nigeria among other places.

Judaism

2.27   Appointment of a Leader in Judaism

There is no king or spiritually elected leader in Israel where the Jews are living today against the background of the quoted guideline;

'When thou art come unto the land which thy Creator giveth thee, and shalt possess it, and shalt dwell therein, and shalt say, I will set a king over me, like as all the nations that are about me;
Thou shalt in any wise set him king over thee, whom the Creator shall choose: one from among thy brethren shalt thou set king over thee: thou shalt not set a stranger over thee, which is not thy brother'.

Det 17 vs 14-15,

The technicality that arise over the appointment of a leader is that the appointment is by the Creator upon the Hebrews communicated through a priest, the Jews have no priests to communicate with the spiritual realm, and the king or leader has to be a Bona fide Hebrew for no stranger can be a king in Israel.   Appointing a non-Hebrew to be king and sit on the Hebrew throne would be fatal and the Jews are well informed, for the Creator would smite that stubborn 'king'.

African or Hebrew Culture, 1 Sam 11 vs 14-17, 1 Sam 16 vs 1-13, 1 King 2 vs 12

2.28   In Battle the Creator Fights for the Hebrews

David, a Hebrew, defeated the entire Philistine army by use of a sling and a stone for the reason that the Creator was with him which conforms to the following;

'Then said David to the Philistine, thou come to me with a sword, and with a spear, and with a shield: but I come to thee in the name of the Creator of Hosts, the Creator of the armies of Jacob, whom thou has defied'.

1 Sam 17 vs 45,

Yet today the heavily armed Jews, armed with modern weaponry supplied by their kin in America are losing battles against unarmed stone throwing children of the Philistines that David defeated single

172

Jewish Culture / Judaism

handedly. The reason is that the Creator is not with the Jews in their Zionist causes. The Africans have won several wars against the imperial armies while barely armed, this they achieved through the might of the Creator, who guided their fore bearers in all their trials and tribulations.

The author had close encounter with Jewish Zionist brutality when their soldiers brutalised minor Palestinian boys; the Jews have set a new record of savagery and barbarism. A fully grown adult soldier cannot use weapons over and above muscular advantage to brutalise a little boy so young that has not even come of age. If you are an army on brutal rampage of the innocent children you will for sure lose the moral war which matters more this day and age.

African or Hebrew Culture, Det 20, Det 31 vs 5-8, 1 Sam 7 vs 8-14,
1 Sam 13 vs 22, 1 Sam 14 vs 12-16, 1 Sam 23 vs 27-29

2.29 Jewish Cultural Dances

Africans by the nature of their bodywork have the dancing prowess that can match that of King David. An African can easily synchronise with any music and come up with a perfect dance in the shortest possible time;

'And David danced before the Creator with all his might; and David was girded with a linen ephod'.

2 Sam 6 vs 14

The readers of this work who have not seen Africans at play should make an effort to watch them do so, they dance well and with might. The African bodywork can support any form of dance required. The Jewish dances which have a resemblance of ballet dancing or northern dances, are nowhere near the dancing skills of King David for the reason of a non-Hebrew bodywork in them, and such dances do not require might to execute save for African dance.

African or Hebrew Culture, 2 Sam 6 vs 14-16

2.30 Enquiring of the Creator at War

During the times of Samuel, the Hebrews pleaded with Samuel to keep on supplicating on behalf of the people not because the people could not do it but that priestly duties require the Bona fide Hebrew priests who are well versed with the procedures;

'And the children of Jacob said to Samuel, cease not to cry unto the Creator for us, that the Creator will save us out of the hand of the Philistines'.

1 Sam 7 vs 8

And Vanhu/Abantu in the last century while fighting against the European settlers from the north, through the priests would enquire of the Creator to seek advice and guidance at war. The same is not happening among the Jews in their wars against the Hebrew children of Ishmael and against the children of the Philistines (Palestinians). The Jews cannot enquire of the Creator because only Bona fide Hebrew or African priests can do that. Thus when they go to war the result to them is a probability, win or lose, whereas the Africans or Hebrews will be told before the battle is fought that it will be a win or not for clear reasons.

Prior to independence, the priests from Zimbabwe told the liberation fighters of the future day of victory and even if Vanhu/Abantu were getting weary they knew victory was certain and so they fought even harder.

African or Hebrew Culture

Jewish Culture / Judaism

2.31   Nehemiah Introduces Amen from Exile

In the entire Hebrew Scriptures, from Noah, Abraham, Isaac, Jacob, Moses, Aaron, Samuel, Saul, David up to Solomon and exile, an offering of either a simple supplication or animal offering was not terminated with the name of an Egyptian deity Amen contrary to what was given by Ezra;

'And Ezra blessed the Creator, the great Creator. And all the people answered, Amen, Amen, with lifting up their hands: and they bowed their heads, and worshipped the Creator with their faces to the ground'.

Neh 8 vs 6,

Such a salutation apart from few instances in the Books of Moses, began to gain prominence after the return of the Jews from exile. Amen had been an unknown term to Africans up until the advent of Christianity which terminates every prayer to Joshua the mortal son of Joseph with Amen.

An African offering or supplication is concluded by clapping one's hands unto the Creator. The term Amen which the Jews have introduced into their vocabulary to mean 'so be it' is not of Hebrew etymology/origin, but rather a salutation of an ancient Egyptian deity as he was thought to be the giver of all by the associated worshippers that included the Canaanites (HaC'naani).

1 Kings 8, Det 27, Judaism

2.32   Tishah b'Av Commemorating of the Fall of Jerusalem

The Rabbis have instituted the 9th of the fifth month of Ab as the day of lamentation by the Jews to commemorate Jewish calamities with special attention to the fall of Jerusalem to Nebuchadnezzar in 586 BCE, yet it was recorded well that Jerusalem fell around 7th of Ab and not the 9th. The Rabbis deliberately coincided the fall of Jerusalem with the pagan day of the commemoration of the fall of Tammuz by the earlier Sumerians as clear testimony of how Judaism was influenced by other cultures while fundamentally deviating from Hebrew Culture as kept by Vanhu/Abantu.

2 Kings 25, Sumerian Culture

2.33   Addition and Subtraction to the Law

Ezra added the incense offering which in Hebrew Culture is an abomination unto the Creator. Ezra also introduced Amen and the Jews have upheld him and the Jews changed the lineage law to suggest that a Jew is Jewish only if the mother is Jewish against the following statute;

'Now therefore hearken, O Jacob, unto the statutes and unto the judgments, which I teach you, to do them, that you may live, and go in and possess the land which the Creator of your forefathers giveth thee.
You shall not add unto the word which I command you, neither shall you diminish ought from it, that you may keep the commandments of your Creator which I command you'.
Det 4 vs 1-2

2.34   The Purim Festival

While all festivals in African Culture kept by Vanhu/Abantu like the Reed Dance, Mukwerere, Bira among many others all conform to the Hebrew or African Culture, the Purim Festival kept by the Jews is a non-Hebrew festival that traces the life of the Jews in the Persian empire. The book of Ester was written by a Hebrew maid Hadassah who changed her name to Ishtar (a virgin mother of a pagan deity), who breached the Hebrew custom of marriage by marrying Achashverosh, the King of Persia. The manner of the marriage itself was not Hebrew, where the maid had to prepare and parade herself like a northern model to make herself attractive to the suitor. The Jews instead of condemning the forbidden marriage

Jewish Culture / Judaism

between a Hebrew woman and a stranger, have glorified the marriage because it is one of the origins of the Jewish people - children born out of Hebrew women and strangers to the culture and faith. If the Hebrews were to enact a holiday or festival against every Hebrew miracle then it will mean that each and every day of the year will be a holiday. One holiday would be perhaps in remembrance of how Lot was saved from Sodom and Gomorrah destruction – Lot's day, another holiday would be in remembrance of how Ishmael was saved from thirst in the wild – Ishmael festival, another holiday would be in remembrance of the miraculous birth of Isaac when Sarah conceived in old age – Isaac festival, another holiday would be in remembrance of the miraculous survival of Moses against Pharaoh's decree to new born Hebrew boys – Baby Moses holiday, another holiday would be in remembrance of the Korah – Datan rebellion, another holiday would be for the Waters of Meribah, and so on.

The holidays that were taught by Moses that include the Sabbath, the Passover, the fast of the seventh month - the day of atonement (Yom Kippur/ Musi weKupupura) among others were ordained by the Creator, they were not as a result of a quorum of elders sitting down and picking a day to commemorate an event in their life. The danger in doing so would run the risk of misleading the Hebrew congregation in that the holidays would be declared to commemorate mortals or idols as the north have done in the Sun Day, in Christmas day, St Michael's day and sooner it would be Sodomite's day where all sodomites would meet and commemorate their gender preference disorder.

In Hebrew Culture, holidays are awarded not in lieu of human's achievement nor to exalt humanity or an idol but purely for the Creator, and the children of Abraham are well informed about that and in that regard, when the north came to Africa, they found the Africans keeping the Sabbath (Chisingarimwi) and all other Hebrew holidays as shown earlier except the day of atonement for this required the administration of the Chief Priest, who was untraceable among the Hebrews at that time.

The book of Esther, Judaism

2.35   The Messianic Concept / Ben David/ HaMoshiach

The messianic concept is purely a Jewish concept and non-Hebrew. The concept of the Messiah started with the people who were born and came from Babylon and Persia who were now called Jews as opposed to Hebrews, not because they were descendants of Judah, but that they were children born out of strangers conceived by captured women of largely tribes of Judah and Benjamin. The demarcation between Hebrews and Jews start after the fall of Judah to Babylonians around BCE 586, (The Hebrews or Vanhu/Abantu went to Africa when a stooge of Babylon was assassinated) and when the children of Babylonians returned around BCE 536, they were now Jews as opposed to Hebrews, the Bona fide Hebrews did not return to this day. When these people came to Canaan around BCE 536 under the leadership of Ezra and Zerubbabel (which means the seed of Babylon), the Jews upon conversion to part of the culture of the Hebrews, were confronted with matters concerning the prophets, the priesthood and the Hebrew monarch/leadership to which they could not qualify for reasons of them being converts and children born out of strangers. In that regard, the things written about the Hebrews, the successes at war, the blessings and many others did not come as prophesied, the reason for that was very clear to the Jews. So many things or miracle lives of Hebrews prophesied of the Hebrews as in successes at war or angelic guidance did not happen to them because they were not original Hebrews, they could not enquire of the Creator because there were no Levites (masvikiro/ amadlozi) among the Jews, they could not appoint a king because there was not a son of David or children of Judah or any other Hebrew, so in the middle of such tribulations the Jews longed for a messiah, - a true Hebrew or a true son of David who would lead the Jews as it was with Moses, Saul, David and Solomon among others.

The Jews knew that successes could only happen when the original Hebrew takes the lead or centre stage. Thus came in the messianic concept, a true Hebrew who would administer the affairs of the Jews at war, in the temple offerings and prophets to enable all the prophecies that have been written about the children of Abraham to come to fruition. The Hebrews from the times of Abraham, have always had a leading figure who led the congregation in all aspects of the Hebrew Culture up to the fall of Jerusalem, but thereafter and upon the return of the Jews from exile, there lacked a spiritual person of

Jewish Culture / Judaism

Hebrew descent among the Jews to inspire them. The Jews then picked the messianic concept from those tribulations, for thousands of years they have been waiting for the messiah, and he has not been forthcoming.

Readers need to note that after the return of the Jews from exile under the leadership of the children of Babylon like Zerubbabel (seed of Babel), there has never been a substantive Hebrew king, for the reason that the Jews knew well what it meant for a stranger to impose himself or herself on the Hebrew throne. When the Jews longed for a messiah, they did not look forward to a god falling from the sky to lead or redeem them, but that they longed for the leadership of a 'Ben David', son of David - Mwana/ Umntwana waMudavadi or simply an original Hebrew to lead them at war and in matters of spirituality. And so when Joshua the son of Joseph came who was a Jew like them, they rejected him because they knew that he was a Jew like them and not a Ben David or Hebrew.

The Greeks picked the messianic concept of the Jews which they did no have a clue about and used it to sell their script globally. The messianic concept was totally Jewish and all benchmarks belonged to the Jews. So when Jesus (Joshua the son of Joseph) came, the Jews noticed that he was not a Hebrew and they rejected him because he did not meet their benchmarks but the Greeks did not care, they amplified Jesus and deified him and today some quarters of Christianity worship not the Creator but a man called Joshua the son of Joseph who is now late. The Greeks deified a man they presumed to be a messiah and today a mortal is being worshipped not only by the Greeks but by the Hebrews themselves, the amazing feat of religious propaganda. If the messiah was to be son of a deity, how would he qualify to be son of David 'Ben David'? Maybe David must be converted into a 'father deity' perhaps. Due to ignorance, the messianic thesis has been picked by Vanhu/Abantu and they are running with the thesis looking for a Hebrew like the Jews without the basic understanding that, them are in fact the Hebrews who are now worshipping a nephew.

An expectation by humankind of a perfect and pure being, the one who will fill this world with peace, justice and love is a declared reluctance by humankind to seek peace and justice from their own effort, meaning men have accepted their pre-occupation with greed and vices to an extent that they will not make an effort to make a personal soul-search as to the requirements of world peace, justice and love, but would rather delegate that to the 'messiah'. People are making barbaric arms of war like atomic or nuclear, chemical and biological to sell for profit while marketing their war equipment by insinuating conflict like America in which the Jews are share holders in those factories of barbarism with the naïve belief that the messiah will bring peace. It is time that humankind realise that the realisation of goodliness, the end of greed, cruelty, barbarism, racism and other world vices will not require a super being and none else save for the people alone. For as long as humankind insist on greed, barbarism and other world vices; peace, justice and prosperity for all shall remain more elusive than ever.

The messiah is a willing and determined heart in pursuance of the above peace objectives among all nations of the world. Jews can allow Zionism to grow with the expectation that in the middle of the created hostilities the messiah will bring peace, for sure they will find themselves burying their own children for an effortless peace and the associated messiah will come at the end of six score eternities.

Isa, Jer, Zach, Judaism

2.36   The Culture of Arrogance

A Jewish prayer (Aleynu leshabeach) has the following recitation; the Creator 'has not made us like the gentiles of the lands, and has not emplaced us like the families of the earth' which in Jewish Hebrew is ('Shelo asanu kegoyey haaratsot, velo samanu kemishpechot haadamah.')

This assertion is the overzealousness of a convert or a fake. A fake coin would want to glitter or shine brighter than a genuine coin. A simple lesson for the Jews is that no human being was created more special than the others for all people or races are all the same and fashioned the same way, Abraham was chosen among many for the reason of his good deeds and humility. How does such a statement

Jewish Culture / Judaism

qualify the Jews to be the example of the world? Such a statement can only do one thing, create unnecessary hostilities against the Jews. Such a statement is synonymous with what fellow people of the north have written about the Pharisees (Jews living in Canaan around first century CE, for the Hebrews had left for Africa five to seven centuries earlier) who professed spirituality based on race and not on deeds while praying in the presence of non Jew. African or Hebrew Culture requires the sincerity of a stranger for him to be part of the culture and not his/her race.

Judaism

2.37 Adonay the God of the Jews' Resemblance to Adonis of the Babylonians

Adonay the god of the Jews which means our master bears close resemblance among other things in nomenclature to Adonis the god of the Babylonians, so are the beliefs and the people themselves, one people with one culture. In African Culture, the Creator as mentioned earlier is called by a designation synonymous with the awesome work of creation 'Musikavanhu', the Creator of heaven and earth or among other designations Unkulunkulu – the Great One without comparison and not by a similitude of Babylonian deity in terms of name or nomenclature.

Babylonian Culture

2.38 The Use of the Term Saint

The term 'saint' is introduced in the book of Daniel;

'But the saints of the most High shall take the kingdom, and possess the kingdom forever, even forever and ever'.

Dan 7 vs 18

Saint is a Christian term, which means one who is holy from the act of canonisation. Meaning the writer/ translator of the book of Daniel had a Christian bias with the prime aim of converting Hebrews or Africans to the culture of the north.

Christianity, Judaism

2.39 The Appearance of the Names of Angels

While angels (mhondoro) feature quite often in the Hebrew or African Culture even from the times of the fore bearers, there have not been names associated with the appearance of an angel. In fact angels do not necessarily come only in the human form but they do take any form that depends on the situation;

'Yea, while I was speaking in prayer, even the man Gabriel, whom I had seen in the vision at the beginning, being caused to fly swiftly, touched me about the time of the evening oblation'.

Dan 9 vs 21

An angel can take the form of a lion, snake, fire, hailstorm, mist or any other natural phenomenon. As an example, when a man who fears heaven is hard pressed with the enemy in battle, a mist may appear to give him cover and enable him to escape and by definition that is an angelic entity at work.

Due to foreign influence, Daniel brought in the name Gabriel (which means El the Canaanite god is my power/hero). Similar names of angels like Michael (Who is like El) have been written about by prophets of the time neighbourhood of exile.

In more recent experiences, angelic entities have appeared in the life of Africans usually in their trials and tribulations and there have not been names associated with those messengers because usually when they come as human, their presence is surpassed by the act they do. A saved person will only realise after the angelic being has gone that he/she has had an encounter with an angel or when elders tell him/her judging by the manner of events surrounding it that it was an act of an angel.

Judaism

Jewish Culture / Judaism

2.40   End of Times Prophets and Prophecies

Hebrew or African Culture does not teach of the end of days for after Noah's flood, the Creator pledged never to destroy the earth again. What ends is the individual's life;

'And he said, behold, I will make thee know what shall be in the last end of the indignation: for at the time appointed the end shall come'.

Dan 8 vs 19

Prophets with a lot of Jewish content of the likes of Zechariah, Daniel and a few others have spoken of the end of days, a subject also dealt with extensively by Christianity. What will happen to the human civilization and their habitat will come out of human savage schemes against their environment or habitat.

Judaism, Christianity

2.41   Non Hebrew Terms

In Hebrew or African Culture there is neither god, son of god, nor god of gods, there is the Creator of heaven and earth and is one;

'And the king shall do according to his will; and he shall exalt himself and magnify himself above every god and shall speak marvellous things against the god of gods, and shall prosper till the indignation be accomplished: for that that is determined shall be done'.

Dan 11 vs 36,

The term god of gods by Daniel occurs often in the Jewish prayer book and is of the form 'Who among the gods is like our master'? (Mi chamochah baelim keAdonay?). It is a statement of acknowledgement or belief by the Jews that there are plenty gods in existence, not in African or Hebrew Culture where Musikavanhu/ Umvelinqangi/ Mudzimu Mukuru/ Unkulunkulu cannot even be compared to anything.

Judaism, Dan 3 vs 25

2.42   Resurrection of the Dead

Hebrew or African Culture acknowledges death but very little is known about the after-death, meaning not much has been revealed in this culture about the after-death save for the reclamation by the Creator of the soul which the Creator breathed in human at birth/creation;

'And many of them that sleep in the dust of the earth shall awake, some to everlasting life, and some to shame and everlasting contempt'.

Dan 12 vs 2

Any variation to this effect of resurrection and life after death is external the Hebrew domain. In Hebrew or African Culture life is a precious gift from the Creator, the longer and more successful one's life here on earth, the greater is the blessing. Theories on heaven and the heavenly mansions are non Hebrew or non African beliefs.

2.43   Purity, Righteousness, Peace and Evil have no Colour

Peace, purity, righteousness and wickedness or evil have no colour. The following scriptural reference shows the race of people who authored/translated the book of Daniel - Caucasian;

'Many shall be purified, and made white, and tried; but the wicked shall do wickedly: and none of the wicked shall understand; but the wise shall understand'.

Dan 12 vs 10

Jewish Culture / Judaism

Then the racist perception that whiteness was associated with purity, righteousness and peace while wickedness was associated with blackness was already established, all of which were a racial fight against the dark skinned Hebrew or African whose dark skin was likened to evil.

2.44   Pitum Haktoret/ Jewish Incense Offering or Recitation

While the Hebrews were strongly admonished not to perform the abominable incense offerings as demonstrated on that law to this day in Africa, the Jews cannot conclude a service without the incense offering recitation.

'And the children of Jacob did secretly those things that were not right against their Creator, and they built them high places in all their cities, from the tower of the watchmen to the fenced city.
And they set them up images and groves in every high hill and under every green tree:
*And there they burnt **incense** in all the high places, as did the heathen whom the Creator carried away before them; and wrought wicked things to provoke the Creator to anger'.*

2 Kings 17 vs 9-11,

The incense offering is a trademark of non-Hebrew cultures for which the two Hebrew priests Nadab and Abihu fell before the Creator. The case of the sons of Aaron was; 'I gave you a law to keep and teach other races including the Hebrews but even you priests, sanctified for My holy service dare join the heathen worshippers in offering the abominable incense offering? - then you must surely die'. Thus Aaron, the Chief Hebrew Priest lost his two eldest sons by the hand of the Creator and the Jews are well informed on that but they do carry on with the 'pitum pitum' for baalim.

As if pungency is a pre-requisite of an incense offering, a Jewish scholar by the name Rabban Shimon ben Gamliel suggested that Pitum Haktoret (Incense mixture formulation) which is a cocktail of ingredients must include soaking the onycha, which is one of the ingredients, in Cyprus wine or excretory non-sweat body water to make it pungent and competitive on the incense stench or rotten smell index. The author is by no means mocking the Jews but is inviting them to embrace African or Hebrew Culture and not the abominations of the Canaanites. African converts to Christianity are not even discouraged by the horrendous smell of the incense offering of the likeness of rotten eggs plus sulphur. The Jews love the incense offering recitation as no Jewish service can go without the recitation of the incense formulation called 'Pitum haktoret' in the Jewish Hebrew dialect.

2 Kings 12 vs 3, 2 Kings 15 vs 4, 2 Kings 23 vs 5, Judaism

2.45   Chanukah

The Jews have ordained a holiday by the name Chanukah commemorated around December each year in remembrance of the miracle of light oil sufficient for one day that burnt for eight days that occurred in the days of the fellow Maccabean Jews.

Maccabee, Judaism

2.46   The Pharisees and Sadducees

Hebrew or African Culture has not had any hierarchy other than the original structures made up of the king, priests, prophets, war generals, heads of a thousands, hundreds and tens, elders, scribes and the ordinary people. The offices of the Pharisees and Sadducees who stood in as the Supreme Council or the Sanhedrin were foreign to Hebrew Culture and can be categorised as follows;

2.46.1   The Pharisees (Farsi) of Jesus Time

The Pharisees of Jesus time were Jewish converts to Hebrew Culture who originated from Persia (Farsi) where Farsi or Pharisees means Persian and these Jews knew the law but did not live the law/culture and were at each other's throat with their contemporary Joshua the son of Joseph for their unparalleled

Jewish Culture / Judaism

hypocrisy. These Persian converts did not separate into a different sect altogether but eventually became like any other Jew of their time who now constitute part of the modern Jews. The Pharisees were overzealous converts who wanted to sound more Hebrew or more authoritative than the Hebrew law itself who wanted to change the law to which they were converts by application of overzealousness. The Rabbis, like the Pharisees, Sadducees and Sanhedrin are a non Hebrew office who have changed a lot of original Hebrew laws to suit their need and situation.

Judaism

2.46.2 The Farsi in Iran, Afghanistan and Pakistan

The Farsi people outside the Jews of Israel today are settled in parts of Iran, Afghanistan and Pakistan and they speak modern Farsi or Persian but are converts to Islam. Religiously what distinguishes the old Pharisees and the modern Farsi is that while the former knew the Jewish law but did not live it, the later Farsi both do not know Islam to which they are converts and they do not keep it not even a figment of it but what they are experts in is to detonate themselves in their kindergarten schools at every minor difference or opportunity.

2.47   Zionism (Tsiyoniyut) / Tsaona / Disaster

Zionism is an atheist Jew's passion for the land of Israel. The term Zionism is derived from the Jewish Hebrew term Tsiyon (Zion), which means patched land, desert or waste. From the years of its founding around 1948, Zionism has not risen in stature proportional to the passion or lobby that it has been accorded over the years by the atheist Jews which corresponds to the holiness associated with Mt Zion (Har Tsiyon). Zionism has earned for itself reproach internationally which is not directly related to the spirituality it has been accorded by the Jews. The rendering in African dialect of Tsiyon (Zion) is Tsaona which means catastrophe, disaster, horrendous experience or serious accident. The rendering in African dialect says it all what the unsuspecting Jews have earned from their passion for Zionism because like a disaster, Zion has been quite horrendous in the eyes of the Jews who came to Israel expecting milk, honey and eternal peace only to discover horrendous experiences in the land - when the land refused to be occupied and began to consume the settler.

Tsaona or Tsiyon (Zion) is a concept very misunderstood by the contemporary Jews, David wept in the neighbourhood of Mt Zion as a result of insurrection by his beloved son Absalom, who later died for it was a disaster for the king to scurry for cover in fear of his son. Later when Nebuchadnezzar ransacked the temple and took them in exile, the Hebrews remembered the calamities of Zion not with the overzealousness of the Zionists but with pain as Zion was a disaster known in Vanhu/Abantu language as Tsaona (Tsiyon) and so when they remembered that disaster in exile they wept. Zion meant disaster manifested by the savage destruction of Jerusalem and the subsequent exile of Hebrews to Babylon which when they remembered in Babylon caused them to cry. In life, weeping is caused by catastrophe but a momentary laugh can come when you remember good moments in life. As an example, if there was a childless couple who later were blessed with a child, they rejoiced exceedingly. When the child dies young, the parents cry bitterly but during those moments of despair if they remember the good days when the child was born, they laugh and rejoice as if the child has come back again. So when the Hebrews sat and wept by the rivers of Babylon in exile, it was in remembrance of Zion the disaster and to this, the Zionists in Israel today need to be enlightened on the subject of Zion or Zionism, a disaster.

The fall of Jerusalem to Babylon, the subsequent ransacking of the temple and the exile of the Hebrews from Canaan remain the greatest calamity in Hebrew history and Psalm 137 vs 1-3 summarises that calamity;

'By the rivers of Babylon, there we sat down, yea, we wept, when we remembered Zion.
We hanged our harps upon the willows in the midst thereof.
For there they that carried us away captive required of us a song; and they that wasted us required of us mirth, saying, Sing us one of the songs of Zion'.

Jewish Culture / Judaism

And so Zion symbolises the fall of Jerusalem to Babylon and so the Hebrew exiles in Babylon wept when they remembered the fall and not the good of Jerusalem for remembrance of the good things by someone in distress causes him/her to smile and cherish the good times.

On the same note, it is worthwhile to remind the Zionists that enemies are easy to make, but once made they start eating their maker and they are not easy to destroy. The patriarchs had a good rapport with their neighbours. Abraham lived quite well with the priest of Salem, Melchizedek. David and Solomon had great friends out of their neighbours in Tyre, but the Zionists have multiplied enemies out of their neighbours including the great friends of the Hebrews.

On the same level, the author observes that HaPelishtim are now laying claim over the city of Jerusalem but from the days of the Hebrew kings, Saul, David and Solomon, wars were fought between the Hebrews and the Philistines among others over certain pockets of land in Canaan but explicitly not over Jerusalem.

Judaism

Jewish Culture / Judaism

Blank Page

Linguistics

Chapter 3   Linguistics

3.0   Language and Culture Linkage

Note: Vanhu/Abantu are the people of Africa while Vanhu/Bantu language was the original language spoken by the founding fore bearers of Africa which today consists of the Vanhu/Bantu dialects spoken in mainland Africa, Jewish Hebrew spoken by the Jews (Bney Yisrael) and Arabi spoken by the Arabs (Banu Arabia) in which case the Vanhu/Abantu identity is visible even in the names of people—Vanhu/Abantu/Banu/Bney.

It is an accepted fact that the link between a language and a culture is that a culture is executed in its language of origin and that a culture survives in its language of origin. If a fundamental language transformation occurs or when a language dies and so will its culture.

And based on the established fact that a culture only survives in its language of origin, as long as a culture is alive then the language in which it is thriving and being executed is the language of its origin.

It is also fact that when both language and culture die, the culture will do so first then followed by the language but not the other way round. Practically a language like Hebrew or Vanhu/Bantu lives longer than Hebrew or African Culture and not the other way round that Hebrew or African Culture outlives the Hebrew or Vanhu/Bantu language.

The faculties or the building blocks of a culture are stored in its language and if a language is destroyed, the same will automatically happen to the culture. Logically, a language is like the blood or soul of a culture in which case the culture is like the physical body. When blood or soul is removed or severed, the body will not live, it will be as good as dead whereas the removed blood (language) can still survive as long as it is kept well. Major facets of a culture are made up by a particular language, in other words given any transform in language by a group of people; the linguistic transformation cannot be extended to the culture. In that regard the culture dies off. A typical example is what happened to Vanhu/Abantu who were taken from Africa for reasons of slavery to the west. They were abruptly subjected to a foreign language and the African Culture that was imbedded in their life died off. The foreign language that they were exposed to could not carry their culture along. Thus Africans today who are still adherent to the Hebrew Culture are rightfully speaking the language spoken by the Hebrew fore bearers thousands of years back. It also follows that the Greek Scriptures 'New Testament' originally recorded in Greek are in summary, northern culture especially in aspects such as virgin birth, begotten of god, human sacrifice and resurrection among other issues discussed therein. In fact the entire 'New Testament' is non-Hebrew but Greek.

The object of this linguistic analysis is to show the linkages between the Vanhu/Bantu dialects and Jewish Hebrew spoken in Israel among the Jews on one side and on the other side show linkages between the Vanhu/Bantu dialects and Arabi (noun) also known as Arabic (adjective) spoken by the Arabs or the children of Ishmael in Arabia (the Middle East). The linguistic analysis will link the three language entities namely Vanhu/Bantu dialects, Jewish Hebrew and Arabi as one group of language called the Vanhu/Bantu language or simply the Bantu language of one people, one culture, one history and one immediate origin.

The culture and language analysis will conclude that since African Culture kept by Vanhu/Abantu and Hebrew Culture lived by the Hebrew patriarchs are mirror images of each other, it means the Vanhu/ Bantu language spoken by Vanhu/Abantu today in Africa while executing African Culture, consisting of the Vanhu/Bantu dialects is the language which is closer to the language spoken by the Hebrew fore bearers than Jewish Hebrew of the Jews and Arabi of the Arabs and the basis of that conclusion is as explained above. In like manner, the language of the Hebrew fore bearers from Abraham is the same medium of communication that the same Africans have used to communicate while executing the Hebrew Culture for the reason that in the dynamics of a people in respect of their culture and language, a culture is the first casualty of any change or adaptation by a people followed by the language of the

Linguistics

people.

Linguistic analysis and comparison can only be possible if there is a writer who understands Vanhu/ Bantu language made up of the various dialects spoken across Africa, Jewish Hebrew spoken in Israel, Arabi of the Arabs and any of northern languages; English, French or even Latin. It was from this understanding that the author made this analysis but there are very few folks with that level of understanding.

3.1 Vanhu/Bantu Dialects – Jewish Hebrew Shared Roots

3.1.1 The African Language - The Vanhu/Bantu Language

The African (Vanhu/Bantu) language is made up of dialects called the Vanhu/Bantu/Banu/Bney dialects. These are variations that occurred to the original Vanhu/Bantu language due to various adaptations as Africans or Hebrews travelled from the north of Africa and sometimes adapted to different habitats, where they picked or dropped a syllable or so to result in the present dialects spoken this day by the various tribes including the Arabs and Jews. When the Vanhu/Bantu dialects are analysed, they share root words, and that same root is the language that was spoken by the patriarchs. Readers fluent in Vanhu/Bantu dialects can easily identify the original words spoken by African or Hebrew fore bearers by a simple test. The test is that any word that is common in most African or Hebrew dialects is the very same word that was spoken by the fore bearers thousand of years back. Africans can identify these words by interacting with fellow Africans of a different dialect; they will note key words, which will be spoken by the other Africans in a different dialect, which they can be able to understand. None common words are likely to be words that developed later as tribes separated and adapted slightly to different habitats.

The African (Vanhu/Bantu) language now in the form of the various dialects is rich and explicit. In construction it consists of syllables all with vowels. Syllables may be of multiple consonant in nature but they have a vowel. When an analysis is made on African dialects today in this respect, it will be noted that all syllables have vowels and on the other side, other languages especially northern languages, have sometimes consonants which carry no vowels as in cry, fly xylem, rhythm, rhyme, krypton and psychology among others. When Arabi (Banu Arabia dialect) and Jewish Hebrew (Bney Yisrael dialect) are analysed in this respect, some syllables have lost vowels as a result of interactions with northern languages. Considering Arabi as an example, the Arabic names that existed around the times of Muhammad had by that time lost a vowel, syllable or so as in Bakr, Umar, Karim, Yamur, Uwaimir and Basra, which originally looked like Bakiri/Bakira, Umari/Umhare, Karimi/Karima, Yamura, Uwaimiri and Basara respectively. Thus by adding a missing vowel the original meaning of the name is not lost but is actually made clearer. Speakers of Vanhu/Bantu dialects will find this easier to understand. Or alternatively in Jewish Hebrew, Ezra recorded the following names, Avraham, Yaakov, Aaron, Mosheh, David, Shlomoh, Ezra, Manna and Kippur among others which are understood in African dialects in their origin as Abarahama/Babarehama, Yakovo, Haruna, Musheche/Munzizi, Mudavadi, Chiromo, Wezhira, Manana and Kupupura respectively while making a clearer meaning as explained later in this work.

Among the African dialects spoken in Mainland Africa today, some names have lost a syllable or so, as a result of a spelling notation that is in synchronization with the languages of the north especially in West Africa where the French had quite some influence. Vanhu/Bantu dialects spelling inconsistencies like the same name in different dialects being given two spelling notations like a word for cloth which has the following names in Vanhu/Bantu dialects – 'mucheka', and 'motshekga' only help to confuse the African people.

3.1.2 The Linguistic Identity of People of African or Hebrew Descent

The speakers of the African group of dialects including Arabi and Jewish Hebrew are referred to as Banu/Bani which in Arabi means 'the people of', Abantu/Batu/Vanhu/Vatu which in Vanhu/Bantu dialects

184

Linguistics

means 'the people/ the people of' and 'Bney' which in Jewish Hebrew means 'the people of/ the children of' as in Banu Arabia – Arabs, Abantu beAfrica / Vanhu veAfrica – Africans and Bney Yisrael – the children or people of Israel - The Jews.

3.1.3   Unhu/Ubuntu Moral Code of Conduct

The speakers of the Vanhu/Bantu group of dialects are the people who keep a human or moral code of conduct called Unhu/Ubuntu or the African or Hebrew Culture – the moral blue print which in summary stipulates what humankind are expected to do morally and what humankind are forbidden to do. The people are supposed to abide by the culture; circumcise their male children, eat a particular diet, keep the Sabbath among other requirements and the code of conduct forbids, heathen worship, adultery, fornication, human sacrifice, nudity, sodomy, incest among other requirements. These are the people who get terrified morally, shocked or shudder with disbelief when they behold other people practising nudity, sodomy and other immoral episodes of their lives. An African who fails the requirements of the Unhu/Ubuntu code is referred to as a dog, not for reason of walking on four legs and with a tail like a dog but for reason of lacking the human moral code of conduct.

Today if a person was to walk near nude or in under garments on a beach in Brazil or Spain, it will not raise a single eyebrow for the reason that those people have not embraced the Unhu/Ubuntu code – African or Hebrew Culture, but should an African or Arabic woman do so, heaven will collapse on her. It is taboo for one who is governed by Unhu/Ubuntu code to do so. Even other nations will find it improper for an African/Arab to do so, they may say 'things are changing quite fast'.

The Vanhu/Abantu people are well written about by northern historians or linguists but the same did not make a mistake of reconciling the speakers of Vanhu/Bantu dialects into one people. The northern scholars who did research on the Vanhu/Bantu language did not mention that Vanhu/Abantu not only refers to people from mainland Africa, but also includes the Arabs and the Jews. What they managed to do was to split Africa into Mainland Africa and what they have termed the Middle East – notwithstanding the fact that the Middle East could be the Equator anywhere along the line. Northern scholars did not make public announcement of their observation that Jews, Arabs and Africans are one people for fear of African Unity. What they have publicised is the un-fact that Africa is made up of so diverse people and multiple languages, yet some African dialects differ in one consonant like the use of 'R' instead of 'L' as in 'pay – bhadhara' used by one dialect and 'bhadala' used by another dialect'. A threat to other nations is that unity among Africans would mean better management of their huge resources and better prosperity among Africans and so any information that brings Vanhu/Abantu closer had to be edited out.

Therefore the linguistic variations in the African language have been termed dialects and not languages in this book for the term African languages is improper as it unnecessarily divides the African people along tribal lines when in fact there is one language in Africa, which is made of dialects largely called the Vanhu/Bantu dialects. In the north, in countries like Britain, Germany or France as examples, the north have unified themselves by speaking a unified English language, Deutche language and Francais in that order and by the same token Vanhu/Abantu must unify themselves for no nation will come to Africa to emphasize the significance of African Unity if Africans do not take the initiative. Readers of African or Hebrew descent need not validate the linguistic classification of 'African languages' undertaken by northern scholars of the form 'Niletic, Ethiopic, Congo-Niger among others,' for these do not speak any of the African dialects and are not reasonably informed and qualified to make any meaningful studies on the African dialects or the African language.

3.1.4   Spectacular Terms of African Dialects in the Hebrew Scriptures

The Hebrew Scriptures as recorded by Ezra has spectacular terms of African dialects especially in the recording of events or names of places as encountered by Moses and Jethro and people of their time neighbourhood. What these instances of Vanhu/Bantu dialects symbolise is the fact that Ezra who then wrote the Scriptures as taught by Moses using a dialect of Hebrew more inclined to Jewish Hebrew and that of his peers than that of the Hebrews who lived those events, wrote of names of places or events

Linguistics

that had lost synchronisation to the Hebrew dialect of his kindred and the present day Jewish Hebrew. The names of places such as Meribah, Chidon, Taberah are among many that mean in African dialects as written by Ezra, and at the same time do not strike a typical meaning in Jewish Hebrew proving without doubt that Moses and Jethro taught the Hebrew Culture as recorded by Ezra centuries earlier in a language closer to what the Africans are speaking today, proving also in clear terms that Africans indeed are the Bona fide Hebrews of the Books of Moses. A story about Africa today can be written in foreign languages namely English, French, Portuguese, German or others and still remain a coherent story outline in those languages but the names of places, objects or people in the African story will not be convertible into the said languages but will stick out foreign to the language of recording like Mount Nyangani, Mapungubwe, Mount Kilimanjaro, Malindi, Ibadan and many other names in their original languages to an extent that the writer may not know the meaning of such words except the owners of the language or their descendants. Such is the story depicted by instances of clear African dialects in the Hebrew Scriptures recorded by Ezra in a Jewish Hebrew dialect. If such an African story is written in a language which is not the language of origin of the story, names of places, people or instances will stick out in the original language either in their original form or in the corrupted form of the language as shall be seen in the Ezra script.

3.1.5 Jewish Hebrew Dialect

The Hebrew dialect spoken by the Jews today, is a combination of parts of the original Hebrew and the languages of the pre-Hebrew inhabitants of Canaan, Persians, Babylonians, Assyrians and that of the north. The sum total of the effects of these foreign languages gave the Jewish Hebrew dialect a more inclination to what it is today, more divergent from the African dialects yet forms part of the group of African or Hebrew dialects which are also known as the Vanhu/Bantu dialects. The Jewish Hebrew dialect possesses traits that are remarkably absent in African or Vanhu/Bantu dialects. These traits arose from the origins of the Jews; they are the children born out of Hebrew women captured by the strangers; Babylonians and Persians in ancient wars fought between the Hebrews and the strangers. The Hebrew women taught the children born out of those marriages two languages, namely Hebrew and a foreign language, the combination of which languages gave birth to the present dialect spoken by the Jews. The Jewish Hebrew dialect combines myths from Babylon, Persia, Assyria, Canaan and the north as shown in the Culture of the Jews in Chapter 2 - Jewish Culture/ Judaism. Paramount in the Jewish Culture which is also linked to the assertion above is the fact that according to the Jews themselves, Hebrewness or Jewishness comes from the mother; it is for the same reason that some Jews have traces of Hebrew blood that came through the mother. The Jews have changed the inheritance law from the father as given in the Hebrew Scriptures to the mother for that reason.

3.1.6 The Ultimate Linguistic Milestone

The ultimate linguistic milestone in learning and understanding the connection among African dialects is to derive the original language of the African or Hebrew fore bearers before the original family of Abraham separated and adapted to different habitats and became different tribes speaking slightly divergent dialects.

African, Arabic and Jewish professors of languages and their students need to sit down and trace the original language based largely on common words and their variances still spoken among these tribes and common syllables and their variances. The resultant language will be produced in text books and associated dictionaries and taught to the entire continent. Technology terms can be encrypted into the language if at all they are not there. Such a language will foster tremendous unity among Vanhu/Abantu and will bring economic and political co-operation among the Africans. The use of foreign languages in schools, business and social communication will die a natural death.

The Hebrew or Vanhu/Bantu language, the language of the patriarchs, the language of high spirituality cannot disappear and yield against other languages of sodomy. The language of peace, compassion, morality, goodliness, hospitality, spirituality, prophecy among other virtues spoken by Abraham, Ishmael, Isaac, Jacob, Moses, Jethro, David, Solomon, the Queen of Sheba,

Linguistics

Mwene Mutapa, Nzinga, Tshaka, Nehoreka, Chaminuka, Mulimo, Nehanda among others to communicate with Heaven cannot yield or succumb to the languages of the world while the descendants of the African or Hebrew fore bearers are still alive. The imperial languages cannot triumph over the language of peace and hospitality.

The people of Africa have no history of conquest; hospitality and goodliness is encrypted in the language through the culture whereas nuclear/atomic, chemical and biological arms of war are designed in English, Russian, German, French and Chinese languages over and above the unethical sciences like human stem cell, gender conversion, abortion are researched and executed in the same laguages and these cannot surely triumph over the moral language Vanhu/Bantu. The Jews though have translated the referenced immoral sciences and technologies into their Hebrew dialect.

3.1.7   Linguistic Medium of Communication and Worship

It is critical for an African to understand, communicate and worship in his/her language. The use of foreign languages has degraded African spirituality to unprecedented low levels not for the reason of a fundamental problem with the culture but because of lack of self belief and identity. An African today would feel more inspired by just mentioning a phrase like 'holy spirit' but would shudder with dislike when the same phrase is transformed into an African dialect to 'mudzimu unoyera' and pagan labels would be attributed to the speaker of that sort of linguistic phrasal translation. The author saw an African pastor of Pentecostal incline rejecting prayers to be made in Vanhu/Bantu dialects, his argument was that such prayers in the gentile language will not invoke the holy spirit.

3.1.8   Trace Similarities Between Vanhu/Bantu Language and Northern Languages

There are indeed linguistic similarities between Vanhu/Bantu dialects, Arabi and Jewish Hebrew group of dialects on one side and northern languages on the other side. The extent of similarities is limited and confined to roughly a single syllable or so. Most early technological terms are common which were invented by ancient civilization which originated from Africa where the north carried with them the technology and the terms involved. When they later returned with the repackaged African technologies, the understanding by most linguistic scholars was that Africans borrowed the term from the north. Besides the technology terms that northern languages borrowed from African civilization is the word 'Prayer' in English, 'Tefila/fila or pilul' in Jewish Hebrew and 'Pira' in African dialect. Vanhu/Abantu were among the first few people to understand and apply prayer. Earlier in Hebrew Culture, people like Enoch and Noah lived well without blame but their articulate application of prayer/supplication/offering was not given in greater detail. Other nations have therefore learnt the essence of prayer from people of Hebrew descent. When Abraham first prayed/offered to the Creator of heaven and earth, other nations outside the Hebrew domain were moulding clay into objects of worship and their form of worship at that time was roughly showing off to their compatriots the physical attributes of their handmade images/deities – 'my god is most polished and brighter than yours, my god is more beautiful than yours, my god has a bigger head than yours and therefore a greater thinker'. Therefore during that time when Abraham was offering to the Creator, other nations had no idea of prayer and the associated supplication to the Creator for blessings. Later other nations then learnt the monotheist way of worship from the Hebrews where prayer, offering and supplication to the Creator were well defined and that is then that they also carried with them the term prayer from the Hebrew 'pira' or 'fila'. Thus the etymology/origin of the word 'prayer' emanates from Hebrew and not from the north.

3.1.9   Reasons for Linguistic Differences Between Vanhu/Bantu and Jewish Hebrew Dialects

1. The fall of northern Israel to Assyria around 721 BCE and that of Judah to Babylon around 586 BCE, brought in foreign influence. The occupation brought in a breed of people called Jews as contrasted to the Hebrews or Vanhu/Abantu. The Jews were paternal children of Assyrians, Babylonians and Persians to Hebrew women who were the war loot/boot of the wars that preceded the said occupations. Later there was also the incorporation of the strangers into the Hebrew land as recorded in the book of Chronicles. The incorporated

Linguistics

strangers combined with the indigenous Canaanites and recently Euro strangers (Khazars) who have converted to Judaism to become the people known today as the Jews whose language is neither that spoken by Africans today nor that spoken by the patriarchs thousands of years ago but a cocktail of languages of people that make up the Jews.

2   When the Jews returned to Canaan from captivity, the Hebrews who had gone to larger Africa (recorded as Egypt in the Hebrew Scriptures) did not return and to this day Vanhu/ Abantu do not share names of deities, culture and any other attributes of the Canaanites or pre-inhabitants of Canaan. The Jews led by Ezra and Nehemiah, did not find it difficult to share language, culture and deities with the Canaanites on their return to an extent that the Jewish god shares the same name as the Canaanite chief god named EL, whereas the Africans or the Bona fide Hebrews have maintained to call upon the Creator of heaven and earth (Musikavanhu/ Mudzimu Mukuru/ Umvelinqangi/ Unkulunkulu) ideally as given in the story of creation. The Africans or Hebrews are the only ones who call their Creator as it is supposed to be. The Jews have in their language a term of 'to create' - 'bore' as in *Gen 1 vs 1; 'In the beginning the Creator created the heaven and the earth',* which in Jewish Hebrew is *'Bereshit bara Elohim et-hashamayim ve-et-haerets'.* To create in Jewish Hebrew means 'bore' and therefore to make the Creator of heaven and earth as distinct as the Africans or Hebrews have done, the Jews could have called the Creator 'HaBore' or any designation synonymous with the work of creation as Africans have done in Musikavanhu (the Creator of humanity, heaven, earth and all), but they did not.

Instead when the Jews documented Hebrew or African Culture by the hand of Ezra the Jewish scribe from captivity, they put in names such as Elohim (which means gods), meaning in their culture, there could be other gods and the Hebrew or African concept of monotheism disappears. The Jews have given the name of their deity identical to the god of the Canaanites El, for the reason that the two people, Jews and Canaanites are/were one people. In fact El is like any other name given to the deities of the world like Tammuz (Babylonian deity), Zeus (Greek deity), Mars (Roman war deity), Apollo and many others. The Jewish Hebrew and Canaanite meaning of 'El' is 'to' as in heading towards some destination or it means 'nothing', which in all have no link to creation. Such words similar to El have found their way into the Jewish Hebrew dialect due to foreign influence. When the Jews returned from exile they inherited the culture of the Canaanites and there was both way assimilation; Jews to Canaanites and Canaanites to Jews and that is why Ezra, when he wrote the Hebrew Scriptures, he exhorted people against the abominations associated with Canaanite culture, which at that time had taken a heavy toll on the Jews. The Africans did not fall prey to this culture because they did not stay long with the Canaanites for the reason that when they went to Africa, (referred to as Egypt in the second book of Chronicles), they did not return to this day for Africa is their land as promised to the fore bearers. The dialects spoken by practising Africans have no substantial traces of Canaanite or northern languages.

The Jews were heavily influenced by Canaanite Culture in their language to the extent that attributes of the Canaanite El is very visible in Jewish spirituality and even language today. Hebrew names that appeared originally as Dan, Nathan, Suma as examples later morphed to Daniel (El has judged me), Nathaniel (Gift from El), Samuel (apprise El). Today the Jews have added 'son' to most Hebrew names like Abraham, Jacob, David to Abrahamson, Jacobson and Davison respectively as a result of influence from the north from which some of them originate and these names have mutated to Abrahamsburg, Jacobsburg and Davisburg as a result of interaction with Netherlands. Vanhu/ Abantu are therefore critical in maintaining the original language and spirituality for the reason that they have lived separately without external influence for a very long time.

Adonizedek (my master is righteous) and Melchizedek (my king is righteous) are names shared linguistically between the pre-Hebrew inhabitants of Canaan (the Canaanites)

188

Linguistics

and the Jews which link them as the same people linguistically and culturally as keeping the same abominations of the Canaanites like incense offering to the same deity El.

3.1.10 Septuagint Mis-transliteration

Though similarities between Jewish Hebrew names, words and general language construction on one side and Vanhu/Bantu dialects on the other side, are without doubt and suggest dialects stemming out from one language, those similarities were deliberately suppressed by the Septuagint translators of the Jewish Hebrew copy of the scriptures that was recorded by Ezra. Prime in the Septuagint translation was the deliberate transformation of names likes Isaac, Jacob, Esau, Moses, Aaron, Jochebed, Jethro, David, Solomon and many others that were made to sound more northern and not like their original form of Sekai, Yakovo, Aisave, Musheche/Munzizi, Haruna, Ochivedi, Yitiro, Mudavadi, Chiromo in that order. The primary motive of that deliberate mis-transliteration was to synchronize the names of the Hebrews to their schemed Caucasian Hebrews. Moreover, today's Jewish names of the following format Abrahamson, Jacobson, Davidson which try to mutate Vanhu/Bantu names from Abarahama/Yako/ Mudavadi to Abraham/Jacob/David and further to Abrahamson/Jacobson/Davidson and possibly to Abrahimovic/Jacobville/Davingic until the original Vanhu/Bantu name is lost.

Linguistics

3.1.11 Common Syllables for Jewish Hebrew and Vanhu/Bantu Dialects

Linguistic table 1 below shows substantial similarities between Vanhu/Bantu and Jewish Hebrew at syllable level. Higher order syllables in African dialects are made by combining two or more consonants like 'nzw-', 'tsv-' to make the following words; 'kunzwa' which means to hear, and 'tsvina' which means dirt. In construction, the Hebrew alphabet forms African syllables better than the ABC taught by the north. Therefore there is more syllable agreement between the Hebrew dialect spoken by the Jews today and the dialects spoken by Africans today as compared to Northern-African syllabic similarities. What has complicated a better understanding of African dialects among Africans is the issue of spellings and accents which were directly linked to the language of particular invading European settlers. North Africans have a French spelling bias in their dialects, Central African countries have a British spelling bias while Southern African countries have Dutch and Portuguese spelling bias in their dialects. A common African syllable like 'kwe' may be spelt 'que' - British bias or may be given the Dutch bias 'koe'. Another syllable 'te' may be spelt 'the'. Such a linguistic maze may confuse African linguistic students and may give an impression that African dialects are as divergent and unrelated as Dutch and Hutu, yet in fact the African dialects are the same and from one language— the Vanhu/Bantu language.

Common Syllable Table for Hebrew and African Dialects

Hebrew Consonant	Hebrew Syllable	Alphabet Consonant	Vanhu/Bantu Syllable
Bet - ב	Ba	B	Ba
Vet - ב	Ve	V	Ve
Gimel - ג	Gi	G	Gi
Dalet - ד	Do	D	Do
Hay - ה	Hu	H	Hu
Zayin - ז	Za	Z	Za
Chet / Chaf - כ	Che	Ch	Che
Tet / Tav - ט / ת	Ti	T	Ti
Yod - י	Yo	Y	Yo
Kaf / Kof - ק	Ku	K	Ku
Lamed - ל	La	L	La
Mem - מ	Me	M	Me
Nun - נ	Ni	N	Ni
Samech / Sin - ס / שׂ	So	S	So
Peh - פ	Pu	P	Pu
Feh - פ	Fa	F	Fa
Tsadi - צ	Tse	Ts	Tse
Resh - ר	Ri	R	Ri
Shin - שׁ	Sho	Sh	Sho

Table 1

Linguistics

3.1.12 Structure of the Vanhu/Bantu or Hebrew Language

Like the African dialects, Jewish Hebrew is a structured language with direct pronunciation found in African dialects. African dialects and Jewish Hebrew have formulae to generate various language constructions. It is much easier for an African to learn to speak the Hebrew dialect spoken by the Jews today than northern languages; the reason being that the dialects in question stem from one language, the language spoken by the fore bearers in old times.

Language Construction

a) The Adjective

In English, a phrase like '*good boy*' has the noun (*boy*) preceded by the adjective (*good*), but in Jewish Hebrew and African dialects the reverse is true that the noun comes before the adjective.
E.g.

English	-	Good boy
Jewish Hebrew	-	Yeled (boy) tov (good)
African dialect	-	Mukomana (boy) akanaka (good)
Arabi dialect	-	Walad (boy) 'tayib' (good)

b) The Preposition

In English for example, the preposition is a separate word that introduces an object or links nouns, pronouns or phrases (objects) e.g. 'in the house', has the equivalent in Jewish Hebrew of 'babayit' and the equivalent in African dialect of 'pamba/ mumba', thus in the Jewish Hebrew and African dialects above, the prepositions form part of the word that describes the entire English expression 'in the house'.

c) Use of singular and plural

In English for example, the verb associated with the subject does not take the plurality or singularity of the subject.

E.g.
English
Everyday I eat (eat takes the same form as below).
Everyday we eat (eat takes the same form as above).

Jewish Hebrew dialect
Yom yom (everyday) ani (I) ochel (the singular form of eat).
Yom yom (everyday) anachnu (we) ochlim (the plural form of eat).

African dialect
Musi nemusi (everyday) ini (I) ndinodya (singular form of eat).
Musi nemusi (everyday) isu (we) tinodya (plural form of eat).

d) The Gender Pronoun

Original Hebrew/African language did/does not have gender specific pronouns 'he' and 'she'. While 'he' is 'hu' in Jewish Hebrew and 'huwa' in Arabi and 'she' is 'hi' in Jewish Hebrew and 'hiya' in Arabi, there are no equivalences for gender pronouns in original Hebrew/African language (Gender equality in the language). In Hebrew/African language, objects are either referred to in their actual noun as in 'the man' which is 'ish' in Jewish Hebrew, 'rajul' in Arabi, 'malume, murume, ndoda' in African dialects or they are referred to by way of a pronoun which is common to all male or female as in 'uyo' meaning 'that one'. So 'hu, hi, huwa, hiya' are some of the common terms between

191

Linguistics

Jewish Hebrew and Arabi on one side and northern languages on the other side which are non-existent in the Hebrew/African language.

e)   The Possessive

In Arabi and Jewish Hebrew, the possessive suffix which gives ownership of an object to the second person is '-ak' and '-cha' respectively while in Vanhu/Bantu dialect, the equivalence is '-ako'.

'Your house' becomes 'baitecha' in Jewish Hebrew,
'Your house' becomes 'baytak' in Arabi, and
'Your house' becomes 'imba yako' in Vanhu/Bantu dialect, the possessive is not a suffix of the noun but a separate word albeit with the same root format '-ak'.

'Our father, our king and our house' is 'avinu', 'malkenu' and 'baytenu' in Jewish Hebrew
'Our father, our king and our house' is 'baba vedu/bethu','mambo wedu' and 'imba yedu/yethu' in Vanhu/Bantu dialects and the possessive is clear '-u' which is suffix to a Jewish Hebrew noun but a separate terminal word in Vanhu/Abantu dialects. In all these language constructions, Vanhu/Bantu dialects terms are longer while Jewish Hebrew and Arabic term are shorter or truncated forms of the original language as proof that the languages changed from the original form.

3.1.13   Similarities Between Jewish Hebrew and Pre-Hebrew Languages of Canaan

Jewish Hebrew dialect	**Other language**
Avimelech (my father is king)	Avimelech (King of Gerah)
Melchizedek (my king is righteous)	Melchizedek (the king of Salem)
Korach (a Levite)	Korach (an Edomite duke)
El (Jewish deity)	El (Canaanite deity)

The above linguistic scenario of shared names/terms is a result of shared culture, language and values embedded in the common terms or names by more or less the same people. Readers need to note that a name shared between Jewish Hebrew and Canaanite languages does not cross over to African dialects, cementing the argument that Africans or the original Hebrews did not stay long in North East Africa, long enough to be influenced culturally and linguistically.

Readers need to take note of the fact that words which are common among African dialects may not necessarily retain the same type of usage; verbs, nouns, idioms but may interchange with usage in another dialect.

3.1.14   Jewish Hebrew and Vanhu/Bantu Dialects Names Agreement in the Hebrew Scriptures

Note: In African or Hebrew Culture, most people are not necessarily called by their birth names, but by names that they acquire later in life from works of virtue, courage, resilience, diligence and sometimes notoriety that they achieve in life.

There is remarkable concordance between Jewish Hebrew names recorded in the scriptures and the contextual meaning of the Hebrew Scriptures as understood in African dialects, as most names which do not make sense to the Jews today are straightforward in African dialects as illustrated below:

1.   Abraham is the name of the Hebrew patriarch which according to the Hebrew scriptural context means father of the nations, agrees with Vanhu/Bantu dialects which understand Abraham as Abarahama which means he who has begotten his people or kinsmen or alternatively 'Aba/Abu' is father while 'ra/re' means for or of and 'hama' means kinsmen/kins/related people in African dialects. In Jewish Hebrew the same name is given as Av-ra-ham where Av means father, (ra)/la means for and ham has no meaning, at best it (ham) can mean they or them or those; thus giving a full meaning of 'father for those/they/them', alternatively 'ham' may be modified in Jewish Hebrew to give the patriarchal name a meaning that relates to the context in the Hebrew Scriptures to become

Linguistics

'ha-am' which means the people thus giving indirectly the full meaning - 'Father of the people'.

2. Sarai is the name of the Hebrew mother which means in African dialects, goodbye, which agrees very well with what Sarai could have said to her people when they left Ur for Canaan. In Jewish Hebrew the meaning of Sarai given as 'a princess' is not original and is not related to the possible contextual meaning as articulated by African dialects.

3. Isaac or Yitzchak in Jewish Hebrew means to laugh, agrees with the African name Sekai given to a child in the same context as that used in the Hebrew Scriptures.

4. Hagar in Jewish Hebrew means to wander and in African dialects it means a declaration by person to a third party who shall never linger or stay (Haagari) as was the fate of Hagar as pronounced by Sarah (She will not stay in my backyard and share my husband, she will have to go away - wander).

5. Esau which in Jewish Hebrew is Esav has no direct meaning, may mean in African dialects Aisave (he who was not the heir to the inheritance), which agrees well to what became of the first born of Isaac who though was first born but never got the inheritance due to the firstborn.

6. Jacob, Yakov in Jewish Hebrew has no direct meaning but the Jews have associated it with supplanter borrowed from what Jacob did to Esau. In African dialects the name is Yako/Yakovo which means your (Esav) inheritance and not my mine.

7. Yocheved, the mother of Miriam, Aaron and Moses has no direct meaning in Jewish Hebrew but in Vanhu/Bantu dialects is Ochivei/Yochivedi/Yochivei which means 'what can she covert' when her child has been saved by the daughter of the Pharaoh and is made to grow up like a prince when other children are slaves to the Pharaoh.

8. Jethro in Jewish Hebrew is Yitro and has no direct meaning while in African dialects the name is Yitiro or Maitiro meaning the way do to things or the way to govern which agrees with the role played by Jethro in teaching Moses the way to govern by instituting the African traditional leaders; the chiefs and headmen as they obtain in the African governance system to this day.

9. Aaron in Jewish Hebrew has no direct meaning but in Vanhu/Bantu dialects is Haruna which literally means 'he who is without' (for the children of Levi have no inheritance).

10. Moses (Mosheh) - drawn out of the river/ water Exo 2 vs 10 - The meaning given in the context is from Pharaoh's daughter and in Jewish Hebrew there is no suggestion and in Vanhu/Bantu dialects is Munzizi (in or from the river/s), Musheche means 'in the sands of the rivers/river' which has a link to the river where Moses was picked.

11. David in Jewish Hebrew is derived from the word 'davad' which means shrewd or cunning which also agrees with African dialects which have a name Mudavadi which means cunning, shrewd and with exceptional ability, a name that agrees with the abilities of King David. 1 Sam 16 vs 16, 1 Sam 21 vs 11-15

12. Solomon in Jewish Hebrew is Shlomoh, which may indirectly mean peace (shalom) or friend (shlomi), which may agree with the achievements of Solomon who made peace, without many battles with his neighbours. However the concordance is more powerful in African dialects which have the name Chiromo for Solomon which means he who has oratory powers or a negotiator. This can be seen from his songs, his proverbs and from the peace that prevailed during his reign, when one does not fight a battle to achieve peace, it must be due to power of speech (oratory) or charisma. Chiromo was full of philosophy and wisdom, and out of that came peace to the world during his time. And if King Solomon was to appear today with that philosophy of peace to the manufacturers of arms of barbarism (atomic/nuclear/chemical/biological) in Asia, the north and west,

Linguistics

would there be any taker of that wisdom today, when everyone thinks power is a measurement of the size of your bomb and not the brain or philosophy?

13. Yedidiah (King Solomon) which means loved by the Creator in Jewish Hebrew, in Vanhu/Bantu is equivalent to 'Diwa' or 'Tadiwa' which means we have been loved and the fundamental agreeing syllable is 'da' which in African dialects means to love.

14. Barzillai (Batsirai) (2 Sam 19 vs 32) in Jewish Hebrew has no direct meaning and in African dialects it means to help, which agrees with the contextual meaning of 'he who helped the king with sustenance'.

15. Taberah (Num 11 vs 3) was a place where a number of Hebrews perished by a fire from the Creator. In Jewish Hebrew the associated verb is 'boer' or 'bvoer' which means burn. In African dialects there are two possible verbs 'tabvira' and 'tapera' which mean respectively we are burnt and finished. The later combination gives a better meaning of the contextual sense of the event at a place called Taberah. Thus there is an agreement between the African dialects and the Jewish Hebrew sense.

16. Achor (Josh 7 vs 21,26) was a valley named after a man who had coveted. In Jewish Hebrew 'achor' means to disturb, to trouble or muddy. This therefore does not have a direct meaning to the context at Achor. In African dialects there is a word called achochora or achiva, which means he who has coveted, which agrees well with the sense of the context.

17. Perez-Uzzah (2 Sam 6 vs 7,8) has a contextual meaning of a place where a man called Uzzah died. In Jewish Hebrew, the nearest contextual meaning is severe judgement upon Perez and in African dialects the word is Pera-Uzzah or Pakaperera/Pakaparara Uzzah, meaning a place where Uzzah died and there is an agreement.

18. Ichabod was a name given to a child which meant that the glory of the Creator had departed the Hebrews (1 Sam 4 vs 21). In Jewish Hebrew, 'I' on Ichabod may mean 'not' or 'where' and chavod means glory, thus the entire name in Jewish Hebrew becomes 'no more glory or where is the glory?' The same word in Jewish Hebrew may also mean go out or extinguished which tallies with the African dialect sense of the context which means the glory of the Creator will depart the Hebrews (Mbiri yaMusikavanhu **Ichabuda**), there is therefore an agreement. Readers need to note that the agreement is sometimes not verb to verb or noun to noun but may be limited to the general sense of the context.

19. Channah or Hannah (1 Sam 1 vs 2) was a barren woman who despite her barrenness was the favourite wife of a man called Elkanah out of his two wives. In Jewish Hebrew Channah may mean favour or rest. Thus favour seems to agree with the context for the reason that Elkanah the husband favoured Channah, however, such a meaning does not seem original but might have been deduced from that context in the Jewish Hebrew. In African dialects, contextually Channah may mean child which is the subject of the context that a woman called Channah was barren and had no child, or it may mean she who is without (haana - without), a preposition describing the subject called Channah who is/was without child.

20. The waters of Meribah was a place where Moses and Aaron were instructed by the Creator to *'Take a rod, and gather thou the assembly together, thou, and Aaron thy brother, and speak you unto the rock before their eyes; and it shalt bring forth to them water out of the rock: so thou shalt give the congregation and their beasts drink'*. Num 20 vs 8. Moses and Aaron did not follow that instruction, instead Moses hit the rock twice, thus he disobeyed, rebelled or rejected to perform an instruction from the Creator which in African dialects takes the forms 'Muribe/Maramba kuita zvandati muite' - You disobeyed or rejected to perform my instructions. There is no clear linguistic concordance between African dialects and the Jewish Hebrew which interpret 'Merivah/meribah' to mean a quarrel or strife. Moses and Aaron did not quarrel with the Creator for there were no

Linguistics

exchange of disagreeing words but they objected/ rejected/ disobeyed/ did not follow the instruction, which sense agrees spot on with the African dialects. The actual Jewish Hebrew term for rebellion/mutiny is 'Meridah' which stretches further the linguistic disagreement, in favour of the African dialects.

21. Samuel was the name of Hannah's long awaited son named after the following circumstances; *'Wherefore it came to pass, when the time was come about after Hannah had conceived, that she bare a son, and called his name Samuel, saying, because I have asked of the Creator.'*

1 Sam 1 vs 20

The original rendering in Hebrew terms of the name Samuel is Samu/Suma/Sumai for Hannah apprised/informed her problem to the Creator or petitioned the Creator of her childlessness and the Creator answered by way of giving her a son. See 'suma' in Table 2 Jewish Hebrew - Vanhu/Bantu dialects similarities. Readers need to note how the Jews have terminated the name Samu with El the Canaanite cult to give the meaning 'apprise or petition El' and you will be answered. In Hebrew spirituality it is not the Canaanite cult of the Jews that answers/blesses/creates humankind but the Creator (Mudzimu Mukuru - the Source of all souls, life and all creation).

22. The Day of Atonement - Yom Kippur - Musi weKupupura

According to the Hebrew Scriptures, on the 10th day of the seventh month is a solemn day of atonement. A day in which every adult would come before the Chief Priest, confess his/her sins and supplicate before the Creator for forgiveness of sin. In African dialect the meaning of Kippur and Kupupura is the same - to come open with/confess one's transgression in anticipation of forgiveness. In linguistic terms, the Jews have lost two vowels on 'Kippur', one on the first 'p' and the other on 'r' from the original 'Kupupura' which further reinforces the argument that Jewish Hebrew has lost a lot of the original language of the Hebrew fore bearers compared to Vanhu/Bantu dialects.

The day of Atonement was one of the few tenets that the Hebrews or Africans could not keep for the reason that the Chief Priest had become untraceable among the Hebrews because of the Vanhu/Abantu or Hebrew movements or Diaspora among other reasons, for the solemn day of atonement could only be administered by the Chief Priest and not any other priest and in the neighbourhood of the holy of holies of the central oracle/shrine.

23. Manna (Miracle Bread) - Manana

On the occasion of bread falling from the sky, '*And when the children of Jacob saw it, they said one to another, It is manna: for they wist not what it was. And Moses said unto them, This is the bread which the Creator hath given you to eat*', Exo 16 vs 16, the Hebrews called it Manna for the reason that they did not know what it was exactly but they knew that it was a miracle provision which agrees with Vanhu/Bantu understanding of miracle which is 'Manana'. In essence Manna did not mean bread but miracle as it was a miraculous appearance which the Hebrews linked with providence but Moses to whom it had been revealed by heaven knew that there would be bread raining from the sky, and so Moses told them that it was bread well after they had called or known it as a miraculous appearance, manna – manana. And again and again Jewish Hebrew 'Manna' lost a vowel 'a' between the two 'n's proving yet again that Vanhu/Bantu dialects spoken by Africans this day are therefore closer to the language spoken by the patriarchs thousands of years back.

Linguistic Inference

When the names above, among others are analysed, they make more sense and are more meaningful contextually when taken from the Vanhu/Bantu dialects sense or point of view than what has been assigned to them by the translators of today's Hebrew Scriptures in respect of Jewish Hebrew.

Linguistics

The names or words like Sarai, Haagari (Hagar), Sekai (Yitzchak), Ochivei/Ochivedi (Jochebed), Musheche/Munzizi (Mosheh), Mudavadi (David), Chiromo (Solomon), Batsirai (Barzillai), Yitiro/Maitiro (Yitro), Sumai (Samuel), Haruna (Aaron), Manana (Manna), Kupupura (Kippur) and Tapera (Taberah) among others, are still in use in Africa today among Vanhu/Abantu and they still make the same sense, logic or meaning as that obtaining in the Hebrew Scripture context or as used by the Hebrew fore bearers.

It is important to note that shared words between Jewish Hebrew and languages of the pre-Hebrew inhabitants of Canaan (Amalekites, Amorites, Philistines, Moabites, Canaanites, Hittites, Hivites, Jebusites, Girgashites, Perizzites and all) are not often the common words between Jewish Hebrew and Vanhu/Bantu dialects. Common words between Jewish Hebrew and African dialects are exclusive to that domain and the common words between Jewish Hebrew and Canaanite dialects are exclusive to the other domain.

The language of the Hebrew fore bearers could not have been closer to the languages of the Canaanites as close as Jewish Hebrew is for the reason that a language carries a cultural content of the speaker, therefore the culture of the pre-inhabitants of Canaan could not have been similar to that of the Hebrew fore bearers given what has been recorded about them especially the Canaanite Culture - an abomination unto the Creator. It is for the reason of that abomination that they lost Canaan to the children of Abraham. If Abraham had the same culture as the Canaanites, then the land of Canaan would not have been given to him and his children.

Linguistics

3.1.15 Linguistic Similarities - Vanhu/Bantu Dialects and Jewish Hebrew

Linguistic Similarities Table 2

English	Jewish Hebrew Dialect	Vanhu/Bantu Dialect/s
Father	Aba	Baba - used by nearly all African/Hebrew tribes
Father is/has come	Aba ba	Baba vauya/babuya
Behind	Acharei	Mashure/mushure
He who has coveted	Achor* Josh 7 vs 21-26	Achochora (Achiva)
Land/earth	Adamah	Munda, reversed syllables
Lessen	Ader	Derera/deredza
Me/I	Ani	Ini
	Can be the interrogative and the response to the interrogation 'Is it Me/I?' (Ani?) and 'Yes it is Me/I' (Ken ani).	'Ani' is the interrogative of 'Ini' as in Ani' (who)? And the response being 'Ini' (me).
I live here	Ani gar po (truncated)	Ini ndinogara apa/pano (Full wording)
I am Tonderai/Vusi	Ani Tonderai/Vusi	Ini (ndini) Tonderai/Vusi
To do work	Asah	Ita ba**sa**
To put	Asah	Isa
Keep back	Atsor	Dzora
Sad	Atsuv	Suva/asuva
Sad/sorrowful/dejected	Atsuv/atsev	Asuva (being sad)
Crucked/wicked	Aveh	Mavi
Father of all nations	Avraham	Abarahama/babarehama (he who has begotten his people)
Then (adv)	Az	Asi
Listen/hear	Azen	Izwa/Inzwa/Zwana
Lion	Ari	Hara
Come	Ba-a/Va-a	Vuya/buya
Come and dig a pit here	Ba-a ucherah gumah po	Vuya/Buya uchere gomba apa/pano
Deity	Baal	Mwari/Bari
		The 'Mwa' syllable is the same as the 'Ba' while the 'ri' is the 'I'. In African dialects, the designation 'Mwari' does not constitute a known verb commensurate with the attributes of creation as the spot on Musikavanhu (the Creator), in fact the 'Mwari' designation is known never to be used in African or Hebrew offerings for the elders have an idea of the lack of spirituality in associating themselves with Baal. The same interchangeability of 'ba' and 'mwa' in - friend - chabar - shamwari - is seen here, where the syllable 'bar' in chabar becomes 'mwari' in shamwari.
Four people	Baana	(Vanhu) vana
Beget children/children	Banah	Bara vana/vana
At home	Babayit	Pamba
Invent	Bada	Buda (come from one's mind)
Divide	Badol	Badura
Rotten, worn out	Balah	Vora
Run away	Barach	Kuita **bara** (idiom)
He who provided the king with sustenance	Barzillai (2 Sam 19 vs 32)	Batsirai A name in African dialect which means help

Linguistics

English	Jewish Hebrew Dialect	Vanhu/Bantu Dialect/s
Meat (flesh)	Basar	Vusavi
House	Bayit	Imba
At/in	Be	Pa
Child/ son	Ben	Bwana/ mwana/ vana
Strong drink/alcohol	Bira	Bira is the entire Thanks Giving offering in which beer or alcohol is a component. The Jewish Hebrew rendering is like calling the entire aviation industry, jet fuel. Like such other terms as 'bake' and 'prayer', beer is derived from the Hebrew/African term 'bira'. Bira is both a spiritual and technological term with a Hebrew/African origin (etymology).
Children of	Bney	Bwana-a/ vana-a
People of	Bney	Banu, Bantu, Vatu, Vanhu This term is the linguistic pointer to the Hebrews of the Books of Moses – See Banu/ Bani in Table 3
The children of inheritance	Bney nachal	Vana venhaka
Ablaze/alight	Boer (bvoer)* *The bracketed Hebrew term gives the actual word construction when the consonant 'v' (vav) that is used to construct the vowel 'o' in boer is taken into consideration.	Bvira/ bvura
Create/ found/ form	Bore	Bara, bereka
Friend	Chabar/ Chaber	Shamwari* * This is yet another instance of the interchangeability of the syllables 'mw-' and 'b-' to give Shamwari from Chabar. The same syllable interchangeability occurs on the term Baal to transform to Mwari.
Carve/ engrave	Chake	Cheka
Wish	Chamud	Chamada
An object of miraculous occurrence/ appearance	Chanukah A lighting oil miracle now celebrated by the Jews as a holy day. It emanates from the miraculous burning of a day's equivalent lamp oil for eight days of the Maccabean times.	Chanyuka From root verb nyuka – miraculous appearance
Barren woman	Channah (Hannah) 1 Sam 1 vs 2	(Asina) chana The woman who was barren and had no child (chana) gives the sense of a child.
Cutting/ hewing/ bite	Charika	Cheka
Sinner, evil	Chata	Shata
Dig thoroughly/ to dig through	Chatet	Teta , chateta This implies the thorough scratching done by a hen/fowl in search of food.

Linguistics

English	Jewish Hebrew Dialect	Vanhu/Bantu Dialect/s
Digging/ scraping	Chatita	Chateta
		Clear one on one linguistic concordance here because in Vanhu/Bantu dialect/s, 'chateta' also means to scrap the surface of ground or any object in search of something as done by a fowl in search of food.
Grass	Chatsir	Sora
Fold/ to make fold	Chefet	Kupeta
	F and P are interlinked in Hebrew, they are one letter with the P having a dot inside to make it sound harder as in chepet (kupeta). The first syllable 'ch-' (chet) is interchangeable with 'k-'.	
Anger, wrath	Chema	Chema means 'to cry' as result of anger
Dig a pit here	Cherah gumah po	Chera gomba apa
Dig here	Cherah po	Chera apa
Lame (disabled in the feet)	Chigere	Chigere
		The sense given by Vanhu/Bantu dialects of this term implies one who remain seated permanently by reason of disability.
Bamboo	Chezer	Chenjere/ shenjere
Desire	Chimud	Chido/ chamada / mushenjere
Snake	Chivey, chivya	Chiva (puff adder)
Sand hill	Cholah	Churu
Speak to	Daber	Taura
To step along; to lead a child to walk	Dade	Dhe-dhe
To sound alarm	Darea	Dare is the bell used to sound alarm
Tinker, skilled, shrewd, cunning, innovative person	Davad	Mudavadi (King David) One with extra skills, cunning, innovation, shrewdness or with extra ability
Exact, precise	Dayek	Diko
If - else	Dei	Dai
Perspiration	Diyut	Dikita
		There is a double linguistic concordance between Vanhu/Bantu dialects and Jewish Hebrew when a different word (ziya) for perspiration is considered as shall be seen later in this table and such cannot be coincidence but clear proof that Jewish Hebrew is part of the Vanhu/Bantu language.
In my opinion	Dati	Ndati (I am saying/I said)
Amphibian	Ducha	Dacha (frog)
Esau	Esav	Aisave (muridzi wenhaka)
		He who was not the heir to the inheritance
Eye/ look/ glance	Eyna	Einai/ onai/ bona/ vonai
Rise, mount, to be high up	Ga-a, yig-e	Gara, (ushe) kana bhiza
To make great, to bring up	Gadel	Gadza
Big/ large	Gadol	Guru
To cease, to end	Gamar	Guma/ gumira
Live/ stay	Gar	Gara

199

Linguistics

English	Jewish Hebrew Dialect	Vanhu/Bantu Dialect/s
Barber	Gara	Mugeri
To shave off, to cut, raze off	Gara or yigra	Gera
		The existence of such technological terms so long ago in Vanhu/Bantu disproves the northern propaganda of associating civilisation with their arrival in Africa.
Wasp	Gaz	Go/igo
Scissors	Gerah	Chigero
		These are technologies which have existed within the African Culture but would now sound as if they have been introduced/ invented by of the north.
Hero	Gibor	Gamba
Break, break into pieces, cutting off	Gidua/ gada	gadura/ gwedura
End, finish	G'mira	Guma/ gumira/ mira
Pit	Gumah	Gomba
Gulp	G'muyah	Gomera
Rob	Gonav	Ganyavhu/ ganyabvu
Gifted with genius, talented	G'oni	Mugoni (from kugona - ability)
Hebrew (One from the other side of the river)	Habiri/ Habiru/ Abiru (Ivri)	Abira, Vabiri (Vemhiri)
To answer	Hader	Daira
Emigrate	Hager (Hagar)	Haagari
To harden one's heart/ to offer defiance/harsh /hard hearted	Haksha	Hukasha
This	Halah	Iri
Dress, clothes, dressing	halbasha	Mbasha/ mbatya
To rejoice, to give thanks, to praise	Halel	Herere/ halala/ mhururu
		Africans today instinctively praise the Creator and rejoice at family gatherings or at shrine occasions, they do so by chanting halala in some tribes or herere in other tribes, however other tribes ululate (mhururu).
The bird sings songs	Ha-of (the bird) shar (sings) shirim (songs)	Shiri inoshaura - Shiri ine mushauriro wayo
		The term bird in African dialects is shiri is the same as the term 'song' in Jewish Hebrew and the two terms are interconnected by the statement 'The bird sings songs'.
Hill/ mount	Har	Harare is name of a hill in Zimbabwe Haarari/harari.
Hillman, dweller of the mountains	Harari	Spectacularly Harari/Harare is the capital city of Zimbabwe named after a hill/mount by the name Harari/Haarari which was the residence of a king who dwelt in that hill/mount. In African dialects Haarari means he who does not sleep, a title befitting a mountain dweller who will not sleep for two reasons namely of him being fully alert because he will be his people's sentinel/nharirire or for the reason that as a mountain dweller, there are predators in the mount, and sleeping would be dangerous.

Linguistics

English	Jewish Hebrew Dialect	Vanhu/Bantu Dialect/s
Lion mountain	Har ari	Harari
Bring forth	Hatsi	Unza/ Hunza
Desire, lust or eagerness	Havah	Havi
This	Hazeh/hazot	Izvi
Overweight	Hechra/hekra	Kora
Marriage feast	Hilulah	Mabiko **eroora/roora/lobola**
Here is	Hineh	Heino/ ona
Here he is	Hino	Heuno
Murmuring, grumbling	Hitonenut	Nyunyuta
Publication	Hitparismut	Paridza
The glory is departed from Jacob (Name of a new born baby)	Ichabod (1 Sam 4 vs 21)	Ichabuda (Mbiri) yaMusikavanhu
Mother	Ima	Amai/ mai (syllable reversal)
Mother is/has come	Ima ba-a	Amai vauya/babuya
Rob/ defraud	Kaba / Yikba	Kuba
Receive/ accept/ take in	Kabel	Kabira
To stand/ to rise up	Kam	Kumira/ muka (syllable reversal)
Wither/ die away	Kamal	Kuoma
Vault/ room/ chamber	Kamar	Kamuri
Draw in/out	Kamet	Kama
To make angry/ to rival /displease	Kane	Kona/ Konana
Past	Kaleh	Kare
Longing/ yearning	Kalut	Kuruta
Fat sheep , ram	Kar In African dialects the 'kar' is an adjective 'fat' that describes the sheep.	Kora / fat (adjective)
Dig up (wells)	Kar/ yakur	Kura/ fukura (mufuku)
Axe	Kardom	Kademo/ demo
Cool down/ calm down	Karer	Kurara
To clack/ rattle/ shake for a movement	Kashkesh	Kashikashi/ kasikasi (idiom)
Small	Katan	Katiki/ kadiki
To exhale/to breathe /fragrance	Katar	Kutura befu
Tiny / very short	Katikton	Katikitiki
Uttermost end or part, section, border	Katseh	Kutsi
To be angry	Katsof	Kutsamwa
Like	Ke	Se
According to measure	Kedey	Kede/ gede
Agreement/ contract/ vow	Ketsitsah	Kutsidza/ chitsidzo

Linguistics

English	Jewish Hebrew Dialect	Vanhu/Bantu Dialect/s
Scald, plucking feathers	Keviyah	Kuvhiya
		Is an example of a misapplication of the original Hebrew by the speakers of Jewish Hebrew. In Vanhu/Bantu dialects, 'kuvhiya' refers to the skinning of an animal to result in the skinned carcass and its hide, where as the term scald in Vanhu/Bantu dialects has a specific meaning 'kuundura' where the process of scalding results in a scalded carcass (applicable to birds) and its feathers. As the second language speakers of the original Hebrew, the Jews that started off with Ezra from exile in Babylon did not master the finer and richer details of the original language of the Hebrew fore bearers which obtains in the Vanhu/Bantu dialects today. What compromised the Jew's ability to do that were the challenges associated with the capturing of both father and mother languages, when the mother and the father were of different cultural and linguistic backgrounds, Hebrew and Babylonian respectively.
For it is cruel	Ki kashatah	Kuti/ nekuti zvakashata
Engaged/ betrothed	Kilulot	Kuroorwa
Atonement (Day)	Kippur (Yom)	Kupupura (Musi/nyamusi/zuva)
		In Hebrew Culture, this day is/was the day for one to come open with the Creator and divulge all his or her sins and repent as a precondition for atonement. The ceremony was solemnized by the High Priest (Cohen Gadol) Svikiro Guru. Upon the loss of trace of the High Priest because of the number of movements as detailed in Chapter 4 History segment of this work, so was Musi weKupupura (Yom Kippur) lost among the Africans.
Tying together/ joining/ union	Kishur	Kosha/ kotya tyava
Anger/ wrath/ rage	Kitsafon	Kutsamwa
Holy	Kodesh	Kosha
Gather	Kohel*	Kohwa
	The Hebrew Kohel here is used for the purpose of gathering people.	The African sense of Kohwa is that of gathering grain - harvest.
Baboon	Kof gadol	Gudo
Haughtiness/ pride	Komah zekufah	Kuoma zvekufa/ kuoma musoro zvekufa kana zvekupedzisira. Stubbornness or hardening one's head is attributed to gross arrogance or pride. Any person who swallows his pride in decision making is never stubborn nor hard headed.
To read	Koreh	Kurava
Point/ end of thread	Kots	Kutsi
Shortness	Kotser	Kutsonga
Drunk/ intoxicated	Kur/ shikur	Koriwa/ kora

Linguistics

English	Jewish Hebrew Dialect	Vanhu/Bantu Dialect/s
Surname	Kuzit	Zita
Eat greedily	Laat	Ruta
For, belonging to, concerning	La/le	Le/ ra/ re
For us	Ianu	Lethu/ edu/ zvedu
Yours	Lecha	Lakho/ rako
To/ for your children	Levanecha	Revanaako / revana vako
Priestly family	Levi	Rozvi - masvikiro kwete n'anga kana mashavi
Place	Makom	Kumakomo yo (yonder place)
Cloth	Mapa	Mhapa
Miracle provision	Manna	Manana (miracle)
Waterfall	Mapal mayim	Mapopo/ mapopoma
Fall/ defeat/ end	Mapelah	Mapera/ Maparara
Cure, healing	Mar'pe	rapa
Aim, objective	Matarah	Maturo
Load/ burden	Matul	Mutoro
One who robs neighbour's field	Mav'eh	Mbavha
Water	Mayim	Manzi/mati
Bless	Mebarech/mevarech	Komborera/ mubereki (can bless or curse)
Physician/ doctor	Merape	Murapi
Refuse/ reject/ rebel	Meribah	Muribe/ maramba
		Num 20 vs 8 Linguistic discordance between Jewish Hebrew and the context, concordance in favour of African dialects as explained earlier, thus supporting the fact that African dialects spoken today are closer to the root language that the Hebrew fore bearers spoke than Jewish Hebrew is.
Bitterness, sorrow, grief	Merira	Mariro (bereavement).
Singer	Meshorer	Mushauri
Molar	Metal-a	Matadza
From	Mi	Mu
Tents	Mishkan	Misha/ misasa
Divine law	Mitsvot	Mitemo
Bride price	Mohar	Roora (muroora)
Teacher/ Instructor	Moreh	Murairi
		The presence of an instructor/teacher in the Hebrew or African Culture proves that education had been in existence before the north claimed to have brought it to the Africans.
Raised/ elevated	Muram	Mira
Roar, growl	Naar	N'ara
Inheritance	Nachal	Nhaka
Our inheritance	Nachlenu	Nhaka yedu
Innocent/ guiltless	Nakah	Naka
Guiltless, pure, innocent	Naki	Naka (munhu akanaka)
Bark (n)	Navicha	Nhava

Linguistics

English	Jewish Hebrew Dialect	Vanhu/Bantu Dialect/s
The king of Babylon	Nebuchadnezzar	Nebuchatinetsa

A believer of an eastern deity Nebu/or the deity Nebu itself of the Babylonians has troubled us as transliterated into Vanhu/Bantu dialects, rendering of Nebuchadnezzar which agrees with what the king of Babylon did to the Hebrews, his desecration and ransacking of the holy shrine, was an unimaginable act by a mortal. The reason for Nebuchadnezzar's success was that the Hebrews had been overtaken by sin and had defiled the land and effectively the oracle.

English	Jewish Hebrew Dialect	Vanhu/Bantu Dialect/s
Pleasant/ nice	Nicha	Naka
Hoeing/ digging	Nikur	Sakur
Lazy	Nirpeh	Nyope
Stand	Omed	Mira
Do (work)	Oseh/asah	Ita (basa)
Dagger, knife	Pagyon	Panga/ banga
Part, separate, divide	Parad	Paradzana
Bear fruit/be fruitful	Parah	Bara
Destroy/ break	Parats	Paradza
Part, disperse	Pared	Paradzira
Publicity	Parhesya	Paridzira
Crumble	Parer	Parara
Stirred/ mixed up	Paror	Pararira
Announce/ publish	Parsem	Paridzira
Break/ crack	Patsecha	Putsika - interchangeability of 'cha' and 'ka'
Split/ separate	Patsel	Patsura / Patsanura
Scatter	Pazer	Paradzira
	There is an interchange of the second and third syllables z_ and r_ but the similarity is discernible.	
Praying	Pilul	Pira

Due to northern brainwash onto the Africans, this term was almost extinct as it was associated with heathen worship when it was the same method of worship which was done by the Hebrew or African fore bearers as practised in Africa today by the Africans themselves.

English	Jewish Hebrew Dialect	Vanhu/Bantu Dialect/s
Fissure/ aperture	Piritsah	Buritsa/ rutsa
Place where Uzzah died	Perez-Uzzah (2 Sam 6 vs 8)	Paka**pararira** Uzzah
Here	Po	Apa
Break/ shatter	Porer	Parara
Hurl/ throw	Pots	Potsa/ Potsera
Shatter/ dash to pieces	Potsets	Putsa

.

Linguistics

English	Jewish Hebrew Dialect	Vanhu/Bantu Dialect/s
Wine press	Purah	Mupuro
	The case of Purah in African dialects is not Necessarily synonymous with wine pressing but rather with small grain Pressing (threshing) and etymology of the verb is Hebrew African.	
See/ look/ read/ perceive/ observe/ view/notice	Raah	Rava/ ringa
Ill	Raah	Rwara
View/ look/ read	Raavah	Rava
Enlarge/ increase	Rabeh	Reba
To ride	Rachav	Chovha
To spread/ to beat flat	Raded	Radada (ideom)
To be weak/ sink/ let go/ spiritless/ lose heart	Rafah	Rafa
Embroidered/ fashion /formed	Rakom/raken	Rukwa/ruka
Raise objections, confute	Ramah	Ramba
Heal	Rape/ rapa	Pora/ rapa
		The senses rendered by the above Vanhu/ Bantu dialects terms complement each other in the healing sense, 'pora' means heal and 'rapa' means treat medically. African dialects separate the terms 'treat medically' and 'heal' as 'rapa' and 'pora' respectively, whereas the Jewish Hebrew renders otherwise for heal, a phenomenon common with a second language speaker who fails to grasp the intricacies and specifics of a language.
To flow	Rar	Erera
Sin/do evil	Rasha	Resva
Hurl/ throw down	Ratesh	Rasha
Trembling/ fear/ fright	Ratet	Teta
Fight/ defend/ punish	Rav	Rova
Wagon/ cart/ chariot	Rechev	Chovha/chovha mubaiwa *Proof of technology presence in the African or Hebrew Culture
Fear/ terror	Rehut	Huta (tremble with fear)
Vehicle	Richuv	Chovha/ chovha mubaiwa *Proof of technology presence in the African or Hebrew Culture
Noise/ sound	Rishrush/ rigshah	Ruzha
Evil/ wickedness	Roa	Roya
Upright	Romah	Ruramah
Head	Rosh	Musoro – syllable reversal
Adjust	Sader	Swedera/ swededza
Put/ place	Sam	Isa
Goodbye (stay behind)	Sarai	Sarai
Choose/ appoint a ruler	Sarer	Sarura
Laughing/ mocking	Sechok	Seka

Linguistics

English	Jewish Hebrew Dialect	Vanhu/Bantu Dialect/s
Fasten	Segor	Sunga/ sungira
Different/ otherwise	Shaani	Siyana
Remain/ to be left behind	Shaar	Sara
		A linguistic pointer to the fundamental meaning of the name Sarai and not 'princess' which Jewish Hebrew infers.
Sabbath, day of rest	Shabat	Usabata
		Desist from doing/or from handling something. The term gives a sense of a high prohibition as in 'thou shalt not do or handle something' as implied in the Sabbath commandment in the same way the Sabbath is understood in African Culture.
Lion	Shachal/ Koari	Chikara
Worship	Shamer	Shumira
Change/ alter/ differ	Shanah	Shandura
Singer	Shar	Mushauri
Sing	Shar	Shaura
Drink	Shata/ yishte	Svuta
Cry out for help	Shavea	Shevedza
Abandon/ desert/ leave	Shayah/yishye	Siya (leave)/ yisiye (leave it)
Intoxicating drink/ alcohol	Shechar	Chikari
Intoxicating drink/ beer	Shekar/bira	Chikari/ bira/ doro
Call out/cry	Shema	Shama (kwama)/chema
Tooth	Shen	Zino
Drink	Shoteh	Svuta/ sveta
Appraisal/valuing	Shumah	Shuma
Apprise/inform	Sumah/ samu	Suma
Dress, put on	Simlah	Simira
Mount Sinai	Sinai	Sinai (miraculous appearance especially of a liquid, agrees with miracles of Mt Sinai.
Thorn bush/ Thorn grass	S'neh	Sine/ tsine
Unclean/ dirty	Sov/Svob*	Sviba
	*The consonant 'v' in svob has been derived from converting the vowel 'o' in sov to its constituents while the b is another form of the consonant 'v'.	
Prison, cage, muzzle, fasten,	Sugar	Sungira, sunga, musungo
Weed	Sur	Sora
Mistake/ go astray	Taa	Taika/taya
Go astray	Taay	Taya (rasika)
We are finished	Taberah* (Num 11 vs 3)*	Tapera
Fire	Tabverah	Bvira* (or tabvira)
		Is in actual fact a verb for 'to burn' caused by the act of a fire. This is yet another instance or evidence of a learner or second language speaker of the original Hebrew. The student could not understand the intricacies of the rich language in which case gave both fire and the burning effect the same term.
Young girl	Talyetah	Taita

Linguistics

English	Jewish Hebrew Dialect	Vanhu/Bantu Dialect/s
Rise up young girl	Talyetah kam	Taita muka
To rise straight	Tamer	Tamira/ mira
Cock	Tangol	Jongwe
Debate, argue	Tarah, taryah	Taura
We are all burnt up	Tav'erah (Num 11 vs 3)	Tabvira
Prayer	Tefilah/(tepilah)	Topira/mupiro/kupira
		Which in African dialects means 'making an offering or supplication'.
Immersion/ bathing	Tibul/ tivila	Tiva
Picture	Timna	Tamuona (we have seen him/her)
		The sense given here is not that of a noun for a picture perse but is what people say when they see the image of someone in a picture, 'we have seen him' though he may not be there physically with them but the picture is showing him - Tamuona.
Flight	Tisah	Tiza
Thank you	Todah	Tenda/ tatenda
Lost/ mistaken	Toe	Taika
Lose one's way	Toeh	taika (rasika)
Take away	Tol	Tora
Burden	Torach	Mutoro
Row/ order/ line	Tor	Mutaro
Swallow/ feed	Tsaad	Svada
Neighing/ shout/ cry	Tsahalah	Hotsira
		Interchanged syllables
To fast	Tsam/ tsom	Tsanya
Dry up	Tsamek/tsamak	Tsemuka
		Is the cracking effect of drying up.
To settle/ revenge	Tsave	Tsiva
Dirt/ filth/ mud	Tsea/ tse	Tsvina
Keeping/ store	Tsepunah	Tsapi
Envy/ jealous	Tser	Tsere
Thorn/ prick/ hook /thorn grass	Tsinah	Tsine
Needle	Tsinorah	Tsono
		This technology term in African Culture indicates an early breakthrough in textile and related technologies such as steel works, a position that renders invalid the northern propaganda that civilisation was brought to Africa by the north
Pillow slip	Tsipah	Mutsipa
	In African dialects, the pillow or pillow slip is a head and neck rest and not the neck perse as suggested by the 'tsipah' term above which again is an instance of language mix up synonymous with a second language speaker who took up a language without sufficient instruction.	Is the neck which rests on the pillow

Linguistics

English	Jewish Hebrew Dialect	Vanhu/Bantu Dialect/s
Head rest/ pillow slip	Tsipah	Mutsago
Messenger/ herald	Tsir	Tsuri
Young girl/ young woman	Tsira	Tsiru
		In Vanhu/Bantu dialects, the term tsiru applies to a heifer but the fundamental sense of a young female is discernible.
Hair lock/ fore lock	Tsitsit	Mhotsi
		Is a physical Hebrew pointer for only the African race have hair that can lock, other hairs do not lock.
Waste, parched, deserted, relating to the grave or sepulture (Zion)	Tsiyon - relates well to the trials and tribulations associated with the children of Jacob around Mt Tsiyon	Tsaona
		The sense of the meaning of Tsiyon in 'waste', 'parched', 'deserted and relating to the grave or sepulture' concurs well with the African dialect meaning of 'tsaona', which means disaster, catastrophe, death and related matters.
Laugh	tsochek	Toseka (we laugh), seka
Pregnant woman	Ubara	Mubereki / mubari
		The Jewish Hebrew term here implies not the pregnancy as understood in African dialects but 'the woman who shall bear for the reason that she is pregnant'.
Eat	Uchal/ ochel	Uje/ udye/
Advise	Uts	Udza
Long for and return	Uteshuvah	Shuva
We beseech thy mercy/ we hereby supplicate	Utetila	Tateterera
Your children	Vanecha	Vanaako (truncated form) / Vana vako
Children	Vanim/ banah/ vanah	Vana/ bana/ bantwana
And	Ve/ u	Vuye/ uye
And now, and thus	Vehineh	Vuye hino, hino
Schemer* (Jacob)	Yaakov	Yakovo/Yako (belonging to you)
Not the original meaning – for it was the mother who preferred Jacob than Esau, who was the schemer.		
Wish, desire	Yaav	Yeva
Heavy (fat*)	Yakar	Yakora*/kora*
Wail/ lament	Yalel	Rira/ yarira mhere
Suck milk	Yanak	Yanwa/yamwa
To flow	Yarir/ rir	Yerera
Initiative	Yazam	Zama
Creator fearing/ fear of heaven	Yera	Yera / yeresa denga
Sanctified	Yera	Yera
Sweat, perspiration	Yeza	Ziya
	Syllable reversal	
Decay	Yibol	Yavora/ vora/ bora*
		* consonants 'b' and 'v' are one and can be used interchangeably.
To hide, to put away	Yignoz	Viga
Revere/ fear	Yira	Yera/ Yeresa
To laugh (Isaac)	Yitzchak	Kuseka (Sekai)

Linguistics

English	Jewish Hebrew Dialect	Vanhu/Bantu Dialect/s
Male / female	Zachary is male and if terminal '-ana' is added to zachary then it becomes female 'zachariyana'.	Zakariyana is a mythical dream wife sang in African children songs - 'Pote-pote, Zakariyana; ndinotsvaga wangu, Zakariyana; musuki wendiro, Zakariyana; anodzichenesa, Zakariyana; semwedzi wagara, Zakariyana'.
Day	Yom	**Nyam**usi/ musi
Maker of skin bottles /to force	Zakak/ hazkek	Kukaka matovo (Working in animal hides.)
Ginger	Zangevil	Tsangamidzi
To stream/ to flow	Zaram	Zara (Rwizi rwa**zara**) - the river is overflowing
Sweat, perspiration	zea/zeya	Ziya
This	Zeh	Izvi
Little, small, tiny	zer	Zera (age) diki (small/young)
Beget/ bear	Zera	Zvara
Inferior soil	Zivurit	Zivhu
Legendary bird (owl) - the horn legend -	Ziz	Zizi
This	Zu	Izvi
To shake/ to move	Zua	Zuwa
To stir/ to move	Zuz	Zuza/ zunza

It is clear from Table 2 above that Jewish Hebrew is part and parcel of the Vanhu/Bantu language and that this language is fundamentally different from the language of the north among others comprising English, French, Dutch, Swiss, Italian, German, Greek, Spanish, Russian which are the languages of the strangers in relation to the Hebrew Culture. There are sporadic similarities between Vanhu/Bantu dialects, Jewish Hebrew and Arabi included on one side and the languages of the strangers on the other side, these are minor and are a result of assimilation/borrowing of usually original African technology terms as the north invaded Africa around the times of Egyptian civilization or as a result of linguistic synergies from earlier interactions.

The Jewish Hebrew dialect spoken today by the Jews is not the language that the Hebrew fore bearers Abraham, Ishmael, Isaac and Jacob spoke, in fact, the fore bearers spoke original Hebrew, which is the root of Vanhu/Bantu, Arabi and the Jewish Hebrew dialects spoken today. The Jews have lost nearly the entire Hebrew Culture by reason of their origin and other cultural influences. A culture can only be executed in its language of origin; any language transform will kill the culture. A typical example is what happened to the Africans who were taken into slavery by the north in the west and elsewhere; on arrival, they were subjected to a foreign language and the African family was destroyed, and so was the culture. A culture will not survive in a foreign language. A people can make a transform in their day to day language of communication, but it is not possible to transform the facets of a culture into a foreign language, a lot of material will die off on the onset of the language transform. If there are substantial similarities in today's Jewish Hebrew to the dialects of the African people of the Hebrew Culture in terms of vocabulary, construction and all other facets of the language, then there are closer ties between the language of the patriarchs to the dialects of the people of the scriptural culture (Africans).

Linguistics

3.1.16 Hebrew or African Common Spiritual Vocabulary

a) **Fear of Heaven - Yira (Jewish Hebrew) - Yera (Vanhu/Bantu dialects)**

In matters of spirituality, Africans were/are guided by the fear of heaven as exemplified in the day to day vocabulary that they used even before the advent of Christianity on the African continent. The same sense of fear of heaven that was experienced by the patriarchs is still in Africa and spectacularly uses the same word to express that respect of the Creator from the basis that common words/syllables in use today in African dialects, Arabi and Jewish Hebrew were the words that constituted original Hebrew of the fore bearers.

b) **Worship - Shamer (Jewish Hebrew) - Shumira (Vanhu/Bantu dialects)**

The sense and method of worship as taught by Moses that was lived by the patriarchs as in the Sabbath, fear of heaven, praying, lock in the hair, holiness and general offerings for the Creator (bira), were/are still being practiced and understood by the Africans in the same sense and word as the Hebrew fore bearers, not by coincidence, or by general biblical origins but by the fact that the two, Hebrew and African people are the same people.

c) **The Sabbath - Shabat (Jewish Hebrew) - Chisi/ usabata basa (Vanhu/Bantu dialects)**

The sanctification of the Sabbath among Africans is of the same sense and format as that practised by the Hebrews before Christianity converted the Hebrews to Sun Day worshipping in reverence of the northern pagan Sun deity.

d) **Praying - Pilul (Jewish Hebrew) - Pira (Vanhu/Bantu dialects)**

The African or Hebrew praying or offering referred to in their dialects as 'pilul' and 'pira' respectively exemplified by animal, first fruit, first born sanctification are still being said in the same terms as used by the Hebrew fore bearers and practised the same way by Africans today.

e) **Liquor offering - bira (Jewish Hebrew) - Bira (Vanhu/Bantu dialects)**

These remain intact in language and manner of offerings as practised by the Hebrew fore bearers in comparison to what Africans are doing today.

f) **Lock of hair or cloth - Tsitsit (Jewish Hebrew) - Mhotsi (Vanhu/Bantu dialects)**

Africans still keep a spiritual lock, which is referred to in a similar term in Jewish Hebrew dialect to this day.

g) **Holy - Kodesh (Jewish Hebrew) - Kosha (Vanhu/Bantu dialects)**

The holiness of any item of spirituality is being understood in a similar term to the 'kodesh' of the Jewish Hebrew dialect.

h) **Supplicate/beseech - ut'tilah - (Jewish Hebrew) - teterera (Vanhu/Bantu dialects)**

The term relating to supplicating before heaven is still shared by Jewish Hebrew and Vanhu/ Bantu dialects as evidence that they stem from one language of origin.

i) **The day of atonement - Yom Kippur (Jewish Hebrew) - Musi weKupupura (Vanhu/Bantu dialects)**
On the term 'Yom kippur', the Jews have lost two vowels from the possible original terms still in use among Vanhu/Bantu dialects but the synergies are without doubt and also not coincidental.

Linguistics

The argument used by the north to justify their settlement in Africa so as teach Africans the supposed 'proper spirituality' through Christianity that is based on the untruth that Africans are the gentiles who needed salvation by baptism to be part of the 'New Covenant' is irrelevant and was just religious propaganda for the Africans are the Bona fide Hebrews of the Books of Moses who need to remain in their culture for them to remain relevant in matters of spirituality and survival.

3.1.17 Linguistic Divergence Upon Return From Exile

There are more linguistic similarities between Jewish Hebrew and Vanhu/Bantu dialects in writings of pre-exile literature and proceedings than those that happened after exile. This was a result of foreign influence that encroached and played a role on the culture of those taken into captivity. The Hebrew women taken by the Babylonians to mother Babylonian children now known as the Jews today taught their children the original Hebrew that was mixed with Babylonian language, for that reason the Hebrew spoken by the Jews sounds like an original Hebrew language being spoken by a learner, stranger or by one heavily influenced by foreign languages and cultures. Even names of children born in Babylon (Babel) said it all, one such name was Zerubbabel which, in African dialect means born in Babel or originating from Babel (Babylon) - ZvoruBabel, which is the fundamental origin of the Jews, their language, culture and general beliefs. The children of Babylonians born to captured Hebrew women (ZvoruBabel is a combination of 'zvarwa - born' and Babel or 'zera' in Jewish Hebrew means beget/bear or seed and so such children were the seed of Babylon or 'zera' in Vanhu/Bantu dialects also means the age which also mean the Age of Babylon).

El the Canaanite deity in Judaism

El was a Canaanite chief deity and the worshipping and reverence accorded to El by the Jews is a non-Hebrew and non-African concept. The term El was widely used by Ezra when he compiled the Hebrew Scriptures as they obtain to this day. However it is important to note that from the times of the patriarchs, El was not an object of worship among the Hebrews themselves but was quite popular among the other cultures among which the Canaanites were top of the list. In that regard it became appropriate for the believers of El to inscribe his names, art and culture in a document. Ostensibly to date, the Jews have maintained the use of the name El in their names and in worshipping. That connection points to the origins of the Jews as Canaanite among other origins and not Bona fide Hebrews as explained earlier. If the Canaanites lost their land Canaan for the reason of such abominations in favour of the Hebrews, it becomes highly ironical for the Jews who claim to be Hebrews to do exactly as done by the Canaanites and still expect the mercy of the Creator.

Instances of El in the Hebrew Scriptural Names

a) Bethel

When analysed from the times of the patriarch Abraham, El was not used as an attachment to names in honour of him apart from the name of a place Bethel which was a result of the author's influence (Ezra). Bethel which in Jewish Hebrew means the house of El is in contrast to the beliefs of the patriarchs who called upon the Creator and not upon El who as mentioned earlier came in at the moment of recording of the law by Ezra who like any other Jew or any other person within the neighbourhood of Canaan had a heavy influence from a belief system based on El, while on the other side the patriarchs had known all the abominations associated with El of the Canaanites but were not party to that.

b) Amraphel

In Gen 16 vs 11, the king of Shinar (Babylon) by the name Amraphel used the 'El' termination to his name. In Hebrew culture, this did/does not pose any contradiction for the reason that the Babylonians were not Hebrews.

Linguistics

c) Ishmael

Indeed Ishmael was a Bona fide Hebrew and so are his children (the Arabs – Banu Arabia), and the name 'Ishmael' means in Hebrew terms god will hear (my afflictions). Though it was the Creator of heaven and earth who heard the afflictions of Hagar (Ishmael's Egyptian mother), to Hagar who was of non-Hebrew (Egyptian) faith before Muhammad taught Islam or revived Hebrew Culture, El was what she knew in matters of spirituality and providence.

d) Rachel

In Gen 29, Laban, son to Bethuel, son to Nahor who was brother to Abraham named his daughter with a salutation of El which he saw on his father Bethuel. Readers should remember that Abraham had been called from Ur to go to the land of Canaan, his kinsmen had remained under the pagan influences of the surrounding people.

e) Reuel

In Gen 36, Esau who had married Canaanite women against his parents' advice, gave his son the name Reuel ostensibly due to the Canaanite influence from his wives. The name had earlier appeared as Reu in Gen 11. The Edomites, the children of Esau from then have vanished into the Canaanites.

Other names in honour of El

The names bearing the name of the Canaanite deity El continued among others with Samuel (apprise El), Ezekiel, Daniel (El is my judge/El has judged me), Gabriel (El is my hero/strength), Nathaniel (my gift from El or El has given me) which was Nathan originally and Michael (Who compares to El). It is important to note that while all this worshipping of El was happening, none of that was/is in occurrence in Africa among Vanhu/Abantu.

When Assyria overran northern Israel around 721 BCE, a few Hebrews who remained after the fall of northern Israel to Assyria blended their language with the invading non-Hebrews. Upon return of the Jews from captivity of Babylon much later, the Jews of that time further blended with neighbouring languages to an extent that a new dialect came into play which differed from that spoken by the bulk of the Hebrews (Africans) who had migrated down to Africa/or those who never returned to Canaan with Moses (referred to as the Lost Tribes of Israel). It was not only the language that was blended with the languages of the neighbouring people but also the culture as shown earlier under Chapter 2 Jewish Culture - Judaism. Among Vanhu/Abantu in Africa, El is non-existent and there are no traces of the name of El in African names. In fact all names of praise and tribulation that Africans give to their children or use in their culture reference the Creator of heaven and earth. If El was the most detested abomination of the Canaanites by the Creator, there is no reason of spirituality by any other people to carry on the matter of El. It is important to note here that the Hebrews (Africans) who had migrated to Africa maintained their original culture to date unadulterated.

The 'Jew' title

The names 'Hebrew or children of Jacob' slowly began to be substituted by 'Jew' from events around 2 Kings 16 vs 6, '*At that time Rezin king of Syria recovered Elath to Syria, and drove the Jews from Elath: and the Syrians came to Elath, and dwelt there unto this day*'.
At that point in time, all the two states of Israel (northern Israel and Judah) were still under the control of the Hebrews themselves as that time was a couple of decades before northern Israel fell to Assyria.

Scriptural Names in Concordance with Vanhu/Bantu Dialects

A close analysis of names overleaf given in most genealogies of the Hebrews show them embedded today in various African dialects spoken today either in their names or in general spoken language.

Linguistics

Readers fluent in Vanhu/Bantu dialects would note that this concordance slowly disappears from most books recording events likely to have occurred towards and after exile of the Hebrews and after the return of the Jews.

Table 3   Hebrew Scripture Names Concordance with Vanhu/Bantu Dialects

Hebrew Scripture Name	Vanhu/Bantu Dialect Possible Equivalence
Ham	Hama
Put (Ptah - ancient Egyptian ruler)	Puta/ Peta
Shem	Shama/ Chema
Seba	Seva/ Save/ Sabi
Havillah	Vira/ Abira/ Chavira/ Mavirira
Raama	Raamai
Sheba	Shava/ Shuva
Aram	Aramba/ Aruma
Eber	Abara
Jerah	Jira/ Jera
Ophir	Aphiri/ Pfura/ Sofala
Shelah	Shara/ Shura
Terah	Tera/ Teera
Abraham	Abarahama/ Babarehama
Isaac	Sekai/ Aiseka
Dumah	Duma
Hadad	Haadadi
Tema	Tema
Keturah	Ketura/ Keta/ Kutura
Medan	Madana/ madanha
Shuah	Shuva
Abida	Abuda
Korah	Kora
Zerah	Zera
Shammah	Shama
Mizzah	Misa
Hori	Ora
Cheran	Chera/ Chereni
Zavan	Zava/ Zavani
Jakan	Jaka / Jakani
Bela	Bela/ Bira
Shaul	Shaura/ Shuro
Onan	Onana/ Anani
Tamar	Tuma/ Tumira
Dara	Dara
Achar	Achera
David	Mudavadi
Zeruiah	Ziruvi
Uri	Uri
Atarah	Atora
Shammai	Shamai
Jada	Yada
Zaza	Zadza
Attai	Itai
Zabad	Zvabuda
Sisamai	Sisamai
Mesha	Musha
Mareshah	Marasha/ Maresva/ Marasha

Linguistics

Hebrew Scripture Name	Vanhu/Bantu Dialect Possible Equivalence
Tappuah	Tapuwa
Shema	Shama/ Chema
Maon	Maona
Ephah	Ipa/ Ifa/ Upfu
Tirhanah	Tirivana
Sheva	Shuva/ Seva
Talmai	Tamai
Solomon	Chiromo
Anani	Anani
Ahumai	Ahumai
Hushah	Hasha
Gedor	Godora
Socho	Soko
Chozeba	Choziva
Tochen	Tochena
Ziza	Zizi/ Zeza
Amasai	Amasai/Masai
Beera	Bira
Zia	Ziya
Huri	Huri/ Ura
Guni	Guni/ Huni
Manasseh	Manatsa
Merari	Marara/ Murara/ Mirira
Izhar	Izhara/ Zhara/ Zhira
Shimmei	Shuma
Tolah	Tora
Puah	Puwa
Gaza	Gaza
Jamai	Yaamai
Gezer	Geza/ Gezera
Gera	Gera
Baara	Bara/ Boora
Moza	Muza
Ziba	Ziva
Dodai	Dadai/ Danai
Gath	Gate
Maresha	Maresva
Azeka	Azeka/ Aseka
Zorah	Zora
Manna	Manana
Kippur	Kupupura
Hushai	Ushai
Azaziah	Azaziya / Azviziva
Mahli	Mahli
Beno	Buno
Mattaniah	Matanya
Mallothi	Malothi / Muroti
Simri	Simira
Kedar	Kudaro
Mishna	Mushana
Massa	Musasa
Kedemah	Kadema/ Kademo
Omar	Umhare
Adlai	Adlani

214

Linguistics

Hebrew Scripture Name	Vanhu/Bantu Dialect Possible Equivalence
Timna (picture)	Tamuona
Chelubai	Chelubai
Shimna	Shimuna
Abishai	Bishi/ Bisai
Asahel	Asahwira
Amasa	Amasa
Azubah	Azuba / Azuva
Hur	Huru
Maachar	Maachari
Temeni	Temeni
Zanoah	Zano
Amaziah	Maziva
Jaanai (Yaanai)	Yanai
Jachani	Jachani
Hanani	Hanani
Baasha	Baasha
Levi	Lozi / Rozvi
Chenaanah	Chenaana
Uzzi	Uzzi
Bukki	Buka
Jaziz (Yaziz)	Yazizi
Zadok	Zadoka / Zuvadoka
Mushi	Mushi/ Musha
Zimmah	Zema
Uzziah	Ziya
Uzza	Udza
Toah	Tova
Bani	Bani
Shamer	Shumira
Yephuneh	Yepfune
Geba	Geba / Gava
Daberah	Dabera
Yericho	Yiriko
Tola	Tola / Tora
Iri	Iri
Zemira	Zemira
Chennanah	Chenani
Jezer	Jezera
Ahera	Hera
Machir	Machira
Maachah	Maacha
Shemidah	Shemida
Sethulah	Sethula
Sherah	Shara
Taanack	Tanaka
Dor	Doro
Ishuai	Ishwa
Beri	Beri
Aharah	Hara
Rapha	Rafa
Geza	Geza
Addar	Dara
Shimhi	Shimhi
Tarea	Tareva

Linguistics

Hebrew Scripture Name	Vanhu/Bantu Dialect Possible Equivalence
Pashur	Pashure
Maasiai	Masiya
Zur	Zuro
Jarah	Jara
Dodo	Dodo
Ira	Era / Yera
Naarai	Nerai/ N'arai
Baanah	Vana
Shiza	Shizha
Maaseiah	Masiya / Maseva
Mekonah	Makona
Tzipora (Zipporah)	Chipo/ Chipora

Names not in concordance with Vanhu/Bantu dialects (Foreign names among the Jews)

1. The Book of Ezra introduces foreign names or names which were/are not in concordance with African dialects such as Bigvai, Mordecai, Maghish and Sisera among the Jews.

2. The book of Nehemiah introduces in Neh 2 vs 13 a dragon well. The patriarchs used names such Beersheba (seven wells), but Nehemiah wrote the term dragon, an insect/animal worshipped in eastern cultures, which is not typical with Hebrew or Vanhu/Bantu names.

3.1.18 Further Analysis of Vanhu/Bantu Terms in the Hebrew Scriptures

The following cases of pure Vanhu/Bantu terms shall serve to provide linkages between Vanhu/Bantu Dialects and the language of the Hebrew Culture. This evidence will conclude the linguistic facts and arguments to link Africans and the Hebrews of the Books of Moses. And for a reader to understand, no prior knowledge of Jewish Hebrew is required, what is simply required is an understanding of any African dialect and then try to make sense out of the English transliteration, what will be detected by a reader is spectacular similarity between the original Hebrew and most Vanhu/Bantu dialects.

1   **Taberah**

> 'And when the people complained, it displeased the Creator: and the Creator heard it; and the anger of the Creator was kindled; and the fire of the Creator burnt among them, and consumed them that were in the uttermost parts of the camp.
> And the people cried unto Moses; and when Moses prayed unto the Creator, the fire was quenched.
> And he called the name of the place Taberah; because the fire of the Creator burnt among them'.
>
> *Num 11 vs 1-3*

The name of the place associated with the incident above is called Taberah, which corresponds in Vanhu/Bantu dialects with two meanings of Taberah, which are in them closely linked. The first meaning is Tabvira which means 'we are burnt up', and the second meaning of Taberah is Tapera which means 'we are annihilated, destroyed, exterminated or finished'. This set of words are one thing and they linguistically mean the same and this language coherence can never be termed coincidence. This is testimony to the fact that the language that Abraham, Ishmael, Isaac, Jacob, David, Solomon up to exile spoke is closer to the Vanhu/Bantu dialects of Africans practising the Hebrew Culture today.

2   **Achor**

> 'And Achan answered Joshua, and said, indeed I have sinned against the Creator, and thus and

Linguistics

thus have I done:

When I saw among the spoils a goodly Babylonish garment, and two hundred shekels of silver, and a wedge of gold of fifty shekels weight, then I coveted them, and took them; and, behold, they are hidden in the earth in the midst of my tent, and the silver under it'.
'And Joshua said, why hast thou troubled us? The Creator shall trouble thee this day. And the children of Jacob stoned him with stones, and burned them with fire, after they had stoned them with stones.
And they raised over him a great heap of stones unto this day. So the Creator turned from the fierceness of anger. Wherefore the name of that place was called the valley of Achor unto this day'.   Josh 7 vs 20-26

Achor has an equivalence in African dialects of Achochora or achiva which all mean he who has coveted, thus Achor is completely in agreement with the application above.

3 Hannah (Channah)

'Now there was a certain man of Ramathaimzophim, of mount Ephraim, and his name was Elkanah, the son of Jeroham, the son of Elihu, the son of Tohu, the son of Zuph, an Ephrathite: And he had two wives; the name of the one was Hannah and the name of the other Peninnah: and Peninnah had children, but Hannah had no children'.
                                                                                 1 Sam 1 vs 1,2

The name Hannah as given in the transliteration would in Vanhu/Bantu dialects mean, she who does not have, and if the transliteration is taken correctly, becomes Chana, which in African dialect means small child on the part of Elkanah's wife who could not mother a child for some reason, or may mean she who did not have a child (chana), as the child was the subject of the matter or problem.

4 Ichabod

'And his (Eli) daughter in law, Phinehas' wife, was with child, near to be delivered: and when she heard the tidings that the ark of the Creator was taken, and that her father in law and her husband were dead, she bowed herself and travailed; for her pains came upon her.
And about the time of her death the woman that stood by her said unto her, fear not; for thou hast born a son. But she answered not; neither did she regard it.
And she named the child Ichabod, saying the glory is departed from Jacob: because the ark of the Creator was taken, and because of her father in law and her husband.

And she said, the glory is departed from Jacob: for the ark of the Creator is taken'.
                                                                                 1 Sam 4 vs 19-22

In African dialect, Ichabod is the same as 'ichabuda' meaning the glory (mbiri)
of the Creator will depart (ichabuda) from Jacob for the reason of the ark.

5 Chidon

'And they carried the ark of the Creator in a new cart out of the house of Abinadab: and Uzzah and Ahio drove the cart'
'And when they came unto the threshing floor of Chidon, Uzzah put forth his hand to hold the ark; for the oxen stumbled'.
                                                                                 1 Chr 13 vs 7,9

In the above context, applying the Vanhu/Bantu dialects when the oxen had stumbled i.e. partially fallen caused by mis-stepping of the oxen's feet, Uzzah had thought the ark had fallen

Linguistics

(Chadonha, in African dialects), which tallies perfectly with the sense of the context.

6　　**Perez-Uzzah**

'And the anger of the Creator was kindled against Uzzah, and the Creator smote him, because he put his hand to the ark: and there he died before the Creator.
And David was displeased, because the Creator had made a breach upon Uzzah: wherefore that place is called Perez-Uzzah to this day'.　　　　1 Chr 13 vs 10,11

The context above in Vanhu/Bantu dialects is pakaperera or pakararira Uzzah (the place where Uzzah died), which tallies well with the context. The Hebrews thought the Creator had made a breach on Uzzah, the appropriate explanation was that Uzzah did not have the right sanctity to hold the ark of the covenant, so he died.

7　　**Barzillai**

'Now Barzillai was a very aged man, even four score years: and he had provided the king of sustenance while he lay at Mahanaim; for he was a great man'.
　　　　　　　　　　　　　　　　　　　　　　　2 Sam 19 vs 32

In African dialects, to provide sustenance means to help and the term for that is Batsirai which tallies well with the name of the helper in the verse given.

8.　　**Meribah**

Meribah was a place where Moses and Aaron were instructed by the Creator;

'Take a rod, and gather thou the assembly together, thou, and Aaron thy brother, and speak you unto the rock before their eyes; and it shalt bring forth to them water out of the rock: so thou shalt give the congregation and their beasts drink'.
　　　　　　　　　　　　　　　　　　　　　　　Num 20 vs 8.

Moses and Aaron did not do that, instead Moses hit the rock twice, thus he rebelled or rejected to perform an instruction from the Creator which in African dialects takes the forms 'Muribe/ Maramba kuita zvandati muite' - You rejected to perform my instructions. There is more linguistic concordance between Vanhu/Bantu dialects and the scriptural context.

3.1.19　Conclusion on Vanhu/Bantu and Jewish Hebrew Dialects Analysis

The linguistic presentation made so far clearly shows Vanhu/Bantu terms in the Hebrew Scriptures recorded by Ezra which demonstrate how both the language of Africa and the African or Hebrew Culture they have executed in that language has not changed at all to warrant a recordable difference. The African dialects depicting events that happened during the times of the patriarchs even up to David and Solomon have remained conspicuous despite the fact that Ezra recorded the Hebrew Scriptures in the Jewish Hebrew which was/is a more divergent dialect to that spoken by the Hebrew fore bearers which reinforces the author's assertion that the Hebrew fore bearers spoke nearly a language closer to the present Vanhu/Bantu dialects than Jewish Hebrew and Arabi, no wonder names recorded by Ezra in Hebrew Scriptures fail to make sense to the Jews when in Vanhu/Bantu dialects the meaning would be very clear and unambiguous.

The Jewish Hebrew Dialect Spoken Today in Israel

The Jewish Hebrew that is spoken by the Jews today in Israel is not the original Hebrew spoken by the patriarchs Abraham, Ishmael, Isaac and Jacob. The language has changed remarkably among the Jews in line with the origins of the Jews and has remained more or less intact among the Africans as shown in

Linguistics

the tables 1, 2 and 3 for the following reasons;

1. The Jews, as explained in Chapter 4.2, History of the Jews, were a result of assimilations of the pre-Hebrew inhabitants of Canaan and surrounding nations as well as conversion of the north into the Hebrew Culture. The assimilation of strangers into the culture brought with it linguistic and cultural changes to the Hebrew Culture and the dialect that were adopted by the Jews.

2. The Jews that came out of the Babylonians and Persians also brought in a blend of culture and language to that already spoken by the captured mothers in exile.

The fundamental of culture and language is the fact that the two are inter-linked. The loss of a culture is the first thing that occurs to a civilisation followed by the loss of a language. This is the order of events and not the reverse that is to say, language is not lost earlier than the culture for culture is embedded in the language and is executed in its particular language.

In other words the culture of the north can not be executed in Vanhu/Bantu dialects or in any other foreign language to it for the reason that in a culture there are basic facets that are not translatable into other languages.

The African people having preserved the Hebrew Culture to the last bit by a high factor are indeed the ones speaking the language of the patriarchs by a much higher factor than that of the Jews. The Jews having lost most of the original culture so have they lost a larger aspect of the language than Africans.

What is seen in the Jewish Culture are instances of Canaanite gods, words, names, myths and Babylonian months, festivals, Persian or Assyrian names and words and northern culture and languages and this is in total contrast to Vanhu/Bantu dialects. Though remarkable similarities are seen linguistically between Vanhu/Bantu dialects and the Jewish Hebrew spoken today, there are no similarities between Vanhu/Bantu dialects and those cultural and linguistic aspects that the Jews inherited from the north, Assyrians, Babylonians, Persians and from the Canaanites, the reason for this is that the bulk of Africans had not been under the influence of any civilization up until the coming of the Arab traders and the northern missionaries and setters who came around the middle of the second millennium common era.

What is noticeable in Africa are traces of Egyptian culture and languages in some and not all of the African tribes, all this is a result of the history of the Hebrews and the routes and options they followed when they left Canaan under siege from Assyria, Babylon and besides, some Hebrews (the Lost Tribes) never reached Canaan from Egypt with the prophet Moses and Joshua.

3.1.20 Morality in Vanhu/Bantu Dialects and the Original Hebrew

While northern languages show indifference to obscene terms or terms associated with gender or excretory organs in speech, Vanhu/Bantu dialects are very clear on those terms which pertain to organs of gender, excretion or the acts of interacting with the opposite gender for purposes of conception or otherwise, are referred to indirectly. There is no use of direct terms for the scenarios above as done in northern languages where sometimes all the hard words in the above context are uttered over a family evening dinner without blinking of the eye. It is taboo in African or Hebrew Culture to do that. The threat to the morality of Vanhu/Bantu language is the inception of African dictionaries by African scholars brainwashed in the north that depict hard words in African dialects that were never part of speech or vocabulary but were simply derived so as to give equivalents in northern languages especially for use in science. Who said science must be taught in immoral terms? Not the science that the Africans understand and originated is taught in sub-moral language. Over and above the fundamental cultural differences between the north and Africa, in linguistic terms the northern languages as examples do not agree in syllables, words and names to any extent in contrast to agreements between Vanhu/Bantu group of dialects which include Jewish Hebrew and Arabi which clearly separates the speakers of Vanhu/Bantu language as one closely related group of people of Hebrew descent.

Linguistics

3.2   Vanhu/Bantu Dialects – Arabi Shared Roots

3.2.1   Linguistic Similarities - Vanhu/Bantu Dialects and Arabi of Banu Arabia (Arabs)

Arabi is the Hebrew or African dialect spoken by the children of Ishmael, the Arabs (Banu Arabia/ Bantu beArabia/ Vanhu veArabia) in North East Africa (referred to as the Middle East) and Africans in North Africa, and Arabi is a Vanhu/Bantu dialect. Like Jewish Hebrew, Arabi has also been influenced especially by the north and east as a result of chiefly trade interactions between the Arabs, the north, and the east from the subsequent intermarriages that ensued those interactions before Muhammad taught Islam or revived bits of Hebrew Culture among the children of Ishmael.

Arabic Names of the Time of Muhammad

Arabic names of the time neighbourhood of Muhammad bore closer resemblance to Vanhu/Bantu dialects as spoken in Africa today than contemporary names of the children of Ishmael. The names itemized below are identical to African names in their construction, fundamental meaning and application or context of use but the majority of these names have disappeared from among Banu Arabia. The children of Ishmael have also lost the Hebrew or African respectful addressing system. Adults or elderly people, men or women are given a title Abu/Baba or Um/Amai when addressing them even when they are not one's biological or foster parents like Abu Bakr or Abu Huraira as was done by Banu Arabia even at the time of Muhammad. In Hebrew or African Culture, a boy or girl is not addressed in the same manner as an adult. Today elderly men and women among the children of Ishmael are now addressed directly without a respectful title as is done by the north as in Adnan, Ahmed, Karim or Saud. Where have the ways of the Hebrew fore bearers gone from among the children of Ishmael?

The dialect and contemporary names of the children of Ishmael have changed over the years due to interaction with the north and east that started in the time neighbourhood of the patriarch Ishmael whose children were traders. The trade involved substantial travel and need for communication with strangers of the north, east and others for better business bargains. In the process, there were intermarriages resulting in the mixed race that prevails among the Arabs (Banu Arabia) this day. Today prevalent among the names of the children of Ishmael are syllables that are foreign to the language of the patriarchs. Arabi now bears names or words without vowels in much contrast to the original names or words below.

Bakr, Huraira, Khuwaisira, Quraishi, Anzari, Hudhaifa, Marwani, Umawi, Sasa, Salama, Zainabi, Umari, Makah, Jariri, Bara, Hudaibiya, Usama, Ghazwa, Juhaifa, Kuniya, Adi, Mina, Munaf, Ghifar, Shami, Dhari, Qama, Bahira, Muzaina, Usauya, Urwa, Muawiya, Bukhari, Ubada, Ashari, Marwa, Maisama, Samura, Haiya, Azizi, Ghaba, Zama, Kufa, Makhrama, Kunya, Hera, Khatab, Hamza, Dhakwani, Hunai, Kinama, Ubai, Maghala, Khalasa, Kabsa, Ghazi, Umaiya, Shuba, Musaiyabi, Rumalisa, Lubaba, Hakam, Khababa, Habiba, Uyaina, Maruri, Zuraira, Shama, Tafila, Abwa, Khaula, Luai, Wada, Rifa, Kinda, Walima, Umama, Raba, Maula, Muawadh, Murara, Buwaira, Siba, Musailama, Barira, Hanzala, Huyai, Bashiri, Kuda, Mudarrab, Bajaila, Bukair, Musalima, Muali, Mijanna, Kabsha, Bairuha, Maimuna, Mualla, Rabadha, Mulaika, Humaidi, Hairur, Haraiuriya, Shaiba, Hamna, Amiri, Hamudi, Uwaimiri, Muadha, Mughaffal, Mughira, Hunifa, Mujashi, Shaibani, Masud, Tauba, Buwairi, Zubairi, Hatibi, Atiya, Kuraibi, Subai, Mubarak, Bajali, Sauda, Saidu, Duba, Thuwaiba, Banani, Ashiri, Haida, Musalla, Ruma, Thalaba, Khushani, Shabi, Muri, Ujara, Taiba, Muqana, Ukasha, Mutamari, Khaulani, Hukaim, Basara, Zaura, Mundhiri, Auzai, Makhul, Aghaniya, Laila, Mazini, Musaba, Haushabi, Rawaha, Mughala, Khuzai, Khudri, Makhad, Khadira, Tarwiya, Kada, Namira, Khadija, Marur, Qutaiba, Buhaina, Uzza, Shuraik, Bakali, Abida, Qilaba, Haraura, Khazira, Salima, Tuhama, Nakhla, Mutimu, Salul, Ghanawi, Muanaqa, Shurai, Hudaira, Khuza'a, Awana, Nakhai, Ashasha, Tamima, Bunani, Karima, Thaqafi, Muzahim, Yamura, Zurara, Utabiyya, Miswar, Muchaiyisa, Mutim, Buzakha, Aziba, Kalim, Uwaimir, Taliba, Munkadir, Khattab, Muzani, Khuzaima, Musaiyaba, Taimullah, Makarama and Munawara among others.

3.2.2   Vanhu/Bantu Reference Dialects

In the Arabi – Vanhu/Bantu dialects linguistic linkage analysis, Swahili was not included among the

Linguistics

reference Vanhu/Bantu dialects for the reason that Swahili is not an original African dialect but a composite language made up of words from a group of Vanhu/Bantu dialects, Arabi and northern languages. There are thus a lot of words that Arabi and Swahili share on that basis and such would not be an original linguistic concordance which is in line with the aim of this work, to show the oneness of African people by an analysis of the one original language, culture, spirituality, history and race.

Contemporary Arab Cities

The contemporary Arab cities in Arabia like Manama, Dubai, Abu Dhabi, Doha, Muscat and Sana'a among others are Vanhu/Bantu names which conform to syllabic syntax as well as their meaning in African context.

Old names in Arabi like Hera, Munawara, Makah, Makarama among a few others that have retained their original form were a result of old records that were made of them.

3.2.3   Linguistic Similarities Comparison Table - Vanhu/Bantu Dialects and Arabi

Linguistic Similarities Table 4

English	Arabi	Vanhu/Bantu Dialects
Cross/ wade through/ swim across/ traverse	Abir	Bira The origins of the name Hebrew (English rendering) of Abiru/ Habiri /Ivri which means 'one who has crossed a river or one who crosses a river or One who resides on the other side of the river, is Mubiri or Abira or Wemhiri in Vanhu/Bantu dialects.
Son/ daughter	Abna/ ibna	Vana – inter-changeability of b and v
Virgin	Adara	Mhandara
Call	Adhan	Dana
Obliteration/ extinction/ ruin /fall/ pass out of use/fall into disuse	Afa	Ifa
Strong	Agwiya'a	Gwinya
Ocular/ eye	Aini (noun)	Ona (verb - see)
Yes	Aiwa	Aiwa (which means Yes or No depending on the context of use)
Come	Aja/ haiya	Uya/ buya/ huya
Food	Akal	Chakula/ kudya
Plough/ till/ cultivate	Akara	Kura/ sakura
Eat/ consume/ swallow	Akara	Kara/ kukara – greedy or consume greedily
Voracious/ gluttonous/ hearty eater	Akkal	Akara/Anokara
Yesterday	Ams	Nyamusi (another day)
I/ me	Ana	Ini
Elegance	Anaka	Naka/ Akanaka
Barren/ sterile/ render barren (womb/woman)	Aguma / aquma	Aguma/ guma (cease to be fertile)
Read	Araa/ iraaya	Rava/ raa
Lively/ happy/ merry	Arisa	Farisa
Lets go	Asahab (singular)	Asambe
Possess/ appropriate/ take	Atara	Tora

221

Linguistics

English	Arabi	Vanhu/Bantu Dialects
Dust or one with dust	Aurab	Uruva/ huruva/ guruva
Refuge/ place of refuge /retreat/ asylum/ sanctuary	Awad	Awanda/ avanda/ vanda, One who has gone into hiding, or hide
Befall/ affect	Awira/ awir	Wira
Firm will / firm intention /energy	Azama	Dzama (firm)/ zama (intention)
Tremendous/ immense /significant	Azama	Dzama
Come/ return	Ba'a	Buya/Vuya
Father	Baba/ aba/ abu	Baba - used by majority of people of Hebrew descent
Spring up/ arise/ come out /bring out	Bada'a A term that the speakers of contemporary Arabi have called primitive which helps sustain the author's point that earlier, the dialects were one language.	Buda
Replace/ compensate /exchange/ trade/ barter	Badala	Bhadhara/ Bhadala
Enormous sums of money	Badra	Bhadhara means pay (v)
First signs/ firstlings /early vegetation/ indications	Bakura	Bukira
Decay/ deteriorate/ decline	Bala	Vora Inter-changeability of b and v, l and r
Wife	Bali	Mubari/ mubereki
To look/ peer at/ see through /see clearly/ perceive /notice/ discover	Bana	Bona/ vona/ ona
The people of/ the people	Bani/ Banu	Bantu/ Vanhu/ Vatu The Vanhu/Abantu or Hebrew identity of people of Hebrew or African Culture of the moral code of conduct called 'ubuntu' or 'unhu'.
Create	Bara	Bara
No matter/ no worry /will not harm	Basa	Hazvina **basa** (no matter)
Only	Basi	Basi
Spend a night/ put up for the night	Bata	Vata
Grasp, seize, hold with hand, understand	Batsha	Bata
Withdraw/ quit/ go away	Bauda	Buda
Children	Ben/bani	Vana
Son/ child	bin	mwana, syllable b– and mw- are Interchangeable.
Cry/ weep/ mourn	Buka	Buka Is a condition of extreme fright in children that causes them to cry uncontrollably
Burn	Byihri	Bvira
Take off (clothes)	Byishlat	Bvisa
Dismiss/ fire	Byizal	Bvisa
Affection/ love/ fondness	Chadab	Chido

Linguistics

English	Arabi	Vanhu/Bantu Dialects
Pierce/ penetrate with a sword	Chaka	Cheka
True/ sure/ right/ correct	Chaqqa	Chokwadi
A handful/ five	Chamsa	Chanza/ shanu
Keep away/ abstain/ avoid /avoid/ God forbid	Chasa	Chisi
Detain/ restrain/ limit /contain/ confine	Chasara	Chasara An item left due to confinement, detention, containment
Sin/ offence/ misdeed	Chauba	Chivi
Viper/ serpent/ snake	Chayya	Chiva (puff adder)
Grab/ grasp/ seize/ catch /arrest/ detain/ take hold /control/ keep down/subdue	Dabata	Bata or ndabata (I have caught)
Belly/ Stomach	Dabba	Dumbu
Frequently or constantly laughing/ laughter	Dahuk	Dauka
Molest/ bother/ trouble	Daka	Daka (noun)
Bang/ knock/ beat/ hammer /throb/ demolish/ destroy	Dakka/ daqqa	Taka
To humble oneself/ submit /implore/ beg/ beseech	Dara'a/daru'a	Dura - open up as a sign of submission/ admission
City or court	Dar	Dare
Harm/ impair/ prejudice /damage/ injure/ force /compel/ coerce	Darra	Dara/ dare
To make know	darra	Dura
Invitation	Dawa	Daiwa/danwa
Calling up/ summoning /demand	Dawa	Daiwa (being called, summoned)
Little/ tiny/ minute	Dikk/ diqq	Diki
Restriction/ limitation /shortage/ scarcity	Diq/ dik	Diki
Like/ alike/ similar	Dir/ dahiy	Dero/ daro/ dai
House/ building /structure/ edifice	Dura/ diyar	Dura
Come in	Fada	Pinda (p is interchangeable with f)
To open/ open wide	Fagara/ fugra	Fukura/ fugura
Joy/ gladness/ glee /happiness/ merriment	Farah	Mufaro/ Rufaro
Merry/ cheerful/ glad/ happy	Farih	Fara
Break-up into fragments /fall apart/ disintegrate	Fasaka	Putsika Inter-changeability of 'f' and 'p'.
Present/ Available	Fi There is no 'p' in Arabi and so 'f' is used in its place	Po, pana, pane, panapo
Offering (in form of food) /animal/ snuff	Fidya	Fodya (snuff offering)
Wash	Ghasal	Geza
Laundry / washing place	Ghasila/ ghasala	Gezero
Warrior	Ghazi	Gazi Is blood – synonym with the effect of war or the work of a warrior
Dust/ dust cloud	Gubara/ gabara	Guruva/ huruva Syllable reversal

223

Linguistics

English	Arabi	Vanhu/Bantu Dialects
Crow/ raven	Gurab	Gunguvo
		A typical example of how certain original terms have changed into different forms as tribes moved separately and adjusted to different habitats. The first and last syllables agree, but the middle syllable is out.
Fog/ mist	Gutaita	Guti
Wish/ want/ like /love something	Habba	Havi
Mine, belonging to me	Hagi	Changu
Come here	Haiya khuni	Uya kuno/ Huya kuno/ buya kuno
So big	Halad	Huru
Senile/ advanced in age /aged/ old/ old man	Haram/harama	Harawa
Here	Hina/ huna	uno
Son/son of	Ibn	Mwana/ vana (plural)
Wood/ stick/rod/pole /stem/twig	Idan	Danda
Administration	Idara	Dare
Possibility/ potential/ likelihood	Imkaniya	Mukana
I have (in possession of)	Indee	Ndine
Bring about/ creation /origination/ setting up /establishment	Insa	Unza
Woman	Insana	Nyamazana
We	Ittna/nittna	Tina
Standard measure /gauge of measures and weight	Iyar	Yera/ muyero
Come to a place/reach	Ja'a	Buya/ uya
Young man/ young fellow	Jada	Jaya
To be happy	Jadila	Jabula
Corpse	Jifa	Mufi (noun) or Kufa (verb - to die)
Swindle/ impostor	Kabb	Kuba
Submit/ obey	Kada	Kuda
About to/ to be on the point of doing something/be about	Kada	Kuda
To munch (with a mouthful) /bite	Kadama	Kadama – (n) cheek or mouthful
To moisten/ wet	Kadira	Kudira To pour a liquid onto
Similar/ equal/ measure up /matched/ at par/alike	Kafa'a/Kuf	Kufana
Greed	Kalab	Kurura/kara
Dull/ dim/ exhausted fatigued/ tired weary	Kalala/Kulul/Kulula	Kurara (to sleep/rest and is linked to / fatigue)
To perform marriage ceremony	Kalala/kulul	Kuroora
Talking/ speech /speaking/ language	Kalam	Khuluma
Talk to me	Kalim ni	Khuluma lami
Repetitious in one's speech /repeat one's self in speaking	Kalama	Khuluma (speak)
Limp/ walk with a limp	Kama'a	Kamhinha
Leaven/ ferment/ yeast	Kamara	Kumera/chimera

Linguistics

English	Arabi	Vanhu/Bantu Dialects
Finished/ complete/ done /accomplished/ concluded	Kamala/ kamila/ kamula	Kumira
Speak nasally/ twang	Kanna	Kwama
Want/ need/ lack	Kara	Kara
To dig/ digging/ excavation	Kara	Kura / kwara
Trouble/ torment/ torture	Karaba	Kurova
Nobility/ heartedness/ esteem /respect/ mark of honour	Karama	Kururama
To be noble/ revered/ honourable/ respectable /dignified	Karuma	Kurema
To miss a shot/ miss a target /err/ mistaken	Kata	Kuta
How are you?	Kayf Halak	Kufara here/ Muno fara here?
Overfilled/ overstuffed	Kaziz	Kuzaza/ Kuzadza
Like this/ similar to this	Kida	Kudai
Bridge	Kubri	Kubira (To cross a river or road)
At this place/ here	Kuni/ khuni	Kuno
Return/ come/ comeback	Kurur	Urira/Kuurira
Left over/ a discard/ remain	Kusara	Kusara (verb– to be left)
Idle talk/ joke/ jest	Kuzabala	Kuzavaza
For/of	Lil	Ra
Evening , night	Laila	Ravira/raira Which means the sun has set or Rara which means sleep
To take food/ consume food	Lamma	Ruma (bite)
To you	Likum	Kwamuri (syllables 'li=ri' have changed positions.
Blemish/ fault/ defect/ flaw /shortcoming/ failing	Ma'ab	Mavi/ chivi
Abode/ dwelling/ habitation	Maba'a	Mumba
To reveal/ to disclose	Madila	Dura (reveal) / Madura – you have revealed
Sprinkle about/ pour/ spread	Madira	Dira
Take one's time /be slow/ tarry/ dawdle	Mahala	Mira
Aquatic/ water/ liquid/ fluid	Mai/ moya	Mati/ manzi/ mvura the core syllable is m_
To prevent	Mana'a	Mana (restrict)
Well-to-do/ wealthy/ solvent	Mali	Imali/mari (money)
Weary /tired/ to tire	Malla	Mira (cease)
Galaxy	Majarra	Gwara
Commissioned/ official /in executive capacity	Mamur	Mumiriri
Not available/ not present	**Mafi**	Hapana, hapapo, Haapo Inter-changeability of 'f' and 'p', in fact there is no 'p' in Arabi
Noble trait/ excellent quality /noble characteristics/ noble traits of character	Makaram	Makarurama/ rurama
Hinder/ refrain/ bar/ block	Mana	Mana
Throat/ neck	Manhar	Muhuro
Stopping place/ way station /campsite	Manzil	Munzira

Linguistics

English	Arabi	Vanhu/Bantu Dialects
Suck/ bite one's fingers	Marata	Ruta/ maruta
Seat/ station/ position /official seat	Maqarr/ magarr	Magaro/ chigaro
Ailment/ sickness	Marad	Marwadzo
Fight/ struggle/ contend with each other/ be at odds	Marasa	Marwisa/ rwisa
Incredible/ wonderful /miraculous	Mashalla	Mashura
An elderly/ venerable gentleman/ old man/ elder	Mashyak/ mashayik/ mashaik	Musharukwa
Dwellings	Maskan/ maasanin	Misha/ misasa
Airport	Matar	Matara, are air-born or off the ground drying platforms for household utensil The link with airport is that airport should be airborne park for aircrafts and not ground based park.
Who?	Minhu?	Munhui?
Appointed time/ date /deadline/ time/ season	Miqat	Sikhati
Gouge/ round form cutting or digging device	Migwara/ miqwara	Mugwara
Water/ drink/ juice	Miya/ amwah	Imwa (drink, (verb))
Like/ alike/ similar	Mudari	Daro / dero
To be chewed/ bite/ bit	Mudga	Mudya (n) Eater or chewer/ kudya (to eat/chew)
Teacher/ instructor	Mudris	Mudzidzisi
Knife	Mudya	Mudya asingakori African idiomatic expression for an eater who does not gain weight - knife
Caller	Muadhin	Mudani
Agreement/ accord/ treaty /commutative contract	Muahada	Mwada/ Mada
Help/ aid/ assistance/ relief /support/ backing	Muawana	Mawana You have found 'help'
System of exchange of goods for goods or barter trade	Mubadala	Mubhadharo / Kubhadharana
One who blesses or source Of blessings	Mubarak	Mubereki (parent) is source of blessing
Gladdening/ cheering /joyous/delightful	Mufrih	Mufaro
Trust/ trustworth	Muhana/ hana	Muhana (in the heart/ hana (heart) which are all associated with trust
Engineer	Muhandis	Mhizha
The ideal of manhood /manliness/ valour	Murua'a/muruwa	Murume (man)
Flowing through/ flow	Murur	Yerera
Problem/ concerns/ worry	Mushkila	Matyira
Numerous/ extensive /manifold/ multiple	Mutakatir (vowel 'a' is lost)	Mutakatira
Rising/ ascending of vapours	Mutasa	Tasa, Idiom for the rising of something
Fall down/ sink down/ collapse	Na'a	Naya (rain)/ nyura (sink)

Linguistics

English	Arabi	Vanhu/Bantu Dialects
Clamouring/ roaring /rabble rousing/ noisy	Na'ar	N'ara
Bee	Nachl	Nyuchi
Gold (pure)	Nadar	Ndarama
Drip/ ooze/ leak/ trickle	Nadda	Donha – syllable reversal
Blow/ puff/ inflate/ fill with air	Nafaka	Fakha
Smell of breath/ fragrance /smell/ scent/ aroma	Nakha	Naka
Purity	Naqa/ naka	Naka
Cause damage/ do harm /prejudice/ impair	Nala	Nera
Purity/ clearness/ clarity	Nasa	Natsa
Fall out/ withdraw/ pull off	Nasala	Sara
A watch/ guard	Natara	Mutariri /Mutarisi
Guest/ stranger/ lodger /boarder	Nazil	Muenzi/ wenzira
Arrows	Nussab	Miseve
Lion	Osama	Ashumba/ shumba
Throw/ cast/ fling/ hurl/ toss	Qadafa/ kadafa	Kanda
A floating impurity/ speck /foreign body in eye /thorn in the flesh	Qadan	Kadanda
Weed out/ uproot /root-out/ pull-out	Qala'a	Kura
Belch/ burp/ spew out/ eruct	Qalasa	Kurasa/ kurutsa
To rise up/ stand /rise from death	Qama	Muka Syllable reversal
Abide/ dwell/ live/ reside /stay/rest/settle	Gara/ qara	Gara/ kara
To read	Qara'a	Kurava
To gnaw/ nibble	Qarama	Kuruma
To cut/ clip/ prune/ trim	Qarama	Kuruma – a similitude
To eat something dry /crunch/ nibble	Qarmasa	Kurumisa
To gnaw/ bite/ nash one's teeth	Gargada/ qarqada	Geregeda/ karakada
Fellow tribesman/ kinsfolk /kindred/ tribe/ race	Qaum	Ukama/ hama
Ape/ monkey	Gird/ girada/ gurud	Gudo
Consult	Raaja	Raya
Wish/ covet/ desire /want to have	Rada	Rudo
To develop/ to grow (a youth)	Rara'a	Rera
Wet/ moist/ dump/ humid	Ratib/ Ratiba	Tiva Swim or submerge in water
Repent/ amend	Rawa/ Ra'a	Rewa/ Reurura/ reva
Usury	Riba	Riba – Literally an item derived from theft
Aggrieved /sad/ go through rugged times	Sa'a	Suwa/ Suwa/ Suva
Friend	Saahib	Sahwira
To strive for/ aspire /desire/ long	Saba	Suva (interchangeability of b and v)
To rest/ to desist from work keep Sabbath	Sabata	Kusabata basa - the theme of the Hebrew day of rest - Sabbath

Linguistics

English	Arabi	Vanhu/Bantu Dialects
Dissuade one from his desires /hinder/ prevent/ resist /oppose/ turn away/ stay away	Sadda	Kusada/ sada
Speak the truth/ be sincere /tell the truth/ hold true /credible	Sadaqa/ sadq/ sidq	Diko
Bump/ knock/ dash/ collide	Sadama	Dhumha/ Dhumhira
To elevate, lift	Saida	Simudza
Remain/ be left/ remnant /left over	Saira/ su'ra	Sara
Rub/ scrub/ scour/ clean /polish/ brush	Saka	Suka
Laugh/ scoff/ jeer /mock/ ridicule	Sakira/ sakar/ sakr/ sukur	Sekera/ sekerera/ seka
Pull out/withdraw/ escape / lip away/ remove gently	Salla	Sara
Rise high/ elevated /raised/ tower up	Sama	Sumuka/ sumu
Lion	Sama	Shumba
Bare	Sama	Shama
Present a matter for someone to hear/ cause someone to listen	Sami/ sumu	Suma
Make someone hear	Samma	Suma
Fabricate/ hand-make/ craft (with skill and artisanship)	Sana	Sona Or alternatively shanda (work)
Work	Sana	Shanda
Epilepsy	Sar	Pfari
Quick/ fast/ prompt/ urge to hurry/ speed up/ rush	Saru'a/ sira	Kasira
Cut/ sever/ cut off	Saruma	Ruma
What you did	Sawwayta	Zvawaita
Apparition/ phantom /ghost/ spirit	Shaba	Shavi
Cling/ cleave/ hold on to	Shabata	Bata/ chabata
Young woman/ young girl	Shabba	Svobi
Appetite/ desire /satisfy desire/ saturate	Shabi'a	Shuva
To occupy/ fill/ hold /have (office, seat position)	Shagala	Gara/ chigaro
Craving/ desire/ longing /ardent wish/ yearning /passion	Shahwa	Shuwa/shuva
Worried/ troubled/ grieved /distressed/ sad	Shajawi	Suwa
Woody/ wooded /abounding in trees	Shajir/ mushjir	Jiri
Jab, thrust, stab with a weapon	Shakka	Cheka
To hang (something on the gallows)	Shanaqa/ shanq	Sunga/ shunika (hold upside down)
Hook up/ to trip up	Shankala	Sungira/ sunga
Fair complexion/ light skinned	Shaqira/ Shuqra	Tsvukira
Misfortune/ distress/ misery	Shaqwa	Shangwa
Road, way	Shari	Zhira/ nzira

Linguistics

English	Arabi	Vanhu/Bantu Dialects
Bad/ evil/ wicked /vicious/ malicious	Sharra	Shura
Go astray/ deviate/ err	Shatta	Shata

This verb together with the pronoun 'I' explains the absence of the Devil or Satan in Hebrew Culture. African Dialect rendering of 'I have gone astray /evil/wicked' is 'Ndashata ini' which in short is Shatani. Arabic rendering of 'I have gone astray/evil/ wicked' is 'Shatta ana' and Jewish Hebrew rendering of I have gone astray /evil/ wicked' is 'Chatati' which is short for 'chata ani', which was a confession made by David before Nathan the prophet on the sin of Uriah and Bathsheba. David did not say a character called Satan has caused him to sin, but he put the blame on himself and he obtained all the mercy of the Creator to end up being one the most faithful servants.

English	Arabi	Vanhu/Bantu Dialects
What is it / what is the thing?	Shay?	Chii?
What is it / what is the thing?	Sheikh?	Chiiko?
Stick used to defend/ cudgel	Shuma	Shamhu
What?	Shuu?/ shinhu?	Chii?/ chinhui
To age/ grow old/ attain a venerable age	Shaka/ Shayak	Sharuka or shayika(die)
Teeth/ fang/ prong	Sinn/ asunn	Zino
Odour emanating from armpit	Sinna	Tsvina
Speedy/ fast	Sira'a	Kasira
Mourning/ graveness/ sadness	Suhum	Svimha
Market/ market place	Suk	Musika
With haste/ quickly	Sura sura	Kasira kasira
Melancholy/ sadness/ gloom	Suwaida	Suwa
Next/ then/ after	Taali	Teera
Follow/ go after/ pursue	Taba'a	Tevera (b and v are inter- changeable)
Fixed/ immovable/ firm /hold out/ hold out one's ground	Tabata	Tabata/ bata
Treat medically /give medical treatment	Tabba	Tova
To cook/ get cooked	Tabaka	Bika/ tabika

Again here as applied to 'pray', the etymology of 'bake' is African/Hebrew for reason of being the originators of technology, Africans or Hebrews had long used fire in their offerings, that time the residents of Caucasus mountains were eating raw flesh.

English	Arabi	Vanhu/Bantu Dialects
Set in a swinging motion	Tadaldala	Tenderera/ tenderedza
Spit	Tafala	Pfira (spit)/ tapfira (we have spit)

Linguistics

English	Arabi	Vanhu/Bantu Dialects
Arrive uninvited or at inconvenient time/ disturb /intrude/ obtrusive	Tafiqqa/ tafika	Isifike/ Svika (arrive)/Tasvika (announcement of one's arrival at the moment of arrival)
Feeding/ nourishment	Tagdiya	Tadya Literally means we have eaten
Fierce struggle/ dog fight /free for all/ brawl	Takalub	Takarova/ takarwa
Quarrel with/ fall out with	Takhaana	Tukana
Follow/ to follow	Tala	Teera /tevera
Three	Talata	Tatu
Annihilated/ destroyed/ damage	Talifa	Ifa (die)/Tafa (We are dead, finished)
Take	Talla	Tora
Increase/ proliferation /multiplication	Takatur	Takatira/ Takashira
To load/ to burden something	Takura	Takura
Hanging/ suspending	Taliq/ Talik	Turika
Talk rumour or gossip	Taqawwul	Kuhwa
Throw up/ vomit/ disgorge	Tarasa	Rutsa (vomit)/ Tarutsa (we have vomited)
Snatch away/ carry away /carry off	Tara	Tora
Knock/ rap/ bang/ blow	Tarqa/ tarka	Taka
Hurry/ haste/ hastiness /rushness	Tasarru	Tasara – 'we are left behind' which is always the feeling of one who is in haste.
Repentant/ yielding	Tauba	Tiva – inter-changeability of 'b' and 'v'.
Straying/ wandering	Tayyah	Taika
Available (remaining)	Tayassar	Sara
Waist band	Tikka/ dikka	Mutika
Repetition	Tikraar	Dzokorora
Die/ pass away	Tiwaffa	Kufa/ wafa/wafi (one who is dead)
The name of a mountain where great battle was fought	Uhud	Hondo (war), which means that the mountain was given the name after the battle.
Comfort/ rest	Ulala	Lala/ Rara (sleep)
Motherhood	Umuna	Umai
Mother	Um	Mai
Molar teeth	Urram	Ruma (v) Which means to bite as done by the teeth
And	Wa	Uye
Admonish/ warn/ caution /advise	Wa'aza	Uza/ udza
To like/ want/ love/ be fond	Wadda	Wada
Love/ friendship/ good term	Wadd/ mawada	Wadiwa
Decrease/ demise/ death /death certificate	Wafah	Wafa (dead)/ Ifa (die)/demise
Stay/ remain/ establish	wagara/ waqara	Gara/ wagara/ wasara
Break/ fracture/ crack especially bone	Waqara/ waqr/ wagara	Gura/ wagura (break) Wakuvara – Injured
Paper	Waraga/ waraqa	Verenga, read and the link is reading Is done on script written on paper.

Linguistics

English	Arabi	Vanhu/Bantu Dialects
Wills and testaments usually associated with the departed	Washaya /Wasaya	Washaya Means the departed and 'siya' means leave something behind, which could be an item of inheritance or any other item 'Wasiya' means He who has left something
Manner/ way/ mode/ fashion /procedure/ method/ style	Watiro	Maitiro/yitiro
Day	Yom	**Nyam**usi/ musi
Kill instantly	Zaafa	Ifa (die)/zvafa (dead)
Come out / appear	Zabada	Zvabuda
On the verge of death	Zahafa	Zvaakufa
Remain	Zali	Sara
Darkness/ pitch-dark night	Zalma	Zarima/ rima
Thought/ opinion/ idea /view/ belief	Zann	Zano/ Zanhi
Sow/ scatter/ plant/ cultivate	Zara	Dyara
To plant	Zarayizra	Dyara / dyariridza (replant)
Shake/ rock	Za'za'a	Zuza/ zunza

3.2.4   Conclusion on Vanhu/Bantu and Arabi Dialects Analysis

Table 4 clearly shows substantial similarities between Vanhu/Bantu dialects and Arabi of Banu Arabia as proof that indeed these are dialects stemming out from one language; Vanhu/Bantu language which is the language of African or Hebrew Culture.

When Muhammad taught Islam among the Arabs, there were many Hebrew practices that were already lost at that juncture and over and above those loses, Muhammad abolished other aspects like the strong drink offering (Bira) which meant that all the language associated with those Hebrew cultural practices were lost as well to result in the current Arabi spoken by the Arabs this day.

Clear in table 4 is the fact that most words in Arabi have lost vowels like Jewish Hebrew and in doing so, there are many permutations of language that are lost when just one vowel is lost and those losses were a result of trade that was done by the Arabs to survive and entailed a lot of travelling, learning languages of their trading partners and the ensuing intermarriages that stole the dark skin to result in the mixed breed that the Arabs are this day.

It is pertinent to note that when Arabs ventured into slave trade and wars of conquest, that aspect of life involved a lot of **brutality, savagery and general heartlessness,** and in that regard they lost a lot of vocabulary that dealt with morality, Unhu/Ubuntu. In Tanzania, the point of no return to slavery to Arabia was called Bagamoyo which meant that if a person was at that point towards slavery to Arabia, the recommendation was for him/her to take out the heart from within and leave it in Africa for the place that he/she was going was so savage that to survive there, one needed no heart like a piece of rock. And the Arabs were a heartless bunch even to this day, their business practices are so full of vices and not only businesses but their disrespect for human life, how it is so easy killing another person in Arabia, as easy as killing a coach roach and the general aspect of Unhu/Ubuntu is one item that is extinct despite their highest prayer per capita among all nations of the world and what is the use of prayers if you remain one of the most savage? Why go into the mosque five times a day when prayer is not changing the compassionate aspect of humanity? Some Moslems even walk into the mosque to pray and then detonate themselves thereafter. And if a system has no regard or respect for human life, then all other moral faculties of a culture are non-existent as they all support human life. The author will not digress into the lack of respect for human life in Arabia for that is graphically in the public domain, some Arabs even play football or pray as usual when dead bodies are all scattered in their streets or backyards.

Linguistics

Blank Page

History

Chapter 4   History

4.1   History of the Hebrews or Vanhu/Abantu

4.1.1   Introduction to Hebrew or African History

After analysing Hebrew Culture in relation to African Culture in Chapter 1, and the subsequent comparison with Jewish Culture/Judaism in Chapter 2 plus the Linguistic analysis in Chapter 3, the whole picture of the link between Vanhu/Abantu and the Hebrews of the Books of Moses as one and the same people is getting clearer and to this clarity, the History of Vanhu/Abantu in relation to Hebrew History or the Diaspora is added.

The history of the African people used in this work is not the history written by the third party about Africans or that written by an outsider about Africa. The African history given herein is not the 'when we brought civilization to Africa, the Africans were eating raw cereals and living in mountains like baboons' history - his (northern historian) story about Africans which in fact was an insult story (Instory) on African people. Instory is notwithstanding the fact that when Africans were designing and constructing the pyramids of Egypt, the mortarless pure stone architectures at Great Zimbabwe and related technologies more than three thousand years ago, the same north (Caucasians) were living and eating raw flesh in the Caucasus mountains – unable to make a fire at the least. Today the north claim to be leaders and originators of technology such as high rise architecture, tall and long bridges cast in steel and concrete that the Africans had known and used over thousands of years back. Who is really in the lead, them or Africans? A good question for kindergarten school final year examination.

African technology lead can be measured by making a comparison of Egyptian Pyramids and Great Zimbabwe mortarless pure stone architectures on one side against northern piles of raw rough stones (Stonehenge) and the sand and clay hill (Silbury) on the other side. These were northern works that were done about the same time neighbourhood of the African technologies mentioned herein. Through their history television channels, the north have uplifted those disorderly heaps of raw stone, clay and sand to the equivalence of apex technologies of all time through massive propaganda. For a fair evaluation, the north can take copies of Stonehenge, Silbury hill, Egyptian Giza Pyramid and the Great Zimbabwe into any of their kindergarten schools and there they will be told by their unbiased innocent children the essence of technology.

The purpose of this work is to undo the Instory and provide the summary of the unwritten African story that links all the people of Africa including the Arabs and Jews into the giant Vanhu/Abantu family. And naturally thereafter, any untruths written about Africans can be deleted. Popular African history has depicted Vanhu/Abantu as a myriad of dark skinned tribes devoid of a spirituality who frequently worship animals (animism) and also very capable in using muti or witchcraft in general. The agenda of the Instory was to negate or delete all known information or leads on African works of ingenuity, de-spiritualize the African people by portraying them as a heathen race as basis for teaching them Christianity. The story obtained in this work is an African story being told by an African and is the story embedded in the African Culture, language and heritage about the African or Hebrew people. Readers should not therefore say but a northern historian who wrote the 'best' history about Africans wrote otherwise because this is an internal African script and no reference shall be made to any work of an outsider.

Africa needs to be wary of who teaches them what for the reason that there is a northern network bent exclusively on Africa to confuse the people. A misinformed nation even when made up of one people will always run into conflict. In that regard, over the years, the doctrinal material that has been authored by external historians, linguists, anthropologists, etymologists, genetic scientists and ethnologists among others, had one resounding theme of African misinformation. The historians wrote Instory to be taught to African children while linguists claimed that Africa had millions of languages spoken by equally divergent people resident in Africa. Ethnologists while grouping ethnological origins of languages have grouped only African dialects, not as African dialects but as Congo-Niger languages while all other language groupings have been given their grouping terms at continental level as European Languages, Asiatic

History

and it is only Africans who have been deprived of that unity of continent. What kind of classification is it that which mixes fundamental groups and sub-sub groups like grouping a cup of water with the seas of the earth?

If African children are to be taught the Instory continuously for generations, it is highly certain that the great grand-grand African children of the later generations will have it imbedded in their heads that when other nations brought civilization to Africa, the African fore bearers were baboons then living in mountains and eating raw cereals. Effort must thus be made by African elders to begin teaching their children their story and their spirituality without fail. African children schooled along such former lines would aspire to be Caucasian when they grow up and they may start even bleaching the dark skin in preference of other skin colours as a clear sign of lack of self belief, esteem and identity.

4.1.2   The Domain Land of Hebrew or African Culture

Chapter 1 describe Africa as the domain land of Hebrew Culture with boundaries defined by Gen 2 vs 10-14 which includes the entire span of the African continent and the key issue is that before the Hebrew Scriptures describe the Hebrew Culture, the boundaries of the land in which that culture is practised are given first. If there was no link between Africa, Africans and Hebrew Culture then the entire Hebrew Scriptures would not have given so much space about Egypt, Ethiopia, Africa, its resources and its rivers. The Hebrew Scriptures give no direct mention of Mexico, Japan or Siberia for the reasons that Hebrew Culture was not prevalent there and that there was no immediate link between Hebrew Culture and Mexican, Siberian or Japanese Cultures. The Hebrew Scriptures therefore start by describing Africa of all places, not because Africa is first on the Alphabet but because Africa is the heartland of Hebrew Culture. In fact, other areas like those around the rivers Hiddekel and Euphrates are mentioned later after the lands around river Nile and southern rivers.

The land with the referenced boundaries was the land given to the Hebrews, a land with gold, and unparalleled mineral wealth, good land of rich soils, yielding good grain, animals, milk and honey, a land of oil, fresh waters, good rains that can support and sustain the most natural agriculture. The only land which if it closes its borders to the entire world can sustain itself.

The scriptural land mentioned in Gen 2 vs 10-14, is present day Africa including the now called 'Middle East'. The referenced scriptural verse geographically describes the land of Africa from the south (Cape Province in South Africa) to Iraq/Iran. Havilah is the southern and western parts of the African continent called in African dialects Mavirira or Chavira (where the sun sets), where there is gold and this includes the gold rich countries of South Africa, through Zimbabwe, Congo, Angola up to Ghana (formerly the Gold Coast). The river Pison describes any of Orange, Limpopo (Vhembe), Zambezi (Kasambavezi) or the Congo rivers. The land within this region has all the precious minerals of the earth in abundance, diamond, gold, silver, uranium, platinum, manganese, cobalt, chrome, coal, oil, natural gas just to mention a few. The north have made explorations and extractions of Africa's minerals for centuries and continue to do so today, have built a majority of their infrastructure (roads, bridges, cities and industries) using the mineral resources of this land (Africa) but they have not exhausted any of it, even by a small fraction. There is no other part of planet earth where there is greater mineral wealth than Africa. This region is the earth's gem and there is agreement between scripture and what is obtaining on this part of Africa. The second river is Gihon (Nile) which starts off from Ethiopia or Central Africa.

In the translation to suit their story, the Septuagint translators have made Pison and Gihon one river, the White and Blue Nile so as to exclude the most southern parts of Africa which are known to be the land of dark skinned people and if they were to take centre stage as given in the Hebrew Scriptures, it would then be more difficult to prop up the Caucasian Hebrew theory when every verse is pointing to Africa.

The third river is Hiddekel and fourth is Euphrates in Iraq. Apart from Africa, the land of the Hebrews or Africans, other lands like the present day Europe and Asia are mentioned indirectly in the Hebrew Scriptures and they only became prominent when the north wrote their own culture and script - The Greek Scriptures popularly known today as the New Testament wrote of the Greeks, Romans,

History

Corinthians, Galatians, Ephesians, Philippians, Colossians and Thessalonians among others of largely European origin and in the New Testament and there is no book for the Egyptians, nor for Ethiopians nor for Persians, nor for Assyrians, nor for Lebanese, nor for Babylonians.

4.1.3   The Grand Scheme of the New Testament

The successes of the Hebrews under the leadership especially of Moses, Joshua, David and Solomon cut across the entire globe like a mythical legend. All nations that heard of the Hebrews admired that fame and there were some that tried to fight them like the Babylonians in order to replace the Hebrews as world leaders but there were some like the north, Greeks and Romans in particular who knew that the Hebrews, with their ark and spirituality were invincible and so then came the New Testament.

The New Testament aimed to nullify Hebrew Culture as the things of the past or shadow of the later so that all the people who had been rallied together under the Hebrew fame and envelope would automatically fall under the Greek Testament and effectively the Greeks especially under the background that Greek Culture had come to replace Hebrew Culture, would result in the Greeks rising to the apex of the world without firing one cannon.

The Greek philosophers sat down to write the Greek Scriptures and therein they turned the tables. All the heroes of the New Testament were northern characters, the warriors like Nicodemus, the centurions, the leaders Pontius Pilate, among others while the names of the Hebrew patriarchs were made the villains chief among them were Judas the betrayer or sell out and Simon the forsaker. And by comparison Hebrew and Greek spirituality are fundamentally far apart that one cannot supersede the other without deleting the superseded culture altogether.

4.1.4   The Hebrew Links with Africa

4.1.4.1   Abram in Africa

After a misunderstanding between Abram and Pharaoh over Sarai his wife, *'And Abram went up out of Egypt, he, and his wife, and all that he had, and Lot with him, into the South.*
And Abram was very rich in cattle, in silver and in gold.
And he went on his journeys from the south even to Bethel, unto the place where his tent had been at the beginning, between Bethel and Hai'.

Gen 13 vs 1-3

The south is referred to as 'up' for the reason that it is higher where the Nile river originates. The land of Egypt where Abraham had come to sojourn in times of famine represent Africa, the land of promise made by the Creator to Abraham's children. It is in the same land, his land that he was blessed with cattle, silver and gold. Thus Abraham made explorations into Africa before he returned to Bethel in Canaan. And always when Abraham or any other Hebrew had a problem of famine as an example, the solution always came from Africa and there is no talk of Abraham travelling to Rome or Corinth but Africa showing that there were closer links between Hebrews and Africa that were either over looked at recording the Hebrew history or those in charge of recording were totally unaware of.

4.1.4.2   The Hebrews Sustained by Africa During Famines

In famine the Hebrews who had more knowledge about Africa than any other place preferred Egypt in search of food and Egypt, not Rome nor Corinth or any other land, played a very pivotal role in the sustenance of the Hebrews, for the reason that there were ties between the people and the land. When Joseph sojourned in Egypt, his brothers did not know that he was in Egypt and their choice of going to Egypt was not influenced by the presence of Joseph in Egypt. If there was no Egypt (Africa) in the life of Hebrew Culture, then there was not going to be anything worth noting about the Hebrew fore bearers and the Hebrew Culture for all have a very strong African foundation.

Gen 42

235

History

4.1.4.3   Midia and Sheba Home to the children of Abraham

The Hebrews have always had a link with Africa represented mainly by Ethiopia, where Abraham travelled as mentioned earlier and he gave this land to the children of his wife Keturah;

'Then again Abraham took a wife, and her name was Keturah.
*And she bare him Zimran, and Jokshan, and Medan and **Midian,** and Ishbak, and Shuah.*
*And Jokshan begat **Sheba** and Dedan'.*

Gen 25 vs 1-3

The mention of Ethiopia in the Hebrew Scriptures did not discount the other tribes but that Vanhu/ Abantu did not have many national identities and so by mentioning Ethiopia that implied all the people of Africa outside the Egyptian domain. The above link explains why Moses preferred to escape to **Midian** from the Pharaoh and not to Canaan, and why Jethro (Yitiro) played a very important part in teaching together with Moses, the Hebrew or African Culture, the culture was already there when Moses was born, the children of Abraham including Ishmael, father to Banu Arabia (Arabs), lived by it. The above link also explains why Solomon (Mambo Chiromo) teamed up with the Queen of **Sheba** (Makada) to build a Hebrew Shrine in Zimbabwe (The Great Zimbabwe), the two were Hebrews, no other wife to Solomon is associated with the enhancement of the Hebrew Culture. And when the Hebrews fled to Africa upon the fall of northern Canaan to Assyria and Jerusalem to Nebuchadnezzar, there were already Hebrews in existence there.

Oral Tradition,

4.1.4.4   Moses Fled to Ethiopia from Pharaoh in Egypt

Moses ran away from the Pharaoh to Central Africa when he had killed an Egyptian who was abusing his fellow Hebrew. Moses did not run to Corinth or Galatia but that he went deep into Africa and if he was Caucasian at that time, he would have confronted a lot of issues but he did not at all, instead he was well received and was allowed to marry one of the daughters of Jethro, the Ethiopian priest;

'Now when Pharaoh heard this thing, he sought to slay Moses. But Moses fled from the face of Pharaoh, and dwelt in the land of Midian: and he sat down by a well'.

Exo 2 vs 15

Generally Moses had an idea from oral tradition that the patriarch Abraham had made explorations in the land of promise, and so to Moses Africa was not a strange land but home. That is why he had to seek refuge from thence. He could not go anywhere where he was not sure of; he had to go where his people knew about. This is the reason Jethro received him well without any suspicions or any possibility of informing Pharaoh of the presence of Moses in Midian.

4.1.4.5   The Hebrew Nation Founded in Africa

The referenced scriptures show how a family of seventy souls grew to six hundred thousand and three thousand and five hundred and fifty men, discounting women, children and the elderly, who were the men of age between twenty (20) and forty (40), those capable of going to war;

'And the sons of Joseph, which were born to him in Egypt, were two souls: all the souls of the house of Jacob, which came into Egypt, were three score and ten(70)'.

Gen 46 vs 27

'These are those which were numbered of the children of Jacob by the house of their fathers: all those that were numbered of the camps throughout their hosts were six hundred thousand and three thousand and five hundred and fifty'.

Num 2 vs 32

History

The readers are free to statistically compute the population of the Hebrews at Exodus. These people exited Egypt with a total African Culture and upbringing. Such a sizeable population was bred in Africa from paltry seventy (70) souls. When the same population growth is computed statistically as a function of time to the present day suits well the African population of over a billion people (the stars of heaven) and not a paltry one or two dozen million Jews of largely Caucasian and non Hebrew origins scattered across the entire face of the earth.

4.1.4.6   At Exodus the Hebrews Craved for Egypt (Africa) - The Return

Though Egypt made the Hebrews endure hard labour, it had its glories like plenty of food and water for the Hebrews and they had a natural bond with Africa. Thus when the Hebrews were confronted with hunger, thirst and war while they travelled to Canaan, they yearned for Egypt, quite a number did return to Egypt. Those that returned did not return exactly to fall subservient to Pharaoh because the Egyptians were still angry of the plagues especially the death of their first born children and so the Hebrews to them brought bad fortunes;

'And the whole congregation of the children of Jacob murmured against Moses and Aaron in the wilderness:
And the children of Jacob said unto them, would to the Creator we had died by the hand of the Creator in the land of Egypt, when we sat by the flesh pots, and when we did eat bread to the full; for you have brought us forth into this wilderness, to kill this whole assembly with hunger'.

Exo 16 vs 2-3

With the scenario above most Hebrews upon crossing the Red Sea backwards, travelled down south where Abraham had travelled and explored before. Most Hebrews by now had knowledge of the place where Moses had sought refuge when he ran away from the Pharaoh. Thus there was a kin connection between the Hebrews and the Africans of upper Nile in the Present day Ethiopia and surroundings.

The Hebrews or Africans who took this route are the people who were never influenced by Babylonians, Canaanites, Assyrians or Persians because these never reached Canaan. The bulk of this people are found in Africa and have kept the law of Moses to the last tenet through oral tradition because then the law was not yet recorded on paper, it was recorded down by Ezra upon the return of the Jews from exile a couple of centuries later and besides the copy that had been recorded by Moses for the Ark was carried along to Canaan at that time.

4.1.4.7   Hebrews Team up to Return to Egypt (Africa).

When the Hebrews were confronted with the warring Amalekites, Canaanites, Philistines, Girgashites, Hittites, Amorites, hunger and thirst and also for the need to be somewhere free from the Egyptians, the Hebrews went deep into Africa (Guruuswa) and West Africa;

'And wherefore hath the Creator brought us unto this land, to fall by the sword, that our wives and our children should be prey? Were it not better for us to return into Egypt?
And they said one to another, let us make a captain, and let us return into Egypt.
And Moses and Aaron fell on their faces before all the assembly of the congregation of the children of Jacob'.

Num 14 vs 3-5

On returning from Babylon much later, Ezra and the Jews that accompanied him did not include in his writing the fact that those Hebrews who teamed up with an aim of returning to Egypt (Africa), did not return indeed to Canaan partly for the reason that Ezra and his generation were many centuries later than the founding generation from Egypt and that information may not have been in the domain of the scribes.

History

4.1.4.8   The Lost Tribes of Israel

The lost tribes of Israel define;

a)   The Exodus Group

During exodus, not everyone reached Canaan. The Hebrews who found conflict and hunger on the way too challenging did not aspire to travel further to see the promised land for some returned to Africa and some truly got lost.

b)   The Fall of Jerusalem Group

The group that included the ten tribes that went to Africa were also considered as the lost tribes and these also included the tribes of Judah and Benjamin that were not taken into captivity in Babylon.

And so when the Babylonian generation returned under the leadership of Ezra, Nehemiah and Zerubbabel to found the Jews, the former tribes did not return and the Babylon generation could not account for them and so were called the lost tribes.

The theory of the 'lost Hebrews' must also have wanted it to appear that the so called lost Hebrews have become unaccounted for forever for the reason that the same sources knew the race of the Hebrews, dark skinned and to then make headlines upon their discovery would invite more questions on the origins of the Jews. For that reason, the matter of the 'lost Hebrews' was rested in the affairs of humankind to cover up for the Jews when in fact it is known that the Bona fide Hebrews of the Books of Moses, the suppliants beyond the rivers of Ethiopia are alive, thriving and still abide by the Hebrew Culture and its associated language a couple of thousand of years later deep in the heart of the African continent. Honestly how would millions of people vanish from this earth without trace, now with forensic laboratories that are unearthing roaches that died several centuries earlier?

4.4.4.9   The Dispersed Beyond the Rivers of Ethiopia

The Hebrew Scriptures explicitly record Hebrew tribes beyond the rivers of Ethiopia;

'For then will I turn to the people a pure language, that they may all call upon the name of the Creator, to serve with one consent.
From beyond the rivers of Ethiopia my suppliants, even the daughter of my dispersed, shall bring mine offering'.

Zephaniah 3 vs 9-10

The land beyond the rivers of Ethiopia is inhabited by Vanhu/Abantu and these are the suppliants, the children of the dispersed who will bring the offerings. The referenced script by Zephaniah provides one of the verses that support the fact that the Bona fide Hebrews of the Books of Moses were dispersed beyond the rivers of Ethiopia, and what became known as the Vanhu/Bantu Migration to northern historians, was part of the dispersion of the Hebrews from Canaan through North Africa and to that effect, the Vanhu/Bantu Migrations did not emanate from Guruuswa.

The people from the land beyond the rivers of Ethiopia will also bring a pure language to the world in the sense that the language that has preserved Hebrew Culture to its purest extent is the original and unadulterated language of the culture and to support that, Chapter 3 Linguistics clearly shows the specifics of Vanhu/Bantu dialects that make them pure in comparison to Jewish Hebrew or Arabi.

4.1.4.10   The Spiritual Wise Counsel from the Land Beyond the Rivers of Ethiopia

Despite the deliberate attempt to twist the scriptures by the Septuagint at the beginning of the quotation

238

History

where they put 'woe (or destruction, catastrophe) unto the land shadowing with wings, which is beyond the rivers of Ethiopia', to distort the message of wise counsel being given to the world from the people from beyond the rivers of Ethiopia;

'Life (or existence, or essence) unto the land shadowing with wings, which is beyond the rivers of Ethiopia:
That sendeth ambassadors by the sea, even in vessels of bulrushes upon the waters, saying, go, you swift messengers, to a nation scattered and peeled, to a people terrible from their beginning hitherto; a nation meted out and trodden down, whose land the rivers have spoiled!
All you inhabitants of the world, and dwellers on the earth, see you, when he lifts up an ensign on the mountains; and when he blows a trumpet, hear you'.

Isa 18 vs 1-3

The referenced prophecy by Isaiah is connected to the earlier prophecy by Zephaniah relating to the people beyond the rivers of Ethiopia. **Hebrew Culture has never at any one point instructed the world to seek counsel from another people who are external to Hebrew Culture for the reason that people who are external to Hebrew Culture will teach the world other cultures that are forbidden in the Hebrew Scriptures. And so when Isaiah teaches of counsel from the people from the land beyond the rivers of Ethiopia the assumption was that those people to give the counsel were the Hebrews.**

With reference to the quoted mistranslation, how can destruction be extended to the people beyond the rivers of Ethiopia, a people who will lift up an ensign on the mountains; and when he blows a trumpet, the world would hear? In that context the world will not hear any trumpet and will not see the ensign because those who are to lift the ensign and blow the trumpet would have been destroyed. The fundamental meaning of scripture is totally lost at every mistranslation in the Hebrew Scriptures by the Septuagint, like Numbers 12 vs 12 relating to the condition of Miriam after she made an unsavoury comment of Zipporah as given in Chapter 5 Hebrew Scriptural Race Evidence.

The translators wanted to downplay the fact of wise counsel emanating from the land beyond the rivers of Ethiopia, the land of the Hebrews, the Africans. They knew as stated earlier what became of the Hebrews when they dispersed from Canaan, and to write things as they were during translation was going to make things more obvious thus exposing the Jews.

It is certain that the Jews have not written anywhere authentically to say that they came to the lands beyond the rivers of Ethiopia, sojourned in those lands, fulfilled prophecy by lifting up the ensign or blowing trumpets and then returned to Canaan. Though there are myths in Judaism about Solomon having built the Great Zimbabwe but the Jews do not take ownership of that theory for the reason that they have nothing with them to vouch that line of their history and the obvious thing that the world is not comfortable to accept is that Vanhu/Abantu are the people of Hebrew Culture.

4.1.4.11   The Link Between Hebrews and Vanhu/Abantu

Amos links the Ethiopians (Africans) and Hebrews as the same people but the same prophet does not link the other people in that neighbourhood like Philistines or Canaanites to the Hebrews;

'Are ye not as children of the Ethiopians unto me, O children of Jacob? saith the Creator. Have not I brought up Jacob out of the land of Egypt? and the Philistines from Caphtor, and the Syrians from Kir'?

Amos 9 vs 7

There is no difference between Vanhu/Abantu and Hebrews, they are all one family with one cultural, historical and geographical origin and Amos did not explicitly group the Egyptians in the same Hebrew domain as he did the Africans (Ethiopians) for the reason that though the Egyptians were dark skinned and totally African, they were in fact a different ethnic group.

History

4.1.4.12   The Hebrew Population and Projected Growth

The population of the Hebrew army by the time of David about 400 years after exodus was one million three hundred thousand men (1,300,000) and at exodus were 600,000 men capable of going to war – age range twenty to forty years. The total population of that time could be computed statistically. Projecting that population to this day, 3000 years later should give a much higher figure that corresponds to the African population, and is a more appropriate modern population of the Hebrews and not the paltry Jewish population of two or so dozen million people around the world compared to the stars of heaven promised to the patriarch Abraham.

4.1.5   The Vast Mwene Mutapa Empire and the Great Zimbabwe Shrine

African Oral Tradition teaches that even the Egyptians were ruled by Mwene Mutapa directly or indirectly and as their custom, they gave him the title Amenhotep, a name or title that corresponds with Mwene Mutapa/ Munhumutapa, the founder of the vast African empire that stretched for thousands of kilometres across Africa, from the Cape in South Africa to Memphis in Egypt up to the great river Euphrates. The language spoken by the people bound by this region supports this historical fact in that the African people including those in Canaan and Arabia today speak dialects directly understandable/ intelligible sometimes without need for an interpreter. African history records that Mwene Mutapa (The emperor of the vast mineral rich empire) built the Great Zimbabwe, which was his spiritual capital under the strict supervision of the priestly tribe - the Rozvi or Levites who naturally would administer the services of the oracle. That position agrees with the African story that the same Mwene Mutapa was King Solomon, known in Vanhu/Bantu dialect as Chiromo which means good orator, negotiator or peace maker who together with his wife, the Queen of Sheba built the Great Zimbabwe shrine.

If Pharaoh of Egypt had more influence in Egypt and Africa than King Solomon, then the Queen of Sheba would not have paid her tributes to King Solomon when the Pharaoh was nearby. This would have made Sheba more vulnerable to the Pharaoh than ever.

The Great Zimbabwe shrine is over 3000 years old, and this agrees well with the ancient Persian and Babylonian artefacts that were excavated at the shrine by the northern historians who took the pieces to the north to their home museums to hide the facts about Africa from Vanhu/Abantu.

African and northern historians have recorded that the Great Zimbabwe shrine was a result of Iron Age technology, which is not correct and is misplaced. The stones that were used to build the shrine were not cut by iron. An analysis of the architecture at the shrines requires not only the knowledge of history to deduce the kind of the technology used more accurately, but also it requires an engineering perspective. The Great Zimbabwe shrine was/is a shrine of very high spirituality where Africans/ Hebrews within the region would communicate to the Creator through a priest (svikiro/dlozi). What is done today at Great Zimbabwe is exactly what the biblical fore bearers did more than three thousand years back - enquiring and thanks giving unto the Creator of heaven and earth and not appeasing spirits of the dead as written by the northern historians.

Northern historians claim that the Great Zimbabwe was undergoing construction by the year 1000 CE when in fact the edifice was already in its decline. The edifice is so old and in the absence of record, not many people understand when the Great Zimbabwe was constructed. Some history sources say that the Great Zimbabwe was built by the Jews, if so, where did they go after the construction and how did they lose the Hebrew Culture, language, race and how did the current inhabitants of the Great Zimbabwe pick Hebrew Culture, language and race? The Great Zimbabwe is in fact centuries older than the Jews.

The Great Zimbabwe

The Great Zimbabwe is the greatest pure stone shrine of high level spirituality in the world. The shrine was constructed along the same lines of Solomon's original Temple of pure stone and not along the remains of the stone and mortar structure built by Herod around 0CE. Up to now it still remains a place

History

where Africans still consult the Creator of Heaven and Earth/Musikavanhu/ Umvelinqangi/ Mudzimu Mukuru/ Unkulunkulu through a priest (svikiro/dlozi) and communicate directly with the Creator as done by Moses or any other Hebrew priest.

The northern historians have deduced the date line relating to the construction of the Great Zimbabwe from a dating system that uses their standards and benchmarks and a lot of assumptions so as to suit their story and moreover, they have also concluded that the Great Zimbabwe was built by the Phoenicians who were also recorded in the Hebrew Scriptures as having built the temple of Solomon in Jerusalem. The Portuguese traders who came across the Great Zimbabwe around the middle of the second millennium Common Era thought that the Oracle had been in existence only for a few centuries earlier because to their scope and within the sphere or extent of their civilization, they did not think that the local people could have performed such a technological feat two to three millennia earlier. The extent of architectural technology exhibited by Africans especially at the Great Zimbabwe and also at Giza pyramids in Egypt among other African technologies was/is beyond modern engineering applications and capabilities. The knowledge of stone work and engineering of mass weight lifting in use today has not come to the extent that existed in Africa more than three thousand years back. Therefore in the process of writing the African history, the African truth embedded in the African Oral Tradition was not important for the northern historians.

In fact, the Great Zimbabwe shrine was constructed around 1000 BCE by King Solomon (Mambo Chiromo known as Shlomoh in Jewish Hebrew the son of Mambo Mudavadi known in Jewish Hebrew as King David) and the Queen of Sheba, Makada. African Oral Tradition and not history recorded by the north supports that assertion fully. Historical excavations made at Great Zimbabwe shrine found pottery of oriental origin of the same period as lived by King Solomon but most of that evidence was stolen by the north. The north reject that the Great Zimbabwe was built 3000 years ago also for the reason that they want to support their propaganda which they have churned out for centuries, that they brought civilization to Africa and accepting the hard facts that three thousand years earlier when the north still used to live in mountains and eating raw flesh unable to at least make a fire, cook or roast food, Africans were designing inspired pure stone and mortarless architectures which have stood the test of time and weather, would without doubt expose them.

The Great Zimbabwe technology was attributed to the Phoenicians by the north in the same way that the xylophone (Marimba) has been attributed to South America even with its clear Vanhu/Bantu name of origin, the assumption being that Vanhu/Abantu are not capable of anything. The staple food in Africa is a thick porridge of ground cereal which was consumed for so many thousands of years and whose preparation is a combination of viscosity and thermodynamic engineering done by largely all women without a reference manual or guide. The summary of northern historian's account of Africa is always to try and time undercut the technology from its actual time of origin to the present day or to always try to dissociate Vanhu/Abantu from ownership of their technologies, culture or even land.

And to the enemies of the Great Zimbabwe, they need to understand that the Great Zimbabwe stood shoulder to shoulder with Babylon and other empires and it still lives and so the contemporary adversaries of the Great Zimbabwe will extinct just like the others before.

It is important to note that during King Solomon's reign, most states paid tribute to him proving his dominance in the domain land of Hebrew Culture. The Hebrew Scriptures record that the Queen of Sheba paid tribute to King Solomon, from Midia or present day Ethiopia/ Eritrea/ Somalia (or the horn of Africa that naturally should have fallen under the control of the Pharaoh of Egypt) including Yemen and the southern parts of Saudi Arabia. This was possible for the reason that it was King Solomon who ruled the entire land of the Scriptures. In that respect, though Solomon was not Egyptian but had influence over the rule of Egypt, the Egyptians referred to him as Amenhotep, which translates to Mwene Mutapa or Munhu Mutapa in African dialects and the same is the founder of the vast state that stretched from the Cape to North East Africa and which had nothing to do with the Jews because then they had not converted to African or Hebrew Culture. Today the Mwene Mutapa Empire is characterized by a number of pure stone shrines that were used by Africans or Hebrews to communicate with the Creator of heaven

History

and earth/ Musikavanhu/ Umvelinqangi/ Mudzimu Mukuru and not El or Elohim of the Jews and Canaanites or Adonis of the Babylonians or Zeus of the Greeks.

The same pure stone shrines found in the Mwene Mutapa Empire were of the same form as King Solomon's pure stone shrine built in Canaan during his reign and not the mortar pasted stone Wailing Wall of the Jews erected by Herod, the Edomite around 0CE. The King who founded the Mwene Mutapa Empire was a dark skinned Hebrew king who naturally also led the services of the shrine together with the priests (masvikiro/amadlozi). The same king Chiromo spoke a language as spoken by most Africans around the same region (Great Zimbabwe and the whole of Africa) today, as shown in Chapter 3 Linguistics.

The name of the country Zimbabwe is founded from the shrine, meaning a house of stone and the entire country is ideally like an African or Hebrew oracle and Zimbabweans are like priestly children and for them to start teaching foreign myths or cultures as done by the European missionaries is terrifying.

Ideally Zimbabwe and other African countries need to keep the culture and are ruled by theocracies in consultation with priests and the angels (mhondoro) of the Creator. Failure to abide by this has seen Africans tailing the entire world. Zimbabwe is a small country, which has very strong influence internationally. Pertinent in the area of international influence is the Land Reform where the leaders of Zimbabwe have taken land from the European settlers and given the land back to the rightful owners. The land issue and the return to African or Hebrew Culture are to set a precedent (as prophesied by Ezekiel about the land between two rivers) in Africa among all the Africans oppressed by the northern army for reason of iniquity in line with Det 28 and Lev 26.

Zimbabwe, the land between the two rivers Vhembe (Limpopo) and Kasambavezi (Zambezi) has at least three places namely Chirorodziva (Chinhoyi Caves), Mount Nyangani and Matonjeni where experiences beyond the ordinary are known to occur, not only by the local populace but even visitors are now aware.

The Zimbabwe Bird

The cherubims referenced herein are mentioned in the Hebrew Scriptures in close proximity to the temple in the same manner as the Great Zimbabwe birds are in relation to the oracle. The stories that revolve around the cherubims and the ark in Jerusalem in the times of David are the same stories that are heard concerning the Great Zimbabwe birds. It is written that when the Philistines had defeated the children of Jacob in battle, they took the ark, but soon they returned it for they could not stand the misfortunes that happened to them because of the ark.

'And thou shalt make two cherubims of gold, of beaten work shalt thou make them, in the two ends of the mercy seat.
And make one cherub on one end, and the other on the other end: even of the mercy seat shall you make the cherubims on the two ends thereof.
And the cherubims shall stretch forth their wings on high, covering the mercy seat with their wings, and their faces shall look one to another; toward the mercy seat shall the faces of the cherubims be'.

Exo 25 vs 18-20

In the history of Zimbabwe, the same happened concerning the Great Zimbabwe birds which were taken to the north by explorers, later one northern power collapsed in the second world war, the birds were then taken by another northern power which also collapsed in the cold war, and the birds were later surrendered back home, as done by the Philistines.

The Great Enclosure in the Great Zimbabwe Oracle

The dimensions of the central shrine in Jerusalem given herein in relation to the population of the

History

Hebrews who had a standing army of more than one and half million soldiers capable of going to war (1,500,000), meant that it was for seasonal pilgrimage services and daily offerings;

'He overlaid also the house, the beams, the posts, and the walls thereof, and the doors thereof, with gold; and graved cherubims on the walls.
And he made the most holy house, the length whereof was according to the breath of the house, twenty cubits, and the breath thereof twenty cubits: and he overlaid it with fine gold, amounting to six hundred talents'.

'And in the most holy house he made two cherubims of image work, and overlaid them with gold'.

2 Chronicles 3 vs 7,8,10

On pilgrimage services, the entire Hebrew population would gather except for some women and men who at that time would be unsuitable for shrine work, for the reasons of the manner of women, and those with newly born children or few men defiled by burying the dead among other reasons. The dimensions of the shrines were not meant to accommodate all the congregation, like the Great Enclosure at the Great Zimbabwe, it was regarded as the holy of holies, a place where the chief priest (svikiro guru/ cohen gadol in Jewish Hebrew) would make offerings for the expiation of sins or enquire of the Creator on behalf of the congregation who would be gathered outside.

Africans are powerful when they fully abide by their culture, they become weak and frail the moment they start calling themselves Dutch, Romans or English.

A close observation of Zimbabwe's history will show that it had one of the bloodiest liberation wars, the reason was that the occupying northern army knew more of the spirituality of Zimbabwe than some of the Zimbabweans, and thus during the war the northern army enquired of the Creator using the African or Hebrew way by forcing an African priest and that is why for example in Zimbabwe the former colonial northern ruler/occupier named his office with an African patriarchal name Mwene Mutapa Building but on each war enquiry, the northern army was told in clear terms that Zimbabwe belonged to the children of the inheritance. The north had wanted Zimbabwe to be one of the selected African territories to be eternal homes for their kindred, lands which were never meant to be freed but this was rejected resoundingly by the Creator (Mudzimu Mukuru wakaramba).

The occupying northern settlers including the missionaries approached the points of African power - the shrines and defiled them by either burying a dead body there or otherwise so as to break the communication channel between the Africans and the Creator of Heaven and earth thus impeding their speed at war.

4.1.6 King Solomon Explorations in Africa

1. The land of Ophir - Aphiri, Sofala,

As stated in Chapter 3 Linguistics, the Hebrew Scriptures were written by Ezra who for reason of exile was then speaking a Hebrew dialect with a more foreign blend. He did not speak original Hebrew and therefore some terms, names of places and the contextual sense of the script he wrote were sometimes unclear and incoherent to his dialect but understandable by Vanhu/Abantu of what he was trying to write.

The exact location of the land of Ophir as recorded in the Hebrew Scriptures is along the lines of Pfura district (Zimbabwe) south of the Zambezi River, where minerals were purified. The land of Ophir tallies also with the Sofala province in Southern East Africa in which Pfura district is part. Early northern explorers observed such peculiarities between the scriptural land of Ophir and Sofala but this was downplayed by the bulk of northern perception on Africa;

243

History

'Then went Solomon to Eziongeber, and to Eloth, at the sea side in the land of Edom.
And Huram sent him by the hands of his servants' ships, and servants that had knowledge of the sea;
and they went with the servants of Solomon to Ophir, and took thence four hundred and fifty talents of
gold, and brought them to king Solomon'.

2 Chr 8 vs 17,18

The referenced directions depict people exiting Canaan at the north end of the Red Sea travelling south towards either the horn of Africa into Ethiopia, Eritrea, Somalia or travelling further down the sea to enter Africa's gold countries of South Africa, Zimbabwe, Congo and Ghana through the eastern lower coast. Chapter 9 of 1 Kings (or 2 Chronicles 8) ends with a description of the land of Ophir where Solomon took gold without war while chapter 10 of 1 Kings (or 2 Chronicles 9) starts with the Queen of Sheba making linkages with Solomon as a result of explorations by King Solomon in the land of Ophir. The two chapters are one continuous story which was split by the Septuagint inconveniently thereby disconnecting Sheba and Ophir which confuses the readers when in fact Solomon and Sheba got to know more of each other because of explorations of his navy into Ophir, the domain of Sheba.

African politicians especially those in Zimbabwe have a problem in supporting this Oral Tradition story for the reason of ignorance. What troubles them is the fact that if they agree to that story, then they are giving away Zimbabwe to the Jews. The Hebrews and Africans are one people. The story of the land of Ophir as described herein becomes more understandable to an African if the issue of linguistics is viewed in the context of communities which speak Vanhu/Bantu dialects around the Great Zimbabwe and Africa in general as detailed in Chapter 3 Linguistics. A pertinent question at this point is, if it were the Caucasian Jews who built the Great Zimbabwe as claimed by Instory, where did all the Jewish builders vanish to without any trace?

2.   **The Mineral Explorations of King Solomon/ Mambo Chiromo/ Melech Shlomoh**

The African Oral Tradition story about the explorations by King Solomon in the land of Ophir in search of gold are supported by the fact that there are mines that are known by Africans to have belonged to King Solomon but have not been regarded as imperial at all because King Solomon was an African King who was collecting tribute from among his people in the land of his sovereign for the purposes of erecting the holy shrine and moreover there is no story relating to wars that King Solomon fought in Africa while mining the gold.

3.   **King Solomon and the Queen of Sheba**

King Solomon and the Queen of Sheba shared substantial classified information on the basis of Hebrew to Hebrew confidentiality;

'And Solomon told her (Queen of Sheba) all her questions: there was not anything hid from the king, which he told her not'.

1 Kings 10 vs 3

When the Queen of Sheba visited Solomon, the king told a fellow Hebrew (the Queen of Sheba) all the secrets of the empire of their forefather Abraham. If the Queen of Sheba was a stranger as recorded by most historians, King Solomon as a wise man would not have confided all secrets of the empire to a stranger. Upon being told of all the secrets of the empire by King Solomon, there is no tale of security breach by the queen for they were one people, with Solomon as the sovereign Hebrew King and the queen as one of the governors of the vast Hebrew/ Mwene Mutapa Empire. And to prove that the discussions and secrets shared by King Solomon and the Queen of Sheba were confidential Hebrew to Hebrew empire material, there is no information that has been recorded in the public domain about what issues they talked about. The Arabs do not have any serious content on the discussions shared between the two subject royalties except for some unsavoury and disrespectful material about the Queen of Sheba for the reasons that the Arabs have no women priests or leaders for lack of respect for their women among themselves. Actually women are considered as low class citizens and in that

History

regard, the Arabs tried to demean the queen in order to discourage their women from rising to the top perhaps.

4.   Menelik

While the relationships between the patriarch Abraham and his wives Sarah, Hagar and Keturah are well recorded in the Hebrew Scriptures, the children begotten and their blessings as well as Ishmael, Isaac, Esau, Jacob and other Hebrews in relation to their wives, but not much information is given in the same writings on the relationship between King Solomon and the Queen of Sheba, no mention is made of their son Menelik and what became of him. The reason was that since there was no argument among northern scholars on the race of the Queen of Sheba and other inhabitants of Africa which was/is dark skin, if the story of Menelik was to be told by the same, readers would expect a coloured race in Ethiopia and surroundings which was home to the Queen of Sheba where Menelik grew up. The same writers would fail to justify the absence of any race save African and that would also undo the earlier untruth that the Hebrew patriarchs were Caucasian.

Menelik was the son of King Solomon and the Queen of Sheba. African Oral Tradition teaches that Menelik opted to travel from Canaan to Ethiopia to his mother. Solomon who wanted him to be his successor had problems with this position by his son. After some consideration Solomon allowed Menelik to go accompanied by a number of princes of the twelve tribes and the priest Azariah. Menelik and his entourage is thought to have carried with them the original Ark of the Covenant and the original copy of the law to Ethiopia; that is why nothing of the ark is heard of after David and Solomon and neither of its presence in Babylon. Menelik being in line with the throne of David is the fore bearer of the late deposed Emperor Haile Selasie (Tafari Makoneni) who happened to be a dark skinned African without a single trace or hint of Caucasian descent. Flowing hair and some trace of pale colour among Ethiopians today was a result of interaction with Banu Arabia much later than King Solomon and the Queen of Sheba.   The Jews in charge of writing the scriptures those days downplayed an outright relationship between dark skinned people as it is clear in all books of history that the Queen of Sheba was African, and linking King Solomon to her in that regard would expose the untruth that King Solomon was of Caucasian descent, when in fact he was a true dark skinned African who related well even to the extent of parenting an African prince (Menelik) with the African Queen of Sheba.

The ark of the Covenant was mishandled by the Ethiopian Hebrews who later preferred to convert to Christianity than keep the culture. A curse has not departed from Ethiopia for that reason, there is hunger, droughts, disease, war and all sorts of tribulations for that fault of the ark and forsaking the covenant. However, for the sanctity of the Creator, the land of Ethiopia did not fall to the uncircumcised imperial north among all the nations of Africa.

Moreover, the majority of Vanhu/Abantu have Hebrew Culture encrypted in their day to day way of life to the extent that a practising African will not require a written reference to the culture because everything they do on a day to day basis is Hebrew. How they manage their families, how they marry their daughters, how they make offerings, how they ask for the rain, how they do agriculture, how they abstain from work on the seventh day (Chisingarimwi) of the week, just about every aspect of their life, yet they never had a copy of the law itself. On another hand, to try and keep the culture of the Hebrews, the Jews read a manual on daily basis - 'Shochen ad marom vekadosh shemo....., An'im z'mirot veshirim e-erog...', every morning, afternoon and evening and it just does not become part of their system for the reason that they are strangers to Hebrew Culture yet for Vanhu/Abantu, all matters of Hebrew Culture and spirituality - songs, festivals, details of an offering and supplications all come from the head, they are not written anywhere but are an intrinsic part of African Culture and no wonder it was not easy for other nations to copy Hebrew Culture detail from Vanhu/Abantu because the culture was not written anywhere. And the objective of missionaries in Africa was to delete Vanhu/Abantu of the Hebrew Culture that they were living without any book because they knew that Hebrews or Africans lose their power when they live outside the culture and are like fish out of water, any nation can overtake them or use them for no reward, or destroy them without a fight as has happened in the past millennium for the Hebrews had forsaken the covenant of their Creator and they have fallen prey to anything in

245

History

want of prey. A touching example on how the Hebrews or Africans are rendered powerless and tactless before their adversaries is what happened during slave trade and later during imperialism that a single northern soldier holding a manual and inefficient gun would hold ransom about a thousand (1,000) able bodied African men capable of going to war without a single one of them opting to disarm the careless soldier who would sometimes sleep and assign his gun to one of the Africans with an instruction to shoot any colleague who encourages insurrection! May the Creator of heaven and earth have mercy on the children of the forefather and pity them and forgive their transgressions of forsaking the covenant. - Tateterera Mukuruwe.

5.   **The Reappearance of Pharaoh after the Reign of King Solomon**

During Solomon's reign, he made explorations deep into Africa into the land of Ophir/Sheba without any hindrances from the Pharaoh. Moreover, the Queen of Sheba could travel up to Jerusalem from Sheba without fear of the Pharaoh for the reason that Egypt was a vassal state to the Hebrew empire but when the reign of Solomon ended, the Pharaoh rose;

'In his days Pharaoh Nechoh king of Egypt went up against the king of Assyria to the river Euphrates: and King Hosiah went against him; and he slew him at Megiddo, when he had seen him'.

2 Kings 23 vs 29

'And Pharaoh Nechoh put him (Jehoahaz) inbands at Riblah in the land of Hamath, that he might not reign in Jerusalem; and put the land to a tribute of an hundred talents of silver, and a talent of gold. And Pharaoh Nechoh made Eliakim the son of Josiah king in the room of Josiah his father, and turned his name to Jehoiakim, and took Jehoahaz away: and he came to Egypt and died there'.

2 Kings 23 vs 33-34

The absence of a substantive Pharaoh was very conspicuous in the reign of King Solomon for the reason that King Solomon had influence from Mandela Island to Euphrates. No wonder when Solomon died Pharaoh rearmed Egypt and started the conquest as described herein that involved killing Hebrew kings and levying a tribute on them, when in fact in the days of King Solomon, states as far as further down into Africa like Sheba and Midian, paid tribute to King Solomon, where was the Pharaoh at that time? The power struggle in the Hebrew family that followed Solomon's death and the subsequent split encouraged the Pharaoh.

6.   **The Great Women of Sheba**

Bathsheba was a fair Ethiopian woman who was wife to Uriah the Hittite who was later taken by King David to wife. Bathsheba (which means daughter of Sheba in Jewish Hebrew) later became the mother of King Solomon. And during his reign, King Solomon married not just a woman of Sheba but the Queen of Sheba, out of which marriage came a son called Menelik who was to become Solomon's heir to the throne of the Hebrews. The Queen of Sheba ruled a land now modern horn of Africa and Central to East Africa west of the Red Sea and on the east of the sea parts of present south of Arabia.

7.   **Why Africans Do Not Call themselves Hebrews**

The term Hebrew is the English transliteration of the terms Abiru, Abira, Vemhiri or Habiru, which mean a resident of the other side of the river or a person who crosses or has crossed a river. The referenced terms originate from Egyptian history where the Egyptians referred to the Hebrews as Abiru, Abira, Vemhiri or Habiru which are all Vanhu/Bantu terms which all mean 'one who has crossed the river or a resident of the other side of the river'. The subject identity was more of an informal name that was used by other people to refer to Vanhu/Abantu of the scriptural culture. The Africans did not refer to themselves as those who have crossed the river or those who reside on the other side of the river because to them it did not make sense, it only made sense from the third person (he/they) referral sense

History

to do so. Vanhu/Abantu called themselves various names that revolved around their totems, regional groupings or simply Vanhu/Abantu. Then the Africans were more united and more closely knit as one family than they are today.

4.1.7   The Vanhu/Bantu Migration—The Hebrew Diaspora

The history of the movement of Africans down the continent as written by some African historians was premised on the theory of evolution. And further to the theory of evolution, African historians claimed that due to geographical constraints on the land that man had inhabited continuously for millions of years, the Africans migrated from West Africa to Eastern Central Africa (Guruuswa) and eventually downwards to Southern Africa. If the horn of Africa was the origin of humankind as theorized by a northern historians as part of the Theory of Evolution, the observation that Vanhu/Abantu began their migration from West Africa leaves a blank on the earlier position on East Africa as the origin of humankind. If their theory of apes to humankind is allowed to stand for argument's sake, why did some people choose to migrate from a rich Africa, with a warm climate into a poor and frozen cold north? If the first humankind had lived in Tanzania millions of years back, why is it that when northern historians make discoveries of remains of dinosaurs, the location of those discoveries are not around Tanzania, but some places in Asia or America? What the northern historians do not say in the same context is how they found themselves in barren, poor and cold lands of the north. However with respect to African movements, there is no evidence on the ground that say indeed there were among other constraints, ecological that could have caused people to begin to move in relation to the problem. All this movement is supposed to have happened a near dozen centuries back, a time when the southern part of Africa had been in proven existence for nearly two dozen centuries earlier by the authentic African Oral Tradition.

In fact, Vanhu/Bantu migration began not in West Africa nor a dozen centuries ago, but started in Canaan about two thousand five hundred years ago and the following movements were the most notable;

1.   The Early Returnees to Egypt at Exodus

En route to Canaan, the Hebrews who left Egypt with Moses found the journey too dry, hungry and full of war and some of these people returned to Egypt and its glories where some chose to be subservient to the Pharaoh and rejoined the Egyptians while the rest of the returnees chose to travel further down into Africa and stay as a separate and independent people.

2.   The Lost Tribes

At exodus from Egypt, not everyone reached Canaan. Some Hebrews failed to find their destination for they got lost along the way and could not proceed to the Canaan that they were not familiar with but traced their way to Africa (Egypt) which they knew about and were confronted with the options similar to the early returnees above.

3.   The Fall of Northern Canaan to Assyria
Out of the total population of the ten tribes that were counted a couple millions about four centuries earlier by David, it is on record that slightly over two dozen thousand people were taken captive to Assyria, the rest shifted downwards to Judah and subsequently to Africa upon fall of Jerusalem to Nebuchadnezzar around 586 BCE. Assyria was situated hundreds of miles north east of Samaria, and when the Assyrians approached Hebrews from that direction, the bulk of the Hebrews found it much easier to escape westwards to Egypt (Africa) through Judah for the reason that there are oceans on the north (Mediterranean), the Red Sea in the south and from the east to north east came the Assyrians. The Assyrians besieged Samaria for three years before overpowering the Hebrews, it meant that during that time the Hebrews were moving en masse to Africa or south to Judah while some were trying to resist;

History

'Then the king of Assyria came up throughout all the land, and went up to Samaria, and besieged it three years.
In the ninth year of Hoshea, the king of Assyria took Samaria, and carried the Hebrews away into Assyria, and placed them in Halah and in Habor by the river of Gozan, and in the cities of the Medes.
For so it was, that the children of Jacob had sinned against their Creator, which had brought them up out the land of Egypt, from under the hand of Pharaoh king of Egypt, and had feared other gods'.

2 Kings 17 vs 5-7

The expeditions of Abraham to Africa, Moses in Midian and Menelik's departure to Ethiopia provided the Hebrews with guidelines and directions to rich Africa. The same land became to the Hebrews a safe haven from predator kings that included Babylon, Assyria, Persia and Pharaoh, and besides Africa was the land promised unto the Africans, the children of the patriarch, and that is why no stranger has claimed the deeds of Africa.

And to prove that when Assyria overran Samaria, the Hebrews dispersed and none was left, is vouched by the following scripture;

'And the king of Assyria brought men from Babylon, and from Cuthah, and from Ava, and from Hamath, and from Sepharvaim, and placed them in the cities of Samaria instead of the children of Jacob: and they possessed Samaria, and dwelt in the cities thereof.
And so it was at the beginning of their dwelling there, that they feared not the Creator: therefore the Creator sent lions (mhondoro) among them, which slew some of them'.

2 Kings 17 vs 24-25

'Then the king of Assyria commanded, saying, carry thither one of the priests (masvikiro/amadlozi) whom ye brought from thence; and let them go and dwell there, and let him teach them the manner of the Creator of the land.
Then one of the priests whom they had carried away from Samaria came and dwelt in Bethel, and taught them how they should fear the Creator'.

2 Kings 17 vs 27-28

And so when there were no Hebrews in Samaria, the strangers found none to instruct them on the rules of the land to the extent that the Creator sent spiritual lions (mhondoro) that slew the strangers whereupon the strangers had to take a few of the priests that they had carried away from Samaria to teach Hebrew Culture to the strangers. And if Samaria was awash with Hebrews, the king of Assyria would not have brought the few of the priests that they had carried away to Assyria which confirms indeed that the Hebrews shifted downwards en masse to Judah and Egypt when Assyria overran Samaria.

Even Prophet Isaiah during his time, castigated Hebrews who were going to Egypt to take counsel or refuge from the Pharaoh in times of distress in Canaan as implication of serious flow to Egypt (Africa) which were the part of Vanhu/Bantu migrations. Then the term Africa was not yet in place and its etymology is quite recent.

Isa 30-31

In the history given above, it is clear that after the Hebrews had left their land, strangers were brought in their stead among which were the Sepharvaim who are today still in Israel and are called the Sephardim who constitute about 20% of the Jewish population. Among also the Jews resident in Israel this day are people known as Samaritans with a slightly variant culture to that of the Jews but they remain Jews in every respect and with similar origins as Jews and are definitely not the original Hebrews of the Books of Moses. These Samaritans were the people Joshua the son of Joseph was quite clear of their non Hebrew origins in his times. Samaria, being the land of the Hebrews given unto them by heaven was holy land, which had to be inhabited by people who had to uphold the spiritual laws governing the land. The strangers did not abide by the rules of the land wherefore spiritual lions (mhondoro) were sent to

History

slaughter them whereupon the King of Assyria instructed the new governor of Samaria to bring from captivity a Hebrew priest (svikiro/dlozi) to Samaria and teach the new inhabitants the ways of the land and this is how the people in Israel today know some selected basics in African or Hebrew Culture.

In 1948 when atheist Zionists and other strangers to the land occupied Israel, they were confronted with hostilities from all angles for the sake of the Hebrew or African inheritance; today they are repeating what the King of Assyria did then. The Jews (strangers and converts in Israel) who have discovered that the land without the presence of the proper Hebrews is inhabitable, are bringing Ethiopian Hebrews, the Yoruba of Nigeria, the Changani of Zimbabwe, the Lemba (vaRemba) of Southern Africa and others to Israel in the same manner as above to sooth the land with the presence of its bona fide people and avert yet more Jewish calamities/tragedies or curses.

4. The Fall of Jerusalem to Babylon

Nebuchadnezzar besieged Judah around 586 BCE and took captive only about four thousand and six hundred Hebrews, and the bulk (millions) escaped into Egypt (Africa);

'In the three and twentieth year of Nebuchadnezzar, Nebutsaradan the captain of the guard carried away captive of the Hebrews seven hundred forty and five persons: all the persons were four thousand and six hundred'.

Jer 52 vs 30

And after the conquest by Nebuchadnezzar, Canaan has been under occupation by strangers until this day. The Bona fide Hebrews migrated to Africa as detailed in the following scripture:

'And as for the people that remained in the land of Judah, whom Nebuchadnezzar king of Babylon had left, even over them he made Gedaliah the son of Ahikam, the son of Shaphan, ruler.
But it came to pass in the seventh month, that Ishmael the son of Nethaniah, the son of Elishama, of the seed royal, came, and ten men with him, and smote Gedaliah, that he died, and the Hebrews and the Chaldees that were with him at Mizpah.
And all the people, both small and great, and the captains of the armies, arose, and came to Egypt (Africa): for they were afraid of the Chaldees'.

2 Kings 25 vs 22,25,26

When Nebuchadnezzar overpowered Judah and ransacked the temple, the Ark of the Covenant was not among the items of his boot or loot. The ark was therefore not carried into exile for it was already off the picture and was a high price artefact which Babylon would have celebrated publicly. When Ezra returned from exile, after having spent quite some time there with two generations who had grown up in exile in Babylonian culture, he lacked the original Hebrew reference record by Moses. The Ezra script then got substantial material from exile; Babylonian, Sumerian and also Canaanite cultures which he had known as he grew up in a Hebrew restricted/censored foreign land where the Jews could not sing a Hebrew song by the rivers of Babylon for the Babylonian habitat was not in favour of the maintenance of the Hebrew Culture.

The siege of Jerusalem by Babylon marked the climax of the movement of the Hebrews into the middle and lower Africa in what was recorded a few centuries ago by the northern historians as the Vanhu/ Bantu Migration. African historians, given the account of the northern historians have not attempted thereafter to assert the accuracy of that story, they did not trace the movement backwards from Egypt and Canaan.

A number of African traditional chiefs, the custodians of African or Hebrew Culture, have it through African Oral Tradition that their fore bearers migrated from Egypt round about the times of the Pharaohs, yet they do not exhibit ancient Egyptian culture but they keep Hebrew Culture to this day. One such African traditional chief among many others is Chief Nyashanu who inhabits the land located in central Zimbabwe today and a knowledgeable leader he is.

249

History

The children of Ishmael (Banu Arabia/ Bantu beArabia/ Vanhu veArabia), who are also Bantu in respect of their origin, language, culture, history and other aspects of Vanhu/Abantu, did not move from Arabia within the same timeline as that of the bulk of Vanhu/Abantu, they only moved much later for Islamisation and slave trade with the Quran and rosary in one hand, and the whip in the other while the slave buyers were holding the bible with holiness overflowing all over the show first at the slave points-of-no-return like Bagamoyo and US Goree Island and later at slave auctions in Arabia and the west and to this day that level of holiness has not changed among the Arabs, it has simply morphed to the work place with enslavement of foreign workers especially from Africa and Asia.

5. **Prophet Jeremiah Part of Vanhu/Bantu Migration to Africa**

After the fall of Jerusalem to Nebuchadnezzar, Johanan the son of Kareah led the major Vanhu/Bantu Migration to Africa with prophet Jeremiah;

'So Johanan the son of Kareah and all the captains of the forces, and all the people, obeyed not the voice of the Creator, to dwell in the land of Judah.'
'Even men, and women, and children, and the king's daughters, and every person that that Nebuzaradan the captain of the guard had left with Gedaliah the son of Ahikam the son of Shaphan, and Jeremiah the prophet, and Baruch the son of Neriah.
So they came into the land of Egypt: for they obeyed not the voice of the Creator: thus came they even to Tahpan-hes'.

Jer 43 vs 4, 6-7

Prophet Jeremiah migrated to Egypt (Africa) with the bulk of the Hebrews where he continued to do his work as a Hebrew prophet to exhort them to abide by the Hebrew Culture, as is being practiced in Africa to this day. As a result of the fact that the Hebrews who came to Africa did not return to Canaan, so Jeremiah also died in Africa, doing his job as a Hebrew prophet among Vanhu/Abantu, his compatriots.

War captives to Babylon were only four thousand people (4600) who went into captivity in Babylon out of a possible population of about six million counted by David at his time which was hundreds of years prior to the fall of Jerusalem to Babylon and the bulk went to Egypt with Prophet Jeremiah and there was no report of Hebrew health or war catastrophe that could have exterminated those millions.

6. **The Return of the Jews**

When Ezra and Nehemiah returned fifty years later from Babylon with the Jews (paternal grand children of Babylon, Persia, Assyria and converts), Vanhu/Abantu did not return, they remained in Africa until this day. These are the ones who have preserved the culture of their fore bearers intact.

Returnees to Canaan from exile were Jews under the leadership of Ezra, Nehemiah and Zerubbabel from Babylon and Persia, but the Bona fide Hebrews that had gone to Egypt (Africa) did not return (Jer 44 vs 14), Vanhu/Abantu stayed in Africa to this day with unadulterated Hebrew Culture for Africa was a peace haven until it was invaded a century ago by the north while the Jews returned with most names and culture of Persian and Babylonian origin. Ezra was the post exile scribe of the law of Moses (Ezra 7 vs 6) because the original copies of the law were at large and could not be traced, which in fact bore closer linguistic, spiritual and cultural resemblance to African Culture and language today and that is how fundamental changes were made to the original script of the Books of Moses

Jewish Return Assisted by Persia and Babylon – Why?

The kings of Cyprus, Persia and Babylon played a very crucial role to facilitate the return of the exiles back to Canaan for the reason that they knew that those children were their descendents, for Hebrew men who went to Babylon or Persia were killed or eunuched and so to these kings, assisting Ezra and Zerubbabel to return was like a latent or hidden take-over of Canaan or extending their empires to include Canaan. If the Hebrews that had gone to Egypt (Africa) had sought to return, both Babylon and Persia would have resisted their return in much the same way as they fought the Bona fide Hebrews in earlier conflicts prior to exile. The zeal with which the Persian and Babylonian kings assisted the Jews especially in the reconstruction of Jerusalem was very mischievous as those Hebrew adversaries especially Babylon and Persia, had fundamental vested interests in the Jews.

7. Foreign Influence on the People of North East Africa – the Middle East

North East Africa, also known as the Middle East has been a land of a diversity of activities. Tracing back to as far as the Sumerians, Acadians, Assyrians, Babylonians, Persians, Greeks, Romans, Turks, British and now Americans, the land has been subject to diverse civilizations. Many foreign wars have been fought on that land and many cultures have been tried on that land. Substantial trade was made on the land between the inhabitants largely consisting of the children of Ishmael and the Jews on one side and different civilizations. Out of that political, social, economic and cultural interactions came influences on;

1. Language Spoken in the land

As explained in Chapter 3 Linguistics, both Jewish Hebrew and Arabi, bear substantial northern and eastern terms that have come out of the civilizations that have been at play in the region. While similarities are without doubt overwhelming between Vanhu/Bantu dialects, Jewish Hebrew and Arabi, the other shared terms between Jewish Hebrew and Arabi terms are remarkably absent in African dialects which were a result of foreign influence. The Jews in Babylon were taught the language of the Babylonians on the instruction of the king, it was compulsory for the exiles to learn of the culture and language of their host.

2. Intermarriages and the New Race

The influence above together with trade between the children of Ishmael and other races caused intermarriages, which resulted in the mixed breed that obtains within the children of Ishmael to this day, but the African or Hebrew features are clearly visible among Banu Arabia especially the males by virtue of the succession of the male gene visa-vis the female gene.

3. Cultural Exchanges and New Culture

The Interaction above also brought in cultural exchanges and reasonable attributes of non-Hebrew Culture that have come up high among which include the treatment of servants or strangers among the children of Ishmael, the matters of resurrection, paradise, the end of the world, inheritance laws, death at war, temporary marriage (male prostitution), the strict understanding of money and profit that saw them sell their kindred (Vanhu/Abantu) to the west like grocery pieces, and the interpretation of death in children in their youth among other issues.

Dan 1.

8. The Apostolic Sects in Africa

These are groups of people who have formed their form of belief system based on African or Hebrew Culture with some traces of Christianity. They all hail from Africa and their founders when analysed in terms of their priestly and prophetic capabilities are without any doubt Hebrews of the tribe of Levi but most of them are not aware of this.

Apostolic sects are Arabic in dress (thobe) and hairstyle (umrah) coupled to an Arabic greeting 'salam alaikum' which is 'Peace unto thee' and 'Rugare kwamuri Mapostori' in Vanhu/Bantu dialect, Christian in religious philosophy and African in terms of culture, a melting pot of schisms. The greetings 'salam alaikum' (Arabic) and 'shalom aleichem' (Jewish) presuppose a war zone where any persons meeting each other had to declare peace else war. Vanhu/Abantu do not have such a greeting for Africa was a peace, and to this day Arabia and Israel are still a war zone and peace is quite some distance to go.

History

4.2 History of the Jews

The people known today as the Jews are not the original Hebrews, the Jews are in fact a result of the following movements, conversions and relationships:

1. **Conversion of the Strangers when Samaria fell to the Assyrians**

   Around 721 BCE, when Samaria fell to the King of Assyria, about two dozen thousand Hebrews were taken into captivity in Assyria while strangers occupied the land;

   'And the king of Assyria brought men from Babylon, and from Cuthah, and from Ava, and from Hamath, and from Sepharvaim, and placed them in cities of Samaria instead of the children of Jacob: and they possessed Samaria, and dwelt in the cities thereof'.

   2 Kings 17 vs 24

   When the Hebrews were displaced from Samaria, the bulk of them went to Judah and some to Africa (Egypt), where Abraham had visited during his time (Gen 13 vs 1), where the Hebrews had lived in Egypt and where the other children of Abraham, through Midian and the Hebrews of Sheba lived.

   Principal among these strangers were the Sepharvaim who now call themselves Sephardim who occupy Israel today and constitute about twenty percent of today's Jewry. When the strangers came, they defiled the land which caused the Creator to send spiritual lions (mhondoro) that mauled them;

   'And so it was at the beginning of their dwelling there, that they feared not the Creator: therefore the Creator sent lions among them, which slew them.
   Wherefore they spoke to the king of Assyria, saying, the nations which thou has removed, and placed in the cities of Samaria, know not the manner of the Creator of the earth: therefore the Creator has sent lions among them, and behold, they slay them, because they know not the manner of the Creator of the earth.
   Then the king of Assyria commanded, saying, carry thither one of the priests whom ye brought from thence; and let them go and dwell there, and let him teach them the manner of the Creator of earth'.
   2 Kings 17 vs 25-27

   Thus slowly the strangers/ non-Hebrews were taught some aspects of Hebrew or African Culture and these are among the people in the land this day. These are some of the overzealous converts who are making more declarations about their 'Jewishness' and 'Hebrewness', more than the Bona fide Hebrews (Africans).

2. **Children Sired by Babylonian Fathers**

   When Judah fell to Nebuchadnezzar around 586 BCE (Nebuchatinetsa - in Vanhu/Bantu dialect which means 'Nebu has troubled us' - for the besiege of Jerusalem and the ransacking of the Holy Temple done by Nebuchadnezzar was beyond the imagination of any Hebrew prophet, king or layman), the bulk of the Hebrews fled to Africa under the leadership of Johanan with Prophet Jeremiah, 2 Kings 25 vs 26, Jer 43 vs 4, 6-7.

   The specialists and artisans were taken into captivity, eunuched and were used to enhance Babylonian technology while Hebrew soldiers were killed. The loot/boot, which consisted of temple expensive utensils less the ark, made by King Solomon and Hebrew women were taken. It is the same Hebrew women who bore children sired by Babylonian fathers. These mothers were very important in the preservation of parts of the Hebrew Culture and

History

language that the Jews enjoy today, for it was the Hebrew mothers who did wonders in the land of captivity. Males who were not killed were eunuched and laboured for the Chaldeans while Hebrew women mothered children for Babylon. The Jews today have honoured those Hebrew mothers by incorporating in the Jewish Culture a change to the genealogy tree, Jewishness comes from the mother and not the father, because it was the mother who carried the Hebrew Culture in exile or it was the mother who had the correct blood of the Hebrew fore bearers and not the Chaldean fathers. Thus when a Jewish man marries a non-Jewish woman, the children born are non-Jewish; the children can only be Jewish if the non-Jewish mother converts to Judaism. The children born out of a Jewish mother and a non-Jewish father are Jewish by default. Such changes by the Rabbis were against the background that the genealogy given in Chapter 1 Hebrew or African Culture, follows the father as in Terah begat Abraham, Abraham begat Isaac, Isaac begat Jacob and not through the mothers as in Sarah begat Rebekah, Rebekah begat Leah. There is no lineage among the mothers for the reason that Rebekah was the granddaughter of Milcah and not Sarah as an example. Thus in making such fundamental changes, the Rabbis were evading clear Hebrew genealogy laws so as to qualify their fathers born out of strangers into the Hebrew inheritance. And as given in Chapter 3 Linguistics, even the names of children born in Babylon (Babel) said it all, one such name was Zerubbabel which, in Vanhu/Abantu dialects mean born in Babel or originating from Babel (Babylon) - ZvoruBabel, which is the fundamental origin of the Jews, their language, culture and general beliefs. The children of Babylonians born to captured Hebrew women (ZvoruBabel is a combination of 'zvarwa - born' and Babel (Babylon) or simply the seed of (Zeru) Babylon (Babel). Further, priestly children of Barzillai and other ordinary people could not be recognized in terms of genealogy, they were polluted in exile just like any other person in exile.

3. **Intermarriages between Hebrews and Persians - The Book of Ester**

In exile in the times of the conquest of the King of Persia, Ester (known as Hadassah in Jewish Hebrew), married the King of Persia Achashverosh in what became an opener to the discouraged intermarriages between Hebrews in exile in Persia and strangers thereof. The book of Ester will give in detail the manner of the discouraged marriages and the Jews today have made Purim a holiday to remember a near catastrophe that almost occurred to the Jews. Such intermarriages between Hebrews and non-Hebrews resulted in cultural and linguistic changes to the culture and language of the Jews today, which are at variance with the majority or mainstream Hebrews in Unhu/Ubuntu continent (Africa).

4. **The Assimilation of the Pre-Hebrew Inhabitants of Canaan**

When Joshua began the conquest of Canaan, one of his first achievements was the assimilation of the Gibeonites into the Hebrew family in Joshua 9. However when the Hebrews fell to Assyria and Babylon such people as Amorites, Perizzites, Hittites, Amalekites and any other inhabitants of Canaan who had been defeated by the Hebrews, were quick and more comfortable to identify with or switch to the new victor as opposed to clinging on to their defeated former victors (Hebrews), these pre-Hebrew inhabitants of Canaan in times of exile did not migrate to Africa, they remained in the land and are invariantly some of the people that are in Israel today. Famous among these are the Philistines (Palestinians); these remained an issue for the Hebrews from the times of Joshua, Saul, David, Solomon and later kings of the Hebrews. The Philistines have remained a distinct people who did not largely assimilate into the Hebrews then or into the Jews today but have nevertheless converted to Islam or Hebrew Culture version of the Arabs which was revived by Muhammad among Vanhu veArabia/ Banu Arabia/ Bantu beArabia.

History

5. **The Conversion of the Khazars (European Strangers) to Judaism**

Around the middle of the eighth century Common Era, the Khazars, or East European people converted to Judaism for political reasons out of the three choices of Christianity, Islam and Judaism. The former two mainly dominated the politics of that time and the King of Khazar preferred Judaism for the reason that he did not want to fall subservient to the former two major powers. Today the descendants of the Khazars call themselves the Ashkenazi. These are the descendants of people who had no idea about the Jewish Hebrew learnt by their children (Jews) later nor the culture itself but have over the years learnt bits and pieces of the culture. The Ashkenazi Jews constitute about eighty percent of the Jews of today. These are pure descendants of the north, there is no bit of Hebrewness in their blood, and they are converts - the blond hair and blue eyed Caucasian Jews. These do not qualify for priesthood, because they are not Levites, they cannot be kings in the land of the Hebrews for the same reason that they are strangers, no wonder the Jews have authored the messianic theses, for they know it is only a pure Hebrew who can rebuild the temple, a pure Hebrew who can offer the sacrifices, thus having authored those messianic theses, they are waiting for his coming, not from among themselves, but from the Bona fide Hebrews - Vanhu/Abantu, though of course they do not tell the world the later specification of the messiah (Ben David - Mwana waMudavadi), but deep in their hearts, they know it for sure.

4.2.1 The First Return of the Jews from Exile

By the time of the fall of Samaria to Assyria, the population of the Hebrews were a couple of millions, and by the time the Hebrews fell to Babylon about one and half centuries later, the population was quite substantial. When the Jews from Babylon returned to Jerusalem about fifty years after the fall of Jerusalem to Nebuchadnezzar, just a few dozen thousands returned. Those that returned marked the beginning of the Jewish people with the origins explained herein. Later Ezra and Nehemiah led more Jews from Babylon; again these were a few thousand returning Jews. The Hebrews that went to Egypt (Africa) never returned to this day.

4.2.2 Anti-Semitism, the Blessings and the Number of the Jews

The blessings of all the nations were given through Abraham and his children;

'And I will make of thee a great nation, and I will bless thee, and make thy name great; and thou shalt be a blessing':

Gen 12 vs 2

The Jews in material terms have done very well like any other descendant of the imperialist north, this they derived from their day to day works, but primary in the acquisition of their wealth has been the use of cheap labour of the Hebrews or Africans and access to African resources. Cheap labour of the Hebrews has built international capitals, it has also made the north generally richer than their counterpart Africans, and the Jews have thus derived part of their wealth through brutality and not by way of the blessings of the Hebrews. The entire population of the Jews is a few dozen millions, and the Africans are numbered in billions, they tally well with the promise made to Abraham in relation to the numbers of his children that they shall be as many as the stars of the sky.

Anti-semitism is quite prevalent in this world today and it is not a blessing at all, the Jews (the world's most hated) must make a thorough reflection on their life to see where the Creator of heaven and earth may be at variance with them in the same token as the Creator may be at variance with the ways of the Africans or Hebrews (the world's most used, despised and impoverished) who have 'become an astonishment, a proverb, and a byword among all nations'. The gardens boys, the farm labourers, the slaves, the tea boys, the housemaids, the caddies at golf tournaments, the general assistants of other nations (including that of the Jews).

History

The Jewish Slave Masters

Slavery saw nearly the entire human race that includes the north, Jews and the Arabs exploiting free labour of the Africans or Hebrews in spectacular agreement with the prophecy of Moses in Det 28 and Lev 26;

'Therefore shalt thou serve thine enemies which the Creator shall send against thee, in hunger, and in thirst, and in nakedness, and in want of all things: and he shall put a yoke of iron upon thy neck, until he have destroyed thee'. Mudzimu Mukuru chirege chinya.

Det 28 vs 48

In the middle of the second millennium common era, all nations assisted by the children of Ishmael, fellow Hebrews, exploited Vanhu/Abantu in slavery and Jews were also beneficiaries of this iniquitous, callous, cruel, vicious, barbaric, savage and inhumane system against the Africans, the Bona fide Hebrews in accordance with the referenced scripture and that does not absolve the perpetrators of that brutality of guilt but that heaven assign evil assignments to the equally evil people.

4.2.3   The Second Return of the Jews - the Search for a Jewish Residence

As a reward for contributions made by Jews to the north in their expansionist barbaric wars, the Jews were issued with the promise of a homeland in Canaan. It is critical to note that Vanhu/Abantu from Abraham to the present day fought or have gone to war only to protect their territorial integrity and to defend their women and children, heritage and rights and they have not fought a single expansionist or barbaric war.

An alternative homeland for the Jews had been suggested before Canaan as Uganda, deep in the middle of Africans. The argument presented was that since Uganda had known descendants of the Hebrews, it was thought to make a perfect home for the Jews who claimed to be the Hebrews. A problem arose on the integration of the two totally different peoples, the friction that might arise across Africa given the fact that the Africans are generally one people of one culture, one race and therefore dropping Jews (of mostly Caucasian origin) in the middle of the Vanhu/Abantu family was for sure going to cause trouble as what happened during imperialism. Canaan then known as Palestine was therefore thought more suitable for a Jewish residence than Uganda. Thus eventually in 1948, Israel was granted independence as a state for the Jews. While it can be acknowledged that the Jews who returned under the leadership of Zerubbabel and later under Ezra and Nehemiah were direct or indirectly descendants of the Hebrews from the maternal side, the Jews that returned to Canaan around the later days towards 1948 CE and much later were not by and large related to the Hebrew fore bearers by genealogy, culture, language nor by any standard whatsoever because plenty of the lobbyists of a Jewish residence were simple atheists, they were children of the Khazars, European vagabonds or wandering wanderers or destitutes in economic stress in search of a homeland. **While that is a known fact about the Jews, they still remain part of the inheritance among them who have chosen to abide by the Hebrew Culture for the law caters for them, Exo 12 vs 48-49,** they should know their position and role in the Hebrew Culture hierarchy.

While the strangers that occupied Samaria upon its fall to Assyria and the Jews that returned from Babylon in the first return of the Jews under the leadership of Ezra, Zerubbabel and Nehemiah lived reasonably well with their neighbours, but the later Jews referenced herein, that came in the second return were totally different in conduct and belief to the earlier Jews. The second group of Jews turned the moral tables upside down, failed to co-exist with the traditional Hebrew neighbours and exerted that level of brutality to the neighbours to give an impression to people who do not know the relationship between the Jews and the Hebrew fore bearers that perhaps the Hebrew patriarchs were a bunch of savages probably worse off than the Jews, when in fact Abraham was like an angel and ancestor to the guiltless Vanhu/Abantu, whereas the Jews are the descendents of the famed Babylon for notoriety which is clearly manifesting in their children in Tel Aviv this day. When the Hebrews fought the Philistines or any other adversaries, women and children of the defeated adversaries were incorporated

History

into the Hebrew family, the Jews do not follow that tradition, they detonate the women and children into bits and pieces like uncivilised and valueless savages with the full blessings of America.

Recent Jewish Movements

After 1948, there have been inflows of Jews to Israel from many parts of the world including Russia and its neighbourhood. The Jews who have come to Israel through these inflows include complete strangers in Hebrew Culture who have brought the complete swine industry and its accessories in the land.

There is talk of genetic tracing of Hebrews and today there is research on Hebrew descent and the reference gene that is being used is the Y-Chromosomes of priests (HaCohanim) when it is known that Jews largely descent from the women or are simply converts from Khazars and trying to link Vanhu/ Abantu with Khazar Y-chromosome is seriously subjective.

4.2.4 Peace in Israel

As it was with the Assyrian conquest of about 721 BCE;

'And so it was at the beginning of their dwelling there, that they feared not the Creator: therefore the Creator sent lions (mhondoro) among them, which slew some of them'.

2 kings 17 vs 25

So shall it always be with the state of Israel each time it is inhabited by strangers who are not of fear heaven kind. The land has its laws that govern anyone who shall endeavour to dwell therein. The laws of the oracle, the Levites, the offerings, treatment of a stranger, the neighbours, sanctity of human life (do not take it anyhow on the land), these are laws which if not performed or performed the wrong way will defile the land and a defiled land will invite heaven to send spiritual lions (mhondoro) to consume the inhabitants. The Jews since 1948 have fought endless battles, but they have not won the war against the Philistines, those that fell to David by way of a sling and stone. Temporary and half peace initiatives can be entered into between strangers and whoever, but for as long as the Bona fide Hebrews, the children of Abraham are not involved, peace shall continue to be quite elusive. The strangers shall continue to lie in wait against each other in battle, if they are not careful they will exterminate each other to the last man, and the Bona fide Hebrews will just walk into their uninhabited land, for the Creator fights for the Hebrews.

An earnest start in the search for peace in Israel would be by changing the name of the country from the Canaanite identity to an original Hebrew name followed by total forfeiture of Canaanite Culture and casting away the spirit of Nebuchatinetsa (Nebuchadnezzar) and associated notoriety and savagery inherent in Judaism and among the Jews, the son of the legend of the Great Zimbabwe, behind the pen, will give the finer details if the children of Babylon (Zerubbabel) want peace in the first place.

Chapter 5   Hebrew Scriptural Race Evidence

5.1   Introduction to Hebrew Scriptural Race Evidence

The Hebrew Scriptures have up to now been manipulated for centuries by the north and the Jews, to portray Caucasian Hebrews and not the true dark skinned Hebrews, who are the African people as at this day.

The Hebrew people starting from the patriarch Abraham to the present day Vanhu/Abantu, have always been dark skinned people. In the biological domain, skin colour that is not dark lacks the dark pigmentation called melanin. Melanin gives human skin the shield, texture and resilience that the skin requires to counter the effects of ultra violet radiation from the sun that normally causes skin cancer and most skin related ailments. In the African context within the African family, the skin condition that lacks melanin is not a new thing. There are children who were born to African mothers and fathers with a skin condition called albinism and whose trials and tribulations with regards to the sensitivity and vulnerability of their skin which lacks melanin are known. The race problem is what happened over centuries and centuries ago when the north played race with the aim of trying to make their skin pigmentation that lacks melanin superior to that of the dark skinned African when in real terms, without necessarily gloating over it, dark skin is in fact the benchmark. Dark skin is more resilient, robust and less prone to any skin condition of the family of cancers and many others. When so much was said by the north of the superiority of the pigmentation of their pale skin which is in the same domain or neighbourhood of albinism they forgot to uplift the condition of albinism to Caucasian status.

The theory that melanin in Vanhu/Abantu (dark skin) is a result of exposure to excess sun radiation and not necessarily an original skin colour from creation is an unproven theory in that no dark skinned people who have lived in the cold northern climates devoid of high solar radiation have mutated to pale skin like Caucasian people, neither have there been any pale skinned people who have lived in African climate for centuries who have turned dark skinned. Some Caucasians who came to Africa through the Cape in South Africa and have lived there continuously for centuries are still the usual pale skinned Caucasians without any figment of dark skin though some of them spent so much time sunbathing but none have turned dark skinned.

It is also known that some animals like monkeys, lions or hippopotami that are naturally born pale skinned (deficient in melanin) have often died of skin cancers in the heat of Africa, but similar animals have done well in Asian cold climates, suggesting that the pale skinned were born from dark skinned animals with a pigmentation disorder but moved to colder climates to survive.

The race issue is like a tale of two people, one owning a broken legged donkey and the other an able bodied healthy donkey. The owner of the broken legged donkey told the able bodied healthy donkey owner the following; 'My donkey is the best donkey, see it cannot move and so it will not pose the risk of straying into the neighbour's field of corn, it will not kick the owner at all and it will not scare the children while they play'. The gullible able bodied healthy donkey owner believed the story and opted to break his donkey's legs notwithstanding the fact that an able bodied donkey is a source of livelihood, transport and not a feeding liability among other benefits, illiterate African women are bleaching their melanin.

African Identity and Self Belief

That is why uninformed Africans will marvel at what they perceive to be the wonders of creation when they behold Caucasian people and at the same time shudder on the sight of their brother, the child of their own mother and father who is with albinism, yet the two, the former and the later have a similar skin condition. The author is trying to demonstrate what foreign brainwash, propaganda, abominations and cultures will do to the African family. These foreign influences will definitely tear down the African family bond by creating pseudo barriers in the family similar to members of same family beginning to identify individually as Anglican, Roman, Dutch among others in accordance with northern religious schism when in truth people who call themselves with such foreign identities are original Vanhu/Abantu with no

European descent, no European passport nor nationality, have never been to Europe, have never owned a square inch of land or property in Europe and do not speak a single European language. From the perspective of Vanhu/Abantu who converted to northern religious schism, it is impossible to have self belief due to identity crisis when an African living deep in an African village, tries to call self a Roman. This is now an opportunity to de-brainwash fellow Africans who, for reasons of racial propaganda, have been made to believe that the race of the north which is usually attached to the colour of their skin is more superior to that of the dark skinned people, the Africans. The de-brainwashing shall be done   without inflicting harm to the fellow Africans with a similar skin condition, but will put them at par with those who have a similar skin condition.

Paying particular reference to the Hebrew Scriptures, readers are advised to make an effort of their own to establish the reaction of people who were temporarily or permanently given/cursed with a skin condition similar to that of pale skin. These include Moses when he was given instructions to confront the Pharaoh, Miriam when she murmured against Moses for marrying Zipporah, Gehazi the assistant of Elisha, when he was cursed and what generally happens to a wholly healed leprous patient. Except for Moses, the others received a skin condition that they could not be comfortable with demonstrating that pale skin, which is also associated with leprosy was not the default skin colour of the people mentioned in this context.

It is against this scriptural background that those with a similar skin condition, the north, have worked tirelessly for centuries from especially the Septuagint Translation, to try and conceal the real race of the Hebrews of the Books of Moses and paint the untrue picture that the Hebrews were of the same skin condition as the north. **Having achieved that, the north would down play all abnormalities associated with their skin condition to the extent that the entire world as it is today would begin to accept the tailing pale skin condition as top of the range. These are the amazing feats of propaganda.** The same have done similar things in science, in every instance that they discovered the power of the dark or black colour, they have downplayed it, typical example is the composition of light spectra. They have declared that the spectra of light is made up of all nice colours except black for the reason that they thought black was as empty as darkness as 'African people' perhaps. Today there are discoveries of black light (spectra), which is more powerful several multiples of white light, now they have to restart and reconcile their racially formulated half theories.

Some northern genetic scientists have classified some Ethiopian African tribes as Caucasian to try and undo the African oneness while trying to evade the hard fact that some dark skinned Ethiopian tribes are direct descendants of Hebrew Kings David and Solomon who the north have declared were Caucasian. It would not have made sense to state that David and Solomon sired dark skinned African children in Ethiopia, without having to qualify the normal dark skinned Ethiopian Africans as Caucasian to suit their story. The Ethiopian tribes in question are there in Ethiopia this day for everyone to see and they are true Africans both from the cultural and race perspectives. What is not there to see are the Hebrew kings David and Solomon, but what is agreed about them is that they sired African dark skinned children in Ethiopia among other places on the continent and what becomes obvious out of those facts is that the two kings were African. Africans living abroad who are in the process of tracing their African origin need to be wary of dubious genetic tests that trace them to Europe so as to confuse them and divide their oneness where a whole dark skinned Hebrew or African (those who exited Africa into slavery from Senegal coast among other points, in the middle of the second millennium CE) is told that he/she originates from the Netherlands. The dubious genetic tests of northern laboratories will declare, 'your father's father's father of the tenth generation was a Dutch and not Senegalese, nor Gambian, nor Angolan, nor Kenyan. Further to that, the same northern genetic scientists have handpicked blood samples of a few African tribes chief among them are the Lemba of Southern Africa. The scientists have compared genetic information of the Lemba to that of the Jews and have found similarities. Picking a tribe out of many African identical tribes is not unusual of the north. The similarities between the Lemba or any other African tribe and the Jews are normal and obvious for the reason that the Jews are part of the Hebrew family as stated in earlier parts of this work. If among the African tribes there are some who claim to be Jews or to have used the bible of Ezra from the beginning of Hebrew movements, that is misrepresentation of facts. Vanhu/Abantu have lived Hebrew Culture taught through African Oral

Tradition from the fore bearers. A written copy of the bible which is exhorting humankind to call upon the name of El and Joshua the son of Joseph only came with the north as one of the gold exploration manuals in the land of the Hebrews. Some African tribes who claim to be Jews are doing so out of poverty. The Jews are dishing out lots of monies to the Hebrews to convert to Judaism and start chanting 'nodeh leloheynu....', 'adonay hu eloheynu', and more Jewish religious songs. **It is amazing irony of this time for a convert with meagre or less appreciation of Hebrew Culture, to convert an original Hebrew to Judaism, which is a bouquet of a few meagrely understood and adulterated Hebrew tenets.**

Prophet Isaiah could never have been more accurate when he prophesied of the Hebrews that an ox was better and far advanced keeper of an instruction of its owner than the Hebrews.

5.2 **Scriptural Race Evidence**

1. **Abraham and the Link with Africa**

In times of famine, Abraham did not travel anywhere else save for Egypt/Africa, for reason of easy identification with the people of the same race namely dark skinned Egyptians, wherein he was referred to simply as a stranger and not as a 'white man' or Caucasian suggesting that the difference between the Egyptians of that time and the Hebrews was language and culture and not the colour of their skin.

Gen 13 vs 1-3.

2. **Abraham Took Hagar for Wife**

Abraham was given Hagar, a dark skinned Egyptian maid of Sarai his first wife for a second wife, and no argument was raised by Abraham along the lines of racial problems arising from inter-race marriages for the reason that Hagar was dark skinned, and the same was Abraham's race. At the time that Abraham took Hagar for wife, marriage did not transcend races which means people used to marry their kindred and there was no tale of Caucasian and dark skinned people coming together to raise a family. **Actually, the coloured or mixed breed of people is quite a recent development for race relations did not go to the extent of intermarriages.**

Originally the children of Ishmael who came out of the referenced marriage were dark skinned as the rest of Africans from mainland Africa. The children of Ishmael later became famous traders who plied their trade in much of Europe, Africa and parts of Asia. As a result of that trade coupled to extensive interaction with the north, the children of Ishmael intermarried with Caucasians to result in the mixed breed that they are today. A close look at Banu Arabia will reveal all the features of an African save for the colour of their skin. As also explained in Chapter 4 History, another influencing force in the way the children of Ishmael have interacted with the north in the manner above was for the reason of political, social and economic activity that took place in the land of the children of Ishmael. North East Africa also known as the Middle East was influenced by entirely all civilizations from Sumerian, Acadian, Babylonian, Persian, Greek, Roman, Turkish, British up to the Americans as at this day. These civilizations have brought diverse influences among the children of Ishmael in their Arabi dialect, history, race and to some crucial aspects, culture especially the Turks where the city of Istanbul has serious artefacts showing cross-cultural linkages between the Arabs and Turks not excluding intermarriages and deeper language integration. Arabs were totally dark skinned but today are quite racist against the dark skinned, the travesty of race relations.

Gen 16

3. **The Birth of Esau and his Peculiarities**

When Esau and Jacob were born, the complexion of Esau was an anomaly from the rest of the family, for over and above his gender, the colour of his skin and body features were mentioned, he was born ruddy and being ruddy (light of skin), Esau was different from other dark skinned Hebrews for it to be noticeable that he was ruddy, he could have had some aspect of albinism.

Hebrew Scriptural Race Evidence

When a child is born, when the message of birth is passed on, it is only the gender of the child and sometimes the method of birth (normal or breach) that is mentioned or transmitted. Other features like the race of the child and features associated with that race are assumed and therefore are not mentioned at all. One cannot pass a message concerning a child born out of a northern couple, of the form; 'Mr. and Mrs. Sinclair have been blessed with a male child of Caucasian race' because they are Caucasian and therefore mentioning the race of their child is unnecessary. It only becomes necessary to mention race when the same couple, per adventure, are blessed with a dark skinned child that resembles perhaps an African. Further to that readers must note that the descriptive term 'ruddy' is one of the most misapplied, misunderstood and manipulated terms in the Hebrew Scriptures.

Gen 25 vs 25

4. Joseph not Different from other Egyptians

Joseph in Egypt as an assistant in the house of Potiphar was referred to as a Hebrew, and no mention of his race was made nor was any other racial feature mentioned during his entire stay and the stay of all the Hebrews in Egypt, implying that their colour (Hebrews and Egyptians) was the same - dark skinned.

Gen 39 vs 14

5. Hebrews and Egyptians indistinguishable

In search of food in Egypt, the ten Hebrew brothers, the sons of Jacob could not recognize Joseph in that with the same dress code and hairstyle as the Egyptians and without any colour difference, Joseph looked just like an Egyptian, who were dark skinned.

The remains of Pharaoh Tutankhamun in Egypt today will tell scholars the race of the original Egyptians. Joseph's brothers thought he was an Egyptian or looked just like Tutankhamun, for there was no distinguishing feature between him and Egyptians. Today there are distinguishable features between dark skinned Vanhu/Abantu and the children of Ishmael. The differences emanated from pre-Islamic extensive travelling of Banu Arabia in pursuit of trade that promoted intermarriages between them and strangers as well as influences on Egyptians from conquests of Greeks and Romans especially between 350 BCE and 500 CE. When Muhammad taught Islam or revived Hebrew Culture, such intermarriages were abolished, which almost deleted the Hebrew or African identity of the children of Ishmael, the African brothers.

African historical artefacts in Egypt that depicted dark skinned Africa and its features were the subject of vandalism especially when the north ransacked Egypt in the initial stages where for example, the Sphinx's undisputable African nose was vandalized but the whole structure still stands today but without its African nose.

Gen 42 vs 8

6. The African Connection with the Hebrews

Earlier in his life, Abraham had been shown in a dream that his children would be slaves in Egypt for 400 years suggesting a latent link between Hebrews and Africa, the land of the Hebrews, (the African connection) and not with the Corinthians nor Galatians among others, for later the entire Hebrew or African populace was brought up/bred in Africa and not in the north.

Gen 46 vs 27, Exo 12 vs 37

7. Hebrews Referred to as Egyptians

When Jacob died, he was brought back for burial in Canaan and the Canaanites referred to the Hebrews as the Egyptians for there was no distinguishing features between the Egyptians and the Hebrews.

Gen 50 verse 11

Hebrew Scriptural Race Evidence

8. The Resilience of the Hebrews or Africans in Egypt

There is no human strength which matches the resilience of Africans or Hebrews and history of the people is well documented to illustrate that resilience.

Hebrew Scriptures records that the more afflicted the children of Jacob were, the more they multiplied and grew as an ethnic group and against the odds. The Hebrew or African people were gifted with fertility and ability to multiply under any circumstances of hunger, poverty or any form of suppression. One would hear of fertility problems from elsewhere but not from Africa. In spite of the AIDS scourge, the population of Africa continues to grow. The circumcision barrier, the traditional African diet and culture will kill off the AIDS scourge and not the retro-viral. The retro-viral will create a frail and defenceless dark skinned person who will soon die off without fail.

In modern times African women in slavery in the sugar plantations of America made wonders, went to the fields of slavery on the last day of pregnancy, toiled in the field until the birth minute, would go to a nearly tree, give birth by themselves, breastfeed immediately after giving birth, put the infant to sleep under the tree and came back to the field of slavery to resume their work and the northern slave masters were shocked, they thought if these people are so strong without arms, what will happen if you give them the same arms of war as the north had, they felt insecure no wonder they have gone nuclear or atomic savagery or barbarism.

Exo 1

9. Moses Indistinguishable from the Children of the Pharaoh

When Pharaoh's daughter picked baby Moses by the river she said *'This is one of the Hebrew's children'*, this deduction she obtained from the odd place the baby was picked in the background of Pharaoh's decree against Hebrew male infant children and not from the race of the child because they were all dark skinned.

Later Moses grew up in the house of the Pharaoh with no suspicion from the Pharaoh himself that Moses could be in fact a Hebrew. The truth only came out after Moses had killed an Egyptian whom he had caught smiting a Hebrew. The puzzle for Pharaoh was; how could an Egyptian kill a fellow Egyptian for the sake of a Hebrew slave. That is how Pharaoh discovered that Moses was not an Egyptian but a Hebrew, and prior to that incident there was no other ground for suspicion.

Exo 2 vs 6,15

10. Moses in Ethiopia was Addressed to as an Egyptian

Moses in Midian was addressed to as an Egyptian and there was no mention of him being a Hebrew. The Midianites who were the descendants of Abraham, were in fact Hebrews, if a Hebrew could be distinguished from an Egyptian, the Midianites would have welcomed Moses as a fellow Hebrew for which he was and not as an Egyptian. Thus the people of Midian, Egypt and Hebrews were all dark skinned. What the Midianites picked from Moses was his speech, which of course had a more Egyptian bias. If Moses was Caucasian, the Midianites would not have referred to him as Egyptian.

Exo 2 vs 19

11. Jethro the Dark Skinned African Priest (Svikiro/Dlozi) - a Descendant of Abraham

There is so much consensus among scholars on the fact that Jethro (Yitiro) the priest of Midian (Moses' father in law) was dark skinned African. The same school does not go a step further to explain how a 'Caucasian' father Abraham would sire dark skinned children. Jethro was a descendant of Midian the son of Abraham to Keturah. Abraham could not have fathered a dark skinned race if he was Caucasian. Midian and Sheba were son and grandson respectively of Abraham through Keturah, the same are the founders of Ethiopia where the great Queen of Sheba descended. Jethro was a Hebrew, so versed in the culture that among other things, he taught Moses the manner of African or Hebrew traditional governance, Jethro made offerings the Hebrew way in front of Moses and other Hebrews and **not only a simple offering but a burn offering;**

'And Jethro, Moses' father in law, took a burnt offering and sacrifices for the Creator: and Aaron came, and all the elders of Jacob, to eat bread with Moses' father in law before the Creator'.

Exo 18 vs 12

Zipporah, Moses' wife, had to circumcise her son when Moses for some reason had kept on dragging the matter, this is testimony to the fact that even the girl child Zipporah daughter of Jethro, the African or Hebrew priest of Midian born and bred in a Hebrew family knew that a boy child had to be circumcised without fail. However the Jews have deliberately and stubbornly portrayed Jethro as a dark skinned African pagan or heathen priest who converted to their 'Judaism' when Moses married his daughter!

The Creator actually appeared to Moses when he was in the heart of the land of the Hebrews, and Jethro played a very pivotal role in transforming Moses from a prince brought up in the court of the Pharaoh to a seasoned Hebrew priest like Jethro himself.

Exo 3 vs 1, Exo 4 vs 24-26, Gen 25 vs 2

12. The Glitter of Aaron's Beard

'Behold, how good and how pleasant it is for brethren to dwell together in unity!
It is like the precious ointment upon the head, that ran down upon the beard, even Aaron's beard: that went down to the skirts of his garments;
As the dew of Hermon, and as the dew that descended upon the mountain of Zion: for there the Creator commanded the blessing, even life for evermore'.

Psalms 133

The goodness and pleasantness of unity is being compared to the glitter and sparkle in both Aaron's hair and beard especially against a dark skinned background upon application of oil whose glitter compares to the dew of mountains Hermon and Zion.

Pertinent to observe in this comparison is the presence of an overwhelming sparkle or glitter when oil is applied to black hair and black beard which compares well with a sparkle or glitter in the mountain dew against the sunshine. Caucasian hair and beard will not give that glitter as implied by the Psalmist, Aaron like any other Hebrew or African was dark skinned, black haired and black bearded.

13. The Effect of Leprosy on Dark Skin

It is incorrect to say leprosy causes changes in the colour of skin from normal to white, but from darker skin to pale skin. If Moses was pale skinned, then the effect of leprosy would not have been clearly demonstrable on him and would not have attracted the sensation that was required to deal with the Pharaoh. In fact, his skin changed from dark to pale due to leprosy. The sense of 'his hand was as leprous as snow' did not imply the colour of snow, but it implied the unevenness, and multiplicity of wounds associated with leprosy, which resembles the physical form of snow and not necessarily the colour. In fact, the danger associated with leprosy, as a disease is not necessarily a colour change from dark skin to pale but the deformation, the wounding effect. The change of the colour of the skin is a secondary after effect which would not have made an impact of making an impression on Pharaoh for what scare would a healed 'pale' looking hand of Moses have done to the Pharaoh. The unevenness of the skin due to the wounding effect of leprosy would have made an impression on the Pharaoh.

Exo 4 vs 6

Hebrew Scriptural Race Evidence

14. A Mixed Multitude Departed Egypt at Exodus

A mixed multitude of Hebrews and Egyptians departed Egypt after the Passover; these people were indistinguishable for the reason that they were all dark skinned.

Exo 12 vs 38

15. Only African Hair Develops into a Nazarite Hair Lock

Naturally African hair is the only hair that develops into the sort of lock that is referenced in the scripture ;

'And all the days of the vow of his (Nazarite) separation, there shall no razor come upon his head: until the days be fulfilled, in which he separates himself unto the Creator, he shall be holy, and shall let the locks of the hair of his head grow.
All the days that he separates himself unto the Creator he shall come at no dead body'.

Num 6 vs 5-6,

Other hairs of other races are sorts of hair that flow or form curls lightly as they grow as opposed to the locks. A lock is a hair development that locks hair into each other as it grows to an extent that the locks once formed, cannot be undone but have to be shaved off while a curl is the slight coiling of flowing hair as it grows which can be undone by a comb. Some Caucasian enthusiasts of the Nazarite hair lock often apply sticky chemicals in the hair to lock the hair but African hair need no chemicals to lock.

Jud 13 vs 5, Jud 16 vs 19

16. Miriam's Comment on Moses' Wife

'And Miriam and Aaron spoke against Moses because of the Ethiopian woman whom he had married: for he had married an Ethiopian woman'.

Num 12 vs 1

The matter of Moses' marriage was that Miriam had expected Moses to marry a woman who hailed from within the near Levite community as is with the Hebrew or African Culture (kuroorerana vematongo). In fact Moses who ran away from the Pharaoh to Ethiopia found himself unable to fulfil that part of the culture, however his wife Zipporah was a Hebrew, a daughter of Jethro the Hebrew priest of Ethiopia, a descendant of Abraham through Midian who was born to Keturah. The issue that Miriam raised with Moses was not of race differences, for the reason that Zipporah, Miriam and Moses were all dark skinned for Hebrews have no other colour. In those early days, there were no cross racial marriages.

17. Racially Biased Septuagint Translation of Hebrew Scriptures

When Miriam murmured against Moses for marrying Zipporah, a Hebrew from Midian, a descendant of Abraham who beget Midian through to Jethro, the Creator punished Miriam by a curse of leprosy and thus Aaron pleaded with heaven through Moses for the restoration of Miriam;

'Let her not be as one dead, of whom the flesh is half consumed when he comes out of his mother's womb'.

Num 12 vs 12

The quoted scripture is not the correct translation of Num 12 vs 12 whose Jewish Hebrew is;

'Al-na t'hi kamet asher b'tseto merehem imo vayeachel chatsi b'sharo'.

Hebrew Scriptural Race Evidence

The script that was written by Ezra did not have vowels and resembled something as shown below:

'Al-n t'h kmt ashr btst mrhm im vyachl chts bshr'.

Readers should note that the vowel 'a' is a consonant in the Jewish Hebrew vowel-less text above. Thus the task of translating Ezra's script into northern languages was not easy for the reason that in the first place, Ezra was born many generations after the Hebrew fore bearers and Moses generation, and his culture and dialect had changed. Ezra's script was limited by remarkable cultural differences between him and the generations of Moses and that of the fore bearers if the vowels had been inserted by that time. The culture of Moses and higher generations was not very familiar to Ezra because he had grown up in a strange land (Babylon where they could not sing an original Hebrew song) with a culture of its own. The matters that were implied by Moses are best understood by Vanhu/Abantu, the Bona fide Hebrews who have not departed from the culture. When the Septuagint translated the vowel-less script, the biggest challenge was to choose the right vowels from the aleph-bet (Jewish Hebrew alphabet), under the background of yet another different culture from that of Ezra which was highly influenced by Babylonian culture, which in turn was different from that of Moses and the Hebrew fore bearers.

Weaknesses of the Septuagint translation

1.   The translation makes reference to the condition of human skin several days after death, a time at which Hebrew or African Culture has no access to the body for the reason that by that time the body would have been buried and would be in the decomposition process, though known to Hebrews or Africans, it is not a subject of reference in day to day lessons or illustrations. Such reference is not synonymous with African or Hebrew Culture because it has no respect for the dead. It is therefore a making of a person without a deep knowledge of the rich and spiritual Hebrew Culture, like the Septuagint.

2.   The subject of the verse is the state of Miriam when the curse of leprosy was upon her. Her flesh is likened to a half-eaten newly born child. Reference is made again in a manner that is not in line with Hebrew Culture. When a child is born, whether the child is born still or alive, it is always in the care of her mother, and therefore the probability of a predator eating the baby is rare, the most probable thing is for the mother to be eaten first and not the baby itself. In other words, the reference of a half-eaten baby is cannibalistic, human eat human, which is not unusual in other cultures. Biologically a newly born child will never look half-eaten, under what circumstances?

Possible translations of Num 12 vs 12

a)   *'No please, she has repented long of her impurity, as she looks like one whose flesh is as half burnt when he comes from his mother's womb'.*
b)   *'No, she is as half-burnt with her impurity, as one whose flesh is as half burnt when he comes from his mother's womb'.*

The earlier mistranslations referenced herein may serve to tell the readers, the race of the people who constituted the Septuagint at the time of translation. They were of Caucasian origin who either did not know that the effect of leprosy on a dark skinned person was akin to a skin complexion of a newly born child of the dark skinned mother or they deliberately twisted the facts to conceal the race of the Hebrews. The complexion of a newly born baby of a dark skinned mother is lighter than that of the mother herself. It is only an African or dark skinned mother that gives birth to an offspring whose complexion is lighter than the mother herself, the child only darkens much later as part of growth. A Caucasian newly born baby has a complexion identical to its mother, and thus this knowledge may not have been obvious to the Septuagint translators. When an adult dark skinned person is half burnt and not half eaten, the outer dermis of the skin peels off, the exposed inner skin resembles a leprous patient and also looks like a newly born child of a dark skinned person or half burnt. Thus the issue of being half-burnt did not make sense to the translators of Caucasian origin, who with a different set of vowels on the vowelless word '*vyachl*' gave half-eaten and not half-burnt. Readers should note that in Jewish Hebrew Aleph-bet (alphabet), the vowel-less consonant word for half-burnt and half-eaten is the same (*vyachl*). It is a matter of knowledge and prudence that causes the translator to choose the right set of vowels to produce the correct Hebrew sense that suits the cultural context. The half-eaten concept that was followed fails Hebrew or African Culture fundamentally.

The plague of leprosy has an effect on the skin, like the effect of half-burning. Leprosy like half burns, deforms the outer skin and sometimes may go slightly deeper than the skin. However the consumption of a body goes beyond the skin surface into the flesh and bones depending on the type of predator. Depending on the type of the eater, sometimes bones can be consumed, that form of consumption bears no comparison at all to the effect of leprosy on the skin of a person and is not in relation to a newly born baby. Miriam thus looked more half-burnt from the effects of leprosy than half-eaten. For as long as the comparison is referencing a newly born child, the question of being half eaten naturally falls off and half burnt becomes the appropriate descriptive phrase.

And so Aaron, Moses, Miriam and other Hebrews were dark skinned like Vanhu/Abantu this day.

18. The Propensity for Imitation

While Hebrew or African Culture is clear on the consequences of imitating other cultures or breaking the cultural taboos among other cultural prohibitions, the same laws are broken often. Northern races are known for their millennium old abominations, these they have lived with them, they have even gone on to teach the vulnerable Africans their northern traditions, culture, customs, abominations, fashion or lunacy and Africans have fallen for it in large numbers. Africans are indeed the people who were given a statute concerning never to imitate anything they see from any nation, but will still do so regardless of severe consequences, for imitation is part and parcel of their gene. There were prohibitions against imitating the Canaanites, the Egyptians and other civilizations, all of which were broken.

Det 7 vs 1-6

19. David Described as Handsome and Light Skinned

David was described as handsome and light skinned ('shaqir' in Arabi dialect and 'tsvukira' in Vanhu/ Bantu dialect). The description of handsome may fit any race, dark skinned or pale skinned, but that of light skinned describes dark skinned people only. Light skinned description to Caucasian or pale skinned people is inapplicable as a majority of the people are pale skinned or light. Those who slightly differ from this general description are in fact tan. More often pale skinned women spend hours in the heat of the sun trying to acquire the right tan, a deviation from pale skin. Most skin care products for Caucasian people aim at giving them the right tan, that is some degree of dark skin, because a majority of them if not all are light skinned or pale and that black/dark skin is beautiful and a blessing of good health - a heavy duty label. On another side due to high levels of brainwash, the dark skinned women/Africans have worked so hard and bought so many skin products to change the colour of their skin from dark to light or even pale, and this has sometimes caused fatal effects to the faces of dark skinned women who got burnt by the effects of chemicals to the extent that they have lost all their beauty all in the search of pale skin whose original and informed owner, on the other hand, is busy trying to do away with.

The lightness of David was relative and the benchmark was dark skin, he was in fact some degrees from absolute dark skin - Mudavadi aiva mukomana mu**tsvuku** (David was light skinned boy). David was also described as ruddy in 1 Sam 16 vs 12, for the same reason that the majority Hebrews were dark skinned and he was lighter.

20. King David's Dancing Ability or Prowess

King David's ability to dance is well recorded in the Hebrew Scriptures. The bodywork that supports such ability suits an African anatomy more than any other. Besides being flexible, the body of an African

Hebrew Scriptural Race Evidence

is highly resilient to any load or form of stress, is heavy duty, full of life and overwhelmingly healthy.

And as mentioned in Chapter 1 African or Hebrew Culture, David danced with might which is typical of most African dances for African dance is spiritual, relaxing and good exercise, there is no single African dance that is soft.

2 Sam 6 vs 14-20.

21. Foot-sole Skin Demarcation of Dark Skinned People

Asahel is described as exceptionally of light in complexion as of foot or as a wild roe. This description is only applicable to dark skinned people as it is only them whose foot sole or foot is lighter in complexion than the entire body which is darker whereas Caucasians have the complexion of their skin the same as that of the foot-sole;

'And there were three sons of Zeruiah there, Joab, and Abishai and Asahel: and Asahel was as light of foot as a wild roe'.

2 Sam 2 vs 18

A roe is an animal of light brown to brown colour and in that context, a Caucasian cannot be described as light but dark or tan as the complexion of a roe in relation to the Caucasian is like sun tanned colour which is darker than the normal pale skinned Caucasian. A dark skinned person with a complexion as that of a roe is considered of light complexion and thus Asahel and all other Hebrews or Africans were/ are dark skinned people. **Light of skin is not a special and applicable descriptor within the Caucasian domain**.

In fact, the other Hebrews had the dark skin complexion comparable to the contemporary Nigerians and South Sudanese and in that domain, Asahel being as light of skin as a wild roe was considered quite light of skin and unlike others and the same applies to David and a few others.

22. The Blackness of King Solomon's Skin Colour

King Solomon confirmed his blackness in terms of skin colour and not in terms of sin. The association of sin or evil with blackness only came much later in the form of racism where paleness and its associated frailness to skin cancer, high sensitivity and lack of resilience has been labelled the superior and appropriate pigmentation and has also been associated with righteousness and peace notwithstanding more weaknesses associated with it. The dark skinned people have never made an issue out of the higher merits of their skin until recently when it became necessary to de-brainwash the dark skinned people as it was realized that those segregated against, were spending too much of their productive time trying to change their skin colour from the ideal dark to otherwise.

Peace, righteousness and evil have no colour. Caucasians are not white but pale skinned. Black skin mentioned in Lamentations as a result of famine is unimaginable to all readers that if Hebrews were Caucasian, surely famine would not blacken their skin. – *'Our skin was black like an oven because of the terrible famine'*. At translation, there was tremendous effort to conceal the race of the Hebrews of the Books of Moses. *Lam 5 vs 10*

SOS 1 verse 5-6

23. Known Descendants of King Solomon and the Queen of Sheba

When King Solomon married the Hebrew Queen of Sheba, Makada (you loved/liked), they bore among other children a son by the name Menelik, a pure dark skinned African who is great ... grand father to Emperor Haile Selasie (Tafari Makoneni) of Ethiopia. The Emperor and his family bear no Caucasian trace in them; they are all African people. The other Ethiopians, who like other Africans are children of Abraham born to Keturah including Midian and Sheba and the children of Isaac, are being relocated to Canaan by the Jews to make the land habitable as was done by the King of Assyria when lions

Hebrew Scriptural Race Evidence

(mhondoro) came from the Creator in Samaria and mauled the strangers in the land.

African Oral Tradition

24. The Dispersed Hebrews Inhabiting Lands Beyond the Rivers of Ethiopia

The Hebrew prophets were spot on and knew that, Africa would be inhabited by Vanhu/Abantu who would keep the entire Hebrew Culture and its associated Vanhu/Bantu language in its near original form (pure language);

'For then will I turn to the people a pure language, that they may all call upon the name of the Creator (Musikavanhu, Mudzimu Mukuru), to serve with one consent.
From beyond the rivers of Ethiopia my suppliants, even the daughter of my dispersed, shall bring mine offering'.

Zephaniah 3 vs 9-10

The history of the African continent from Mandela Island to the river Tigris, has never been wholly inhabited by other races (pre, during and postcolonial era). It is only parts of Canaan that are now inhabited by converts of largely Caucasian origin. The lands beyond the rivers of Ethiopia or rather the land beyond all banks of the rivers of Ethiopia, are all inhabited by the African people, the Bona fide Hebrews of the Books of Moses, the same are the children of the dispersed Hebrews as prophesied herein by Zephaniah and not the Jews.

Until the middle of the second millennium common era, Vanhu/Abantu lived in isolation from the whole world in the serenity of the domain land of Hebrew Culture while practising the full Hebrew Culture and speaking the Vanhu/Bantu dialects, the language of Hebrew Culture. And when the first Europeans settlers (missionaries) came, Africans thought that the settlers were ghosts or spooks (madhunamutuna) while some thought that the European settlers was another human genome with no knees as a result of the trousers that the settlers wore which concealed the knees.

And in that context of isolation, a pure language as written by Zephaniah was spot on that Vanhu/Abantu today speak the language spoken by the Hebrew fore bearers, **to the extent that if the echoes of the sounds made by Abraham, Ishmael, Isaac, Jacob, David and Solomon were to be reproduced, the African tribes will understand them without the need of a translator.**

Hebrew Scriptural Race Evidence

Blank Page

Prophecy

Chapter 6   Prophecy

6.1   Introduction to Prophecy

Prophecy as revealed to the Hebrew prophets had/has the aim of exhorting the Hebrews to abide by their culture that was given unto their fore bearers for an everlasting covenant. By adhering to their culture the Hebrews would be blessed in all that they put their hand in, in agriculture, at war, in the fruit of their bodies and in many other matters of their life. At any one time in the life of the Hebrews, at least one pious man/woman would be inspired to prophesy and lead, inform, advise the Hebrew family on the requirements of keeping the law and the curses that may befall the people in the event of their failure to abide by the culture. Any deviation from the culture to any abominations will bring curses, misery and suffering of all sorts pursuant to Det 28 and Lev 26; that is to say, closely attached to the blessings is a culture or a set of guiding tenets (unhu/ubuntu) to abide by and failure to abide by those tenets would result in the misfortunes as prophesied by Moses as detailed in the referenced scripture and the following verse which emphasized that;

'This book of law (culture or guiding tenets) shall not depart out of thy mouth; but thou shalt meditate therein day and night, that thou mayest observe to do according to all that is written therein: for then thou shalt make thy ways prosperous, and then thou shalt have good success'.

Joshua 1 vs 8

Africans or Hebrews have often failed to abide by these laws (culture) due to among other reasons, foreign influence. Failure to abide by these tenets does not justify the proliferation of other myths external to Hebrew Culture in the land of the Hebrews (Africa) as normally given by the teachers of Christianity. The law was given forever and will remain. If the Hebrews fail to abide, there is no provision necessarily to amend it to cater for their frail hearts, but what would simply be done to them would be like the fate of those that perished in the wilderness, till such a time when there would be born out of their children's children, an obedient generation that would come and live peacefully on earth and enjoy the fruit of the land. Proof of African spiritual failures can be seen on what is happening today, many of the people, in the middle of their iniquities have opted for other cultures and the end result has not been the amelioration of events but the worsening thereof, implying without doubt that Vanhu/Abantu are spiritually lost as a people this day.

This work will show the readers where the Africans have failed on the law and the consequences thereof in relation to what was prophesied about the Hebrews of the Books of Moses. A comparison will be made on what has happened to the Jews and also on what the Jews have done to the Hebrews that shall clearly show the readers who in real terms are the Bona fide Hebrews of the Books of Moses. Readers will find that the Jews are not in a position to fulfil the prophecies of Moses because they are actually part of the world vices in which the Bona fide Hebrews are mercilessly caught in.

6.2   Modern Day Prophecies

It is fact that there are no prophets in Israel today, a land now inhabited by among others the Caucasian converts to the culture of the African or Hebrew fore bearers. Prophets have not arisen from the Jews for the reason that these are not Hebrews by origin but by conversion, all the known prophets have been Hebrews, for it is written in the Hebrew Scriptures as an address to the Hebrews;

'Thy Creator will raise up unto thee a Prophet from the midst of thee, of thy brethren, like unto Me; unto him you shall hearken'.

Det 18 vs 15

The referenced portion of the Hebrew law is not the only one that precludes others to abide by certain tenets. There are laws on priesthood (masvikiro/amadlozi); one has to be of the tribe of Levi (Vaera Mwoyo - VaRozvi - VaLevi) to be a priest. A stubborn non-Levite who will insist on doing the services of

Prophecy

the shrine (Dzimbahwe) will face the fate of Korah and Dathan or Saul. One is literally swallowed by the earth on which he/she stands. The Jews are well informed on that and that is why they cannot rebuild Solomon's shrine unto the Creator. The Hebrew leadership as obtaining in African Culture comes back to the descendants of the Mwene Mutapa, whose founder was King Solomon (Mambo Chiromo) or any other Hebrew deemed fit to lead the Hebrew family by the Creator. These can rule the entire African continent, with the assistance of the chiefs, headsmen in place today and the governance law which was taught to Moses by Jethro (Yitiro) in close liaison and consultation with the priests.

That is why there is no king in Israel, even a less executive one, there is none among the Jews with the direct lineage of Judah or Hebrew in general.

Among Africans were people of great renown and prophets among them who made prophecies that have come to pass and which were identical to already existing Hebrew prophecies yet these African prophets never had set sight on the recorded law of Moses, chief among them were:

6.2.1   **The Prophecy of Chaminuka**

Before the advent of the European settlers in Africa from the north, an African by the name Chaminuka, a true prophet of Musikavanhu/ Umvelinqangi/ Mudzimu Mukuru/ Unkulunkulu, (the Creator of Heaven and Earth) who resided between the great rivers Vhembe (Limpopo) and Kasambavezi (Zambezi), made a revelation to his fellow people that;

'Soon there would come strangers from afar, such as Vanhu/Abantu have never seen before, whose language the Africans will not understand and these strangers would take away the African land, cattle and stock and would make Africans slaves for Africans shall work for them. The same strangers would profane the shrines of the Africans where they communicate with the Creator of heaven and earth. The same strangers would teach Africans foreign abominations (Christianity).'

Chaminuka

The quoted prophecy was made known to Africans before the north arrived in the land between the two rivers. What surprises adherent Africans is the fact that high profile Africans, chiefs and headsmen who have more knowledge of Prophet Chaminuka and his prophecies have in fact become the mouthpieces of foreign religious schisms at the expense of the highly spiritual African or Hebrew Culture, with resultant consequences as outlined in Det 28 and Lev 26.

During his time, Prophet Chaminuka was popular with a bull sanctified to the Creator which he lived with and talked to on daily basis like a personal friend, something not actually recorded in the Hebrew Scriptures in relation to any of the prophets.

The prophecy of prophet Chaminuka is Det 28 vs 48-52 given herein:

'Therefore shalt thou serve thine enemies which the Creator shall send against thee, in hunger, and in thirst, and in nakedness, and in want of all things: and he shall put a yoke of iron upon thy neck, until he have destroyed thee.
The Creator shall bring a nation against thee from far, from the end of the earth, as swift as the eagle flies; a nation whose tongue thou shalt not understand;
A nation of fierce countenance, which shall not regard the person of the old, nor show favour to the young:
And he shall eat the fruit of thy cattle, and the fruit of thy land, until thou be destroyed: which also shall not leave thee either corn, wine, or oil, or the increase of thy kine, or flocks of thy sheep, until he have destroyed thee.
And he shall besiege thee in all thy gates, until thy high and fenced cities come down, wherein thou trustedst, throughout all thy land: and he shall besiege thee in all thy gates throughout all thy land, which thy Creator has given thee'.

Det 28 vs 48-52

Prophecy

6.2.2　　　**The Prophecy of Nehanda**

When indeed the northern army had come and occupied the land pursuant to the prophecy of Chaminuka and Det 28 vs 48-52, a prophetess arose in Africa from the same geographical boundaries between the rivers Vhembe (Limpopo) and Kasambavezi (Zambezi) and declared the following before the noose set up by the enemy to take her life in her quest to liberate the land and the African inheritance that had been taken by the north;

'I depart today and as I lie subdued for now as one that is dead before the enemy, but my bones will rise up and conquer again this land of my inheritance, the inheritance of my fore bearers and the inheritance of my children'.

Nehanda

The prophecy of Nehanda was fulfilled about a hundred years later when Africans reclaimed their sovereignty from the imperial north.

The prophecy of Nehanda is very much related to Ezekiel 37 vs 1-10;

'The hand of the Creator was upon me, and carried me out in the spirit of heaven and set me down in the midst of the valley which was full of bones, And caused me to pass by them round about: and behold, there were very many in the open valley; and, lo, they were very dry.
And the Creator said unto me, son of man, can these bones live? And I answered, O Musikavanhu/ Umvelinqangi/ Mudzimu Mukuru/ Unkulunkulu thou knowest.
And again the Creator said unto me, prophesy upon these bones, and say unto them, O ye dry bones, hear the word of Musikavanhu/ Umvelinqangi/ Mudzimu Mukuru/ Unkulunkulu.
Thus saith the Creator unto these bones; behold, I will cause breath to enter into you, and you shall live:
And I will lay sinews upon you, and will bring up flesh upon you, and cover you with skin, and put breath in you, and you shall live; and you shall know that I am the Creator.
So I prophesied as I was commanded: and as I prophesied, there was a noise (African consciousness movements), and behold a shaking (liberation wars), and the bones came together, bone to his bone (political independence).
And when I beheld, lo, the sinews and the flesh came up upon them, and the skin covered them (economic independence): but there was no breath (African or Hebrew spirituality) in them.
Then said the Creator unto me, prophesy unto the wind, prophesy, son of man, and say to the wind, thus said Musikavanhu/ Umvelinqangi/ Mudzimu Mukuru/ Unkulunkulu; come from the four winds, o breath, and breathe upon these slain, that they may live.
So I prophesied as the Creator commanded me, and the breath came into them, and they lived, and stood up upon their feet, an exceeding great army'.

Eze 37 vs 1-10

Interpretation of the Prophecy

1. **Dry bones in the Valley**

The dry bones in the valley are the oppressed, enslaved and colonised children of the Hebrews fore bearers, the Africans scattered and settled in the land surrounding the rift valley.

2. **A Noise**

A noise symbolises African consciousness about their Africa or their inheritance and rights.

3. **A Shaking**

A shaking symbolises African liberation wars/struggles fought between Vanhu/Abantu and the imperial north to liberate the land.

Prophecy

4. The Coming Together of Bones

The coming together of bones were the liberation (political independence) of the African people from the yoke of imperialism, oppression and slavery by the north.

5. Sinews and Flesh

The free Africans who were blessed by the Creator through their fore bearers were given the richest continent, Africa, but on the onset of Uhuru, they are without the riches (sinews and flesh) for the riches were in the hands of the strangers. The act of giving muscles to the children of Abraham is the restoration of the blessings promised to the patriarch back unto his seed in the form of the land, industry and general economic empowerment.

6. The Final Breath of Life

The final breath to be breathed unto the body with sinews and flesh symbolises the restoration of African or Hebrew spirituality and culture as it was in the beginning with the fore bearers before mythologies such as human sacrifice and incense taught in Christianity of the north, had caused Africans or Hebrews to lose spiritual focus.

6.3 The African Union

The steps above lead to the African Union where the entire continent of Africa, home to the children of Hebrew fore bearers will unite, and given the resources of the vast African continent from the Cape to the Euphrates, the Africans will without doubt, be the champions of the entire world. It is important to note that powers have risen; Sumerian, Acadian, Assyrian, Babylonian, Persian, Greek, Roman, Turkish, British and today it is American. The children of Abraham are yet to rise to become a force of renown. The steps being done by the African people pursuant to the African Union are in the right direction. Africans should not leave out North East Africa in the African Union, which is now known as the Middle East of the children of Ishmael – Banu Arabia. When the African children rise, it will be forever for no nation on this earth will surpass or conquer Africa again. All that Africa needs is to unite, and when that is so, Africans will not even need to fire one pellet to go to the top. The unity, resolve, resilience and robustness, culture and huge resources will put a trillion men capable of going to war standing before Africa, to flight. **The atomic or nuclear arms and other devices of war of barbarism and savagery will fail to detonate on holy ground as happened to the arsenal fired on Chaminuka, which were to no effect.**

The matters of African sub-boundaries like ECOWAS (Economic Community of West African States), SADC (Southern African Development Community), OPEC (Organization of Petroleum Exporting Countries), PTA (Preferential Trade Area), COMESA (Common Market for East and Central Africa), GCC (Gulf Co-operation Council) and others are trivial and divisive. The African people if they unite under the background of such vast resources as the giant African Union with a single currency and no border from the Cape to the Euphrates, the northern currencies will fall spot on and the success pendulum will swing this time in favour of Africa. The north know it in clear terms that their greatest threat of all time is a United Africa from the Cape to the Euphrates with a single currency and one external boundary. That is why today a lot of money is spent on dividing the Africans through a variety of forums or sponsoring civil wars or terrorists.

The Setbacks to the African Union

Some Africans are entering into 'special' exploitation treaties with other nations in favour of those nations especially in oil and other mineral extractions. Cartels of oil processing countries will eventually benefit other nations who buy in super bulk and have made in roads and penetrated the continent and set up large oil extraction companies in the middle of Africa, at the expense of fellow African brothers. Africans wonder among themselves, in what way are other states advancing the welfare of Africa.

Prophecy

Considering that the African continent is a zero import continent, for all what hearts long for is in Africa. It is the only continent that can sustain itself if a science high wall were erected around it. However, due to lack of co-ordination on production quotas of commodities and the assessment of the import and export market off Africa, Africa end up a net importer and the trade deficit and debt for now will continue to grow.

6.4   The Common Wealth

The north should never be the benchmark for African governance, technology, culture, spirituality, business ethics or beauty for Africans have standards that are best suitable for their people. Civilisation, technology, writing, education, spirituality and all other virtues of life began in Africa, with the sophisticated African fore bearers, therefore there will not be a moment when the African lead will be lost should the Africans stick to the culture of their fore bearers as an eternal reference. Africans can drink, get merry, dream, fantasize, but they must not depart from the reference set up between the Creator and their fore bearers - the eternal covenant.

Leaders of Africa need to note that a benchmark for African governance should not translate to abuse of office by the leader and oppress his/her subjects. An African leader should remain nearly faultless in the eyes of his or her subjects though he remains an ordinary mortal, who is like any other citizen, an object of creation.

The African people especially those who were oppressed by the northern queen, should not continue to aspire or to be identified as the former slaves of the northern queen, they should not continue to gloat in the so called 'Common Wealth' for the reason that the wealth of the African children is not common, though the north may have had an opportunity to extract it for centuries, but it remains the exclusive inheritance of Vanhu/Abantu and none else. Any statement to the effect that the African wealth is common to any race is mischievous and is a survival threat to Africa and all generations to come. The wisest thing the African heads that are still in the 'Common Wealth' can do is to break off the chains of neo-oppression, neo-imperialism and neo-slavery and begin to identify themselves as African people and expedite the African Union. Northern imperialism was necessitated by poverty in the north and so when the north lost their imperial conquest, they put measures like the Common Wealth that seek to maintain their strangle hold on Africa by qualifying the wealth as common when it is not but exclusive to Vanhu/Abantu.

6.5   African People Fulfilling Hebrew Prophecies of the Books of Moses

1.   Hebrew Blessings and Victories

The conquest of Canaan by Joshua, Saul, David and Solomon, and the fortunes associated with that time were without doubt the blessings that came along adherence to the law of the Creator. However such prosperity was soon overtaken by sin. When the Hebrew fore bearers deviated from the culture, in place of prosperity came the fall of the Hebrews to Assyria, Babylon, Persia and the north.

Destiny is a non-Hebrew concept. Every human being is born with the possibility of excelling in life or the possibility of living a long and comfortable life and none is predestined to die young, poor, disabled or of low caste but that all calamities that fall humanity are avoidable and depend on goodliness. Goodliness is rewarded with good life and not only necessarily after death, but while people are still alive and evil receives curses.

What causes these curses are iniquities by humankind. A person can be born able bodied with a complete functional anatomy, but when he chooses to steal or rob, he may lose his right hand as punishment or may sustain injuries in the process of theft. A newborn child may be born with disability if the parent was not behaving ideally, a smoking mother may cause disability on the child, a promiscuous parent may catch gender diseases and the children born may inherit the diseases – 'visiting the iniquities of the fathers upon the children'.

273

Prophecy

Humanity are given the freedom to choose between right or wrong, when they choose to be good and obedient, blessings will come, when they choose disobedience, the curses will come.

Det 28 verse 1-14

2. Meat for Fowls of the Air

Over and above the Hebrews of age twenty years and above that fell in the wilderness for the reason of stubbornness and stiff neckedness, large numbers of them have fallen in the later days as a result of slavery, imperialism and from subsequent wars that were waged by the African people to liberate themselves in accordance with;

'And thy carcass shall be meat unto all the fowls of the air, and unto the beasts of the earth and no man shall fray them away'.

Det 28 verse 26

Modern history has overplayed the six million Jewish casualties to the Nazi while nearly saying nothing about hundreds of millions of Hebrews or Africans who have fallen to the cruelties, savagery and barbarism of this world. In recorded or unrecorded events of this world, there have never been any people that have surpassed the casualties of the African people to this world's vices. The casualties incurred by the African people are the grim realities of Moses' prophecy pursuant to the verse in question. Indeed the African people were never buried at all, they never got a proper burial, for the birds of the air literally fed on them or they were swallowed by sharks on their way to the west to slavery when they were thrown in the sea by brutality, as a result of a departure from the spiritual culture.

3. Oppression

The African continent is the richest continent, yet the African people whose inheritance it is are not prosperous. All means of production are in the hands of the strangers and the Bona fide Hebrews over centuries has been the subject of oppression, slavery, racism and imperialism;

'And thou shalt grope at noonday, as the blind gropes in darkness, and thou shalt not prosper in thy ways: and thou shalt be only oppressed and spoiled evermore, and no man shall save thee'.

Det 28 vs 29

A quick reflection on the events of the world people are living in today, will show that the bulk of the underpaid farm workers of the sugar plantations, tobacco farms and other industries of this world are the African people or the dark skinned people mostly of African origin and others. The Africans or Hebrews constitute the bulk of this world's downtrodden. In the homes of the north and west, the Africans or Hebrews are the housemaids, the garden boys, the animal nurses, the horse-cleaners; in the sporting world they are the caddies at golf tournaments, the lawn keepers, the grounds men and the toilet cleaners or the janitors.

4. The Fruit of the Land to be Eaten by a Stranger

The Hebrews dating back to the days of their fore bearers were blessed with livestock, sheep and goats and they also had vast vineyards full of fruit. All these resources have been reduced to not by the designs of imperialism;

'Thine ox shall be slain before thine eyes, and thou shalt not eat thereof: thine ass shall be violently taken away from before thy face, and shall not be restored to thee: thy sheep shall be given unto thine enemies, and thou shalt have none to rescue them'.

'The fruit of thy land, and all thy labours, shall a nation which thou knowest not eat up; and thou shalt be

Prophecy

only oppressed and crushed always'.

Det 28 vs 31,33

Vanhu/Abantu had thousands of animals prior to the advent of European settlers, but were later restricted to few cattle per family on flimsy grounds of 'proper animal husbandry management' when in fact the Africans had vast skills in that respect especially the ability to balance the ecosystem. The excess stock was sold to the north at give away prices, like a clearance sale or were simply taken away.

The fruits of the land lie in the hands of the strangers while the children of the inheritance wallop in abject poverty. Hunger and malnutrition are rampant among the Africans yet every day of their life they produce export quality food and other merchandise to feed other nations back at their homes.

5. **Slavery**

The African children were taken away from their longing parents into slavery, and the Jews were also beneficiaries of slave trade, they were slave masters who used the Bona fide Hebrews of the Books of Moses to work their industries using free labour of the children of Abraham as foretold by Moses;

'Thy sons and thy daughters shall be given unto another people, and thine eyes shall look, and fall with longing for them all the day long; and there shall be no might in thine hand'.
'Thou shalt beget sons and daughters, but thou shalt not enjoy them; for they shall go into captivity'.

Det 28 vs 32,41

Today the former slaves constitute a sizeable dark skinned people in the north and west. They were stolen by force from Africa and sold to the north and west to provide free labour in the sugar, citrus and tobacco plantations of the north and west. Today most of the former slaves have lost the African or Hebrew identity, the language and culture but the dark skin is clearly visible. The African resources and African free labour were used to develop the barren and cold lands of the north. Now the inheritance of the African people is scattered across the face of the entire earth.

The spiritual meaning of slavery was that, when Abraham was chosen from among all nations for reasons of his deeds, piety and righteousness, a covenant was entered into between the Creator and Abraham. The terms and conditions of the covenant were that Abraham and his children and any other willing people would follow a specific code of conduct – the Hebrew Culture, unhu/ubuntu, to guide humankind while the Creator would in turn bless the keepers of the covenant. In the covenant were obligations for Hebrews to keep and get blessed and failure to keep those laws, the Hebrews would be chastised, thus all parties to the covenant were quite informed. Prime in the conditions of the covenant was the need by the Hebrews to keep the laws, to keep them and be obedient and loyal to the Creator and be blessed with abundance in food, shelter, peace in the land and general prosperity among the Hebrews.

In the event of not keeping the requirements of the covenant, the Hebrews would be confronted with the trials and tribulations of hunger, poverty, illness and war from enemies among others. Slavery then came to Hebrews as one of their tribulations in that the people had rejected subservience to the Creator. The Hebrews were to be subjected to a mortal because they had rejected divine guidance and associated blessings. The demeaning episodes of belonging to another mortal, working for another mortal providing free labour was going to be the motivation for the Hebrews to begin to search for divine guidance and associated blessings.

Readers need to note that when the Hebrews were subjected to slavery at the hands of the north and west, it did not imply that the slave master nations were righteous but that the Creator with all the wrath would not punish by all that anger for if that had happened none would have survived. The Hebrews were better punished by other means that would not cause total decimation of their kind. And so if the Hebrews were made to confront humankind in war or any other vice like slavery for example, they stood

Prophecy

a better chance of survival. It follows that if the Creator causes the Hebrews to confront another people as punishment, it is better for the Hebrews and quite lenient and considerate for the Creator to do so because man on man brawl/encounter will not kill all, but if the Creator with all the wrath and anger was to confront the Hebrews each time they transgress, they would be extinct by now, the children of Abraham would be no more, but at the same time, the Creator will not forsake the covenant with Abraham. The appointment of another nation as an adversary against the Hebrews in times of sin as chastisement is an act of Great Mercy and Compassion for if the Creator was to come in full anger against the people, that will be full catastrophe as happened to the people of Sodom and Gomorrah who perished before a fire from heaven.

6. **An Astonishment, a Proverb and a Byword**

Any people today who are hearing that the African people are indeed the Hebrews of the Books of Moses will be shocked, for the African people are a shadow of their former, for they are the same people who in about three thousand years ago, were the originators of civilisation and the owners of technologies and architectures of the complexity of the Great Zimbabwe, the Pyramids and the Shaduf of Egypt, technologies which have overwhelmed the test of time for quality, ingenuity and endurance;

'And thou shalt become an astonishment, a proverb, and a byword among all nations whither the Creator shall lead thee.'

Det 28 vs 37

The same people are today the downtrodden of the entire world. They abandoned the culture of their fore bearers, and the blessings that were associated with the culture vanished with the culture itself. The restoration of the culture among the African people as in the olden days will bring the blessings back, a great incentive indeed.

7. **Toiling for no Yield**

In the absence of the technology lead that Vanhu/Abantu had in the old times, Africa as rich as it is, is not giving sufficient yield for its poverty stricken people;

'Thou shalt carry much seed out into the field, and shalt gather but little in; for the locust shall consume it'.

Det 28 vs 38-42

The African continent, which has very rich soils, is now characterised by droughts, locust attacks and sometimes floods. The results of these weather patterns have seen little yield for the hard working Africans. Restoration of the culture is fundamental to address the issue of food abundance in Africa. The Africans need to approach a priest (Svikiro/Dlozi) and find out the causes of all these misfortunes and make redress.

8. **The Stranger among you will Lead**

The European settlers from the north among other destinations came to Africa, the land of the Hebrews as strangers without anything at all; they had neither skill nor the wherewithal, now they own everything, properties and the means of production. Africans borrow from them, they lead in all material aspect, and Africans are the tails as foretold by Moses;

'The stranger that is within thee shall get up above thee very high; and thou shalt come down very low. He shall lend to thee, and thou shalt not lend to him: he shall be the head, and thou shalt be the tail'.

Det 28 vs 43,44

The biggest banks in Africa and the world-over largely belong to other nations, which have been capitalised from years of exploitation of the inheritance of the African children, mineral exploration, farm produce and free or cheap labour. The north and west are what they are today because of Africa and the Africans. Now when an African or Hebrew wants to venture into business, he does not walk in the same banks and claim a share of his/her inheritance that the north or west extracted over the years from the land of his/her inheritance. The Hebrew or African has for now lost that privilege, these are the costs or misfortunes associated with abandoning the spiritual culture of the fore bearers, the blessings that go with the culture. Instead, the prospective African businessperson will go to the bank and beg for a loan to finance his/her business.

He/she will be required to produce a laborious list of papers including his/her creditworthiness that will be assessed based on rules designed by the now rich strangers and purely on their discretion. He/she has been dispossessed of his wealth and in real terms he/she has no collateral, while collateral is a critical requirement for him/her to access the loan. More often an African after presenting the requisite papers, pursuant to a loan application and having waited for nearly a lifetime, will finally be told 'your loan application has not been successful, next', with the failed papers being flown to his/her face. No convincing reason will be given as to the failure of his/her application. This is a curse that shall live by Africans for as long as they do not return to the covenant of their fore bearers and enquire of the requirements of the Creator. While the Hebrew remain under stress, other nations will continue to dominate, they will continue to lead while the Hebrews continue to tail.

9. **The Yoke is upon the African**

The African people now have nothing for themselves, and for them to get even little food to feed their children, they must work for other nations, for other nations own the means of production. Literally other nations put a yoke on African necks to pull their machinery for the African to earn that little food. Sometimes an African, a head of the family has worked for the northern settlers as a farm labourer for forty years, yet the property he has acquired from those services are a single bed for him and his wife and a few pots for his wife, and nothing more;

'Therefore shalt thou serve thine enemies which the Creator shall send against thee, in hunger, and in thirst, and in nakedness, and in want of all things: and he shall put a yoke of iron upon thy neck, until he have destroyed thee'.

Det 28 vs 48

The African children will not go for an education because an Africa salary is hardly enough to guarantee a descent meal for family; an education becomes a luxury. The children born out of this family will not evade the vicious poverty cycle for generations and that is decisively destruction as quoted.

Mudzimu Mukuru chirege chinya; Tateterera Mukuruwe.

10. **The Coming of the Imperial North to the Land of the Hebrews Foretold**

The following is the prophecy about the coming of the Imperial North to the land of the Hebrews and the loot they inflicted on the continent for centuries;

'The Creator shall bring a nation against thee from afar, from the end of the earth, as swift as the eagle flies; a nation whose tongue thou shalt not understand;
A nation of fierce countenance, which shall not regard the person of the old, nor show favour to the young:

And he shall eat the fruit of thy cattle, and the fruit of thy land, until thou be destroyed: which also shall not leave thee either corn, wine or oil, or the increase of thy kine, or flocks of thy sheep, until he have destroyed thee.

And he shall besiege thee in all thy gates, until thy high and fenced walls come down, wherein thou

Prophecy

trusted, throughout all thy land: and he shall besiege thee in all thy gates throughout all thy land, which thy Creator hath given thee."

Det 28 vs 49-52

The referenced prophecy is not about the Assyrian, Babylonian or Persian conquests, for these besieged Canaan from the East and took away the Hebrews to their lands and in the place of the Hebrews they put in their own people. Africa which is in the south as a reference, the far end of the earth is the north and therefore the European settlers being talked about indeed came from the north, around the time neighbourhood of modern days of aviation, for their speed is likened to '*as swift as the eagle flies*'.

At the time of the advent of the European settlers on Africa, it was clear that the Africans or Hebrew fore bearers had erred on the covenant to allow the Creator to bring an enemy onto the land. If the people had not defaulted on the law, the invading north, by the power of heaven would not have found their way onto the land but would have ended up lost elsewhere, Alaska shores or Siberia or African tropical diseases would not only have killed ninety percent of the settlers but would have transferred the diseases back to the north to kill more than hundred percent of the settlers. The African fore bearers who were invaded by the north did not understand the northern language for African dialects and the northern languages are as different as the people themselves as explained in Chapter 3 Linguistics. With regard to '*A nation of fierce countenance, which shall not regard the person of the old, nor show favour to the young*', the African people do remember how the European settlers would refer without respect or with degrading terms to elderly Africans, 'hini wena lo,' in accordance with northern culture.

Sometimes the European settler would give their pets more dignity than that which they gave to the Africans where they would put certain public notices in their exclusive places such as '**no African allowed except when accompanying a dog**'. It was not just an ordinary dog that an African had to accompany to have access to the exclusive places of the European settlers, but had to be a northern dog. Dogs had higher privileges than Vanhu/Abantu in the eyes of the European settlers in spectacular agreement with the prophecy of Moses.

Mudzimu Mukuru chirege chinya; Tateterera Mukuruwe.

11. Blossoming of Witchcraft among the Hebrews

Witchcraft is unquestionably quite deep rooted among the Africans; men and women literally eat their own children as foretold by Moses. The women and men who do this are indeed so delicate, so presentable that one will not suspect they practice witchcraft;

'*And thou shalt eat the fruit of thine own body, the flesh of thy sons and of thy daughters, which thy Creator has given thee, in the siege, and in the straitness, wherein thy enemies shall distress thee:*
So that the man that is tender among you, and very delicate, his eye shall be evil toward his brother, and toward the wife of his bosom, and toward the remnant of his children, which he shall leave:
So that he will not give to any of them of the flesh of his children whom he shall eat: because he has nothing left him in the siege, and in the straitness, wherewith thine enemies shall distress thee in all thy gates.
The tender and delicate woman among you, who would not adventure to set the sole of her foot upon the ground for delicateness and tenderness, her eye shall be evil toward the husband of her bosom, and toward her son, and toward her daughter.
And toward her young one that comes out from between her feet, and toward her children which she shall bear: for she shall eat them for want of all things secretly in the siege and straitness, wherewith thine enemy shall distress thee in thy gates'.

Det 28 vs 53-57, Lev 26 vs 29

Men and women of Hebrew Culture, for reason of poverty at the hands of imperialism, have developed hate and do plan evil designs against their few successful brothers. Baby dumping is happening among

Prophecy

the Africans with the same proportions as foretold by Moses. It is nowhere else in the world where women throw away their children soon after birth for reason of stress from poverty, it is a heartless act that can only be done by one who was cursed in that respect, for a child is a blessing from the Creator and those blessed must rejoice and not dump the baby. Baby dumping can be likened to a man being blessed with great wealth, but along the way he sins and loses all his wealth and later becomes so poor to the extent of not being able to afford a meal, but has to survive by scavenging, for most women, who dump their babies or abort pregnancies, normally have problems in conception when they want children.

12. Diseases not Written in the Book of Law

Acquired Immune Deficiency Syndrome and Ebola are examples of those diseases foretold by Moses that were not written in the book of the law or were unknown to the Hebrews;

'Moreover the Creator will bring upon thee all the diseases of Egypt, which you were afraid of; and they shall cleave unto thee.
Also every sickness, and every plague, which is not written in the book of this law, them will the Creator bring upon thee, until thou be destroyed.
And you shall be left few in number, whereas you were as the stars of heaven for a multitude; because thou would not obey the **voice** of thy Creator'.

Det 28 vs 60-62, Lev 26 vs 21

The **voice** as the Voice heard at Matonjeni / Mabweadziva.

Some of the diseases ravaging Vanhu/Abantu resemble more of designs by the enemies of the Africans or Hebrews than natural diseases. Indeed these diseases are inflicting a heavy toll among the Hebrews and not necessarily on other races yet promiscuity is more rampant among the north and west than among Vanhu/Abantu. The African people are dying in large numbers to these diseases and indeed their numbers are diminishing as foretold by Moses, but the keepers of African culture will remain, those that are circumcised will get a added immunity benefit, and those that will maintain a Hebrew/African diet in their homes, that abstain from among other things, cholesterol swine, will have a better health.

Mudzimu Mukuru chirege chinya; Tateterera Mukuruwe.

13. The Hebrews to Serve Gods

Today the African people are calling upon the names of Baal (Mwari or Bari), Amen, Elohim (the gods), the late Joshua the son of Joseph and the three Christian deities that form the trinity, which were all unknown to their fore bearers in accordance with following prophecy but the Jews have called upon El and Adonay (Adonis) from the beginning derived from their Canaanite and Babylonian fore bearers and have not deviated;

'And the Creator shall scatter thee among all people, from one end of the earth unto the other; and there thou shalt serve other gods, which neither thou nor thy fathers have known, even wood and stone'.

Det 28 vs 64

The African fore bearers have known Musikavanhu/ Umvelinqangi/ Unkulunkulu/ Mudzimu Mukuru (the Creator) and have called so. Such designations as Mwari or Bari were not known to them, a priest (svikiro) who enquire of the Creator on behalf of the people will acknowledge that Baal (Mwari) is not the terminology used in matters of spirituality. The designation Mwari normally comes in trivial matters, trivial talk or when a Hebrew makes a false oath or to confirm a lie as in 'O ndinopika naMwari O', meaning its quite easy to take the name of Baal in vain and not Mudzimu Mukuru.

Each and every prayer made today now conclude with the name of Amen, as a seal to confirm deliberately or in ignorance that the prayer is for Amen, the ancient Egyptian State deity. The conclusion or seal of a prayer with Amen is a salutation made by a blessing seeker to Amen to give a response. Africans are declaring today in the name of the 'father, son and holy spirit', matters that were never taught in the African or Hebrew spiritual realm. The Creator, Musikavanhu/ Umvelinqangi/ Unkulunkulu/ Mudzimu Mukuru is never known to have a son, nor to work with a helper nor is the actual form of the Creator known among Vanhu/Abantu. These are descriptive matters pertaining the Creator that have not been revealed to humanity, yet the north posture in public, telling myths such as the existence of the trinity to the Creator. Yes the trinity may exist when pagan deities are mentioned, but not when the Creator of heaven and earth is mentioned. The Oneness of the Creator is unquestionably without doubt. The partitioning of that Oneness into three by the north is testimony to their insatiable search for multiple deities as generally taught in cultures external to Hebrew or African Culture.

14. The Fear of the North or West

As explained in Chapter 5 Scriptural Race Evidence, the dark skinned people are anatomically more robust, resilient and enduring than the other races. They can withstand harsh conditions of hard labour or tough battle. During slave trade, they were packed like logs in ships, which were bound to the west among other destinations, but a great number did not die, most of those who died were finished off upon sustaining injuries of ill treatment along the way. Thus Africans being such strong people, are capable of handling hard battles and winning them, however during that time thousands of Africans were frog matched by a single northern soldier wielding a non-automatic riffle, with no African revolting at all. When the northern soldier would want to sleep, he would give the gun to one of the Africans with an instruction to shoot any riotous African colleague. Today a youngster, child to a northern farmer resident on the land of Africans, will put a thousand African men to flight on the farm in fright. If a group of chatting Africans today are approached by even a harmless northerner, they remain submissively quiet till he has passed by in agreement with the following prophecy;

'And among these nations shalt thou find no ease, neither shall the sole of thy foot rest: but the Creator shall give thee there a trembling heart, and failing of eyes and sorrow of mind:
And thy life shall hang in doubt before thee; and thou shalt fear day and night, and shalt have none assurance of thy life'.

Det 28 vs 65-66, Lev 26 vs 36-39

Africans or Hebrews, were given a trembling heart for their sins. The trembling heart comes ironically under the following background in the event of abiding by the culture;

'And you shall chase your enemies, and they shall fall before you by the sword.
And five of you shall chase an hundred, and an hundred of you shall put ten thousand to flight: and your enemies shall fall before you by the sword'.

Lev 26 vs 7-8

But today when Africans are living outside their culture, they are now like fish out of water and anyone can catch and eat.

15. The Desecration of African Shrines

When the north came to the land of the Hebrews, they penetrated the Hebrew people and learnt that desecration of African shrines would break the communication link between the Hebrews and the Creator and so they desecrated or defiled the shrines or spiritual connection points or gateways;

'And I will make your cities waste, and bring your sanctuaries unto desolation, and I will not smell the savour of your sweet odours.
And I will bring the land into desolation: and your enemies, which dwell therein, shall be astonished at it'.

Lev 26 vs 31,32

Prophecy

The north literally took their women during the time of their manner for a swim in pools that were located at African holy shrines thus defiling them. The north brought northern soaps (detergents) and perfumes made out of swine and related unclean products and sprayed themselves and walked through African shrines thus defiling them. The north have buried their dead in Hebrew shrines, and the voice of the Creator that normally would answer some of the African problems at such sites upon enquiry has disappeared.

To make matters worse, the breed of African leaders that emerged at Uhuru/ independence were an inconsequential brainwashed bunch like one from the Great Zimbabwe who prides in being a Roman Jesuit instead of rallying his flock to the Hebrew shrines in liaison with masvikiro/amadlozi to revive Hebrew Culture and often flies to the Vatican to kneel before a celibate priest of another competing system or civilization.

And what is fundamentally missing in Africa is true African or Hebrew leadership to steer the African flock from poverty, dilapidation, deleted identity and spirituality to re-establish the lead that the fore bearers had when the north were lagging in the Caucasus mountains while eating uncooked rodents or dogs (hot dogs).

6.6 African or Hebrew Salvation

There are volumes of literature and teachings on salvation that have been made to the African people by the north based on human sacrifice and human blood but the requirements of an African or Hebrew to get salvation is in accordance with the referenced scripture, to return to the covenant, the laws of the knowledge of good and bad **kuti Mudzimu Mukuru unozorangarira sungano yeMadzitateguru**, (then the Creator will remember the covenant made with the African or Hebrew fore bearers);

'If they shall confess their iniquity, and the iniquity of their fathers, with their trespass which they trespassed against Me, and that also they have walked contrary unto Me;
And that I also have walked contrary to them, and have brought them into the land of their enemies; if then their uncircumcised hearts be humbled, and they then accept of the punishment of their iniquity:
Then will I remember my covenant with Jacob, and also my covenant with Isaac, and also my covenant with Abraham will I remember; and I will remember the land'.

Lev 26 vs 40-46, 2 Chr 7 vs 14

Thus the theories of salvation based on the mythologies of other cultures will not solve the problems that Africans confront this day. Such theories external to Hebrew Culture will only help the Hebrews to sink deeper and deeper into oblivion. The 'Salvation Army' consisting of clergies from the north and west preaching the spirituality of the trinity, human sacrifice and expiation of sins by use of human blood will not advance the welfare of the people of the Books of Moses nor bring salvation.

The application and use of human blood and human sacrifice is the fundamental etiquette and sustenance of Christianity, witchcraft, sorcery, life of goblins and the general underworld and will not harmonize humankind and their Creator for it is an abomination that will invite the full anger/wrath of the Awesome Creator.

Prophecy

Blank Page

Index

Ab	89, 162, 174	animism	105
Abarahama	184, 213	anointing oil	117, 136
Abida	220	Anzari	220
Abrahamsburg	188	apartheid	44
Abrahamson	188, 189	apartheid laws	102
Abrahimovic	189	Aphiri	243
Abu Bakr	220	Apollo	81, 94, 188
Abu Dhabi	221	apotera avanda	150
Abu Huraira	220	arms of barbarism	2, 4, 28, 107
Abu Shia	19	Ashanti	17
Abu Sunni	19	Ashari	220
Abwa	220	Ashasha	220
Acadian(s)	32, 251, 259, 272, 278	Ashiri	220
Acholi	17, 27	Ashkenazi	254
Achor	194, 216, 217	Assyria	5, 16, 32, 42, 43, 168
Adar	89, 162		186, 187, 212, 236,
Adi	220		246, 247, 248, 249,
Adja	18		250, 251, 252, 254,
Adnan	220		255, 256, 266, 273
Adonay	80, 160, 177, 178, 279	Assyrians	84, 159, 167, 170, 186
Adonis	177, 242, 279		187, 219, 235, 237,
Adonizedek	188		252, 272
adultery curse	74	Atiya	220
adultery detection	74	Auzai	220
Afara	18	avenging spirit	12, 15, 27, 51, 67, 68
Afghanistan	172, 180		71, 91, 95, 96, 130,
African American	6, 134		152
African Anthem	12	Avraham	184
Afro-Asiatic	6	Awana	220
African Union	3, 18, 19, 32, 272, 273	Ayar	89, 162
African Unity	185	Aziba	220
Aghaniya	220	Azizi	220
Ahmed	220	baal/bari	155, 156, 279
Aisave	66, 189, 193	babamudiki	32, 137
Akan	18	Babarehama	184
Alaska	278	Babylonian	32, 83, 84, 89, 160,
albinism	257, 259		162, 168, 170, 177,
aleynu leshabeach	176		186, 187, 235, 237,
Amen	154, 155, 174, 279, 280		240, 242, 249, 251,
Amenhotep	107, 240, 241		252, 253, 272, 278
Amen-Ra	81, 155	Bagamoyo	231, 250
America	256, 261	Bahira	220
American	32, 251, 259, 272	Bairuha	220
Amhara	17	Bajaila	220
Amiri	220	Bajali	220
Anamongo	18	Bakali	220
ancestors	12, 13, 14, 15, 63, 64	Bakira	184
ancestral spirit	12	Bakiri	184
angelic entity	42	Bakr	184, 220
angelic guidance	86	Balanda	18
angelic sounds	92	ballet dancing	153
Anglican	6, 99, 257	Bambara	18
Anglicanism	1, 87	Banani	220
Angola(n)	36, 234, 258	Banda	18

Index

Bantu Migration	5, 247, 248, 249, 250
Bantustan	102
baptism	65, 66
Bapunu	18
Bara	220
barbaric technology	31, 46
Bariba	18
barika	39
Barira	220
Barzillai	194, 196, 197, 218, 253
Basara	184, 220
basa rasekuru	137
basa revakuru	97
Bashiri	220
Basoga	18
Basra	184
Bateke	18
Batsirai	194, 196, 197, 218, 253
Baya	18
Belgium	17, 20
Bemba	17
Ben David	175, 176, 254
bereavement	78
Bereshit	160
Beta	122
big bang	9
biogenetics	28, 45
Bioko	18
biological arms of war	4, 187, 193
bio-modified food	31, 84, 107, 108
biotechnology	31
Bira	10, 15, 82, 124, 135, 174 210, 231
Bire	87
birth right	65
bitter water test	74
blackmail	3
black market	3
Black Monday	3
black sheep	3
blood group A, B, O	3
blood money	27
Blue Nile	16
bney nachal	107
Bney Yisrael	3, 5, 183, 184, 185
Bobo	18
Boer	18
Botswana	18, 33
brass serpent	140
breast cancer	40
Brent	17
bride price	55, 60, 169
Britain	185
Briton	65

British	32, 190, 251, 259, 272
Bubi	18
Buddha	94
Buddhism	94
Buhaina	220
Bukair	220
Bukhari	220
Bulala	18
bulala muthakathi	101
Bunani	220
Buwaira	220
Buwairi	220
Buzakha	220
bwana bwenhaka	107
Caesarean Section	79
Cameroon	18
Canaanite University	92
Cape	19, 30, 39, 65, 234 240, 241, 257, 272
Caribbean Islands	138
Caspian	19, 30, 65
casting lots	130, 165
Catholic	99, 117
Catholicism	1, 24, 87
celibacy	116
census	115
Chaga	17
Chaminuka	64, 104, 270, 271, 272
Changani	17, 249
Channah	194, 198, 217
Chanukah	179, 198
Chavilah	16
Chavira	16, 234
cheka ukama	137
chembere mukadzi	116
chemical arms of war	4, 187, 193
Chernobyl Nuclear Stn	108
cherubim	111, 112, 242, 243
Chevra Kadisha	166
Chewa	17
chibako	120, 125
Chidon	186, 217
chief priest	92, 115, 175, 195, 243
Chief Rabbi	37, 136, 168
chigero	137, 200
chikanganwa hama	114
chikuva	32
chimandamanda	47, 53, 54
chimbadzo	103
Chimurenga War	153
chimutsa mapfiwa	75
Chinese	187
Chinhoyi Curves	242
chiratidzo choumhandara	53, 54

Index

chirikadzi	102	Dubai	221
Chiromo, Mambo	106, 107, 147, 184, 189, 193, 196, 236, 240, 241, 242, 244, 270	Dutch	1, 6, 48, 85, 91, 96, 98 99, 154, 190, 209, 243 257, 258
Chirorodziva	29, 49, 125, 242	Dzimbahwe Guru	106
chishava	47, 53	dzinza	64
Chisingarimwi	21, 22, 105, 106, 110, 143, 175, 245	Ebola	279
		ECOWAS	18, 272
chisionekwe	136, 137	eden	16, 30
chisvo	137	egyptology	51
chitsidzo	48	El	11, 12, 66, 67, 80, 81 159, 160, 177, 188, 189, 192, 211, 212, 242, 279
Christmas Day	175		
circumcision	5, 41, 42		
Cleopatra	88		
cohen gadol	202, 243	El Elyon	80, 160
Colossia	2	Elohim	12, 80, 81, 160, 161, 188, 242, 279
Colossians	235		
Colossus	94	El Shadai	80, 160
COMESA	18, 272	Elul	89, 162
Common Wealth	273	Embu	18
Congo	3, 16, 17, 19, 31, 234 244	Ephesians	235
		Eritrea	241
Congolese	18, 19	Ester	89, 174, 253
Congo-Niger	6, 185, 233	Ethanim	89
Congo River	16, 234	Ethiopia	2, 5, 16, 18, 90, 104, 128, 234, 235, 236, 237, 238, 239, 241, 245, 246, 248, 258, 262, 263, 266
Corinth	2, 235, 236		
Corinthians	235, 260		
courtship	54, 55		
crude oil friendship	32, 100		
cultural dynamism	143	Ethiopian	258, 263
Cupid	94	Ethiopic	6, 185
D-Day	3	Euphrates	3, 16, 39, 234, 240, 246, 272
Dagomba	18		
dare	157	European Union	18
Darfur	19	Ewe	18
Davisburg	188	familiar spirit	13, 82, 113, 134, 135, 139
Davison	188, 189		
Davingic	189	Farai Cooper	64
Day of Atonement	102, 136, 195, 202, 210	Farsi	179, 180
Deborah	81, 88	fear of heaven	46
demon casting	130	first born	38
Deutche	185	Francais	185
devil	118, 156	France	17, 185
Dhakwani	220	French	18, 186, 187, 190, 209
Dhari	220	Fukushima	108
dhiyabhorosi	118	Fulani	18
Dinka	18	Funi	18
dinosaur	9	Gabriel	43, 86, 159, 177, 212
Distress Call	141, 142	Galatia	2, 236
Doha	221	Galatians	235, 260
dominus vobiscum	113, 155	Gambian	258
D. R. Congo	17, 30	Ganyire	87
Drakensberg	30	Garaginya	6, 18
Duba	220	Gata	101

Index

GCC	18, 272	Haagari	193, 196
Gehazi	45, 129, 258	Habiba	220
gender conversion	4, 107, 187	HaBore	12, 118, 160, 188
genealogy	64, 170	HaCnaani	12, 55, 174
gentile	84, 163	Hadassah	89, 174, 253
German	186, 187, 209	Haida	220
Germany	17, 185	Haile Selasie, Emperor	104, 245, 266
Ghaba	220	Haiya	220
Ghana	16, 154, 234, 244,	Hajj	49
Ghanawi	220	Hakam	220
Ghazi	220, 223	halal	123
Ghazwa	220	Hamitic	6
Ghifar	220	Hamna	220
ghost	267	HaMoshiach	175
Gihon	16, 234	Hamudi	220
Gio	18	Hamza	220
Giza	9, 79, 132, 233, 241	Hannah	194, 195, 217
GMO	31, 108	Hanzala	220
god particle	9, 46	HaPelishtim	112, 181
Gogo	17	Haraiuriya	220
Gola	18	Hairur	220
Gold Coast	16, 234	Harari	200, 201
gonan'ombe	120, 125	Har Tsiyon	180
gore remhashu	89	Haraura	220
gore renzara	89	Haruna	184, 189, 193, 196
Gorani	6, 18	Hatibi	220
goy	163	Hausa	3, 6, 17
graven images	94	Haushabi	220
Great Enclosure	106, 242, 243	Havilah	16
Great Zimbabwe	9, 20, 29, 31, 32, 37, 49	Haya	17
	79, 106, 107, 108, 110	Hebrew Diaspora	5, 16, 247
	111, 112, 154, 164, 233	Hebrew identifier	22
	236, 239, 240, 241, 243	Hebrew marker	22
	244, 256, 276, 281	Hebrew Salvation	281
Great Zimbabwe Bird	111, 112	Hebrew University	92
Gregorian	163	Hellenic	2
Greece	16	Hera	220, 221
Greek(s)	1, 32, 85, 138, 176, 183,	Herero	6, 17
	209, 234, 235, 242, 251,	Herod	240, 242
	259, 260, 272	Herod's Temple	164
Greek Orthodox	1	Hiddekel	16, 234
Greek Philosophers	2	High Priest	14, 136, 202
gudzadungwe	109	Hitler	159
gumbwa	101	hoko	147
gupuro	151, 152	Horus	81
Gurima	18	hosho	99, 119, 157
Gurunsi	18	Hudaibiya	220
Guru	18	Hudhaifa	220
Guruuswa	237, 238, 247	Hudaira	220
guvi	109	Hukaim	220
gwenyambira	157	Humaidi	220

Index

human cloning	107
human sacrifice	119, 121, 183
human stem cell	4, 107, 108, 187
humwe	158
Hunai	220
Hunifa	220
Huraira	220
Hutu	3, 17, 190
Huyai	220
hyssop	139, 166
Ibadan	186
Ichabod	194, 217
Igbo	3, 18
igwe	163
incense	120, 125, 174, 179, 189
incest	137
induna	152
Instory	233
inxwala	26, 109
Iran	3, 19, 30, 65, 180, 234
Iraq	3, 234
Ishe Komborera Africa	12
Ishtar	89, 174
Islam	6, 21, 37, 80, 81, 150 160, 171, 180, 212, 220, 231, 253, 254 260
Islamic Conversion	171
Islamisation	250
Isis	66
Israel	5, 37, 49, 66, 92, 122 129, 145, 159, 162, 163 167, 170, 172, 180, 183 184, 187, 212, 218, 248, 249, 251, 252, 253, 255, 256, 269, 270
Israelites	159
Istanbul	259
Italy	17
Italian	99, 113, 209
Jacobsburg	188
Jacobson	188, 189
Jacobville	189
jakwara	158
Jamaica	138
James Muti	64
Japan	234
Japanese	234
Jariri	220
Jephtah	26, 63
Jeremiah	5, 16, 37, 64, 250, 252

Jihad	29, 37, 38, 62, 148
jinda ramambo	150
Jochebed	189, 193, 196
Johanan	5, 16, 250, 252
Jola	18
Joseph Hill	2
Juba	18
Judas Iscariot	2, 235
Juhaifa	220
Julian	163
Jupiter	81, 94, 161
Kabah	49
Kabiye	18
Kabsha	220
Kabsa	220
Kabwe	49
Kada	220
Kaguvi, Sekuru	64, 153,
Kalanga	18
Kalenjini	18
Kalim	220
Kamba	18
Kanembo	18
Kaonde	17
Karim	184, 220
Karima	184
Karimi	184
Kasambavezi river	16, 87, 140, 234, 242, 270, 271
Kennedy Space Centre	108
Kenya	3, 30, 77, 113, 133
Kenyan	258
Khababa	220
Khadija	220
Khadira	220
Khalasa	220
Khatab	220
Kattab	220
Khaula	220
Khaulani	220
Khazar(s)	5, 160, 161, 168, 188, 254, 255, 256
Khazira	220
Khudri	220
Khumbulani	60
Khushani	220
Khuwaisira	220
Khuza'a	220
Khuzai	220
Khuzaima	220
Kiblah	6

Index

Kikuyu	3, 6
Kilimanjaro Mt	30, 186
Kinana	220
Kinda	220
Kippur	136, 184, 195, 196, 202 214
Kisii	18
Kislev	89, 162
kosher	123
Kotoko	18
kuba	97
kubata maoko	130
kubvisa tsapata	79
kubvisa umhandara	67
kubvumwa kwemupiro	124
Kuda	220
kudya kwevakuwasha	56
kudzana	153
kudzinga mhepo	129, 165
kudzingisa vanakomana	41
kueresa denga	46
Kufa	220
kufa nechigumbu	69
kufumura nyika	141
kugadza mutungamiri	145
kugadzwa kwesvikiro	113
kugara kwemwedzi	140
kugara nhaka	25, 38, 70, 71, 72, 170 171
kugiya	153
kukanda hakata	130, 165
Kukutendai	60
Kunama	18
Kuniya	220
Kunya	220
kuoma kwenyika	33
kuomba kwemhondoro	92
kupa Mbereko	40
kupa zita	60
kupfimba	55
kupfimbirwa nevabereki	51
kupinduka kwetsika	143
kupira	10, 25, 37, 143
kupira Mudzimu	14
kupira n'ombe	162
kupupura	136, 184, 195, 196, 202 214
kuradza minda	110
Kuraibi	220
kuraira nhaka	77
kurasira	129, 130, 165

kuroodza	101
kuroora	10
kuroora mhandara	52, 168
kuroorerana vematongo	51, 263
kurova guva	10, 13, 70, 71, 72, 83, 124
kurova manda	152
kusuma nyikadzimu	76
kusungira	10, 85, 161
kutambira vakuwasha	55
kutanda botso	95
kutanga kwemwaka	83
kutanga kwenyika	9
kutanga kwezuva	9
kutema ruhau	125
kutema ugariri	55, 60, 169
kutevera	128
kutsvetsva	55
kutungamirirwa nemhondoro	86
kuvhunzira	10, 134, 138, 166
Kuyu	17
Laila	220
land sabbath	110
Lango	18
Latin	113
Laughter Mwanga	64
Lebanese	235
Lebanon	2
Lemba	249, 258
Lesotho	33
Libya	3, 31
Limpopo	16, 234, 242, 270, 271
Lingala	18
Lobi	18
lobola	55, 60, 169
Lomwe	17
London	131
Lost Tribes of Israel	212, 219, 238, 247
Lot	43
Lozi	17
Luai	220
Luba	18
Lubaba	220
Lucy Sibanda	64
Luganda	18
Luhya	18
Lunda	17
Luo	3, 18
Luvale	17
Luxemburg	17, 20

Index

Maba	18	masungiro	47
mabiko emhuri	47	masvikiro echikadzi	87
Mabua Smith	64	Matonjeni	29, 33, 37, 49, 110
Mabweadziva	110, 164, 279		125, 164, 242, 279
madhunamutuna	267	Maula	220
madzishe	90, 163	mavirira	16, 234
madzitateguru	14, 15, 63, 64, 281	Mazini	220
Mafia	58	Mbaka	18
Maghala	220	mbatya dzemasvikiro	113
magic enchanters	135	mbereko	10
Maimuna	220	mbira	99, 119, 157
mainini	32, 75	Mediterranean	247
Maisama	220	Mein Kampf	143
Maitiro	193, 196	melanin	3, 257
mai vemba	56	Melchizedek	181, 188, 192
Makada	236, 241, 266	Melech Shlomoh	107, 244
Makah	220, 221	Memphis	240
Makah Makarama	6, 32, 49	Mende	18
Makarama	220, 221	Menelik	244, 246, 248, 266
Makate	89, 90	merape	135
Makhad	220	Meribah	90, 175, 186, 194,
Makhrama	220		203, 218
Makhul	220	messiah	175, 176
Makhuwa	17	messianic concept	175, 176
makomo anoyera	111	Mexico	16, 234
makunhakunha	137	Mexican	234
makuva	50	mhepo	119
Malawi	33	mhiko yerufu	63
Malindi	30, 186	mhondoro	42, 43, 63, 87, 159,
Malinke	18		177, 242, 248, 252,
mambakwedza	142		256, 266
mamhepo	130	mhosva inoripwa	67
Manama	221	Michael	43, 86, 159, 177, 212
manana	61, 184, 195, 196, 203	Michael James Williams	2
Mande	18	Mijanna	220
Mandela Island	246, 267	Mina	18, 220
Mandinga	6, 17	mitemo yemaDzimbahwe	92
Mandja	18	mitupo	77, 171
Manjakwa	18	Miswar	220
Manna	53, 195, 196, 203	Monokutuba	18
mapira	15, 82, 87, 115, 143, 157	Mono reMasvikiro	117, 136
Mapungubwe	29, 32, 37, 49, 110, 164	Morocco	18
	186	Mosheh	184, 193, 196
Marimba	241	moshiach	175
Marur	220	Mosi-a-tunya	30
Maruri	220	Moslem	171, 231
Marwa	220	Mossi	18
Marwani	220	motshekga	184
Mars	81, 94, 188, 161	Mozambique	30, 33
masadunhu	90, 163	Muadha	220
Masai	18, 77	Muali	220
mashavi	13, 135	Mualla	220
Masud	220	Muanaqa	220

Index

Muawadh	220
Muawiya	220
Mubarak	95, 220
mubereki	95
Muchaiyisa	220
mucheka	184
Mudarrab	220
Mudavadi, Mambo	106, 147, 153, 164, 176
	184, 189, 193, 196, 213
	241, 265
mudzimu	12, 64
Mudzimu Mukuru	9, 11, 12, 13, 14, 15, 33
	66, 80, 86, 93, 144, 155
	156, 157, 159, 160, 164
	178, 188, 195, 241, 242
	243, 255, 267, 270, 271
	277, 278, 279, 280, 281
mudzimu unoyera	187
Muera Shumba	107
Mufti	37
Mughaffal	220
Mughala	220
Mughira	220
Muhammad	6, 29, 37, 41, 81, 82
	212, 220, 231, 253, 260
mukadzi wekwanhingi	25
mukunda	53
mukwerere	109, 124, 126, 174
Mujashi	220
Mulaika	220
Mulimo	64, 153, 187
Munaf	220
Munawara	220, 221
Mundhiri	220
Munhu Mutapa	107, 240, 241, 242, 243
Munkadir	220
munyai	55
Munzizi	184, 189, 193, 196
muperekedzi	57
mupiro	49
mupoteri	150
mupupuri	48
Muqana	220
Murara	220
murarabungu	27
murapi	135
muroyi	101
Muri	220
Musaba	220
Musailama	220
Musaiyaba	220
Musaiyabi	220
Musalima	220

Musalla	220
Muscat	221
Musheche	184, 189, 193, 196
Musikavanhu	9, 11, 12, 13, 15, 66,
	80, 81, 87, 91, 93, 94,
	95, 144, 155, 156, 159
	160, 161, 177, 178,
	188, 194, 241, 242,
	267, 270, 271, 279,
	280
Musi weKupupura	102, 136, 175, 195,
	202, 210
Mutamari	220
Mutare	88
muteyo	74
muthakathi	101
muti	50, 120, 233
Mutim	220
Mutimu	220
Muti Usina Zita	20, 21
Mutoko	89
mutorwa	102
Muzahim	220
Muzaina	220
Muzani	220
muzeze	139
muzvere	128
mvura yekuchenura	139, 166
Mwana waMudavadi	176, 254
mwana wedangwe	38
mwari	155, 156, 279
mwedzi wembudzi	89
Mwene Mutapa Building	243
Mwene Mutapa Empire	107, 187, 240, 241
	242, 244, 270
mweya	12, 64
Mweya Mukuru	12
n'anga	13, 134, 135, 152
Nakhai	220
Nakhla	220
Namibia	18, 33
Namira	220
Nazarite	41, 119, 133, 136, 137
	138, 263
Nazi(s)	3, 150, 274
Ndebele	3, 17, 18
Ndiro yeDzimbahwe	112
Nebuchadnezzar	5, 84, 89, 161, 164,
	174, 180, 204, 236,
	247, 249, 250, 252,
	254, 256
Nebuchatinetsa	204, 252, 256

Index

Nehanda, Mbuya	64, 81, 88, 153, 154, 187, 271	Ophir	243, 244, 246
Nehoreka	64, 89, 187	Orange River	3, 16, 234
Nether	91	Oromo	18
Netherlands	17, 94, 188, 258	orphan(s)	102
ngoma	99, 119, 157	Ovambo	17
ngozi	12, 27, 51, 67, 69, 152	Ovimbundu	18
Ngugi waBotha	64	Palestine	255
nguva yezhizha	83	Palestinian(s)	43, 148, 150, 173, 253
Nhamoinesu	60	Pakistan	172, 180
nhapwa	100	Paris	131
nhekwe	120, 125	Passover	175
nhenhere	83	Paul	116
nhimbe	158	Pentecostal	36, 117, 125, 130, 154, 187
nhoroondo	98		
Nherera	102	Perez-Uzzah	194, 204, 218
Nicodemus	235	Persia	2, 5, 64, 168, 175, 179, 186, 250, 273
Nigeria	3, 18, 31, 154, 172, 249		
Nigerian	266	Persian(s)	32, 84, 160, 166, 170, 174, 179, 180, 186, 187, 219, 235, 237, 240, 251, 253, 259, 272, 278
Niletic	185		
ninga	50, 87		
Nisan	89, 162		
Nkosi Sikelela Africa	12		
Nkululekho	60	Peter McIntosh	2
n'ombe yakapirwa	104	pfumvute	83
n'ombe yemudzimu	104	Pfura	243
n'ombe yeumai	47, 86	Pharisees	177, 179, 180
nuclear arms	2, 31, 62, 187, 261, 272	Philippi	2
nuclear arms of barbarism	193	Philippians	235
Nwankwo Martins	64	Philistine(s)	112, 148, 150, 172, 173, 237, 242, 253, 255, 256
Nyadenga	80, 155		
Nyakyusa	17		
nyama yezvirango	114	Phoenicians	106, 241
Nyaminyami	140	pira	187, 204
Nyamwezi	17	Pison	16, 234
Nyangani Mt	45, 49, 111, 125, 164, 186, 242	Pitum Haktoret	125, 159, 179
		polygamy	39
Nyanja	17	Pontius Pilate	235
Nyarwanda	18	Pope	120
Nyashanu, Chief	249	Portugal	17
Nyikadzimu	12, 72	Portuguese	65, 186, 190, 241
Nymex	17	prayer per capita	1, 62, 231
nyora	133	priestly portions	114
nzara	156	PTA	18, 272
Nzebi	18	Pungwe	88
Nzinga, Queen	187	Purim	174, 253
nzvimbo dzinoyera	91	pwanyaruzhowa	67
nzvimbo yekupira	49	Qama	220
oath of death	63	Qilaba	220
Obamba	18	Qutaiba	220
Ochivedi	189, 193, 196	Quraishi	220
Ochivei	193, 196	Quran	250
OPEC	18, 272	Ra	66

Index

Raba	220	satan	118
Rabadha	220	satani	118, 156, 157
racism	3	Saud	220
Ramadan	84	Sauda	220
rare earth metals	30	Saudi Arabia	31, 241
Rawaha	220	scapegoat	129, 130, 165
reed dance	54, 174	Sefuno	18
religious schisms	1	Sekai	189, 193, 196, 213
resource ratio	30	seka urema wafa	132
Rift Valley	271	sekuru	137
Roman Catholicism	87	Sena	17
Roman Jesuit	281	Senegal	258
Roman(s)	1, 6, 32, 48, 85, 91, 96, 98	Senegalese	258
	120, 154, 234, 235, 243,	Sephardim	248, 252
	251, 257, 258, 259, 260,	Sepharvaim	42, 248, 252
	272	Septuagint	189, 234, 238, 244, 258,
Rome	2, 16, 155, 235		263, 264
roora	55, 60, 169	Serengeti	30
Rozvi	240	Shabi	220
rufu	69	Shaduf	132, 276
rukoto	109, 124	Shahadah	171
Ruma	220	Shaiba	220
Rumalisa	220	Shaibani	220
runyanhiriri	142	Shalom Aleichem	251
runyoka	74	Shama	220
Russia	256	Shami	220
Russian	187, 209	Shangela	18
Ruth	25, 78	Sheba, Queen	81, 88, 90, 186, 236, 240
Ruvarashe	89		241, 244, 245, 246, 262,
ruvhunzavaeni	142		266
SADC	18, 272	Shebat	89, 162
Sadducees	179, 180	Shia	3, 19, 35, 37
Saharawi	3, 18	Shlomoh	184, 193, 241
Saho	18	Shona	3, 6, 17
Saida	220	showera	131
Saidu	220	Shuba	220
Salama	220	Shul	110
Salam Alaikum	251	Shurai	220
Salima	220	Shuraik	220
Salul	220	Siba	220
Salvation Army	281	Siberia(n)	16, 234, 278
Samson	46, 138	Silbury Hill	233
Samura	220	Sidamo	18
Sana'a	221	Simba	60
Sanctified bull	104	Simon Peter	2, 235
Sangha	18	Sinai Mt	14, 64, 92, 93, 111, 169
Sango	18	Sinclair	260
sangoma	13, 134, 135, 152	Sivan	89, 162
Sanhedrin	179, 180	snuff	120
Sara	18	snuff dish	120
Sarahule	18	Sofala	243
sara pavana	71, 73	Somali	18
Sasa	220	sodomy	44, 51

Index

Somalia	3, 18, 177, 241, 244	Temne	18
Soninge	18	Thalaba	220
Sotho	17	Thaqafi	220
Source Soul	12, 14, 47, 80, 93, 142, 160, 164	Thembinkosi van der Mer	64
		Theory of Evolution	9, 105, 247
South Africa	3, 16, 18, 19, 30, 31, 33, 45, 62, 65, 102, 112, 113, 164, 234, 240, 244	Thessalonians	235
		Thessalonica	2
		thobe	251
South Sudanese	266	Thukela River	94
Spain	17	thummim	123
Spaniard	65	Thuwaiba	220
Spanish	209	Tibet	16
Sphinx	260	Tibetan	16
spook	267	Tigrinya	18
Star of David	163	Tishret	89, 162
Statue of Liberty	94	tithe merchant	36, 117, 154
Stonehenge	233	tithe revenue	117
stone laver	112	token of divorce	151
Subai	220	Tonga	17
succah	109	totems	77, 78, 171
succot	109	Trans-Atlantic	61
Sudan	3, 133	Trans Frontier Park	30
Sukuma	17	Trevor Sutherland	2
Suma	188, 195	tsaona	180
Sumai	195, 196	Tshaka, King	94, 187
Sumerian(s)	32, 162, 174, 251, 259, 272	Tsiyon	180, 208
		Tsiyoniyut	180
Sunni	3, 19, 35, 37	tsvimbo dzababa	75
Svikiro Guru	136, 202, 243	tsvimborume	11, 116
Swahili	220, 221	Tswana	6, 17
Swazi	17	Tuhama	220
Swaziland	33	Tumbuka	18
Swiss	209	Turkish	259, 272
Switzerland	17	Turks	32, 251
Syria	2	Tutankhamun	260
Taberah	186, 194, 196, 206, 216	Tutsi	3, 17
Tadiwa	193	Ubada	220
Tafara	60	Ubai	220
Tafari Makoneni	245, 266	Uganda	3, 27, 255
Tafila	220	Uhuru	272, 281
Taiba	220	Ujara	220
Taimullah	220	Ukasha	220
tale bearing	132	Ulunyoka	74
Taliba	220	Umaiya	220
Tamima	220	Umama	220
Tammuz	89, 162, 174, 188	Umar	184
Tanzania	30, 33, 231	Umari	184, 220
Tarwiya	220	Umawi	220
tattoos	133	Umhare	184
Tauba	220	Umhlanga	54
Tebit	89, 162	umhondi	96
Tefila	187, 207		
Tel Aviv	255		

Index

Unkulunkulu	9, 11, 12, 13, 15, 66, 80, 93, 94, 95, 155, 156, 160, 177, 178, 188, 241, 270, 271, 279, 280	White Nile	16
		widow(s)	102
		Winston Khumalo	64
		witness	48
Umrah	251	Xhosa	3, 6, 17, 18
Umvelinqangi	9, 11, 12, 13, 15, 66, 80, 93, 94, 95, 155, 156, 160, 178, 188, 241, 242, 270, 271, 279, 280	xylophone	241
		Yaakov	66, 184, 208
		Yahveh	160
		Yako	66, 189
ungochani	44	Yakovo	66, 184, 189
United Africa	18, 31	Yakoma	18
United Kingdom	17	Yamur	184
upombwe	96	Yamura	184, 220
urim	123, 134	Yao	18
urombo uroyi	33	Yedidiah	194
Urwa	220	Y gene	38
Usama	220	Yemen	241
Usauya	220	Yitiro	189, 193, 196, 236, 261, 270
US Goree Island	250		
usury	103	Yitro	193, 196
Utabiyya	220	Yitzchak	193, 196, 208
utongi	146	Yochivedi	193
Uyaina	220	Yochivei	193
Uwaimir	184, 220	Yom Kippur	102, 136, 175, 195, 202, 210
Uwaimiri	184, 220		
Uzza	220	Yoruba	18, 249
Vaera Bere	77	Zachary	209
Vaera Beta	77	Zaghawa	18
Vaera Dziva	77	Zainabi	220
Vaera Hove	77	Zakariyana	209
Vaera Mwoyo	26, 77, 269	Zambezi River	16, 87, 140, 234, 242, 243, 270, 271
Vaera Shumba	77		
Vaera Mbizi	77	Zambia	33
VaHosi	39, 41	Zaura	220
vakuru	157	Zeus	81, 94, 161, 188, 242
VaLevi	269	Zimbabwe	16, 30, 31, 110, 113, 125, 146, 154, 200, 234, 236, 242, 243, 244, 249
Vana veNhaka	107, 142		
VaRemba	249		
VaRozvi	26, 92, 106, 269		
Vatican	109, 116, 146, 281	Zimbabwe Bird	242
vazukuru	67	Zion	180, 181
Venda	18	Zionism	163, 176, 180
Vhembe River	16, 234, 242, 270, 271	Zionist(s)	66, 173
Vhumba Mt	30	zita rasekuru	28
virgin marriage	52, 168	Zodiac Sgns	68, 133, 162
Virunga	30	Zubairi	220
vow	48	Zulu	3, 6, 17, 18
Wada	220	zunde ramambo	36, 91, 136, 151
Wailing Wall	164, 242	Zuraira	220
Walima	220	Zurara	220
Wanano	24	zvinoera	45
water of separation	139, 166	zviroto	68
Western Wall	107	zvisipiti	88
Wezhira	184	zviumbwa	94

Reference / Bibliography

1. African or Hebrew Culture and Spirituality

2. African Oral Tradition

3. The Hebrew Scriptures

4. Hadith Al-Bukhari

5. ArtScroll Siddur – Rabbi Nosson Scherman

Made in the USA
Middletown, DE
25 July 2017